The Last Afrikaner Leaders

Reconsiderations in Southern African History
Richard Elphick, Editor

HERMANN GILIOMEE

The Last Afrikaner Leaders

A Supreme Test of Power

UNIVERSITY OF VIRGINIA PRESS

CHARLOTTESVILLE AND LONDON

To Annette

Published jointly by
Tafelberg
An imprint of NB Publishers
40 Heerengracht, Cape Town, 8000
South Africa
www.tafelberg.com

University of Virginia Press
P.O. Box 400318, Charlottesville, VA 22904-4318
USA
www.upress.virginia.edu

Printed in the United States of America on acid-free paper

First University of Virginia Press edition published 2013

9 8 7 6 5 4 3 2 1

Library of Congress Cataloging-in-Publication Data

Giliomee, Hermann, 1938–
    The last Afrikaner leaders : a supreme test of power / Hermann Giliomee.—First University of Virginia Press edition.
        pages   cm. — (Reconsiderations in southern African history)
    Includes bibliographical references and index.
    ISBN 978-0-8139-3494-5 (pbk. : alk. paper)—ISBN 978-0-8139-3495-2 (e-book)
    1. National Party (South Africa)—History—20th century. 2. Politicians—South Africa—20th century. 3. Apartheid—South Africa—20th century. 4. Power (Social sciences)—South Africa. 5. South Africa—Politics and government—1948–1994. 6. South Africa—Race relations—20th century—Political aspects—History. I. Title. II. Series: Reconsiderations in southern African history.
    JQ1998.N2G55 2013
    320.968—dc23
                                                                                        2013015101

Set in Minion / Book design Nazli Jacobs / Index Sanet le Roux

Excerpt from a poem Robert Burns wrote in 1785
as an apology after accidentally overturning a
mouses's house in a cornfield:

But, Mousie, thou art not thy lane [you are not alone],
In proving foresight may be vain;
The best-laid schemes o' mice an' men
Gang aft agley [often go awry],
An' lea'e us nought but grief an' pain,
For promised joy!

Contents

Introduction

A Tragic Dilemma

IN THE SECOND HALF OF THE TWENTIETH CENTURY, SOUTH AFRICA WENT through two 'revolutions'. The first was the implementation of the apartheid policy, accompanied by massive social engineering, which more comprehensively segregated races than any other racial policy in the world. The second was the unprecedented handing over of power by whites to blacks, although the state, based predominantly on the white minority, was neither defeated nor bankrupt. This book is about five white leaders – Hendrik Verwoerd, John Vorster, PW Botha, FW de Klerk and Frederik van Zyl Slabbert – and their roles in one or other of these revolutions.

Writing well before apartheid was fully introduced, Alan Paton published two novels, *Cry, the Beloved Country* (1948) and *Too Late the Phalarope* (1953), about the unfolding political drama of what he called the 'tragic dilemma' of the white man. 'A man is caught on the face of a cliff,' Paton writes. 'As he sees it, he cannot go up and he cannot go down; if he stays where he is, he will die. All those who stand watching have pity for him. But the analogy, alas, is obviously incomplete, for the world's spectators of our drama are seldom pitiful; they are more often reproachful. From their point of vantage they can see which way we ought to go, but they see us taking some other way which will lead us to our destruction. And the world looks at us in astonishment, wondering what madness has possessed us.'[1]

In the mid-1960s British journalist Douglas Brown remarked that apartheid had no counterpart in history and that 'no race has ever been so universally condemned for preserving its identity' than South African whites.[2] Pulitzer Prize-winning American novelist and commentator Allen Drury observed that the white community, which had established one of the world's most sophisticated and viable states, 'cannot understand why they must be expected to give it up. They will not do so.'[3]

There was a reason why Brown and Drury were so certain there would be no surrender of power. The people in power were Afrikaner nationalists who, more than the English-speaking community, were rooted in the land. They controlled a state

---

1 Alan Paton, 'The White Man's Dilemma', *The Saturday Review*, 2 May 1953, p. 12.
2 Douglas Brown, *Against the World* (London: Collins, 1966), p. 9.
3 Allen Drury, *'A Very Strange Society': A Journey to the Heart of South Africa* (London: Micheal Joseph, 1968), p. 451.

on which they made a major imprint. They considered the state and the army their state and their army, and were driven by the conviction that they had nowhere else to go. By 1975 the state that had been built up could – in terms of economic indicators – be considered a successful state. On a world rating list South Africa had the 18th largest economy and it was the 15th largest trading country. Thirty years later it would fall to 28th and 37th respectively on the list.[4]

To most informed commentators writing in the 1960s and 1970s it was inconceivable that Afrikaners, with such a large stake in the state, would give up power voluntarily. From the early 1960s Afrikaners had begun to dominate the senior levels of the civil service, security service and public corporations. They would be the first targets of a new government committed to racial transformation.

Also likely to be affected was Afrikaans, enjoying equal status with English as an official language as part of an English-Afrikaner pact in the drafting of the Union Constitution of 1909. Afrikaans – along with Hindi, Malay-Indonesian and Hebrew – became one of only four languages in the world that were standardised in the course of the twentieth century and came to be used in all branches of life and learning, including postgraduate studies and science and technology. In 1990 a commentator considered Afrikaans the strongest language in South Africa as it was used countrywide, both formally and informally.[5] Given the haste with which newly independent African states elevated the colonial language to the status of the only national language, it could be expected that a new government in South Africa would waste little time in doing the same.

There were also fears that the overthrow of the government could be accompanied by attempts at retribution. In early 1973 the United Nations General Assembly declared apartheid a crime against humanity and agreed to the drawing up of an 'International Convention on the Suppression of the Crime of Apartheid'. An obvious attempt on the part of the Soviet Union to embarrass the West, the Convention was ratified first by twenty countries in the Soviet bloc that had no record of protecting human rights themselves. Although leading Western nations openly refused to endorse the resolution or ratify the Convention, the African National Congress (ANC), through skilful propaganda, manufactured the impression that the entire world considered apartheid a crime against humanity.[6]

The four National Party (NP) leaders featured in this book all believed the power

---

4   RW Johnson, *South Africa's Brave New World: The Beloved Country since the End of Apartheid* (London: Allen Lane, 2009), pp. 598. The figures are from the World Trade Organisation.

5   Lawrence Schlemmer, cited in Hermann Giliomee et al., *Kruispad: Die toekoms van Afrikaans as openbare taal* (Cape Town: Tafelberg, 2001), p. 117. See also Hermann Giliomee, *The Rise and Possible Demise of Afrikaans as a Public Language* (Cape Town: PRAESA, 2003), p. 3.

6   Hermann Giliomee, *Liberal and Populist Democracy in South Africa: Challenges, New Threats to Liberalism* (Johannesburg: SA Institute of Race Relations, 1996), pp. 8-9.

they held conferred on them the huge responsibility not to put at risk Afrikaner political power and the prospects for Afrikaner survival, which they closely linked. From the early 1960s they increasingly blamed 'agitators', 'communists' or 'black nationalists' for any resistance to apartheid. The fifth leader discussed here, Van Zyl Slabbert, never held political power, but would in my opinion have reached the highest political position in the land if, during the mid-1960s, he had chosen the career path that the Afrikaner nationalist establishment – aware of his remarkable abilities – had marked out for him.

Slabbert was fully aware of white fears, both rational and irrational, but argued that apartheid, not communism, was the real cause of the conflict. He became the most formidable critic of the policy, using a unique combination of intellectual, economic and moral arguments. Like some of his academic contemporaries, Slabbert was gripped by the ideas of NP van Wyk Louw, the pre-eminent Afrikaner poet and essayist, who had argued in a book published in 1958 that the challenge for the Afrikaners was 'not merely to survive, but to survive in justice'.[7]

In the first half of the 1990s the second revolution occurred. Afrikaners did what few expected: they accepted majority rule without having suffered a defeat at the hands of the subjugated population. The army and the police remained intact and loyal to the NP government. There is no other example in recorded history of such a surrender of power without defeat. It is true that sanctions, black opposition and white demographic decline (whites as a proportion of the total population sank from 19% in 1951 to below 10% by 2005) put strong pressure on white minority rule. Yet a government determined and bloody-minded enough could, through skilful cooptation of both black and business leaders, have held on for quite some time. This was one thing on which FW de Klerk and Van Zyl Slabbert agreed.

The argument that financial considerations forced the NP government to surrender power is implausible. Derek Keys, finance minister from 1992 to 1994, observed that though conditions were tight, the government, financially speaking, could go on.[8] After the transition was completed, the white community found itself without effective representation in government. This despite the fact that, by the end of the 1980s, it paid 90% of the personal tax (31% of the total revenue) and most of the sales tax (27% of the total revenue).[9] There is no similar case in recorded history of a peaceful transfer of power from the propertied classes to those without property, paying a relatively small proportion of tax.

---

7 Hermann Giliomee, 'Survival in Justice: An Afrikaner Debate over Apartheid', *Comparative Studies in Society and History*, 36, 5, 1994, pp. 527-48.

8 Interview with Derek Keys, 17 October 2010.

9 *Finansies en Tegniek*, 23 September 1988, p. 21. These figures were based on the calculations of JL Sadie.

The last three decades of the twentieth century saw a veritable avalanche of books on apartheid. They tend to stress the social processes and the abstract forces that first shaped the construction of the system and later worked to bring about its erosion and overthrow. Some of these studies have produced major insights, but they have done so without giving full weight to human agency.

This book is different. It does not deal with the apartheid policy in all its manifestations, the resistance against it by individuals and organisations, the role of business leaders and trade unions, nor with the influence of the popular press.[10] It also does not discuss the social or economic policy of the NP government. Instead, it focuses on the political schemes the various NP leaders proposed – and Slabbert's criticism of these schemes. In a certain sense this work is a companion to my book on the Afrikaners, but with a much greater focus on political leadership.[11]

Social scientists in particular are inclined to underestimate the role of leadership. It is when they enter politics that they realise how wrong they were. After talking to Anwar Sadat, Golda Meir and other leaders on one of his shuttle missions in the Middle East in 1974, Henry Kissinger said: 'As a professor, I tended to think of history as run by impersonal forces. But when you see it in practice, you see the difference personalities make.'[12]

An embattled ethnic or national group such as the Jews or the Afrikaners, fearing not only the loss of their power but also of their cultural heritage, attaches great weight to leaders to secure the group's survival and material welfare. In the mid-1970s a large opinion survey found that 60% of Afrikaners would support their leaders 'even if they acted in ways they did not understand or approve'.[13] In 1992, with white civil servants feeling very insecure about their career prospects, a poll was taken to measure their trust in politicians. It found very low levels of trust in politicians in general, but more than three quarters of NP- or DP-supporting respondents trusted De Klerk to negotiate a settlement that they could endorse.[14]

Although not even the most charismatic of leaders can prevail over unfavourable structural conditions, political leadership remains of vital importance, particularly in ethnic parties. All the NP leaders discussed here were acutely aware of the trust they enjoyed and felt an enormous responsibility weighing upon them. For better

---

10   A definitive study is the work of David Welsh, *The Rise and Fall of Apartheid* (Johannesburg: Jonathan Ball, 2010).

11   Hermann Giliomee, *The Afrikaners: Biography of a People* (Cape Town: Tafelberg, second edition, 2009).

12   Cited by Walter Isaacson in Michael Leventhal (ed.), *The Hand of History* (London: Greenhill Books, 2011), p. 69.

13   Theo Hanf et al. *Südafrika: Friedlicher Wandel?* (Munich: Kaiser, 1978), pp. 421-22.

14   JS Wessels and A Viljoen, *Waarde-oriëntasies en toekomsverwagtinge van die Vereniging van Staatsamptenare* (Pretoria: HSRC, 1992), pp. 6-7, 44.

or worse, they left a far greater imprint on the course of history and the Afrikaners' fate than is normally assumed.

How does one isolate and evaluate the role of leadership? The great American diplomatic historian George Kennan, who produced seminal perspectives on the Soviet Union's capacity for reform, observed that the historian has to go beyond the *what* of history to consider the *how*. Historians have to ask how leaders saw the facts and how they related to them. This leads to other questions: What did they think they were doing and what did they in fact achieve? What motivated them and what was their vision? What role did this vision play in the outcome? Finally, in the light of the historical perspective, how did their efforts relate to the ultimate results of their behaviour?[15]

This book tries to answer these questions about five South African leaders. How did they build up their power, what motivated them and what did they achieve (and not achieve)? Did they rely on sage advice and to what extent did their health or personal circumstances affect their decisions? The first half of the book covers the period from September 1958, when Hendrik Verwoerd took office, to June 1984, when PW Botha, at the height of his power, paid official visits to eight countries in Europe.

The book attempts to reassess the grand scheme of apartheid as envisaged by Hendrik Verwoerd (Chapters 2 and 3). An academic in politics, he was a systematic thinker who in numerous speeches held up apartheid and integration as two competing systems. He first outlined the likely course of integration – and from the vantage point of 2012 one can concede that some of his predictions were quite astute – before concluding that apartheid offered a far better future, not only to whites but to all the other communities. He envisaged as the final stage of apartheid a 'commonwealth' of 'nations' and 'states', with leaders deliberating and cooperating with each other on an ongoing basis. He introduced a system of mass public education for black and coloured pupils that emphasised primary education with a focus on the acquisition of basic skills. At that stage the labour market demanded unskilled and semi-skilled black labour rather than well-educated school leavers expecting white-collar jobs.

John Vorster is presented as a leader in thrall to Verwoerd's grand scheme (Chapter 4). Trained as a lawyer, Vorster made the fatal error of believing that by denationalising blacks he had developed a legal bar to their vote. He authorised an ill-conceived incursion of South African troops into Angola in the vain hope of bringing Jonas Savimbi, who controlled a large region of Angola, into a 'constellation of states'. Politically speaking, Vorster's years in office were arid, lost years.

Two main interventions characterised PW Botha's term. He began to de-racialise parliament and brought black workers, through their own unions, into a common

---

15   Robert Ulan, 'The US and the World: An Interview with George Kennan', *New York Review of Books*, 12 August 1999, p. 6.

system of bargaining in industrial councils. The reason for this latter step has long been poorly understood, especially in view of the fact that this bold instance of reform stands in such strong contrast to the timid attempts at political reform.

The section on the work of the Wiehahn Commission on labour reform offers the first extensive exposition, based largely on interviews, of the dynamics of the labour reforms. It shows that the commission was conceptualised as a conservative intervention. The aim was to deflect pressure from overseas on both government and employers over poor wages by allowing workers to negotiate, at the same time regulating and controlling black unions, which until 1979 was not recognised.[16] By mid-1985 the labour system had led to an outcome no one had anticipated (Chapter 6).

The second half of the book, covering the years from 1984 to 1994, attempts a reinterpretation of the years of transition. It presents an in-depth account of the NP leadership as they grappled with the greatest-ever challenge faced by the Afrikaner people and the larger white community. It offers a fresh account, based on interviews, of PW Botha's ill-fated Rubicon speech of August 1985 (Chapter 8). It also describes how Van Zyl Slabbert, with passionate conviction and telling arguments, became the man in Alan Paton's parable who told whites to get off the cliff if they did not want to be destroyed. Chapter 9 on the last year or two of Botha's term discusses Nelson Mandela's initiative, while still in jail, to start negotiations.

Finally, the book suggests a new interpretation of FW de Klerk (Chapters 10 to 14). He is presented as someone who had the courage to start formal negotiations, but was too idealistic in his assumption that parliamentary democracy could readily be restored to glory. He was not a good strategist in negotiations. He postponed resolving the contested issue of power sharing until after the ANC had mobilised sufficiently to reject it. At the same time, however, it was De Klerk's demand for a constitutional state that provided to minorities and minority parties some leverage against an all-powerful dominant party.

A brief word on apartheid. Irish historian Roy Foster, writing on a different subject, remarks on coming to grips with the collective misdeeds of the past: 'Apology is easier than explaining.'[17] I believe the major duty of historians is to explain rather than to apologise. The challenge is to explain apartheid in the context of the time when it was introduced and enforced. The international context has changed dramatically since then. As late as 1944 Gunnar Myrdal's massive study entitled *American Dilemma* could state: 'Segregation is now becoming so complete that the white Southerner practically never sees a Negro except as his servant and in other standardized and formalized caste situations.'[18]

---

16   Interview with Piet van der Merwe, 27 January 2011.

17   Roy Foster, 'Fashion for apology can invite danger of amnesia', *Sunday Independent*, 25 July 1999.

18   C Vann Woodward, *The Strange Career of Jim Crow* (New York: Oxford University Press, 1974), p. 118.

When Eben Dönges introduced the Prohibition of Mixed Marriages Bill in 1949, he mentioned that there were 30 states in the United States that had similar legislation. When, in 1961, the woman who would give birth to Barack Obama married a black man from Kenya, there were still nearly two dozen US states that prohibited such marriages. Dwight Eisenhower spoke with sympathy at a presidential news conference about the fears of Southern whites seeing 'a picture of the mongrelisation of the race'.[19] As late as 1970 the state of Louisiana passed a law that made $\frac{1}{32}$ the fraction of 'Negro blood' that constituted the dividing line between white and black. It was repealed in 1983 after a woman, generally regarded as white, had taken legal action following a decision of the state Bureau of Vital Statistics to label her coloured.[20] It was only in 1965, a year before Verwoerd's death, that the United States abolished racial discrimination nationwide.

Apartheid was fundamentally undermined by four developments no one could have foreseen in 1948. First, between 1946 and 1996 the black population would multiply by more than four times, from 7.8 million to 32.1 million, while the white population did not even double (2.3 million to 4.4 million). Second, the Second World War and decolonisation would fundamentally undermine the traditional notions of white supremacy in the United States and Europe. Third, during the Cold War the European powers, in their competition with the Soviet Union and the Eastern bloc, would increasingly turn against South Africa to side with the African states. Fourth, the rapid growth of the South African economy in the 1960s and 1970s would lead to a skills shortage that only the training of black and coloured workers could fill.

The second half of the book is to a large extent based on interviews. Between 1988 and 2012, I interviewed virtually all the white political leaders. I also draw on the texts of lengthy interviews conducted by two other writers on the transition, Patti Waldmeir and Padraig O'Malley. Except where indicated otherwise, I conducted all interviews cited in the footnotes. I found that most of the people interviewed, especially members and officials of the NP government, were willing to talk much more frankly than they were in the turbulent 1990s. The sad disappearance of the craft of letter writing means that increasing emphasis will be put on e-mail communications and interviews to construct a credible history of the past.

Autumn 2012
Stellenbosch

19 William L O'Neill, *American High: The Years of Confidence, 1945-1960* (New York: The Free Press, 1986), p. 253.
20 Virginia R Dominguez, *White by Definition: Social Classification in Creole Louisiana* (New Brunswick: Rutgers University Press, 1994), pp. 1-2.

Chapter 1

An Extraordinary Country

'WHAT SPECIAL INTELLECTUAL OR SPIRITUAL TASK DO YOU SUGGEST TO THE Afrikaner nation, which as a young West European nation, is only now reaching its spiritual maturity?'[1] In 1951 this was a question the young and upcoming member of the Afrikaner nationalist intelligentsia Piet Meyer asked some leading Western intellectuals after the unexpected National Party victory in the 1948 election.

Arnold Toynbee, one of the Anglophone world's most prominent historians, responded. A single-volume abridgement of his ten-volume *A Study of History* had appeared four years earlier. In 1949 *Time* magazine had featured Toynbee on its cover, with a cover story urging the government of the United States – the leading nation of Western civilisation – to learn the lessons of earlier civilisations in recorded history. Toynbee's views had stimulated as much publicity and discussion as Samuel Huntington's article 'The Clash of Civilizations?' would do 40 years later.

Toynbee's reply deserves to be quoted at length: 'My personal feeling is that the Afrikaner nation is confronted with a most difficult, and at the same time most important, spiritual task, which it is bound to undertake, without having any choice of refusing. It seems to me that, in South Africa, you are faced already with a situation that is going very soon to be the common situation of the whole world as a result of the "annihilation of distance" through the progress of our Western technology ... There will never be room in the world for the different fractions of mankind to retire into isolation from one another again.'

Toynbee continued: 'Now, in South Africa, the accident of history has put the native, coloured and white people of the country into this difficult situation at an early date: History – or God – has given you the honourable mission of being the spiritual pioneers in trying to find the solution of a spiritual problem that is soon going to face the rest of the human race as well.'[2]

'A unique combination'

Why did Toynbee assign to Afrikaners a major role in dealing with the problem of the annihilation of distance? The reason can best be found by looking at three fea-

---

1 PJ Meyer, *Nog nie ver genoeg nie* (Johannesburg: Perskor, 1984), p. 64.

2 Meyer, *Nog nie ver genoeg nie*, pp. 64-65.

tures that make South Africa exceptional, according to economic historian Charles Feinstein. As he formulates it, South Africa represents a unique combination of the way in which the indigenous population, European settlers and mineral resources were brought together in a process of conquest, dispossession, discrimination and development to promote rapid economic growth.[3]

The country's history was indeed extraordinary. First, virtually alone in the history of Western colonisation, substantial numbers of the indigenous population survived. The numbers of Khoisan and Africans by the beginning of the nineteenth century can be put at 1.5 million, rising to 4 million by 1904. Second, Europeans settled in much larger numbers than in other European colonies not founded as settlement colonies. At the time of the 1904 census they totalled over a million. There also was a third difference: while other colonies also had rich mineral resources, there was nothing that could be compared to the vast mineral wealth of the Witwatersrand. The discovery of gold in 1886, together with the earlier discovery of diamonds, transformed South Africa.[4]

The substantial rise of the gold price in the early 1930s sustained high growth for nearly 40 years, but many of the constraints on development remained. The historian CW de Kiewiet singled out three major factors that hampered the country's growth: 'its low-grade ore, its low-grade land, and also its low-grade human beings'.[5] Much of South Africa's low-grade gold ore sold at a low, fixed price and could only be mined by very cheap labour. Low-grade land, together with poor and uncertain rainfall, was responsible for many of agriculture's problems. There also were 'low-grade human beings' – the product of low spending on education and the great distances many rural children had to travel to school. The education for coloured and black children, provided by church or missionary societies, was in most cases inferior to what white schools provided.

Between 1929 and 1933 the worldwide economic crisis changed the shape of white politics in South Africa. The ruling National Party (NP), under the leadership of General JBM Hertzog, and the South African Party (SAP), under the leadership of General Jan Smuts, merged in 1933–34 to form the United Party (UP) under Hertzog's leadership. Nineteen members of the Cape NP, led by Dr DF Malan, rejected this Fusion and formed the *Gesuiwerde* National Party (NP), which became the official opposition in 1934.

Between 1910 and 1936 a system of rigorous segregation between whites and blacks was implemented. This culminated in the 1936 legislation that removed

---

3 Charles H Feinstein, *An Economic History of South Africa* (Cambridge: Cambridge University Press, 2005), p. 3.

4 Feinstein, *An Economic History*, pp. 1-2.

5 CW de Kiewiet, *A History of South Africa* (Oxford: Oxford University Press, 1941), p. 212.

Cape Africans – about 3% of the total number of voters – from the voters' roll. They would have to vote on a separate roll for three whites to represent them in the House of Assembly. Four white senators, elected by electoral colleges, would represent other blacks in South Africa. There would also be a Natives Representative Council to discuss issues affecting Africans in both the reserves and the common area. An additional 7.25 million morgen of land would be bought up for the reserves. Once that was completed, 13% of the country's land would be in black hands.

In discussing the rise of a harsher form of racial exclusion in the American South during the 1890s, which would last until the 1960s, C Vann Woodward, an outstanding historian of the region, made an important point. While economic and social changes paved the way for a more extreme form of segregation in the American South, the basic motives were political. The new system of segregation was instituted mainly to gain or perpetuate power. Far from being the work of 'rednecks', the policy of segregation ought to be considered as 'the subtle, flexible, complex fabrication of sophisticated elites'.[6]

In South Africa, too, it was sophisticated elites in the Afrikaner community who placed South Africa on the road towards a more severe form of segregation and later of apartheid. They, too, were spurred on more by the drive to win power through the ballot box and use it for the advancement of their community than by deep-seated racist convictions. In the 1929 election, when Hertzog's NP contested the election alone, the party message on racial policy was much harsher than in 1924, which had been fought in alliance with the Labour Party. While some Nationalist politicians enthusiastically wooed the coloured vote between 1910 and 1929, they switched to propagating a rigorous form of segregation in the early 1930s. This was because the UP occupied the middle ground in white politics, leaving the NP little hope of attracting coloured support. To win over the Afrikaner intelligentsia the NP tried to present its racial policy as something better than segregation, which it claimed was merely interested in 'walling off' the coloured and the black population in their 'locations'.

Social segregation

In the 1930s and 1940s all the major parties strove to maintain social segregation. In 1931 leading liberal philosopher Alfred Hoernlé wrote that both whites and blacks properly valued 'race purity' and 'racial pride'. It was part and parcel of 'the best public opinion, the most enlightened racial self-consciousness, of natives no less than of whites'.[7] In 1936 he remarked that a visitor from Mars would immediately be struck by the pervasiveness of racial exclusion and discrimination in South

---

6   C Vann Woodward, 'The Edifice of Domination', *New Republic*, 17 December 1982.
7   *The Star*, 25 September 1931; *Die Vaderland*, 18 June 1935.

Africa. Such a visitor could come to only one conclusion: '[There] was a dominant urge towards segregation, which has moulded the structure of South African society and made it what it now is.'[8] *Forum*, a journal founded to support Jan Hofmeyr's liberalism, stated that it was 'revolted' by miscegenation.[9]

The UP retained the elements of liberalism that had characterised the Cape Colony since the 1850s. There was still no law that restricted coloured people or Africans from living where they wished or from buying property in the Cape Colony. From the early 1930s government policy was to build separate coloured townships, but by 1950 almost a third of coloured people in Cape Town still lived in mixed areas, often called the *onderdorp*. There was no ban on sexual intercourse between white and coloured people, though in 1927 a ban had been placed on marriages between whites and blacks. Coloured-white marriages were rare. Between 1943 and 1946 only 100 such marriages per year took place on average, compared to 30 000 intra-white marriages per year.

There also was no statutory population registration. During the 1930s a select committee of parliament found that a population register was impracticable. That was also Jan Smuts's view. It was, he said, an attempt to classify what was unclassifiable. When the NP government introduced the Population Registration Act in 1950, he pleaded: 'Don't let us trifle with this thing, for we are touching on things which go pretty deep in this land.'[10]

Political segregation

Before 1910 political segregation was policy in the Transvaal, Orange Free State and Natal provinces, but the policy was more fluid in the Cape. Coloureds and Africans could vote along with whites since the introduction of the liberal Cape Constitution in 1853. Essentially, electoral politics involved the Afrikaner and English sections of the white population, but between 1910 and 1929 coloured voters held the balance of power in the rural seats of Stellenbosch and Paarl and several other constituencies in the rural western Cape.[11] In Paarl and Stellenbosch their share of the vote was estimated at between a quarter and a fifth of the total vote.

While some leading Cape NP members pressed for putting coloured voters on a separate roll from 1915, the alternative of a qualified vote was hardly ever proposed. Generals Hertzog and Smuts discussed it in 1928 at a time when the African National Congress (ANC) demanded 'equal rights for all civilized men'. But the two

---

8   RF Alfred Hoernlé, *Race and Reason* (Johannesburg: University of the Witwatersrand Press, 1945), pp. 96-97.

9   Alan Paton, *Hofmeyr* (Cape Town: Oxford University Press, 1971), p. 232.

10 *House of Assembly Debates*, 1950, col. 2534.

11 Hermann Giliomee, *Nog altyd hier gewees: Die storie van 'n Stellenbosse gemeenskap* (Cape Town: Tafelberg, 2007), pp. 114-40.

white communities were at quite different levels of socio-economic development. English-speakers earned an income of at least half more than that of Afrikaners and nearly a quarter of Afrikaners were deemed to be 'poor whites' – people so destitute that they could not maintain what was called a white living standard. A qualified vote could well exclude large numbers of poor Afrikaners, threatening to relegate the NP to the fate of a permanent opposition. Increasingly, leaders of the Cape NP began arguing that coloured voters had to be put on a separate roll.

The first major weakening of the coloured vote occurred as a result of the electoral reforms of 1930–31. The franchise was extended to white women, but not to coloured women. Virtually all qualifications were removed in the case of whites, but not in the case of coloured people. The law allowed anyone to challenge the registration of a voter. The onus of proof rested on the voter in court – a humiliating and time-consuming procedure. Invariably, it was coloured voters who were challenged. General Hertzog denied that he had promised coloureds the vote on the same basis as whites; he had only promised they would 'eventually be included with us politically'.[12]

Overall, coloured people lived in a grey area in which there was neither integration nor mandatory segregation. Municipal offices in the Western Cape did not have segregated counters. There was very little organised mixed sport, but coloured people were admitted to performances in the Cape Town City Hall. A few cinemas in the inner city of Cape Town sold tickets to coloureds and seated them at the back or on the balcony. The South African Library was open to all, as were the Art Gallery and the Museum. There were no beaches or municipal gardens or parks marked 'Europeans only'. In 1948 the coloured newspaper *The Sun* summarised the situation: 'In the past it had been the accepted thing for the semi-whites to keep themselves to their places of employment, businesses and entertainment and wherever else it was expedient for them to keep the false flag flying.'[13]

'Bright young men'

Anthony Delius, an outstanding liberal commentator, pointed out that in proposing solutions to the racial problem, the nationalist intelligentsia appropriated the good things in Afrikaner history, particularly the quest for cultural pride, group autonomy and freedom.[14] In defending what became known as apartheid, they argued that they 'granted' (the Afrikaans word *gun* carries much more weight) to the black and coloured communities what they valued themselves. In their view,

---

12 Gavin Lewis, *Between the Wire and the Wall: A History of South African 'Coloured' Politics* (Cape Town: David Philip, 1988), pp. 144-48.

13 *The Sun*, 27 August 1948, editorial.

14 Anthony Delius, 'The missing liberal policy', *Forum*, 1952, pp. 40-41.

coloured or black separateness would imbue these communities with a sense of ethnic pride and purpose.

The first printed record of the term 'apartheid', used in its modern sense, dates back to 1929. In addressing a conference of the Free State Dutch Reformed Church (DRC) on missionary work, held in the town of Kroonstad, Reverend Jan Christoffel du Plessis said: 'In the fundamental idea of our missionary work and not in racial prejudice one must seek an explanation for the spirit of apartheid that has always characterized our [the DRC's] conduct.' He rejected a missions policy that offered blacks no 'independent national future'.[15] By 'apartheid' Du Plessis meant that the Gospel should be taught in a way that strengthened the African 'character, nature and nationality' – in other words, the *volkseie* (the people's own). Africans had to be uplifted 'on their own terrain, separate and apart'. Blacks and whites had to worship separately to 'ensure the survival of a handful of [Afrikaner] people cut off from their national ties in Europe'.

Du Plessis's main concern was finding a policy that concentrated on the *eie*, or that which was 'one's own', and which promoted what he called the *selfsyn*, or being oneself.[16] Implicit was the view that only identification with one's own ethnic community was authentic. Du Plessis envisaged the development of autonomous, self-governing black churches as a counter to English missionaries, whose converts tried to copy 'Western civilization and religion'.[17]

Apartheid as a term caught on slowly. It was only in 1943 that it first appeared in an editorial in *Die Burger*, when it was referred to as the 'accepted viewpoint of the Afrikaner'. A year later DF Malan became the first person to use it in parliament.[18] Stellenbosch academics and a few politicians with seats in the Boland promoted it in Malan's small circle, which dominated the NP. Academics and clergymen with links to Potchefstroom and people in the executive council of the Afrikaner Broederbond, whose head office was in Johannesburg, also played a role in developing the apartheid ideology, but their contribution was not of the same order as that of the members of Malan's inner circle.

Among the most prominent supporters of Malan in the western Cape were Albertus Geyer (editor of *Die Burger*), Paul Sauer (son of JW Sauer, who had been one of the leading Cape liberals at the turn of the century) and Eben Dönges (a senior advocate). Closest to Malan was Sauer, born in 1898. A key experience in

---

15 An earlier, eccentric use of the word 'apartheid' is recorded by Irving Hexham, *The Irony of Apartheid* (Toronto: Edward Mellen Press, 1981), p. 188.

16 JC du Plessis, 'Die ideale van ons kerk in Sendingwerk', *Die NG Kerk in die OVS en die naturellevraagstuk* (Bloemfontein: Nasionale Pers), pp. 22-25. I wish to thank Richard Elphick for pointing me to this pamphlet. See also Louis Louw (compiler), *Dawie: 1946-1964* (Cape Town: Tafelberg, 1964), p. 49.

17 Hermann Giliomee, *The Afrikaners: Biography of a People* (Cape Town: Tafelberg, 2009), pp. 454-55.

18 Giliomee, *The Afrikaners*, p. 475.

his career was his defeat as NP candidate in the Stellenbosch seat in 1924. In a by-election in 1923 Sauer narrowly lost the Stellenbosch seat by 21 votes, but in the general election of 1924 he lost by 470 votes after the SAP had registered 600 additional coloured voters. Sauer's biographers recorded his reaction: 'He hates this dishonesty, this abuse.' He accused the SAP of opportunistically registering as many coloured voters as was necessary to ensure victory and of forgetting about them afterwards.[19]

Assuming power, Hertzog's Pact government, made up of the NP and the Labour Party, tried to consolidate its coloured support. It increased spending on coloured education by 60%, which caused the number of coloured children in school to grow by 30%. Formally the Pact's 'civilised labour' policy had to give coloureds as well as whites preference in public works and on the railways, but invariably whites were favoured over coloureds. The Pact also refused to remove the disparity in pay between whites and coloured people. Despite the increased spending on coloured education, the differential in the spending on whites and coloureds remained the same. It introduced an old-age pension for coloureds, but the maximum was only 70% of that of whites.

In 1929 the NP won both the Stellenbosch and Paarl seats with the help of coloured support, but attracted less than 10% of the coloured vote in the Cape Province. Sauer said after the election: 'The services of the government during the past five years had merited better support from the coloured community.'[20] Sauer strongly urged Dr Malan to put coloured voters on a separate electoral roll. After its establishment in 1934, the NP under Malan's leadership decided to abandon the canvassing of coloured voters. Bruckner de Villiers, who won the Stellenbosch seat in 1929, strongly disagreed with this. He thought his 1929 campaign, which included targeting spending on the coloured voters, showed the NP could win coloured support. After the 1938 election, in which he lost the Stellenbosch seat by 30 votes against the UP's Henry Fagan, he commented scathingly on the 'bright young men' in parliament whose 'clever plans' cost the party several Cape seats, while winning only one seat in the Transvaal.[21]

Another influential figure was Albertus Geyer, who received his doctorate in history in Berlin and became editor of *Die Burger* at the age of 35. Responding to Fusion, Geyer proposed that the NP build an opposition out of 'the [Afrikaner] working class, the republican Afrikaners and the Afrikaner intelligentsia'.[22] The

19   Dirk and Johanna de Villiers, *Paul Sauer* (Cape Town: Tafelberg, 1977), pp. 33-34.
20   Thelma Shifrin, 'New Deal for the Coloured People: A study of NP policies towards the coloured people, 1924-1929', BAHons dissertation, UCT, 1962, p. 62.
21   Gert Pretorius, *Bruckner de Villiers: Man van die daad* (Cape Town: HAUM, 1959), pp. 116-17.
22   At van Wyk, *Die Keeromstraatkliek* (Cape Town: Tafelberg, 1983), p. 117.

rapid expansion of the white educational system in the first 25 years of Union had produced an Afrikaner intelligentsia much larger and more self-assured than the one that had joined Malan and Hertzog in 1914–15, when they founded the NP. Between 1924 and 1948 Geyer earned the nickname of *Ysterman* (Iron Man) for his tough criticism of Fusion, the United Party programme and liberal alternatives to segregation and apartheid.

A third key figure was Theophilus Ebenaeser (Eben) Dönges, son of a Dutch Reformed Church minister. He received an MA degree in philosophy with distinction from the University of Stellenbosch, and went on to the London School of Economics where he received a doctorate in law before he turned 26. On his return to Cape Town, he accepted an offer to be editor of *The South African Nation*, published by Nasionale Pers. The journal strongly supported Hertzog's racial policy, in which the political and economic integration of whites and coloureds was an important part, calling it 'an act of statesmanship'.[23] Dönges was admitted to the Cape Bar as advocate and soon co-authored a book on municipal law. John Vorster, whom he lectured in civil law at Stellenbosch, stated that he was 'captivated by his silver tongue'.[24] After 1933 Dönges rejected his earlier view that white and coloured people belonged together. He now regarded as social evils all forms of racial levelling, ranging from the common voters' roll and mixed marriages to *saamwonery* (racial cohabitation).[25]

NP leaders showed the same lack of consistency in the way they expressed themselves about blacks. In 1921, after the police near Queenstown had shot dead 163 blacks who were members of a religious sect, DF Malan sent a telegram to an assembly of blacks gathering there. 'No race has shown greater love for South Africa than the Natives. Therein he, the Native, assuredly is a pattern of true patriotism and is entitled to take his place side by side with the Nationalists in the common political arena.'[26] In the election campaign of 1929, however, the NP yielded to pressure from the right wing and made the main issue the 'preservation of a white South Africa'. It became known as the 'Black Peril' election.[27]

As leader of the UP, Hertzog pushed ahead with his plans to remove Africans from the voters' roll. In the 1936 debate Malan as leader of the *Gesuiwerde* NP opposed the purchase of more land for the African reserves, proposed as a form of compensation. Funds should go instead to buying land for white tenants, share-

---

23 Anton Bekker, *Eben Dönges: Lewe en loopbaan tot 1948* (Stellenbosch: Papirus, 1988), pp. 55-56.

24 John D'Oliveira, *Vorster – The Man* (Johannesburg: Ernest Stanton, 1977), p. 33.

25 Bekker, *Eben Dönges*, pp. 143-45.

26 Eddie Roux, *Time Longer than Rope: A History of the Black Man's Struggle for Freedom in South Africa* (Madison: University of Wisconsin Press, 1966), p.184.

27 Henriëtta Lubbe, '*Die Burger* en die "Swart Gevaar" – propaganda in die parlementêre verkiesing-stryd, 1928-29', Master's dissertation, University of South Africa, 1991.

croppers and *bywoners*. The acquisition of land by blacks had to happen 'on their own initiative and according to their own real needs'.[28] With the doubling of the reserves a fait accompli, Malan and his followers reconsidered their view. They soon proceeded to make a new claim: the land set aside for blacks was sufficient to deny them representation outside these areas. Such attitudes confirmed the liberal belief that, as Jan Hofmeyr observed in 1937, 'constructive segregation' was not practical in view of white obduracy.[29]

Verwoerd and race

Hendrik Frensch Verwoerd did not move in Malan's circles, but his work among the poor whites soon became widely known. Born in Amsterdam in 1901, Verwoerd was the son of Dutch immigrants who settled in Cape Town in 1903. His father was a building contractor who did missionary work among the coloured people in Wynberg in his free time. He soon took his family to Bulawayo, where he served as a missionary under the auspices of the local DRC congregation.

Verwoerd enrolled at the University of Stellenbosch in 1919 and received a doctorate in psychology with distinction at the age of 23. He quickly established a reputation as a man with a brilliant mind and strong personality. In 1925–27 he visited some German and US universities on a postdoctoral study tour. German academic life did not make any particular impression on him, but he returned from the United States impressed with the work social scientists were doing. By the mid-1930s many leading South Africans had developed such a fascination with the United States that Lord Hailey noted in his diary, 'South Africa regards itself as the USA in the making.'[30] Verwoerd would be no exception in thinking that South Africa could become a dynamic state that could successfully deal with major problems like poverty and racial conflict through research and planning. He adopted the positivist approach of the time that rejected speculative thought in favour of research based on empirical inquiry, the identification of social patterns, and the drafting of legislation that anticipated future trends and possible conflicts.

Back in Stellenbosch Verwoerd was appointed professor of psychology in 1927 and professor of sociology in 1931. He soon turned his attention to the so-called 'poor white' problem that had begun to dominate the national agenda. It was to a large degree an Afrikaner problem. The number of Afrikaner poor was put at 250 000, or a quarter of the Afrikaner population. Verwoerd made his name

---

28 PW Coetzer and JH le Roux, *Die Nasionale Party, 1V: 1934-1940* (Bloemfontein: INEG, 1986), p. 57.

29 Saul Dubow, *Racial Segregation and the Origins of Apartheid in South Africa* (London: Macmillan, 1989), p. 170.

30 Roberta Millar, 'Science and Society in the Early Career of HF Verwoerd', *Journal of Southern African Studies*, 19, 4, 1993, p. 646.

nationally by his speech to the *Volkskongres* on the problem held in 1934 in Kimberley. In his analysis he put a premium on the role of the state in targeted intervention, particularly in establishing a department of social work and providing for the professional training of social workers. The state had to coordinate its activities with those of local organisations founded to promote social welfare and health.[31]

Verwoerd also started grappling with the racial issue. There has been speculation that he was influenced by Nazi ideas during his visit to Germany, but there is no evidence of this. He visited Germany before the Nazi party had established itself as a major contender for power. In his class notes, prepared after his return from Germany, he dismissed the idea of biological differences among the 'big races', adding that because there were no differences, 'this was not really a factor in the development of a higher civilization by the Caucasian race'. He also rejected the notion of different innate abilities. He observed that what appeared to be differences in skills in the case of Europeans and Africans were simply differences in culture due to historical experience.[32]

Between the two World Wars white South Africans were strongly race conscious. Some, like Verwoerd, rejected racism defined as a belief in the inherent biological or genetic superiority of whites. But his thinking could be considered racial because he believed that biological descent, along with culture, were immutable attributes of social identity.[33] In this he did not differ fundamentally from most of the white intelligentsia in South Africa or, for that matter, opinion formers in Europe or the European colonies in Africa or Asia.

Testifying in 1935 to the Wilcocks Commission on coloured people, Verwoerd still showed no inclination to draw a sharp line between the white and coloured communities. Considering the problems of the white poor and the coloured poor as interrelated, he advocated a single department of social welfare to deal with white and coloured poverty. When asked if there ought to be a policy of equal opportunity or segregation between white and coloured, he replied: 'I believe you cannot lay down a firm principle. Sometimes you must differentiate because you cannot always provide the same thing for both.' He supported job reservation for the poor whites, but only as a temporary measure.[34] There was little evidence of the politician of later years with his belief in the most rigid form of apartheid.

---

31 Giliomee, *The Afrikaners*, pp. 349-52.

32 Millar, 'Science and Society', pp. 638-46.

33 For a discussion see Christoph Marx, 'Hendrik Verwoerd's Long March to Apartheid; Nationalism and Racism in South Africa', Manfred Berg and Simon Wendt (eds), *Racism in the Modern World: Historical Perspectives on Cultural Transfer and Adaptation* (New York: Berghahn Books, 2011), pp. 281-302.

34 Giliomee, *Nog altyd hier gewees*, p. 100. Verwoerd's testimony is in Union Government 54-1937, *Report of the Commission of Enquiry regarding the Cape Coloured Population of the Cape Colony*, pp. 2941-52.

The white intelligentsia in general shared a rejection of miscegenation, but while UP leaders and their supporters in the press wanted to curtail this by way of social sanctions, Verwoerd and Dönges insisted on a legal ban on all mixed marriages. In the campaign for the 1938 election Verwoerd – now a newspaper editor – had a hand in an election poster that was later called the 'Bastard poster'. Under the banner 'Vote for South Africa and protect the *volk* and its descendants from mixed marriages', it showed a white woman and black man with two coloured children sitting in a state of despair in front of their dilapidated house. There was an outcry and some people argued that the poster sullied the honour of white women.

Verwoerd was unrepentant. In language that foreshadowed that of the NP of the 1950s, he insisted it was his duty to warn against dangers that threatened the *volk*. One of them was the incidence of mixed marriages that sprung from racially mixed slums where the poor of all races lived. He displayed something of his future relentless demand for avoiding 'the thin end of the wedge' by arguing that 250 000 people would be produced in three generations if the 1 300 couples who had entered into mixed marriages between 1926 and 1936 all had at least four children who also married across racial lines.[35]

Verwoerd had joined Malan's NP, which he viewed as the only party that took the problem of white poverty seriously. He had accepted the editorship of the Johannesburg daily *Die Transvaler*, believing he could use it as a vehicle for tackling Afrikaner poverty and slum conditions in the cities. Almost 40% of adult male Afrikaners in Johannesburg were clustered in four job categories: unskilled labourer, mineworker, railway worker and bricklayer.

In Verwoerd's view 'every Afrikaner, rich or poor, must feel that they belong to a single *volk* and were their brother's keeper'. When government adopted a policy that allowed 'decent' blacks to be served in coffee rooms on stations, he objected. 'There should be no separation between "raw" and "decent" blacks.' The better educated or trained blacks, just like their Afrikaner counterparts, should learn that they are their poorer brothers' keepers and should oppose any effort to impose segregation between the rich and the poor.[36] He stressed the duty of serving one's community above almost everything else.

Verwoerd and nationhood

Verwoerd was a child of immigrants from Europe. There was a strange abstract quality in his tendency to see South Africa through the prism of the community of nation-states in Europe, where the boundaries of states were fixed and the authority

---

35 Dioné Prinsloo, 'Die Johannesburg-periode in Dr HF Verwoerd se loopbaan', doctoral dissertation, Rand Afrikaans University, 1979, pp. 477-85.

36 Prinsloo, 'Die Johannesburg-periode', p. 327.

of national governments undisputed. For him, whites in South Africa had the same rights to their own country as the Dutch or the French.

A biographer makes the valid point that while nationalism tends to come easily for those who interpret it as an extension of family and community, for immigrants and their children it is a willed action and a deliberate choice.[37] Verwoerd consciously willed to be an Afrikaner. He was the first student in South Africa who completed his studies from undergraduate level to doctoral dissertation in Afrikaans, although he spoke and wrote English well. As a politician he extolled Afrikaner history in a way that irritated his cabinet colleague Ben Schoeman: 'He always spoke of our ancestors, our glorious past . . . It was as if he wanted to convince himself and his supporters of his *Afrikanerskap*'.[38] Yet Verwoerd's views on nationhood were not as rigid as many of his critics claimed. During the 1930s he generally avoided terms like the 'organic' Afrikaner *volk* with its own *volksiel*, fixed identity, unique calling and separate destiny.[39] For him the Afrikaners were a distinct segment of the white nation whose two white communities had to stand together.

While Verwoerd mainly used secular arguments to justify apartheid, he realised that the support of Afrikaans churches for apartheid was indispensable for spreading the message that the policy was just. When the synod of the Transvaal Dutch Reformed Church accepted a report that used the Tower of Babel and the Old Testament history of Israel as justifications for apartheid, Verwoerd wrote that 'the Afrikaners' survival struggle against millions of non-whites would become ever more difficult. Afrikaners would prevail if they clung to a single idea: "It was in accordance with God's will that different races and *volke* exist".'[40]

'A people rescues itself'

Both Dönges and Verwoerd played a key role in the *Ekonomiese Volkskongres* of 1939, a congress held to mobilise Afrikaner capital and capture a share of industry and commerce for Afrikaners. The spark for this was the 1938 centenary celebrations of the Great Trek. Free State church leader JD 'Father' Kestell suggested at one of the meetings that the best tribute to the Voortrekkers would be to save poor Afrikaners through a *reddingsdaad*, or act of rescue. He stressed that only limited help could be expected from the state or the corporate world. His call that *'n Volk red homself* (a people rescues itself) captured the popular imagination.

The idea of holding a congress quickly gained momentum. Both Dönges and

37   Henry Kenney, *Architect of Apartheid: HF Verwoerd – An Appraisal* (Johannesburg: Jonathan Ball: 1980), pp. 20-22.

38   Ben Schoeman, *My lewe in die politiek* (Johannesburg: Perskor, 1978), p. 288.

39   AN Pelzer (ed.), *Verwoerd Speaks* (Johannesburg: APB, 1966), pp. 206-11.

40   *Die Transvaler*, 16 February 1947; Johan Kinghorn, 'Groei van 'n teologie', Johan Kinghorn (ed.), *Die NG Kerk en apartheid* (Johannesburg: Macmillan, 1986), pp. 102-03.

Verwoerd were members of the 1939 *Volkskongres*. Here Dönges propagated an Afrikaner finance house, and Verwoerd made the case for an Afrikaner consumer association that could assist Afrikaans enterprises and offer a service to Afrikaans customers. The *Volkskongres* created three institutions: a finance house, a chamber of commerce and an organisation to assist in a 'rescue action'. The most important was the finance house, Federale Volksbeleggings (FVB), controlled by Sanlam. Afrikaners were asked to participate in conventional investment in shares in sound Afrikaans enterprises. One of FVB's first loans to a small Afrikaner enterprise was to a company belonging to a young entrepreneur, Anton Rupert.

The mobilisation of Afrikaner savings and capital was received unfavourably in some influential English quarters. The *Rand Daily Mail* declared that 'the sponsors of economic segregation in trade and industry cannot ultimately avoid the charge that they are fanning the flames of racial bitterness in South Africa'.[41] In 1941 Dönges entered parliament as an NP member representing a Free State constituency. He used his new member's speech to defend the economic mobilisation of Afrikaners. He cited figures showing that in 1934–35 Afrikaners earned only one third of the total national income and that the average income of white non-Afrikaners was 40% higher than that of the average Afrikaner.

Dönges argued that it was not in the general interest for a large section of the population not to have its legitimate share of commerce and industry. It would be much sounder if both white communities were properly represented in every area of the economy. The commercial and industrial sectors would also benefit because there would be a better understanding of the problems in these sectors if Afrikaners played a larger role. The 'race' conflict between the two white communities would be mitigated if there were a more equal division of the economic cake and if white poverty was not restricted to Afrikaners.

He stressed that Afrikaners were determined to act as a group to increase their share fairly and peacefully. In his words: 'The Afrikaners had no right to expect others to help them and were too proud to ask for help from others to work out their economic salvation.' But, he added, they also had the right to ask English-speakers to maintain at least a 'benign neutrality' to allow Afrikaners to undertake their economic initiatives.[42]

Between 1939 and the mid-1970s Afrikaners made strong economic advances. Their share of the private sector grew from less than 10% in 1939 to over 20%. The star entrepreneur was Anton Rupert, who expressed himself in the classic idiom of the *Volkskongres*. He defined his firm's goal as that of furthering 'our nation's progress'

---

41 *Rand Daily Mail*, 15 July 1941, cited by GD Scholtz, *Die ontwikkeling van die politieke denke van die Afrikaners* (Johannesburg: Perskor, 1984), vol. 8, p. 61.
42 *Debatte van die Volksraad*, 15 April 1941, col. 6364-69.

and of helping Afrikaners to gain 'their rightful place in industry and their future as employers and employees'.[43] The economic profile of Afrikaners changed dramatically. By 1939 only one third of Afrikaners were in white-collar occupations, but by 1970 this figure had risen to more than two thirds.

Johannesburg days

A formative period in Verwoerd's career was between 1937 and 1948 in Johannesburg, when he was the founding editor of the morning paper *Die Transvaler*. Here he was exposed at first hand to the rapid urbanisation of blacks fleeing destitution in the reserves. In 1939 Verwoerd wrote: 'Reform has to start today . . . Tomorrow will be too late.' At the end of 1945 he called for action against the 'reign of terror' of criminals at a protest meeting. Two years later he wrote that tackling crime was not enough. 'What is obviously necessary is that the government should return large numbers of natives and their families to their places of origin. The government and the country are confronted with a crisis.'[44] He deplored the fate of poor Afrikaners having to bear the brunt of the black influx in the appalling slums of the western suburbs of Johannesburg. *The Star* also warned about an uncontrolled influx and the potential dangers of slums.[45]

The stream of rural blacks to the towns and cities accelerated after the end of the war. Dismal squatter camps mushroomed as a result of poor planning. Crime was rife as desperately poor people scrambled for some means to live. HV Morton wrote: 'There is no doubt that the increased crime on the Rand is due to the wartime over-crowding and the bad housing conditions in these locations [Pimville, Orlando and Sophiatown]. But what a problem it is. Where does the reformer begin?'[46]

Verwoerd backed the call from a member of the Natives Representative Council who asked for black traders to replace whites and Asians, who were allegedly exploiting their black customers. He wrote that the policy of segregation offered blacks protection and care, but it also rejected any form of social levelling. 'It gives the native a chance to develop that which is his own and to develop pride and self-respect instead of being humiliated in an effort to mimic whites.'[47] Here were the seeds of Verwoerd's stand against using white private capital in the development of the reserves.

---

43   WP Esterhuyse, *Anton Rupert* (Cape Town: Tafelberg, 1986), pp. 24-25.

44   GD Scholtz, *Dr HF Verwoerd* (Johannesburg: Perskor-Uitgewery, 1974), vol.1, pp. 112-13: Prinsloo, 'Die Johannesburg-periode', pp. 333-34.

45   *The Star*, 28 April 1947.

46   HV Morton, *In Search of South Africa* (London: Methuen and Co., 1948), p. 307.

47   Scholtz, *Verwoerd*, vol.1, p. 113.

Conflicting policies

From the early 1930s the growing numerical preponderance of blacks and the steady urbanisation of blacks dominated the political debate. Between the 1936 and the 1951 census, the total number of blacks increased by nearly 25%, from 6.59 million to 8.56 million, against the 8% increase in the population of whites, whose numbers grew from 2 million to 2.64 million. Between 1936 and 1960 the total black urban population would increase by nearly half.

At the root of the rapid rate of black urbanisation was the failing ability of the reserves to feed their inhabitants and the poor wages many farmers paid. Shortly after the Second World War Donald Molteno, one of the Native Representatives in parliament, depicted the conditions among the black population in bleak terms: 'Our whole African population has been uprooted. They have been proletarianised, pauperised and demoralised. Those – as yet comparatively few – that have acquired some measure of education are denied occupational opportunities and effective civil and political rights. Their consequent bitterness bodes ill for the future of the relations of black and white.'[48]

The Smuts government (1939–1948) had to deal not only with a white population divided over the country's participation in the Second World War, but also with the effects of rapid urbanisation. In 1942 Smuts said that large-scale black detribalisation and urbanisation were 'as great a revolution as has ever happened on this continent ... Segregation has fallen on evil days ... [Any] policy that had originated in fear was bound to fail.'[49] The government recognised the permanent status of urbanised blacks and began to provide better social services and education for all the subordinate communities. Blacks were paid old-age pensions and disability grants, and were included in unemployment insurance. Education for blacks was expanded. By 1945 the financial provision for blacks in secondary education was three times as much as it had been in 1936. In the primary standards free education, free books and free school meals were introduced.

By 1944, however, with the Allied powers sure to win the war, the tide of reform had begun to turn. Initially Native Affairs Minister Piet van der Byl and Secretary Douglas Smit decided to accept the permanence of a section of the black urban population. They rejected migrant labour, except in the mining industry.[50] But, as Van der Byl noted, a crucial question remained unresolved: was the government's policy still the traditional one of segregation, or had it been replaced by integration? Unwisely, he raised the issue in the UP caucus and a predictable battle broke

48 Phyllis Lewsen, *Voices of Protest: From Segregation to Apartheid* (Johannesburg: Ad Donker, 1988), p. 266.
49 Cited by P Smit and JJ Booysen, *Swart verstedeliking* (Cape Town: Tafelberg, 1981), p. 24.
50 Piet Meiring, *Tien politieke leiers* (Cape Town: Tafelberg, 1973), p. 209.

out between the liberal and conservative factions. Smuts was furious and hardly spoke to him for several months.[51] After the war the government renewed the policy of limiting black urbanisation to a minimum. In 1946 Van der Byl announced that the sale of railway tickets to blacks in the reserves would be restricted to those who could prove that they had previously been employed in urban work.

At a loss for a way forward, Smuts appointed Henry Fagan, a former UP cabinet minister and now a judge, to head a commission to investigate the issue of African urbanisation. Born in 1889, Fagan was a graduate of the University of Stellenbosch who followed Hertzog into the UP. Fagan's report, published early in 1948, challenged the idea that blacks could be confined solely to the reserves. It argued that from both a moral and economic point of view it was imperative to allow migrant labourers' families to join them in the city in order to stabilise the labour force. The stream of blacks to towns and cities could be 'guided and regulated, and may be perhaps also limited . . . but cannot be stopped or turned in the opposite direction'. Any policy based on the proposition that Africans in towns were all temporary migrants 'would be a false policy'. The reserves were so overcrowded and overstocked that it was unrealistic to believe they could accommodate urban blacks as well.

Instead of advocating a final and definite solution, the commission recommended neither integration nor segregation, but the 'in-between option' of parallel structures for white and black communities. The approach had to be an evolutionary one: 'The relationship [between whites and blacks] will always be fluctuating and changing, for life is dynamic and never stands still – and a cut-and-dried solution is therefore something that cannot be.' What was needed was 'the constant adaptation to changing conditions, constant regulation of contacts and smoothing out of difficulties between the races so that all may make their contribution and combine their energies for the progress of South Africa'.[52]

This recommendation did not exclude using the reserves as part of a solution. Fagan would later refer to an extensive study of the territories by the Social and Economic Planning Council, which stated that the policy 'should be directed towards the ideal of the Reserves as the home of the settled, stable Native population'. However, the latter report added an important rider: 'No Reserve policy will make it possible for South Africa to evade the issues raised by the presence of Natives in European farming areas and urban areas. This must be considered on its own merits.' Fagan calculated that at least a million of the 2.3 million blacks who lived in the urban areas, according to the 1951 census, had been there for a generation or more.[53]

In its 1948 election manifesto the UP made no reference to the reserves as part

51   Meiring, *Tien politieke leiers*, p. 208.
52   UG 28-48 *Report of the Native Laws Commission*, see esp. pp. 4, 13, 18-29, 45-50.
53   Henry Fagan, *Our Responsibility* (Stellenbosch: Universiteitsuitgewers, 1960), pp. 29-30.

of the political system. It pledged the extension of the rights and functions of the Natives Representative Council (NRC) and 'other native bodies' and 'their general equipment with powers to run their own affairs'. It also committed itself to provide proper accommodation to a stable black urban labour force and the opportunity for blacks to participate to an increasing extent in their own local government in their own townships.[54] But the party also rejected a policy of 'equality and assimilation'.[55]

A watershed election

The Second World War and the anticipation of freedom for subordinate nations made the black leadership in South Africa more assertive. By 1946 the NRC, established in 1936 as a mouthpiece for black opinion, had become increasingly exasperated with its lack of power. It rejected the defence of government policies by Jan Hofmeyr, deputy prime minister and the leading liberal in cabinet. It declared that the government had made no attempt to deal with the pass laws, the colour bar in industry or political rights, and still had not recognised the African Mineworkers' Union.

For Smuts, political power for Africans was an unthinkable concession. In 1947 he tentatively proposed to the NRC the establishment of 'an all-Native elective body', which would be given increasing 'executive authority in the development of the Native Reserves'. The council rejected this, demanding black representation at all levels of government from municipal councils to parliament.[56] Smuts told Edgar Brooks that 'our native policy would have to be liberalized at a modest pace but public opinion has to be carried with us'. Until this was secured, his approach was 'practical social policy away from politics', carried out as finances permit.[57]

The NP under DF Malan appointed a committee led by Paul Sauer to prepare a report on which it could base racial policy for the 1948 election. The report of the so-called Sauer Commission reflected all the ambiguities of the leadership's thinking. It spoke of 'total apartheid' between whites and 'natives' as the eventual 'ideal and goal', but added that it was unrealistic. The thrust of the report was the elimination of 'surplus' black labour, not black labour, and the channelling of sufficient labour to the mines, farms and industry.[58]

The report wanted the reserves to be turned into 'the true fatherland of the Native'. 'Prestige and status' had to be accorded to the 'natives' in every sphere in the

54   WA Kleynhans, *SA algemene verkiesingsmanifeste* (Pretoria: Unisa, 1987), p. 314.
55   Alexander Hepple, *Verwoerd* (Harmondsworth: Penguin Books, 1967), p. 113.
56   Gwendolen Carter, *The Politics of Inequality: South Africa since 1948* (London: Thames and Hudson, 1958), p. 358.
57   Rodney Davenport, *South Africa: A Modern History* (Johannesburg: Macmillan, 1987), p. 343.
58   Kleynhans, *SA algemene verkiesingsmanifeste*, p. 327.

reserves. Leaders there had to become the 'spokesmen of the Bantu'. A greater variety of economic activities had to be established in these areas.[59] The report urged the retention of the 'white character' of the cities. Blacks in urban areas had to be treated as visitors who could never claim equal political and social rights with whites. The state had to provide a form of education to blacks based on their own national character and cultural level.[60]

The NP's election manifesto presented apartheid as 'the guarantee for racial peace'. Territorial segregation between whites and blacks had to be introduced. The 'native reserves' had to be developed as the true fatherland of blacks. The economic development of these territories had to be promoted. Schools had to be provided here rather than in the townships. A 'Christian-National' curriculum, anchored in the ethnic character of the child, had to be introduced. All urban blacks had to be located in townships. They were to be regarded as visitors who could never enjoy equal political rights with whites.

For coloured people, who were seen as occupying a middle position between whites and blacks, the Sauer report recommended social, residential, industrial and political segregation. They had to be encouraged to develop their own national pride and self-respect. It recommended the establishment of a Coloured Representative Council for the Cape Province, consisting mostly of elected representatives, and a special state department. The report saw Indians as an alien community, who had to be repatriated as far as that was possible.[61] The NP's manifesto for the 1948 election was largely based on the Sauer report. The coloured community would be given the opportunity to develop on its own and would be offered protection against unfair competition with blacks.[62]

The NP in alliance with the Afrikaner Party won the election with a narrow margin of just five seats. It had captured only 40% of the votes cast. The result strengthened the NP's resolve to remove coloured voters from the electoral roll. Between 1937 and 1945 the number of coloured voters had doubled, turning many constituencies into marginal seats. In the constituencies of Worcester (where Eben Dönges won), Paarl and Malmesbury, the NP's margin of victory was less than 1 000 votes.

A fork in the road?

In 1948 the NP took power and soon began to introduce its policy of apartheid. The question is whether 1948 represented a fork in the road – one where South Africa opted for increasing strife, isolation and repression instead of gradual ac-

---

59 Kleynhans, *SA algemene verkiesingsmanifeste*, pp. 314, 345.
60 BM Schoeman, *Parlementêre verkiesings in Suid-Afrika* (Pretoria: Aktuele Publikasies, 1977), p. 276.
61 Kleynhans, *SA algemene verkiesingsmanifeste*, pp. 320-23, 331.
62 Kleynhans, *SA algemene verkiesingsmanifeste*, p. 316.

commodation, mutual understanding and a peaceful resolution of the conflict, laying the foundation for high growth and the rapid reduction of poverty. There is a debate among historians whether apartheid should be considered as part and parcel of the policy of racial segregation or whether it represented a much more draconian form of racial oppression. Many assume that while racial discrimination did exist before 1948, it was not poisonous and that if the UP had remained in power it would have been able to expand social welfare and progressively broaden the franchise across racial barriers.[63]

As with all counter-factual discussions, the safest rule is to avoid wishful thinking. Incremental reform leading up to a non-racial, progressive order would have required exceptional leadership of the kind provided by Abraham Lincoln in abolishing slavery in the United States. Lincoln became president after drawing only 40% of the popular vote – as did the NP in 1948. Initially Lincoln had no intention of establishing racial equality, preferring emancipated slaves to be shipped out to be settled in other countries.

Gradually, and playing his cards exceptionally well, Lincoln managed to establish the broadest possible antislavery coalition to bring about emancipation and what he called 'the freedom of the free'. It was a development no one could have predicted in the mid-1850s. But ultimately it was the war that his government launched against the South that created an intense state of emergency. It allowed Lincoln to make his progressive moves and construct reform coalitions strong enough to abolish slavery as an institution.[64]

Could the end of segregation in South Africa have been achieved in similar fashion in the 1950s? To start with, there was no leader in the UP ranks as dynamic as Lincoln. Smuts was 80, exhausted and without vision. Hofmeyr was 54 in 1948, three years older than Lincoln was when he became president, but had no personal power base to speak of. While Lincoln had a reasonably solid base in the Republican Party, any reformers in post-1948 South Africa would have had great problems putting together a platform for reform. Smuts led a ruling party that had come to power purely on the contentious issue of South Africa's participation in the Second World War.

After the election of 1943, and with the Allies clearly on the winning path in the war, the enthusiasm for reform in the UP waned, as the experience of Piet van der Byl with the UP caucus in 1944 showed. At the same time, the radicalised urban

---

63 The view that a UP government could have established a substantially reformed social order is expressed in several chapters of the collection edited by Saul Dubow and Alan Jeeves, *South Africa's 1940s: Worlds of Possibilities* (Cape Town: Double Storey, 2005).

64 Eric Foner, *The Fiery Trial: Abraham Lincoln and American Slavery* (New York: WW Norton, 2010), p. 237.

black leadership was in no mood for modest concessions. Chapter 3 tells the story of Hendrik Verwoerd offering members of the Natives Representative Council 'the greatest possible measure of self-government' for urban blacks (see pp. 54-55). They rejected it because they demanded representation, along with whites, on all levels of government. Privately General Smuts conceded that his constituency was far from ready for it.

The only hope for liberals was that economic and social pressures would have forced recognition of the permanence of urban blacks and of the need to grant them political rights. But liberals had no theory of incorporation except a liberalism based on the rights of the individual, which was imported from the homogeneous British society. Liberals also had no electoral base. With Afrikaners making up close to 60% of the electorate and with the electoral system skewed in favour of rural constituencies, the UP would have needed to win between a fifth and a quarter of the Afrikaner vote. In 1958 the NP would win 103 out of 156 parliamentary seats on the basis of drawing 80% of Afrikaner votes and only 1% of English votes.[65] Dominated by English business and other middle-class English speakers, the UP had little to offer white workers and farmers, or lower-class English speakers, who shared the racial prejudices of the Afrikaner working class.

There was much those working to mobilise the NP as a party reaching out to all classes in the Afrikaner community could exploit. There were many grievances, real or imagined, about the way government treated Afrikaners during the war, and the scaling down of Afrikaans as an official language by government. It helped that Afrikaners were a homogeneous group. According to the 1946 census, some 89% of Afrikaners were concentrated in the income group R0–R6 000, with 9% in the class of R6 000–R12 000. Only 1% earned more than R12 000 (in 1980 prices). The Nationalist alliance that came to power in 1948 consummated the alliance of the Afrikaner intelligentsia and the workers, which Albertus Geyer had fifteen years earlier seen as the only possible basis for an NP victory (see p. 23).

Apartheid as a policy programme was a trade-off between the intelligentsia and the workers. The workers would tolerate the intelligentsia's vision of black homelands and an ideology purged of racial rhetoric. The intelligentsia would indulge the workers by accepting them as full members of the movement, bestowing on them public deference and protecting them from competition from black or coloured workers. What Afrikaner nationalists (along with probably most whites) wanted was a leader who could impose his scheme for systematic apartheid, regardless of

---

65   Jan Sadie, 'Politiek en taal: 'n Ontleding', *Die Burger,* 29 August 1958; Jan Sadie, 'Die demografie van die blanke Afrikanergemeenskap', *Journal for the Study of Economy and Econometrics,* 1998, 22, 3, pp. 17-24.

the intricate racial interdependencies, and who could explain and justify it in modern terms. Such a leader would soon appear. His name was Hendrik Verwoerd.

Chapter 2 will discuss the rise to power of Verwoerd and the crushing of his main source of opposition in the Afrikaner community, the Cape Nationalists. Chapter 3 will focus on Verwoerd's policies and their results.

Chapter 2

An Extraordinary Professor and the 'Cape Nats'

WHEN HENDRIK VERWOERD WAS APPOINTED TO DF MALAN'S CABINET IN 1950, he joined Eben Dönges, a leading figure of the group that Transvaal conservatives would later label the 'Cape Nats'. Although Verwoerd and Dönges had known each other from their student days at Stellenbosch and often shared platforms in building the Afrikaner nationalist movement, they were never close personally. Their contribution to the apartheid order was also different.

With his legal background, Dönges erected the statutory framework in which group areas and other forms of communal apartheid could be imposed without legal challenge. It was he who introduced the three bills dealing with population registration, group areas and the removal of the coloured vote – the bills that constituted the very foundation of what can be called communal apartheid. Verwoerd, a sociologist and an authority on social work, introduced the legislation dealing with black education, self-government for the homelands and a tougher form of influx control that constituted the basis of NP policy on blacks. He was the first leader who held up the vision of independent homelands for separate nations, which would form the core of apartheid ideology from the early 1960s.

There were also other major differences between the two men. For Dönges apartheid was a response to the immediate needs of the NP's Afrikaner constituency in the aftermath of the Second World War. In 1946 more than 40% of Afrikaners occupied blue-collar jobs. Without protection, the unskilled or poorly skilled Afrikaner workers would face tough competition from black and coloured workers. Also needing assistance was the farming community. Some 40% of Afrikaners were in farming in 1946, but within fourteen years this proportion would plunge to 16%. The majority of those who left farming had been unable to cope with the demands of commercial farming. Less than a third of Afrikaners were in white-collar jobs.[1]

Shortly after the NP's victory in 1948 Dönges told a foreign journalist that apartheid was intended to protect the present and next two generations against the dangers posed by a growing black and coloured population.[2] The implicit assumption

---

1   JL Sadie, *The Fall and Rise of the Afrikaner in the South African Economy* (University of Stellenbosch: Annale 2002/1), p. 54.
2   John Hatch, *The Dilemma of South Africa* (London: Dennis Dobson, 1953), p. 93.

was that whites, forming a small minority, would have to prepare themselves for the day they had to survive without a monopoly on power. In such an approach, policy was about process; the task of the policy maker was to keep the process alive and to leave enough room for manoeuvre through reforms.[3]

For Verwoerd, by contrast, apartheid was a political system based on clear and specific principles. Strong leadership had to ensure the system remained intact despite formidable challenges. Minor concessions or deviations constituted the thin edge of the wedge. To allow them would threaten the coherence of the system. Accordingly, Verwoerd wanted to force churches in white areas to apply for a permit to hold services attended by both whites and blacks. He also refused to accept black diplomats or Maoris as part of the New Zealand rugby team.

Someone who took a dim view of such actions was Ben Schoeman, a Transvaal colleague who sat with him in cabinet for sixteen years. He had started his career as a stoker on the railways and went on to become minister of labour. He believed Verwoerd's Achilles heel was race and that he was 'unbelievably short-sighted' on the issue.[4]

Earlier Schoeman also took Verwoerd on when they served in Strijdom's cabinet. He believed Verwoerd's suggestion to permit no black workers in the western Cape was utterly impractical. At a private meeting of cabinet ministers a furious row erupted when Verwoerd advocated holding up to the voters the ideal of complete territorial separation, although he realised it was unrealistic. Schoeman called this blatant fraud and wanted nothing to do with it. Tempers flared and Strijdom had to make peace.[5]

Verwoerd fought with leaders of the Cape Nats much more often. The NP was a federation of four provincial parties and most members of parliament were in the first place loyal to their respective provincial leaders and parties. Despite spending nearly twenty years in Stellenbosch, after his move to Johannesburg Verwoerd identified himself with the Transvaal NP and its radical policies. 'Provincialism', and in particular the Cape-Transvaal conflict, caused serious trouble in the NP. Tensions also existed between Nasionale Pers in Cape Town, with *Die Burger* as its flagship, and the NP-supporting papers in the north. Although Cape Afrikaners had secured funding for *Die Transvaler*, there was little love lost between Verwoerd and his close ally and Transvaal NP leader JG Strijdom on the one hand and, on the other, the Cape's NP leadership and senior managers and journalists at Nasionale Pers.

As editor of *Die Transvaler* Verwoerd made several serious errors of judgment.

---

3   The distinction between defending a fixed system and managing a process is taken from Samuel Huntington, 'Reform and Stability in a Modernizing, Multi-Ethnic Society', *Politikon*, 8, 1981.

4   Ben Schoeman, *My lewe in die politiek* (Johannesburg: Perskor, 1978), pp. 246-47.

5   Schoeman, *My lewe in die politiek*, p. 224.

In the very first issue he published a long article attacking Jewish 'over-representation' in business and the professions and proposing a quota system to enable Afrikaners to win their rightful share. This undoubtedly contributed to the paper's failure to attract advertising, which cast a shadow over its viability. Then in 1943 Verwoerd, in his private capacity, sued the editor and proprietor of *The Star* for defamation. The paper had alleged Verwoerd deliberately falsified news about the World War so as to promote the German cause.

In what was generally considered to be a poor judgment, Justice PA Millin, who understood no Afrikaans, found that Verwoerd did support Nazi propaganda in his paper and knowingly made it a tool of the Nazis in South Africa. The judge dismissed the libel action with costs. It was a heavy financial setback for Verwoerd, but there was no one in Johannesburg ready to help. DF Malan expressed sympathy, but added that Verwoerd was 'unwise' to sue without first consulting his board of directors. In the end Nasionale Pers decided to provide financial assistance to Voortrekkerpers in order to help Verwoerd. As is so often the case, the favour did not win friends.

In 1947 Verwoerd refused to publish any reports on the visit of the British royal family to South Africa, of which he strongly disapproved. The editors of *Die Burger* blamed Verwoerd's dominance of *Die Transvaler* for the paper's continuing financial troubles. Phil Weber saw Verwoerd as a charming man, but added that he 'becomes the victim of his own unbounded self-righteousness when he sits down in front of his typewriter'.[6] In an effort to counter provincialism and to get sufficient unity on contentious issues during the 1940s, NP leader DF Malan and the Nasionale Pers board of directors tried to set up a committee of party leaders and Nationalist editors. The historian of Nasionale Pers questioned the wisdom of trying to get the Nationalist papers to speak with one voice, adding 'Verwoerd would in any case not go along'.[7] Piet Meiring, his news editor at *Die Transvaler*, remembered his dogmatic self-assurance: 'He usually spoke the first and the last word. Those who thought differently did not easily put him off. I have never met anyone more convinced of his own case and ideas.'[8]

Provincial tensions were at their most severe in the decade after the 1948 election. Under JG Strijdom's leadership, the Transvaal NP won half of the NP's seats in 1948 and six more than the Cape NP, but received only two minor cabinet posts (Labour, and Lands and Irrigation). Malan curtly dismissed a memorandum from a number of Transvaal MPs asking for the appointment of Verwoerd to his cabinet. To Verwoerd, this must have been a blow. Malan relented some two years later after he had heard him speak in the Senate.

---

6 JC Steyn, *Penvegter: Piet Cillié van* Die Burger (Cape Town: Tafelberg, 2002), p. 100.

7 CFJ Muller, *Sonop in die Suide* (Cape Town: Nasionale Boekhandel, 1989), p. 680.

8 Piet Meiring, *Ons eerste ses premiers* (Cape Town: Tafelberg, 1972), p. 124.

There were other issues that rankled. The editor of *Die Burger* attended the meetings of the NP parliamentary caucus, a privilege not extended to the two northern Afrikaans press companies. Planning to enter the northern newspaper market, Nasionale Pers applied to government for an increased supply of newsprint. Strijdom, who became prime minister in 1954, made certain it was turned down.[9] As prime minister later, Verwoerd would keep a beady eye on Nasionale Pers. Although it was improper to do so, since he was a director of the two northern Afrikaans press companies, he tried to block the press group when in the mid-1960s it announced its plan to publish a Sunday paper in Johannesburg.[10] It was seen not only as competition from the more efficient Nasionale Pers, but also as a challenge to Transvaal dominance after 1954 when power in the NP shifted to the north.

A leader in the making

In 1950 Verwoerd became Minister for Native Affairs. He soon established a reputation as intellectually gifted and hard working, but he was not widely tipped as a future NP leader. The child of immigrants, he had arrived in the country when he was just three months old. There were no sources of wealth or family connections that could smooth the road to political power. To Cape Nationalists he came across as dogmatic, inflexible, rash and impervious to argument. Although he gave as good as he got in polemics or parliamentary debates, Verwoerd in many ways remained a professor. After Verwoerd's election as prime minister Stanley Uys, who served as parliamentary correspondent for a group of English-language newspapers in the 1950s and 1960s, wrote: 'Dr Verwoerd differs from you and me in this important way: we allow ourselves the conceit of thinking we are right; he *knows* he is right.'[11]

Looking back 50 years later, Uys emphasises Verwoerd's detachment, even aloofness: 'Verwoerd's personality did not fit into the general parliamentary personality. He was aloof with his thoughts and philosophies ... Hence his relative calmness.' Uys continues: 'The people around him (and in the outer-world) were his pupils. He knew all the answers and it was just a matter of explaining the details to his pupils. I don't recall him losing his temper and flaring up. The only times he seemed to be a little agitated was when he felt his message was not getting across – the pupils were too dumb to understand the message. Then he would put an extra vigour into his speeches, perhaps raise his voice a little.'[12]

By the end of the 1950s Verwoerd had developed enough standing in the Afrikaner nationalist movement to enable him as an outsider to defeat Dönges, one of the

9 Steyn, *Penvegter*, p.100.
10 Schalk Pienaar, *Getuie van groot tye* (Cape Town: Tafelberg, 1979), pp. 45-48.
11 Alex Hepple, *Verwoerd* (Harmondsworth: Penguin Books, 1967), p. 136.
12 E-mail communication from Stanley Uys, 10 November 2010.

most senior cabinet ministers, in the contest for the NP's leadership in 1958. According to Piet Meiring, a well-informed journalist who worked closely with Verwoerd, only three cabinet ministers voted for him. It was the solid support from 'Young Turks' from the Transvaal that clinched the victory. By the time Verwoerd died in 1966 he had built up a formidable reputation as a visionary leader that extended far beyond the shores of South Africa. Meiring remarks that he had a remarkable ability to instil confidence in people, even those outside NP ranks. Few could resist him if he turned on his 'charisma taps'.[13]

The qualities that above all forged the image of Verwoerd as leader were his unshakeable convictions and his willingness to wager his personal or political fortune in pursuing the things he believed in. To put the poor whites on the national agenda, he sacrificed the security of a tenured professorship in Stellenbosch to become a newspaper editor in Johannesburg. He had no training in journalism and the funds for the paper still had to be found. Sometimes, some of the staff's salaries could not be paid. Yet this did not deter him from continuing to express his ideas bluntly and uncompromisingly, making the tough task of attracting advertisements even harder. In 1948 Verwoerd had entered politics confident of being appointed to cabinet if the NP won the election. He performed well, but narrowly lost in the Alberton constituency, deemed to be a safe United Party (UP) seat. To his disappointment Malan did not appoint him to his first cabinet. He accepted a senatorship, but the board of directors of Voortrekkerpers turned down his offer to do the job of senator and editor simultaneously.

As a politician he displayed the audacity that characterised his early career. He did not hesitate to change his mind if the situation required it. In 1951 he did not envisage independent black states in the homelands, stating that 'self-government within one's own area is something entirely different from saying that South Africa is to be divided into a series of states'.[14] In 1959 he changed course sharply. He now promised independence to the homelands without consulting the NP caucus. In 1960 he called a referendum on a republic when there was no evidence of majority support. In 1961 he withdrew South Africa's application for continued membership of the Commonwealth although he had promised white voters he would fight for it. There seemed to be nothing he would not dare if he were convinced that daring was demanded.

Verwoerd as minister showed tremendous drive and energy. He was no ivory tower intellectual dabbling in politics. He sometimes put in eighteen hours' work in a day, routinely taking a carload of files from his office to study at home. He spent long hours discussing issues with his officials until he mastered the finest details.

---

13 Meiring, *Ons eerste ses premiers*, pp. 120-22.
14 *Debatte van die Volksraad*, 1951, col. 8361.

He travelled indefatigably to talk to African chiefs or headmen who supported his policies. He combined the work of an academically trained social engineer and a fact-finding journalist – all within the apartheid framework. But a fundamental flaw plagued his approach: he never spoke to even moderate black activists.

Verwoerd served as a cabinet minister at a time when concern was beginning to mount in NP leadership ranks about the apparent disarray over policy and ideology. DF Malan was unenthusiastic about self-governing homelands. According to his son, he was quite happy to stick to 'group areas apartheid'.[15] Dismay over the lack of leadership is particularly evident in the correspondence between two of his stalwart supporters, Albertus Geyer, ex-editor of *Die Burger* and at that point the High Commissioner in London, and *Die Burger* editor Phil Weber. 'What really is the conception that old Doctor [Malan] has of apartheid?' Geyer asked in a letter in January 1953. 'It seems as if it consists of nothing more than adopting a series of laws with a negative character ... Do we really want to have apartheid as something that is more than making our current position temporarily more secure?' Weber replied: 'We have to make haste with the implementation of the positive aspects of apartheid in order to win over the more conservative blacks, otherwise we are doomed. We cannot over the longer run govern black masses who are actively hostile to us.'[16]

Weber and Geyer were unhappy not only with the emphasis on 'negative apartheid', but with the fact that African urbanisation was continuing despite much tougher influx control measures. In 1953 Weber wrote to Geyer: 'We say that economic integration will lead to the granting of political rights and our downfall, but in the meantime we have been integrating faster than ever over the past ten years. It cannot go on this way. We must realise that apartheid is not separate entrances and counters. Our intelligentsia will probably force us to look facts in the eyes, if *Die Burger* does not do so. I sometimes think that we shall get apartheid but only after horrendous riots, as in India and Pakistan.'[17]

Ironically, in the light of his reputation in contemporary South Africa as the supreme racist of the NP era, Verwoerd, at least on the ideological level, actually tried to get away from race as the core feature of the political system. He told his son that individual-based liberalism had become the dominant ideology in the Western world and South Africa had to move away from traditional segregation to avoid being 'mauled by the millstones'.[18] He believed that one of the core principles

15   US Library, DF Malan Collection1/1/3268, 'Herinneringe aan my vader' by Daniël Malan, 1965, p. 48.

16   US Library, Weber Collection, Geyer-Weber, 31 January 1953; Weber-Geyer, 6 February 1953.

17   US Library, Weber Collection, Weber-Geyer, 6 February 1953.

18   WJ Verwoerd, 'Vader', WJ Verwoerd (compiler), *Verwoerd: So onthou ons hom* (Pretoria: Protea Boekhuis, 2001), pp. 52-54.

on which to rest an alternative to segregation was one recognised by the West – namely, national self-determination, which accords primacy to a distinctive *volk* with its distinctive state.

In an article published in a Stellenbosch magazine in 1950, he wrote that whites had to accept that 'non-whites, with their own national consciousness and ambitions, would refuse to live forever as subordinates while being integrated in the white community'.[19] But Verwoerd also stressed another principle that had become discredited in the West: explicit white privilege and exclusivity. He wrote that the government had to maintain and defend white or Western civilisation and had to ensure that there would be no economic or social levelling.[20]

For Verwoerd the prime duty of Nationalists was to devise a policy that took these facts soberly into account. They had to 'retain the tried and tested and natural Western outlook with respect to the advantages of individualism and to developing along one's own lines'. At the same time they had to pursue ways along which both whites and non-whites could exercise their rights separately in their circle without devouring each other or destroying their own nature.[21] As Henry Fagan pointed out, this line of thinking symbolised the fusion of two main principles in Afrikaner nationalist thinking: republicanism and apartheid, both propounding the separateness of people.[22] Better than anyone else Verwoerd could combine these two principles in a single forceful message.

In the course of the 1950s the idea of separate homelands where the different black 'nations' could realise their highest political and economic aspirations became the hub of NP ideology. Although the policy's application constantly reinforced racial inequality, racist rhetoric itself became taboo. MC de Wet Nel, who in 1958 succeeded Verwoerd as minister of native affairs, challenged a meeting to name a single instance where a white South African leader had recently said that the black man was doomed to permanent racial inferiority or could be deemed morally a lesser creature in the eyes of God.[23] The apartheid system spawned in growing measure its own black politicians and civil servants, whose courteous treatment was assured because they did not compete for power with or challenge their white counterparts.

It is difficult to conceive of apartheid as it took form in the 1960s without the immense impact of Verwoerd. Interviewing him just after he became prime minister, perceptive *Die Burger* journalist Rykie van Reenen was struck by 'his immense

---

19   HF Verwoerd, 'Waarom is ek 'n nasionalis?', *Stellenbosse Student*, 4, 1950, pp. 13-15.
20   Verwoerd, 'Waarom is ek 'n nasionalis?', p.14.
21   HF Verwoerd, 'Die Akademies-opgeleides en die toekoms', *Koers*, xxiv, 6, 1957, pp. 229-36.
22   HA Fagan, *Our Responsibility* (Stellenbosch: Stellenbosch University Press, 1960), p. 27.
23   MDC de Wet Nel, 'Waarom die beleid van apartheid?', *Tydskrif vir Rasse-aangeleenthede*, 11, 4, 1960, p. 174.

charm', his 'razor-sharp brain power' and his lack of even a modicum of self-doubt. When she asked him whether he could sleep at night, given the awesome responsibility of executing his policy, he replied that he slept very well, adding: 'You see, one does not have the problem of worrying whether one perhaps could be wrong.'[24]

Respected journalists writing in the 1960s saw Verwoerd as a political leader seriously grappling with daunting challenges in a way that did not benefit whites alone. The correspondent of the *Christian Science Monitor* wrote after Verwoerd became prime minister: 'There can be no doubting the sincerity of his belief that ultimately his actions will benefit the African people as a whole.'[25] Douglas Brown, a well-regarded British journalist writing for the *Daily Telegraph* during the 1950s, wrote that Verwoerd 'is seeking ways to avoid a racial clash, but too many publicists in the West seem to be trying to keep race antagonisms alive'.[26] Pulitzer Prize winner Allen Drury interviewed Verwoerd just before his death and wrote: 'I found him to be extremely intelligent, extremely competent, much superior in brains and ability to most of his noisy critics abroad . . . [He was] the only man who could possibly have continued to lead his people and his nation to a gradually more reasonable, and ultimately more humane, accommodation with other races.'[27]

Verwoerd never made any effort to hide that for him white interests were paramount and that he considered these interests legitimate. Addressing parliament, he said that he would do nothing 'in the interests of the Bantu at the expense of the White, because I would not take up a spade to turn the first sod in digging the grave of the white man'.[28] But he believed his actions would also benefit black people. This must be understood in the context of his view that blacks at that point were unable to compete against whites.

DF Malan was convinced that the lesser-skilled whites could not survive competition with blacks, but Verwoerd turned it around: whites would hold the stronger position for a long time, and blacks would be 'defeated in every phase of the struggle'. This was sure to give rise to an increasing sense of 'resentment and revenge' among them. The only possible way out was 'to adopt a development path divorced from each other'.[29]

---

24 *Die Burger,* Byvoegsel, 14 June 1957.
25 A report of 17 October 1958 cited by Garry Allighan, *Verwoerd, The End* (Cape Town: Purnell and Sons, 1961), p. xxxv.
26 Douglas Brown, *Against the World: A Study of White South African Attitudes* (London: Collins, 1966), p. 212.
27 Allen Drury, *'A Very Strange Society': A Journey to the Heart of South Africa* (London: Michael Joseph, 1967), p. 407.
28 Hepple, *Verwoerd,* p. 105.
29 *Senate Debates,* 1948, col. 227; AN Pelzer (ed.), *Verwoerd Speaks* (Johannesburg: APB, 1966), pp. 14-24.

Verwoerd had in mind the more skilled jobs for which very few blacks were trained. During the 1950s the level of black education was very low. In 1958 a mere 5% of university students were black, against 89% who were white. Although there was a massive expansion of black primary education in the 1950s and 1960s, very few blacks initially made it to secondary school. By 1970, 93% of rural blacks had not attained Standard 6 or higher, compared with a mere 4% of the white labour force.[30]

Verwoerd did not expect his policy to remain static. He told Carel Boshoff, his son-in-law who was about to become a missionary: 'You young men must do your job as thoroughly as possible, because there would be such an awakening of national consciousness among blacks in the next twenty years that whites won't enjoy much influence in their churches.'[31] When someone questioned the wisdom of establishing new black university colleges, Verwoerd replied: 'We shall have to negotiate frequently with [blacks] in the future over many issues, including education and politics. It will be better to negotiate with people who are well informed and educated.'[32] He hoped that these colleges would produce proponents of the policy of separate homelands for separate black national groups, while whites retained the bulk of the land. In this he was utterly mistaken.

Verwoerd's fundamental error, apart from basing his policy on flawed population projections (see pp. 58-59), was his assumption that his policy would ignite the enthusiasm of the main black ethnic groups for a state of their own instead of working for an inclusive, black-ruled South African nation. He believed there was no single African nation, but seven or eight nations, each eager to pursue a separate political destiny in its own state. It was a policy that served white interests particularly well, and most of his white contemporaries strongly believed in it. Drury recorded the conventional wisdom after an extended tour of South Africa: 'Indians, Coloured and Bantu all hate and fear one another, [whites] feel they must act as barriers between, and controllers of, the other races or see a dreadful and apocalyptic outbreak of a racial war of all kinds, not only Black against White, but all races against all races.'[33]

While such a white perspective was clearly biased, ethnic division in other parts of Africa was serious enough to spark serious conflict. Right to the end of the 1980s reputable scholars working on South Africa based their constitutional proposals for a post-apartheid government on the assumption that the black community would split up into different parties. A 1983 poll showed that close to half of

---

30 Charles H Feinstein, *An Economic History of South Africa* (Cambridge: Cambridge University Press, 2005), p. 160.

31 E-mail communication from Wynand Boshoff, 20 January 2012.

32 G van de Wall, 'Verwoerd, die hervormer', WJ Verwoerd (compiler), *Verwoerd: So onthou ons hom*, p. 166.

33 Drury, *A Very Strange Society*, p. 451.

rural Xhosa and rural Zulu indicated that they would feel 'weak and insecure' if other groups were to have more power than theirs in a future government.[34] Such concern was much weaker in Soweto, which would become the engine room of the black struggle.

Cape Nats at bay

Stellenbosch academics using the platform of the South African Bureau for Racial Affairs (Sabra) to propose a more idealistic form of apartheid greatly irritated Verwoerd. Shortly after he became minister of native affairs in October 1950, he received a Sabra delegation asking him to discuss a memorandum it had prepared. Verwoerd, who could explain the logical consistency of apartheid better than anyone else – even if his premise was flawed – declared at the outset: 'I have read the document. Let me state what you wanted to tell me, and then say what you actually should have told me and then I shall give you my reply.' Understandably, the academics were furious.[35] Ten years later Verwoerd supporters in the Afrikaner Broederbond's executive council purged the Sabra of Stellenbosch reformists, turning the body into an echo chamber of Verwoerd's views.

After the election of 1953 the Cape Nats began to develop doubts about the wisdom of removing the coloured vote. An NP electoral defeat seemed increasingly remote, and the UP had made no effort to register large numbers of new coloured voters. Coloured voters themselves had become apathetic in the face of their circumscribed political rights. From a high of 54 000 in 1945 the registered coloured voters dropped to 38 000 in 1954. In 1953 Weber wrote to Geyer that high qualifications for all new coloured voters on a common roll would be a wiser alternative. He had voiced this opinion to senior Cape NP leaders, Dönges and PW Botha, and he took their silence to mean that they agreed.[36]

Verwoerd's fortunes improved dramatically after the 1953 election when the NP's centre of gravity shifted to the north. There were now twice as many Transvaal and Free State members in the NP caucus as Cape members. In 1954 his close ally, JG Strijdom, became prime minister. Weber resigned himself to the new reality and wrote to Geyer: 'We shall have to make the best of it, although I do not know if we shall be consulted much. For the sake of [party] unity we shall have to be prepared to accept a lot.'[37]

Strijdom quickly demonstrated that the Transvaal was now in control. Dönges's

34 Hermann Giliomee and Lawrence Schlemmer, *From Apartheid to Nation-building* (Cape Town: Oxford University Press, 1989), p. 168.
35 Fanie Botha, 'Leier en vriend', in WJ Verwoerd (compiler), *Verwoerd: So onthou ons hom*, p. 107.
36 US Library, Weber Collection, Weber-Geyer, 8 November 1953.
37 US Library, Weber Collection, Weber-Geyer, 17 October 1954.

hope of becoming Strijdom's minister of finance was dashed. While Dönges lauded the recommendation of the Tomlinson Commission for the dynamic development of the homelands, Verwoerd poured cold water on it, favouring a much more modest pace of development. But by the end of the 1950s Dönges was endorsing the homelands policy as something that 'opened new windows'. He also stated: 'We don't want to have the Bantu as co-owner of the same house or as partner in our lounge, dining room and bedroom.'[38]

The 1958 leadership election was the last chance that the Cape Nats would have to retain their dominant position. The day after Strijdom's death *Die Burger* reported that there were three candidates: Cape leader Dönges, Free State leader CR Swart, and Verwoerd. To block Verwoerd's ascent to power, Dönges had to make a deal with Swart and some northern MPs. The English press reported that several Cape MPs were so opposed to Verwoerd that, if he were to come to power, they could break with the NP and forge an alliance with the UP under Sir De Villiers Graaff.

A few days before the election Dönges was offered significant support if he promised to appoint three specific people to his cabinet: PK le Roux, Jan Haak and Albert Hertzog. Balking at appointing the right-winger Hertzog, Dönges refused. Devoutly religious, he was revolted by the political deals typical of climbing the greasy political pole to the top. Weber called on him in his office but could not persuade him to change his mind. Turning to leave, Weber said to Dönges: 'Remember, Eben, only a saint stands alone.'[39] In the first round of the voting Verwoerd attracted 80 votes, Dönges 52 and Swart 41. In the second round Verwoerd defeated Dönges by 98 to 75 votes.

The Cape NP's fears were soon realised. Verwoerd agreed to Dönges's request to be appointed minister of finance, but insisted that Haak become his deputy minister. When Dönges refused, Verwoerd threatened to withdraw the offer. Only after a warning from Dönges that he would go public did Verwoerd relent. Verwoerd also effectively demoted Paul Sauer, who had recruited him in 1936 in Stellenbosch to become the founding editor of *Die Transvaler*. He offered PW Botha, a strong Dönges supporter, only a deputy minister post, which was refused.[40] Referring to Verwoerd's humiliating treatment of Sauer and Botha, Geyer wrote to Weber: 'I have no confidence at all in Verwoerd.'[41]

Tensions came to a head in October 1960, when the NP leadership in each province had to submit names of senators to the new, reduced Senate. It was conven-

---

38   Anton Bekker, *Eben Dönges, Balansstaat* (Stellenbosch: Sun Press, 2005), p. 182.
39   Communication of Sarel du Plessis, private secretary to Dönges, to Una Ramsey, Dönges's daughter, 10 September 2008.
40   Bekker, *Dönges*, pp. 136-37.
41   US Library, Weber Collection, Geyer-Weber, 13 October 1958.

tion in such situations that nominations of the respective provincial leaders were accepted without opposition. But Verwoerd rejected the two names Dönges proposed on behalf of the Cape and insisted on retaining two sitting senators. Dönges became red in the face and said it would have serious implications for the Cape if Verwoerd's proposal went through. Afterwards, PW Botha, Sauer and FC Erasmus urged Dönges to make a stand and offered to resign along with him, but Dönges decided not to resign 'in the best interests of the Cape NP'. Afterwards he said that 'something died in him'. He felt the failed attempt on Verwoerd's life six months earlier had exacerbated his 'dictatorial tendencies'. For a long time the two men did not speak to each other.[42]

One can only speculate about what would have happened if Dönges rather than Verwoerd had become prime minister in 1958. The Sharpeville massacre in March 1960 and its aftermath prompted some Nationalist politicians to seriously reconsider the fundamentals of apartheid policy. *Die Burger* spelled out in its influential 'Dawie' column what informed Nationalists had long known: the policy virtually ignored urban blacks. The column remarked that whites' future depended on the policy towards the urban blacks.[43]

Verwoerd was still in hospital when Sauer, with the backing of senior ministers Dönges and Ben Schoeman, stated publicly that the government had to soften the pass laws and offer greater security to urban blacks. He pleaded that 'the Native has to be given hope for a happy existence, free of fear of oppression and the concept of *baasskap* (boss-ship) of whites over non-whites'. The wages and living conditions of urban blacks had to be improved.[44] Yet, soon after he recovered, Verwoerd issued a statement that there was no need to change the policy.

In December 1960 there was another near-revolt when delegates of Afrikaans churches belonging to the World Council of Churches accepted several resolutions critical of apartheid at Cottesloe, Johannesburg. One stated there could be no principled objection to the direct representation of the coloured community in parliament. *Die Burger*, under the editorship of Piet Cillié, backed this call. But at Verwoerd's urging, the synods of the respective Afrikaans churches quickly condemned the Cottesloe resolutions. Verwoerd also rejected Cillié's call in *Die Burger* to permit coloured MPs.

Burnt by previous clashes, Dönges was unsupportive on the issue of coloured representation. He told Weber that Cillié had become 'too excited' about it. He would not comply with Cillié's request to take a stronger stand. It would be better, he said, to be circumspect. On 21 January 1961 the NP Federal Council gave their unani-

---

42 Bekker, *Dönges*, pp. 206-07, citing an interview with Dönges's widow.
43 Louis Louw (compiler), *Dawie, 1946-1964* (Cape Town: Tafelberg, 1965), p. 175.
44 Piet Meiring, *Tien politieke leiers* (Cape Town: Tafelberg, 1973), p. 144.

mous support to Verwoerd. Weber noted sadly that the Cape ministers, including Dönges, Sauer and Erasmus, had completely capitulated to Verwoerd.[45]

Considering Cillié the great culprit in the story, the executive committee of the NP's Federal Council met with the board of directors of Nasionale Pers to discuss the issue. Two directors, Weber and Recht Malan, spoke up strongly for Cillié and *Die Burger*. The paper had not deviated from policy and had the right to 'adult thinking'.[46] Cillié felt that Dönges and some of the church leaders had left him in the lurch. To the surprise of many, Cillié made his peace with Verwoerd shortly afterwards. The man with probably the best mind in Afrikaans journalism had bought into Verwoerd's scheme.

Someone who retained his intellectual independence from Verwoerd was Schoeman. In his memoirs he wrote that he was unable to stand Verwoerd for many years, but once Verwoerd became prime minister the situation changed. He found Verwoerd 'a completely different person', someone 'with much charm and an attractive personality'.[47] Nonetheless, Schoeman was prepared to stand up to Verwoerd. When the prime minister mooted the possibility of removing the last vestiges of coloured representation in parliament, Schoeman stated that in such a case he would have to reconsider his position in cabinet. Verwoerd dropped the matter.[48] It could well be that Verwoerd's antagonism to the Cape Nats had its roots in his bitter battles of earlier years against the power elite of the south.

By the mid-1960s Verwoerd's main critic in the Nationalist press was Schalk Pienaar, editor of *Die Beeld*. Pienaar thought Verwoerd's dominance in all policy making and in the debate among Afrikaners had created 'a false sense of security'. He always believed that Afrikaners' strength lay in a 'group leadership' with a sense of collective responsibility. He believed that Verwoerd's ascendancy to the position of sole decision maker represented a threat to Afrikaners' survival in a hostile world.[49] He would later declare: 'As if it was the most natural thing in the world, Verwoerd considered himself the leader of the Afrikaners and the arbiter of what was good and bad for the Afrikaners.'[50] In his memoirs Pienaar told of a friend's remark that pulled him out of his state of shock after hearing of the prime minister's assassination: 'How much longer could the country have endured Verwoerd?'[51]

Verwoerd's remarkable rise to power was due to his rare ability to attract disparate

---

45 Steyn, *Penvegter*, pp. 176-79.
46 Steyn, *Penvegter*, p. 183.
47 Schoeman, *My lewe in die politiek*, pp. 246-47.
48 BM Schoeman, *Van Malan tot Verwoerd* (Cape Town: Human & Rousseau, 1973), p. 249.
49 Alex Mouton, 'Reform from within: Schalk Pienaar, the Afrikaans press and apartheid', *Historia*, 45, 1, 2000, p. 156.
50 Pienaar, *Getuie van groot tye*, p. 50.
51 Pienaar, *Getuie van groot tye*, p. 65.

constituencies: blue-collar workers requiring protection against cheap black labour, farmers demanding cheap labour, and the Afrikaner intelligentsia insisting on a policy that was defensible. He came to power on the shoulders of the 'Young Turks' of the north demanding a rigorous form of white supremacy, but also won over the intelligentsia. As Helen Suzman observed, 'He convinced the Nationalists that the policy of apartheid was ethical and not based on naked racism. The breakthrough for him was being able to convince the Afrikaner academics of this. Without them the policy would not have been able to survive.'[52]

Verwoerd impressed Prime Minister Harold Macmillan of Britain and Secretary-general Dag Hammarskjöld of the UN. After 1961 he increasingly began to win over English speakers, who voted in considerable numbers for the NP in 1966. But the black, coloured and Indian intellectual elites, believing in an inclusive South African nation, rejected his scheme. In the long run his scheme had no hope of succeeding without them.

---

52 Cited in 'Some Hated Me', *The Argus*, 14 July 1977.

Chapter 3

'The Most Terrific Clash
of Interests Imaginable':
Hendrik Verwoerd's Response

HENDRIK VERWOERD SPELLED OUT HIS VIEWS ON THE RACIAL QUESTION IN South Africa in his maiden speech in parliament in 1948. These views had been moulded by his experience and observations in Johannesburg during the preceding decade. He sketched a picture of Europeans and non-Europeans living mingled across the whole of South Africa. Not only blacks, but also coloureds and Indians were 'swarming everywhere, uncounted and uncontrolled'.[1] They were mixing in the trams and trains, and were 'taking possession of the theatres and the streets'. If this 'mixed development' continued, he would say a few years later, 'it would lead to the most terrific clash of interests imaginable'. He remarked that while complete separation between white and black would have been ideal, history had taken a different course. For Verwoerd the challenge was to come as close as possible to the best solution of the problem.[2]

A senator during his first ten years in parliament, Verwoerd was spared the chores of constituency work and worries over fighting the next election. In addition, the Senate's schedule was much less rigorous than that of the House of Assembly. But there was a downside. His salary of £700 a year was much lower than that of a newspaper editor, and Verwoerd's family continued living in Johannesburg. He used his time to immerse himself in the literature on the issues the new government had to grapple with.

When he became minister of native affairs in October 1950 he hit the ground running.

Pressing problems

Assuming power in 1948, the NP government faced formidable pressures and challenges. Rapid industrialisation was changing the face of the country and the racial composition of its cities. In the mid-1940s the number of black people overtook the number of whites in the cities, which whites had traditionally considered their domain. By 1951 there were 2.38 million urban blacks, representing a quarter of the total black population. The backlog in urban black housing was appalling. Less

---

1 Fred Barnard, *13 Jaar in die skadu van Dr Verwoerd* (Johannesburg: Voortrekkerpers, 1967), p. 44.
2 AN Pelzer (ed.), *Verwoerd Speaks* (Johannesburg: APB, 1966), pp. 14, 24.

than a fifth of the more than 800 000 blacks on the Witwatersrand lived in formal houses.

Early in 1948 a report of a commission under the chairmanship of Henry Fagan made it clear that black urbanisation was irreversible, and that in the urban areas there were not only migrant labourers but also a settled black population (see p. 32). In the same year the Board of Trade and Industries issued a warning: 'The detribalisation of large numbers of Natives . . . [together with] rootless masses concentrated in the large industrial centres is a matter which no government can sit back and watch . . . [Unless] these masses of detribalised Natives are effectively and carefully controlled, they will become more of a burden than a constructive factor in industry.'[3] Investors were wary of South Africa under an NP government, aware of the anti-capitalist noises the party had made while in opposition. With more than a third of capital investment coming from foreign sources, firm measures were needed to assure investors of political stability and labour peace.[4]

Several issues required the government's urgent attention, with political rights for blacks the most important. The Natives Representative Council had become defunct after virtually disbanding itself in its frustration with the United Party government's poor response to its submissions and pleas. Revitalised by the founding of a Youth League by Nelson Mandela, Oliver Tambo and Walter Sisulu in 1949, the ANC leadership attacked the new government's policies. In 1952 it wrote to government that apartheid had less to do with the preservation of white identity than 'with the systematic exploitation of African people'. Calling apartheid laws an insult to the African people, it demanded direct representation for Africans in parliament and all other legislative bodies.[5]

The ANC, together with the South African Indian Congress, staged largely peaceful protests, with volunteers courting arrest by defying apartheid laws. Although the state punished the offenders harshly, the ANC's membership mushroomed from 10 000 to 100 000. After the government restricted most ANC leaders, its finances and volunteers dwindled. In 1956 the police arrested 156 people, including leading ANC activists, and put them on trial for high treason. All were given bail pending trial, but the charges against most of the accused were later withdrawn, suggesting that the primary purpose was to suppress agitation. In this the state was largely successful. By the end of the 1950s ANC-led mass resistance had fizzled out; the state's repression greatly weakened its organisational structures and the linkages between leaders and masses.

---

3   Deborah Posel, *The Making of Apartheid* (Oxford: Clarendon Press, 1997), p. 38.
4   Jill Nattrass, *The South African Economy* (Cape Town: Oxford University Press, 1981), p. 85.
5   Leo Kuper, *Passive Resistance in South Africa* (New Haven: Yale University Press, 1957), pp. 233-41.

Groping for a policy

The NP platform for the 1948 election described the reserves as the true home of blacks. The party promised its supporters that urban blacks would be treated as visitors who could never claim equal rights with whites. Yet influential NP-supporting Afrikaners continued to debate alternatives. Privately Albertus Geyer, ex-editor of *Die Burger*, mooted the idea of the black authorities forming a Central Council to discuss matters common to all reserves. He also suggested introducing machinery for 'close contact and consultation' between such a council and the government. Verwoerd, who was appointed minister for native affairs on 19 October 1950, rejected the idea because he felt competition would develop between such a council and parliament.[6]

But Verwoerd also explored an approach that differed starkly from his subsequent single-minded focus on the homelands as the only places where blacks could express themselves politically and fulfil their career aspirations. Six weeks after becoming a cabinet minister, he addressed a meeting of the Natives Representative Council (NRC). There was an unreal quality about this meeting. The councillors demanded direct representation at all levels of government, which Verwoerd was determined to resist. It is strange that he wanted to address the NRC, knowing that there was so little common ground.

In his speech he was brutally frank in telling the NRC that the policy of his government was for whites to be master in their own areas, but to allow blacks to dominate in their areas. Agricultural and industrial development would be promoted there, while industries would be established on the reserves' borders to supplement the available job opportunities. He hoped many urban blacks would relocate to the reserves if sufficient development occurred, to exercise their talents as artisans, traders, clerks or professionals, or to realise their political ambitions.

Over the next 35 years, NP leaders would increasingly voice this mantra, but the significance of Verwoerd's proposition has been largely overlooked by historians. He stated that, even as he hoped black people might return to the reserves, he expected large numbers would remain in the cities for many years, and he announced that government planned to give these blacks 'the greatest possible measure of self-government' in urban areas. All the work in these townships would have to be done by their own people, enabling blacks to pursue 'a full life of work and service'. For this reason blacks had to be educated to be sufficiently competent in many spheres, the only qualification being that they would have to place their development and their knowledge exclusively at the service of their own people. Verwoerd invited the NRC members to meet him after the session for a 'comprehensive interview' about

---

6   JP Heiberg, 'Dr AL Geyer as Suid-Afrika se Hoë Kommissaris in die Verenigde Koninkryk', doctoral dissertation, University of Stellenbosch, 2001, pp. 211-13.

these matters and to put forward proposals, offering a prompt reply from government to their representations.[7]

This was a fateful turning point. A new field for black politics could have been opened up if this offer had been accepted – particularly if it set in motion a political process that entailed talks between government and the urban black leadership on the election of urban black councils, the formula for the allocation of revenue, the staffing of the local councils' bureaucracy, property ownership and opportunities for black business. It would have opened up a whole new area for the development of black managerial and administrative capacity, something that the country would sorely lack when whites handed over power in 1994.

The NRC did not take up the offer and it is easy to see why. The urban black elite demanded representation at all levels of government in common with whites. Verwoerd's proposal fell far short of that. It was made in the context of complete segregation and Verwoerd represented a government they viewed with grave suspicion.

NRC councillors who spoke after Verwoerd explained why they rejected the offer. Councillor ZK Matthews said: 'As long as a policy is a unilateral policy, conceived, worked out, and applied by one section of the population, it will not meet the needs of all sections of the population.' Councillor Selope Thema, who, like Matthews, was a member of the ANC, said that there could be no agreement if the minister and his party insisted on telling blacks where they should live. If there had to be apartheid, it had to take the form of two states, including one where blacks would make their own laws.[8]

Verwoerd disbanded the council. He also discarded the idea of establishing a meaningful form of black local government. In a letter to the prime minister the ANC demanded direct representation at all levels. In a reply that Verwoerd probably drafted, the ANC was brusquely told that the government would under no circumstances entertain the idea of giving any power to 'non-Europeans over Europeans'.[9]

The NP government was well prepared to crush opposition. It targeted communists, both white and black, and in particular left-wing trade unionists who appeared to be making some headway among black labourers. In 1950 parliament passed the Suppression of Communism Act, banning the SA Communist Party, and giving the government the power to ban publications that promoted the objectives of communism. It could also 'name' people, who could then be barred from holding office, from practising as lawyers or even from attending meetings.

The view that there could be no settled black population in the 'white' towns and cities was not held from the outset. Verwoerd initially pursued the possibility

---

7   Pelzer (ed.), *Verwoerd Speaks*, pp. 28-30.
8   Margaret Ballinger, *From Union to Apartheid* (Cape Town: Juta, 1969), pp. 210-11.
9   Kuper, *Passive Resistance in South Africa*, pp. 233-41.

of promoting a privileged black stratum through his urban labour preference policy. The objective was to limit the use of migrant labour until optimal use had been made of settled blacks already qualified to be in the cities.

The policy failed. Black urbanites often refused to take menial jobs and employers did not like employees who had an 'attitude'. They considered them expensive, 'cheeky' and difficult to control. Overwhelmingly, employers opted for migrant labour, despite the high cost of a frequent turnover in their workforce. Migrant labour was cheap, and large numbers were employed – often wastefully.[10]

Still largely dormant was the idea of de-nationalising blacks. In 1953 Prime Minister DF Malan used his New Year's message to talk of the 'beacons of peace and happiness' for the citizens of the country. 'Living as we do in a multiracial society we must recognise each others' right of existence unreservedly. South Africa is our common heritage and belongs to all of us.' (Two years later the latter phrase appeared in the Freedom Charter, which united most of the liberation movements.) Malan went on to say that South Africans must not live in camps in which one section would find it necessary to defend itself against another. Every population had to feel secure in the maintenance and development of what is particularly its own. South Africans 'must in the first place regard themselves as children of South Africa to which they must give their primary love and commitment'.[11]

A few weeks later, Werner Eiselen, secretary for Native Affairs, cited Malan's words in opening the congress of the Municipal Advisory Board, attended by black councillors. He told the meeting a new deal was in the offing that would depart from the old concept that the 'Bantu' constantly needed white help as 'some sort of sub-community that was sub-economic and sub-moral'.[12] The words of Malan and Eiselen highlight the degree to which apartheid as a policy to regulate white-black relations was still in flux in the early 1950s.

It was in the field of education that the government confronted one of its greatest dilemmas. During the last ten years of United Party rule there had been a considerable improvement in state funding of black and coloured education. Consistently stressing that apartheid would provide something better than segregation, the NP government could hardly try to reverse this expansion, but it was keen to remove the control of black and coloured schools from the churches and missionary societies, which it believed imparted the wrong educational message. In its place it would introduce a state system of mass-based basic education.

The question was what political effect a greatly extended education system

10   Posel, *The Making of Apartheid*, p. 186.
11   *Die Burger*, 3 January 1953.
12   Archive for Contemporary Affairs, Bloemfontein , PV93/1 /31/ 1/1, Verwoerd Papers, Address by W Eiselen, 195.

might have. JG Strijdom, Verwoerd's provincial leader, was openly sceptical about the political wisdom of black education on a mass scale in a system of white supremacy. In 1947 he wrote to DF Malan that 'the ever greater extension of education to blacks, without granting equal rights, will inevitably lead to bloody clashes and revolutions. It will erode the distinguishing line of colour and would, step by step, bring about equality.'[13] The NP government decided that an expanded education system would have a stabilising effect only if the pupils received what was called Christian National education, leaving school committed to improving the condition of their community.

Flawed assumptions

In the early 1950s Verwoerd began to develop elements of his grand scheme, which he would expound with such conviction by the end of the decade. Some of his assumptions were badly flawed. One of them, relating to the carrying capacity of the homelands, the keystone of his scheme, will be discussed later (see p. 104). The other main incorrect assumptions relate to the historic claim to the land and the projected growth of the black population over the next 50 years.

Verwoerd often spelled out his view of how South Africa was settled. One such occasion was his impromptu reply to a speech by Prime Minister Harold Macmillan of Britain in parliament in 1960. He declared: 'We [the whites] settled a country that was bare. The Bantu too came to this country and settled certain portions for themselves. It is in line with the thinking on Africa to grant them there those rights, which . . . all people should have. We believe in providing those rights for those people in the fullest degree in that part of Southern Africa which their forefathers found for themselves and settled in.'[14]

This historical claim to the land was not as preposterous then as it sounds today. In 1957 a new edition of the standard and most widely read general history of South Africa was published. Written by Eric Walker, professor of African history at Cambridge University, this book of nearly a thousand pages had fewer than ten on southern Africa before the first European voyages around the coast. About settlement by Africans, he stated: 'In some parts of the present-day Union and Southern Rhodesia their occupation is not much older than that of the Europeans, and in the western half of the Cape Colony it is more recent than theirs.'[15]

Walker's view would soon be radically revised. In the course of the 1950s archaeologists and anthropologists gathered a growing body of evidence that Bantu speakers had reached as far south as the Transkei by the sixteenth century and probably

---

13 HB Thom, *DF Malan* (Cape Town: Tafelberg, 1980), p. 179.
14 Pelzer (ed.), *Verwoerd Speaks*, p. 338.
15 Eric Walker, *A History of South Africa* (London: Longman, 1957), p. 7.

much earlier. In the course of the 1960s radiocarbon dating of artefacts from the Transvaal showed that people who were almost certainly Bantu speakers had occupied the northern part of the region by the eleventh century.[16] But by the time Verwoerd died in the mid-1960s these new perspectives had not yet filtered into the public domain.

Then there were flawed demographic projections. Demographic trends started to haunt Verwoerd and other leading members of the Afrikaner intelligentsia. In the 1936 census the black population was 6.5 million. By the 1946 census, this had grown by more than 2 million to 7.8 million (later revised to 8.5 million). The proportion of blacks who had urbanised increased from 13.8% to 18.5%. Against this, the white population grew by less than 400 000 from 2 million in 1936 to 2.4 million in 1946.

Jan Sadie was a member of a group of young Stellenbosch academics who belonged to the NP-aligned think tank, the South African Bureau for Racial Affairs (Sabra). He used the figures for 1936 and 1946 in an article published in 1950, pointing out that numbers are of the essence in democracy, where one person means one vote. 'The population, its growth or its decline, [its] births and deaths, [and its] racial composition, are the basic data of politics . . . In the long run numbers must count . . . If whites did not want to be swamped they would have to face up to the fact there was only one way out: complete separation [between white and black] over the long run.'[17]

Sadie projected a figure for the year 2000 of 19 million blacks compared to 5.7 million whites. There would then be 13.2 million more blacks than whites compared to only 5.4 million in 1946. Breaking the population of blacks down into the different areas where blacks lived, Sadie projected the following figures for 2000. The table below shows his projected figures and the actual figures for 2000.

BLACKS IN DIFFERENT AREAS

	1950 projection	Actual 2000 figures
'White' urban areas	2–3 million	15 million
'White' rural areas	3–4 million	4 million
Reserves	10–12 million	15 million
Total	19 million	34 million

---

16   Monica Wilson, 'The Archaeological Background', M Wilson and LM Thompson (eds), *Oxford History of South Africa* (London: Oxford University Press, 1969), vol.1, p. 37.

17   JL Sadie, 'The Political Arithmetic of the South African Population', *Journal of Racial Affairs*, July 1950, p. 152.

As the right-hand column shows, Sadie greatly underestimated the growth of the black population. He admitted later that in 1950, when he wrote his article, demography as a discipline was as yet unable to provide accurate projections of predominantly rural groups.[18] Verwoerd's thinking was shaped by these flawed projections. In 1952 he wrote in a private letter that the black population was expected to reach 19 million by 2000, while the white population would top 6 million. His aim was to work towards a situation in which more than 10 million blacks would live in the reserves by 2000. This would leave 2–3 million living in the 'white' towns and cities and 3–4 million in the 'white' rural areas. In his words, 'white civilisation' would be saved because 'six million against six million' in both the cities and rural areas would be 'infinitely better' than if the flow to the cities continued uninterrupted.[19] These figures turned out to be hopelessly wrong.

Influx control

Verwoerd's main concern was the introduction of tough curbs to slow down the flow of blacks to the cities. During the 1930s black and coloured workers began to leave the rural areas in large numbers to seek a better life in towns and cities. Farmers complained vociferously about labour shortages. The main reason was low wages that remained stagnant in real terms. Even average mine wages (including the value of food) were twice those of farm wages.[20]

To clamp down on the influx the Department of Native Affairs instructed native commissioners to withhold travel permits, noting that many rural blacks arrived in Johannesburg, Pretoria and elsewhere in a desperate condition and without passes of any kind. To placate the farmers who were demanding an increased supply of labour from the reserves, both the UP and the NP governments postponed the transfer of additional land to the reserves as was required in terms of the 1936 legislation. Land transfers would be completed only in the 1970s.

After 1948 the NP government introduced a host of even tougher influx control measures than those already on the statute book. Its framework was one originally proposed by the Stallard Commission of 1922: that cities were white creations and blacks should be allowed there only if they served white interests. In 1952 the government prohibited any black person from being in a white urban area unless specifically exempted. The so-called 'Section Ten exemptions' applied to those who were born in the city, had worked for different employers for fifteen years, or had worked

---

18   JL Sadie, 'The Political Arithmetic of Apartheid', P Hugo (ed.), *South African Perspectives* (Cape Town: *Die Suid-Afrikaan*, 1989), pp. 150-57.

19   Barnard, *13 Jaar*, p. 38.

20   Francis Wilson, 'Farming', Monica Wilson and Leonard Thompson (eds), *Oxford History of South Africa* (Oxford: Clarendon Press, 1971), vol. 2, p. 146.

uninterruptedly for one employer for ten years. Verwoerd saw these exemptions as a device that conferred 'guarantees, security and stability'.[21] In contrast, a migrant needed a permit to have his wife and children live with him in the town or city, which he rarely got. Those who had lost their jobs could be removed to the reserves by force.

There were some disastrous misconceptions in the NP's thinking, which was underpinned by the strong belief that rapid black urbanisation could be turned around. By 1950 more than a million of the 2–3 million urban blacks had lived in the cities for more than a generation. But to white politicians and officials the other 1–1.5 million seemed to be temporary and without any firm roots in the city. The cry 'Send them back' went up from the voters. Henry Fagan made the wry comment: 'There appears to be a belief that every black man had a home somewhere in the reserves that longed to welcome him back.'[22]

Apartheid as an authoritarian system was imposed not by generals and foot soldiers but by civil administrators, using bureaucratic means. Apart from the pass laws, their key instrument of control was a system of labour bureaus, operating on three tiers: a central labour bureau in Pretoria at the top, regional labour bureaus on the second tier and, on the third tier, district and local labour bureaus located in the municipalities or reserves. The first two tiers were required to coordinate the overall flow of labour, while the local bureaus had to control the flow of labour into, within and outside their area.[23] Any prospective worker residing in the reserves had to ask permission from a labour officer to move to an urban area. The purpose was to ensure enough labour for low-paying sectors such as farming.

In one of his first speeches as minister of native affairs Verwoerd warned that the dependence on black workers in the cities could mean 'the death of white civilisation'. He added that white survival was more important to him than expanding industrial development.[24] Publicly he said he would not arrest economic growth in order to curb black numbers, but in cabinet in the mid-1950s there was a clash between him and the minister of labour, Ben Schoeman. When Verwoerd wanted to impose a total ban on blacks entering the Witwatersrand area, particularly Johannesburg, Schoeman objected. He argued that it would stifle industry and kill economic growth.[25] Verwoerd had to back down. While he was minister of native affairs the government failed to stem the rapid increase of urban blacks or to change the preference of employers for cheap migrant labour. It undermined all

21 Posel, *The Making of Apartheid*, p. 113.

22 HA Fagan, *Our Responsibility* (Stellenbosch: Stellenbosch University Press, 1959), p. 20.

23 Ivan Evans, *Bureaucracy and Race: Native Administration in South Africa* (Berkeley: University of California Press, 1997), pp. 86-90.

24 *House of Assembly Debates (HAD)*, 1951, col. 3797.

25 Ben Schoeman, *My lewe in die politiek* (Johannesburg: Perskor, 1978), p. 147.

efforts to create an urban black elite that would acquiesce in white domination in return for favoured treatment by the state.

Verwoerd did not give up the attempt to stem black urbanisation. Influx control was originally meant to regulate the movement of male migrant labourers, but the influx of women from the reserves and farms changed things substantially. The ratio of black men to black women in the Johannesburg area had dropped from 23:1 in 1910 to 5:1 in 1927 and 2:1 in 1960. In 1956 government imposed the pass laws on black women as well.

In the 1950s, pass laws were applied much more stringently. Prosecutions increased sharply from 214 000 in 1951 to 418 000 in 1959. But despite all these interventions, the proportion of urbanised blacks rose from 27% to 30% between 1951 and 1960. In the second half of the 1960s even stricter regulations managed to curb the flow, but only temporarily. The number of black workers employed in the manufacturing and commercial sectors kept increasing dramatically.[26]

BLACK EMPLOYMENT IN MANUFACTURING AND COMMERCE

Year	Manufacturing	Commerce	Total blacks (both sectors)	All workers (both sectors)
1950	267 070	69 281	336 351	843 326
1960	357 700	138 240	495 940	1 055 457
1970	617 200	186 300	803 500	1 615 700

Source: Stanley Greenberg, *Race and State and Capitalist Development* (New Haven: Yale University Press, 1980), pp. 425-26.

Urban segregation

Verwoerd became minister at a time when black people in the reserves and in urban locations were under severe pressure. At the same time, black farm labour was very poorly paid. Speaking in the Senate in 1952, he undertook to show how the various acts, bills and public statements he had made 'all fit into a pattern and together form a single constructive plan'. For urban black communities he planned to build houses and provide an orderly life. For the reserves he envisaged economic farming units, development projects for non-farming communities and border industries to cut down migration to the cities. His department was also 'training the Bantu for possible forms of self-government'.[27]

Urban segregation was Verwoerd's highest priority. Between 1919 and the early

---

26 For an extended discussion on the conflicts over policy within the NP, which effectively debunks the notion of a single grand plan, see Deborah Posel, *The Making of Apartheid* (Oxford: Clarendon Press, 1997).

27 Pelzer (ed.), *Verwoerd Speaks*, pp. 31-52.

1950s, uncoordinated attempts to segregate residential areas characterised government policy. In 1945 the Smuts government passed a law decreeing that 'all natives within the limits of any native area or any specified portion thereof shall reside in a location, Native village or a Native hostel'.[28] During the time Verwoerd was minister and prime minister, urban space was ordered much more rigorously than before, entrenching segregation.

Verwoerd's department also embarked on large-scale construction of dwellings for urban blacks. By the end of the 1950s the government had cleared most of the slums and had built about 100 000 houses. As in most township developments, the houses were small and the township architecturally monotonous, with few public amenities. The doctrine that all blacks were only temporary sojourners in the 'white' towns and cities increasingly affected urban planning, the provision of services and township administration. The policy stressed the marginal character of the urban black population: they were in but not of the city.[29]

Verwoerd, keenly interested in urban security, ordered that every black township be clearly demarcated, with buffer zones separating it from the residential areas of other population groups. Entrances by road were limited to two or three and township streets were purposely wide so that police could control movement more easily. Roads from the townships to places of work were planned not to pass through white suburbs.

The true destiny of all blacks was their respective homelands. It became policy to build new secondary schools for blacks only in the homelands. The policy tried to prevent the growth of a black trading class in the townships. Until 1976 the law prevented the forming of partnerships or the setting up of companies.

Black residents could not put their own stamp on their houses, since the state built nearly 90% of them. This leverage gave the state the opportunity to construct new townships in a way that placed specific ethnic groups together, often along the spokes of the wagon-wheel pattern that characterised many townships. The state's argument was that this made it easier for planning of mother-tongue schools. But the policy failed to win acceptance. A study undertaken at the end of the 1970s showed that more than four fifths of the younger generation of blacks rejected the stress on ethnicity in planning the townships.[30]

By the early 1960s the government had removed almost all blacks living in 'white' residential areas or the inner cities, and cleared up squatter camps. The policy

---

28   P Smit and JJ Booysen, *Swart verstedeliking: Proses, patroon en strategie* (Cape Town: Tafelberg, 1981), p. 74.

29   Smit and Booysen, *Swart verstedeliking*, pp. 73-75.

30   Smit and Booysen, *Swart verstedeliking*, p. 76.

entered a new phase when it was decided to locate new townships as far as possible in the homelands.[31] In 1960 the government announced measures to promote border industries, allowing homeland workers to commute. Concessions were offered to industrialists prepared to establish labour-intensive industries just beyond the homelands' borders. Between 1960 and 1965 border industries succeeded in employing on average 8 200 black workers per year, compared to an average entry of 40 000 black workers into secondary industries each year. The numbers employed rose considerably after 1965, but the border industries scheme undermined the economic development of the reserves. The primary goal was not economic; it was to stem black influx into the cities.

In 1956 Verwoerd declared that the stream of blacks to the cities would start reversing in twenty years' time as the socio-economic development of the reserves improved. By the mid-1960s this assumption had become so unrealistic that Schalk Pienaar, Verwoerd's main critic in the Afrikaans press, mocked the idea. When De Wet Nel, Verwoerd's successor as minister of native affairs, suggested that the date ought not to be taken literally, Pienaar wrote that the party had bid farewell to an old friend. Verwoerd publicly reprimanded Nel.[32]

Henry Fagan called this policy an attempt to increase racial segregation without achieving real territorial separation.[33] In the end these policies were futile. The townships built for commuters in the border areas or the homelands were dysfunctional (see Chapter 4, p. 104). Apart from the many hours the commuters spent in travelling and the effect this had on productivity, the state or employers had to pay huge subsidies that soon became unaffordable. The policy represented a massive project in social engineering that is difficult to envisage without Verwoerd as the architect and driving force.

Propping up the chiefs

Verwoerd designed an elaborate system of administration for the homelands. The authorities introduced here had to help implement influx control and increasingly assume powers to govern the territories. They also had to serve as the focal point for the political aspirations of urban blacks. In 1950 Verwoerd remarked that if blacks had 'ambitions in the direction of full citizenship, then they have to go back to the areas that are theirs'.[34] In 1951 he piloted through parliament the Bantu Authorities Act, providing for three tiers of authority in the reserves, all under his control through the Department of Native Affairs. In opting for tribal authority

---

31 Evans, *Bureaucracy and Race*, p. 122.
32 Schalk Pienaar, *Getuie van groot tye* (Cape Town: Tafelberg, 1979), p. 63.
33 Fagan, *Our Responsibility*, pp. 48-49.
34 Pelzer (ed.), *Verwoerd Speaks*, pp. 10-11.

with power reinforced through revived customary law, the South African government was following the example of the colonial rulers in Africa.[35] They, not the urban black elite, chose the chiefs to prop up their rule. Verwoerd observed that 'tribal authority' is 'the natural ally of government against such rebellious movements'.[36]

By the 1950s the system of traditional rule in South Africa was in an advanced state of decay. Many of the chiefs were already seen as the stooges of white magistrates, but the government favoured subservient chiefs who were prepared to enforce government policy even at the cost of their own popularity. Between 1957 and 1962 the apartheid state had to move in to suppress rural resistance in areas of Sekhukhuneland, the Hurutshe reserve in the western Transvaal, and Pondoland and Thembuland in the eastern Cape.

The government had appointed the Tomlinson Commission to report 'on a comprehensive scheme for the rehabilitation of the Native Areas' shortly before Verwoerd became minister. From the start the relationship between him and the commission was wracked by tension because Verwoerd wanted to develop his own policy. Tabled in 1956, the Tomlinson report proposed the consolidation of the 'Bantu areas' into seven historical 'nuclei or heartlands' based on the linguistic and territorial divisions of the country. Income would come initially from small-scale labour-intensive farms and the remittances of migrant labourers.[37] To sustain the rest of the population, the commission proposed industrial development based on both white private capital and state investment.

The commission's key recommendation was that government should spend £104 million (in 2011 the sum had a purchasing value of R15 billion) over the next ten years to develop the reserves. The report also recommended admitting white private capital to facilitate industrial development. It estimated that by 1981, after 25 years of intensive development and industrialisation, the territories would be able to support 7 million people. Another 2 million could exist on the remittances of migrant labourers. This would provide sustenance for 60% of the reserves' population. Looking further into the future, it suggested that the reserves could carry about 70% of the total black population. Even apart from the fact that the population projections were wrong, this was – in the words of a distinguished economic historian – 'a fantasy'.[38]

The reform-minded Afrikaner intelligentsia welcomed the report enthusiastically.

---

35 Mahmood Mamdani, *Citizen and Subject* (Cape Town; David Philip, 1998).

36 *HAD*, 1956, col. 6617; John Lazar, 'Conformity and Conflict: Afrikaner Nationalist Politics in South Africa, 1948-1961', doctoral dissertation, Oxford University, 1987, p. 213.

37 FR Tomlinson, 'Rejoinders', *Social Dynamics*, 6,1, 1980, pp. 49-52.

38 Charles H Feinstein, *An Economic History of South Africa* (Cambridge: Cambridge University Press, 2005), p. 156.

Leading poet and intellectual NP van Wyk Louw was upbeat: 'A small ray of light has come: what is ethically right is perhaps – if the goodwill is there – not economically impossible.'[39] Roelof (Pik) Botha, then a young diplomat posted in Stockholm, told a critical editor that there was a possibility of a quite different system developing in South Africa. Independent states could come about in which blacks would enjoy full civil rights. Incorporating mineral-rich areas into these territories would ensure their economic viability.[40] Dawie, influential columnist at *Die Burger*, placed his hope for bold action on Verwoerd, a 'man with a sense of calling and a vision'. Whether the territories would develop fast enough to carry the increase of black numbers over the next fifteen years would depend on his driving force. 'No one is fitter for the task,' Dawie argued.[41]

But Verwoerd was determined to devise and implement the policy at a pace set by him, using the resources he saw fit. In the white paper tabled in 1956 Verwoerd rejected the key Tomlinson proposals. Where the commission proposed development expenditure of £104 million, he refused to commit the government to any sum apart from £3 million for the first year. Where the commission recommended a progressive system of land tenure and economic land units, Verwoerd opted for continuing with the outmoded plan of 'one man, one lot'.

Verwoerd also rejected the admission of white private capital. The reserves would have to depend mainly on 'self-aid and . . . the mobilisation of African capital'. To him white private enterprise would make no real contribution 'towards keeping the Native Areas truly Bantu'. Without the involvement of private capital any hope for the development of the reserves was extinguished.

In many ways Verwoerd thought more like an academic than a politician in considering the development of economically depressed areas. To him the right kind of growth and tempo of community development was more important than throwing large amounts of money at the project in the hope that this would compensate, for the lack of black rights and opportunities in 'white' areas. Opening the door to private white initiatives could, in his view, lead to a form of neocolonialism. Blacks should not depend only on financial aid and assistance from outsiders; they should invest some of their own money as well.[42] Verwoerd ignored the reality that very little black capital was available and that the timescale for self-government and independence in Africa had become very short.[43]

His aversion to 'foreign' capital stemmed at least partly from his Johannesburg

39 JC Steyn, *Van Wyk Louw: 'n Lewensverhaal* (Cape Town: Tafelberg, 1998), p. 644.
40 Theresa Papenfus, *Pik Botha en sy tyd* (Pretoria: Litera, 2010), p. 58.
41 Louis Louw (compiler), *Dawie: Bloemlesing van* Die Burger *se politieke kommentator, 1946-1964* (Cape Town: Tafelberg, 1965), p. 114.
42 *HAD*, 14 May 1956, col. 5570-5595.
43 CW de Kiewiet, 'Loneliness in the Beloved Country', *Foreign Affairs*, 43, 3, 1964, p. 415.

experience, where Afrikaners had built up enterprises from scratch without asking for assistance from the English business class. Nor did he want white-black partnership to challenge the apartheid model. Three years later he fell out with cigarette and liquor tycoon Anton Rupert who wanted to start a company in Paarl with a 50/50 partnership between white and coloured people. Rupert had already achieved considerable success in Malaysia, Basutoland and other countries with this model. Verwoerd rejected the plan, because white technical staff would work for a company with non-white directors.[44]

In the NP caucus too there was not strong support for a radical plan. According to his secretary, Verwoerd was 'deeply hurt' by the complaints of party members that because of his policy, the government 'was doing too much for blacks'.[45] Having committed government in 1954 to taking over all the spending on black education, Verwoerd probably knew that cabinet would not agree to any major funding while the government was facing many obligations with limited resources.

Bantu Education

Verwoerd's intervention in black education was the act for which he would become most notorious. Since the early 1970s successive generations of blacks have blamed Verwoerd for the lack of black progress in the modern economy. The suggestion is often made that his education policy was deliberately designed to hold blacks back, but the picture is more complex than this charge suggests. Even allowing that he imposed this system without canvassing the views of parents, his intervention was timely and appropriate in terms of the labour needs of the 1950s.

There can be no doubt that intervention in black education was urgently needed when Verwoerd became minister of native affairs in 1950. Missionary societies or churches – with the Anglican and Roman Catholic churches the most prominent – dominated black education. The state helped by providing salaries for approved teaching posts, but overall state aid was meagre. School buildings were dilapidated and classes overcrowded. Most schools were understaffed and there was a severe shortage of competent teachers.

With the demand for education growing rapidly, schools had to take in far more children than they could teach effectively. Several admirable secondary schools and teachers' training colleges were functioning well but, as one historian commented, the renowned reputation of a few good mission high schools 'should not obscure the fact that most mission schools were poor primary schools with large dropout rates' and that the 'mission system was breaking down at all levels'.[46]

---

44   Ebbe Dommisse, *Anton Rupert: 'n Lewensverhaal* (Cape Town: Tafelberg, 2005), p. 176.
45   Barnard, *13 Jaar*, p. 49.
46   Jonathan Hyslop, *The Class Room Struggle: Policy and Resistance in South Africa, 1940-1990* (Pietermaritzburg: University of Natal Press, 1999), pp. 8-11.

By the early 1950s less than half of black children between the ages of seven and sixteen were attending school, and only 2.6% of black pupils were enrolled in post-primary standards. The average black child spent only four years in school, and just 24.5% of black children of school-going age were enrolled as pupils.

Growing pupil militancy gave rise to several angry confrontations. In 1946 serious troubles rocked the prestigious black schools of Lovedale and Healdtown. Urban youths also became increasingly disaffected. In a presidential address to the South African Institute of Race Relations, Edgar Brookes said: 'In our towns thousands of children are growing up as juvenile delinquents.' He called for 'compulsory education as a preventative against delinquency and crime'.[47] To rectify the situation, government not only had to provide school facilities for the natural increase in the population of school-going age – it came to a considerable 2.8% per annum – but also had to try to accommodate the large backlog.[48]

The primary school syllabus had been devised especially for blacks, but the secondary school syllabus was largely the same as for white pupils. Before the NP took power in 1948, there was a debate among educationists over the contents of the syllabus for black schools, but the question was still unresolved. On the one hand, missionaries and the urbanised black elite were clamouring for a common education system and the use of English after the first three or four years. On the other hand, there were those who supported a differentiated form of education that was less academic and more practical in orientation, using the mother tongue as medium of instruction for at least the first eight years.

Among those who questioned the value of academic training for blacks were some prominent liberals. Leo Marquard and Julius Lewin concluded that, with white and black children growing up in such different conditions, it was not prudent to use the same syllabus.[49] ZK Matthews, a leading black authority on education, called for a separate curriculum for 'Africans and Europeans' so as to preserve the 'African heritage', using the powers of the vernacular to effect social rejuvenation.[50]

Emphasising the training of whites for skilled labour, the United Party government saw no need to train large numbers of black artisans for employment in the common area. Blacks could only expect to do skilled work in the reserves. In terms very similar to those Verwoerd would use later, the secretary of the Department of Native Affairs told the De Villiers Commission on Technical and Vocational Training

---

47 Hyslop, *The Class Room Struggle*, pp. 3, 10-11.

48 JL Sadie, 'Economic and Demographic Aspects of School Education in South Africa', unpublished paper, 2005, p. 15.

49 Leo Marquard and Julius Lewin, *The Native in South Africa* (Johannesburg: University of Witwatersrand Press, 1948), p. 76.

50 Cynthia Kros, 'Deep Rumblings: ZK Matthews and African Education before 1955', *Perspectives in Education*, 12, 1, 1990, p. 35.

in 1947 that 'the unfolding of extensive government development schemes' in the reserves would produce a large number of skilled posts.[51]

Reserving the skilled and even semi-skilled jobs for whites had long been an accepted practice. Employers wanted black youths in a state-controlled education system that provided only basic literacy. A study states: 'The overwhelming demand among urban employers was for workers with basic literacy, who could be employed as unskilled labour. In most cases "tribal labour" was preferred.'[52] There was little demand for blacks who had completed the more advanced standards. During the 1950s the advancement of blacks to more skilled levels previously occupied by whites was still slow. Together, black and coloured workers would take over only 36 000 white jobs in the course of the entire decade.[53]

Verwoerd appointed Werner Eiselen to chair a commission of inquiry into black education. Eiselen was an anthropologist who had served as chief inspector of black education in the Transvaal from 1936 to 1947. Both men were determined to wrest leadership of the black population away from the missionaries and the black urban elite, whom they considered Anglophile.

To Eiselen – and there is no reason to think that Verwoerd disagreed – the main differences among South Africans were cultural rather than racial. His 1951 report found no evidence that 'the intelligence of black children was of so special and peculiar a nature as to demand on these grounds a special type of education'. It also stated: 'The Bantu child comes to school with a basic physical and psychological endowment that differs ... so slightly from that of the European child that no provision has to be made in educational theory or basic aims.'[54]

The Eiselen report was based on the argument that education at school had to meet the special ethnic character and needs of a child, regardless of his or her racial group. It pointed out that African cultures were dynamic and could provide the context for modernising entire peoples. Instead of imitating English and European cultures, the system had to inculcate pride in the *volkseie* – the history, customs, habits, character and mentality of a unique people. The report also showed a strong belief in the superiority of mother-tongue education. As a result, the ethnic language as medium of instruction was made compulsory during the entire primary school phase.

In piloting the Bantu Education Act through parliament in 1953 Verwoerd attacked the previous education policy. In his view, it showed the black man 'the green pastures of the European but still did not allow him to graze there'. By that he meant pupils were provided with skills that employers did not want from black

---

51   Hyslop, *The Class Room Struggle*, pp. 4-5.
52   Posel, *The Making of Apartheid*, p. 186.
53   *Financial Mail*, 14 July 1967, Supplement, p. 43.
54   Union Government 53/1951, *Report of the Commission on Native Education*, pp. 13, 131.

workers. He criticised the existing policy as uneconomic, because money was spent on education with no clear aim. This frustrated educated blacks, who were unable to find the jobs they wanted. He said: 'Education should have its roots entirely in the Native areas and in the Native environment and the Native community . . . The Bantu must be guided to serve his own community in all respects. There is no place for him in the European community above the level of certain forms of labour. Within his own community, however, all doors are open.'[55]

This comment is referred to frequently. It is often distorted by quoting only the first part – 'There is no place for him in the European community above the level of certain forms of labour' – omitting the qualifier Verwoerd added: 'Within his own community, however, all doors are open.'

The most widely read general history of South Africa argued in its fifth edition (published in 2000) that both the Eiselen report and the Act were based on the 'assumption of an inferior potential in African minds' and were 'explicitly designed to prepare blacks for an inferior place in society'.[56] In a previous edition (published in 1987) there is no reference to such assumptions or designs. The 2000 edition is a reflection of the fact that a new government preoccupied with white racism had come to power. Apartheid was no longer seen only as a wrong or misguided policy, but as evil. The latter view is absent in most of the writings of the 1950s and 1960s.[57]

Verwoerd was not arguing that the barrier to blacks rising to higher posts was a supposed racial inferiority. He was not doing much more than referring to the policy – also followed by previous governments – that blacks in 'white areas' could only expect to be appointed to lower-level jobs. Yet his words that 'all doors are open' in their own communities reveal an ideological myopia. The extremely simple economies of the reserves and the depressed state of the townships would for a long time offer very few openings even for qualified blacks.

Verwoerd also remarked that it made little sense to teach mathematics to a black child if he or she could not use it in a career. Probably taking its cue from these words, a recent study alleges that as a result mathematics was no longer taught as 'a core subject in black schools'.[58] In fact, the policy did not change and mathematics continued to be a school subject.[59]

---

55 Pelzer (ed.), *Verwoerd Speaks*, p. 83.

56 Rodney Davenport and Christopher Saunders, *South Africa: A Modern History* (London: Macmillan, 2000), p. 674. Compare TRH Davenport, *South Africa: A Modern History* (Johannesburg: Macmillan, 1987), p. 375.

57 See, for instance, Monica Wilson, 'The Growth of Peasant Communities', M Wilson and Thompson (eds), *Oxford History of South Africa*, vol. 2, pp. 78-79.

58 Francis Wilson, *Dinosaurs, Diamonds and Democracy* (Cape Town: Umuzi, 2009), p. 88.

59 Joubert Rousseau, 'Iets oor Bantoe onderwys', WJ Verwoerd (compiler), *Verwoerd: So onthou ons hom* (Pretoria: Protea Boekhuis, 2001), p. 177. Rousseau spent his entire career in 'Bantu Education' and retired as director-general.

A 1968 study by Muriel Horrell of the SA Institute of Race Relations was critical of Bantu Education, especially its use of mother-tongue instruction, but wrote approvingly of the syllabuses. Those for primary classes were 'educationally sound' and an improvement on the previous syllabuses, while those for the junior and the senior certificate were the same as those used for white children.[60] Ken Hartshorne, noted historian of education, also states that the syllabuses were 'very much the same as those used in white provincial schools and were an improvement on those in use previously'.[61]

The main problem was a lack of qualified teachers in key subjects, particularly the natural sciences and mathematics. Children tended to avoid maths and physical science. From 1958 to 1965 a total of only 431 black matriculants passed mathematics.[62] Nevertheless, the overall impression is of a definite improvement in the provision of mass education and the general standard of literacy, contrary to the popular perception today. Many enthusiastic whites spent their careers as teachers, church ministers, civil servants or agricultural extension officers in the black community. Although many came as disciples of apartheid, just as many were imbued with an enthusiasm that had little to do with party politics.

Verwoerd and Eiselen never hid the fact that black educational advancement, while important, should never come at the expense of the dominant white position. Yet their intent was not 'racist', in the sense of a belief in racial inferiority.

Someone who was in the field himself was Manie Opperman, who taught mathematics during the 1960s and early 1970s at the top missionary schools, Lovedale and Healdtown, before becoming a lecturer at the University of Fort Hare. He states: 'The content and standards were the same [as before 1953]', and adds: 'Thousands of white teachers and officials entered the classrooms and the administrative offices of Bantu education. They realised that the policy was to replace them when suitable black teachers and civil servants came to the fore. It was, however, a slow process. The white teachers, who were mostly Afrikaans-speakers, had to transfer knowledge in their second language to pupils whose English was often of only a rudimentary kind. It required patience, understanding, empathy and perseverance. Despite this some success was achieved. Numerous blacks who are today in government, academic life and business are products of the old Bantu education.'[63]

Why did Verwoerd find it necessary to use such crude, offensive terms in presenting the bill? Verwoerd was doubtless keen to assure the NP caucus that there was

60 Muriel Horrell, *Bantu Education to 1968* (Johannesburg: SA Institute of Race Relations, 1968), pp. 58-59, 71.

61 Ken Hartshorne, *Crisis and Challenge: Black Education, 1910-1960* (Cape Town: Oxford University Press, 1992), p. 41.

62 Horrell, *Bantu Education to 1968*, p.72; Rousseau, 'Iets oor Bantoe onderwys', WJ Verwoerd (compiler), *Verwoerd: So onthou ons hom*, p. 177.

63 E-mail communication from Manie Opperman, 28 September 2010.

no political risk in introducing mass black education. Over the long run, however, his words that there was 'no place for [the Bantu] in the European community above the level of certain forms of labour' did more than anything else to discredit NP education policy.

The growth of education

Black education grew at a rapid rate. The number of places in schools for blacks jumped from 800 000 in 1953 to 1.8 million in 1963, and expanded even more rapidly afterwards. Although most children dropped out at an early stage, there was also an expansion of secondary education. The target the Eiselen report set of doubling secondary school enrolment within ten years was achieved in 1959, the numbers rising from 20 000 to 43 496. Hyslop notes that by bringing the bulk of urban blacks into a few years of basic schooling, black education 'provided a mechanism of social control, which could be used to combat crime and political militancy'. Also, it generated a semi-skilled workforce. 'To a large extent, the Eiselen report met liberal educational demands.'[64]

Controversy nevertheless swirled around the new policy, particularly over mother-tongue education, which was extended well beyond the existing first four years. In 1959 the public examination for Standard 6 (the eighth school year) was written for the first time in one or other vernacular language instead of English. Although mother-tongue education was in line with international practice, the urban black elite strongly opposed mother-tongue instruction beyond Standard 2.

The leaders who had sat on the Natives Representative Council or belonged to the ANC were bitter that they were never properly consulted, but there was such a gulf between them and Verwoerd that it is unlikely a compromise could have been found. Nevertheless, there was some consultation with the community. The Bantu Education Act of 1953 placed the immediate management of black schools in the hands of black school boards. It also introduced the Education Advisory Council, on which leading blacks sat. The council circulated a survey to the governing bodies of schools to test support for the different options for language of instruction in secondary schools. The most popular option was both Afrikaans and English (64%), followed by English only (31%), Afrikaans only (5%) and mother tongue (1%).[65] But once the homelands received a measure of self-government, the respective governments quickly decided to use mother-tongue education only for the first four years.[66]

What was also new in the policy was the potential creation of significant numbers of white-collar jobs in the homelands as the government expanded the provi-

64   Hyslop, *The Class Room Struggle*, p. 199.
65   Rousseau, 'Iets oor Bantoe onderwys', in WJ Verwoerd (compiler), *Verwoerd: So onthou ons hom*, p. 174.
66   Hartshorne, *Crisis and Challenge*, p. 199.

sion of schools, clinics and other services in these areas. In 1958 a well-regarded Africanist from the United States commented without criticism on Verwoerd's vision of the homelands as dynamic areas of political 'self-determination' for blacks, where job opportunities would arise to which they could not aspire elsewhere.[67]

The main black resistance came from the personnel of church schools and training colleges, many of which were soon to be closed down. Although the black urban elite strongly opposed the policy, most parents accepted it because there was such a desperate need for education and no alternatives available. Boycotts failed for nearly two decades.[68]

Strong criticism was directed in later years at the insufficient and discriminatory funding. The amount of money spent, on average, on each black pupil rose from R17 in 1953 to R25 in 1971–72; in the case of whites it increased from R128 to R461. Until the early 1970s the government pegged the state's allocation to black education at R13 million; additional money had to come from direct taxes blacks paid. As a result, the gap in the ratio of white to black per capita spending widened in these years from 7:1 to 18:1.

But it would be wrong to concentrate only on the racial gap in per capita spending. Total spending on black education grew by 14% in real terms from 1952 to 1957, by 2% in the next five years and by nearly 50% from 1962 to 1967.[69] More importantly, there was a major increase in the number of black pupils – from 800 000 in 1950 to 2.75 million in 1970. At the same time, however, the growth rate of black public school teachers remained constant. A recent study passes a measured judgement: 'The experience of black schooling during the 1950–70 period was one of partial modernization, generating a higher enrolment of black pupils, without providing additional teaching resources at a comparable rate.'[70] It is doubtful that the main opposition party in parliament, also subject to white electoral pressure, would have substantially narrowed the gap in per capita spending at a much faster rate.

Taking the entire period of NP rule into account, Sadie states: 'The number of black children enrolled at school grew at an average rate of 5.5% per annum during the period 1948 to 1994, raising the school attendance rate from 24.5% to 84.5%. To provide for a natural increase of 2.8% per year would have strained resources in any economy.'[71]

---

67   Gwendolen Carter, *The Politics of Inequality: South Africa since 1948* (London: Thames and Hudson, 1958), pp. 102-03.

68   Jonathan Hyslop, 'A Destruction Coming In: Bantu Education as a Response to Social Crises', Phil Bonner (ed.), *Apartheid's Genesis* (Johannesburg: Ravan Press, 1993), pp. 393-410.

69   John Kane-Berman. *Soweto: Black Revolt: White Reaction* (Johannesburg: Ravan Press, 1978), p.187.

70   JW Fedderke, R de Kadt and J Lutz, 'Uneducating South Africa: The Failure to Address the Need for Human Capital', *International Review of Education*, 46, 3, 2000, pp. 257-81.

71   JL Sadie, 'Economic-Demographic Aspects of School Education in South Africa', unpublished paper, 2004, p. 15.

Inequalities remained huge. In 1953 government spending per African child was just 14% of that for a white pupil. This was mainly due to the very large intake of black pupils, coupled with the fact that growing numbers of white children were enrolled in the more expensive secondary school standards.[72] Until the early 1970s the system did not do much more than provide very elementary education for black pupils. Analysing the 1970 census data, Feinstein found that 79% of urban blacks and 93% of rural blacks had not attained Standard 6 or higher, compared with a mere 4% of the white labour force. Half of all urban blacks and three quarters of rural blacks had not even passed Standard 3.[73]

Until the early 1970s the department did not insist on Afrikaans as medium of instruction in black secondary schools in Natal, Transkei and parts of the Witwatersrand, where most teachers were not proficient in the language. But the medium of instruction in secondary schools – and insufficient funding – became the targets of the Black Consciousness Movement that rapidly politicised the education system in the early 1970s. At this point Verwoerd's fateful words that blacks ought not to be educated above a certain level if they planned to live and work in the urban areas returned to haunt the system.

The government segregated university education in a move that split the white university community. Coloured, Indian and black students would no longer be able to attend any of the existing 'open' universities, except under special circumstances. In addition to the existing University College of Fort Hare, four new university colleges would be established – two for blacks, one for coloured students and one for Indians.

Verwoerd's 500 days

Verwoerd built up his authority as a leader in a remarkable 500 days, stretching from his response to a speech by Prime Minister Harold Macmillan of Britain on 3 February 1960 to the proclamation of a republic on 31 May 1961, which he considered the highlight of his career. In Macmillan's speech to the South African parliament, he said the British government accepted 'the wind of change' that heralded the rise of national consciousness across the African continent. It hoped South Africa would also confer individual rights on its subject population, and share power in society on the basis of individual merit alone.[74] Although Macmillan did not elaborate, it was generally accepted that the type of inclusive democracy he called for would be based on the liberal Westminster model in which the majority would come to power and rule in a winner-takes-all fashion.

---

72 Jeremy Seekings and Nicoli Nattrass, *Class, Race and Inequality in South Africa* (New Haven: Yale University Press, 2005), p. 134.

73 Feinstein, *An Economic History of South Africa*, p. 160.

74 *Cape Times*, 3 February 1960.

Behind the civilities of diplomacy was an ominous message: in Britain's head-long decolonisation of Africa British morality and British interests considered whites in South Africa expendable. The underlying assumption was that South African whites, like whites in other African colonies, would either accept political subordination to blacks or move elsewhere to live within a white majority society.

Verwoerd welcomed the speech as far as it supported the survival of Western values and Western civilisation. The whites in South Africa, he said, had brought these values and 'civilisation' here, had stimulated African nationalism by bringing education, and had encouraged industry and development. At the same time whites had developed such a stake in South Africa that it had become their only mother-land. Acting as a link between Europe and Africa, they had made themselves in-dispensable. 'We are white,' Verwoerd said, 'but we are in Africa.' In line with the Western policy of decolonisation, South Africa wanted to give Africans full rights in those parts of the country where their forefathers had settled. But whites had to be able to enjoy rights in the parts they had settled.[75] There had to be justice for both blacks and whites.

Speaking on behalf of whites in a follow-up speech a month later, Verwoerd re-jected the notion that only numbers counted. Whites had always been a minority in the world, but had played a dominant role by virtue of their character, initiative, creative urge and intellectual capacity. He added: 'The white man in Africa is not going to be told that because he is outnumbered by black peoples he must allow his rights to be swallowed up and be prepared to lose his say ... The merit which counts is not only that of the individual – even though one recognises such merit in its right and proper place – because that would make it possible for the most capable groups to be outvoted. We who are white will stand, fight and win in Africa on the merits of our white community as an entity.'[76]

When on 21 March 1960 police shot and killed 69 black people who were pro-testing the pass laws in the Sharpeville township, Verwoerd remarked to his bench mate in parliament: 'Now we are going to have great problems.'[77] The wave of pro-tests that followed presented the first major challenge to white rule. ANC leader Albert Luthuli burned his pass and asked people to stay away from work. The stay-away was nearly total and brought many businesses that depended on African labour to a standstill. Many whites were terrified. The stock exchange plummeted, followed by a massive capital outflow. With foreign governments condemning the killings and the harshness of apartheid, the country stood on the brink of interna-tional isolation.

---

75 Pelzer (ed.), *Verwoerd Speaks*, pp. 336-38.

76 Pelzer (ed.), *Verwoerd Speaks*, p. 366.

77 Schoeman, *My lewe in die politiek*, p. 260.

The government's response was swift and ruthless. On 30 March it declared a state of emergency. Over the next few weeks it detained more than 18 000 people. On 8 April it banned the ANC and the Pan Africanist Congress (PAC). Then on 9 April a mentally deranged white man shot Verwoerd in the head and seriously wounded him. The Sharpeville massacre and its aftermath prompted some Nationalist politicians to seriously reconsider the fundamentals of the policy of apartheid, but Verwoerd quickly stamped out the revolt in party ranks (see Chapter 2, p. 50).

The economy quickly recovered from the shocks of the first four months of the year. To stem the flow of money out of the country, the government introduced tough exchange and import controls that proved remarkably effective. Unable to send their money out, investors turned to the stock exchange or speculation in real estate, and industrialists expanded their plants. Order books filled up again. English-speaking South Africans started to look more positively at the prospects for economic growth and stability. De Kiewiet makes the astute comment: 'Considerations of purse and property caused a new thoughtfulness about Dr Verwoerd and his policies.'[78]

Verwoerd soon put his mind to campaigning for a yes vote in the referendum on a republic to be held in October 1960. Before the campaign started, polls showed only minority support for a republic. Verwoerd argued persuasively that establishing a republic was the best way to start uniting the country. Although the English yes vote was small, it probably tipped the scale in favour of a republic. Verwoerd's speeches had been decisive in the victory. His recovery from the assassination attempt and more particularly his against-the-odds victory in the republican referendum elevated him and his policies to an almost untouchable position among his followers.

But Verwoerd was already reformulating his ideology. From the time he became editor in 1937 to his election in 1958 as NP leader, he stressed Afrikaner unity and culture. From 1960 he increasingly stressed white unity and republicanism in place of Afrikaner nationalism and ethnic unity. Toasting the republic on 31 May 1961, the day of the inauguration of President CR Swart, he even spoke of 'the fundamental unity of one *volk* in South Africa'. He also referred to the 'indigenous population', which, unlike other indigenous peoples in the world, had not only survived but had multiplied in numbers. Whites and blacks had to find a way of coexisting alongside each other as friends. It was a far cry from the ideology of orthodox ethno-nationalism that DF Malan had propounded.[79]

---

78   CW de Kiewiet, 'Loneliness in the Beloved Country', p. 419.

79   Pelzer (ed.), *Verwoerd Speaks*, pp. 560-61; T Dunbar Moodie, *The Rise of Afrikanerdom* (Berkeley: University of California Press, 1975), pp. 285-87.

'Full authority' for the homelands

Shortly after becoming prime minister, Verwoerd began to consider the abolition of the indirect representation of blacks in parliament. He believed that the four white representatives in the House of Assembly kept alive the hope that blacks would one day represent blacks in parliament. But this made it necessary to offer some alternative at a time when more and more colonial peoples worldwide were receiving their freedom. Ghana, for example, had become independent in 1957.

Foreign Affairs Minister Eric Louw warned that leaving black people without political rights would have serious consequences for the country's foreign relations. Earlier Verwoerd had shown little enthusiasm when Sabra members and Potchefstroom University's LJ du Plessis had proposed independence for the black homelands. However, in the late 1950s he came round to the idea that conceding the possibility of independence for the homelands could deflect the pressure that had been building up at a time when one African country after the other received its independence. It could also neutralise criticism from the Afrikaner reformists who were disappointed with his response to Tomlinson.[80]

Almost as an aside, Verwoerd stated in parliament on 27 January 1959 that while whites would retain authority over their own territory, blacks would be led in the course of time towards 'full development' and 'full authority' in 'their own areas'.[81] Spotting the significance of Verwoerd's words, *Die Burger* stated in a front-page report that his statement heralded a 'new vision'. Four months later the government passed a law that abolished the system of indirect black political representation in parliament. Introducing the bill, Verwoerd tried to deny the charge that it stripped urban blacks of political rights. A limited form of black local government would be introduced, but these councils would fall under white municipalities, which would continue to own the land on which a township was built. Verwoerd added that urban blacks would also have rights in their respective ethnic homelands – even to vote for the representative bodies in these areas.

The political flagship for the policy was the Transkei, which was granted self-government in 1963 despite an election in which voters showed scant support for the project. Two thirds of Transkei voters cast their votes for Victor Poto's party, which stood for a united, multiracial South Africa where power would be shared. The government only secured a majority for the pro-apartheid party of Kaiser Matanzima by packing the house with traditional leaders it had appointed.

Initially both *The Guardian* and *The Sunday Times* in London commented favourably. The latter described it as a courageous step towards a viable alternative to

---

80   Christopher Marx, 'From Trusteeship to Self-determination: LJ du Plessis – Thinking in Conflict with Hendrik Verwoerd', *Historia*, 55, 2, 2010, pp. 50-75.

81   Pelzer (ed.), *Verwoerd Speaks*, p. 245.

integration. It lauded the £75 million the government had committed in development aid and compared this favourably to the £14 million Britain committed in aid for the British protectorates in southern Africa.[82] But the homelands' economies failed to take off. Their contribution to South Africa's gross domestic product remained insignificant, rising from 2.5% in 1966 to 3.5% ten years later.

Verwoerd's grand scheme

Verwoerd rarely spelled out the ultimate goal of apartheid, though on a few occasions he speculated about some kind of future confederation along the lines of the British Commonwealth. After his withdrawal of South Africa's application to remain part of the Commonwealth, he said in London: 'We prefer each of our population groups to be controlled and governed by themselves, as nations are. Then they can co-operate as in a Commonwealth or in an economic association of nations where necessary.'[83] In a private letter to Robert Menzies, Australia's prime minister, he briefly developed what he called his grand scheme of apartheid. He envisaged a multiracial 'commonwealth' with a conference of premiers as the hub of the system, and black local authorities in 'white' areas linking up with homeland governments. Coloured MPs could one day represent coloured constituencies in parliament on two conditions: that black people accepted they would not be represented in parliament and that coloured people had made good progress with local government.[84] Indian South Africans were not mentioned. It was only in 1963 that the NP government recognised Indian South Africans as full citizens, but it had no plans for their representation, even on local government level.

Verwoerd envisaged the redrawing of the country's boundaries along the northern, north-eastern and north-western borders to facilitate the establishment of a southern African 'commonwealth' or confederation. In 1963 he spoke publicly of the five 'heartlands of the Bantu': Transkei, Zululand, Swaziland, Basutoland and Bechuanaland, and mentioned the possibility of Bechuanaland incorporating the Tswana of the Transvaal.[85] He wanted the British government to work with the South African states to develop southern Africa economically with the aim of consolidating the white and black areas.

Here Verwoerd was following in the footsteps of his predecessors. Since 1910 South African prime ministers had dreamed of incorporating the three British protectorates in order to make the map for a white-black 'division' somewhat more

---

82 Quoted in *Die Burger*, 29 January 1962.
83 Pelzer (ed.), *Verwoerd Speaks*, p. 512.
84 Robert G Menzies, *Afternoon Light: Some Memories of Men and Events* (London: Cassell, 1967), pp. 198-210.
85 BM Schoeman, *Van Malan tot Verwoerd* (Cape Town: Human & Rousseau, 1973), p. 251.

credible. During Macmillan's 1960 visit to Cape Town, Verwoerd asked for permission to speak to the black authorities in the High Commission Territories (Bechuanaland, Basutoland and Swaziland). But this was a dead end. There was no chance of agreement from either the British government or the governments of those territories that they should be swallowed by South Africa.

Verwoerd also spelled out his vision of the direction in which he wanted to take the country to Dag Hammarskjöld, secretary-general of the United Nations, who visited South Africa in January 1961 to investigate charges of human rights violations. Verwoerd considered the visit important enough to arrange six off-the-record meetings with him. According to Brand Fourie, a South African diplomat who accompanied Hammarskjöld on his visit, he was impressed by Verwoerd's intellectual ability, integrity and sense of purpose in pursuing a solution. Verwoerd, in turn, considered the secretary-general a highly intelligent man whose word he could trust.[86]

Hammarskjöld's memorandum of the meetings noted that he told Verwoerd the UN favoured speedy integration in South Africa. Verwoerd said this was totally unacceptable. Hammarskjöld then posed the vital question: was there a chance of apartheid being turned into what he termed a 'competitive alternative' to integration? Verwoerd replied that the homelands policy constituted a key part of the solution.

Hammarskjöld countered that for the homelands policy to be considered a 'competitive alternative', the government had to set aside a sufficient and coherent territory for blacks, publish a plan for their economic development, and introduce institutions based on the will of the people, which would lead to independence if the people so wished. The government also had to accept that the homelands could not be a complete solution. Africans working outside the homelands had to be entitled to similar rights and protection that Western countries gave to foreign workers. In particular, after prolonged residence they had to be entitled to citizenship in South Africa with full civic rights.[87]

Verwoerd had a unique opportunity here to develop a plan that could gather sufficient international support for the 'decolonisation' of South Africa. The indications are that, supremely confident as always, he felt his government could rise to the challenge. Hammarskjöld reported to the UN that Verwoerd indicated he found the talks constructive and intended to invite him again to explore further the matters that were raised.[88]

---

86 Brand Fourie, 'Buitelandse sake onder Verwoerd', WJ Verwoerd (compiler), *Verwoerd: So onthou ons hom*, p. 128.

87 Manuscript of Dag Hammarskjöld's memorandum provided to the author by Brian Urquhart, his biographer. A copy is lodged in the University of Stellenbosch manuscript collection.

88 Chris Saunders, 'Dag Hammarskjöld's Visit to South Africa', *African Journal of Conflict Resolution*, 11, 1, 2011, pp. 15-34.

Tragically, Hammarskjöld was killed a few months later in a plane crash, robbing the South African government of a valuable interlocutor. Nevertheless, later in 1961 the government introduced a form of African local government through Urban Bantu Councils, allowing for the election of representatives on these bodies. With few powers and very limited funds, they failed to win any acceptance and Verwoerd soon seemed to lose interest in them.

A few weeks before his death Verwoerd held up his scheme to an American writer: the 'independent Bantu states', along with the governments of Basutoland, Swaziland and Bechuanaland, could form a common consultative body. 'All will meet as independent states, each having its own personality, dignity and standing ... In this consultative body, Coloureds and Indians along with the Bantu states would also be taken in.' He added: 'If the Basutos or the Swazis did not want to come in, we are prepared to have a consultative body of our own people.'[89]

Radical rejection

Verwoerd symbolised everything the ANC leadership rejected in government policy. Nelson Mandela contributed as volunteer-in-chief to the Defiance Campaign in 1952, in which volunteers in the ANC and allied organisations openly defied apartheid laws and asked the government for African representation on all levels of government. Dismissing the government's position that the legislation was necessary to protect 'the identity of Europeans as a separate community', the letter argued that they were 'man-made laws artificially imposed not to preserve the identity of Europeans as a separate community but to perpetuate the systematic exploitation of the African people'.

Malan's reply, which Verwoerd probably drafted or helped to draft, states that the ANC appeared to argue that racial differences were superficial, rather than 'permanent and not man-made', as Europeans believed them to be. Europeans considered it their right to preserve their identity as a separate community, and the government would never give to 'Bantu men and women' any power over Europeans or 'other smaller non-European groups'.[90]

Mandela started his political career in the ANC Youth League, becoming president in 1951. Initially he strongly supported the idea that Africans had to go it alone. The Defiance Campaign, however, fostered the idea of cooperation between Africans and non-Africans, giving rise to the Congress Alliance. Elites of the coloured, Indian and white community participated in the alliance, along with the ANC leadership. The South African Communist Party (SACP) was banned in 1950 but many

---

89   Allen Drury, 'A Very Strange Society': A Journey to the Heart of South Africa (London: Michael Joseph, 1968), p. 41.

90   Kuper, Passive Resistance in South Africa, pp. 233-41.

members remained active. The link at that stage between the communists and the ANC leadership became so close that a recent study describes it as symbiotic. The communists strongly supported non-racialism and actively supported the ANC as vanguard of the radical struggle against apartheid. At the same time, it encouraged a 'positive class consciousness' against capitalism and for socialism.[91]

The SACP was the first component of the Congress Alliance to launch an armed struggle. For this purpose it founded Umkhonto weSizwe (MK), an underground guerrilla organisation. The first commander was Nelson Mandela. There is a debate on the issue of whether he was a formal member of the SACP at this stage, as historian Stephen Ellis maintains in a recent article, or a 'fellow-traveller' of the communists. Mandela was also the main intermediary who relayed and explained the SACP decision to the ANC. Ellis states that two black SACP members travelled to Beijing where they consulted Mao Zedong about the struggle they planned to wage in South Africa. This shows the extent to which the 'armed struggle was inscribed in the politics of the Cold War'.[92]

Mandela remained interested in dialogue with the Afrikaner nationalists. In 1961 he decided that MK would launch its first attacks on 16 December – the day on which a Voortrekker commando had defeated a large Zulu army 123 years earlier – to demonstrate the dialectic of African and Afrikaner nationalism. In talking to Afrikaners he liked to portray the struggle as between these two nationalisms, which was so bitter because it took place in the same country. He often stressed the parallels between the Afrikaner rebellion in 1914–15 and the ANC insurrection.[93] On other occasions Mandela presented the struggle as a class struggle (Joe Slovo, an SACP leader, would later write that Mandela grasped the 'class basis of national oppression' in the course of the 1950s). At times he even presented it as a struggle between non-racialism and racism (as in his statement from the dock in 1964 during the Rivonia Trial). Mandela was the only person to successfully combine all the different tendencies in the ANC.

It is difficult to say whether Verwoerd and Mandela might have found common ground had they ever met. Verwoerd would have understood the nationalist in Mandela and perhaps even his Africanist tendency, but would probably have been appalled by his identification with communism and his sycophantic admiration of the British culture and traditions. In 1961 Mandela wrote a letter to Verwoerd, calling for a national convention. He received no reply. When he stood trial in August 1963, after being on the run for seventeen months, he said that in any civilised

---

91   David Welsh, *The Rise and Fall of Apartheid* (Johannesburg: Jonathan Ball, 2009), pp 114-16.

92   Stephen Ellis, 'The Genesis of the ANC's Armed Struggle in South Africa, 1948-1961', *Journal of Southern African Studies*, 4, 2011, pp. 657-76.

93   Interview with Nelson Mandela, 12 March 1992.

country this would have been regarded as 'scandalous'. Called as a witness, Verwoerd's private secretary rejected this, saying the letter had remained unanswered because it was aggressive and discourteous. Mandela later commented that 'there may have been something in this'.[94]

In 1962 Albert Luthuli, president of the ANC, described Verwoerd as 'the author of our calamity'. Verwoerd's laws governed every aspect of a black South African's life, from his schooling to the grave. Verwoerd's Bantu Education was a 'huge deceit'. IB Tabata, leader of the Non-European Unity Movement, described Verwoerd's education policy in the title of his book as 'education for barbarism'.[95]

Moderates' doubts

Verwoerd believed that the self-governing homelands would show the world that whites did not want to keep blacks in perpetual servitude. He hoped the West would see his scheme as part of its own attempts at decolonisation and promoting national self-determination for its ex-colonies. Privately, he would later admit he was disappointed by the response of Western governments.[96]

While the homelands, unconsolidated and very poor as most were, could be seen as building blocks of a system – particularly if sometime in the future they were integrated politically with an adjoining white province or region – Verwoerd's scheme offered no real place for urban blacks or the coloured and Indian communities. There was simply nothing that would attract educated urban blacks, from whom the brains trust of the challenge to white supremacy was to come.

Verwoerd insisted he could not offer coloured people any significant alternative to parliamentary representation until he had brought his 'commonwealth' into existence. As an interim measure his government established the Union Advisory Council for Coloured Affairs, but it turned out to be a mere talk shop. He proposed 'full-fledged' coloured municipalities and a Coloured Control Board that would have similar status as a provincial council. The latter could evolve into a 'Coloured Parliament' that would administer education, health and welfare services for coloured people. On matters of common interest he proposed annual 'consultations' between the prime minister (or the minister of coloured affairs) and the executive of the Coloured Board or Council.

The plan was for central government to allocate to these local and 'provincial' bodies the revenue that coloured taxpayers paid directly or indirectly. Verwoerd never dealt with the issue of how the coloured towns, drawing only on the rates and

94 Tom Lodge, *Mandela: A Critical Life* (Cape Town: Oxford University Press, 2006), p. 105.
95 Albert Luthuli, *Let My People Go* (London: Fount Paperbacks, 1962), pp. 176-77; IB Tabata, *Education for Barbarism* (London: Unity Movement of South Africa, 1959, second edition, 1980).
96 Schoeman, *Van Malan tot Verwoerd*, pp. 225-29.

taxes coloured people paid, would escape the fate of becoming mere dormitory towns. Playing on the fears of a vulnerable minority, he urged coloured people to accept a segregated system as a better alternative than a single political system dominated by blacks: 'The coloureds must not think they will be the last to be pushed out of the control of, or the participation in, the advantages of such a mixed community. They might easily be the first. What group might be regarded by the Bantu dictatorship as the least necessary? Will it not be the coloureds? The esteem and help of the whites might still be kept because of the benefit of their knowledge.'[97]

But even the homelands, the putative building blocks of the scheme, showed a dismal lack of development. In 1966 Ton Vosloo, a young reporter at *Die Beeld*, wrote that there was no hurry among businessmen to invest in border industries. He added: 'Economists frankly doubt the viability of most homelands.'[98] Between 1960 and 1972 only 85 554 new jobs were created in the homelands and border areas. This was well below the figure that the Tomlinson Commission considered necessary.

Not much progress was made towards moving the other homelands along the same political path as the Transkei. Asked whether he was going to do this soon, the minister for Bantu administration replied: 'Not too soon. We want to give them more experience first ... put more responsibility on them and see if they can handle it.'[99] There did not seem to be plans for the consolidation of other homelands or the enlargement of the black territories, and their economic development proceeded at a snail's pace.

Yet the Afrikaner nationalist intelligentsia continued to believe in Verwoerd's vision. In a sermon delivered at the time of Verwoerd's death, Danie Malan, a church minister and son of a previous prime minister, spoke for many when he said: 'When JG Strijdom died we were not certain that the policy of apartheid could be implemented, because its extent and complexity seemed overwhelming. Verwoerd brought certainty that the policy could be implemented and was just.'[100] Thirty years after Verwoerd's death Rykie van Reenen, one of the most astute journalists of her time, stressed her belief that Verwoerd's policy was based on idealism. 'He had an absolute certainty and logically saw eventual equality between equal peoples ... I am absolutely convinced that idealism was his point of departure.'[101]

---

97   Pelzer, (ed.) *Verwoerd Speaks*, p. 646.
98   *Die Beeld*, 15 May 1966.
99   Drury, 'A Very Strange Society', p. 55.
100 C Hattingh (compiler), *Hy was groot en gelief: Roudiens-preke by die afsterwe van HF Verwoerd* (Johannesburg: Voortrekkerpers, 1967), p. 94.
101 Judith Tayler, 'With her Shoulder to the Wheel': The Public Life of Erika Theron, 1907-1990', doctoral dissertation, Unisa, 2010, p.73.

One should distinguish between the Verwoerd before he became prime minister and the Verwoerd who established his ascendancy over white politics in the final eight years of his life. There was more than a hint of extremism in his advocacy in 1937 of putting a ceiling on Jewish opportunities in order to enable Afrikaners to advance, refusing to publish any news of the visit of the British royal family in 1947, blocking any integration of coloured people and imposing rigid policies on urban blacks. But there was also a more pragmatic side that became more manifest after 1961.

As Stanley Uys puts it: 'He was no longer determined to enforce the separation of the races, but had begun to seek models in which the race groups could live side by side in harmony. Repeatedly, he presented the nation with new ideas. Would he have been so persistent in ordering his officials to try this plan and then some other plan – all in pursuit of harmony – if he was not also pursuing an ideal?'[102]

It is sometimes argued that Verwoerd's thinking was so rigid and his insistence on *konsekwentheid*, or consistency, so great that if he had lived, his scheme would not have amounted to much. White leaders would still have taken all the decisions at the 'commonwealth' meetings and the pass laws would simply have been replaced by passport controls and the homeland governments would have continued to represent the urban black communities.

Such an interpretation is not necessarily invalid, but one should keep in mind that Verwoerd could come up with the unexpected. Two examples are his 1950 offer to the NRC to open up 'the greatest possible measure of self-government' in the townships, and his willingness in 1961 to discuss 'a competitive alternative' to integration with Hammarskjöld. He could also be stopped, as happened when Ben Schoeman refused to go along with his plan to abolish indirect coloured representation in parliament. Privately he admitted that whites and blacks would have to negotiate often in future.

David de Villiers, a respected senior advocate who led South Africa in the World Court case on its mandate for governing South West Africa, worked closely with Verwoerd for several years. He concluded that while Verwoerd might use expedient political arguments, he was not one to mislead himself on important policy issues. Brand Fourie, secretary for foreign affairs, told him that the legal team found it difficult to defend the policy towards coloured people in South West Africa, since they had no homeland there like the other ethnic groups and shared a culture with whites. Verwoerd's reply was that the policy lacked any logic, adding that coloured and white people had the same destiny. 'But the time is not ripe.'[103]

There is some speculation that Verwoerd may have changed his mind about

---

102 E-mail communication from Stanley Uys, 29 January 2012.
103 Fourie, 'Buitelandse sake', WJ Verwoerd (compiler), *Verwoerd: So onthou ons hom*, p.132.

apartheid in his final days. Nationalist MP and chief whip Koos Potgieter later told business magnate Anton Rupert that a day or two before he died Verwoerd had confessed to him that the existing policy was impractical and impossible to implement. There had to be a change of course, but it could not be done abruptly. Rupert speculated that Verwoerd was impressed by the pragmatism of Chief Leabua Jonathan, who was to become prime minister of Lesotho a month later.[104]

But Jonathan did not seem to share this view. Asked about the leadership qualities of Verwoerd and his successor, John Vorster, he said Verwoerd was 'a bit difficult, indeed very difficult'. He was a philosopher and 'philosophers want you to accept their philosophy'. But he added that Vorster was a lawyer and 'they are more amenable'. This confirms Henry Kissinger's point that a leader's qualities are invariably reinforced by the special qualities of his profession, whether it was law, business or academia.[105] Verwoerd set out as an intellectual, but social forces increasingly challenged the policy he was laboriously constructing.

The spell Verwoerd cast over Afrikaner nationalists was so powerful that for many years after his death there was no attempt to find alternative ways of reaching a more lasting form of political accommodation with blacks. He reminds one of Robert McNamara, an American politician with a 'scientific' approach to waging war in Vietnam, who discovered only later that the number of insurgents killed bore little relationship to the battles on the ground.[106] In a similar way, the projected population figures on which Verwoerd based his policy were seriously wrong. Verwoerd and McNamara come across as two of a kind: both exceptionally intelligent, both completely self-assured and both embracing a mistaken faith in central planning that was fashionable during the 1950s and 1960s.

Two options

During his last five years in office Verwoerd repeatedly insisted that there were only two options for South Africans – segregation or integration – and that segregation was the only choice because integration was so unacceptable to whites. In 1963 he told a largely English-speaking audience: 'You cannot have integration without being prepared to see it through to its logical conclusion ... The majority, whoever they may be, will finally rule. There is no democracy of one big mixed nation possible without at some stage or another the Bantu being in complete control of South Africa ... You may make it difficult for a constitution to be revised constitutionally but the lesson of Africa is clear – constitutions are cast aside sooner than a boot

---

104 Dommisse, *Anton Rupert: 'n Lewensverhaal*, p. 230.
105 Deon Geldenhuys, *The Diplomacy of Isolation: South African Foreign Policy Making* (Johannesburg: Macmillan, 1984), p. 240.
106 John Kay, 'Managers Doomed to Repeat the Mistakes of History', *Financial Times*, 27 July 2009.

grows old . . . Have no illusions, in the black-dominated society it is the white man who will be discriminated against.'[107]

As Henry Fagan observed, however, segregation had serious unacceptable consequences that would become worse over time. He cited leading Mississippi newspaper editor Hodding Carter, who, after a visit to South Africa in the late 1950s, observed that no other nation in the world was as strongly divided as South Africa on language, religious, racial and political grounds. Fagan deplored the removal of the right of Africans to elect representatives to parliament. As the economy became more sophisticated, the need for communication between groups would become ever more pressing. Over the long run, the dominant group would lose most as a consequence of lack of mutual understanding and common loyalty in society. He pointed out that the goal of accommodating most blacks in the homelands could never be realised.[108]

Verwoerd's final five years represented the apogee of the apartheid system. The basic framework and cornerstones of apartheid were in place and state officials zealously guarded against transgressions. Verwoerd prided himself on his *konsekwentheid* that informed his decision to admit no Maoris as part of the New Zealand rugby team in 1965 and led to the tour being cancelled.

In Verwoerd's last month in office *Time* magazine put his photograph on its cover. It was highly critical of apartheid, but observed that South Africa was in the middle of a massive boom. Attracted by cheap labour, a gold-backed currency and high profits, 'investors from all over the world had ploughed money into the country. Production, consumption and the demand for labour [were] soaring'. Verwoerd was 'one of the ablest white leaders Africa has ever produced'.[109]

Two weeks before his death, the *Rand Daily Mail* wrote: 'Dr Verwoerd has reached the peak of a remarkable career . . . The nation is suffering from a surfeit of prosperity.' The day after his death the same paper paid tribute to the leader who had refined the crude ideology of white supremacy 'into a sophisticated and rationalised philosophy of separate development'.[110] In 1967 the *Financial Mail*, South Africa's premier financial magazine, celebrated the period 1961 to 1966 as the 'Fabulous Years', a period in which South Africa's gross national product rose by 30% in real terms.[111]

Some modest redistribution did take place. In 1964 Harry Oppenheimer, head of Anglo American, remarked that in the previous five years the average wages of

---

107 Verbatim copy of speech held in Durban, 26 August 1963, ms. collection of WJ Verwoerd.
108 Fagan, *Our Responsibility*, pp. 28-31.
109 *Time*, 26 August 1966, pp. 20-25.
110 *Rand Daily Mail*, 7 September 1966.
111 *Financial Mail*, 14 July 1967, Supplement, p. 59.

'non-white' workers in secondary industry had risen by 5.4% (against those of whites at 3.7%) per year. This explained why the country was 'so much more stable than many people are inclined to suppose'.[112]

This was of little comfort to blacks living in dire poverty in the reserves. For them the only glimmer of hope was the prospect of a job, albeit one at a very low wage. In 1965, 73.6% of new entrants to the labour market were absorbed into the formal sector, a rate never achieved before. It would rise to 76.6% in 1970, but dropped to 43.4% in 1998.[113]

Assessing Verwoerd and his policies presents a stiff challenge, given that today he is considered the very symbol of injustice. There is an even greater obligation than usual to avoid the perils of judging by hindsight. In 1951, in one of his first speeches as a minister, Verwoerd had said: '[The] survival of white civilization . . . is more important to me than expanded industrial development.'[114] At that point no one could have foreseen the high growth of the 1960s. One of the reasons for the boom must be sought in the fact that investors knew the man at the helm was resolute and would reject all attempts to secure black political and industrial rights. Verwoerd insisted that apartheid was the 'fountainhead' of the economic prosperity that South Africa enjoyed, but although attempts were made until the end of the 1960s to curb the flow of labour to the Witwatersrand, there was no more talk of curbing economic development for the sake of a political ideal.[115]

Two assessments by CW de Kiewiet, published in 1956 and 1964, can still be regarded as among the most perceptive analyses of the difficulties of changing apartheid. In 1956 the respected liberal historian observed that since only whites had the vote, changing apartheid was an exceptionally difficult task. 'Apartheid,' he wrote, 'is no subject for mockery or facile comment. It is very grim, very important, very difficult.'[116] He was not impressed by the proposals of the Sabra academics for the political and economic development of the homelands: 'Out of fact and fancy' Sabra had 'ingeniously concocted . . . a mental toy, operating outside history and economics'. Yet De Kiewiet added: 'Apartheid has within it the basis for re-education and a new recognition of the realities of South African life.'[117]

Verwoerd, like Sabra earlier, accepted that the homelands could develop politically to the point of independence, but he rejected any proposal for large-scale investment. Nevertheless, in 1964 De Kiewiet declared that Verwoerd was confront-

---

112 Anglo American, Chairman's Statement in 1964 Annual Report, p. 2.
113 Personal communication from Jan Sadie, 23 July 2002.
114 *HAD*, 1951, col. 3797.
115 Pelzer, (ed.) *Verwoerd Speaks*, p. 342.
116 CW de Kiewiet, *The Anatomy of South African Misery* (Oxford: Oxford University Press, 1956), pp. 40-45.
117 De Kiewiet, *The Anatomy of South African Misery*, pp. 40-45

ing the country's grave problems with 'boldness, shrewdness and even imagination'. It was, he indicated, by no means absurd to suggest a comparison between Verwoerd and Charles de Gaulle, 'the stern, headstrong but deeply imaginative leader of France'.[118]

Why did De Kiewiet soften his judgement? A clue may be his disillusionment with the newly independent states in Africa. Democracies had been replaced by corrupt dictatorships in Ghana and Sudan; there were ethnic massacres in the Congo; and bloody strife was sapping the prospects of Zanzibar. Most commonly, there was a perversion of the democratic system into one-party rule accompanied by the arrest and expulsion of dissenting leaders without even any pretence of trial by law. One can add a factor that De Kiewiet does not mention. As long as the Soviet Union propagated socialism, which appeared to be working, radical politicians would continue to be attracted to it. There was no reason why they would not want to experiment with it if they unexpectedly came to power.

Implicit in De Kiewiet's assessment is the question: how could voters be persuaded to accept majority rule if there was a good chance that South Africa could follow this negative route? In this context he noted that liberals were showing 'respectful interest' in the concept of Bantustans. His own view was that while the homelands did not offer a major solution to black and white relationships, 'the Bantustan experiment' had some appeal because 'it promises an enlarged political experience and establishes an enlarged area of experiment'. It offered 'some relief from the political rightlessness in the white areas'.[119] De Kiewiet understood that an abrupt and violent change in the political system would disrupt the conditions needed for economic development. The South African liberal, he added, was 'searching desperately to find a way between the two unacceptable alternatives of economic chaos and human despair'.[120]

As late as the 1970s an outcome other than black rule in a unitary state was possible. In 1977 the leading liberal Alan Paton urged the American secretary of state Cyrus Vance to press the South African government to establish a federal state in which the homelands were incorporated. He believed such a federal state could be a stepping stone to an inclusive democracy.[121]

What should not be discounted is the possibility of Verwoerd embarking on a course no one would have anticipated. In November 1950, a month after becoming

---

118 De Kiewiet, 'Loneliness in the Beloved Country', pp. 413-27. 'Oh, you remind me of De Gaulle, you are the same type', British prime minster, Harold Macmillan, remarked in a conversation with him after Verwoerd, on the grounds of principle, refused to concede something. See Betsie Verwoerd, 'Eggenoot', WJ Verwoerd (compiler), *Verwoerd: So onthou ons hom*, p. 50.

119 De Kiewiet, 'Loneliness in the Beloved Country', pp. 424-25.

120 De Kiewiet, 'Loneliness in the Beloved Country', p. 424.

121 Peter Alexander, *Alan Paton* (New York: Oxford University Press, 1994), p. 387.

a minister, he held up the possibility of 'the greatest possible measure of self-government for urban blacks', which was in conflict with the NP's election manifesto of 1948. Verwoerd's presentation of apartheid's goals to UN Secretary-General Dag Hammarskjöld in 1961 impressed the latter sufficiently for him to tell a private meeting: 'I hope you will reach your goal in the way you wish.' Verwoerd's exceptional self-confidence enabled him to gamble with exceeding his authority in order to attain certain goals along the road he envisaged. Liberal Party leader Alan Paton was sufficiently concerned about Hammarskjöld's words to ask him in a telegram to oppose South Africa's polices in the UN until the country's policies were in line with its declaration of human rights.[122]

Verwoerd's main problem was one over which he had no control. He saw his scheme as a plan in the making, but his successors – most notably John Vorster, who admired him greatly – embraced his policy and executed it as if it was the final word and only awaited dutiful implementation. As a result the plan stagnated, something Verwoerd would probably not have allowed.[123]

In an ironic way Verwoerd was the father of the mass democracy that was introduced in the mid-1990s. His introduction of state-funded mass education put South Africa on a new road. Although funding in the first two decades was inadequate and discriminatory, the reform had a dynamic of its own, pushing black children upwards to ever-higher standards. The higher the standards black pupils reached, the more comprehensively they rejected apartheid.[124] Segregated colleges produced the alienated Black Consciousness leadership that would rally the schoolchildren of the townships to revolt in 1976.

---

122 *Die Burger*, 11 January 1961.
123 E-mail communication from Wynand Boshoff, 11 May 2011.
124 Giliomee and Schlemmer, *Apartheid to Nation-building*, p. 119.

Chapter 4

Denying Black South Africans Citizenship: John Vorster's Empire

TWO WEEKS AFTER HE CAME TO POWER IN 1966 BALTHAZAR JOHANNES (JOHN) Vorster made it clear he was Hendrik Verwoerd's disciple, planning to grant political rights to blacks only in their own territories and never in 'white' territories. Two years later he insisted: 'We have our land, and we alone will have the say over the land. We have our Parliament, and in that Parliament we and we alone will be represented.' When his cabinet first met he said: 'Verwoerd was an intellectual giant. He thought for each of us. I am not capable of being a second Verwoerd. From now on each of us will have to know his own field, immerse himself in it and control it.'[1]

In 1976, with the townships ablaze in an urban uprising, Vorster gave the second Verwoerd Memorial Lecture. He recounted how as a young parliamentarian in the 1950s he felt that if Verwoerd couldn't 'find a solution to our problems we must accept that they are insoluble'.[2] Clearly he thought Verwoerd had found the solution. While Vorster would dominate parliament and the NP caucus from 1970, he would fail to introduce any significant political reforms. It was almost as if he felt that he had no responsibility to do so, since Verwoerd in his wisdom had already provided the model. He told a biographer: 'I never saw it as my task to push forward policy either in Parliament or outside. A person can never become a good leader unless he is also a good follower.'[3]

But the world of Verwoerd no longer existed. A major change in the understanding of human settlement before the founding of a Dutch refreshment station had come about. In the 1960s archaeological research revealed a picture of pre-1652 human settlement very different from that of 1959, when Verwoerd first spelled out his apartheid scheme (see pp. 57-58). Informed opinion now accepted that by the 1650s, when whites came to stay in the southernmost part of Africa, black settlement was already widespread in the eastern and northern part of the country.

Vorster never seemed to take note of this fundamental shift in historical knowl-

---

1   BM Schoeman, *Vorster se 1000 dae* (Cape Town: Human & Rousseau, 1974), p. 14.
2   BJ Vorster, *Tweede HF Verwoerd gedenklesing* (Pretoria: University of Pretoria, New Series 109, 1976), p. 4.
3   John D'Oliveira, *Vorster – The Man* (Johannesburg: Ernest Stanton, 1977), p. 225.

edge. He vainly attempted to justify the homeland policy in traditional terms as something that 'history' had imposed. He stated: 'It was not our party's policy to annex the black people and bring them under our control. The British had brought them into the state. If the British had not incorporated them, they would have been independent long ago.'[4] With the historical justification all but gone, the ideological basis of the policy was threadbare.

A second major change was even more far reaching. The demographic projections on which Verwoerd had based his policy were revealed as hopelessly flawed (see Chapter 3, pp. 58-59). In 1969 *Die Beeld* announced 'a new factor' in South African politics: the black population was growing much faster than anticipated. Instead of a projected 19 million black people, there would be 28 million by the year 2000.[5] But even the revised projections were wrong. In reality, by 2000 there were 34 million black South Africans, with some 15 million living in cities instead of the 2–3 million projected in 1951.[6]

The end of the 1960s was perhaps the government's last opportunity to take the initiative and devise a policy that, over the long term, would secure for whites and other minorities at least part of the power, or power in part of the country. Black political organisations locally and abroad were still struggling to recover from the blows of the early 1960s. In 1969 Vorster described the state's battle against its enemies as an 'easy one'.[7] What was called the 'tyranny of numbers' was not yet a decisive factor, but between 1970 and 1995 the black population would jump from 15 to 31 million.

The devolution of power to multiracial authorities in the regions was probably the only step that would have prevented the all-out onslaught of the 1980s against a single seat of power. But Vorster's response was as unrealistic as the talk of seven or eight viable states in the respective homelands. He set out to withdraw South African citizenship from all those blacks whose putative nations had been granted independence. When the Transkei and Ciskei were made 'independent', for instance, all Xhosa speakers lost their South African citizenship. The same would happen to Tswana and Venda people. In 1978 Minister of Plural Relations Connie Mulder formulated the political rationale bluntly: 'If our policy is taken to its logical conclusion as far as black people are concerned, there will be not one black man with South African citizenship ... Every black man in South Africa will eventually be accommodated in some independent new state in this honourable way and there will no

---

4 *Die Burger*, 16 May 1977.

5 *Die Beeld*, 5 and 19 January 1969.

6 E-mail communication from Servaas van der Berg, 21 November 2010. For a detailed demographic study of black urbanisation see P Smit and JJ Booysen, *Swart verstedeliking: Proses, patroon en strategie* (Cape Town: Tafelberg, 1981); according to the 1951 census there were 2.3 million blacks in cities and 614 000 in towns, p. 36.

7 Annette Seegers, *The Military in the Making of Modern South Africa* (London: Tauris, 1996), p. 132.

longer be a moral obligation on this Parliament to accommodate these people.'[8]

Vorster's term of twelve years can be divided into two parts. In the first half there were positive elements, such as the easing of petty apartheid. He also observed conventional etiquette in government-to-government relations. For instance, he had lunch in Pretoria with Chief Leabua Jonathan, prime minister of Lesotho – unlike Verwoerd, who sent officials in his place.[9] His government urged employers to narrow the enormous racial gap in wages, and the public sector set an example. It expanded secondary education for black pupils and steadily narrowed the racial gap in social spending.

A much darker picture marked the period 1974 to 1978. 'Summits' with homeland leaders produced few results. In authorising a military incursion into Angola, Vorster hoped to gain the support of the United States and attract a new black ally in Jonas Savimbi, leader of one of the popular movements. Here Vorster was totally out of his depth, simply failing to understand either American or African politics.

'Relying on his instincts'

Born in 1915, Vorster grew up as one of fourteen children on a farm near the small town of Sterkstroom in the eastern Cape. His father was one of the first people in his district to subscribe to *Die Burger* when it was established in 1915. Vorster prided himself on his political instincts, which he believed he got from his mother, who, he said, 'was very seldom wrong'. He added: 'Let me say outright that I have relied very heavily on my political instincts on a number of occasions and, on balance, I think that I have come out of these decisions on the right side.'[10]

Yet trusting one's instincts could be a high-risk form of decision-making, as revealed by US President George Bush's decision to invade Iraq early in the twenty-first century. Vorster's 'instincts' would prompt him to send the armed forces on an incursion into Angola from which the South African government would extricate itself only with great difficulty and at huge cost.

Vorster studied at the University of Stellenbosch, where he received a law degree in 1938. In 1940 he became an attorney in Port Elizabeth, where he was arrested two years later. He was detained without trial for eighteen months at Koffiefontein. Vorster was active in the anti-war Ossewa-Brandwag movement and made no secret of his support for an authoritarian system to replace the parliamentary one. In 1953 he became a member of parliament and in 1961 Verwoerd appointed him minister of justice.

---

8 *House of Assembly Debates,* 1978, col. 579.

9 Deon Geldenhuys, *The Diplomacy of Isolation: South Africa's Foreign Policy Making* (Johannesburg: Macmillan, 1984), p. 261.

10 D'Oliveira, *Vorster,* p. 266.

Vorster introduced draconian security legislation, warning that he would act against 'agitators' with all the means at his disposal. The security police used these laws to smash the ANC and all other organisations prepared to use violence to bring about a unitary state and universal franchise. In the leadership election of 1966 Vorster was the candidate of the anti-communist right, which applauded his attacks on communists and liberals as subversive elements.

Vorster was reputed to have had the untidiest desk of all the attorneys on the East Rand. Once he became prime minister, it was clear he was a poor administrator. By all accounts, the administrative system underlying cabinet decision-making was primitive: there was no cabinet secretariat and the most junior minister kept a record of decisions in an exercise book. The unfortunate result of Vorster's administrative style was rampant 'departmentalism', with ministers heading out in different directions. This differed starkly from Verwoerd's style.

There were other major differences between him and Verwoerd. Verwoerd's apartheid scheme was a goal in itself, one that did not allow for internal inconsistencies, but for Vorster apartheid was 'merely a method to serve the goal of maintaining Afrikaner identity.'[11] He persuaded his followers that allowing black sportsmen representing other countries or black diplomats in South Africa did not threaten Afrikaner identity or security. He also permitted the so-called *verligtes* (enlightened ones) in the Afrikaner nationalist movement to push for incremental reform.

While Verwoerd protected the faction later known as *verkramptes* (arch-conservatives), Vorster held a protective hand over the *verligtes*. He had to be cautious, though, with surveys showing two thirds of the white political elite were insisting on rigid segregation. Nevertheless, within the elite the feeling had grown that the rigorous application of apartheid was dysfunctional and sometimes downright embarrassing. Helen Suzman, virtually the sole liberal voice in parliament, noted a strange phenomenon in the aftermath of Verwoerd's assassination: 'the eerie absence' of almost any reference to him. 'It seemed as if there was a conscious effort to forget him, to exorcise his memory.'[12]

As a leader Vorster could not have been more different from Verwoerd. Vorster was, as Suzman notes, pragmatic, down to earth and with no pretension to divine missions. In her words, Verwoerd was 'the only man who has ever scared me stiff', but she managed to strike up a working relationship with Vorster on issues such as the treatment of Nelson Mandela and other political prisoners. Verwoerd squashed dissidents with his sharp intellect and force of personality, but Vorster became bogged down by strife inside his party.

While Verwoerd was preoccupied with the future, Vorster disliked speaking about

11 Dirk Richard, *Moedswillig die uwe: Persoonlikhede in die Noorde* (Johannesburg: Perskor, 1985), p. 134.
12 Helen Suzman, *In No Uncertain Terms* (Johannesburg: Jonathan Ball, 2003), p.72.

it. His biographer noted: '[H]e consistently evaded serious discussion of the future.' He was, the author went on, like a chess player, determined not to reveal his moves to anybody.[13] Vorster's style could also be compared to that of the chairman of a board who operated on the basis of consensus. His deliberations were pragmatic, experimental and tentative. The overriding concern was party unity.

Verwoerd was a political entrepreneur, wooing English speakers immediately after winning the referendum on a republic. He was prepared to take his own political life in his hands in announcing policy shifts. He told his family he kept his small farming operations going as an economic safety net, since it was possible to lose political power overnight.[14]

Vorster, by contrast, refused to gamble. No entrepreneur who sought to expand his power base, he considered himself a chess player patiently waiting for opponents to make a mistake and then eliminating them or keeping them safely at bay. Helen Suzman recounted that when Vorster asked the world in 1974 to 'give South Africa six months', those urban blacks she spoke to were captivated. 'If only he had offered something concrete, even if it was only putting blacks in the Senate, he would have turned the process of polarisation around.'[15]

But Vorster had no intention of doing this. In his last year or two he dabbled with the idea of incorporating the black urban elite into a position of semi-privilege, but he could not bring himself to abolish the pass laws.

Empire with a difference

Under Vorster the large 'Native Affairs' bureaucracy set up by Verwoerd expanded further. In 1966 the perceptive British journalist Douglas Brown wrote that South Africa was a colonial empire with a difference: she had her colonies at home. 'The Department of Bantu Administration and Development was what the Colonial Office was to Britain a century ago – if you can imagine the people over whom it ruled milling around in the streets of London.' He went on: 'There was something uncanny about this mighty *imperium et imperio*, which must be one of the biggest and most all-embracing administrative machines on the face of the earth.' It was equally ubiquitous in the towns and the reserves, 'controlling the movement, the labour, the housing, the education and the social welfare of every African in the Republic'.[16]

At 'summits' that Vorster arranged with homeland leaders he was like a Roman emperor, often concerning himself with trivial issues while the barbarians were

---

13   D'Oliveira, *Vorster*, p. 287.
14   E-mail communication from Wynand Boshoff, 3 February 2012.
15   Interview with Helen Suzman, 26 August 2004.
16   Douglas Brown, *Against the World* (London: Collins, 1966), p. 114.

massing on the borders. The summits discussed the finer details of the administration of black affairs, but not the principle of white rule. Vorster heard the homeland leaders' pleas about land, citizenship and influx control – and promptly dismissed them. He acted as if real negotiations had taken place at these meetings, but the leaders had no power. He also held periodic meetings with those coloured politicians who participated in the segregated structures his government had introduced. Just like Chief Mangosuthu Buthelezi, leader of the KwaZulu Territorial Authority, they found these meetings a complete waste of time.

Vorster strongly believed that subordinate communities such as the coloured people should take responsibility for their own 'salvation', just as he believed the Afrikaners had done in escaping from poverty. Offering Dr Richard van der Ross the post of vice-chancellor of the University of the Western Cape in 1976, he told him: 'There was an era when the Afrikaners, even if they performed well, were not recognised as equal to English speakers.' Van der Ross later commented: 'I understood that he was aware of the situation [of the coloured people], but that we would have to do something about it ourselves. We must organise like the Afrikaners had done against the English ... He was implying that we [the Afrikaner and the coloured community] would eventually arrive at the same place.'[17]

Vorster believed that between 1930 and 1960 Afrikaners had saved themselves, and in doing so had provided a model for the coloured and black communities. But this analogy was fatally flawed. Afrikaners struggling to get on their feet economically in the towns and the cities had the vote, were far better educated than coloured or black people, and could increasingly draw on the surplus capital of Afrikaner farmers, who had managed to commercialise their undertakings since the mid-1930s. They received generous government subsidies and other forms of assistance. While it is true that Afrikaners had made the best of their opportunities, their advance occurred at a time when the economy grew faster than ever before or subsequently.

Erika Theron, a staunch Afrikaner nationalist who headed a commission on conditions in the coloured community, rejected the suggestion that coloured people should accept responsibility for their own salvation as the Afrikaners had done. She correctly pointed out that they lacked political and economic bargaining power. There was 'no possible comparison between the position of the Coloureds and the so-called poor-White problem'.[18]

Vorster never got to know well any professional, westernised Africans or members of the black elite. He countered African nationalism with all his might. He

---

17 *Rapport*, 17 February 1991.
18 JA Tayler, 'With her Shoulder to the Wheel: The Public Life of Erika Theron, 1907-1990', doctoral dissertation, Unisa, 2010, p. 317.

disdained liberals, whom he suspected of wanting to 'skim off' the cream of other peoples, but he could be equally contemptuous of those who opportunistically tried to promote Afrikaner chauvinism. He coined the scornful phrase 'super Afrikaners' for elements in the Broederbond who attacked him from the right after his government had made minor modifications to apartheid, trying to counter South Africa's growing international isolation.

Yet Vorster knew the South African state had to modernise and had limited time to do so. International pressure against apartheid was intensifying. By the early 1970s diplomatic and economic sanctions had started to bite, the United Nations had prioritised wresting South West Africa from South African control, anti-apartheid organisations had proliferated, the war in Rhodesia had turned against the Smith government, and the Soviet Union had begun to fish in troubled waters in and around the African subcontinent. For South Africa the glory days of a booming economy had passed and the country was facing rapidly growing black unemployment.

A power base

During his first four years as prime minister, Vorster struggled to find his feet. The rebellion of the *verkramptes* under Albert Hertzog caused him undue concern and there was also friction with Piet Meyer and some other Broederbond leaders. He nearly resigned a year or two after coming to power when the *verkramptes* under Hertzog targeted him with gossip and slander because of his relaxation of social apartheid. Ben Schoeman, the most senior minister, had to tell him bluntly: 'You cannot run away now, since it will have people believe the lies are true. Think of the damage you will do to the party.'[19]

The 1970 election, the first in which the far-right Herstigte Nasionale Party participated, resulted in what was seen as an NP setback, but Vorster soon consolidated his position and emerged stronger after the general election of 1974. The NP not only increased its number of seats from 117 in the 1970 election to 122 (out of 169 seats), but also routed its historical foe, the United Party, which soon began to disintegrate. Even more gratifying to Vorster was the reverse suffered by the Afrikaner right-wing party, the Herstigte National Party: its total votes dropped from 53 504 in 1970 to 44 717.

This was a ringing endorsement of Vorster's attempt to trim the rough edges of apartheid. By the mid-1970s he enjoyed the support of more than 80% of Afrikaners and a considerable proportion of English-speaking whites. When 60% of Afrikaners polled indicated that they would support their leaders even if they acted in ways

---

19   Ben Schoeman, *My lewe in die politiek* (Johannesburg: Perskor, 1978), p. 335.

they did not understand or approve of, it was Vorster they had in mind.[20] But Vorster's popularity had begun to extend beyond the ranks of the white population. When the black paper *The World* invited its readers to evaluate Vorster as prime minister, the majority wrote positive letters. An English daily commented: 'The whole country is on a Vorster kick.'[21] The question was what Vorster might achieve with this substantial support base.

'An appalling wage differential'

Vorster understood that the country's future would be decided in the cities and that there would be no reverse flow to the homelands. He accepted the urgent need for removing petty injustices and narrowing the huge white-black wage gap. George Kennan, who visited the country in 1971 as a guest of the US-South Africa Leadership Exchange, touched on the issue. Esteemed in American academic and diplomatic circles, he had served as a diplomat in Moscow between 1944 and 1946, going on to become perhaps the most distinguished commentator on the Cold War. An article 'The Sources of Soviet Conduct' (also known as 'Telegram X'), of which he was later revealed to be the author, depicted the Soviet system as inherently unstable. He advocated 'containment' and letting time do its work rather than forcing the issue through military confrontation.

His view of the South African 'empire' was essentially the same. He remarked that to anyone raised with traditional American values the situation in South Africa was nothing less than tragic. Nevertheless, he opposed sanctions and other forms of external intervention. He took what he called the historian's view: '[T]here are problems which, at the time they occur, are insoluble.' In answer to some black observers' argument that conditions could not get worse, he referred to his Moscow experience: 'Joe Stalin taught the Soviet people one thing: when you think that life cannot get any harder, it can.'

Kennan believed it was unnecessary for South Africa to be 'homogenised to be happy'. Accordingly, he had nothing against the policy of giving the various black African groups their own territories and extending full economic rights to blacks living there. But he was highly critical of the government's pretence that the presence of millions of blacks in the major industrial centres of South Africa was only a 'temporary condition'. All the people in South Africa, he argued, were caught in a situation none of them had created themselves. Deploring the gap between whites

---

20   Theo Hanf et al., *South Africa: The Prospects of Peaceful Change* (London: Rex Collings, 1981), pp. 401–05.

21   JA du Pisani, 'Die BJ Vorster tydperk', unpublished paper, 2011.

and blacks, he wanted to see it narrowing.[22]

The disparities in the state sector were huge. Between 1947 and the mid-1960s the maximum value of black pensions fell from 25% of the maximum value of white pensions to 13%. This was not enough to cover the minimum food budget.[23] The ratio of white to black per capita income rose from 10.6:1 in 1946/7 to 15:1 in 1970.[24] More than 70% of the national income went to whites, which formed just 15% of the population. One of the main reasons for the huge wage gap was the dual system that characterised industrial relations (see p. 148).

Vorster recognised the irreversible dependence of the economy on a growing black labour force, whose levels of education and skills were becoming one of the main determinants of economic growth. The government accepted that establishing high schools for blacks in 'white' areas had become a priority and that the racial gap in spending had to be reduced. The ratio of per capita spending on white and black pupils narrowed progressively from 16.6:1 in 1968 to 7.2:1 in 1982.[25] Both the state and the private sector were beginning to accept that the enormous wage disparity between whites and blacks was unacceptable.

The Vorster government concluded that with the white community sufficiently well off, the state had to start meeting its obligations to the disenfranchised.[26] It urged employers to narrow the wage gap and undertook to set an example in the civil service.[27] As economist Charles Simkins later observed, this was a development no one could have predicted at the beginning of the 1970s.

In the 1975/6 budget the government reduced the personal income of whites by 7%, but raised that of Indians by 3%, that of coloureds by 19% and that of blacks by 11%.[28] In 1978 Vorster warned whites that the abolition of social and economic inequities would demand significant sacrifices in their living standards and mate-

---

22 George Kennan, 'Three Visitors Report', *Munger Africana Library Notes*, March 1971, p. 2. In the same year as Kennan's visit, Heribert Adam's *Modernizing Racial Domination: South Africa's Political Dynamics* (University of California Press, 1971) appeared. It argued that a revolution was not imminent and that the regime was capable of adapting its labour system pragmatically. The book dominated academic debate for nearly fifteen years.

23 Stephen Devereaux, *South African Income Distribution, 1900-1980* (University of Cape Town: Southern Africa Labour and Development Research Unit, 1983), pp. 56-59.

24 Jeremy Seekings and Nicoli Nattrass, *Class, Race and Inequality in South Africa* (Scottsville: University of KwaZulu-Natal Press, 2005), p. 137.

25 Ken Hartshorne, *Crisis and Challenge: Black Education, 1910-1990* (Cape Town: Oxford University Press, 1992), p. 87.

26 Charles Simkins, *Liberalism and the Problem of Power* (Johannesburg: SA Institute of Race Relations, 1986), p. 16.

27 Devereaux, *South African Income Distribution*, p. 48.

28 For an extended discussion see JL Sadie, 'The Economic Demography of South Africa', doctoral dissertation, University of Stellenbosch, 2000, pp. 316-85.

rial aspirations. Three years later the director-general of finance declared that a drastic increase of state spending on blacks was underway at the expense of whites. It was now government's priority to narrow the racial gap in education and other social services. It would do so by keeping spending on whites constant in real terms.[29]

'Human beings with souls'

The state's example was one that the private sector could not ignore. By the beginning of the 1970s the ratio of white to black wages in the private sector was a shocking 21:1 in the mining sector and 6:1 in the manufacturing sector. In real terms, black mining and farm wages had declined since 1910. On 7 July 1973 *The Economist* reported that Anglo American's pre-tax profit from gold mining in 1972 was more than five times its black wage bill. An outcry over low wages and a rise in the gold price prompted the corporation to increase the wages of its black miners by 26%.

On 9 January 1973 some 2 000 black workers went on strike at the Coronation Brick and Tile Company on the outskirts of Durban, demanding that the minimum weekly cash wage be raised from R8.97 to R20. Although this was abysmally low, some other plants were paying even less. The strike quickly spread to other factories in Durban. Some 75 000 black workers in different sectors embarked on strike action. The *Financial Mail* published a cover story entitled 'Frame's shame' about the Frame Group, a multinational company, which paid its textile workers lower wages than Coronation Brick and Tile. In Britain the growing anti-apartheid lobby seized on these appalling wages to demonstrate the iniquity of the system.

Blacks had engaged in so little industrial action in the 1960s that the Durban strikes immediately attracted huge attention. It puzzled observers that the strikes happened in Durban, with its black population of 400 000, considered much less politicised than those on the Witwatersrand. But the reasons were simple: apart from the seafront, the white city was virtually completely surrounded by black townships. Since the late 1960s informal alliances had been formed between black activists, mainly inclined towards the Black Consciousness Movement, and radical white academics committed to fundamental change.

The strikers also seemed to have received some veiled encouragement from Zulu traditional authorities. Paramount Chief Goodwill Zwelithini had visited the Coronation brick works in the second half of 1972. According to an analysis published shortly after the strike: 'There is little doubt that his speech left many workers with a more or less firm expectation that the new year would bring higher wages.'[30]

29   Hermann Giliomee, 'Afrikaner Politics, 1977-1987', John Brewer (ed.), *Can South Africa Survive?* (London: Macmillan, 1989), pp. 114-16.

30   Institute for Industrial Education (IIE), *The Durban Strikes* (Durban: Ravan Press, 1974), p. 10.

Chief Mangosuthu Buthelezi, appointed leader of the KwaZulu Territorial Authority in 1970, became very involved in helping workers in Richard's Bay and Durban.[31]

In parliament, Minister of Labour Marais Viljoen criticised Buthelezi for 'interfering' in the strikes on the grounds that Durban fell outside KwaZulu's jurisdiction. Buthelezi curtly pointed out that the South African government created the KwaZulu authority for Zulus 'wherever they are'.[32] He supported the founding of the Institute for Industrial Education (IIE) by some academics in Durban (including Lawrence Schlemmer, Rick Turner, who was later assassinated, and Fozia Fisher, his companion. At the invitation of this group and some workers, Buthelezi was made the IIE's 'chancellor'.

The outcry over the shocking pay for workers scrambled some old dividing lines in white South African politics. Historian Alex Mouton remembers his father, a senior police officer in Durban, telling him of a frantic call he received from a businessman demanding that his striking workers be arrested. Unmoved, Mouton asked his caller: 'Why must my policemen be stoned when you do not pay your workers a living wage?' Mouton commented: 'My father was a paternalist who saw himself as the protector of blacks and was revolted by businessmen and farmers who exploited defenceless workers.'[33]

The head of the riot police made it clear there would be no arrests. 'The police have nothing whatsoever against people demanding higher wages,' he said when he flew to Durban from Pretoria. He instructed the police to use minimum force.[34] The government had obviously decided that the strikes posed no challenge to the state – but this proved to be incorrect. The major impact of the Durban strikes was not the higher wages obtained, but the enhanced sense of worker power.

Accustomed to moral outrage over apartheid directed almost solely at the Afrikaners, the Afrikaans press displayed considerable schadenfreude over the embarrassing revelations of extremely low wages paid by local English or British firms. *Die Nataller*, published by the Natal National Party, carried a story deploring the 'shocking wages' under a headline stating 'Employers must take full blame'.[35]

The debate in parliament displayed the divisions within the NP. There was deadlock between those intent on coming down on the strikers with the full might of the law and those who realised that white power had to meet the reasonable demands of the black workforce. In the former camp was the minister of labour, who railed against the 'inciters and the people who are behind the agitators'. Their objective was 'to cause chaos' in South Africa.

31   Interview with Mangosuthu Buthelezi, 15 September 2010.
32   Interview with Mangosuthu Buthelezi, 15 September 2010.
33   E-mail correspondence with Alex Mouton, 6 October 2010.
34   IIE, *The Durban Strikes*, p. 20.
35   *Die Nataller*, 3 February 1973.

By contrast, Vorster did not once refer in his speech to agitators. He declared: 'I do want to say at once that the events there contain a lesson for us all ... We would be foolish if we did not all benefit from the lessons to be learned from that situation.' He also appealed to employers in the private sector. Too many of them 'saw only the mote in the Government's eye and failed completely to see the beam in their own'. They should see their workers not only as units producing so many hours of service a day for them; they should also see them as 'human beings with souls'.[36]

What did Vorster mean by learning lessons from the Durban strikes? Perhaps his instincts told him that starvation wages for workers were detrimental to state security. At the very least his words meant his government would not stand in the way of attempts by workers to improve their wages. But the government's reforms only tinkered with the system. It passed a law that encouraged black workers and their employers to establish either works committees or liaison committees. Works committees were factory-based bodies for which workers elected representatives. They had limited rights of consultation with employers. Much weaker were the liaison committees, which most employers preferred, with a 50/50 workers/management representation that was largely decided by management. Both works and liaison committees fell far short of recognition of black unions, which were still excluded from the industrial councils, where effective bargaining took place.

De-nationalising blacks

Initially Vorster showed little indication that he intended to make haste in granting independence to the homelands. Shortly after he became prime minister the government introduced regional authorities in six of the homelands, but there was no indication of any further constitutional development. In 1968 Minister of Bantu Administration MC Botha laid down prerequisites for independence so stringent that they would take at least a generation to be met.[37] Opposition parties argued that astronomical sums would have to be invested to develop these territories to a level where the stream to the cities could be reversed.[38] Among blacks no strong popular support had developed for the policy.

Early 1970, implementation of the homeland policy was accelerated. The dream of homelands with viable economies had faded, but not the determination to transfer as many blacks as possible to them. Acting as a spur was the news that broke in 1969 that the black population would be an estimated 10 million people larger than projected in 1950 – a projection on which Verwoerd had based his policy. Under

---

36 *House of Assembly Debates*, 9 February 1973, col. 346.
37 South African Institute of Race Relations, *South Africa Survey, 1968* (Johannesburg: SA Institute of Race Relations, 1968), p. 141.
38 JA du Pisani, 'Die ontplooiing van afsonderlike ontwikkeling tydens die BJ Vorster era: Die tuislandbeleid', doctoral dissertation, UOFS, 1989, p. 189.

Vorster the idea caught on that a numerical majority for whites could be artificially engineered by removing South African citizenship from blacks if their putative nation was granted independence.

By the beginning of the 1970s the Vorster government had become willing to grant independence. A 1971 law put all the homelands on the same track as the Transkei for the transfer of political, executive and judicial authority. Over the next seven years Bophuthatswana, Ciskei, Lebowa, Venda, Gazankulu, QwaQwa and KwaZulu all became self-governing. In 1976 Transkei became independent, followed by Bophuthatswana (1977), Venda (1979) and Ciskei (1981).

Along with independence came de-nationalisation. A 1970 law made it possible to deprive Africans of their South African citizenship if the government of the homeland they were deemed to belong to had opted for independence. In terms of the Population Registration Act, the main racial groups (e.g. blacks) were subdivided into ethnic units (e.g. Xhosas or Tswanas). Children whose parents had acquired an exemption to stay in the urban areas – referred to as 'Section Ten' rights – would not inherit the exemption if their parental 'homeland' had become independent before their birth. They would only qualify for residence permits.[39]

In 1976 Transkei was granted independence by the Status of Transkei Act. It provided that, in addition to those persons born in Transkei or directly descended from Transkeians, any person who was a citizen of Transkei before independence or who had linguistic or cultural connections with the Xhosa or Sotho groups in the Transkei 'shall cease to be a South African citizen'. This effectively turned all the people described in the Act into alien citizens who could make no claim to full citizenship of the Republic of South Africa.[40]

When the government of Lucas Mangope decided to take independence for Bophuthatswana he vainly tried to prevent a similar fate befalling Tswana people living outside the homeland. Vorster bluntly rejected the plea because the purpose of his homeland policy was to de-nationalise blacks. He depicted the negotiations as follows: 'Mangope and I agreed about everything as far as independence was concerned. Then Mangope came up with the idea that he wanted to take only those people who were within Bophuthatswana territory.'

Vorster was prepared to wait patiently until his opponent gave way. 'I then said to him the policy of my party is not to make territories independent but to make nations independent. I said to him that if he expected to take only some Tswanas and expected me to take the rest and give them South African citizenship, then I was not prepared to come to an independence agreement with him.'

39   Du Pisani, 'Ontplooiing van afsonderlike ontwikkeling', p. 115.
40   John Dugard, *Human Rights and the South African Legal Order* (Princeton: Princeton University Press, 1978), pp. 94-95.

Vorster went on: 'On the eve of independence Mangope again came with a pro-posal: he was prepared to take all the Tswanas but they should be allowed to exer-cise a choice whether they wanted to accept his citizenship. I then said to him I was not prepared to give to blacks South African citizenship. And that was that.'[41] Vorster appeared to believe that the weight of black numbers could be countered by the 'de-nationalisation' of blacks and by 'resettling' large numbers of blacks in the home-lands. Despite these policies, by 1980 there were only 4.5 million whites in 'white' South Africa compared to 10.1 million blacks.[42]

The land issue

Apart from the issue of citizenship and a lack of economic development, the home-lands policy raised the contentious issue of land. The question uppermost in homeland leaders' minds was getting more land and having the scattered pieces of land that made up their respective homelands consolidated into a contiguous land mass. When the UP government decided in 1936 to remove Cape Africans from the voters' roll, it undertook to buy additional land for blacks, in accordance with pro-posals made by the Beaumont Commission in 1916. Apart from the 10.4 million morgen set aside in the Natives Land Act of 1913, the government undertook to acquire a further 8.3 million morgen to be transferred to blacks. This would raise the black share of the country's territory from 7% to 13%.

Fearing resistance from the farming lobby, the state had not yet acquired the additional land by the early 1970s. Homeland leaders pressed for the transfer of land but also asked a new question: why stick to the 1936 legislation when it came to a fair allocation of the land? Backed by other homeland leaders, Mangosuthu Buthelezi correctly pointed out that when the legislation was passed in 1936, the idea of independence for the black territories was not even contemplated. Blacks had never been consulted about the division of land. Before any homeland govern-ment could consider independence, the issue of a fair division of land between whites and blacks had to be dealt with.

In 1972 Vorster said that while his government was prepared to work for home-land consolidation, it would consider the land issue closed once it had transferred the additional six percentage points decided on in 1936. He warned homeland lead-ers not to demand additional land as a precondition for independence; it would only serve to delay the constitutional process.[43] At a 1973 summit six homeland leaders urged the government to incorporate into the homelands the white farms that broke

---

41   Interview with John Vorster, 1980. An article by me based on the interview appeared as 'BJ Vorster and the Sultan's Horse', *Frontline*, November 1983.

42   E-mail communication from Servaas van der Berg, 4 April 2011.

43   *House of Assembly Debates*, 1972, cols 5366-5370.

up the homeland territories, without the owners losing their property.[44] The leaders brought the issue up again at a 1974 summit. Unwilling to budge, Vorster claimed implausibly that he was bound by the 1936 legislation.

Vorster simply refused to acknowledge that things had changed radically. In 1916, when the Beaumont Commission first suggested 13% of the land should be reserved for blacks, the black population was a mere 5 million and the reserves served only as a home base for migrant labourers and small-scale farmers. By the early 1970s, when Vorster's government decided to stand by Beaumont's 'division' of land, the black population had already reached 18 million, and the homelands were designated as the territorial base of independent states.[45]

In 1975 the government announced its proposals to reduce the approximately 112 blocks of black land to 35. In the case of KwaZulu, 48 blocks would be reduced to 10 and in the case of Bophuthatswana, 19 would become 6. These proposals elicited strong criticism. While the farming lobby bewailed the loss of productive land, homeland leaders pointed out that the proposed land allocation was insufficient to meet the needs of homeland residents. The most telling comment came from economist Dr SP du Toit Viljoen, chairman of the Bantu Investment Corporation, who said that the homelands, with their fragmented territories, had no prospect of becoming viable.[46]

A project in trouble

By the early 1970s the lack of economic development was conspicuous. Between 1960 and 1972 only 85 544 jobs were created in the homelands and border areas – well below the number the Tomlinson Commission had considered necessary. In 1974 Professor Tomlinson remarked that economic development of the reserves had been small-scale and fragmentary.[47] In 1981 he ruefully observed that his commission had been highly successful, but only as an ideological exercise. For fifteen years after the tabling of the report in 1956 hardly anything was done. Yet, he added, 'There has not been a single Parliamentary session since [1956] that the report has not been referred to.'[48]

Tomlinson's words have to be qualified. Under Vorster, spending on the home-

---

44 Du Pisani, 'Ontplooiing van afsonderlike ontwikkeling', p. 77; SA Institute of Race Relations, *Survey, 1972*, pp. 36-37.

45 Anthony Lemon, *Apartheid: A Geography of Separation* (Westmead: Saxon House, 1976), p. 203; Du Pisani, 'Ontplooiing van afsonderlike ontwikkeling', pp. 69-100.

46 Du Pisani, 'Ontplooiing van afsonderlike ontwikkeling', p. 88.

47 *Die Volksblad*, 24 October 1974, cited by JC Steyn, *Van Wyk Louw: 'n Lewensverhaal* (Cape Town: Tafelberg, 1998), p. 1165.

48 Adam Ashforth, *The Politics of Official Discourse in Twentieth-Century South Africa* (Oxford: Clarendon Press, 1991), pp. 152-53.

lands went up significantly, increasing as a proportion of the budget from 6.3% to 8.1%. By 1983 it would stand at 9% of the budget. However, about 60% of this was regular expenditure allocated to provide schools, health care and physical infrastructure for the people living there.

The rapidly growing surplus of labour changed the function of the homelands. Instead of providing alternative places for work, they became places where the 'surplus' population could be settled. A new policy froze the expansion of townships close to any homeland. Blacks looking for accommodation had to move to one of the new towns that were built in the homelands. Government planners based their plans on the estimate that daily commuting was possible within a distance of 113 kilometres and weekly travel was possible within 644 kilometres. By 1965 the department had already erected 38 500 houses in 37 new homeland towns. An acute housing shortage developed in the townships in the common areas. The dormitory towns had little or no hope of growing organically. Two researchers remarked: 'If the borders of independent homelands should ever be closed to commuter traffic, these towns would inevitably die.'[49]

Several categories of removals took place. A million blacks were removed from white farms; another 600 000 from 'black spots' (black-owned land or mission stations in 'white' areas) and 750 000 from cities in the 'white area' under a policy of township relocation. Removals mostly resulted in great hardship. In some of the 'black spots' families had lived peacefully for many decades.

As a result of these resettlement policies and the redrawing of homeland boundaries to include black townships in 'white areas', the proportion of blacks living in homelands increased sharply. From about 39% of the black population in 1960, the figure rose to almost 53% by 1980.

BLACK POPULATION IN WHITE AREAS AND THE HOMELANDS; 1960, 1970, 1980 (PERCENTAGES)[50]

	White urban areas	White rural areas	Homelands
1960	29.6	31.3	39.1
1970	28.1	24.5	47.4
1980	26.7	20.6	52.7

From 1918 to 1955 the average population density in the reserves (later called

49 Smit and Booysen, *Swart verstedeliking*, p. 27.
50 Charles Simkins, *Four Essays on the Past, Present and Future of the Distribution of the Black Population Growth in South Africa* (Cape Town: South African Labour and Development Research Unit, 1983), p. 143.

homelands) was 50 to 60 people per square mile; by 1970 it had doubled to 125. Between 1970 and 1980 the overall population of the homelands rose by another 51%. As a result of this massive inflow of people into the homelands, subsistence farming all but collapsed. By the mid-1950s there had still been what was called a constant 'fragile productivity maintenance' – fragile in the sense that constant output per head depended on substantial net emigration.[51] But by 1970 agricultural production had declined dramatically. Increasingly unable to feed themselves, people from the homelands also found it ever more difficult to enter migrant labour. By the end of the 1970s about half of all migrant workers were not in employment.[52]

Politicians, editors, bureaucrats and academics close to the NP continued to support the homelands scheme until the 1980s, but the rank-and-file NP supporters had long been sceptical about the financial sacrifices required to give substance to the policy. A 1974 poll testing response to the idea of enlarging the homelands to make them more viable revealed that more Afrikaners opposed the scheme than accepted it, while more English speakers than Afrikaners endorsed it. Read together with other responses in the poll, it is clear that Afrikaners preferred the option of a measure of controlled upper-level integration to that of sacrificing for 'separate development'.[53] Not more than a quarter to a third of voters supported the option of partition presented in a poll as 'independent homelands with more land and some of our industrial areas'.[54]

From start to finish the homelands were the obsession of the Afrikaner intelligentsia; the policy did not fool ordinary people. Yet civil servants who worked in the homelands in the 1960s and the 1970s often displayed enormous commitment and idealism in executing their tasks.

'Imperial summits'

Vorster propagated a forum for a 'power bloc' or 'constellation of states' where the prime minister and the minister of Bantu administration and development could meet with leaders of the homeland governments. The idea would be to cooperate without sharing any power and to discuss ways in which disagreements could be resolved. Some homeland leaders participated in the hope that this could become a catalyst for a federation of the homeland governments, with the white government

---

51 Simkins, *Four Essays*, pp. 133-35.

52 JL Sadie, 'RSA-Homelands Relations', *Studies in Economics and Econometrics*, 1, 1977, pp. 35-56.

53 Lawrence Schlemmer, 'Change in South Africa', Robert M Price and Carl G Rosberg (eds), *The Apartheid Regime* (Berkeley: Institute of Commonwealth Studies, 1980), pp. 260-61.

54 Theo Hanf et al., *South Africa: The Prospects of Peaceful Change* (Cape Town: David Philip, 1981), p. 235.

at the centre.[55]

Vorster held seven 'summit' meetings between 1973 and 1977 – with very little result. One of the few 'concessions' was for Pretoria to replace the identity documents of blacks, issued by the South African government, with a travel document issued by the respective homeland governments.[56] Buthelezi was the only homeland leader who directly challenged the system, disturbing the polite talk at these summits. He had built up Inkatha as a mass movement that boasted more than 100 000 paid-up members by the beginning of 1976. More than half were not Zulu speakers. Dressed in a semi-military uniform of black, green and yellow – the same colours as those of the ANC – they made a striking impression of a movement determined to press its cause against huge odds.

Vorster chose not to engage Buthelezi in a serious discussion. Although he did not use any terms that could be construed as racist, he expected black leaders to know their place in the political system. Buthelezi recounts that he had a single one-on-one meeting with Vorster: 'He invited me to his office to chide me. He accused me of being "used" by the English press, particularly the Rand Daily Mail. I asked in what way do they use me and Mr Vorster said: "Why do they always go to you for comments?" I said that I had to comment if they had approached me. He further accused me of being "used" by the Progressive Federal Party. I asked him in what way do they use me? He said that I even address their congresses. I said that if the NP invited me to their congresses, I would gladly accept.'[57]

On 14 March 1976 Buthelezi told a crowd of more than 16 000 people at the Jabulani Stadium in Soweto he had informed Vorster that unless détente began at home, it would not succeed across the country's borders. Whites had to realise that 'the country had to move towards majority rule. It is this single principle that is central to any question that has to do with South Africa's policies.'[58] In the final words of the speech Buthelezi addressed himself to Vorster as much as to the crowd: 'My message to you is that history has overtaken apartheid. There is hope for the future. Justice will prevail and you will be given the opportunity in the building of a better South Africa.'[59]

Vorster failed to see that Buthelezi was a leader the NP government should cultivate, not because he could be controlled but because he was his own man with a genuine support base. Buthelezi recognised the dangers of attempting to force a rapid transfer to black rule, but he was no moderate willing to do the bidding of

55   Deon Geldenhuys, *South Africa's Black Homelands* (Johannesburg: SA Institute of Race Relations, 1981), pp. 16-24, 49.

56   Du Pisani, 'Ontplooiing van afsonderlike ontwikkeling,' p. 272.

57   Interview with Mangosuthu Buthelezi, 15 September 2010.

58   Ben Temkin, *Buthelezi: A Biography* (London: Frank Cass, 2003), p. 179.

59   Temkin, *Buthelezi*, p. 181.

the apartheid system. He told a meeting of followers in Johannesburg: 'History will triumph over apartheid . . . because in the final analysis history is made by majorities and not by minorities . . . Nowhere in the world have minorities prevailed against the majority indefinitely.'[60] In 1977, 44% of a sample of urban blacks named Buthelezi as the black leader they most admired. Of those who admired him, 40% were non-Zulus.

In October 1976, while people in Soweto and other townships were still in open revolt, Buthelezi questioned the very system of rule at one of Vorster's summits. He said the state had called in the riot police because state control of urban blacks had failed. He rejected the policy of 'national self-determination' for black nations. Blacks did not see why the government imposed separate ethnic identities and political vehicles on them while whites, who formed no ethnic group, had a common political vehicle and destiny. He added: 'Our people have not and will never desire self-determination in the framework laid down by whites. To expect them to act differently is to expect them to do what whites, and the Afrikaners in particular, never did during their struggle.'[61]

In Buthelezi's eyes the Vorster government's refusal to transfer more land to the homelands exposed the idea of black states as a pipe dream. In 1974 he said the fundamental choice before the country was between violence and majority rule. He suggested a national convention to negotiate a federal system for South Africa under a multiracial government that balanced majority and minority interests. The political rights of all national groups would be protected and majority rule would go hand in hand with 'power-sharing'.[62] Vorster replied that he saw no merit in a national convention, which he described as the 'baby' of the Progressive Party.

At one summit Vorster tried to drive a wedge between Buthelezi and other homeland leaders by asking the latter what they thought. A biographer sympathetic to Buthelezi said: 'The argument between Vorster and Buthelezi became so heated at one point that [Lennox] Sebe [of the Ciskei] and [Kaiser] Matanzima [of the Transkei] shouted in concert in Zulu, *Pheka Mhlekazi* – "Stop Chief". Afterwards, Buthelezi described the meeting as a "farce" while Lennox Sebe . . . endeared himself to government by describing Vorster as a "great statesman".'[63]

The Vorster government made every effort to keep Buthelezi restricted to his homeland and ethnic base. In 1977 Jimmy Kruger, minister of police, and Gert Prinsloo, chief of the security police, warned him not to expand Inkatha beyond

---

60   Jack Shepherd Smith, *Buthelezi* (Melville: Hans Strydom Publishers, 1988), p. 144.

61   Temkin, *Buthelezi*, p. 189.

62   Gatsha Buthelezi, *White and Black Nationalism: Ethnicity and the Future of the Homelands* (Johannesburg: SA Institute of Race Relations, 1974); Hanf et al., *South Africa*, p. 261.

63   Temkin, *Buthelezi*, p. 190.

the Zulu group or get in touch with leaders of the ANC and PAC abroad. It was a bizarre meeting. The two white functionaries tried to argue that these two banned organisations were racist because they lumped all black people together against whites. Trying to unite blacks against whites was, in Kruger's words, 'against nature'. Buthelezi wanted the 'whole cake' and the government was not going to give it to him. Buthelezi responded that he wanted power sharing in a federal government, but that fell on deaf ears.[64]

Vorster could not make up his mind about Buthelezi. It was not clear to him whether Buthelezi was simply a stalking horse for the ANC, or whether he was someone with whom a deal could be struck to exclude the black forces pushing for a radical redistribution of power and wealth. By early 1977 Buthelezi had given up on Vorster. He said: 'Consultations with Mr Vorster are futile, he does not hear you, he just talks over and round your head, uses the occasion to justify his policies. We talk past each other. Of course, if the right things are not carried through, he is the one who will be judged harshly by history.'[65]

The Soweto uprising

The Soweto uprising that started on 16 June 1976 was rooted in the pass laws, the denial of black political rights, and the lack of any representation in the industrial councils and conciliation boards where wage and other disputes were settled. Black rejection of these structural features of white domination dated back to the earliest days of Union. But some of the acts of the Vorster government during the 1970s precipitated the uprising. In 1972 the government transferred responsibility for the black townships from the city councils and placed it in the hands of sixteen Administration Boards, all reporting directly to Pretoria. Staffed mainly by white government officials, these boards absorbed much of the townships' revenue.

Blacks felt even more alienated from the system of rule than when city councils administered the townships. In addition, they were now even more restricted in moving from one township to another. Thirty years later Piet van der Merwe, who did extensive research for the Riekert Commission of 1978, called the 1972 decision 'one hell of a mistake'. He explained: 'It politicised things even more. Instead of relaxing control, the Administration Boards intensified it. Blacks felt even more alienated than before. They felt cut off from the municipalities and from the entire public administration. The state was faced with a very big problem.'[66]

The most immediate flash point was the enforcement of Afrikaans as medium of

---

64 *Meeting between Chief Gatsha Buthelezi and Mr JT Kruger, 19 September 1977*, pamphlet published by Inkatha, 1978.

65 Anna Starcke, *Survival: Taped Interviews with South Africa's Power Elite* (Cape Town: Tafelberg, 1978), p. 76.

66 Interview with Piet van der Merwe, 18 March 2009.

instruction in Soweto schools. Ideally Vorster's 'summits' should have served as an early warning mechanism, provided he was prepared to listen and give appropriate instructions to his ministers and civil servants. At the 1974 and 1975 summits, the homeland leaders asked for the same medium of instruction to be used in township schools as in the homeland schools. In practice, this was a request for English to replace Afrikaans as the medium of instruction in the townships. At both conferences MC Botha, the minister in charge of black education, promised to investigate the issue, which he called 'complex'.[67] Buthelezi said in an interview 36 years later: 'We actually warned Vorster [in 1974] that imposing Afrikaans in the urban schools outside of the homelands would trigger violence.'[68] The warning was ignored. It is not clear whether the issue was ever discussed at cabinet level.

Early in 1976 the Department of Bantu Administration and Development told inspectors in Soweto and other schools in the southern Transvaal to give instructions that mathematics and arithmetic had to be taught in Afrikaans alone, even though most teachers and pupils probably had no command – or at best a poor command – of Afrikaans. Teacher organisations and black parents on school boards in the townships warned that a volatile situation was building up. When black anger exploded in Soweto, virtually all the Board's liquor stores and beer halls were destroyed. After order was restored eleven months later, the Board's offices had to be ringed with barbed wire. Remarking on how unpopular the Boards were among blacks, a labour adviser to government expressed the hope that with more 'positive services' their image would improve. It was increasingly being questioned whether the Boards were effectively regulating the labour market, and if they were not needlessly antagonising blacks.[69]

Vorster clung to the homelands policy, although time was clearly running out. Even before the Soweto uprising, widely respected Afrikaner editor Schalk Pienaar wrote: 'To think that the creation of homelands offers a solution to the urban black is nonsensical ... [The] urban black man is as important as an independent Transkei and a solution must be found for Soweto when the Transkei becomes independent.'[70]

Yet while the fires of the Soweto uprising were still burning, Vorster informed US Secretary of State Henry Kissinger at a meeting in Germany that his government's policy was that of 'self-determination' for the different peoples of South Africa. He anticipated that the policy would evolve into 'a series of self-governing

---

67 Du Pisani, 'Ontplooiing van afsonderlike ontwikkeling', p. 277.

68 Interview with Mangosuthu Buthelezi, 15 September 2010.

69 Stanley Greenberg, *Legitimating the Illegitimate: State, Markets and Resistance in South Africa* (Berkeley: University of California Press, 1987), pp. 57-58.

70 Cited by Patrick Laurence, *The Transkei: South Africa's Politics of Partition* (Johannesburg: Ravan Press, 1976), p. 13.

black homelands with one or two white homelands, which would be clearly dominant'. Kissinger responded that the United States would never accept such a policy.[71]

Publicly Vorster showed no inclination to abandon the Verwoerd framework.
Ons het klaar gedink (we have done our thinking about a solution), he said on one
occasion in late 1976. Giving the Verwoerd memorial lecture four months after the
uprising started, he insisted the problems confronting government would be much
larger if Verwoerd had not conceptualised and implemented the policy of separate
development. He spent virtually the entire lecture dwelling on the granting of
independence to the Transkei, which he considered – quite implausibly – to be of
major significance in the country's political history.[72] But Transkei's independence
was of no help to the government in attempting to reassert its old hegemony, or to
stem the growing assistance from foreign trade unions and churches to the emerging black unions.

Conferring 'privileges'

From the early 1970s the idea took root among some top people in government and
business that the system could be stabilised by selectively conferring a few privileges
on settled urban blacks. These would include the right to join trade unions and to
move about more freely. They hoped these 'insiders' would accept their privileged
position and refrain from making common cause with migrants, commuters and
other outsiders.

From the outset several factors undermined any scheme that aimed to separate
insiders from outsiders. For instance, deteriorating conditions in the reserves made
it very difficult to restrict the desperate outsiders to those areas. The homelands
provided work for only a quarter of their inhabitants. The average income of urban
blacks was nearly four times that of blacks in the rural areas. Black unemployment
had manifested itself as South Africa's gravest social problem.

The government believed that the only way rural blacks could be kept out was
by imposing the pass laws and other forms of influx control on all blacks.[73] But as
people also subjected to the pass laws, the insiders considered themselves to be
sharing with outsiders the common condition of oppression and humiliation that
the pass laws symbolised. As a Dutch Reformed Church minister with a black congregation in Port Elizabeth observed, the press and radio had created a climate of
pervasive uncertainty among all blacks, including the insiders. They did not see
influx control merely as part of the government's labour policy that put migrants

---

71 Henry Kissinger, *Years of Renewal* (London: Weidenfeld and Nicholson, 1999), p. 963.
72 BJ Vorster, *Tweede HF Verwoerd gedenklesing*, given on 28 October (Pretoria: University of Pretoria,
    New Series 109, 1976).
73 Jill Nattrass, 'The Impact of the Riekert Commission's Recommendations on the "Black States"',
    South African Labour Bulletin, 5, 4, 1979, pp. 80-85.

at a disadvantage, but as part and parcel of the government's big project of reversing the black stream to the cities. It made all blacks feel equally vulnerable.[74] A 1981 survey found that although the urban black middle class might be less affected by influx control, 'the presence of legal restrictions on movement and residence is felt by this middle class as an injury to their personal dignity and worth'.[75]

The state steadily lost its ability to deal with rapid population growth and swelling unemployment. Any attempt to impose influx control could work only if controls were also rigidly enforced at the place of recruitment, but rural labour bureaus were corrupt or inefficient. Government acted on the assumption that the state was still strong and its laws would be obeyed as they were in the 1960s, but the reality was very different. Some work seekers bypassed the labour bureau to stream to the towns and cities. 'We shoot straight', one of them told researchers.[76] Others waited at the recruitment offices in the homelands or just beyond their borders for an offer of work. At a bureau near King William's Town such a large crowd of work seekers regularly assembled that an official had put a fence up – 'not to guard against terrorism, but to keep them from tearing the place down'. One day after he announced a considerable order for labour, 'the blacks just flattened the fence'.[77]

In 1977 Vorster appointed two commissions to examine the legal framework of labour relations that had been laid down over the previous 25 years. One, chaired by Unisa law professor Nic Wiehahn, was asked to review the legal framework of industrial relations (see pp. 152-64); the other, headed by Dr Piet Riekert, chairman of the prime minister's Economic Advisory Council, was asked to make proposals for the training, employment, housing and governance of black workers in industry.

The Riekert Commission was tasked with proposing a policy that avoided discrimination on the grounds of race, colour or sex 'as far as possible', but also kept in mind the need for safety and security. It recommended moving away from the policy of singling blacks out as a category whose affairs were administered separately. Responding to this recommendation, the government began to shift the functions of the Department of Plural Relations – which was the successor of the Department of Native Affairs – to functional departments that dealt with the rest of the population. By the mid-1980s the Department of Plural Relations retained only a fraction of its functions. Its main responsibilities had been parcelled

---

74 JJF Durand, *Swartman, stad en toekoms* (Cape Town: Tafelberg, 1970), pp. 62-63.

75 Lawrence Schlemmer, 'The Fence of Opportunity', Hermann Giliomee and Lawrence Schlemmer (eds), *Up Against the Fences: Poverty, Passes and Privilege in South Africa* (Cape Town: David Philip, 1985), p. 107.

76 Stanley Greenberg and Hermann Giliomee, 'Managing Influx Control from the Rural End: The Underbelly of Privilege', Giliomee and Schlemmer (eds), *Up Against the Fences*, pp. 68-84; Greenberg, *Legitimating the Illegitimate*, pp. 85-122.

77 Greenberg and Giliomee, 'Managing Influx Control', p. 72.

out to the Departments of Manpower, Justice and especially Constitutional Development.

While the Riekert report was critical of the Administration Boards, it did not recommend their abolition. Instead it proposed that they should act as agents for the Department of Manpower. Clearly the government considered their expertise in administering influx control too valuable to discard. The report also recommended that those with 'Section Ten' exemption should be given preference in various ways. Labour bureaus would only allocate work to migrant labourers if it could be shown there was no suitable local labour available in the towns and cities. It also proposed that Section Ten blacks should be allowed to move from one urban area to another, subject to the availability of work and housing, and the approval of the local labour bureau. The government accepted this, but in practice it meant little. Very few houses were available to those who wished to move, given the overall shortage of 141 000 houses, estimated conservatively.[78]

The report proposed two mechanisms to replace old-style influx control: controlled employment and approved accommodation. Controlled employment meant targeting the widespread practice of employers unlawfully employing black workers without 'proper papers'. In response to a Riekert recommendation, the government raised the maximum fine for offending employers from R100 to R500. But this pillar soon turned out to be defective. Used to taking on illegal workers for as long as they could remember, employers refused to comply. A shortage of labour inspectors – seven had to police the entire metropolitan area in Durban – made a mockery of the law. When offenders were taken to court, magistrates refused to impose the maximum penalty.[79]

Approved accommodation was also a nightmare to enforce. Between 1968 and 1974 the state did not build any new housing in townships in the 'white' areas. Even after 1974 the Administration Boards made it a priority to construct houses in the homelands, so a huge black housing shortage developed in the townships. Thousands of blacks lived illegally in the houses of qualified blacks.

The law provided for heavy fines for the illegal occupation of land or houses, and for extended police powers to search premises in the townships. The burden of enforcement would mostly fall on black township officials, who would have to check the houses during the night. In practice this was impossible. A white official remarked: 'In Soweto there are 600 000 people; imagine trying to find the 40 000 illegals. I'll get a fucking riot.'[80] In press interviews Riekert estimated the number of

---

78   Pieter le Roux, 'The Retention of Influx Control', *South African Labour Bulletin*, 5, 4, 1979, p. 107.

79   Greenberg, *Legitimating the Illegitimate*, p. 103.

80   Greenberg, *Legitimating the Illegitimate*, pp. 98, 104.

illegal people in Soweto at 200 000.[81]

Between 1967 and 1982 pass law prosecutions declined from a high of 693 700 to 171 400, roughly the 1945 level.[82] The Riekert report pointed out that the daily scrutiny of passes, together with police arrests of hundreds of thousands of pass offenders every year, 'seriously disturbed race relations between population groups' and caused 'bitterness and frustration'.[83] It suggested releasing urban blacks from the obligation of carrying a pass. 'Outsiders' would still have to prove that they were lawfully in an urban area.

But Vorster failed to douse the burning fuse of resentment over the pass laws. The white paper tabled in response to the report noted that approved accommodation and approved employment as mechanisms of control would require exceptionally strict application. Vorster decided to retain passes as a control mechanism for the time being. Afterwards Riekert frankly admitted that the intention was not to abandon influx control, but to find the 'right mechanism' for influx control. Approved accommodation and controlled employment were fine as colour-blind mechanisms, but Vorster had no intention of sacrificing what Riekert called 'effectiveness of control'.[84]

It took until 1986, with the country in the grip of a widespread rebellion, for the government finally to abolish pass laws and other forms of influx control that had alienated all black South Africans, insiders and outsiders alike.

Schemes for coloured people

Under Verwoerd the cabinet had discussed removing indirect representation of coloured people in parliament, but a single minister put a spoke in the wheel. He was Ben Schoeman, who threatened to resign if this happened. The matter was dropped. [85] Once Vorster came to power, however, he wasted little time in removing the last vestiges of coloured representation in the House of Assembly (four whites elected on a separate roll by coloureds), the Senate, and the Cape Provincial Council. As a substitute his government introduced a Coloured Persons' Representative Council (CPRC) consisting of nominated and elected members with extremely limited powers. Another law passed in 1968 made it illegal for parties to be active in the political affairs of another racial group.

Also in 1968 the South African Indian Council Act was passed to create an advi-

---

81 *Financial Mail*, 22 June 1979, p. 1053.

82 Michael Savage, 'The Imposition of Pass Laws on the African Population in South Africa, 1916-1984', *African Affairs*, 85, 1986, pp. 181-205.

83 Republic of South Africa, *Report of the Commission of Inquiry into Legislation affecting the Utilisation of Manpower (RP 32/1979)*, p. 108.

84 *Financial Mail*, 29 June 1979, p. 1146.

85 BM Schoeman, *Van Malan tot Verwoerd* (Cape Town: Human & Rousseau, 1973), p. 249.

sory, wholly nominated body to deal with Indian affairs. In 1971 all coloured voters were removed from municipal voters' rolls. The next year, the terms of office of coloured councillors in Cape Town and some other towns in the Cape Province ended. The intention to set up segregated coloured municipalities was ill conceived because none was financially viable.

Vorster was badly mistaken in his hope that these moves would bring peace within his party, which was showing increasing strain. Unlike Verwoerd, he could not project himself as a bold leader utterly convinced of his scheme. Instead he offered 'parallel development' for coloured people as a compromise halfway between the two wings of his party. This closed the door to both integration and more extreme segregation. The CPRC, which was supposed to remedy the lack of representation in the main legislative bodies, was doomed to fail. Without significant revenue or powers, it put coloured people in a worse position than homeland blacks. The Labour Party, which won most of the seats, set out to wreck the council. In response, the government fabricated a pro-government majority by appointing nominated members from the ranks of politicians who had been defeated in the election, further eroding the body's status.

Divisions on the coloured issue surfaced in 1972 when a senior Transvaal cabinet minister proposed a more severe form of segregation. Even more serious was the intervention of Gerrit Viljoen, rector of the Rand Afrikaans University and head of the Afrikaner Broederbond, who proposed what sounded very much like a homeland for coloured people. The Cape NP and some of its academic supporters at the University of Stellenbosch vehemently rejected this. To stem the unease in its own ranks, the government in 1973 appointed a commission of inquiry into the coloured population, headed by Erika Theron. For the first time since the NP came to power, a commission included coloured members.

The report signed by the majority of the Theron Commission did not attack the notion of white or coloured self-determination and endorsed some of its principal features, such as residential segregation, population registration and coloured people's removal from the voters' roll in the 1950s. Some of its findings, however, amounted to a strong and devastating critique of government neglect of the coloured population. The chapter on economics spoke of 'chronic community poverty' that affected more than 40% of the population. In the urban labour market coloureds were reported to be suffering from pervasive discrimination, since they could not join mixed trade unions without government permission. The policy failed in its objective of giving coloured people control over their own affairs, since whites, particularly Afrikaners, dominated senior positions in all state institutions that served them.[86] Unable to find answers, Vorster said the next generation would have to tackle the problem.

The main political recommendation of the Theron Commission was that coloured people should have direct representation at all levels of government and that the existing Westminster-based political system had to be changed to accommodate them. When Vorster got wind of the proposal in the final stage of the commission's work, he called in Sampie Terreblanche and Ben Vosloo, two *verligte* members of the commission, on 24 March 1976. Terreblanche told him: 'We at the Theron Commission have made a cost-benefit analysis of the Coloured Persons' Representative Council, and the majority concluded that it cannot work.' Vorster angrily retorted: 'It must be made to work.'[87] The tone of the government's response to the commission's report was so churlish that it pushed considerable numbers of coloured people into participating in the uprising of 1976 and the public demonstrations of subsequent years.

From 1974 foreign policy issues increasingly occupied Vorster's mind. He grappled with the fall of the dictatorship in Portugal, the collapse of the buffer of well-disposed regimes along the northern perimeter of South Africa and increasing United Nations pressure for South Africa to withdraw from South West Africa. It was a field completely new to him and it was one in which his inexperience soon showed.

86   JMM Barnard, 'Die Erika Theron Kommissie, 1973-1976', Master's dissertation, University of Stellenbosch, 1999.
87   Interview with SJ Terreblanche, 8 April 2011; Tayler, 'With her Shoulder to the Wheel', p. 331.

Chapter 5

Moving out into Africa:
John Vorster's Foreign Schemes

BETWEEN THE ELECTION OF 1974 AND HIS RETIREMENT IN SEPTEMBER 1978, John Vorster fell from a position where he was widely hailed as a bold and even courageous leader to one over whose head darkening clouds of failure and scandal were gathering.

Apart from the 1976 Soweto uprising, the turning points were the military coup in Lisbon on 25 April 1974 followed by the new government's decision to grant independence to Portugal's two colonies, and the weakening of Ian Smith's government in Rhodesia after sustained attacks by the liberation movements. The external wing of the South West African People's Organisation (Swapo) had also been making steady progress in its battle to win diplomatic recognition for its struggle to bring independence to South West Africa/Namibia. Faced with the collapse of protective buffer states on South Africa's northern border and a hostile Carter administration in the White House in Washington, Vorster battened down the hatches and put any significant reforms on hold.

Deflecting pressure

After coming to power in 1966 John Vorster considered different initiatives to deflect the mounting pressure on South Africa. First, he proposed détente with the states in southern Africa in an attempt to dissuade them from assisting the liberation movements or allowing troops from Cuba or other communist-leaning countries in the region. One of his first steps was to establish diplomatic relations with Malawi.

Second, he embarked on what was called an 'outward movement' or dialogue with states in West Africa to win their support for any actions he might initiate in southern Africa. By meeting in West Africa with President Leopold Senghor in Senegal and President Houphouët-Boigny in the Ivory Coast, he hoped to demonstrate that respected African leaders were willing to talk to the South African government despite the reigning African consensus that it was illegitimate.[1] Third, he approved a campaign of unconventional propaganda that would soon degenerate into bribery and the illegal publication of a newspaper with government funding.

The NP-supporting press tried to present 'deténte' and the 'outward movement'

---

1 Deon Geldenhuys, *The Diplomacy of Isolation: South African Foreign Policy Making* (Johannesburg: Macmillan, 1984), p. 118.

as an integral part of the fundamental transformation of South Africa away from a society based on race. But Vorster had no such grand idea. Later he confessed he did not know where the term 'outward movement' originated. He stated bluntly that South Africa had to move outward to tell the world that the entire population of South Africa – white, black and coloured – accepted 'separate development'.[2] By the mid-1970s this outward movement had faded away and South Africa became more isolated than before. It was barred from most United Nations' activities, the world ecumenical movement and most international sport. Official inter-governmental contact was limited to what was necessary.

A period of unconventional diplomacy began in 1974. Eschel Rhoodie, who had become secretary for information two years earlier, persuaded Vorster that conventional methods of propaganda were ill suited to selling apartheid to an increasingly hostile world. The only approach that would work was circumventing the regular channels in favour of unorthodox methods, bordering on the irregular and the illegal. In 1974 he allegedly told Vorster: 'I would not like to work under a misconception. Are we in agreement that we are not talking about an intensification of the current Department of Information activities but in fact of the launching of a no-holds-barred war free of government rules or regulations. Is that the case?'[3] Vorster said yes and agreed to provide substantial secret funding.

Two important results flowed from this development. Firstly, it undermined diplomats abroad and corrupted the channels of information to Pretoria from Washington and other Western capitals. Two diplomats commented: '[It] was virtual parallel diplomacy with projects covertly hatched, authorized, and financed away from the scrutiny of the auditor-general and parliamentary oversight, and behind the back of the Department of Foreign Affairs.' Individuals from 'the Department of Information, and the security and intelligence agencies, were at the centre of some of the controversial projects'.[4] If Vorster had relied on his Washington-based diplomats he would have discovered at an early stage that any South African military involvement in Angola would cause a storm in Congress, particularly if it became known that the CIA was aiding and abetting it.

A second result of this 'unconventional diplomacy' was the establishment of a secret committee, sometimes called a 'cabinet within a cabinet', to oversee the unconventional or irregular projects. Apart from Vorster, it consisted of Minister of Finance Nico Diederichs, Minister of Information Connie Mulder, Eschel Rhoodie

2 *Dagbreek*, 26 August 1967, cited by Japie Basson, *Raam en rigting in die politiek*, (Cape Town: Politika, 2002), p. 152.

3 Eschel Rhoodie, *Die ware Inligtingskandaal* (Pretoria: Orbis, 1984), p. 66.

4 Neil van Heerden and Herbert Beukes, 'Foreign Policy: Captive to Domestic Policy', Pieter Wolvaardt et al. (eds), *From Verwoerd to Mandela: South African Diplomats Remember* (no place: Crink, 2010), p. 46; see also www.crink.co.za.

and General Hendrik van den Bergh, head of the secret service.[5] Vorster made little use of the top military officers as advisers. He preferred to work with security police and in particular with Van den Bergh, an ally and trusted adviser, who had been detained with him in Koffiefontein for their support of the Ossewa-Brandwag during the Second World War. Van den Bergh became the first head of the Bureau for State Security (BOSS) when it was established in 1969.

A Rhodesian settlement

In November 1974 Vorster made an enigmatic comment that stirred hopes for substantial change: 'Give South Africa six months ... and you will be surprised where South Africa stands then.'[6] The previous month he had declared that southern Africa had 'come to the crossroads' between violent upheavals and negotiation, adding that the alternative to a peaceful settlement was 'too ghastly to contemplate.'[7] President Kenneth Kaunda of Zambia hailed his speech as the 'voice of reason', but this was mainly a response to Vorster's policy of détente with Africa – and in particular his attempts to bring about the end of white rule in Rhodesia.

By 1974 Vorster had developed a good working relationship with Kaunda, who was in frequent contact with President Mobutu Sese Seko of the Democratic Republic of the Congo (also called Zaire). Both were strongly opposed to the spread of communism in southern Africa if leaders with little or no mass support came to power through Soviet backing. Vorster's most ambitious hope was to create an anti-communist bloc of states in southern Africa. South Africa would be prepared to give generous development aid in return for acceptance of its domestic policies – homelands and all.

Together Vorster and Kaunda agreed to impose their own plan for a settlement in Rhodesia on Ian Smith and the black nationalist leaders. Vorster's first step was forcing Smith to release these leaders, including Robert Mugabe and Joshua Nkomo, from detention in December 1974. Eight months later Vorster and Kaunda hosted a conference at the Victoria Falls to help broker a settlement between Smith and the main black leaders. It failed, but Vorster emerged with enhanced status as leader. This was captured by a photograph of a young Zambian holding up a poster with the words 'Vorster becomes great today.'[8]

Knowing that Rhodesia was seen as a major test for his commitment to détente, Vorster pushed ahead.[9] He withdrew South African forces from Rhodesia and slowed

---

5   Japie Basson, *Politieke kaarte op die tafel* (Cape Town: Politika, 2006), p.147.
6   BJ Vorster, *Select Speeches* (Bloemfontein: Institute for Contemporary Archives, 1977), p. 231.
7   Vorster, *Select Speeches*, p. 221.
8   John D'Oliveira, *Vorster – The Man* (Johannesburg: Stanton, 1977), between pp. 240-41.
9   Robert Jaster, *South Africa's Narrowing Security Options* (Washington: Adelphi Papers, No.159, 1980).

down rail traffic to the country. Given the popularity of the Smith government among South African voters, he showed political courage in taking these initiatives. But he faced a formidable adversary in President Julius Nyerere of Tanzania, who persuaded some other African presidents that peaceful change in Rhodesia was no longer attainable and that the strategy of intensified guerrilla war should be pursued. With Jimmy Carter in the White House (1976–1980) there was no chance the United States would recognise the results of an election in which the main liberation movements did not participate.

Why did South Africa accept an election in Rhodesia/Zimbabwe in 1980 in which the liberation movements participated and scored a runaway victory? In an election held by the internal parties in 1978, which attracted a poll of 63%, the party led by Bishop Abel Muzorewa had scored a handsome victory. The South African government put substantial amounts of money and other resources behind Muzorewa and his party in that election and in the internationally recognised election held in 1980. In the latter, it expected Muzorewa to win or, at worst, to form a coalition with Joshua Nkomo, leader of the less militant liberation movement.[10] The sweeping victory of Robert Mugabe and his party was a huge disappointment, but the Botha government quickly adapted to the reality of the Mugabe government, which was initially quite circumspect in its dealings with its neighbours.[11]

'Fighting with Africa?'

Sometime in 1974 or 1975 Vorster and his minister of defence, PW Botha, began toying with the idea of a new scheme. With the homeland policy approaching a dead end, the idea took root of a South Africa that would 'fight along with Africa' against communism in the region. They hoped that engaging the heads of African states in a common venture would make it impossible for local black parties to reject cooperation with the South African government. Tired of local politics, Vorster found it exhilarating to engage in top-level 'diplomacy' to combat the spread of Soviet influence in the Third World.

Vorster was convinced that, if unchecked, the Cubans and the Russians would attempt to secure a whole row of Marxist states from Angola to Dar-es-Salaam. They might even have an more audacious plan up their sleeve: 'to stand astride the Cape sea route and to act at will ... to the detriment of the Free World and the West.'[12] The presidents of Zambia, Senegal, Ivory Coast and Zaire shared Vorster's concerns.

Exhausted after fighting a losing war for more than ten years in Vietnam, the

---

10   E-mail communication from Jamie Miller, 19 November 2011.
11   E-mail communication from Neil van Heerden, 28 November 2011.
12   *The Guardian*, 13 January 1976.

United States was not expected to become involved again in a Third World trouble spot. Africa was the continent that least attracted its interest. Early in 1975 Donald Easum, assistant secretary of state for Africa, told the South African ambassador in Washington that there was so little American interest in Africa that it would take a major 'sales job' to get people interested in programmes there.[13] But the ball game changed swiftly when Washington learned that the MPLA, with the assistance of Cuban forces, had embarked on a plan to seize power in Angola. Realising that Congress would block any overt US action, the Cold War warriors in Washington, and in particular Henry Kissinger, secretary of state in the Ford administration, and the CIA's William Colby, looked around for a proxy force that could check a Cuban-backed seizure of power in Luanda.

By the early 1970s some African governments had also become concerned about the spread of communism in sub-Saharan Africa and Angola in particular. They did not care too much if South Africa helped to thwart it, provided the intervention was of a covert kind. After South Africa sent troops to Angola in 1975 PW Botha declared: 'South Africa did not enter helter-skelter into the war. We reacted to requests from impeccable sources.'[14] Apart from President Kaunda and President Mobuto Sese Seko of Zaire, the strongest pleas came from Jonas Savimbi, the guerrilla leader controlling the southern third of Angola. He quickly made a favourable impression on Vorster and PW Botha, and spent 10 November 1975, the day before Independence Day for Angola, in a secret meeting with Vorster in Pretoria.

What they discussed remains secret, but in all probability it included the creation of an anti-communist bloc of states. A little more than four years later, when PW Botha tried to convince Buthelezi of the merits of a 'constellation of states', he mentioned Savimbi's willingness to be part of such a constellation and join 'a common stand against communism'.[15] General Johan van der Merwe (who would become head of the security police during the 1980s and later of the police force) attended several meetings where Savimbi was present, along with PW Botha and other senior officers in the security forces. There was a feeling in these circles that Savimbi would become the African leader who could 'save Africa'. Van der Merwe later commented that the political leadership 'totally misjudged' African politics and politicians.[16]

---

13   Odd Arne Westad, *The Global Cold War: Third World Interventions and the Making of our Times* (Cambridge: Cambridge University Press, 2005), pp. 229-30.

14   *Die Afrikaner*, 30 January 1976.

15   Archive for Contemporary Affairs (ACA), Bloemfontein, PV357 Kobie Coetsee Papers, File 1/A1/5 Minutes of Consultative Meeting, 29-30 October 1979, London; Interview with Mangosuthu Buthelezi, 15 September 2010; Jack Shepherd Smith, *Buthelezi: The Biography* (Johannesburg: Hans Strydom, 1988), p. 141.

16   E-mail communication from Johan van der Merwe, 29 March 2011.

It is unlikely that Vorster's September 1975 decision to send combat troops into Angola was part of a well-conceived scheme. His intervention in Angola resembled that of a sleepwalker groping around in a strange house. Using South Africa's military prowess and economic muscle, Vorster and his successor, PW Botha, attempted a form of geopolitical engineering on the subcontinent to bolster white rule. The plans would go awry. All of South Africa's neighbours rejected the 'constellation of states' and in 1980 formed their own bloc, the Southern African Development Co-ordination Conference, which was committed to reducing their economic dependence on South Africa.

The march to war

In mid-1975 the normally cautious and slow-moving Vorster got South African forces embroiled in a civil war in Angola. This came after hints from sections of the Ford administration in the United States that South Africa's participation in the effort to rebuff the Marxist forces would be welcomed. For the Vorster government, which had long campaigned on an anti-communist platform, the opportunity of working with President Gerald Ford and Secretary of State Henry Kissinger in combating the spread of Marxism in Angola was too tempting to resist.

Despite opposition from PW Botha and the military, Vorster allowed the Frelimo movement under Samora Machel in Mozambique, with its strong popular base, to come to power without putting any obstacles in its way. Angola was different. It had three minority movements contending for power. Two were aligned to the West: the Frente Nacional de Libertação de Angola (FNLA), a northern-based nationalist movement led by Holden Roberto; and Savimbi's União Nacional para a Independencia Total de Angola (Unita), which was based on a large ethnic group in the central highlands. A third, the Movimento Popular de Libertação de Angola (MPLA), led by Agostinho Neto, was a movement of indigenous Marxists looking to Cuba and the Soviet Union for military assistance to seize power. Strong in Luanda and surrounding areas, it controlled less than a quarter of the country's territory by mid-1975.[17]

In January 1975 the Portuguese government and the three movements in Angola drew up the Alvor Agreement in terms of which Portuguese troops would be withdrawn by 30 April and a new army would be formed from recruits of the three movements. The respective leaders of the movements would form a coalition until elections took place for a new government of national unity in October, followed by the transfer of power on 11 November. Zambia and Zaire, backed by Senegal and Ivory Coast, strongly supported the idea of a government of national unity. These countries did not seem to have any principled objection to South Africa helping bring this about, provided it did so discreetly.

---

17   Chester Crocker, *High Noon in Southern Africa* (New York: WW Norton, 1992), p. 49.

The Alvor Agreement soon unravelled. Although the three movements formed a coalition, clashes between the FNLA and the MPLA in and around Luanda led to the FNLA's withdrawal from the coalition, followed later by Unita. The FNLA and Unita on the one side and the MPLA on the other squared up for a military showdown.

Which party was most responsible for the war that soon broke out is a complex question. The MPLA had little intention of honouring the Alvor Agreement. In all probability it had planned from the outset to install itself as the sole party in government. In response to MPLA pleas, Cuba sent some 250 advisers to help combat the FNLA. From the start the MPLA also expected help from the Soviet Union. In the second half of October newspapers reported the arrival of Soviet and East German ships in Angola. On board were 10 000 tons of war material and 750 Cuban uniformed troops.[18] By 11 November there were approximately 2 800 Cuban soldiers in Angola. By the end of the year the figure had risen to somewhere between 4 000 and 6 000, according to US President Gerald Ford.

Some sources believe that Fidel Castro only increased the number of his troops after the South Africans had entered the fray. Others stress that by the end of August Castro had already decided on a full-scale invasion as a glorious showcase of his concern for the nations of the developing world. The question was whether he could rely on the Soviet Union to test the United States' resolve in Angola as one of the hot spots in the Cold War.

South Africa soon got sucked in. It is unlikely that it would have penetrated deep into Angola had no Cuban troops arrived in Luanda and had the CIA and senior members of the Ford administration not egged it on. It had no idea that the Soviet Union would get involved in a major way.

The US involvement

The Ford administration in the United States was unwilling to concede victory to the MPLA and its allies in an area it considered part of the Western sphere of influence. In January 1975 it approved a request from the FNLA for assistance. France also feared that the MPLA would unilaterally declare independence. It projected its power by persuading eleven Francophone African countries not to recognise such a declaration and it sent nine planeloads of arms and equipment to Kinshasa, to be distributed to the FNLA.[19]

Henry Kissinger, secretary of state in the Ford administration and former national security adviser, considered Soviet-backed intervention in Angola a serious violation of the ground rules of détente between the two Big Powers. He noted: 'Our

18 Robin Hallett, 'The South African Intervention in Angola 1975–76', *African Affairs*, 77, 303, 1978, p. 364; FJ du Toit Spies, *Operasie Savannah: Angola, 1975–76* (Pretoria: SA Weermag, 1989), p. 52.

19 Spies, *Operasie Savannah*, p. 55.

concern [in Angola] is not the economic wealth or the naval base. It has to do with the USSR operating 8 000 miles from home with all the surrounding states asking for our help.'[20] He strongly believed that Soviet intervention in other African countries was a real possibility if the Soviets were allowed to get away with interfering in Angola.[21]

In April 1975 President Kaunda visited Washington to tell President Ford that Cuban help and Soviet arms deliveries to the MPLA were assisting the movement to seize power. He convinced Ford that American assistance was essential to frustrate Soviet designs.[22] Kissinger wrote in his memoirs that this was one of the rare occasions when a visit by a foreign head of state produced a change in US foreign policy, but this must be taken with a pinch of salt. In the Ford administration it was Kissinger who had been actively propagating the same view as Kaunda. He now used Kaunda's plea to get Ford to accept the necessity of weakening the MPLA enough to force the formation of a government of national unity on Independence Day.

On 16 July Ford authorised the small sum of $14.7 million – later increased to $25.7 million – for covert supplies of arms to the FNLA and Unita. By the end of the month the first planeload of arms left for Zaire, used as a rear base. Kissinger wrote in his memoirs that both President Ford and the national security adviser, General Brent Scowcroft, sided with him in strongly favouring American intervention, but that it turned out the three of them were 'spread far too thin' to bring this about.[23] In effect, it meant they would be unable to defend the intervention if Congress got wind of it. Kissinger faced particularly stiff opposition from the African desk in the state department. In his view, they had developed 'a kind of siege mentality, casting themselves as defenders of American idealism'.[24] For its part, the African desk argued that the American public had no stomach for US intervention in Angola.

Kissinger authorised the training and deployment of 300 CIA-backed operatives to support the FNLA, and the supply of arms and military equipment. He also set up a working group (known as the Forty Committee) as a National Security Council ad hoc sub-committee consisting of representatives of the CIA, defence, the state department and other departments. John Stockwell, a CIA agent who was a member of the working group, later described the operation in a revealing book.[25]

For the CIA, a covert South African force in Angola would greatly help to counter

20 Martin Meredith, *The State of Africa: A History of Fifty Years of Independence* (London: Free Press, 2006), p. 316.
21 See Kissinger's speech quoted in Hallett, 'South African Intervention in Angola', p. 356.
22 Henry Kissinger, *Years of Renewal* (London: Weidenfeld and Nicholson, 1999), p. 791.
23 Kissinger, *Years of Renewal*, p. 811.
24 Kissinger, *Years of Renewal*, p. 800.
25 John Stockwell, *In Search of Enemies: A CIA Story* (London: André Deutsch, 1978).

Soviet-Cuban involvement in Angola. It soon discovered that the Vorster government did not need much encouragement. Stockwell succinctly sums up the way in
which the CIA viewed the inclinations of Pretoria. 'They felt their troops, even
though white, would be more acceptable to most African leaders than the non-
African Cubans. They also expected to be successful, understanding that the Ford
administration would obtain US congressional support for an effective Angola pro-
gram.' Stockwell comments that on both these points the South Africans 'were
disastrously wrong'.[26]

American military assistance turned out to be laughably inadequate. Jannie
Geldenhuys, who became head of the defence force in the late 1980s, had the task
of drawing up a list of arms and equipment the United States was supposed to
supply to the FNLA. Very few supplies arrived. He said later: 'I doubt if they received
more than a hundred semi-automatic machine guns.'[27] General Constand Viljoen,
director of military operations at the time and also a future head of the defence force,
described the US help as 'pathetic'. He recounts: 'One evening at Kinshasa Airport,
while we were overseeing the unloading of arms from the US planes, [FNLA leader]
Roberto expressed his bitter disappointment. "These arms are only fit to hunt rab-
bits," he said.'[28]

Vorster was primarily concerned about the growing role that Cuban soldiers and
Soviet advisers were playing in the conflict. In June 1975 he agreed to a request from
both the FNLA and Unita for aid. On 4 July he sent General Viljoen and Gert Rothman (deputy head of BOSS) to meet Savimbi, Roberto and President Mobuto in
Kinshasa to ask what help was needed. Viljoen and Rothman recommended a substantial increase in the supply of military equipment to the two movements. Vorster agreed.[29]

South Africa sucked in

What prompted Vorster to send South African troops deep into Angola has been
the subject of much speculation. Up to that point he had handled his détente and
outward movement initiatives skilfully and acted with a sure hand in dealing with
Rhodesia and Mozambique. South Africa's immediate concern was the Calueque
hydroelectric and water supply project on the Cunene River some 16 kilometres
inside the southern Angolan border, which it co-funded and helped to operate.
Water from the dam was used for agriculture, industry and hospitals in northern
South West Africa; any interruption would have had serious humanitarian conse-

26 Stockwell, *In Search of Enemies*, p. 186.
27 E-mail communication from Jannie Geldenhuys, 27 May 2008.
28 Fax message from Constand Viljoen, 18 May 2011.
29 Hilton Hamann, *Days of the Generals* (Cape Town: Zebra Press, 2001), p. 23.

quences. To guard the installations and workers against guerrillas operating in the area, South Africa stationed a platoon of South African troops at the dam. This carried the tacit approval of both the Portuguese government, which was still the de facto authority, and the secretary-general of the United Nations to whom Ambassador Pik Botha explained the situation on 5 September.[30]

In August and early September 1975 the MPLA forces captured the city of Nova Lisboa and the ports of Benguela and Lobito. They pushed down far south, sweeping Unita aside and threatening Calueque. South African troops had earlier begun training Unita fighters as a matter of urgency.

Viljoen explains the steady slide towards ever-greater involvement: 'The Unita guerrillas knew very little of conventional defence and attack. This was a serious situation since the Cuban and Russian advisers of the MPLA had been focusing from the start on arming and training men for conventional war. With their help the MPLA captured city after city, with both Unita and the FNLA unable to mount a defence. The latter's guerrilla fighters were used to running away to return later and stage a hit-and-run operation.' But the South African instructors could not train the Unita fighters soon enough in a steadily deteriorating situation. To deal with the crisis, South African troops and the Unita guerrillas were combined in units under South African officers.[31]

But what was the government's larger strategic purpose?

In a new study that uses both primary sources and interviews with some of the leading participants, Jamie Miller argues that PW Botha and Magnus Malan used the dam at Calueque as a pretext for their grand strategic design. General Constand Viljoen told Miller: 'I always had the impression that it was a handy way of explaining an operation that did not have the intention [in the first place] of protecting Calueque and Ruacana.'[32]

Botha was playing for much larger stakes: to establish a South Africa-controlled, communist-free zone in southern Angola. This would block Swapo guerrillas and help turn South Africa into 'part of Africa instead of the colonial powers', as General Constand Viljoen phrased it.[33] Two African states, Zambia and Zaire, had asked South Africa to stem the spread of communism in sub-Saharan Africa by preventing the Cubans and Soviets from installing an MPLA government in Angola.[34]

---

30 Speech of Jeremy Shearar to the World Affairs Council, Grand Rapids, 14 February 1976, incorporated in an e-mail communication to the author, 20 May 2011.

31 Fax message from Constand Viljoen, 18 May 2011.

32 Jamie Miller, 'Into the Quagmire: Reassessing South Africa's Intervention in the Angolan Civil War, 1975', unpublished paper, 2012, p.19.

33 Hamann, *Days of the Generals*, p. 15.

34 Annette Seegers, *The Military in the Making of Modern South Africa* (London: I.B. Tauris, 1996), pp. 212-13.

Being approached by the CIA and two African states in the region was heady stuff for Botha and Vorster. As Miller writes, 'Botha utilised a minor incident to justify a long sought presence in Southern Angola.'[35] From accepting the need for training and supplying weapons to guerrillas, Botha cajoled Vorster into approving an incursion of an army contingent into Angola. On 24 September the Vorster government instructed the defence force to prepare for action in Angola in what was to be called Operation Savannah.

Early in October a force of not more than 2 500 troops and 600 vehicles penetrated into the country to secure the Calueque project. But the aims soon expanded: it had to help Unita and the FNLA to keep those areas they had once controlled, clear the south-western part of Angola of Swapo guerrillas, and assert control over the Benguela railway line.[36] To monitor Operation Savannah, Vorster established a small sub-committee under his chairmanship, which included Hendrik van den Bergh and the minister of defence, PW Botha.

Chester Crocker, who later became US assistant secretary of state for Africa, stated that up to that point the United States and other Western governments had done nothing to discourage Operation Savannah. With Portugal on the point of withdrawing, there was now a rough balance of power. This created the conditions for installing a government of national unity that the West desired.

The Soviets had other plans. According to Kissinger, they had decided to arm the MPLA as early as December 1974.[37] A Soviet official states that they began supplying the MPLA with arms and training even before the Cuban involvement. Advisers and instructors were sent to Luanda immediately after independence.[38] It is still unclear if the decision to escalate Soviet involvement occurred because of the South African incursion or because it wished to consolidate MPLA power after the latter had installed itself as the government of the People's Republic of Angola on 11 November. It is nevertheless clear that the Soviets had been upping the ante since the beginning of 1975.

It was on 11 November that the real test between the West and the Soviets and its allies began. Crocker tells the story: 'Havana and Moscow promptly raised the ante again, mounting "Operation Carlota" to surge additional forces and hardware. Havana and Moscow were determined to shore up the MPLA position and enable it to beat back the FNLA-Unita-Zairean-South Africa coalition that may still have challenged the MPLA's hold on Luanda.' He adds: 'The Cuban force was doubled in the next six weeks. In Washington, meanwhile, the Ford administration's position was rapidly unravelling.'[39]

35   Miller, Into the Quagmire', p.19.
36   Spies, *Operasie Savannah*, p. 70.
37   Kissinger, *Years of Renewal*, p. 795.
38   Vladimir Shubin, *The Hot 'Cold War': The USSR in Southern Africa* (London: Pluto Press, 2008), p.53.
39   Crocker, *High Noon*, p.50.

In a massive operation – its first effort of this kind – the Soviets transported more than 12 000 Cuban soldiers and advanced military hardware to Angola during the final months of 1975 and the early months of 1976. The Soviets hoped to extend their power and influence in Angola at the expense of a West that clearly dreaded getting tied up with South Africa in a common venture. They expected little resistance from the South African force. From Moscow the Angolan adventure looked like a walk in the park. Vorster was suddenly confronted with a situation he had not anticipated in his worst dreams.

Conflicting goals

Working closely with Vorster in overseeing the incursion into Angola was PW Botha, a security hawk who favoured bold action bordering on the reckless. It was above all he who pressured Vorster to instruct the South African troops to drive the Cuban and MPLA forces far back and penetrate as far as 700 kilometres beyond the border. Strangely enough, both Vorster's sub-committee and the CIA rarely consulted the South African military on South Africa's strategic objectives and the means of attaining them. General Viljoen stated: 'Only once did the CIA ask us strategic advice and information on ways in which we could succeed in a joint operation.'[40]

Vorster also never fully informed Viljoen of his strategic objectives, although he was director of operations. Viljoen was under the impression that the goal of the operations was quite limited and did not extend to capturing Luanda. The idea was simply to help Savimbi and Roberto retain control over their respective areas and to get the Organisation of African Unity (OAU) to endorse a government of national unity. Viljoen elaborated: 'Our goal was a federal type of government.'[41] In his memoirs Magnus Malan, who was head of the army, states emphatically that there was no plan to install a specific government or for the South African force to move as far as Luanda.[42]

This was also the view of Brand Fourie, departmental head of foreign affairs, who later stated: 'To my knowledge our ambitions did not extend beyond securing the southern part of Angola until the meeting of the Organisation of African states, where we hoped the moderate states would prevail in installing a government of national unity.'[43] But PW Botha had other plans. A biography written with his co-operation states that he was anxious to prevent Luanda from falling into the hands of 'Marxists'. The cabinet, however, turned the plan down when it heard that capturing the city could mean the death of 30% to 40% of a force of 1 500 men.[44]

---

40 Fax message from Constand Viljoen, 18 May 2011.
41 Fax message from Constand Viljoen, 9 May 2011.
42 Magnus Malan, *My lewe saam met die SA Weermag* (Pretoria: Protea, 2006), pp. 120-23.
43 Brand Fourie, *Brandpunte* (Cape Town: Tafelberg, 1991), p. 200.
44 Dirk de Villiers and Johanna de Villiers, *PW* (Cape Town: Tafelberg, 1985), p. 264.

Looking back much later, General Viljoen makes the point that for the Vorster government the fighting in Angola was never a military war in the traditional sense of the word. Its military objectives were always subordinate to political objectives. Viljoen concludes: 'It was a Cold War game played with very little integrity – a text-book example of how it should *not* be done.'[45] CIA agent John Stockwell shares this view: 'Vorster's plan – putting in a small, covert force – violated the cardinal rule of military strategy: the clear definition of a desired objective.'[46]

The key figure in the contacts between Vorster and the hawks in Washington was General Van den Bergh. He later claimed he had been against the operation in Angola, but it was he who urged Vorster to provide arms to the anti-MPLA forces and to give BOSS the task of coordinating the operation. He found the new relationship between the CIA and BOSS quite exhilarating. General Hein du Toit, head of military intelligence, was scathing about Van den Bergh: 'They manipulated him just as they liked. He was thrilled at being seen by them as so important.'[47]

The new channels of communication bewildered the South African embassy in Washington, which found itself bypassed on the Angolan war until December 1975. JSF (Frikkie) Botha, ambassador in Washington from 1971 to 1975, recalls: 'South Africa's diplomatic isolation and lack of normal communications had made the Vorster government hungry for friends, sometimes at all costs. It was easy prey for false friends who abused us for their own purposes.' He added that, apart from the strong ties between the CIA and BOSS, a channel had also opened between the top military officers in the United States and South Africa.[48] He later stated that it was 'far from realistic' at the outset to think a majority in Congress would be willing to openly support any action by the United States that could be beneficial to the South African government.[49]

Operation Savannah

The South African venture, called Operation Savannah, resembled a covert CIA expedition. Soldiers did not wear their regular uniforms or insignia, and the government informed neither parliament nor the NP caucus. It made no information available to the South African public for several months, although most of the troops were conscripts. Because the public was kept in the dark, the government instructed the military to do everything in its power to prevent too many South African casualties. While successfully hiding the incursion from its electorate, the government had no means of preventing a flood of information appearing in the foreign press.

---

45 Fax message from Constand Viljoen, 9 May 2011.
46 Stockwell, *In Search of Enemies*, p. 232.
47 Hamann, *Days of the Generals*, p. 24.
48 E-mail communication from JSF Botha, 30 March 2011.
49 E-mail communication from JSF Botha, 5 April 2011.

The South African contingent split in two after entering Angola. A column code-named 'Foxbat' linked up with Savimbi's troops in eastern Angola and then moved northwards. A column codenamed 'Zulu' moved rapidly up the coast where it captured several towns, including the port of Benguela. It only stopped some 200 kilometres from the capital where, as some claimed, they could see the lights of Luanda. As a British historian notes, its performance amounted to 'a series of dramatic successes that must have induced a considerable euphoria'.[50] At the same time a contingent of FNLA and Zairian troops drove from the north on to Luanda.

By early November the South Africans had assisted the FNLA and Unita to assume control over the areas they respectively claimed, but it was clear that holding on to these territories would be expensive. At that point the MPLA and its Cuban allies did not control more than the capital, Luanda, and a broad zone extending to the east. Polish journalist Ryszard Kapuscinski, who was in the capital, described it as in a state of utter *confusão* – an untranslatable word that in Angola means 'confusion, a mess, anarchy, and disorder . . . a state of absolute disorientation'. He added that almost all the Portuguese citizens had departed. 'Every so often someone came into the hotel shouting: "They are coming! They are coming!" and announced breathlessly that the armoured vehicles of the Afrikaners were already at the city's edge.'[51]

No elections were held on the scheduled day in October, so all minds were fixed on Independence Day scheduled for 11 November. The MPLA was widely expected to install itself as the sole party in government. Holden Roberto, the FNLA leader who still dreamt of leading the government of national unity, was desperate to prevent it, but Cuban reinforcements poured into the capital.

MPLA-Cuban forces anticipated an attack by FNLA forces under Roberto from the north, where a single tarred road over a large morass provided the only access to the city, so they dug themselves in at the northern outskirts. Roberto's plan was for FNLA infantry and some Zairian troops to advance on Luanda immediately after an artillery bombardment. Early in November Roberto asked the Vorster government for two cannons and a small artillery crew to assist in the attack. When PW Botha ordered General Viljoen to comply with the request, Viljoen objected, saying this was not part of the military plan. Botha insisted: 'Look here, General, if we Afrikaners get a request from Africa we cannot say no. It is a matter of honour.'[52] A contingent of 26 artillery troops and a few cannons were promptly sent to reinforce Roberto's force.

Viljoen later remarked: 'Militarily I realised the operation would not work, but politically I was forced to do it . . . I said to PW Botha: "This is wrong: we are now

50   Hallett, 'The South African Intervention in Angola', p. 376.
51   Ryszard Kapuscinski, *Another Day of Life* (Harmondsworth: Penguin Books, 1987), pp. 118-120.
52   Interview with Constand Viljoen, 16 April 2011.

deviating from a principle that was laid down right at the beginning."' Many years afterwards he said: 'The attack on 10 November was the only attack on Luanda and it was a PW Botha attack – there is no doubt about it.'[53]

At 5:40 on the morning of 10 November the South African artillery began to rain shells onto the MPLA positions at the northern entrance of Luanda, causing the MPLA and the Cubans to flee. Roberto and his men had to use this critical moment to attack, but they only arrived at 6:05 and were clearly not ready. Roberto had not yet explained the battle plan to his troops, and he insisted they have breakfast first. Viljoen remarked later: 'That breakfast was the cause of Roberto's defeat in Luanda.'[54]

Roberto's force began its advance only at 7:40. By this time the enemy troops had taken up their previous positions, from where they soon began to rain 122-milli-metre rockets on the FNLA and Zairian troops. Their retreat was a stampede, effec-tively ending the attack on Luanda and the FNLA's participation in the war.[55]

The path was now clear for the MPLA to take over the government. On 11 Novem-ber the Portuguese high commissioner held a ceremony in which he handed over power to the Angolan people without a single Angolan being present. At midnight, MPLA leader Agostinho Neto proclaimed the People's Republic of Angola. Fierce fighting continued for several weeks, but the arrival of thousands of Cuban troops and arms, airlifted by Soviet planes, dramatically changed the balance of power.

Neither Portugal nor any member of the OAU recognised the new government. On 29 November Kissinger still stated: 'We would support any move that keeps out-side powers out and we would participate in such a move. President Ford voiced his concern over the "millions and millions" the Soviets were pumping in and the presence of 4 000 to 6 000 Cuban soldiers.' The Ford administration proposed the amount of $28 million to be earmarked for the battle in Angola.[56]

But the tide was running rapidly against all those in Washington who were back-ing US intervention. On 2 December a meeting of the Forty Committee took place in Washington to review the situation. It sought ways to keep the United States engaged in Angola despite growing signs that Congress would cut off all aid. The meeting decided to send an official to get guidance from Kissinger before he flew to Peking. The official reported that Kissinger had just grunted. 'Was it a positive or a negative grunt?' the meeting anxiously demanded to know. The hapless official shrugged. 'It was just a grunt . . . it did not go up or down.'[57]

Vorster had made his decisions in the strong expectation of US assistance in

53   Hamann, *Days of the Generals*, pp. 36-37.
54   Interview with Constand Viljoen, 16 April 2011.
55   Spies, *Operasie Savannah*, pp. 135-38.
56   De Villiers and De Villiers, *PW*, p. 265.
57   Stockwell, *In Search of Enemies*, p. 22.

Angola. It was only in mid-December it dawned on him that South Africa would get no assistance. On 14 December 1975, three months after a South African force had entered Angola in significant numbers, Vorster phoned Pik Botha (who had replaced Frikkie Botha as ambassador in mid-1975) to ask whether there was anything to the story that the Senate would cancel all aid to Unita and the FNLA. When the ambassador replied in the affirmative, Vorster said he was told 'on the highest authority that we had the support of the American government'. He instructed Botha to visit Congress urgently to do some 'homework' on the Capitol and give him feedback.[58] Two days later Botha reported that no assistance could be expected.

Who was the 'highest authority' that promised the assistance of the US government? General Hein du Toit, head of military intelligence, asserted that he met Pik Botha in Washington while Operation Savannah was in progress. The ambassador asked the general to report to the government that 'the greater majority of the Senate supported us and [General] Scowcroft said we must carry on because the US will support us'. Du Toit considered the information important enough to report it to the State Security Council.[59]

Ambassador Pik Botha flatly denied ever having made the statement that General Du Toit attributed to him.[60] Jeremy Shearar, the deputy head of mission, confirmed this view: 'If General Du Toit really believed he was advised by the Embassy that we had the majority of the Senate, it was his own interpretation ... what might have been said to him can only be speculation.' He recounted: 'I accompanied Pik to many, if not most, meetings on the Hill and cannot recall reaching such conclusions. If the Prime Minister told Pik that he had this [information about US assistance] on the highest authority, then clearly Pik could not have been his informant.' He added: 'This is not to say that we did not receive some encouragement, but none went as far as actual promises of support or gave us ground for hope. In fact, as time passed, the climate worsened and Pik [Botha] so informed the Prime Minister.'[61]

Interviewed recently, both ambassadors JSF Botha and Pik Botha expressed the conviction that Van den Bergh played a key role in getting Vorster to assume that 'the highest authority' in the United States backed South Africa's action.[62] The evidence suggests that the CIA, perhaps even Director William Colby himself, encouraged Van den Bergh to think that Ford and some of his highest officials were in a position to help South Africa prevent a communist takeover. Public statements by Secretary of State Kissinger also fed this expectation. His memoirs leave little doubt

---

58 Fourie, *Brandpunte*, p. 201; Theresa Papenfus, *Pik Botha en sy tyd* (Pretoria: Litera, 2010), p. 470.

59 Hamann, *Days of the Generals*, p. 41.

60 E-mail communication from Pik Botha, 18 May 2011.

61 E-mail communication from Jeremy Shearar, 20 May 2011.

62 E-mail communication from JSF Botha, 5 April 2011.

that he wanted to thwart the Cubans and Soviets in their military venture and would have been happy if the South Africans were to do it.

On 19 December the US Senate decided by 54 votes to 22 to cut off any aid to the two Angolan movements. To a large extent South Africa's game was up. Its involvement had turned on the hope of US backing – hopes that had now been dashed. Pik Botha told Vorster the American giant was 'sick' and that all South African planning had to assume nothing would come of American promises.[63] Summoned by Vorster, Botha flew to his seaside home at Oubos to brief him, the ministers of defence and foreign affairs and the top military command on the situation in Washington. In his memoirs General Magnus Malan writes that Pik Botha told the meeting unambiguously that it would be disastrous for South Africa to stay in Angola. The force should be withdrawn before any soldiers got caught and before the UN Security Council took action.[64]

General Brent Scowcroft, national security adviser to President Ford, urged Pik Botha to ask the South African government to keep its troops in Angola, warning that an 'early' South African withdrawal would leave the door wide open for the MPLA backed by the Cubans and Soviets. While he wished the South African troops to stay until the OAU decided on Angola, he also indicated that if they did, 'no logistical help will be forthcoming from the US and South Africa should approach the Republic of China for arms'. [65]

It soon became clear that the United States would not even sell arms to Unita. Botha told a US official that his prime minister 'had begun to suspect that America wished to use South Africa as a doormat'. Vorster reluctantly agreed that the South African troops should stay until the OAU took a decision on Angola. On 10 February the OAU recognised the MPLA government.[66] South Africa immediately withdrew to its pre-independence position in southern Angola.

Is there a possibility that South Africa secretly demanded a quid pro quo from the United States? Citing cables from South African diplomats in Washington, a highly acclaimed history of the Cold War observed: 'Pretoria expected great returns from the Americans for – as they saw it – helping the Ford administration out in Angola.' It is alleged that Pretoria made four demands: US acceptance of independence for the homelands; an end to the US weapons embargo; no US interference with the rapidly accelerating South African nuclear weapons programme; and American support for Vorster's scheme to get rid of Ian Smith's regime in Rhodesia

---

63 Papenfus, *Pik Botha*, p. 471.
64 Malan, *My lewe saam met die SA Weermag*, p. 41; e-mail communication from Pik Botha, 18 May 2011.
65 Papenfus, *Pik Botha*, pp. 474 -77.
66 E-mail communication from Pik Botha, 20 May 2011; Papenfus, *Pik Botha*, pp. 474-75.

(later Zimbabwe) and replace it with an African-led coalition government beholden to South Africa.[67]

But in truth the documents to which the history refers tell a quite different story. Written by diplomats in February 1976, they all warn that no help at all could be expected from the United States and that the relationship between Washington and Pretoria was seriously strained. They explain that the Watergate scandal and Vietnam had left severe scars on the American psyche, so there was a feeling of revulsion towards being drawn into any conflict ostensibly opposing communists. The Ford administration was isolated and Congress was investigating the CIA. These developments were 'extremely harmful' to South Africa. The cables make it clear why Pik Botha advised Vorster at the Oubos meeting that South African troops should be withdrawn promptly.

South Africa's participation in the Angolan war was a costly venture, leaving it worse off than before. The Russians and Cubans now massively stepped up aid to African countries. A Soviet functionary who worked closely with the ANC notes that after the war in Angola the African states took a more positive view of the ANC's ties with the USSR.[68] The ANC would soon move most of its bases to Angola.

Afterwards Kissinger frankly warned Pik Botha not to count on America. '[The] American people in certain situations become divided, like after Vietnam, and then there will be no action taken by them.' John Chettle of the South Africa Foundation's Washington office put it in even stronger terms: the United States had become a 'truly unpredictable and potentially revolutionary force' in southern African politics. It was influenced by volatile public swings, a yearning for idealistic action, and the feeling that white rule in southern Africa was doomed.[69]

The Vorster government had entered the war in Angola with very little understanding of the hazards and the fickleness of Western support. 'Unconventional diplomacy' – eagerly practised by the secretary of the Department of Information, Eschel Rhoodie, and General Van den Bergh – had fatally disrupted the flow of dependable intelligence and analyses. The affair showed up the weakness of the Vorster government's decision-making system. It was sheer folly to depend on people like Van den Bergh for advice on the possibility of US assistance and to undertake a costly incursion without setting clear military objectives. The CIA estimated that by February 1976 the Soviet Union had spent $400 million and the military venture had cost South Africa $133 million. The United States would end its Angolan programme after spending less than $26 million.[70]

---

67 Westad, *The Global Cold War*, pp. 232, 438. Most of the cables cited by Westad can be found under CV 1/33/3 vols 31-33 in the archives of the Department of Foreign Affairs in Pretoria.

68 Vladimir Shubin, *ANC: A View from Moscow* (Johannesburg: Jacana, 2008), p. 122.

69 Westad, *The Global Cold War*, p. 238.

70 Stockwell, *In Search of Enemies*, pp. 232-33.

On the eve of the opening of parliament early in 1976 *Rapport* wrote that 'the shadow of Angola lay black and heavy'.[71] Nationalist MPs told journalist Stanley Uys that the West, in particular the United States and France, had left South Africa 'scandalously in the lurch'. But voters, who tended to consider communist penetration in Africa a real threat, were remarkably forgiving. In a May 1976 poll two thirds approved of the government sending troops into Angola; only 18% thought it wrong.[72]

To understand this response it is necessary to look at an earlier poll conducted among the white elite. Respondents were asked: 'Which of the following factors do you consider the greatest threat to South Africa?' More than 84% ticked the option 'lack of understanding' in the West and more than 73% endorsed 'international communism'. Only 9% endorsed 'black nationalism within the Republic'.[73] It was in such a context that the Soweto uprising took almost all white South Africans by surprise.

Limiting commitments

While Vorster was determined to limit South Africa's regional commitments to a minimum and defend only the South African border, Minister of Defence PW Botha was willing to project South African power far beyond its borders to create a buffer zone against penetration by guerrilla fighters. For Vorster, South Africa's continued control of South West Africa (now Namibia) was not decisive for white supremacy. South West Africa was less a security issue than a political one; there were nearly 75 000 whites in the country, the great majority Afrikaners. The South African government feared a severe voters' backlash if Swapo came to power in an election marred by large-scale violence and intimidation, all sanctioned by the UN and by poll observers. That could put a damper on all further reform initiatives in South Africa.

The government was also very concerned about the proliferation of arms. Fighting had intensified in southern Africa from the mid-1970s and explosives, rockets and automatic rifles had poured into the region. The security establishment in South Africa wanted permission to hit guerrillas as far beyond the border as possible. It also wished to put pressure on neighbouring states to refuse sanctuary to ANC guerrillas. Vorster agreed – reluctantly, in view of the failed 1975–76 intervention – to cross-border operations against Swapo guerrillas operating from neighbouring states, particularly Angola.

---

71 *Rapport*, 25 January 1976.

72 Hallett, 'South African Intervention in Angola', pp. 364-65.

73 Heribert Adam, 'The South African Power-Elite', H Adam (ed.), *South Africa: Sociological Perspectives* (London: Oxford Press, 1971), p. 91.

In February 1978 the Vorster government committed itself to independence for South West Africa before the end of 1978, and two months later accepted a plan drawn up by Western powers (the United States, Canada, Britain, France and Germany) for a settlement. This plan would be presented to the UN General Assembly after all the parties had agreed. South Africa would remain in control until April 1979, when an election would be held for a government to steer South West Africa to independence. The cabinet accepted the following position: 'If SWAPO won an open [sic] election under circumstances where we were essentially in control over the territory, it would be clear proof that it enjoys majority support.'[74] Minister of Defence PW Botha was a dissenting voice in the cabinet, but he got permission to attack a large Swapo base in Cassinga, Angola, 250 kilometres north of the South West African border, where fighters lived along with women and children. In the battle as many as 600 Swapo fighters and other followers died.

The cabinet was poised between two quite different roads. The military hawks were confident of their ability to bludgeon the guerrillas into submission and to build up a moderate counter to Swapo in South West Africa through a hearts and minds strategy. The doves felt that cross-border operations might trigger further sanctions and some doubted the possibility of building up a moderate black force. Vorster could have held the line for the doves, but he was worn down by the 'information scandal' that threatened to become public at any moment. He was also angered by the fact that UN Secretary-General Kurt Waldheim presented the Western Five plan with details going well beyond what South Africa had agreed to. He resigned as prime minister in September 1978 and was succeeded by PW Botha.

The hawks under PW Botha now set the agenda. South Africa pulled out of the UN plan and announced that it would sponsor internal elections in South West Africa in December 1978 with the aim of building an internal counter to Swapo. As in 1975 with the Angolan invasion, the military hawks believed that moderate African states backed a 'moderate' solution, which meant the exclusion of a Swapo government in South West Africa/Namibia on account of its presumed communist sympathies.[75]

Vorster's fall

Vorster brought about his own fall by granting Secretary for Information Eschel Rhoodie permission in 1974 to wage an unconventional propaganda war with secret state funding.[76] A small cabinet committee consisting of Vorster, Nico Diederichs and Minister of Information Connie Mulder authorised the amounts of money allocated to the different projects.

---

74 Fourie, *Brandpunte*, p. 169.
75 Geldenhuys, *Diplomacy of Isolation*, p. 227.
76 Mervyn Rees and Chris Day, *Muldergate* (Johannesburg: Macmillan, 1980), p. 171.

Over the next five years, as numerous secret projects were launched, sleaze, corruption, violation of exchange control regulations, murder and lies in parliament accumulated. The Department of Information established a front that brought out the pro-government newspaper *The Citizen*, funded by the state. It employed secret state funds and falsified its circulation figures. The department also tried to buy *The Washington Star*, the French journal *L'Equipe*, and a British investors' journal. A fictitious club of businessmen called the Club of Ten placed advertisements in overseas publications.

A gruesome incident occurred. On 22 November 1977 Robert Smit and his wife were murdered in their home. Smit was due to stand as an NP candidate in the general election a few weeks later. Immediately afterwards it was speculated that Smit, an employee of the World Bank in Washington, was about to reveal his discovery of funds in secret foreign accounts to be used for payoffs and bribes to twenty American politicians, journalists and businessmen. Investigative journalism by American newspaper *Sunday News Journal* sketched a picture of BOSS and DINA, its Chilean counterpart, using CIA-recruited terrorists from Cuba to carry out assassinations. It is alleged that BOSS instructed three of these Cuban operatives to murder Smit to prevent him from releasing details of sums laundered to foreign banks.[77]

A recent study by RW Johnson links the late Taillefer 'Tai' Minnaar to the murders. Minnaar had allegedly worked undercover in Cuba alongside the CIA in the mid-1970s. According to Johnson, Minnaar murdered Smit, who had discovered that a senior cabinet minister had creamed off millions to a Swiss bank account. Johnson also asserts that Minnaar became remorseful about the hit in his later years, saying his orders had 'come from the very top', but he now regretted 'the whole dirty business'.[78] Recently Johan van der Merwe, head of the South African security police during the 1980s, refused to comment on the theories – and they are still nothing more than that – but expressed doubt about the Minnaar link. 'If BOSS was involved, Minnaar was the last person they would have used.'[79]

The Smit murders remained unsolved and the attention of the press at the time quickly shifted to the secret campaigns and unauthorised spending. Vorster and Hendrik van den Bergh, together with Connie Mulder and Eschel Rhoodie, desperately tried to stem the tide of exposés in the English-language newspapers. They would have succeeded at least partially had there not been a leadership race in the NP, pitting Mulder against PW Botha, who benefited from the exposés.

77 James Myburgh, 'The Lost Theory of SA's Greatest Unsolved Political Crime', www.politicsweb. co.za, 7 June 2010.

78 RW Johnson, *South Africa's Brave New World: The Beloved Country since the End of Apartheid* (London: Allen Lane, 2009), p. 25.

79 E-mail communication from Johan van der Merwe, 24 November 2010.

As more and more secrets were exposed, Vorster claimed he had been unaware of the financial arrangements for the Department of Information's secret projects until May 1978. A few days later Eschel Rhoodie said that a secret cabinet committee had approved the funding. In parliament, Connie Mulder denied that *The Citizen* was published with state funding. Vorster was present, but kept quiet. Senior ministers quickly abandoned him.

In September 1978 Vorster resigned as prime minister to become state president. Before the election of a new leader, Vorster told Pik Botha: 'The choice is between a babe in the woods [Connie Mulder] and a bull in a china shop [PW Botha].' He had become estranged from Van den Bergh, on whom he had relied so strongly in the case of both the Angolan and Information debacles. 'I never want to see that *wetter* [utter scoundrel] in my life again,' he told Pik Botha.[80]

Mulder would soon be forced out of the cabinet and the party. After a commission found Vorster had been aware of the financial irregularities, the PW Botha government asked him to resign as state president. Deon Geldenhuys perceptively noted that there were remarkable similarities between the Angolan and Information debacles: 'an obsession with secrecy, the confinement of political decision-making to very few people; the lack of a range of various interested parties – notably foreign affairs – and the corresponding absence of a system of inter-departmental checks and balances, and the prime minister's lack of firm direction and control.'[81]

A fatal contradiction

There was a fatal contradiction in Vorster's policy. Under his watch the offering of secondary and tertiary education to blacks was greatly expanded, the racial gap in salaries and pensions was narrowed and the private sector was urged to follow suit. All of this raised the expectations of urban blacks. At the same time, however, Vorster made no attempt to meet the political aspirations of the black or coloured people. Instead he intensified the feelings of insecurity with the policy of removing the South African citizenship of those blacks, such as the Xhosa, whose 'nation' had accepted the government's offer of 'independence'. He made half-hearted efforts to reform the pass laws and to allow blacks to form trade unions.

Providing slightly improved socio-economic conditions while keeping the clamps on political expression was a recipe for a political explosion. The higher that black or coloured children moved up in the school standards, the more pronounced their rejection of apartheid was. Vorster thought his security forces would squash any challenge, but he failed to fathom the depth of the alienation, particularly among the educated elite, children in high school and large numbers of unemployed people.

---

80 Telephonic communication from Pik Botha, 18 May 2011.

81 Geldenhuys, *Diplomacy of Isolation*, p. 89.

Eli Louw, who entered parliament in 1977 and ten years later would become minister of manpower, captures Vorster's qualities as a leader well: 'He was an outstanding speaker, and he was superb in summarising a debate in parliament and then formulating his view and reasserting his authority. To top it all, he had a sharp sense of humour.'[82] Asked in 1977 by his wife what his main impression of his first parliamentary session was, Louw replied: 'Two things: the enormous power and influence of John Vorster and the fact that he does nothing with it. It looks as if things have come to a standstill, have become stuck. There is no dynamic movement.'[83]

After leaving politics in disgrace in 1979, Vorster spent his bitter final years in virtual seclusion, occasionally denouncing the NP's 'liberal' reforms. During the 1983 campaign for a white referendum on the tricameral parliament, he supported a 'no' vote and made a rare public appearance at the University of Pretoria to address a student audience of 2 000. In his grave voice he first told the students that a new constitutional dispensation was about to dawn: 'There will be an Indian chamber,' and then, after a pause, 'there will also be a coloured chamber.' He paused to ask: 'Will there also be a white chamber?' After another pause he laconically answered: 'For your peace of mind: the answer is yes.' The students roared with laughter.[84]

Vorster represented a strange case: a leader who dominated parliament, led his party to resounding victories at the polls, and enjoyed the trust of his people, yet was unable to provide any leadership to extricate his country from a system that had become dysfunctional, threatening the very possibility of peaceful change.

Vorster died on 10 September 1983. The family told a single cabinet minister that he would be welcome at the funeral. Vorster remains the most enigmatic and contradictory of all the modern Afrikaner leaders.

---

82   Interview with Eli Louw, 30 December 2010.
83   Interview with Eli Louw, 30 December 2010.
84   Koot Jonker, *Vegters teen politieke boelies* (no place: Griffel Media, 2009), p. 32.

Chapter 6

PW Botha and 'Power Sharing without Losing Control'

IN AN ARTICLE PUBLISHED IN 1959 UNDER THE TITLE 'HISTORY'S WARNING TO Africa' historian Arnold Toynbee considered the different roads open in an empire to a dominant minority that is suddenly confronted by a majority which for centuries had placidly resigned itself to subjugation. He had in mind Greco-Roman rule over the subordinate populations in southwest Asia. For nearly 1 000 years the dominant minority made no real attempt to socially integrate the native populations. This implacable hostility to absorbing the subordinate classes gave the Arab-Muslim invaders their opportunity to overthrow Roman rule and bring about integration.

Toynbee pointed to the contrasting case of the Spanish empires in Latin America. The Spanish also exploited the native peoples, but here the division between first-class and second-class citizens did not follow racial lines, and barriers to the top were not racial, and hence not impermeable. The result was continued Spanish predominance even after independence. So too the people of European descent (or predominantly European descent) in the former Portuguese colony of Brazil, forming just over half the population, still dominate society on virtually all levels.

In stark contrast stood the colonies that the Dutch and the British founded in Africa. Upward mobility for subordinate races was difficult and intermarriage was virtually ruled out. There was, Toynbee noted, 'no easy way of entry into the . . . dominant caste for an able and adaptable Bantu'. He warned: 'The Greco-Roman precedent shows that even after a thousand years the roots of domination may still be as shallow as they were in the first generation.'[1] Demography was important. If the dominant minority was ahead in technology and culture, the struggle would be more drawn out and more morally complex than in the case of a clear-cut military struggle. But 'the dénouement may be more tragic'. Sooner or later ruling minorities had to accept the status of 'an unprivileged minority' among a majority they considered culturally inferior. The alternative was to hold on to their present supremacy by sheer force against a rising tide of revolt.

He warned that holding on against the tide was fatal for the minority. 'Even if its belief in its own cultural superiority was justified, numbers would tell in the long run, considering that culture is contagious, and that an ascendancy based on cultural

---

1   Arnold Toynbee, 'History's Warning to Africa', *Optima*, 9, 2, 1959, pp. 56-57, 59.

superiority is therefore a wasting asset.' He expressed sympathy with the dilemma of minorities: voluntary abdication in favour of a majority 'whom one feels to be one's inferior is a very hard alternative for human pride to accept'.[2]

A growing challenge

In South Africa a small but significant stratum of black and coloured people in white-collar jobs had begun to form by the end of the 1970s. The proportion of people in white-collar jobs in the coloured community rose from 12% in 1970 to more than 20% in 1983. In the Indian community it went up from 38% to over 50% in the same period. In the case of black people it was still below 10%, but in numerical terms the figures were substantial.

The most successful members of this aspirant middle class moved into suburbs still classified as white, sending their children to formerly white private schools and to the universities, which were rapidly desegregating. Mixed sport, first on an international level and then on a provincial and local level, slowly became acceptable in place of sports apartheid. But apartheid South Africa nevertheless provided very few places or positions where people could escape the burden of colour.

Opinion surveys revealed the alienation of the disenfranchised. A 1981 survey found that fewer than half of coloured people felt proud to be South Africans, only a third were prepared to condemn terrorism outright, and only a quarter (compared to 80% of whites) were willing to fight for their country. Surveys undertaken in the early 1980s found that urban blacks in South Africa overwhelmingly supported Robert Mugabe as leader in Zimbabwe, based on the perception that he was a successful freedom fighter promoting black interests. A 1981 poll in KwaZulu and Natal revealed that nearly half of blacks were prepared to provide covert aid to the ANC if it infiltrated the country. The notion that white power was too formidable to confront directly was fast becoming discredited.[3]

By the early 1970s there still was no radical organisation capable of challenging the state. The implementation of draconian security measures left the liberation movements in disarray. Vladimir Shubin, an official of the Soviet Union with close ties to the ANC, wrote in revealing terms about the state of the ANC and its allies, the South African Communist Party (SACP) and the South African Congress of Trade Unions (Sactu). Inside South Africa their structures were crushed and most of the leadership had to go into exile.

Things were not much better abroad. The Tanzanian government compelled the external missions of the ANC and the SACP to move from Dar es Salaam to Moro-

---

2   Toynbee, 'History's Warning to Africa', pp. 55-56.
3   Deon Geldenhuys, *The Diplomacy of Isolation: South African Foreign Policy Making* (Johannesburg: Macmillan, 1984), pp. 201-202.

goro, a minor provincial town. Here Moses Kotane and JB Marks shared a small office and slept in two adjacent rooms. In London, Joe Slovo and Yusuf Dadoo manned a modest office. Acting ANC president Oliver Tambo, based in London, formed the Revolutionary Council in 1969 to conduct covert operations. Although he travelled widely, Tambo could show few tangible achievements. In 1971 the main success noted in his report was a series of leaflet bombs that had been distributed in a number of South African cities.[4]

The Black Consciousness Movement (BCM) that sprang up in the late 1960s made an inclusive black identity the focus of black pride and assertion. Flourishing in its first five years, it succeeded in politicising black and coloured high school pupils and university students, but failed to establish ties with the black workforce. In the adult urban black community, particularly on the Witwatersrand, ethnic divisions remained and the state did its best to reinforce them through housing and education policies.

Considering white power unassailable, urban blacks focused on wages and salaries. Since these were still quite low, the state and business thought they could buy most of them off with improved remuneration.[5] The Soweto uprising that erupted on 16 June 1976 caught the government and the ANC by surprise. A few thousand people fled the country, many flocking to ANC offices. But as a Soviet analyst noted, there were myriad problems in exile, 'such as a relative lack of commitment to the ANC, poor discipline, and errors in selection for the various kinds of training available'.[6]

'Adapt or die'

In August 1979, twenty years after Toynbee's warning, PW Botha – who had become prime minister a year before – made a speech that attracted much excitement. It seemed to signal that the moment of truth for white supremacy had finally arrived. Opening the NP congress in Durban he said: 'The world does not remain the same . . .We have to adapt our policy to those things that make adjustment necessary, otherwise we die.'[7] A bold newspaper headline promptly turned his words into the dramatic slogan 'Adapt or die'. In parliament, Botha denied that he had posed such a stark choice but, whether he meant it or not, South Africa had embarked on a journey for which there was no prescription or precedent. Gone was

---

4   Luli Callinicos, *Oliver Tambo: Beyond the Engeli Mountains* (Cape Town: David Philip, 2004), p. 304.

5   Edward Feit, 'Conflict and Cohesion in South Africa', *Economic Development and Cultural Change*, vol. 14, 1968, pp. 490-91.

6   Vladimir Shubin, *ANC: A View from Moscow* (Johannesburg: Jacana, 2008), p. 128.

7   Robert Schrire, *Adapt or Die: The End of White Politics in South Africa* (London: Hurst and Co., 1991), pp. 29-47. This brief study remains the best analysis of Botha's term in office.

John Vorster's paddling about in a pool of complacent white supremacy. The cry went up that South Africa had to change radically before a civil war erupted.

Botha's background did little to prepare him for incorporating coloured and black people into the political system in a way that would foster a multiracial middle class loyal to the system. Born in 1916, he went to school and university in the Orange Free State, abandoning his university studies in 1936 to become the Cape NP's organising secretary. The next year the 21-year-old secretary proposed a motion at the party's congress warning about the 'dangers of communism', a theme that would run through his entire career.

Botha entered parliament in 1948. He strongly opposed white parties competing for the coloured vote. He was driven by the winner-takes-all ethos of the Westminster electoral system, demolishing the opposition rather than building alliances and consensus. When he became minister for community development in 1961, he made no secret of his enthusiasm for imposing the policy of group areas. His rationale was that segregated suburbs would end a situation where black or coloured people lived as 'appendages' and where they had developed 'a sense of inferiority'. He argued that living in their 'own' townships would provide them with a greater sense of dignity and self-worth. He was oblivious to the pain, suffering and humiliation of forced removals.

In 1966 Botha became minister of defence, a portfolio he would hold for thirteen years. He oversaw the rapid build-up of the South African army, based on a relatively small permanent force and a large annual intake of white conscripts. Like the top military officers, he was influenced by the work of counter-revolutionary strategists. Highest on his reading list were John J McCuen's *The Art of Counter-Revolutionary War* and the books of the French strategic thinker André Beaufre, as well as the major French intellectual Raymond Aron. From his reading he took the view that the South African state had to defend itself against communist subversion not only by military means but also by combating political and ideological attacks.[8]

'Setting ourselves free'

In the year after he became prime minister in September 1978 Botha hit South Africa like a storm. In contrast to Vorster, who acted like a potentate inviting the homeland leaders to come to his office for occasional 'apartheid summits', Botha reached out to black people. He called them 'fellow South Africans', visited Soweto with 'a message of hope', and toured all the homelands to meet the leaders. He urged Afrikaners to study the lessons of their own history. 'The moment you start oppressing people . . . they fight back. We must acknowledge people's rights and . . .

---

8   Interviews with Niel Barnard, 21 April 2002, and with Johan van der Merwe, 21 November 2002. The latter headed first the security police and then the police force during the 1980s.

set ourselves free by giving to others in a spirit of justice what we demand for ourselves.'[9] Great changes seemed to be under way. After his first year in office, the *Washington Post* noted that the changes astonished blacks and kindled hopes of an alternative to violence and despair.[10]

Yet it was still inconceivable that the white community would yield all its political power. Botha wanted a more rationalised, efficient, white-controlled system; at the same time, however, he also made it clear that parliament would not be elected on the basis of one man, one vote while he was NP leader. 'We are not prepared to accept black majority rule ... We are not prepared to hand over power in such a way that our children would not have a future in South Africa.'[11] He was determined not to be sucked by stealth into reforms he rejected. According to Magnus Malan, minister of defence in his cabinet, Botha would crush any person who tried to bypass him instead of being open with him.[12] Jannie Roux, director-general in his office and cabinet secretary, sums up Botha's hold on power: 'He was not afraid of taking decisions and he disliked long discussions in cabinet. He looked people straight in the eyes and told them just what he thought. He had no secret agenda and never pulled any punches.'[13]

Under Vorster the state resembled a ramshackle family firm struggling to cope with radically changing demands and threats. With Botha came a radical rethink of the way in which the state should be administered. He was impressed with the professionalism and can-do mentality of the military, sharing its dismay with the tardy way in which some of the state departments implemented policy.

Lacking Vorster's ability to personally attract people to him, Botha built up his power through much improved control over his party, the cabinet and the state administration, greatly boosting the oversight capacity of the head of government. He reduced the number of state departments and introduced a cabinet secretariat that could keep minutes effectively and supervise the execution of decisions. Standing at the apex of the system, Botha soon established a well-earned reputation as an effective administrator who came to every meeting well prepared.[14] His power was direct and personal; he was a straight talker, tough, brutal, overpowering and at times thuggish, vindictive and petty.

9   Merle Lipton, *Capitalism and Apartheid* (Aldershot: Wildwood House, 1986), pp. 51-52.

10 Dirk de Villiers and Johanna de Villiers, *PW* (Cape Town: Tafelberg, 1984), p. 152.

11 JJJ Scholtz, *Vegter en hervormer: Grepe uit die toesprake van PW Botha* (Cape Town: Tafelberg, 1988), p. 29.

12 Interview with Magnus Malan, 9 February 2008.

13 Interview with JR Roux, 30 November 2007.

14 Interview with JR Roux, 30 November 2007.

Countering security threats

Botha soon realised that one of the state's main weaknesses was a lack of professionalism in gathering and analysing data related to security threats and to a fast changing external environment. In 1975 a small committee under John Vorster, of which Botha was a member, decided to launch an incursion into Angola without clearly defined military objectives and without asking the advice of diplomats in Washington. In 1979 Foreign Affairs blundered by predicting that the party of Bishop Abel Muzorewa would win the election in Rhodesia (later Zimbabwe) by a handsome margin.[15]

Botha and his military strategists concluded that a national security strategy could only be pursued successfully by bolstering the State Security Council, acting under the leadership of civilian politicians. It had to be assisted by a bureaucracy consisting of senior military officers and civil servants able to review security threats, coordinate intelligence reports and devise proper responses.[16] In 1979 it was announced that a National Security Management System (NSMS), in which the military had an important voice, had become fully operational. The NSMS would not only coordinate the gathering of information but would also coordinate the implementation of policy. It would play an important role in the state's response to the urban revolt of 1984–86.

Botha created a special agency, the National Intelligence Service (NIS), to perform the task of gathering and assessing intelligence professionally. To head up the organisation, he hand-picked political scientist Dr Niel Barnard, who recruited some very capable staff. It was a far cry from Hendrik van den Bergh, the head of the Bureau of State Security, and his unsophisticated, often brutal methods. David Welsh gives an acute portrait of Barnard: 'a quiet, studious and self-effacing person with impeccable Afrikaner nationalist credentials', who quickly built up a sophisticated and professional organisation.[17] An ex-NIS official noted: 'Barnard believed in stealth, diplomacy, outwitting and outthinking the enemy. He placed a high premium on intelligence analysts within the service and on the value of validated information.'[18]

Barnard concluded that a fight to the bitter end was no option for white South Africans. Sceptical of the 'total onslaught' doctrine propagated by the military, he established formal contacts with the Soviet Union in the mid-1980s. He steadily gained Botha's trust. Mike Louw, his understudy at NIS, described his growing influence: 'Barnard started off being very much of an outsider but somehow his

---

15   Annette Seegers, *The Military in the Making of Modern South Africa* (London: IB Tauris, 1996), pp. 161-62.

16   Seegers, *The Military*, pp. 132-34.

17   David Welsh, *The Rise and Fall of Apartheid* (Johannesburg: Jonathan Ball, 2009), p. 251.

18   Riaan Labuschagne, *On South Africa's Secret Service* (Alberton: Galago, 2002), p. 23.

character clicked with PW despite their being two utterly different persons . . . Within a couple of years he was already one of the most trusted and over the last years he was really trusted above all his other advisers.'[19]

Adapting an ideology

At the core of Botha's political ideology was the assumption that racial and ethnic groups formed the building blocks of the political and social system, and that there could be no interracial democratic competition.[20] Another core belief was that Afrikaner leadership alone could bring about orderly change. He knew full well that Afrikaners would lose most by ceding control over the state, so the government had to retain their trust in every move it made. He told two biographers: 'You can only lead when you make it possible for people to trust you.'[21]

Having started his career as a party organiser, Botha kept a close watch on swings in the white electorate – and among Afrikaner voters in particular. But he was not inclined, as Vorster was, to maintain unity at all costs. He was acutely aware that reform was eroding his Afrikaner base. The proportion of Afrikaners supporting the NP dropped from more than 80% in the 1977 election to just over 60% in the early 1980s. In the early 1990s it would drop to approximately 50%. Botha sensed that power sharing with blacks was a bridge too far for his supporters.

He strongly believed that the Soviet Union, using Third World surrogates in its rivalry with the United States, caused most conflicts in the developing world. He even suspected it of pursuing a master plan for bringing South Africa and all its mineral riches under Soviet control. In his view it was not apartheid that was causing the conflict in South Africa, but communists who had infiltrated black political organisations and the ANC in particular. In 1977, when he was still minister of defence, his department published a White Paper spelling out the belief that South Africa faced a 'total onslaught' in virtually every area of society.[22]

But new realities marked the political scene. Until the Soweto uprising of 1976 Hendrik Verwoerd's project of enforcing separate development of the racial communities had held extraordinary sway over the minds of the Afrikaner nationalist elite. It imbued them with a mixture of self-confidence, self-righteousness and high morale. But the policy had failed to produce viable black states, curb the flow to the towns and cities, or persuade urban blacks to see their political destiny as lying in the homelands. In the place of complacency and rectitude came a sense of crisis,

19   Interview with Mike Louw by Patti Waldmeir, 29 May 1995.

20   Koos van Wyk and Deon Geldenhuys, *Die groepsgebod in PW Botha se politieke oortuigings* (Johannesburg: Randse Afrikaanse Universiteit, 1987), p. 47.

21   De Villiers and De Villiers, *PW*, p. 367.

22   C Alden, *Apartheid's Last Stand: The Rise and Fall of the South African Security State* (London: Macmillan, 1996), pp. 41-50.

ideological confusion and what commentator Conor Cruise O'Brien called 'the unexpected force of guilt'.[23]

Another reality was that after the Soweto uprising blacks were more resolute and openly angry about the system. The proportion of Witwatersrand blacks who were 'angry' and 'impatient' about conditions in South Africa jumped from 39% in 1977 to 56% in 1981, when two thirds of Soweto residents expected that South Africa would change radically in about six years. They believed the struggle against oppression would be successful. Half of black people indicated they would be prepared to secretly assist the ANC, which had stepped up its sabotage attacks. Whites got the message. In 1980 two thirds of Afrikaners and three quarters of English speakers expected war and internal violence.[24]

A further reality was that major demographic shifts were severely eroding white domination. During the early 1950s the NP government introduced the apartheid system on the assumption that whites could continue to fill all the top and middle positions on the labour ladder. At that stage whites formed 20% of the population. By 1980 the proportion had sunk to 13%, and it would sink to below 10% by the turn of the century. So NP-supporting business leaders started telling the political leadership that the economy would suck whites into ever-higher positions on the job ladder and that blacks would fill the posts they had vacated.

By the early 1970s it was already clear that whites could not supply the entire demand for skilled labour. Between 1947 and 1977 the proportion of whites in the manufacturing sector dropped from 33% to 22%, while in the construction sector it declined from 25% to 14%. Between 1971 and 1977 whites made up only a quarter of the increase in fully employed, skilled workers. In the latter year nearly half of a sample of leaders in the manufacturing sector thought a lack of skilled labour was causing bottlenecks.[25] A senior official in the Department of Labour recounted: 'We had reached a point where all the available white labour had been absorbed and the number of vacancies was multiplying. Employers told the department: "We want to build a factory but we do not know where to get labour. Allow us to train black labour and employ them on merit as skilled labour."'[26]

From this followed the policy of greatly stepping up the provision of secondary education to black and coloured children. They now rose to educational and occupational levels their parents could only dream about. In a mere ten years, from 1978

---

23   Conor Cruise O'Brien, 'South Africa: An Ominous Lull', *New York Review of Books*, 27 September 1979, p. 28.

24   Hermann Giliomee, *The Pattern of Politics* (Cape Town: David Philip, 1982), pp. xi-xiii.

25   Hermann Giliomee and Lawrence Schlemmer, *From Apartheid to Nation-building* (Cape Town: Oxford University Press, 1989), pp. 110-11.

26   Interview with Dennis van der Walt by Naas Steenkamp, 7 October 2008. Van der Walt served as the full-time secretary of the Wiehahn Commission on labour policy.

to 1988, black high school graduates increased from 13% of the total to 51%, while the proportion of blacks enrolled at universities jumped from 11% to 35%. This shift had enormous political consequences. A 1981 study showed that the higher the level of education, the stronger the rejection of apartheid. While half to two thirds of blacks with low educational qualifications (Standard 2 or below) accepted the segregation of schools and residential areas, fewer than 15% with Standard 10 or higher were prepared to do so.[27]

'Sharing power'

Reforms of labour policy (see pp. 152-164) and the attempt to incorporate coloured and Indian representatives in parliament (see pp.167-174) quickly gave rise to questions. Were the reforms initiated by the Botha administration sham or real? Were they fundamentally changing South African society or merely restructuring apartheid? A prominent Afrikaans business leader ventured an opinion that was widely quoted: 'We Afrikaners are trying to find the secret to sharing power without losing control.'[28] There were some chuckles at the obvious contradiction, but the business leader was quite serious – and not without reason. Almost unwittingly, he had captured the real paradox of the reforms that emanated from the Botha cabinet.

Afrikaner nationalists were determined to retain control while trying to spread income and resources more widely than before, and bringing blacks into decision-making structures. Here they would have *inspraak*, which meant they would have a say but certainly not the decisive say. Chris Heunis, minister of constitutional affairs, said in a speech in October 1981: 'It is in the long-term interest of South Africa that the Afrikaner should always have the privilege of the leadership role. This role of leader will be accompanied by ever greater responsibilities.' The great task was 'to formulate and implement a new political and socio-economic dispensation for South Africa'. Afrikaners, he said, would have to embark on it with others, 'but to a large extent it will be their responsibility'.[29]

Indeed, a new ideology could be said to have sprung up alongside apartheid since the late 1970s. It accepted economic growth, training, job creation and food production as primary goals, but always based on maintaining political stability, which was seen as making all these things possible. Reform depended on firm control of the state by a fairly unified Afrikanerdom as the stable 'centre' of South Africa. If this centre lost its cohesion, everyone would suffer.

This was the scheme that inspired the NP under Botha. In some cases, as in

---

27 Schrire, *Adapt or Die*, pp. 15-17.
28 Hermann Giliomee, 'The Botha Quest: Sharing Power without Losing Control', *Leadership SA*, 2, 3, 1983, p. 27.
29 Giliomee, 'The Botha Quest', p. 27.

implementing the reforms recommended by the Wiehahn Commission, the leadership was prepared to 'share power' in common institutions such as a unified system of industrial bargaining. Likewise the tricameral parliament, but in the case of the black homelands Botha could come up with nothing more than the idea of a 'constellation of states', which was no advance on the scheme mooted by Verwoerd in 1961 after withdrawing South Africa's application to remain in the Commonwealth.

Black unions

After the Durban strikes of 1973 (see Chapter 4, pp. 98-99) the Vorster government introduced works and liaison committees. It thought these would provide an acceptable channel to communicate workers' grievances and would deprive black unions of 'their life's blood and necessity for existence'. In later years unionists would refer to these committees as 'dogs without teeth'.[30] In terms of the law regulating industrial relations that was passed in the 1920s, black workers did not qualify as 'employees' as defined in the Act. As a result, they were not represented on industrial councils, where equal numbers of employer and employee representatives met to resolve disputes. Under the Bantu Labour Act of 1953 blacks were forbidden to strike, punishable with as much as three years in jail, while the Bantu Labour Act of 1964 imposed criminal penalties for desertion, breach of contract and disobeying an employer. Blacks could form unions, but these were not recognised.

Until the late 1970s employers were in no rush to accept black unions. A labour activist wrote: 'Big firms were often worse than the apartheid state in denying workers' rights.'[31] Business leaders worried more about the lack of skilled labour, which stood in the way of economic growth. A survey from the early 1970s showed that three quarters of all English-speaking employers opposed job reservation.[32] The government was now willing to phase out job reservation where the white-led unions had agreed to it.

In 1970 activists established the Urban Training Project (UTP) to help black workers build a strong labour movement. It held workshops to discuss the formation of new unions, advise the existing black or multiracial unions, help workers to organise, and assist in developing negotiating skills and strategies. Springing from these workshops was the strategy of bypassing the state, which the workers increasingly followed. At each plant the workers elected their own leaders, who initially raised only issues of immediate concern to the workers. Once they had succeeded in signing up most of the black workers in a union, they would ask the employer to recog-

---

30   Jeremy Baskin, *Striking Back: A History of Cosatu* (Johannesburg: Ravan Press, 1991), p. 18.

31   Donovan Lowry, *20 Years in the Labour Movement* (Johannesburg: Wadmore, 1999), back cover.

32   Heribert Adam, 'The South African Power-Elite', Heribert Adam (ed.), *South Africa: Sociological Perspectives* (London: Oxford University Press, 1971), p. 87.

nise it in an agreement binding both the workers and the individual employer to good faith negotiations.

The unions focused on semi-skilled black production workers and singled out foreign firms less able to impose repressive measures. Some employers resisted the demand for recognition and the police harassed and eventually banned fourteen whites and ten blacks engaged in worker education and black unions.[33] But a process had been set in motion that could not be rolled back. As Tito Mboweni, the first ANC labour minister, would later write: 'By 1976 UTP had launched or revived nine unions and it had begun to fashion the tactics which would make the unions such a force for the achievement of democracy in the country.'[34] It formed the Consultative Committee of Black Trade Unions with a signed-up membership of 19 000.

In Durban the Trade Union Advisory Co-ordinating Council was formed after the Durban strikes. In Cape Town a workers' advice bureau was soon turned into the Western Province General Workers Union and eventually the General Workers Union. Also in the field were the Black Allied Workers Union, with 6 000 members, and the Council of Industrial Workers of the Witwatersrand. The steady strengthening of black labour along with the shortage of white skills made it possible for black workers to press successfully for better wages. The black-white wage gap declined steadily in the course of the 1970s. The ratio of white to black wages on the mines declined from 21:1 in 1970 to 6:1 in 1979; in the manufacturing sector it dropped from 6:1 to 4:1.

The ANC was ambivalent about the prospects of building a black union movement. A union activist later told a researcher: 'We were left alone by the ANC because exiles told me that, quite frankly, we did not have a hope in hell of building unions under such repression.' But in 1974 Joe Slovo told Alec Erwin, an academic soon to become a key trade union leader, to continue building unions.[35]

By 1975 Vorster sensed that the 1973 legislation had not really helped to stabilise the workplace and he began to consider admitting black unions to the regular industrial relations machinery. He first mooted the idea of a new labour framework in mid-1975, in informal conversations with friend and close ally Fanie Botha, minister of water affairs.[36] He was concerned about the steady increase in the number of black unions, the bargaining that often occurred outside any legal framework,

---

33 Loet Douwes Dekker, 'Towards Democratic Practices: South Africa in the 1970s', unpublished paper, 2010, p. 3.

34 Tito Mboweni, 'Foreword' in Lowry, 20 Years in the Labour Movement, p. xv.

35 Dave Cooper, 'War of Position and Movement: Reflections on Central Europe and the South African Trade Union Movement', South African Journal of Sociology, 27, 2, 1996, p. 60.

36 Interview with Fanie Botha by Naas Steenkamp, 4 August 2008.

the growing criticism from international labour federations, and the steady flow of funds from abroad to black workers' committees and trade unions.

Vorster and Botha envisaged a scheme that would combine limited reform with strict control. Black unions would be allowed to enter the formal system of bargaining on the industrial councils, but only so-called 'insider blacks' (people with Section Ten exemption) would be permitted to become members of these unions. They would have to register with the Department of Labour and accept the regulations concerning foreign funding.

In January 1976 Vorster appointed Fanie Botha as labour minister. At that point three quarters of a million white, coloured and Indian workers were members of unions and part of the formal system of industrial relations. Between 55 000 and 70 000 blacks belonged to a total of 27 trade unions, none of which could be registered. In addition, 690 000 black workers were represented by liaison committees and 74 000 by works committees. This meant that a tenth of economically active blacks now enjoyed some form of representation through unions, works committees or liaison committees.

Thoughts of 'Chairman Wim'[37]

From the start Fanie Botha turned for advice to Willem (Wim) de Villiers, chairman of the board of the Afrikaner-controlled mining house Gencor. After completing a doctorate in engineering at the University of Cape Town, De Villiers accepted an offer from Anglo American to become general manager at Rhokana mine in Northern Rhodesia (now Zambia), one of the largest copper mines in the world. He was appalled by the extremely low wages the corporation paid its black workforce. 'It is not much more than the wages the mines paid in the time of Paul Kruger. It is a crying shame,' he told his wife.[38]

After ten years he returned home to work for Anglo in South Africa, with a special responsibility for productivity on the Free State gold fields. He earned a reputation for innovative approaches to black labour management, productivity and labour relations. His book *The Effective Utilisation of Human Resources in the Republic of South Africa* (1974) attracted widespread attention in both business and government circles. He wanted South Africa urgently to pursue the twin objectives of high economic growth and an enhanced standard of living for the subordinate population. These goals could only be achieved through sharp increases in the productivity of workers of all colours.

But while De Villiers wanted to improve the productivity and welfare of the

---

37   This section is drawn from Naas Steenkamp, 'Voorbrand: Die Wiehahn-kommissie as wegbereider vir demokrasie', unpublished ms., 27 August 2008.

38   Interview with Francie de Villiers, Wim's wife, 10 October 2010.

workers, he was sceptical about the ability of trade unions to play a constructive role in organising black workers. On the Copperbelt De Villiers had developed a strong distaste for labour unions organised on the British model. He had witnessed workers organised by British trade unionists waging a decade-long campaign of costly strikes. For the workers in the lower ranks the outcome was disastrous: a reduction of the workforce and increased unemployment. To him the main problem of the British model was the intervention of a third party – the union leadership – in the management-labour relationship. Organised on a national or industry basis, such intervention was detrimental to job creation and productivity.

He believed developments in Britain in the late 1960s and early 1970s provided an object lesson in the dangers of handing power to leftists in the union movement who were bent on attacking the entire political and economic structure of a country. In his view these unionists were not interested in an orderly relationship between workers and employers. They were not even interested in a fair wage for workers, but in the overthrow of the system of production and the social relations based on it.[39]

To De Villiers the lessons for South Africa were clear: extending trade union power to blacks on the British model would lead to the aggressive mobilisation of black political power. While a small minority would benefit from ever-increasing wages, the country would suffer. Unemployment would increase steadily and there would be a declining material standard of living for the great mass of the black population. Inflation would produce an ideal climate for political agitators.

He realised that the British form of trade unionism had become rooted among white workers in South Africa, but he somehow hoped that black workers could be persuaded to accept plant-based works committees as an alternative to unions. He sent Naas Steenkamp, personnel and industrial relations manager in the group, on a tour overseas that included a fortnight in Japan, whose enterprise-based employee model of *kigyubetsu kumiai* particularly interested him. Steenkamp's report recommended that black works committees be used in the Gencor group of companies 'as the basis for structures of communication, negotiation and the settlement of disputes'. The proposal was adopted throughout Gencor's mines and industries.

But there was a major flaw in the De Villiers vision for a modern system of industrial relations: it would further institutionalise the dualism that treated black and non-black workers as separate categories. South Africa was already well past the point where a separate system for blacks or plant-based committees, alongside white and coloured unions, could make any kind of sense.

Self-evidently utopian and inauspicious as these views might now appear, they appealed powerfully both to political and business leaders. They underlined the

---

39 De Villiers sets out his view on unions for black workers in *The Effective Utilisation of Human Resources in the Republic of South Africa* (Johannesburg: General Mining Group, 1974), pp. 86-93.

urgency of providing proper education and training to blacks, improving productivity and raising wages, and introducing effective institutions to facilitate bargaining over wages and working conditions. When the idea of plant-based committees failed to win support, De Villiers quickly accepted the idea of unions as an alternative. To him the priority was effective representation of workers within a framework of industrial relations that avoided the excesses of the British system.

By the mid-1970s Wim de Villiers's views had begun to influence top people in government. They recognised that it was no longer possible to make minor adjustments to the industrial relations framework. It was time for a commission with a well-balanced membership to grapple with the issue.

The Wiehahn Commission

In 1977 Vorster appointed a commission, chaired by Unisa law professor Nic Wiehahn, to review the existing industrial relations legislation, the machinery for dispute regulation and discriminatory practices such as job reservation. The Wiehahn Commission was the most representative commission the NP government had yet put together. Business leaders, employer organisations and white unions expressed extraordinary interest. The commission received 320 written submissions and held evidence-taking sessions in all the major centres.

Only one member opposed black trade unions in principle. He was Attie Nieuwoudt, president of the South African Confederation of Labour, of which the militant white Mineworkers Union was an affiliate. Nieuwoudt argued that the recognised unions would be swamped 'by force of numbers'. Black unions would inevitably become embroiled in politics, and mixed unions would 'disturb the social order and industrial peace'.[40]

The rest of the commission was split roughly down the middle between 'progressives' and 'reformists'. The key issue was this: should unions include as members migrants and commuters from both the independent and non-independent homelands? The progressives wanted to make a clear break with the existing system by opting for freedom of association. This would allow anyone working in South Africa to become a member of a recognised union. It was what the emerging unions wanted and was in line with the key principles of the International Labour Organisation (ILO) and in particular its Convention No. 87 concerning 'Freedom of Association and Protection of the Right to Organise'.

This convention binds ratifying governments (including South Africa) to ensuring that 'workers and employers, without any distinction whatsoever, shall have the right to establish, and, subject *only* to the rules of the organisation, to join organisations of their own choosing without prior authorisation'. Workers had the right to

---

40   NE Wiehahn (ed.), *The Complete Wiehahn Report* (Johannesburg: Lex Patria, 1982), pp. 29-63.

strike and employers the right to dismiss and lock workers out in certain circumstances. Exclusion of certain categories of workers from the right to establish and join trade unions, and limiting the right to strike to certain workers, would undermine the very essence of the convention.

Although members were theoretically serving in their personal capacity, a head-count of ideological commitment took place virtually from the beginning. Looking back 30 years later, Naas Steenkamp, a commission member, gave the following line-up:[41]

NIC WIEHAHN (CHAIRMAN)

Progressives	Reformists	Resisters	Swing vote
Naas Steenkamp	Piet van der Merwe	Attie Nieuwoudt	Arthur Grobbelar
Chris du Toit	Erroll Drummond		
Dick Sutton	Tommie Neethling		
Gopie Munsook	Nic Hechter		
Chris Botes	Wally Grobler		
Ben Mkoatle			

From the outset the progressives, with Steenkamp as their main spokesman, wanted all workers to be included. While agreeing with them on the need for comprehensive change, the reformists had their eye not so much on the ILO but on the NP government, which was expected to reject incorporating in a single step all workers, including the migrants and commuters who formed a large majority. Some of the white-controlled unions and employers' organisations would also object strongly.

Led by Piet van der Merwe, the 'reformists' aimed to exclude migrants and commuters from union membership – certainly as a first stage. They also wanted to make their conditions of employment subject to the treaties between the South African government and the homeland governments in terms of which workers could be given the right to belong to recognised unions. In this Van der Merwe enjoyed Wiehahn's mostly tacit support. But to the progressives this was anathema, since it opened up the possibility of some homeland governments refusing to accept

---

41 Steenkamp, 'Voorbrand', p. 28.

unions. Dick Sutton, one of the progressives, even threatened to resign over this issue.

In a recent interview Van der Merwe explained his position. 'The new labour legislation had to be introduced incrementally. The first step was to incorporate Section 10 blacks, to be followed by the others . . . The minister could not say at the outset: "Trade unions for all, regardless of who and what they are."' He continued: 'I told Fanie Botha the government could give workers from the independent home-lands bargaining rights over the terms of their employment, while refusing initially to give them the right to strike on the grounds that they were not permanent resi-dents. Fanie sat upright in his chair when he heard that and said: "I can sell that to cabinet and the caucus."'[42] But such a strategy clashed with ILO norms and con-ventions, which did not provide for such limitation of the right to strike. Fanie Botha clearly hoped that the commission's first report would recommend the incorpora-tion of black insiders only, but he never revealed his long-term plan.

The swing vote was that of Arthur Grobbelaar, representative of the Trade Union Council of South Africa (Tucsa), who had previously attended many ILO meetings. He had to move cautiously because his federation included unions that favoured the recognition of black unions in the hope of controlling them, while others wanted to squash them. Nic Wiehahn adopted the stance of impartial chairman and was not keen to use a casting vote.

Initially the commission debated the topic under the agenda item 'Eligibility for trade union membership'. Such a formulation implied that certain workers would not be eligible. During the first year of deliberations it looked as if there was a majority for making only the black insiders eligible and deferring a decision on the eligibility of migrants and commuters until negotiations between the South African government and the various homeland governments had taken place. This would give the homeland governments a major say in whether their workers could become unionised. Such a measure would be unacceptable to the unions and clashed with the principle of freedom of association.

The balance of power changed dramatically in the closing stages of the commis-sion's work when Grobbelaar joined the camp of the progressives, who supported freedom of association. Steenkamp recounts a private Sunday morning meeting at which Grobbelaar announced he would now support the principle. He drove home and drew a line through the words 'eligibility for trade union membership' in the commission's draft report and wrote over them 'freedom of association'.[43]

Grobbelaar's decision meant that the commission was now facing stalemate, with seven members in favour of freedom of association; five wanting to limit member-

---

42   Interview with Piet van der Merwe, 18 March 2009.
43   Interview with Naas Steenkamp, 25 May 2011.

ship to urban black insiders; and one (Nieuwoudt) flatly opposed to any form of black unionism. This left chairman Nic Wiehahn in a pivotal position. If he sided with the reformists and used his casting vote, the result would be a 7-7 tie, making the wording of the recommendation to the government highly problematic. Nieuwoudt, however, rejected black unions outright and refused to vote with the reformists who supported the incorporation of the urban black insiders into the industrial relations system. Faced with the fact that supporters of freedom of association now had a clear majority, Wiehahn opted for a resourceful compromise, effectively endorsing elements of both standpoints.[44]

In its first report, tabled on 1 May 1979, the majority recommended acceptance of the principle of freedom of association in line with ILO requirements. All workers should be free, irrespective of race, colour or gender, to join any union of their choice, and unions had to be free to admit or bar any individual. It strongly rejected the view of the minority: 'The phasing in of migrants and commuters into trade union membership implies that there will be an unspecified period of time during which [their] trade union membership will be prohibited and subjecting the question of membership to "negotiation" implies the possibility that in some instances membership will be absolutely prohibited.'[45]

The commission also dealt with a range of other issues. It recommended the United Kingdom's framework of provisional and final registration of employer organisations and unions. It proposed abolishing the principle of statutory work reservation and recommended that the Department of Labour should consult interested parties about phasing out the practice. Any person should be eligible for apprenticeship. It proposed an industrial court to deal with undesirable labour practices and with unilateral changes in labour practices. The government accepted most of these recommendations.

High hopes

Fanie Botha thought it appropriate to table the commission's report on Labour Day (1 May) 1979. It raised high hopes of a start to a genuinely liberal reform of the labour order. But he was now without the support of Vorster, his comrade in arms in the matter. PW Botha, the new prime minister, was never known to be a supporter of the idea of black trade unions.

Both PW Botha and Fanie Botha were determined to prevent the issue from splitting the party. Fanie Botha later told Wiehahn that the issue sailed through cabinet. 'There was no one who objected, in fact no one got a chance to speak.'[46] The confi-

44 *The Complete Wiehahn Report*, pp. 38-62.
45 *The Complete Wiehahn Report*, p. 45.
46 Interview with Nic Wiehahn by Wessel Visser, 30 May 2002.

dential minutes of the NP's parliamentary caucus on the labour reforms, held on 2 May, reveal that only the two Bothas spoke in the meeting. Fanie Botha argued that the job reservation situation had changed radically since its introduction 25 years earlier. Only 28 jobs and one out of every 300 workers were still covered by job reservation. 'The world was crucifying South Africa for a law that did not work.'

He also told the caucus the law would specify that changes in the workplace could only happen after employers and employees had agreed. White workers had recourse to a National Manpower Commission that would be established to keep labour law under constant surveillance. He remarked that black unions, many of which were under sound leadership, were growing and that more would be established. 'We must understand the situation: we cannot refuse to let people talk to their bosses,' he said. The best approach was getting proper control over these unions by forcing them to register. That would enable government to get reports on their finances and prohibit them from participating in politics.

PW Botha said that labour reforms were important to help withstand foreign pressure. Economic growth was essential for stability and to enhance South Africa's position in Africa. 'Black unions have attained a position of power, which could be used effectively against us.' It was essential to maintain labour peace without sacrificing protective measures.[47]

The main stumbling block on the right was the militant and vociferous Mineworkers Union (MWU). It had committed itself to remaining a white union for 'all time' and was doing its utmost to resist further black job advancement. In its submission to the Wiehahn Commission it had strenuously insisted on the retention of job reservation on the mines, depicting this as the only safeguard against 'oppression'.[48] But a strike of 223 MWU members on a copper mine at O'Kiep near Springbok over the appointment of a coloured worker in a 'white' position failed.[49] The Botha government had weathered the first storm.

Dashed hopes

The White Paper tabled by Fanie Botha on 7 May 1979 dashed the progressives' hopes for bold reform, as did the law promulgated on 4 July 1979. The government 'accepted the minority proposal that eligibility for membership be restricted' (although it rejected the notion of subjecting conditions of employment to interstate

47   Archive for Contemporary Affairs (ACA), Bloemfontein, National Party Collection: Minutes of Parliamentary Caucus, 2 May 1979.

48   South African Institute of Race Relations, *South Africa: Survey, 1979* (Johannesburg: SA Institute of Race Relations, 1979), p. 270.

49   Wessel Visser, *Van MWU tot Solidariteit* (no publisher, no date), pp. 229-243.

agreements). Only those black workers 'who are in permanent jobs and therefore constitute a permanent part of the labour force' would be granted the right to join unions. Narrowing the definition of 'employee' to permanent residents, the law specified that registered unions could not admit a non-employee to membership, effectively excluding workers who were commuters or migrants.[50] Unions risked a fine of R500 for each migrant or commuter member in their ranks when they registered. This was almost impossible to implement in a place like Durban where the vast majority of workers were either migrants or commuters. In other cities, too, a large section of the workers were migrants.

The government had managed to placate the fears of white workers and their conservative supporters. Andries Treurnicht and Ferdie Hartzenberg, leaders of the NP's right wing, congratulated Wiehahn on his report when he visited parliament during the discussion of the labour bill.[51] But it had come at a great cost; Wiehahn returned from a trip overseas with the news that there was major disappointment at the half-hearted reform after the commission's report had raised such great expectations.

The government now squared up to the white mineworkers without too much trouble. The main issue was the symbolic one of limiting blasting certificates to whites, as demanded by the white Mineworkers' Union. Some said that blacks with blasting certificates would use the explosives against white miners. The concrete reality was rather different: often blacks did the actual blasting without being rewarded at the rate for the job, because they did not having a blasting certificate. Removing this form of job reservation was nevertheless an excruciating affair. Several talks between the conservative unions and the Chamber of Mines repeatedly broke down.

In the end the minister of labour went back on his promise that the vestiges of job reservation would only be phased out with the consent of the affected parties. Piet van der Merwe, who became director-general of the Department of Labour in 1980, tells the story: 'We were pestered by questions from journalists who wanted to know when job reservation on the mines would be phased out. On my advice we placed a notice in the Government Gazette withdrawing the blasting certificate determination without alerting the media. Three weeks later a journalist phoned me with the question: "When are you going to repeal it?" But the deed had already been done. No one could do anything about it. The critical moment had passed.'[52]

---

50 *The Complete Wiehahn Report*, pp. 56, 132; Foreign Policy Study Foundation, *South Africa: Time Running Out* (Berkeley: University of California Press, 1981), p. 93.

51 Interview with Nic Wiehahn by Wessel Visser, 30 May 2002.

52 Interview with Piet van Merwe, 18 March 2009.

Strategic unionists

Between 1979 and 1993 the membership of the new black unions, also called independent or emerging unions, grew massively from 100 000 to 2 million, to become the best organised force yet to challenge the political order. The architects of the strategy that would outflank the government's scheme came mainly from the executive of the Federation of South African Trade Unions (Fosatu), founded in April 1979 as a broadly based federation of industrial unions. At that point it comprised twelve unions with 45 000 members. It grew rapidly and by 1981 constituted the largest bloc of emerging unions.

Fosatu strategists nevertheless accepted the need for caution while it was still weak, to avoid the government's wrath. It simply did not make sense to use the unions to demand black political rights when black workers' rights were not yet secure. Leading Fosatu official Alec Erwin stated that in the early stages the unions avoided 'dangerous activities' that would 'divert resources and provoke state action against our embryonic movement'. Jay Naidoo, another key Fosatu official, characterised the organisation as apolitical because of its 'continuing weakness and vulnerability'.[53]

Fosatu made the shrewd decision to register in terms of the new legislation – despite its misgivings. It continued to stress that the exclusion of migrants violated the principle of freedom of association as also supported by the majority of the Wiehahn Commission.[54] Membership in the new industrial order gave Fosatu legal standing and a much-enhanced status in entering factories to register workers and oppose victimisation of workers and shop stewards.

While Fosatu did register, it also signalled that it would sign up commuters, migrants and foreign workers, although this was against the law. In doing so, it calculated correctly that the state would find it difficult to police the exclusion of non-racial unions and the signing up of foreign and migrant workers. Publicly, Fosatu asked government to consider lifting the restriction on commuters as a first step.

Another federation of emerging unions, the Council of Unions of South Africa (Cusa), also opted for registration. In its ranks was the National Union of Mineworkers (NUM), with Cyril Ramaphosa as general secretary. Some of the new unions refused to register because migrants and commuters were excluded. This gave Fosatu and Cusa the opportunity to project themselves as moderate voices the state could not afford to suppress. The government's plan to force blacks to limit or eliminate racially mixed unions failed when the Supreme Court ruled in favour of Fosatu's application for registration on a non-racial basis.

---

53   Anthony Marx, *Lessons of Struggle* (London: Oxford University Press, 1992), p. 196.
54   *Critique of the Wiehahn Commission* (Cape Town: SA Labour and Development Research Unit, 1979), p. 36.

Employers, especially those in capital-intensive industries, were unwilling to wage a battle to have the new law strictly applied and soon resigned themselves to having unions recruit their workers. Most of the Fosatu and Cusa unions continued with plant-level bargaining and avoided the Industrial Councils, where clashes with established unions were bound to occur.[55]

Abroad, the government had gained little from its half-hearted reform. At a meeting of the ILO in Geneva in mid-June 1979, representatives from Africa expressed anger and Western delegates were also quite critical.[56] Several of the Wiehahn commissioners attended this meeting in Geneva. Piet van der Merwe recalls the situation at the time: 'In the eighteen months between the first Wiehahn report and the publication of the sixth and last report things had changed dramatically. The external climate got worse and the sanctions threat became much more real. The detention or banning of trade union leaders was causing outrage.' Van der Merwe returned to South Africa from the ILO meeting with an ominous warning: 'You don't know how close South Africa is to being declared a terrorist state.'[57]

At the crossroads

In 1981 labour reforms were at a crossroads. The exclusion of migrants and frontier commuters meant that more than 2 million workers were being left outside the legal framework. On the inside were those black workers who had qualified for permanent residence in the urban areas. The 1979 legislation excluded well over half the workers in the manufacturing sector, in which the number of black workers had soared from 500 000 in 1965 to over 800 000 in the early 1980s.

The state soon came to realise it was no longer in a position to drive a wedge between 'insiders' and 'outsiders' in the black workforce. A major resurgence of strike activity and political resistance had produced a labour force willing to challenge the state on its plans to divide it. The independent unions increasingly ignored the restrictions imposed on unions in terms of enlisting workers and receiving foreign funds. Some sections of industry – particularly mining – began to consider the exclusion of migrants from industrial rights as increasingly problematic.

In the recollection of Fanie Botha, the idea of granting industrial rights to a small section of the black labour force originated in 1975 when he and John Vorster discussed it on a hunting trip. A key assumption was that proper controls and limiting industrial rights to only a section would prevent the unions from becoming politicised. This explains why PW Botha went along with it when he succeeded Vorster. But by now it had become clear to Fanie Botha that the scheme as originally conceived had become unstuck.

55 Cooper, 'War of Position and Movement', p. 64.
56 *Financial Mail*, 22 June 1979, p. 1052.
57 Interview with Piet van der Merwe, 18 March 2009.

A major development was the fifth report of the Wiehahn Commission, published in 1981, which accepted the principle of freedom of association, allowing in migrants and frontier commuters. The majority, now also including Van der Merwe and Wiehahn, argued that accepting this would stabilise rather than destabilise the system, as some had claimed it would. A reduced minority of four commissioners disagreed.[58]

Government response in the form of a White Paper was crucial. A negative re-action could well sink the labour reforms as a major government initiative. A *bosberaad* – attended by the minister, senior officials in his department, and selected officials from other parts of the civil service, like Dr Simon Brand – helped to shore up support for the commission's report. A well-informed source states that a long private conversation between Wim de Villiers and Fanie Botha was instrumental in achieving the vital objective of getting the minister on board.[59]

De Villiers was at the heart of the Afrikaner elite network of political, economic and business leaders that dominated politics in the early 1980s. The Botha govern-ment was particularly responsive to the views of some like De Villiers who easily straddled these three sectors. Moreover, his membership of the Afrikaner Broeder-bond (AB) signalled to cabinet that he considered the Afrikaner nationalist cause to be as important as promoting the interests of business and the welfare of the coun-try. The ideas expressed in his book *The Effective Utilisation of Human Resources in the Republic of South Africa*, published in 1974, became part of the government's economic philosophy.

In June 1975, probably just after Vorster and Fanie Botha first mooted the idea of extending industrial rights to a limited section of the black labour force, the AB's executive decided to appoint an ad hoc committee to study the issue. Among its members were De Villiers, Nic Wiehahn and FW de Klerk, who would later ap-point De Villiers to his cabinet. The minutes indicate that De Villiers's views were influential. The committee felt that satisfying the demands and needs of the black labour force had become essential, but it shied away from advocating recognition of trade unions for blacks. Instead it supported De Villiers's idea of plant-based workers' committees.[60]

In 1980 the AB's executive appointed a new study group, but by now it had become clear that it was impossible to formulate a consensus view on the issue. The politi-cal divisions within the Afrikaner nationalist movement were replicated in the AB. Wim de Villiers had dropped his idea of plant-based workers' committees and now accepted freedom of association.[61]

---

58   *The Complete Wiehahn Report*, p. 464.
59   Interview with well-placed source, 23 February 2012.
60   Ernst Stals, 'Die geskiedenis van die Afrikaner-Broederbond, 1918-1994', unpublished ms., 1998, pp. 604-08.
61   Interview with Naas Steenkamp, 10 March 2012. Steenkamp recounts that De Villiers had given him free rein in the Wiehahn Commission, saying 'Doen wat jy dink reg is.' ('Do what you think right.')

Winning PW Botha over

The main question was what PW Botha's response would be to giving industrial rights to all workers and allowing freedom of association. To discuss this Fanie Botha, Dennis van der Walt (secretary to the Wiehahn Commission) and Niel Barnard (head of National Intelligence) went to see him in his office. Van der Walt recounts that Fanie Botha was 'very tense' and read from prepared notes. PW Botha listened intently and asked for clarification on some issues, but did not offer objections.[62]

It should not be thought that PW Botha and Fanie Botha foresaw the rise of a militant and politicised union movement when they decided to remove the restrictions. They were not alone. Respected labour specialists and political analysts expected the unions to stick to bread-and-butter issues. Even some of the progressives on the Wiehahn Commission did not expect migrant workers on the mines to be much interested in union membership.

The 1981 Labour Relations Amendment Act enshrined the landmark decision to accept freedom of association by allowing migrants and frontier commuters to become members of unions. It also permitted racially mixed membership. The state still tried to impose control by decreeing that unions had to open their membership lists and accounts to the registrar, and by prohibiting unions from any direct association or financial links with political parties. Soon these regulations were flaunted. In 1987 the government tried to prohibit unions from supporting community boycotts and sympathy strikes. This ban was also ineffective.

By the mid-1980s it was clear that the attempt to prevent trade unions from becoming agents for political transformation in South Africa had failed. Increasingly, the government accepted that it could not harass trade union leaders and shop stewards if it wanted industrial peace. It still did not know that the unions would soon become the battering ram of those pushing for fundamental change to the political system.

Labour's advance

Labour quickly assumed a central place in South Africa's new power structure. Now there was shared decision-making on the industrial councils. The unions demanded – and obtained – a say not only on wages, but also on the safety of workers and labour practices. Wages remained the stated reason for most strikes, but there was also strike action against the bills before parliament on matters such as pensions. Increasingly, business began to urge government not to get involved in the new relationship being forged between labour and management.[63]

Membership of Fosatu and other federations of the emerging unions rocketed

---

62   Interview with Dennis van der Walt, 1 March 2012.
63   *Financial Mail*, 24 July 1981, pp. 380-81.

as the new unions proved their ability to press for better working conditions. Where Tucsa unions had once been in the forefront in pushing for change in the workplace, Fosatu and the other new federations now outpaced them in enrolling black members. In December 1985 Fosatu and Ramaphosa's NUM joined in a new trade union federation called the Congress of South African Trade Unions (Cosatu). Whereas in 1979 Fosatu had 95 000 members in 387 organised factories, in its first year Cosatu enjoyed a paid-up membership of 650 000.

The question was how long the new unions would wait before taking explicitly political stands. Since the 1970s the so-called community unions had rejected registration and depended on mass rallies and community action to attract members. For the first five years of their existence the industry-based unions – in which category Fosatu and Cusa can be placed – were reluctant to get involved in direct political action. But in September 1984 the tricameral parliament met for the first time and violent protest broke out in the townships south-east of Johannesburg. These events served as a catalyst for more radical union action. Fosatu formed an alliance with community-based unions and organisations in support of a wide range of student and community demands.[64]

By 1985 Cosatu had aligned itself with the ANC, which saw the federation as a key ally in its campaign 'to make South Africa ungovernable'. The main speaker at the NUM's fifth annual congress was Winnie Mandela, wife of Nelson Mandela who was a symbol of the ANC's struggle. The slogan it chose for the year 1987 was 'The Year Mineworkers Take Control', a deliberate echo of the ANC's 'Year of Advance to People's Power'.

The NUM was now openly associated with the liberation struggle. 'Clearly aching for a fight', as his biographer phrases it, Ramaphosa set a series of impossible demands, including a 30% wage increase for the next year. When the mining companies stood firm, 340 000 workers went out on strike. For once Ramaphosa's judgment had deserted him; the mining houses began dismissing workers on a large scale. The strike turned out to be a violence-ridden failure, with nine workers dead and more than 500 injured. Realising they could do with far fewer workers, the mining companies reduced their workforce drastically over the next fifteen years.[65]

The strike ended in a resounding defeat for Ramaphosa and his union. The blunder of the otherwise cautious and strategically astute Ramaphosa prompted speculation that he had obeyed a decree from the ANC in exile in Lusaka. Marcel Golding, Ramaphosa's second in command, recounts: 'For me it was a very sobering experience about the system and what you were up against. To me that was the most tan-

---

64   Steven Friedman, *Building Tomorrow Today: African Workers in Trade Unions, 1970-84* (Johannesburg: Ravan Press, 1987), p. 447.

65   Anthony Butler, *Cyril Ramaphosa* (Johannesburg: Jacana, 2008), pp. 182-205.

gible expression of the limits of power, I suppose, and also that in the end it doesn't matter what, you must talk. You must settle or you have anarchy.'[66]

In July 1987 Cosatu adopted the Freedom Charter. Eli Louw, who became manpower minister in 1988, said recently: 'I realised from the start that the unions were a powerful political factor. Without them the ANC would never have come to where it did. The state could not arrest or ban trade union leaders. There were too many and they were too radical. They could not be intimidated: they knew they could use the workers standing behind them.'[67]

'Turned on its head'

The story of how South Africa stumbled into a regime of industrial rights for all its workers is a remarkable one. Some see it as a classic case of 'democracy from below', with black workers in great numbers struggling for their rights and strategists in the union leadership shrewdly deploying them in a scheme to gain workers' power step by step.[68] Others emphasise business leaders as the key movers behind the reform.[69]

While it is true that Harry Oppenheimer cautiously called for the emerging unions to be recognised provided they did not become 'political', business leaders had scant influence on the government on this issue. The one exception was Wim de Villiers, whose opinion both Fanie Botha and PW Botha valued. How was it possible that the emerging unions slipped the careful controls built into the government scheme for a new labour order? Fanie Botha's hope was that the state could build the new system on the cumbersome and bureaucratic industrial councils, still dominated by the white unions within and outside Tucsa. But the initiative quickly shifted from bargaining in the industrial councils to factory-based negotiations, in which shop stewards, acting in accordance with mandates given by the workers, played a crucial role. The gains the new unions made by negotiating favourable wage settlements and raising a banner for the voteless black population yielded a rapid increase of members.

Arthur Grobbelaar's Tucsa missed the boat as far as enrolling black members was concerned. When the black unions began entering the industrial councils in the mid-1980s, Tucsa could no longer claim to represent the majority of the workers. It disbanded in 1986. By this stage Attie Nieuwoudt's Confederation of Labour had

---

66 T Dunbar Moodie, 'Managing the 1987 Mine Workers' Strike', *Journal of Southern African Studies*, 35, 1, 2009, pp. 45-60.

67 Interview with Eli Louw, 30 December 2010.

68 Elizabeth Jane Wood, *Forging Democracy from Below: Insurgent Transitions in South Africa and El Salvador* (Cambridge: Cambridge University Press, 2000), pp. 197-212.

69 Merle Lipton, *Liberals, Marxists and Nationalists: Competing Interpretations of South African History* (London: Palgrave, 2007), pp. 47-64.

lost half its members. A scholar writes: 'The Wiehahn strategy was turned on its head: the new unions began to dominate the old and incorporate the old.'[70]

Alienating Buthelezi

After the Soweto uprising, the government tried to devise a somewhat more credible form of black local government in 'white' areas. In 1977 it introduced community councils with limited powers and able to collect very little revenue. In Soweto the election for these councils was a total failure, with a poll of 6%. The NP government also tried to introduce a form of government that would join together the 'white' state with the different homeland governments. But since the bottom line was maintenance of control over all vital issues that affected whites, this meant little in practice.

In 1979 PW Botha invited a large group of business leaders to participate in developing what he called the 'constellation of states' in the southern African region, where leaders would discuss matters of common concern, such as unemployment and poverty alleviation. But business was unlikely to participate enthusiastically unless the plan had broad black acceptance. The three homelands that had taken Pretoria-style independence by 1979 would support it, but the question was whether KwaZulu would also accept independence and become part of the scheme of the homeland leaders. Chief Minister Mangosuthu Buthelezi had by far the most credibility, locally and abroad.

Up to that point Buthelezi had unambiguously rejected the idea of an independent KwaZulu. By 1979 he had carefully positioned himself halfway between the ANC in exile and the NP government. Both the Botha government and the ANC in exile, under the leadership of Oliver Tambo, had difficulty in deciding whether Buthelezi and his 250 000-member-strong Inkatha movement was an ally or a foe in their struggle for future supremacy. Buthelezi issued appeals that made white leaders prick up their ears. He told an interviewer in 1977: 'I would like my people to share in decision-making, to share the goodies . . . Power sharing is a very crucial issue.'[71]

On a tour in his first year as prime minister, Botha visited Buthelezi at Ulundi. Here he raised the issue of KwaZulu independence and the homeland becoming a member of the 'constellation of states'. A row erupted when Buthelezi refused to have anything to do with either, saying he would make a press statement explaining his reasons for rejecting independence. Buthelezi recounted that Botha objected vehemently. 'He did not want me to release it [the memo with the reasons] to the media . . .

70   Cooper, 'War of Position and Movement', p. 65.
71   Anna Starcke, *Survival: Taped Interviews with South African Leaders* (Cape Town: Tafelberg, 1978), p. 76.

PW Botha waved his finger in my face; he was shaking with rage.'[72] Shortly afterwards, Buthelezi told a meeting of ANC and Inkatha leaders in London that Botha had told him Jonas Savimbi was willing to have the region he controlled in Angola included in the proposed constellation. But, Buthelezi went on, he himself had told Botha that KwaZulu was *not* joining such a body. On the copy of a secret report on the ANC-Inkatha meeting, lodged in the papers of Minister of Justice Kobie Coetsee, someone had scribbled in the margin, 'Ons moet hulle daarin forseer' (we must force them into this).[73]

After that Botha met Buthelezi privately only once – when he told him he was not prepared to issue a statement of intent, which Buthelezi had made a prerequisite for negotiations. Meeting in private with Afrikaans journalists, Piet Koornhof, the minister responsible for promoting the constellation, confessed that the idea was stillborn if KwaZulu refused to accept independence or join such a body.[74]

The government's failure to make an effort to recruit Buthelezi as an ally is remarkable, given that he was the only credible internal black leader suitable as a partner for constructing a proper power-sharing scheme against what the government termed the 'revolutionary forces'. The time for that was running out. In the five years since the 1976 uprising the ANC had made remarkable strides, while Inkatha had weakened. A 1977 poll of blacks in Johannesburg, Durban and Pretoria showed 22% support for the ANC and double that for Inkatha. By 1981 a poll in the same cities saw 40% of respondents stating that they would vote for the ANC in a parliamentary election, against 20% who would vote for Inkatha. Nelson Mandela enjoyed 'towering popularity' as a leader with 76% support.[75]

An Inkatha-ANC meeting

Intelligence reports of the Department of National Security (a forerunner of the National Intelligence Service, established in 1980) show that there were strong suspicions in the security establishment that Buthelezi was either a stalking horse for the ANC or plotting on his own against the government. In August 1979, two months before the Inkatha and ANC leaders met in London, a report stated that the ANC in exile had requested Inkatha to use the protection it enjoyed as 'part of the system' to promote the liberation of blacks until the ANC was ready to intervene with violent means. Another report said Inkatha had appealed to the trade union movement to join it in a joint effort to 'mobilise the people'. Yet another

---

72 Jack Shepherd Smith, *Buthelezi: The Biography* (Melville: Hans Strydom Publishers, 1988), p. 231; Interview with Mangosuthu Buthelezi, 15 September 2010.

73 ACA, PV357 Kobie Coetsee Papers, File 1/A1/5 Minutes of Consultative Meeting, 29-30 October 1979, London; Interview with Mangosuthu Buthelezi, 15 September 2010.

74 Interview with Johannes Grosskopf, 27 May 2011.

75 Geldenhuys, *Diplomacy of Isolation*, p. 200.

quoted a statement by ANC leader Oliver Tambo that Inkatha was performing a 'politicising and a conscientising function' that was to the ANC's advantage. However, the ANC had adopted a policy of refusing to cooperate openly with Inkatha 'because it supported only liberation movements, which it deemed Inkatha not to be'.[76]

On 3 October 1979 the Department of National Security issued a top-secret report. It noted that in a meeting arranged by US civil rights leader Jesse Jackson, Buthelezi, Desmond Tutu and Nthato Motlana, chairman of the Soweto Committee of Ten, had agreed to affirm their South African citizenship. Their intention was not to give it up under any circumstances, nor to give up their basic right to universal suffrage. In addition, they pledged not to attack one another in public. In press interviews Buthelezi called for a national convention in which Nelson Mandela and other leaders participated. He said: 'Our brothers in exile and in jail, particularly Nelson Mandela, should be there. I don't think that we can have a meaningful dialogue at a national convention in their absence.'[77]

The leadership of the ANC in exile welcomed the appeals for a national convention in which it could participate, but Buthelezi's espousal of a market-oriented economic policy and of power sharing in a federation was anathema to it. So was his opposition to the armed struggle and sanctions. The ANC's model for the seizure of power was still the one proposed by the SACP, which dominated the strategic thinking of the ANC in exile. Inspired by the Russian Revolution of 1917, the SACP – the ANC's main ally – believed it could overthrow the government in a revolution. The first stage would be a national democratic revolution and the second stage a socialist revolution. In its thinking, Buthelezi had no major role to play in either the violent seizure of power or a future government. At most he could be appointed to the cabinet, but the price would be disbandment of Inkatha and the proscription of any emphasis on tribe or ethnicity in the organisation he led.

At a meeting of ANC and Inkatha leaders in London in October 1979, Thabo Mbeki tried to string Buthelezi and the others along in a manner similar to his tactics in wooing NP politicians and business leaders later. He assured the Inkatha delegation that the ANC believed their movement had 'behaved well in keeping the ANC alive'. For their part, the Inkatha delegation went out of their way to give assurances of loyalty. Frank Mdlalose said that 'Chief Buthelezi regards himself as ANC' and Oscar Dhlomo remarked that the ANC was wrong to think Inkatha was against the armed struggle.[78]

In the end neither Inkatha nor Buthelezi personally got anything concrete for the

76 ACA, PV357 Kobie Coetsee Papers, File 1/133/3, Informasie Rapporte, 8 August 1979.
77 *Rand Daily Mail*, 28 November 1979.
78 ACA, PV357 Kobie Coetsee Papers, File 1/A1/5 Minutes of Consultative Meeting, 29-30 October 1979, London; Interview with Mangosuthu Buthelezi, 15 September 2010.

homage that the movement's leaders paid to the ANC. Buthelezi recounts that the London meeting was cordial. 'It went off very well, even when we agreed to disagree. We did so without being disagreeable. At the end, Mr Oliver Tambo promised that the ANC's executive would respond to some of the issues I raised. It never happened.' He continued: 'The Secretary General of the ANC, Mr Alfred Nzo, launched a blistering attack on me on the 26th of June 1980, in London. After that, I can say that the sluice gates were opened. And the vilification of me by the ANC both at home and later through the UDF [United Democratic Front] and internationally was intensified through Radio Freedom, through their publication *Sechaba* and at many international platforms that they used.'[79]

A part of the explanation for the ANC's hard line was a visit in 1979 of an ANC delegation to Vietnam to learn about the tactics the Vietcong had used against the United States. According to a Soviet expert on the ANC, the delegation was 'deeply impressed by the Vietnamese methods of underground armed struggle, especially the co-ordination between illegal and [legal] mass activities'.[80] It returned convinced of the appropriateness of waging a 'people's war' in the townships with the aim of making them 'ungovernable'. This type of struggle combined high-profile armed attacks by trained units with mass campaigns of civil disobedience.[81]

With the rift between him and the ANC leadership steadily widening, Buthelezi tried to win over whites to his idea of a multiracial federation. In 1981 a commission he appointed proposed integrating the white-controlled province of Natal with the KwaZulu homeland. It would be run by an assembly elected by proportional representation and a multiracial executive making decisions along power-sharing lines. A single body would control education, the local economy and welfare services. These proposals were fleshed out by a multiracial Natal *indaba* in the mid-1980s, and received the backing of the business leadership in the province and the liberal opposition. But the Botha government had no interest in schemes it did not initiate or was unable to control.

A 'power-sharing' parliament

In June 1976 the Theron Commission reported on the coloured community and the youth of Soweto rose up against apartheid. Soon afterwards the government embarked on an attempt to revise the constitution, getting rid of the single all-white parliament and all-white cabinet as its dominant features. The constitutional committee of the President's Council briefly considered including blacks living out-

---

79   Interview with Mangosuthu Buthelezi, 15 September 2010.

80   Shubin, *ANC: A View from Moscow*, p. 194.

81   Anthea Jeffery, *People's War: New Light on the Struggle for South Africa* (Johannesburg: Jonathan Ball, 2009), pp. 25-40.

side the homelands in the new system, but decided it would be 'more sensible' to start with the three minority communities. If this was successful, 'other possibilities might present themselves'.[82]

In the debate over a new constitution, the term 'consociation' – power sharing between communities – often came up. But it was a misnomer for the type of constitution that the committee would recommend to government. Arend Lijphart, the academic who developed consociational democracy as a respectable alternative to simple majority rule, listed several objections to the arguments of the constitutional committee. For instance, a constitution that excluded blacks could not be called democratic. Excluding blacks and forcing people to participate as part of a group classified by government was undemocratic.[83]

In 1977 the NP government had started out with the idea of three separate parliaments for white, coloured and Indian people. Five years later it moved to the idea of a single parliament with three separate chambers whose representatives were elected on segregated rolls. The government and its supporters in the Afrikaans press called this the 'politics of consultation and joint decision-making', but it is more appropriate to call it sharing power without losing control.

There was a marked ambivalence in the way the government tried to sell the idea of the new parliament. To the more *verligte* voters it stated that including coloureds and Indians in a common system was simply 'a step in the right direction', leading to the eventual incorporation of blacks as well. In campaigning for a yes vote in the 1983 referendum on the constitution, Botha called it 'a new basis for national unity upon which reform along evolutionary lines in a stable environment could take place'.[84] To its more conservative supporters, however, the NP projected the tricameral parliament as an effective way of shoring up white power. It maintained that blacks would be accommodated separately through the homelands and the soon-to-be-introduced system of black local authorities.

To give the plan a measure of respectability, the NP had to compromise on its core principle of 'white self-determination'. During the late 1970s PW Botha often said that while a white power monopoly had become outdated, he advocated the *division*, not the *sharing* of power. In July 1979 he declared unambiguously: 'I reject mixed political parties and power sharing because it is Prog policy'.[85] When Alex Boraine, a member of the Progressive Federal Party (PFP, or Progs), asked him two years later if he believed in power sharing, he told him not to talk nonsense.[86]

---

82 Cited by Arend Lijphart, *Power-sharing in South Africa* (Berkeley: Institute of International Studies, University of California, 1985), p. 56.

83 Lijphart, *Power-sharing*, pp. 57-59.

84 Alf Ries and Ebbe Dommisse, *Broedertwis: Die verhaal van die 1982-skeuring in die Nasionale Party* (Cape Town: Tafelberg, 1982), p. 112.

85 *Die Burger*, 29 July 1979.

86 Koot Jonker, *Vegters teen politieke boelies* (no place: Griffel Media, 2009), pp. 11-14; *Die Burger*, 27 August 1981.

But having accepted a single parliament for whites, coloured people and Indians, the government could no longer duck the question of whether the tricameral parliament constituted power sharing. When parliament opened in January 1982, tensions between Botha's followers and the right wing under Andries Treurnicht had reached fever pitch. Early in February Jan Grobler, the editor of *Nat 80s*, a magazine published by the party, listed several new realities. One of them was that whites, coloureds and Indians shared the same geographical territory. He added: 'Logic demands that there could not be more than one government in a country.'

Treurnicht demanded a correction. He wrote to the editor that his words implied coloured and Indian cabinet ministers would 'co-govern' over whites. This, he said, was totally unacceptable. Grobler refused to retract, asking what Treurnicht thought of the idea that the NP should 'at any price get the coloureds, as a bloc of 2.5 million people, to side with the whites in order to broaden their power base and prevent them from being turned over to a "black power" situation'. Privately Botha told a senior reporter that he sided with Grobler. His view was also that in a sovereign country there could not be more than one government or parliament, although there could be different 'instruments of government'.[87]

On 22 February Botha summoned a special cabinet meeting. After an extensive debate he said the government had accepted power sharing, but this should not conjure up 'too many ghosts'. The government used the term quite differently from the official opposition, the PFP. While the PFP did so in the context of a unitary state and a liberal democracy, the NP refused to emasculate 'white self-determination'.[88] But the genie was out of the bottle. For four and a half years the party had tied the concept of power sharing to the PFP; now the NP leader also promoted it.[89]

Treurnicht remained quiet in the special cabinet meeting, but threw down the gauntlet in the NP caucus meeting of 24 February. He said the party had told its followers power sharing was not part of NP policy, and he would stand by the party's policy until the NP congresses changed it. PW Botha responded by asking how the white community could hope to maintain 'peace, freedom, civilised norms if it had to fight both an enemy in front of it and one behind it'. The government's constitutional proposals provided for the division of power in the respective groups' 'own affairs', but for the sharing of power in 'general' affairs.[90]

Suddenly, open revolt loomed large. Senior cabinet minister Fanie Botha proposed a motion of confidence in Botha as chief leader and his right to formulate policy.

87   Ries and Dommisse, *Broedertwis*, pp. 110-13.
88   *Die Burger*, 23 February 1982.
89   Ries and Dommisse, *Broedertwis*, p. 115.
90   ACA, PV408, National Party Collection: Minutes of Parliamentary Caucus, 24 February 1982, pp. 18-24.

When Treurnicht and 21 other members walked out, one of them, JH (Koos) van der Merwe, told journalists waiting outside: 'I am done with the Prog PW Botha.'[91] The Conservative Party that was formed in 1982 under Treurnicht's leadership would soon attract between a third and a half of Afrikaner support.

A controversial system

As we have seen, the Botha government proposed a form of 'healthy power sharing', but it was one in which the NP, as the ruling white party, could not be outvoted by a coalition of the white opposition, coloureds and Indians. There would be a single parliament with a white, a coloured and an Indian chamber elected on separate rolls according to a fixed 4:2:1 ratio that corresponded with population size. An electoral college drawn from all three houses would elect an executive state president. Each house would have its own cabinet and budget to deal with the 'own affairs' of its community – mainly education, housing and social welfare. There would also be common debates about 'general affairs' such as defence, security and economic policy.

All bills would be discussed and passed separately by each house. A power-sharing element was introduced, requiring all houses to approve a bill and stating that the president could appoint coloured and Indian ministers to serve in a general affairs cabinet. (Botha would appoint the leaders of the coloured and Indian chambers to his cabinet.) The lever of white control was retained; as the largest party in the white chamber, the NP would effectively elect the president, who would be able to use a President's Council – a multiracial advisory body of experts mostly supportive of him – to break any deadlocks if a house refused to pass a bill. Power would ostensibly be shared, but there would be no loss of control.

Before the referendum on the draft constitution in November 1983 the NP government ran a brilliant campaign to woo white voters. But it was an abysmal campaign as far as the government's key target was concerned – namely, the elite of the coloured and Indian communities. The more the NP leadership tried to assuage white fears, the more the coloured and Indian elite were convinced they would gain little or nothing from participating in the process. Viewing apartheid as an insult to them, they saw the segregated chambers as yet another mutation of the hated policy. Black leaders in general were outraged by their exclusion from parliament.

Three quarters of the registered white voters went to the polls in the referendum. A third voted 'no'. They were split between followers of Van Zyl Slabbert, leader of the PFP, who rejected the proposed constitution because of the alienating effect it would have on blacks, and followers of the Conservative Party's Andries Treurnicht, who rejected any dilution of white supremacy.

---

91   E-mail communication from JH (Koos) van der Merwe, 6 April 2008.

A total of 1 360 223 or 66% of white voters approved the tricameral constitution in the belief that the new system was a step in the right direction, diluting the white community's superiority and exclusivity. It was expected that it might help whites become accustomed to people who were not white serving in cabinet, and to future black representation in parliament. 'A new foundation for national unity has been laid. South Africa has made a date with destiny,' Botha said in his victory speech.[92]

Unintended consequences

Looking back, Eli Louw, who was minister for the budget in the House of Assembly (the 'white house'), remarked: 'People don't realise how important it was to have the tricameral parliament before we tackled negotiations with blacks. Our voters would never have accepted the latter if there had not been the preparation the tricameral parliament provided.'[93]

From the perspective of the NP and its followers who voted 'yes', the only way the government could go was indeed that of incremental constitutional reform. The unspoken pact between the NP leadership and its followers in 1983 was that the government could go ahead with the tricameral constitution and then proceed with the partial incorporation of blacks. Very few people in South Africa anticipated that eleven years later the NP and the white community at large would find itself with no formal political power at all.

Since losing control was never the NP government's objective, how did the scheme come unstuck? First, the government underestimated the basic forces it was up against, starting with demography. In 1977, when the NP started thinking seriously about the scheme, at most 750 000 people out of a population of 25 million cast their vote for the party in that year's election. It would have been better to seek agreement beyond party ranks on the principles of a new constitution before a start was made with drafting a constitution. The NP, however, still acted on the assumption that it could control the outcome of its reforms.

Second, NP leaders continued to cling to the Westminster system of highly centralised government and a first-past-the-post electoral system. In his political career PW Botha had known no other system and he had never explored alternatives. He remained firmly opposed to electoral competition between whites and people who were not white. As late as 1968 he still recounted the abuses that took place before coloured voters were removed from the common roll in the mid-1950s. He told his biographers in the early 1980s that during the 1960s he favoured the coloured people being represented by coloured representatives in both parliament and the Cape Provincial Council, but out of loyalty to his leader he never spoke up.[94]

92 De Villiers and De Villiers, *PW*, p. 211.
93 Interview with Eli Louw, 30 December 2010.
94 De Villiers and De Villiers, *PW*, pp. 64-73.

Third, the Botha government continued to see South Africa as a single country that could only be governed by a strong central government dominated by whites. In 1982 the Buthelezi Commission – which investigated the future of KwaZulu and Natal – recommended power sharing, with strong guarantees for minorities, as the form of government for a unified Natal and KwaZulu. Here was a last opportunity for the government to avoid losing control over the process of change. If it backed regional integration in this key region without trying to control it, it could spark similar initiatives in other regions of the country. As a next step, properly elected leaders from these regions could be elevated to the national cabinet. The risks to the NP would be counterbalanced by the advantages of powerful, legitimate black leaders in central government. This would stave off some of the internal and international pressure.[95]

But PW Botha's response to these proposals was in the classic apartheid mode. He said Buthelezi was welcome to investigate matters that concerned 'his own country', but had no right to deal with matters under the central government's control.[96]

Constitution on trial

In his memoirs Frederik van Zyl Slabbert, leader of the opposition in the last white parliament, told of a breakfast with Henry Kissinger during which they debated the new constitution. Kissinger volunteered to play devil's advocate, defending the constitution, while Slabbert would oppose it. Slabbert wrote: 'Kissinger was extraordinarily skilful. What came out of his defence was not the need for reform, but how a dominant minority intent on maintaining control could manipulate patronage by co-opting clients to it.'[97]

How should the new constitution be evaluated in terms of such a perspective? From the start it was clear that the scheme was in trouble. In 1982 more than 60% of coloured and Indian people polled were prepared to accept the new dispensation (there was then still the possibility of a single chamber instead of three). Two years later less than a fifth of the voters that could be registered supported it. The promise of a new political dispensation providing for only partial integration was no longer attractive to the prospective 'clients'. The new coloured and Indian middle classes were demanding an open society in which they – like any other middle class – could define themselves and choose where they wanted to live. This was exactly what the new constitution with its imposed group areas and political identities did not offer.

---

95   Lawrence Schlemmer, cited by Roger Southall in 'Buthelezi, Inkatha and the Politics of Compromise', *African Affairs*, 80, 321, 1981, pp. 453-81.

96   Smith, *Buthelezi*, p. 162.

97   Frederik van Zyl Slabbert, *The Last White Parliament* (Johannesburg: Jonathan Ball, 1985), p. 114.

As a result, a boycott was stunningly effective in the top strata of the Indian and coloured communities. The figures for Cape Town were particularly telling. Only 5% of eligible voters in the metropolitan region went to the polls. Whereas in the 1975 election for the Coloured Persons Representative Council some 44 270 people in Cape Town voted, only 25 110 voted in 1984. To the coloured and Indian middle classes, the new system's most objectionable feature was the perpetuation of the two key apartheid mechanisms: residential segregation and race classification. Without coloured group areas and coloured schools, the system could not work, and it soon transpired that no coloured municipality was financially viable.

But the system did offer some benefits. The 'own affairs' administrations made it possible for government to advance qualified coloured civil servants quickly. By 1993 nearly 19 000 posts fell under the House of Representatives (the 'coloured house') and nearly 90% of these posts were filled by coloured civil servants. Between 1984 and 1994, the budget allocated specifically to 'coloured affairs' grew rapidly from R744.58 million to R5.3 billion. By 1993 racial disparities in pensions had been eliminated. Significant progress was made in improving coloured education. The number of children in secondary schools increased by a third and the number of successful matriculants doubled. More than 10 000 new houses were built.[98]

But the time was too short and the changes too small to produce a broad middle class with a stake in the system. By 1990 only 15% of coloured people had an income of more than R2 000 per month, compared to 67% of whites. Many of the most vociferous opponents of tricameralism were teachers, who enjoyed great influence. Coloured teachers considered the new system an assault on their dignity. Matters were exacerbated by the Labour Party, which initially controlled the 'coloured house'. It turned appointments and promotions, long made on professional grounds, into political patronage, giving preference to those who supported 'the system'.[99]

In the 1994 election the NP would attract more than 60% of the coloured vote in the Western Cape. It did exceptionally well among coloured voters with relatively low educational qualifications, who benefited from improved pensions and better opportunities. But it had little success in attracting 'clients', to use Kissinger's term, among the educated coloured classes. This is clear from the following table:

98   MC Dempsey, 'Die geskiedenis van die Raad van Verteenwoordigers as 'n administratiewe komponent van die driekamerparlementstelsel in Suid-Afrika, 1984-1994', doctoral dissertation, University of Stellenbosch, 1999, pp. 234-256.

99   Dempsey, 'Geskiedenis van die Raad van Verteenwoordigers', pp. 239-42.

Party	None	Sub A– Std 6	Std 8	Std 10	Std 10 plus diploma	Degree
ANC	13%	10%	10%	24%	33%	61%
NP	47%	47%	44%	28%	28%	2%

LEVEL OF EDUCATION AND PARTY SUPPORT: COLOURED VOTERS, 1994

Source: NP election data

The attempt to create a bloc of whites, coloureds and Indians against 'a black power situation', as the editor of *Nat 80s* suggested in 1982, enjoyed only limited success.[100] About half the less educated coloured voters became staunch NP supporters, but the elite – those who had successfully completed high school – refused to have anything to do with the NP. The great majority of the coloured elite only defected from the ANC at the end of the first decade of the new century. By that time the NP was dead and buried.

---

100 Ries and Dommisse, *Broedertwis*, p.112.

Chapter 7
A Crossing Suspended:
PW Botha's Rubicon

PW BOTHA REACHED THE PINNACLE OF HIS POWER BETWEEN NOVEMBER 1983 and September 1984. In November 1983 the NP won the referendum for a tricameral parliament that resoundingly ended the symbolic supremacy of whites. Botha did not try to intervene when the labour reforms went well beyond the government's original intentions. In September 1984 he was sworn in as the first executive president in a system that resembled that of France under Charles de Gaulle.[1]

After 1976 South Africa continued to experience political turbulence, but the state seemed remarkably stable considering that almost all the power and wealth were concentrated in the hands of 15% of the population. The security forces exercised control well beyond the borders. During the first years of the 1980s South African commandos bombed ANC facilities in Maputo and Maseru, and supported dissident factions in eastern Zimbabwe, Lesotho and particularly in Mozambique, which had become the main route of ANC guerrillas into South Africa.

In 1980 South Africa took over the Resistência Nacional de Moçambique (Renamo) – originally established by the Rhodesian security forces – to pressure the Frelimo government of Mozambique under President Samora Machel, a Marxist-socialist. Unlike Unita in Angola, Renamo was not based on an ethnic group, lacked a charismatic leader and used a primitive system of command and communications. It was never much more than a band of brigands, but operated successfully because of South African help. It cut railway lines, mined roads, blew up fuel depots, destroyed grain stores and disrupted the export and import routes of the border states. By 1984 a cordon sanitaire had been established along South Africa's north-eastern borders.

On 2 March 1984 PW Botha and Samora Machel signed the Nkomati Accord, its goal the establishment of a 'security commonwealth' in southern Africa. The two governments committed themselves to economic cooperation and to ending all assistance to groups within their borders engaged in violence, terrorism and aggression against citizens of the other country. The heads of the governments of Britain, Germany and the United States warmly congratulated Botha. He must have been

---

1   Robert Schrire, *Adapt or Die: The End of White Politics in South Africa* (London: Hurst and Co., 1991), pp. 41-46.

particularly pleased by President Ronald Reagan's message congratulating him on reaching an understanding with South Africa's neighbours to 'deny opportunities to the Soviet Union, which has sought to profit from violence and confrontation'.[2]

Addressing an American audience, Reagan said the Nkomati Accord offered hope for peace and democracy across southern Africa. RF (Pik) Botha, minister of foreign affairs and one of the main architects of the Nkomati Accord, hoped for similar pacts with the governments of Angola and Zimbabwe. This would enhance the legitimacy of the South African government and reduce the ANC's mobility in southern Africa. The ANC openly admitted that the signing of Nkomati was a serious setback, denying it access to facilities in Mozambique.[3] Oliver Tambo described it as the greatest blow to the ANC since it was banned in the 1960s.[4]

From the end of May to the middle of June 1984 Botha paid official visits to Britain and seven countries on the continent of Europe. He was well received. Journalist John Scott, a member of the press contingent, remarked that the trip would likely influence South Africa's position in the world positively.[5] For Botha the trip was a moment to savour.

Talking to the Soviets

Having concluded that South Africa benefited little from US support in its efforts to contain the spread of communist influence in southern Africa, the Botha government tried to reach an understanding with the Soviet Union. In 1984 Botha signalled to Moscow that his government was prepared to distance itself from the West if Moscow would back its proxies in southern Africa less aggressively.

In August 1984, shortly after the Nkomati Accord was signed, a South Africa-Soviet Union meeting took place in Vienna. Niel Barnard, head of the National Intelligence Service, led the South African delegation. According to a Soviet source, Barnard told the Soviet team Pretoria preferred to pursue an independent foreign policy. It wanted Moscow to stop 'hostile actions towards South Africa' and 'promote peace and dialogue'. The Soviet source mentions that South African officials also broached the possibility of cooperation in controlling the sale of strategic minerals. He states that the Soviets 'rejected the idea of exchanging Moscow's support for its friends for a dubious chance of Pretoria's distancing itself from Washington'.[6] According to the source, the South Africans were disappointed that no deal could be struck.

---

2   Dirk de Villiers and Johanna de Villiers, *PW* (Cape Town: Tafelberg, 1984), p. 363.

3   Theresa Papenfus, *Pik Botha en sy tyd* (Pretoria: Litera, 2010), p. 319.

4   Vladimir Shubin, *ANC: A View from Moscow* (Johannesburg: Jacana, 2008), p. 199.

5   John Scott, *Venture to the Exterior: Through Europe with PW Botha* (Port Elizabeth: Acme, 1984), back cover.

6   Vladimir Shubin, *The Hot 'Cold War': The USSR in Southern Africa* (London: Pluto Press, 2008), p. 254; Shubin, *ANC*, p. 214.

The new Soviet leader Mikhail Gorbachev met Oliver Tambo on 4 November 1986 at the Kremlin. He told the ANC leader that PW Botha had tried to contact Moscow through 'a third, even a fourth party', but that the Soviet government would take no step without consultation with the ANC. Tambo was unable to prevail on Gorbachev to visit southern Africa, which, in the ANC leader's view, 'could transform the situation in the region'.[7]

Although in the initiative of 1984 the South Africans were unrealistic in believing that the Soviet Union might enter into an agreement with Pretoria, it is nevertheless significant that such initiatives were taken. It shows Botha was far from the single-minded Cold War warrior that is normally assumed. His stature in the world had grown. A year earlier UN Secretary-General Javier Perez de Cuellar remarked after a visit to South Africa: 'Two world leaders have made a big impression on me: China's Deng Xiao-Ping and South Africa's PW Botha. They understand power.'[8]

But the progress Botha made in improving diplomatic relations and isolating the ANC would be dramatically undermined by a series of events and developments between September 1984 and September 1985. First, there was a major uprising in the black townships triggered by an ill-conceived form of black local government imposed on urban blacks. Second, Botha suffered a stroke that seriously affected his temper and judgment. Third, he made a speech in August – later known as the Rubicon speech – that constituted nothing less than a disaster for South Africa's diplomatic relations and economic prospects.

Addressing black rights

With the resounding victory in the referendum of 2 November 1983 behind him, Botha faced a formidable challenge. On the one hand he had to get urban black leaders to accept the exclusion of blacks from the tricameral parliament. On the other, he had to persuade them to participate in a negotiating forum on black political rights.

Realising the urgency, Botha appointed a special cabinet committee five days after the referendum. Chaired by close ally JC (Chris) Heunis, minister of constitutional development and planning, the committee was given a circumscribed brief. Botha made his position clear at the outset: he was opposed to a fourth chamber for blacks, but would support regional development, land consolidation in the homelands and the creation of a constellation of states. Unlike John Vorster who remained stuck to the 1936 legislation fixing the black share of the land at 13%, Botha indicated that this law was not 'a holy cow'.[9]

7   Shubin, *The Hot 'Cold War'*, p. 254.

8   Alf Ries and Ebbe Dommisse, *Leierstryd* (Cape Town: Tafelberg, 1990), p. 45.

9   De Villiers and De Villiers, *PW*, pp. 213-15.

The government's options were limited. In 1982 it had assured whites that blacks would not be part of the new dispensation of a tricameral parliament. Heunis had stated that if blacks were to be included 'the protection of minorities would disappear ... This is an issue that is non-negotiable.'[10] The tricameral parliament sent the powerful negative message to black South Africans that they were foreigners in their own country and would have to be satisfied with voting for homeland governments or black local authorities.

The government claimed that the black local authorities about to be introduced would compensate urban blacks for their exclusion from parliament. But the system, introduced in 1984, was seriously flawed. Black local authorities had almost all the powers of their white counterparts, but without a proper revenue base. Few township residents owned property and revenue from rates was limited. Many township beer halls – a major source of revenue – had been destroyed in the Soweto uprising of 1976 and the subsequent turmoil. There was no formula for redirecting to the townships the revenue that neighbouring 'white' towns or cities derived from black spending.

The 1984 black local authorities' elections saw low voter turnout. Many residents had stopped paying rent for houses and rates for water and electricity. Undeterred, some of the new councils sharply increased rental and electricity charges. During the first days of September 1984, as the tricameral parliament was being inaugurated, riots broke out in the Vaal Triangle south-east of Johannesburg. Crowds attacked councillors' houses and police offices in several townships. In Sharpeville a councillor was 'necklaced' by a petrol-doused tyre being put around his neck and set alight. It was not before the second half of 1986 that the uprising subsided.

A stroke hushed up

In March 1985 Botha suffered a stroke caused by the rupture of a cerebral blood vessel. The stroke was kept secret, except from the closest members of his family and a handful of top officials and medical doctors. Even his cabinet colleagues were kept in the dark, although some of them eventually realised what had happened. A symptom that frequently accompanies this condition is the suppression of some sensory stimuli, as for instance in the left visual field. This was reported in the case of Botha, who failed to notice stimuli in the peripheral visual field on his left side.

Neurosurgeon Professor JC (Kay) de Villiers and neurologist Dr Paul Cluver were asked to study Botha's brain scan. De Villiers remarked that the kind of stroke the president suffered is also often accompanied by psychological disturbances, which could include a reduced inhibition of traits such as temper outbursts.[11] This

---

10   *Die Burger*, 21 August 1982.
11   Letter of President PW Botha to Dr P de V Cluver, 3 April 1985; Interview with Prof. Kay de Villiers, 20 March 2008.

was widely reported in Botha's case. Robin Renwick, who took up the post of British ambassador to South Africa in 1987, noted that Botha was 'prone to furious rages' and that 'his ministers were terrified of him'. Through these eruptions, he intimidated any challenger.[12]

De Villiers states that, had he been asked, he would have advised the president to retire rather than continue in such a demanding and responsible post. Botha's erratic performance in the second half of his term may well have been due to his medical condition.[13]

Botha's aftercare was not entrusted to neurologists but to a specialist in another field, now deceased. It is speculated that this was to maintain the highest degree of secrecy. It is not known what medication, if any, the specialist prescribed. Colleagues agree it is likely he advised Botha to rest as much as possible and to avoid emotional strain for six months. He certainly would have been counselled to avoid losing his temper. One of the puzzles described later in this chapter (see pp. 187–192) is Botha's silence in the important meeting of the extended cabinet six months later, two weeks before his ill-fated Rubicon speech. It could well be that Botha was simply following doctor's orders by keeping quiet rather than joining a discussion that could upset him. Addressing American and British officials shortly afterwards, Minister of Foreign Affairs Pik Botha shared his impression that Botha's silence meant approval of the major reforms that were proposed. This was a disastrous assumption.

Machiavellians and quarrelling ministers

In creating a tricameral parliament that excluded blacks, the government had made any future agreement with black leaders much more difficult. Possible solutions were discussed mainly in the Department of Constitutional Development and Planning with Chris Heunis as minister, and in a special cabinet committee that considered the proposals emanating from this department.

In devising the tricameral parliament Heunis – an intelligent and energetic but overbearing politician – made extensive use of the expertise of academics. They included Sampie Terreblanche and Ben Vosloo, respectively professor of economics and professor of political science and public administration at the University of Stellenbosch. Three other academics, Ig Rautenbach and Rassie Malherbe (both law professors at the Rand Afrikaans University) and political scientist Willie Breytenbach, went to work for the government after Botha became prime minister.

In 1984 Heunis appointed prominent legal scholar Andreas van Wyk as director-general in his department. Joh van Tonder, professor of political science at Potchef-

---

12   Robin Renwick, *Unconventional Diplomacy in Southern Africa* (London: Macmillan, 1997), p. 114.
13   Interview with Prof. Kay de Villiers, 8 February 2012.

stroom University, was recruited to become chief director of Constitutional Development and Planning while Fanie Cloete, an academic authority on public administration, became director. Academically qualified people were also appointed in the burgeoning bureaucracy of the presidency. Friction over constitutional proposals soon developed between Daan Prinsloo, head of the political desk in the presidency who kept closely to the president's line on reform, and senior officials in Constitutional Development. After his retirement Prinsloo would write Botha's biography with his close cooperation.

Given Botha's reluctance to accommodate black people in a system where numbers counted, the reformists in the Department of Constitutional Development and Planning followed what Cloete called a Machiavellian strategy.[14] Niccolo Machiavelli (1469–1527) had grappled in northern Italy with the task of building a state strong enough to impose its authority on a hopelessly divided society.

In his study The Prince Machiavelli warns that a precarious moment arrives when a ruler has to embark on reform with the common good in mind. He risks making enemies of 'all those who prospered under the old order', while gaining only lukewarm support 'from those who would prosper under the new'.[15] To succeed, he must first concentrate all power in himself. He may be compelled to use violence and other 'reprehensible actions' but 'their effects' may justify such steps. It is the ruler who uses violence 'to spoil things' who is blameworthy, not the one who uses it to mend things.

For Machiavelli the key question was not whether the prince's actions met the standards of Christian morality; it was whether he took appropriate action in cases where he was 'compelled [necessitato] to act without mercy, without humanity, and without religion'.[16] He warned against the prince lending an ear to different advisers with different agendas. The ideal was a single, astute adviser. Countless regimes faced this challenge in the centuries that followed. For instance, Brazilian elites living under the dictatorship of President Getulio Vargas during the 1960s declared that they wanted the government 'to make the revolution before the people do'.[17]

Huntington in South Africa

The Pretoria reformists admired the contemporary academic authority on reform, Harvard political scientist Samuel Huntington. Huntington, described as an 'ultra-

---

14   Interview with Fanie Cloete, 20 December 2007.

15   Niccolo Machiavelli, The Prince (Harmondsworth: Penguin Books, 1961), p. 51.

16   Niccolo Machiavelli, The Discourses (Harmondsworth: Penguin Books, 1970), p.132; JM Coetzee, Diary of a Bad Year (London: Harvill Secker, 2007), p. 18, citing The Discourses, sections 20, 23.

17   Samuel Huntington, Political Order in Changing Societies (New Haven: Yale University Press, 1968), p. 359.

Machiavellian',[18] argued that substantial reform was possible if two methods, Fabianism and the *blitzkrieg*, were used in combination.

The Fabian method, used by reformers in Britain in the late nineteenth century, was unspectacular and incremental: '[It was] the foot in the door approach of concealing aims, separating the reforms from one another, and pushing for only one change at a time.' By contrast, the *blitzkrieg* was a quick assault on a discredited or dysfunctional institution. Huntington wrote: '[The] reformer should separate and isolate one issue from another, but having done this, he should, when the time is ripe, dispose of each issue as rapidly as possible, removing it from the political agenda before his opponents are able to mobilize their forces.'[19] The reforming government had to retain the initiative at all times. The reform package had to be broken up into distinct elements, introduced separately. New allies had to be sought for each stage of the reform process, culminating in a grand reform coalition of, in South Africa's case, government, moderate blacks, business leaders and key managers in both the civil service and semi-state corporations.

Huntington visited South Africa in 1981 as a guest of the Department of Foreign Affairs. Addressing a conference, he warned that a combination of challenges would make it very difficult for the white minority to hold on to power for more than a few decades. 'Revolutionary violence does not have to be successful to be effective. It simply has to cause sufficient trouble to cause divisions among the dominant group over the ways to deal with it.'[20] To avoid losing the initiative, Huntington suggested that the government had to keep power concentrated in their own hands. For the most part, seeking support for reform had to take place secretly.

To apply Huntington's ideas to South Africa was no easy task. PW Botha and Heunis were Cape-based politicians keen to end the exclusion of the coloured community, but neither knew the black community well. With the exception of Mangosuthu Buthelezi, leader of the Inkatha movement, few black leaders with popular support were willing to talk to Botha or Heunis. Initially they had little idea of the extensive support for the ANC and its internal ally, the United Democratic Front. Also, Botha was accountable to his party, lacking the free hand of a Reza Pahlavi, the shah of Iran, or the military-based dictators of Latin America. He listened not only to Heunis but also to the 'securocrats', particularly Magnus Malan (minister of defence), Pieter van der Westhuizen (chief of the special cabinet committee's secretariat) and Niel Barnard (head of the National Intelligence Service).

18 Dan O'Meara, *Forty Lost Years: The Apartheid State and the Politics of the National Party, 1948-1994* (Athens: Ohio University Press, 1996), p. 263.

19 Huntington, *Political Order*, pp. 346-47.

20 Samuel Huntington, 'Reform and Stability in a Modernizing, Multi-Ethnic Society', *Politikon*, 8, 1981, p. 11.

Heunis and his advisers saw it as their task to delicately steer the debate to a point where PW Botha would buy into their proposals. The situation calls to mind Huntington's observation: 'The problem for the reformer is not to overwhelm a single opponent [in this case Botha, who was lukewarm about incorporating urban blacks] with an exhaustive set of demands but to minimise his opposition by an apparently very limited set of demands.'[21] Alternatively, the proponents of substantial reform had to secure agreement for some abstract principles, hoping Botha and the conservative faction of the cabinet would not discover their concrete implications until it was too late. Heunis prided himself on his ability to 'shift boundaries' by using ambiguous wording for ambivalent proposals. 'Got that one past them,' Heunis once chortled after PW Botha had announced a fairly significant shift in policy in a way that escaped the attention of the Conservative Party.[22]

The name of the game was incremental reform: to engineer a common political system step by step, preferably by forcing the conservatives to accept abstract principles they had previously endorsed without grasping the practical implications. PW Botha once complained to Heunis: 'I only later realised what some of the things you have made me say actually mean.'[23]

The reformers failed to confront a problem far bigger than conservative white resistance. The country's political system was highly centralised, with only slight decentralisation following the introduction of the tricameral constitution. The leadership could tinker with the system but what was needed for South Africa, a large country with a population approaching 40 million, was a decisive move away from the Westminster system, which concentrated all power in the hands of a small group at the centre. The ANC in exile was committed to a highly centralised state, however.

For the NP government, representing whites, the proper devolution of power to multiracial institutions would in the long run be a much more viable strategy than coopting some black and coloured leaders into the centre. But the long exposure of PW Botha, Chris Heunis and later FW de Klerk to the Westminster system, along with their determination to preserve white power, made them averse to any devolution of power.

The special cabinet committee

The special cabinet committee (SCC) began meeting early in 1984 to discuss proposals for addressing black political demands. PW Botha attended the first meeting,

---

21 Huntington, *Political Order,* p. 347.
22 Brian Pottinger, *The Imperial Presidency: PW Botha – The First Ten Years* (Johannesburg: Southern Books, 1988), p. 82.
23 Interview with Joh van Tonder, 11 January 2008.

but did not appear to take a personal interest in subsequent proceedings. Dr Jannie Roux, the director-general in PW Botha's office and secretary to the cabinet, occasionally attended the monthly meetings. No minutes were kept.

The ex-academics in Heunis's department provided position papers and often sat in on meetings. Fanie Cloete formulated their strategy as follows: 'We had to get the politicians to make piecemeal concessions on principles in order to achieve greater openness or flexibility and afterwards to provide concrete details and to make sure that the new principles were irreversible. This process, however, slowed down as the decision on the key principle, namely power sharing with blacks, approached.'[24]

The reformers' best supporting evidence was indisputable demographic and economic data. The white proportion of the population was steadily shrinking and the economy was stagnating. Joh van Tonder recounts their approach: 'We showered the Special Cabinet Committee with data. We got experts from other departments and from the business sector. We even coached them on what to say.'[25] For the handful of cabinet ministers serving on the SCC it would become the key forum for debating black political rights. FW de Klerk considered his membership of the SCC to be as important as his membership of the cabinet or his leadership of Transvaal.[26]

All the cabinet divisions were reflected here. On one side were the reformists – Chris Heunis, Pik Botha and Minister of Finance Barend du Plessis; on the other side, the conservatives either opposed to or sceptical of power sharing – De Klerk, Minister of Police Louis le Grange and Minister of Education and Training Gerrit Viljoen. All the contenders for the office of president sat on the committee. The race to succeed PW Botha would be decided here.

Sharp and combative, Heunis poured words out in torrents, often leaving his listeners suspended in bewilderment as they tried to catch the argument. De Klerk described him as someone 'whose brain worked faster than his tongue'.[27] The academics who worked for Heunis considered him domineering but also quick-witted and more often than not a match for them in debate. Andreas van Wyk deemed him the most *verligte* as well as one of the most intelligent members of the cabinet. 'Intellectually and emotionally he was far more convinced of the need for change than the theatrical Pik Botha, the vacillating Kobie Coetsee and the still reserved FW de Klerk.' But as a reformer Heunis was hamstrung by his strong emotional dependence on his political mentor and leader, PW Botha, who dominated the relationship. Botha was reluctant to walk the road of political rights for blacks, but until the Rubicon speech in August 1985 (see pp. 199–201) Heunis believed he could take Botha along.[28]

24   Interview with Fanie Cloete, 20 December 2007.

25   Interview with Joh van Tonder, 11 January 2008.

26   FW de Klerk, *Die laaste trek – 'n Nuwe begin* (Cape Town: Human & Rousseau, 1998), p. 118.

27   De Klerk, *Die laaste trek*, p. 138.

28   Interview with Andreas van Wyk, 6 May 2008.

While Heunis took care to stick with party policy in public, Pik Botha tested the limits in his call for bold reforms. He was a career diplomat from 1953 to 1970, when he became minister of foreign affairs. He knew better than any of his colleagues how dangerously in conflict with world opinion South Africa was. The government's star performer on television, he was confident of winning over the white electorate to far-reaching reforms. One poll after the other showed him to be whites' popular choice to succeed PW Botha. Although Pik Botha identified with Afrikaner history, his choice to remain an NP member was purely strategic. In many ways he remained the diplomat, not the foreign minister. 'I am not the South African government,' he told a startled American diplomat in 1981.[29] Chris Heunis was fond of referring to Pik Botha as the *foreign* minister.[30]

The third key member of the SCC was FW de Klerk. As someone with an eye firmly on the NP leadership, he positioned himself carefully midway between the conservative and *verligte* wings of the party. Unlike Heunis, who pushed for the extension of general affairs in the tricameral parliament, he pleaded for the principle of 'own affairs'.[31] He rejected a fourth chamber for blacks, pointing out that the NP only accepted the tricameral parliament because the entrenched numerical ratio for representation in parliament ensured white domination.

According to Fanie Cloete and Joh van Tonder, who both sat in on SCC meetings, De Klerk wanted a 'constellation of states' where representatives of the independent and non-independent homelands would meet with the NP cabinet members to take decisions without any votes being taken. Cloete states: 'FW de Klerk was one of the most consistent, rational, goal-oriented politicians I have ever met. But the framework was a very conservative value system. His core values were order, discipline, own affairs and communal self-interest.' 'Self-determination for each ethnic group' trumped all other principles.[32] Van Tonder agreed: 'By 1985 and 1986 De Klerk was still sticking firmly to the fundamental NP policy position of separate nations with separate statehoods.'[33]

De Klerk later claimed he disagreed with Heunis because he opposed what he called reform by stealth and the obfuscation it entailed. He recounted that he and Gerrit Viljoen were often the only SCC members who grasped what Heunis was driving at. De Klerk insisted that proposals for reform should be presented in unambiguous terms, their logical consequences thought through and clearly spelled out. *Verligte* cabinet member Stoffel van der Merwe commented that once De Klerk

---

29   Chester Crocker, *High Noon in Southern Africa: Making Peace in a Rough Neighborhood* (New York: WW Norton, 1992), p. 115.
30   Interview with Pik Botha, 20 November 2007.
31   Interview with Joh van Tonder, 11 January 2008.
32   Interview with Fanie Cloete, 20 December 2008.
33   Interview with Joh van Tonder, 11 January 2008.

had made the implications clear, 'everyone shied away from their proposals'. De Klerk was then considered a 'spoiler'.[34]

But De Klerk's strategy was the classic one employed by conservatives or what Huntington calls 'stand-patters' – leaders who refuse to consider or accept change. By forcing the reformists to spell out their intentions, they could stop reform in its tracks. De Klerk represented the predominantly conservative constituency of Vereeniging, where the Conservative Party (CP) had started to make major inroads. As the 1980s drew to a close, De Klerk, the Transvaal NP leader, not only had to face the CP onslaught in the province, but also had real reason to fear that he could be unseated at some point in the future.

A new approach

From the outset the president laid down clear parameters to Heunis for political reform: 'own affairs' had to stay, 'one man one vote' had to be rejected, and the black community had to be accommodated in a different way from the coloured people and Indians.[35] That meant a confederal model made up of the tricameral parliament, the governments of the homelands and perhaps some councillors as representatives of some black 'city states'.

The president would appoint black leaders, starting with the homeland leaders, to the confederal cabinet. Botha firmly rejected the idea of black representatives appointed to cabinet getting their mandate from voters in a non-racial election. The furthest he would go was to appoint blacks, coloureds and Indians to the executive council of bodies in local and provincial government, which he did in 1986.[36] A cabinet minister recounted: 'Botha often said the government could enter into negotiations with blacks, but his bottom line was clear: there will be no surrender of power.'[37]

From this, Heunis's department had to construct a policy that could be construed as genuine reform. Their planners' first opportunity was in drafting Botha's speech for the opening of parliament on 25 January 1985. They carefully balanced the reaffirmation of existing government policy with proposals for reform. Structures had to be created for black communities outside the homelands, through which they could decide on their own affairs up to the highest level. The same bodies could cooperate with the South African government and homeland structures on matters of common interest. A 'national council' of representatives of the government and

---

34 De Klerk, *Die laaste trek*, p. 119.

35 Daan Prinsloo, *Stem uit die Wilderness: 'n Biografie oor oud-pres. Botha* (Mosselbaai: Vaandel Uitgewers, 1997), p. 211.

36 Interview with Daan Prinsloo, 30 January 2008.

37 Interview with Dawie de Villiers, 6 May 2008.

non-independent homelands and of other black communities would be established to advise on matters of common concern.

Although Heunis and his officials still paid lip service to the idea of independence for the 'self-governing' homelands, their new constitutional goal was to balance cooperation on matters of common concern with 'self-determination' for each population group on their 'own affairs'. The question of black citizenship was reviewed. Full property rights would be given to blacks in areas where they qualified for leasehold rights.[38]

Heunis began preparing the NP's constituency for major reforms. On 29 May 1985 he said Afrikaners shared the land with people who cherished the same ideal of freedom to which the Afrikaner people subscribed. They could no longer be subjugated and had to be granted the same freedom Afrikaners demanded for themselves. On 1 June he pointed out that black communities lacked proper political mechanisms to realise their aspirations. On 20 June he observed that urban blacks could not assert themselves within the context of the homelands policy. In notes for a speech to be given the day after Botha's Rubicon address, he called for negotiations in which the parties had to be prepared to yield on their non-negotiable positions. The ideal was a common political system.[39]

During the first half of 1985 Heunis also held several meetings with homeland leaders after proposing that they work together on common issues. He hoped to widen the scope to include those African leaders operating outside government structures.[40] But Heunis faced stiff obstacles. Mangosuthu Buthelezi, the most important internal black leader, expressed no interest in a confederation and demanded a statement of intent before any negotiations. Like other black leaders with whom Heunis met, he insisted that Nelson Mandela and other ANC leaders had to be released before talks could begin.

By mid-1985 Heunis had become frustrated by the lack of progress. Homeland leaders were not competent to speak for urban blacks, and the real urban leaders were in jail. Part of the problem was the president himself. Twice during the preceding year Minister of Justice Kobie Coetsee had rejected Heunis's request to speak to Nelson Mandela in prison.[41] Coetsee knew the president did not want Heunis to talk to Mandela before Mandela had forsworn violence. He also knew the president viewed Mandela as part of the problem, not the solution.

In mid-1985 Heunis reported to President Botha that he had failed to make any

---

38 *Parliamentary Debates*, 25 January 1985, cols 11-16.

39 Archive for Contemporary Affairs (ACA), Bloemfontein, Amanda Botha, 'Navorsing oor Chris Heunis', 16 January 2007, unpublished memorandum.

40 Interview with Chris Heunis reported by Chris Alden, *Apartheid's Last Stand: The Rise and Fall of the South African Security State* (London: Macmillan, 1996). pp. 199-201.

41 Interview with Chris Heunis by Jan Heunis, undated, ca. 2005.

progress in attracting black leaders to the table. He had complained earlier that the SCC had become deadlocked in 'arguments, hair-splitting and strife'. He despaired of finding a compromise in such an unwieldy committee consisting of people with deep-seated differences. The SCC had not advanced much beyond concluding that blacks could not be accommodated by way of a fourth chamber in the tricameral parliament.[42]

PW Botha offered to call a meeting of ministers and deputy ministers to discuss ways in which the government's offer for blacks could be made more attractive. This meeting would take place in Pretoria on 2 August in a building called the Ou Sterre-wag (Old Observatory), which served as a conference facility for military intelligence. Botha undertook to announce decisions taken there to the congress of the Natal NP in Durban on 15 August. Jannie Roux, secretary of the cabinet, was not asked to attend and no minutes were taken. That omission was largely responsible for the drama that unfolded over the next thirteen days.

Pik Botha's initiatives

In the meantime Pik Botha was trying to remove obstacles to negotiations – sometimes to the chagrin of Heunis and senior officials in his department, who felt he was trespassing on their turf. As minister of foreign affairs, Pik Botha was responsible for the independent homelands and had become exasperated with the financial profligacy of their governments. The Transkei threatened to plunder the Transkei pension fund if the South African government curbed overspending and Ciskei bought a snowplough for the local airport after Chief Minister Lennox Sebe visited Germany.

Pik Botha asked his departmental legal advisers to prepare legislation enabling an independent homeland to apply for reincorporation into the Republic of South Africa and advised their leaders that this would soon be possible. He believed that restoring South African citizenship to homeland 'citizens' would remove one of the major black grievances.[43] But by trying to force this issue, he incurred the displeasure of Heunis's department, which did not consider it a priority.[44]

Pik Botha was also busy trying to secure the release of Nelson Mandela. Early in 1985 President Botha had offered to free Mandela if he renounced violence, but Mandela insisted on unconditional release. Sensing that Mandela held what he called a 'veto power' on both his release and future all-party negotiations, Pik Botha tried to get Mandela to forswear violence, 'if only by implication'. He hit on the

---

42 Interview with Willie Breytenbach, secretary of the special cabinet committee, 4 June 2011; Prins-loo, *Stem uit die Wilderness*, p. 209.

43 Interview with Pik Botha, 30 November 2007.

44 Interview with Andreas van Wyk, 6 May 2008.

idea of getting the leaders of the independent homelands and Buthelezi to give an assurance to President Botha that Mandela would not resort to violence and would respect the law. Pik Botha later wrote: 'Ek onthou dat dié idee PW geval het.'[45] (I remember that PW liked the idea.)

But this was stretching it a bit. The insensitive way in which PW Botha rejected the demand for Mandela's unconditional release in his Rubicon speech suggests that the foreign minister had assumed far too much. It is also very unlikely that Mandela would have approved of this plan. He unswervingly insisted on being set free unconditionally. He knew that accepting the offer before the ban on the ANC had been lifted would tear the organisation apart.[46]

A fateful meeting

As planned, a meeting of the extended cabinet took place at the Ou Sterrewag in Pretoria on 2 August 1985 to discuss constitutional reform. Exactly what happened at this meeting is largely shrouded in mystery. All the participants interviewed described it as a low-key meeting with little participation from the floor. The atmosphere was more that of a party caucus than a cabinet meeting. Some even described it as a team-building exercise. President Botha's ministers knew that he disliked extended discussions in cabinet. As a result, ministers who had a controversial reform initiative to present often cleared it with him before a cabinet meeting. Heunis had clearly followed this route and received Botha's nod.

At the Ou Sterrewag no one challenged Heunis's presentation and Botha kept quiet. His doctor's orders to avoid emotional outbursts may have been the main reason for his silence. He may also have thought his guidelines to Heunis for the limits to reform were clear and did not need restating.

Seven months later, when his government was paralysed by divisions, the president looked back wistfully to the discussion at the Ou Sterrewag. He repeated that he was not in favour of 'one man one vote' in a unitary or federal state. Looking back to the Sterrewag meeting, he almost plaintively observed: 'I thought on August 2 that we had clarity, but I do not think we have it anymore. Because you want me to say we stand for a unitary South Africa, you allow me to say it, you write it in my speeches, and I accept it, but what do we mean by that?'[47]

What was decided? The simple truth is that no one really knew. With no minutes taken, historians can only try to put together the most likely version drawing on available accounts. There are four accounts by ministers. According to Kobie Coetsee's account, influential members of cabinet, including Heunis, Gerrit Viljoen

---

45 *Beeld*, 22 June 2007.
46 Interview with Jannie Roux, 6 June 2011.
47 Verbatim extract from cabinet minutes, published in the *Sunday Times*, 28 August 1994.

and himself, wrote the speech that the president rejected. This version clashes with all the other evidence and can be discarded.[48]

The second account comes from an interview with Chris Heunis recorded by his son Jan some twenty years after the event. Heunis stated briefly: 'I made proposals [at Sterrewag] and responded to questions. In short, it came down to a decision that we would include blacks in cabinet. PW asked me to give him a draft speech that he could use to announce the decisions in Natal.'[49]

Asked whether that meant the unbanning of the ANC and the release of Nelson Mandela and other prisoners, Heunis replied: 'Not at that stage, but it would inevitably lead to that. Once you admit that they [blacks] have to be included in cabinet, you also admit they are part of the South African citizenry and have the right to be part of government.'[50] According to his son, Heunis saw the inclusion of blacks in cabinet as an interim measure pending negotiations with black leaders for a new constitution.[51]

The third account is De Klerk's narrow interpretation of the decisions in his memoirs written ten years later. The most significant change for him was the government's acceptance of the permanence of a section of the black population. The six non-independent homelands would 'not necessarily' be expected to progress to independence. Blacks living in the non-independent homelands and in 'white' South Africa would be treated as South African citizens; and negotiations would take place on how they would be accommodated in a new constitution, including getting a say in decision-making on all levels of government.

According to De Klerk, the Sterrewag decision amounted to the ditching of the ideology of grand apartheid.[52] This view is not correct. Group Areas and the division into 'own affairs' and 'general affairs', based on the Population Registration Act, were all still very much intact and remained part of De Klerk's political creed.

If De Klerk's interpretation was the narrowest, the fourth account – that of Pik Botha – was the most reformist. Looking back more than twenty years later, he commented: 'At the Sterrewag discussions there were not only members of cabinet, but also party leaders and people from the provinces. We were a big group; perhaps double the number of cabinet ministers. If you ask me what the main impact was I would say racial discrimination must be ended, and in principle Mandela must be set free.' Asked if PW Botha's condition that Mandela had to forswear violence was

---

48 O' Malley Archives, Interview with Kobie Coetsee, 26 September 1997. Patti Waldmeir clearly based her interpretation on Coetsee's views: see her *Anatomy of a Miracle* (New York: Vintage, 1997), pp. 54-56.

49 Jan Heunis, *Die binnekring* (Johannesburg: Jonathan Ball, 2007), p. 78.

50 Interview with Chris Heunis by Jan Heunis, ca. 2005.

51 Heunis, *Die binnekring*, p. 82; Interview with Andreas van Wyk, 9 May 2008.

52 De Klerk, *Die laaste trek*, p. 120.

still there, Pik Botha replied: 'It was always there.'[53] A report in the *Sunday Times* of 11 August 1985 was probably based on a source close to the foreign minister: South Africa would revert to being a single constitutional unit, the cabinet would be expanded to include black leaders (who would initially be the homeland leaders), negotiations would take place with the true black leaders, and influx control would be abolished.[54]

Excitement was building in the cabinet that the Sterrewag proposals signified a real breakthrough. On his way to a meeting of a parliamentary sub-committee on black political rights, Van Zyl Slabbert ran into Pik Botha, who said: 'Big things are coming. You must help us.' Slabbert told the committee: 'The government talks of negotiations, but are you going to talk with genuinely representative leaders or are you going to choose the leaders with whom you wish to negotiate?' Heunis replied: 'We shall get to that.'[55]

It is difficult today to determine why there was such excitement among reformers after the Sterrewag meeting. Daan Prinsloo is convinced the president did not waver from his stand: 'He had come to accept the need for including black leaders in a confederal cabinet, but he rejected the idea of elected leaders in a common system.'[56] Speaking 35 years later, FW de Klerk concurred. 'In all probability PW would never have gone further than a kind of overarching body on which cabinet ministers would sit with homeland leaders.'[57]

The mood at the Sterrewag meeting has to be understood in the light of the political climate. The meeting took place after eleven months of violent clashes between protesters and the regime. South Africa appeared to be hurtling towards a cataclysm. The toll of 'political deaths' rose ominously and funerals became highly charged political occasions, often resulting in more deaths at the hands of the police. The uprising put the government under far greater pressure than ever before. In the eyes of many, PW Botha was a hated tyrant who had to be toppled at all costs.

South Africa's international isolation continued apace. On 25 July France recalled its ambassador and suspended all new investments. On 31 July American bank Chase Manhattan decided that the risks of doing business with South Africa had become too high and resolved to call in all maturing loans and terminate borrowing facilities. Although the bank would announce its decision only on 15 August, just after the Rubicon speech, rumours of Chase's imminent withdrawal reached

---

53 Interview with Pik Botha, 30 November 2007.
54 *Sunday Times*, 11 August 1985.
55 Interview with Van Zyl Slabbert, 1 August 2007.
56 Interviews with Daan Prinsloo, 26 and 30 January 2008.
57 Interview with FW de Klerk, 30 May 2009.

Pretoria almost immediately. Pik Botha recalls: 'I will never forget the night of 31 July when Barend du Plessis [minister of finance] phoned me. I still perspire when I think of it. [He said] "Pik, I must tell you that the country is facing inevitable bankruptcy ... The process has started. An American bank has decided to demand the immediate repayment of all its loans to South Africa. Can you help? Is there not someone in the United States who could talk to the bank?"' Botha implored retired secretary of state Henry Kissinger to intervene, but Kissinger called back to say nothing could be done and that other banks would soon follow suit.[58]

Some of the president's advisers failed to grasp the seriousness of the crisis. They told Gerhard de Kock, governor of the Reserve Bank, that all that was required was to imprison a few thousand more agitators and South Africa's problems would be solved. British ambassador to South Africa, Robin Renwick, later wrote in his memoirs that he was convinced the security chiefs had persuaded the president to stand firm and enforce the status quo with strict security measures.[59] Some ministers interpreted PW Botha's silence at the Sterrewag meeting as a sign that he realised the gravity of the situation and was prepared not only to abandon his resistance to the unconditional freeing of Mandela, but also to accept the need for a cabinet truly representative of all South Africans. But they were too wary of his outbursts of temper to ask.

Still deeply shocked by Chase Manhattan's decision to call in its loans, Pik Botha thought the meeting signalled a major breakthrough for reform. Carl von Hirschberg, deputy director-general of the Department of Foreign Affairs, recalls: 'When I met Pik in his office after the Sterrewag meeting, he was bursting with enthusiasm. He could hardly contain himself. It was his account of the policy changes agreed to at the meeting that I used in the draft I prepared as the input [from the Department of Foreign Affairs to Heunis's department] for PW Botha's Durban speech. It was my clear impression that PW had agreed to these changes, so I was not particularly concerned that he might reject them. The most I expected was that he might adapt my wording to suit his own purposes, which usually happened when departments contributed suggestions for his speeches.'[60]

Dave Steward, a senior foreign affairs official who accompanied the foreign minister on his visit to Europe, recounts that there was great excitement in their ranks. It seemed to them that the government had at last managed to extricate itself from the deadlock in which it had been trapped, and had now accepted the idea that whites and blacks shared a common political destiny. It was expected that white

58   Pik Botha, 'Die land was op pad na ekonomiese verwoesting', *Rapport*, 6 June 2010.
59   Renwick, *Unconventional Diplomacy*, pp. 110, 165.
60   E-mail communication from Carl von Hirschberg, 20 April 2008.

and black leaders would soon meet to negotiate a system that would give constitutional expression to this idea.[61]

Selling the 'breakthrough'

After the Ou Sterrewag meeting the president wrote to Chancellor Helmut Kohl of Germany, Prime Minister Margaret Thatcher of Britain and President Ronald Reagan of the United States that breakthrough proposals had been made, to which he was giving serious consideration.[62] It was within this context that he gave Pik Botha permission to travel abroad to brief representatives of these leaders. By using the term 'consideration', the president thought he had kept his options open, but it was a recipe for a disastrous misunderstanding. Why would Reagan and Thatcher send envoys all the way to Vienna to meet Pik Botha if all he would do was to communicate proposals the president could still reject?

Battle-scarred by many encounters with 'the two Bothas', as American diplomats liked to call them, Chester Crocker, US assistant secretary of state for Africa, was not impressed with the South African president's letter to President Reagan. In his view Botha 'remained mired in the concepts and terminology that could not be sold beyond his party'. To prove his point he cited a phrase from PW Botha's letter: 'Structures must be developed for black communities outside the national states [independent homelands] to decide for themselves on their own affairs up to the highest level.'[63]

Crocker suggested that Robert McFarlane, National Security Council adviser to Reagan, should lead the team to meet Pik Botha. The meeting took place in Vienna on 8 August. Crocker had dealt with Botha for five years and knew he would never fail to spin a reform measure in a way that maximised its significance. Furthermore, he did not consider him influential in President Botha's cabinet. Pik Botha and his team, he wrote, 'faced rival agencies [a reference to the military] which were in a position to cook the books seen by the cabinet'.[64]

Crocker was dismissive of Botha's presentation in Vienna: 'Pik Botha was at his thespian best in Vienna, walking out on limbs far beyond the zone of safety to persuade us that his president was on the verge of momentous announcements. We learned of plans for bold reform steps, new formulas of constitutional moves and further thinking relative to the release of Mandela.'[65]

By contrast, McFarlane – who was experiencing Pik Botha's dramatic style of

---

61 Interview with Dave Steward, 21 April 2008.
62 Prinsloo, *Stem uit die Wilderness*, p. 309.
63 Crocker, *High Noon*, p. 275.
64 Crocker, *High Noon*, p. 115.
65 Crocker, *High Noon*, p. 275.

presentation for the first time – reported positively to the White House. According to him, Pik Botha had made four points. First, independent homelands would be given the option to be reintegrated into an 'undivided South Africa'. Second, South African citizenship would be restored to all people in the so-called independent homelands. Third, the independent and non-independent homelands could participate in some federal government, if they wished. Fourth, all citizens would have the ability to influence decisions at the national level. McFarlane explained to President Reagan that this meant blacks could play a role in the formation of their own 'regional' governments, which would then participate 'in a sort of federal system'.

McFarlane considered Pik Botha persuasive, but he stressed that everything would depend on credible black leaders supporting these steps. Botha replied that once the process had begun, the government would start on one or two of the more important black grievances, such as ending influx control and releasing Mandela.[66]

In Vienna Botha also met Ewan Ferguson, a former British ambassador to South Africa and special representative of Prime Minister Thatcher. At this meeting Botha spoke of proposals for 'co-responsibility for decisions on the highest level that affect the entire country, one citizenship, and one undivided South African territory'. He added that because of 'sensitivities in South Africa' terms such as 'power-sharing or a unitary state' had to be avoided.[67] President Botha would give no constitutional blueprint, only guidelines that had to be worked out further by leaders. After the Vienna meetings Pik Botha travelled to Frankfurt to meet the representatives of Chancellor Kohl.

Dave Steward recounts that while Pik Botha spoke of 'big plans', he did not go beyond presenting them as 'strong recommendations'. The final decision was the president's prerogative.[68] Werner Scholtz, a South African diplomat who attended Botha's Vienna briefings, puts it somewhat more strongly: 'Pik presented the proposals as virtually the final draft of the president's speech. The representatives of the Western powers believed Pik Botha because they thought he spoke with his president's full blessing and had cleared everything. It simply was inconceivable that he would try to sell reform proposals that were still half-baked as important policy shifts.'[69]

Neil van Heerden, a senior foreign affairs official who briefed regional African leaders, sums the situation up as follows: 'Pik Botha would definitely try to extract

---

66 Margaret Thatcher Foundation, McFarlane e-mail to White House, 8 August 1985, http:www.margaretthatcher.org/archive/displaydocument.asp?docid=111636.
67 Papenfus, *Pik Botha*, p. 370.
68 Interview with Dave Steward, 21 April 2008.
69 E-mail communication from Werner Scholtz, 15 April 2008.

the maximum political and diplomatic advantage from the Sterrewag recommendations, but he would certainly not lie or deliberately mislead.'[70] Pik Botha was at pains to stress that the president still had to take the final decision, but the emissaries of the Western leaders in Vienna and Frankfurt could well ask why there was such a fuss if the president could still upset everything.

The speech the president eventually gave was a communications disaster. Some of the US emissaries felt they had been misled.

There were two reasons for the disaster. First, the president's silence at the Sterrewag meeting was wrongly interpreted as acquiescence. Second, Pik Botha gave copies of his department's input to Heunis's department and to the president's office, but before he met with US emissaries in Vienna he did not inquire from either office what parts of the input would be included in the president's speech. It seems safe to conclude that in the crisis atmosphere that prevailed, the foreign minister, knowing Mandela's release would impress foreigners and could stave off further sanctions, decided to take a huge gamble to force the president's hand.

'We have crossed the Rubicon'

After the Sterrewag meeting the president asked Chris Heunis to draft his speech for the opening of the Natal NP's congress in Durban two weeks later. Heunis had to incorporate the inputs that Foreign Affairs and other departments had prepared for his consideration and ultimately for the president. Pik Botha instructed Carl von Hirschberg to write the Foreign Affairs input. After listening to Pik Botha's account of the Ou Sterrewag meeting, Von Hirschberg – known for his eloquent style – decided to write it in a language 'acceptable for an international audience rather than for the loyal local political followers'. He handed the minister his draft on 10 August. After reading it, Pik Botha inserted the sentence: 'We have now finally crossed the Rubicon.'[71]

Written with a rhetorical flair rare in official documents, Foreign Affairs' input tried to assuage white fears, meet black demands and satisfy foreign expectations. In a veiled reference to the ANC and its allies, it attacked those who rejected peaceful negotiations for power sharing. The challenge to South Africa was 'to build a better future out of [differences in] cultures, values, and languages, which are demonstrably real in our heterogeneous society'.

It went on to remark that government intended to approach the challenge in two ways. The first was by 'negotiation between leaders ... in which there will be give and take'. The second was by proceeding in negotiations from the basis that 'we are all human beings, created by the same God' and endowed with the 'inalienable human rights of life, liberty, and the pursuit of human happiness'.

---

70   Interview with Neil van Heerden, 6 May 2008.
71   Papenfus, *Pik Botha*, pp. 371-72.

The input offered to the president also assured government supporters that it would never surrender to outside demands: 'South African problems will be solved by South Africans and not by foreigners.' The solution was to be found in 'cooperation and co-responsibility' by means of a system that acknowledged the 'right of each and everyone to share in the decisions which shape his destiny'. It rejected a numbers-based approach with a 'winner-takes-all' outcome. Instead it proposed a system based on 'population groups'.

The government planned to negotiate with the 'black leadership' without deciding who the real leaders were. These leaders would have to take responsibility for decisions on matters of common concern, which had to be taken in such a way that there would no 'domination of one population group over another'. The government respected the independence of the 'independent national states', but they were welcome 'to negotiate with the South African government on the conferment of South African citizenship on their citizens'.

Finally, the Foreign Affairs input stated that the government would also consider Nelson Mandela's release if he or respected black leaders would assure them that he would conduct himself 'in a law-abiding manner'. The vexed issue of the political violence sweeping the urban areas was also mentioned. The government would take up the legitimate grievances of blacks and abolish all discrimination on the basis of colour or race. 'Any reduction of violence will be matched by action on the part of the Government to lift the State of Emergency.' The document ended with a ringing declaration: 'The implementation of the principles I have stated can have far-reaching effects on us all. I believe that we are today crossing the Rubicon. There can be no turning back. We now have a manifesto for the future of our country.'[72]

Director-General of Constitutional Development Andreas van Wyk, together with two other senior officials, Fanie Cloete and Joh van Tonder, wrote the draft speech of the president. Van Wyk recounted that he and the other officials used 'the style rather than the substance' of the Foreign Affairs input.[73] The main concern of the speech writers was to elaborate on the ideas the president had expressed seven months earlier in parliament – accepting the permanence of urban blacks and the need for negotiations about their incorporation into the system. In composing the president's draft speech Heunis's department conveyed a picture of a government that had abandoned old-style white arrogance and was intent on searching for solutions through negotiations with recognised black leaders.

---

72 The State President's Durban Manifesto. This document, which was not signed or dated, was the proposed input from the Department of Foreign Affairs for the president's speech. A copy is lodged in the library of the University of Stellenbosch. Pik Botha discussed this document in detail in an article entitled "'n Feitelike resensie van Jan Heunis se *Binnekring*', *Beeld*, 21 June 2007.
73 E-mail communication from Andreas van Wyk, 19 February 2012.

Heunis intended to give a speech just after the Durban meeting but discarded the draft after Botha had made his Rubicon speech. The draft conveys a sense of the speech the department wrote for the president. The government would negotiate with black leaders about black participation at all levels of decision-making. The speech pledged government to recognise black human dignity, eradicate all forms of discrimination and create equal opportunities. 'The First World component of South Africa had to be prepared to sacrifice some of their rights and vested interests and to make sacrifices in order to meet the demands of political and social justice.' All the legitimate political aspirations of blacks had to be accommodated. This meant that 'as South African citizens they had to be able to realise their political rights up to the highest level'. There had to be 'a search for democratic solutions because they best meet the demands of social justice'. The government was prepared to consider restoring the South African citizenship of black communities 'including that of those living in the independent and self-governing states'.[74]

Neither the president nor Heunis's department at that point considered Mandela's release a priority. By holding this up as a step that the president may announce in his speech two weeks later, Pik Botha was indeed walking on very thin ice.

'Making my own speech'

Between the meeting in Vienna and the speech on 15 August, media speculation both in South Africa and abroad reached fever pitch. *Time* magazine described it as the 'most important announcement since the Dutch settlers arrived in South Africa 300 years ago'. A few days before the Natal congress Gerrit Viljoen, the minister responsible for black affairs, told an audience of Afrikaans women that 'the future position of whites would be radically different from the present and that the country's youth would have to be prepared for drastic changes'.[75]

Viljoen was probably referring to future prospects in a general way, but his words simply increased the excitement. Even *Die Burger*, which rarely deviated from the president's line, wrote that major changes were likely to be announced – until it received word of Botha's furious state of mind. It then promptly published a cartoon depicting 'anti-South African forces' pumping up expectations.[76]

On 10 August President Botha decided to deviate from the original intention to put across a strong and consistent reformist message. In retirement, Botha told a journalist that Pik Botha had deliberately inflated international expectations in order to embarrass him. 'That was his game, that's why he does not come here.'[77]

---

74 ACA, Amanda Botha, 'Navorsing oor Chris Heunis', 16 January, 2007, unpublished memorandum; Heunis, *Die binnekring*, pp. 84-85.

75 This paragraph is based on Prinsloo, *Stem uit die Wilderness* , pp. 346-47.

76 *Die Burger*, 14 August 1985.

77 Waldmeir, *Anatomy of a Miracle*, p. 54.

Heunis later told his son that there had been a report from Europe about Pik Botha's presentation of the proposed reforms, implying that he had exceeded his brief, but there is no other evidence that this had triggered the president's wrath. It is significant that he never reprimanded his foreign minister.

Ters Ehlers, PW Botha's private secretary and aide-de-camp who worked closely with him during those days, rejects any suggestion that Pik Botha's 'over-promising' in Europe had angered the president. In the office he did not once mention his foreign minister as a reason for what he called 'making his own speech'. He said to Ehlers: 'I am not going to let people like Chester Crocker prescribe to me the kind of speech I must make.'[78]

Prinsloo's biography of Botha suggests a more likely possibility. It states that a report by senior journalist Tos Wentzel in the *Weekend Argus* of 10 August provided 'the catalyst' for PW Botha's discarding the most venturesome interpretations of what had been decided at the Sterrewag. The report stated that the president would announce far-reaching changes in his speech and speculated that 'the government was trying to find a power-sharing formula with blacks without stating this too openly for fear of a right-wing revolt'.[79] When Heunis drove to the president's home at noon on Saturday 10 August to hand over his department's input, he saw the posters of the *Weekend Argus* trumpeting the news of imminent bold reforms. The president did not invite Heunis – his closest ally – in. Over the telephone a few hours later he told him he was not prepared to give the 'Prog speech' that Heunis had prepared for him. Heunis replied that it was not a Prog speech, but a draft that reflected 'decisions' taken at Sterrewag.[80]

President Botha was intensely irritated by press speculation that threatened to make almost any reform initiative an anticlimax. Here he was, still contemplating the recommendations of the Sterrewag meeting, but the press had already announced them as his decisions. The term 'power sharing' in the *Weekend Argus* touched a particularly raw nerve, because it was this term that caused the NP to split in 1982 on the much less weighty issue of coloured and Indian participation.[81] His entire career was directed at preventing blacks from gaining a foothold in, and then control over, government. Moreover, the report hinted at radical reforms that had not yet been canvassed in the NP's caucus or provincial congresses. Defence Minister Magnus Malan recalled people in his circle saying it would take at least five years for the NP government to persuade the electorate to accept some of the Sterrewag proposals.[82]

---

78   Interview with Ters Ehlers, 7 June 2008.
79   *Weekend Argus*, 10 August 1985; Heunis, *Die binnekring*, p. 82.
80   Heunis, *Die binnekring*, p. 82; Interview with Chris Heunis by Jan Heunis, ca. 2005.
81   Prinsloo, *Stem uit die Wilderness*, p. 343.
82   Interview with Magnus Malan, 8 February 2008.

There was also a real threat that the speculation might jeopardise future negotiations. PW Botha had just received a letter from Margaret Thatcher, his strongest supporter among Western leaders, in which she suggested: 'We should exchange our ideas as far in advance of your announcement as possible and preferably without attracting attention.'[83] It is also possible that Heunis had mentioned to Botha his unhappiness with all the loose talk about power sharing, since it could undercut his strategy for negotiations. At this stage Heunis wanted to make only his opening move – inviting blacks to serve in the cabinet.[84]

The stakes for the country were very high indeed, but President Botha was not the kind of leader who could be pressurised. He possibly felt trapped by the snares prepared by the Machiavellians and wanted to reassert his authority and control. He did not understand how vulnerable to foreign pressure his government and the country's economy had become. He decided to lash out, regardless of the consequences, and to re-establish his dominance in policy making. He instructed Daan Prinsloo in his office to rewrite the speech he had received from Heunis in a way that he would be comfortable with.

On Monday 12 August he summoned some senior cabinet members to his office. De Klerk would later tell the story. First, Botha asked who had been involved in the draft speech. He then picked up the copy, threw it down on the table and declared: 'I will not make that speech. I will make my own speech.'[85] He humiliated those present by forcing them to listen for nearly 45 minutes to the speech that he would give three days later. The draft speech from Constitutional Development with the inputs from Foreign Affairs had been gutted.

Heunis responded in a dignified way by telling the president that the draft he had handed him reflected the Sterrewag decisions and that he had nothing to add. Later he told his son: 'We sat there like a bunch of small children, listening to him reading his speech to us. No one protested. In fact, everyone nodded in agreement.'[86]

Part of Botha's speech did indeed announce a significant shift in the government's stance. First, the government was willing 'to share its power of decision-making with other communities', and, second, blacks living permanently in 'white' South Africa would be granted political rights in the same system that accommodated whites, coloureds and Indians. But to a foreign audience these reform initiatives would sound insignificant. While the speech President Botha gave incorporated important parts of the draft speech, the tone and terminology were radically different. Von Hirschberg's eloquent formulations in the Foreign Affairs input and the mea-

83 Prinsloo, *Stem uit die Wilderness*, p. 346.

84 Pottinger, *The Imperial Presidency*, p. 330.

85 *Beeld*, 12 November 2007.

86 Interview with Chris Heunis by Jan Heunis, ca. 2005; Heunis, *Die binnekring*, p. 80.

sured academic formulations of the officials in Heunis's department had largely fallen by the wayside; in their place came the harsh and strident tones of a party boss assuring his faithful that he had the situation firmly in hand and would not yield to foreign pressure.

Everything pointed to a major crisis. Although knowing full well that the speech was to be broadcast to a world audience, Botha's highest priority was reasserting his control, a far cry from language that foreign leaders would recognise as part of the democratic lexicon.

Communications disaster

The speech President Botha gave on 15 August was screened live to a world audience of more than 200 million. Instead of a heroic leader renouncing apartheid, they saw 'an old president's twisted, hectoring image', making it difficult to listen to what he was saying.[87] 'Don't push us too far,' he warned at one point with a wagging finger, confirming the stereotype of the ugly, irredeemable apartheid politician. Instead of a short, well-rehearsed statement with a core message, he delivered a long, rambling harangue.[88]

The great irony was that Botha was in fact announcing reforms that at another time would have been recognised as major policy shifts. Influx control was on its way out. Independence for black 'states' was still policy but, as the president put it in his speech, blacks in the non-independent homelands 'remain part of the South African nation, are South African citizens and should be accommodated within political institutions within the boundaries of the RSA'. Structures would be established where all South African communities would attain the goal of 'co-responsibility and participation'.[89]

In calmer times this would indeed have been seen as a Rubicon of sorts that was being crossed. After nearly 40 years the NP finally admitted that black people had to be incorporated into the same system as whites. Here they would be considered full citizens sharing rights with others. At the same time, however, Botha ruled out almost everything his audience would have understood as democracy: he rejected majority rule, 'one man one vote' and a black chamber in parliament.

While calling for negotiations to bring about a system in which all South Africans participated, he bluntly dismissed any suggestion of far-reaching change. He said: 'But let me be quite frank with you . . . I am not prepared to lead white South Africans and other minority groups on a road to abdication and suicide. Destroy

---

87   Waldmeir, *Anatomy of a Miracle*, p. 54.

88   E-mail communication from Dave Steward, 3 May 2008.

89   Verbatim text of the speech, issued by the SA Consulate General, New York, published in Schrire, *Adapt or Die*, pp.147-59.

White South Africa and our influence, and the country will drift into factional strife, chaos and poverty.'

Botha called his speech 'a manifesto for a new South Africa', but almost in the same breath went on to state that 'our enemies – both within and without – seek to divide our peoples . . . Peaceful negotiation is their enemy . . . They wish to seize and monopolize all power . . . Blacks, Whites, Coloureds and Asians . . . shall jointly find solutions acceptable to us. But I say it is going to take time. Revolutionaries have no respect for time . . . because they have no self-respect. Look what they have done to Africa, a continent that is dying at present.'

There were two particularly disastrous aspects. One was his rejection of the unconditional release of Nelson Mandela. He made it appear as if Mandela and his comrades in the early 1960s were motivated solely by communist convictions. There was no reference to grievances widely considered legitimate and he presented no evidence that Mandela was indeed a communist.

The other was that Botha also explicitly refused to issue a statement of intent, which Buthelezi – the major internal black leader – had insisted on as a prerequisite for negotiations. Buthelezi had demanded an assurance that the negotiations would be about 'power sharing' and not just about structures where blacks would merely be consulted. Incomprehensibly, Botha linked this demand to what he termed a 'wish to destroy orderly government'.[90] By refusing to free Mandela unconditionally or to make a statement of intent, Botha stiffened Buthelezi's resolve not to talk about a future constitution before the ANC leaders had been freed or allowed back into the country.

Botha ended his speech with the words: 'The implementation of the principles I have stated today can have far-reaching effects on all of us. I believe that we are today crossing the Rubicon. There can be no turning back.' But these words – and the entire speech – simply mystified the international audience. Dave Steward, who would become President De Klerk's main communications adviser, sums it up: 'PW Botha showed an absolute lack of understanding of modern political communication. Instead of addressing his TV audience of hundreds of millions of viewers in the West, he addressed the NP faithful. Instead of language that his real audience could understand, he used the rough and tumble idiom of South African political meetings.'[91]

Pik Botha was devastated. Earlier he had told audiences the president's speech would be the most important event for South Africa since Jan van Riebeeck's arrival, a turning point from which there was no going back. He phoned *Time* magazine's Peter Hawthorne to apologise. 'What can I do, Peter? What can I do to

---

90   Lawrence Schlemmer, 'Message Received', *Sunday Times*, 18 August 1985.
91   E-mail communication from Dave Steward, 3 May 2008.

get this old bastard to change?'[92] But the 'bastard' had lashed out: he made his own speech.

Andreas van Wyk, who had helped to write the rejected draft speech, later recorded his grave disappointment. 'The manner in which PW Botha gave his speech – the attitude, the body language and the aggressive language – was exactly the opposite of what Heunis and his department had envisaged. The context – a party conference – was totally wrong.' He went on: 'A world audience looked on dumbfounded while PW gave a typically fighting speech for a party congress. The people who saw him on television totally missed the content. What in actual fact happened was that the NP government had finally decided to accommodate blacks in a single, common system. It was a far-reaching step if ever there was one.'[93]

Forced to pick up the pieces, Pik Botha called it 'a speech with which I definitely could live'.[94] He told a press conference that President Botha considered it 'a historical occasion', and added: 'I agree.'[95] Years later he remembered the press conference as 'one of the most difficult tasks of [his] life'. He recounted that he tried to persuade the media that the reforms 'on which we all waited were hidden under all the aggression and kragdadigheid (forcefulness)'.[96]

The foreign press immediately fingered the foreign minister as the man who had created false expectations. The Los Angeles Times reported that the emissaries from foreign heads of government who listened to him in Vienna and Frankfurt were persuaded that his president would announce important steps such as dismantling apartheid, abolishing the homelands, freeing Nelson Mandela and lifting the state of emergency.[97] But this was not a completely accurate portrayal of what Pik Botha had said; he always made it clear that it was the president's prerogative to decide on the Sterrewag proposals.

ANC President Oliver Tambo issued a response from Lusaka, in which he spoke of 'a ruling group who could not help but show itself for what it is – a clique of diehard racists, hidebound reactionaries and bloodthirsty, fascist braggarts who will heed nobody but themselves'. Rather than release and talk to 'the genuine leaders of our people', Botha only wanted to negotiate with his 'salaried employees'. The time had come for the Western world to 'abandon all pretence that it has any say in influencing South Africa other than through the imposition of sanctions. South Africa has crossed her Rubicon.'[98] Tambo enjoyed one of his best days in office.

---

92 Papenfus, Pik Botha, p. 375.
93 Interview with Andreas van Wyk, 7 July 2007.
94 Prinsloo, Stem uit die Wilderness, p. 345.
95 The Citizen, 17 August 1985.
96 Cited by Willem Jordaan, Beeld, 19 August 2005.
97 Los Angeles Times, 18 August 1985.
98 ANC response to PW Botha's Rubicon speech, 16 August 1985, http://www.anc.org.za/ancdocs/pr/1980s/pr850816.html.

A costly speech

The Rubicon speech landed South Africa in deep financial trouble. The country had always been strongly dependent on foreign investment for growth. During the booming 1960s foreign investment, mainly in shares, made up over 20% of all investment. After the oil crisis of 1973 and the collapse of the Portuguese empire there was a sharp fall in portfolio investment by foreigners. The overseas investment that remained was mainly in the form of short-term loans, particularly to the public sector that borrowed money on a large scale. By the mid-1980s investment by the public sector made up nearly two thirds of all investment.[99] In the perception of foreign investors South Africa was unstable, and 'small, unstable countries, unlike large ones, do not borrow money'.[100] With South Africa so financially vulnerable, the Rubicon speech was an unmitigated disaster.

The Western reaction was swift and severe. Chase Manhattan Bank, one of South Africa's main short-term lenders, could perhaps have been influenced by dramatic reforms, but it now announced it would no longer roll over loans to South Africa. Other banks quickly followed suit. With two thirds of its foreign debt short term, South Africa was forced to default and declare a unilateral moratorium on foreign debt. These debts were later rescheduled, but South Africa's ability to raise foreign loans had received a mortal blow.

The rand fell sharply, capital flight accelerated and markets were forced to close. South Africa faced an escalation of sanctions. In late August 1985 the US Congress passed the Comprehensive Anti-Apartheid Act, which banned new investment and loans, withdrew landing rights and severely curbed imports of coal, uranium, iron and steel. The European Community and the Commonwealth imposed a variety of milder sanctions.

South African whites were never more isolated. Governor of the Reserve Bank Gerhard de Kock remarked half in jest that the speech had cost the country billions – at a rate of a few million rand per word.[101] Even a well-packaged, eloquent speech would not have dispelled all the serious doubts about the country's growth prospects. But Botha's speech had made the situation far worse.

Perhaps – and this is speculation – the president was embarrassed that he had not spoken up at the Ou Sterrewag meeting two weeks earlier, when Pik Botha made proposals he would normally have slammed down. Perhaps – and this too is speculation – he was under doctor's orders not to get embroiled in arguments that could

99   CH Feinstein, *An Economic History of South Africa* (Cambridge: Cambridge University Press, 2005), pp. 228-29; 'Dr. Wim [de Villiers] se sakebloudruk vir SA', *Finansies en Tegniek*, 23 September 1988, p. 12.

100 Waldmeir, *Anatomy of a Miracle*, p. 56.

101 De Klerk, *Die laaste trek*, p. 123.

cause him to lose his temper. Whatever the case, Botha's petulant reaction when expectations had begun to build up bordered on irresponsibility. It cost the country billions. It also made the task of finding a settlement that was more even-handed than the one ultimately negotiated much more difficult.

British Ambassador Robin Renwick described it as a turning point.[102] The Rubicon speech signalled the moment when the Botha government lost both the initiative and almost all credibility. In the eyes of the world Botha could not recover.

Picking up the pieces

In the two months following the Rubicon speech, President Botha made some amends for the grave damage he had done. He used the Free State congress to announce that his government was prepared to restore South African citizenship to all blacks resident in 'white South Africa' who had lost it because of the granting of independence to some homelands. At the Cape NP congress he went further, saying his government was committed to an undivided South Africa based on the principles of one state, a common citizenship and universal franchise for all, but within structures that South Africans themselves would choose.[103] At the Transvaal congress, he committed himself to talks with the ANC, provided it forswore violence and detached itself from the SA Communist Party. 'If the ANC makes such an announcement, they could come back to South Africa tomorrow. We shall not act against them. We shall negotiate with them.'[104]

Von Hirschberg, who was not part of Pik Botha's inner circle, remarked recently: 'At the end of the provincial congresses, I called for transcripts of all four speeches of the president and analysed them with a fine-tooth comb. Sentences, even phrases lending them [sic] to a more positive interpretation, I highlighted and extensively redrafted. I was surprised at the end of the process how much positive material the speeches had hidden in them.'

He added: 'I used this material liberally in drafting replies to the letters that poured into the Presidency from Heads of Government like Thatcher, Kohl, Mitterand, Reagan and others. These were all referred to the Foreign Minister, who submitted replies for the president's signature. It is interesting that the president never once altered a single word in the replies. With each wave of responses and replies, we were able to extend the boundaries of Government policy.'

Von Hirschberg went on: 'It is a great pity the proposed changes were so sensationalised before the Durban speech. PW Botha was an enigma if ever there was one.

---

102 Renwick, *Unconventional Diplomacy*, p. 110.
103 Prinsloo, *Stem uit die Wilderness*, p. 215.
104 For a discussion of Botha's speeches at the party congresses see Prinsloo, *Stem uit die Wilderness*, pp. 211-15.

He was indeed a reformer – vide the positive elements hidden in his four speeches that we have already referred to; and his acceptance of the drafts we sent to him in reply to the letters from Heads of Government. They all contained some extension of Government policy.'[105]

PW Botha had indeed moved far. Opening parliament in January 1986, he accepted the permanence of those blacks settled in the white areas. Senior political reporter Peter Sullivan remarked on the president's 'great courage'.[106] De Klerk said in his memoirs that the SCC accepted a new framework containing the following principles: a united South Africa, one man one vote, the removal of all forms of discrimination, and effective protection of minorities from domination.[107]

On the face of it, the Machiavellians in Pretoria had made considerable progress. The reforms announced in the NP's four provincial congresses did indeed amount to a major policy shift. But the 'reform by stealth' strategy backfired when PW Botha decided to make his 'own speech' after the Ou Sterrewag meeting.

Huntington's response

During the last half of the 1980s PW Botha often complained about how little credit he received for the reforms he introduced. His record was in fact much more impressive than that of his predecessor. It included the abolition of the racial sex laws, the pass laws, the dualism in the labour market and the all-white parliament. In more stable times Botha's lament would have been valid, but far more was needed to turn around the trend of growing polarisation.

What had gone wrong with the Botha reforms? The simple answer is that the reform message was too full of contradictions.

In opening parliament in February 1986 PW Botha committed his government to 'equal opportunity' and equal education and declared that apartheid was outdated. However, speaking a few days later, FW de Klerk stated that segregated education would remain, which indicated that apartheid was far from outdated. Botha also announced the establishment of a national council that would include black leaders to advise him on constitutional structures, but he adamantly refused to release Nelson Mandela and other leaders from jail, which these leaders had set as a precondition for negotiations to start. Within the same week the president gave Pik Botha a severe dressing-down for saying he was prepared to serve under a black president. A commentator observed: 'Pres Botha took the political initiative but lost it within the space of a week.'[108]

---

105 E-mail communication from Carl von Hirschberg, 30 April 2008.

106 *Sunday Star,* 6 October 1985.

107 De Klerk, *Die laaste trek,* p.127.

108 Anthony Sampson, *Black and Gold* (London: Hodder & Stoughton, 1987), p. 226.

Samuel Huntington, who in 1981 presented his scheme for reform, was one of the very few academics that cabinet ministers took seriously as a commentator on reform.[109] After a second visit to South Africa in February and March 1986 he made illuminating comments. He observed that while the reforms had changed South Africa, they had failed to restore stability. They had been slow, laborious and full of contradictions. They had raised expectations, but had failed to deliver. The government had not succeeded in controlling the violence; and it had won over no important new constituencies. Instead, it alienated many sectors of society.

Huntington wrote: 'In 1981, the government was very much the only political actor, now there are a large number of other ones. All this will make it very difficult for the government, even if it wanted to, to carry out a programme of substantial reform by unilateral action from above under present conditions.'[110] In effect, South Africa found itself in a stalemate, or to use Huntington's words: 'The government was too weak to impose reform from above – assuming it wanted to – and the opposition was too weak to compel reform from below through negotiation.'[111]

Metaphor for failed courage?

The details of the Rubicon speech have been forgotten but the speech has become a metaphor for a leader failing to seize a golden opportunity. The underlying assumption is that PW Botha's failure to embark on negotiations led to the bloodshed and the polarisation of the next ten years. But is it realistic to assume that negotiations were on the cards? By August 1985 the ANC was definitely not ready to talk. Most of its leaders remained adamant that as long as the regime had not been weakened sufficiently, negotiations had to be ruled out.[112]

For the ANC, the issue of negotiations was fraught with danger. Negotiations could mean a major split on economic policy at a time when many still considered the Soviet model a real alternative. Enjoying large-scale support from the Soviet Union, the leadership of the ANC in exile had little interest in negotiations before white rule showed signs of collapse. Not hampered by police harassment or a funding crisis, it could continue the fight. By 1987 the United Democratic Front considered turning away from a head-on confrontation of the state's forces, but their emissaries to the ANC leadership in Lusaka were told to go back and 'keep the revolution going'.[113]

---

109 Interview with Pik Botha, 30 May 2008.
110 Samuel Huntington, 'Whatever Has Gone Wrong With Reform?' *Die Suid-Afrikaan*, 8, Winter 1986, pp. 20-21.
111 Huntington, 'Whatever Has Gone Wrong With Reform?', p. 22.
112 Shubin, *ANC*, pp. 236, 250.
113 Interview with Joe Slovo by Patti Waldmeir, 14 November 1994.

Looking back 25 years later, General Magnus Malan, minister of defence, said: 'We could have negotiated before 1990, but with the Russians and Cubans behind them the ANC would have refused to do so. Why would they take the chance?'[114] Internationally the climate was not favourable. The Cold War was still a reality. Ronald Reagan and Mikhail Gorbachev had not yet met at Reykjavik for mould-breaking talks and the Berlin Wall had not yet fallen. Ultimately, it was the fall of the Berlin Wall that convinced the ANC that there was no alternative but to negotiate.

In all likelihood the ANC in exile would have responded to a speech that called for negotiations by demanding the release of all political prisoners and setting other tough demands. It is possible that the American banks would not have foreclosed too hastily if Botha had announced Mandela's release, but that would have greatly increased the ANC's anxieties. In exile it lived in a world of suspicion, betrayal and counter-betrayal.

When he made his speech in August 1985 PW Botha had no intention of em-barking on open-ended negotiations. Determined to smash the internal uprising, he was far from convinced that releasing Mandela would restore stability. He was acutely aware of the need to maintain the support of his constituency. Johan van der Merwe, who was head of the security police in the mid-1980s, gave this assess-ment: 'Electorally the NP would have committed suicide by starting negotiations with the ANC. The memory of the ANC bomb in Church Street, Pretoria in 1983, killing 18 people, had produced a strong white backlash.'[115]

Botha's Rubicon speech marked nothing more than his reassertion of white con-trol and paradoxically also his acceptance after nearly 40 years of white rule that no peace was possible without addressing the demands of urban blacks. How far he would have gone if he had embarked on negotiations no one can really tell.

114 Interview with Magnus Malan, 9 February 2011.
115 E-mail communication from Johan van der Merwe, 24 March 2008.

Chapter 8

Van Zyl Slabbert: The Golden Boy
and the Black Prince

IN 1973 THE PROGRESSIVE PARTY (PP) INVITED SOME 30 AFRIKANER ACA-
demics to a conference near Pretoria. Standing for a qualified franchise and the
abolition of racial discrimination, the PP enjoyed little Afrikaner support. Its sole
parliamentary representative was Helen Suzman, who in 1961, 1966 and 1970 won
the Houghton seat with its predominance of middle- and upper-class English speakers. Colin Eglin, elected party leader in 1970, stepped up efforts to reach Afrikaner
voters. Hoping to attract Afrikaner academics, he invited a number of them to a
conference to discuss the idea of an independent think tank that could analyse the
political parties and their policies.

Ray Swart, a leading Prog from Natal, fetched Frederik van Zyl Slabbert – a young
Stellenbosch sociologist – from the airport. On the way to the conference venue
Slabbert observed that he was one of very few invitees who did not hold pro-
government views: 'From the guest list I have seen, most of the people you Progs
have invited are staunch Nats and very anti-Prog,' he said. Afterwards Swart commented, 'He was right, but at least they had accepted our invitation.'[1]

Aged 33, Slabbert had begun to speak up about political polarisation in South
Africa and the injustices of apartheid, but found little support. Afrikaner nationalism had drawn together all classes and strata in the Afrikaner community, and the
enthusiasm generated by the successful struggle for a republic had only just begun
to dissipate. Although prosperity was steadily eroding nationalist passions and convictions, most top businessmen, professional people, university rectors, academics
and civil servants still openly identified with the National Party (NP).[2]

By the early 1970s the United Party (UP) – long-standing foe of the NP – was
showing signs of political sclerosis, offering little to attract a new generation of
university-educated Afrikaans speakers. Afrikaners viewed the Progressives or 'Progs'
as a party of urban middle-class English speakers comfortably tucked away in leafy
suburbs, moved less by a desire for a multiracial democracy than by their distaste
for Afrikaner political domination. They believed the Progs had never thought

---

1 Ray Swart, *Progressive Odyssey* (Cape Town: Human & Rousseau, 1991), p. 119.
2 Albert Grundlingh, '"Are We Afrikaners Getting too Rich?" Cornucopia and Change in Afrikanerdom in the 1960s', *Journal of Historical Sociology*, 21, 2/3, 2008.

through the effects of majority rule in Africa and only rarely spoken up about developments in those independent African states where democracy had become a fig leaf for corrupt, autocratic rule.

Opinion polls, now common, suggested that close to a fifth of the Afrikaner elite was susceptible to the Prog message. A finding published in 1971 showed that 10% of a sample of the Afrikaner elite favoured a qualified franchise, while 5% favoured complete integration with a common franchise.[3] But there was little doubt that Afrikaners in general were conservative, cautious and disinclined to take political risks. A poll published later indicated that what bothered Afrikaner voters most about black domination were threats to order and security (80%), while 37% of respondents feared a loss of job opportunities and job security, and 14% were concerned about possible threats to the Afrikaans language and culture.[4] These were the concerns that Slabbert would have to tackle as a young and enterprising politician.

Slabbert was born in Pietersburg (now Polokwane) in the Transvaal in 1940 and grew up in a broken home. In his first book he tells the poignant tale of his childhood. At seven years old he and his twin sister were taken away from their mother, who later died of alcoholism. At sixteen he first got to know his father and found him an unimpressive man, not the larger-than-life figure his mother had portrayed. But there were loving relatives in the district who took the two children into their care. His mother died in 1974 as he was about to enter politics. Only he and his half-brother attended the funeral. Slabbert entered politics reluctantly – he later wrote that he only became a candidate because he had been assured he could not win – but having experienced politics once, he could not get it out of his system.[5]

In Pietersburg, Slabbert experienced first-hand the most vicious side of white racism. Increasingly his grandfather's 'brutal paternalism' towards some labourers on his farm grated on the young Slabbert. One evening after church he joined some friends who invited him 'to have some fun'. It turned into a vigilante party brutally beating up an innocent black pedestrian who had missed the 21h00 curfew. He wrote: 'I saw the black man bleeding from the mouth and pleading for mercy and I ran away retching and coughing with nausea.'[6]

Slabbert nearly stood as a UP candidate in the 1974 election, but changed to the PP at the last moment. Against expectations he beat a strong local UP candidate in the seat of Rondebosch. Countrywide the Progressives won 6 seats and drew 6% of

---

3   Heribert Adam, 'The South African Power-Elite', Heribert Adam (ed.), *South Africa: Sociological Perspectives* (London: Oxford University Press, 1971), p. 94.

4   Lawrence Schlemmer, 'White Voters and Change in South Africa', *Optima*, 27, 4, 1978, pp. 62-83.

5   Frederik van Zyl Slabbert, *The Last White Parliament* (Johannesburg: Jonathan Ball, 1985), pp. 5-10.

6   Slabbert, *Last White Parliament*, p. 14.

the votes cast, against the NP's 122 seats and 55% of the vote and the UP's 41 seats and 31% of the vote. The chance for a major realignment in white politics seemed remote, but Slabbert believed in himself and in the capacity of charismatic leaders to move mountains. The UP disintegrated in 1977, prompting Japie Basson, Harry Schwartz and a handful of other liberal MPs to join the Progressives to form the Progressive Federal Party (PFP). Slabbert was elected PFP leader two years later.

On the eve of the 1982 election my daughter Adrienne, then eleven years old, came home from school perplexed. She had had an argument with friends at Bloemhof, an Afrikaans-medium school for girls in Stellenbosch, where more than 80% of Afrikaner voters supported the NP. The question had arisen as to which party they would vote for if they could. As could be expected, her friends opted for the NP, but she said she would vote PFP. Her friends exclaimed: 'Oh, silly! Then the blacks will come to power.' She replied bravely: 'No, the Progressives will govern.' She asked me: 'I am right, aren't I?' When I told Slabbert the story, he laughed: 'We shall turn these blacks into Progressives.'

But of course there was a fundamental problem that plagued all those who supported Slabbert and the Progs. What if the blacks were not progressives of the kind Slabbert was?

Sociologists in politics

Unlike Hendrik Verwoerd, Slabbert was never an Afrikaner nationalist, although he did vote for a republic in the 1960 referendum. He was particularly revolted by race classification and the prohibition of sex across racial lines. His opposition, initially an intellectual rejection of the system, developed into a profound emotional revulsion.

As sociologists who would turn to politics, Slabbert and Verwoerd had remarkably similar careers. Both studied at the University of Stellenbosch – Verwoerd in the early 1920s and Slabbert in the early 1960s. Both quickly made their mark on campus as bright and engaging students with leadership potential. Both could smilingly demolish an adversary's argument in a private discussion or a public meeting. Both had formidable persuasive powers.

Verwoerd did his doctorate in psychology under Robert W (Bobby) Wilcocks, while Slabbert did his in sociology under SP Cilliers, author of *An Appeal to Reason* (1971). The book called for full civil rights for coloured people, while keeping largely to the framework of the homelands policy for blacks.[7] (The *Festschrift* for Slabbert, published for his 70th birthday in 2010, is called *The Passion for Reason*).

Both Verwoerd and Slabbert had planned to become ministers in the Dutch Reformed Church, but defected to become lecturers in sociology, that haven for academics whose church had failed them. Both retained a sense of mission: to lead

---

7   SP Cilliers, *An Appeal to Reason* (Stellenbosch: University Publishers, 1971).

people out of what they saw as a political desert – in Verwoerd's case the increasing political and social integration of South Africa and in Slabbert's the increasing polarisation of society as a result of apartheid.[8] Both entered politics in their mid-thirties, Verwoerd as an overtly political editor of *Die Transvaler* and Slabbert as a parliamentarian.

Soon after entering parliament both were elected leaders of their respective parties. Neither seems to have lobbied to get the post. Very few cabinet ministers voted for Verwoerd as party leader (see p. 48), and Slabbert replaced Colin Eglin in the face of opposition from some leading figures in the party. Eglin had come under pressure as a result of a successful diversionary tactic the NP used in parliament to put him and his party on the defensive.

As social scientists, Verwoerd and Slabbert tried to grapple systematically with social problems of their time. When they turned to politics, they favoured policy programmes based on clear principles rather than ad hoc arrangements or gradual change. Wilcocks, Verwoerd's academic mentor, emphasised that social problems had to be identified and defined, and that methods for dealing with them had to be spelled out clearly in advance.[9] From his first major public speech, made in Kimberley in 1934 where he addressed a congress on the poor white question, Verwoerd's approach was relentlessly methodical and analytical.[10] He would also use this approach in developing apartheid ideology during the 1950s.

Before entering politics in 1974 Slabbert took a hard analytical look at the political system. He pointed out that the tradition of white politics was one of 're-orientation and new formations'.[11] This had been true in the case of Verwoerd, who deftly shed the rhetoric of Afrikaner nationalism after the proclamation of a republic and spoke of the two white communities as a *volk* that had put the historic divisions of old behind it and was determined to survive together into the future.[12] This paid off handsomely in the 1966 election, when English voters supported the NP in considerable numbers for the first time. Slabbert, for his part, was constantly looking for a possible realignment in white politics that could catapult him and his party into the position of power brokers.

During the early 1960s, when Slabbert was still a student and lecturer in Stellenbosch, the poor white question that had preoccupied Verwoerd was no longer an issue. By now approximately a third of all Afrikaners were middle class (compared

---

8   E-mail communication from Lawrence Schlemmer, 28 May 2011.

9   RW Wilcocks, 'Die armblanke vraagstuk', *Verslag van die Volkskongres oor die armblanke vraagstuk*, 2-5 October 1934 (Cape Town: Nasionale Pers, 1934), pp. 210-220.

10 For a brief account of his approach to the poor white problem see Hermann Giliomee, *The Afrikaners: Biography of a People* (Cape Town: Tafelberg, 2003), pp. 349-53.

11 Cited by Japie Basson, *Politieke kaarte op die tafel* (Cape Town: Politika, 2006), p. 7.

12 AN Pelzer (ed.), *Verwoerd aan die woord* (Johannesburg: APB, 1963), pp. 664-66.

to less than 10% in 1946). For Afrikaner nationalists the issue now was almost the reverse: 'Are we Afrikaners getting too rich?'[13] Too rich would mean Afrikaners would no longer find it necessary to insist on apartheid, the policy that had kept the nationalists united. In such a context it was conceivable that someone like Slabbert could become a catalyst in building a new multi-ethnic ruling party.

In Stellenbosch Slabbert found a university captivated by the apartheid ideology, reshaped by Verwoerd from a loose set of beliefs into a coherent ideology that followers would believe in with utter conviction. Slabbert would later describe 'the excitement, even the thrill' of academics and students in discussing this ideology. He added that it had 'a coherence and systematic quality which cannot be dismissed as racism pure and simple'. It 'made logical sense and addressed some very prickly issues'.[14]

Here Slabbert witnessed how NP-aligned academics came under the spell of a message. 'Verwoerd was an ideologue with dogmatic confidence,' Slabbert wrote later.[15] Was it possible, he probably asked himself, for an exceptional leader to turn the liberal ideas of non-racialism, non-discrimination and fairness into an ideology that imparted an equally compelling message? As a superb analyst, he could identify the structural elements of society – class, nation, culture and religion – and he knew how to talk to Afrikaners about them.

In his speeches Slabbert stressed again and again that the core apartheid assumption was wrong: the country did not contain 'a plurality of voluntary ethnic minorities', and the statutory groups of apartheid, apart from whites, did not wish to 'govern themselves'. The apartheid laws, starting with race classification, destroyed voluntary association and imposed membership of a discrete statutory group on everyone. The whole scheme was untenable – intellectually, politically and morally.

For Slabbert the key question was: how could South Africa escape from apartheid without a major upheaval that would destroy the conditions for peace and prosperity? He found an answer in the work of Talcott Parsons, a Harvard sociologist on whose work he wrote his doctoral dissertation. Parsons belonged to a then dominant school of sociology labelled 'functionalists', who assumed that a consensus about basic values was a precondition for a functioning society. In the absence of such values, any society would become conflict-ridden and dysfunctional.

Yet critics of functionalism argued that conflict – rather than consensus and equilibrium – is a normal state of affairs. Slabbert sympathised with the 'conflict theorists'. Indeed, South Africa with its deep cleavages proved that a society without a value consensus could still cohere and function, as Belgian-American sociologist

13 Grundlingh, 'Are We Afrikaners Getting too Rich?'
14 Ivor Wilkins, 'This Man Who Guides the Ordinary People', *Sunday Times*, 19 April 1981.
15 Slabbert, *The Last White Parliament*, p. 85.

Pierre van den Berghe – another student of Parsons – argued in his famous 1965 book *South Africa: A Study in Conflict*. Slabbert nevertheless continued to believe that despite the great difficulties, South Africa could work towards a system that sustained a stable social order based on commonly shared values such as commitment to the nuclear family, individual rights, free enterprise and the rule of law. In his view, the apartheid order undermined all these pillars of stability.

For Slabbert the challenge was to rebuild society by building all these pillars anew. Wilmot James, one of the few black students who studied under Slabbert at Stellenbosch, wrote later: 'It was the first time the Harvard sociologist Talcott Parsons sounded like a revolutionary. In what was to become one of his special abilities, Van Zyl Slabbert explained to students how Parsons highlighted what was lacking in apartheid – widespread legitimacy and therefore a sustainable social order.'[16]

Slabbert's only unequivocally academic analysis of apartheid was written in 1973–74, just before he entered politics. It concluded that the NP government was vulnerable in elections only from the right, but would increasingly have to deal with 'non-electoral pressures in the form of black demands and economic fluctuations'. He expected the NP to become increasingly intolerant of 'liberal' non-parliamentary opposition. It would try to force all forms of dissent into government-sanctioned organisations or institutions.[17]

In parliament

Soon after he became Prog leader in 1979 Slabbert showed he was not interested in a party resigned to a prolonged period in opposition. He wanted to win enough seats to bring about a balance of power and a ruling coalition strong enough to embark on the urgent task of building a society based on individual freedom. Because he realised there was no electoral support for a system that reduced whites to permanent exclusion from power, he was attracted to 'consociationalism' – commonly called power sharing.

Slabbert was genuinely interested in people and made a strong impression on others even before he became a public figure. 'He was not the prototypical politician. He was both a thinker and a doer and was not much interested in the frills attached to political leadership,' Ray Swart wrote.[18] Eglin, who recruited him to politics, recounts that Slabbert did not like the ritual of parliament and the restrictive agenda within which it debated. 'While superb in his analysis and indict-

---

16   Wilmot James, 'Van Zyl Slabbert: Sociologist at Work in Advancing Democratic Politics', Alfred Le-Maitre and Michael Savage (eds), *The Passion for Reason: Essays in Honour of Frederik Van Zyl Slabbert* (Johannesburg: Jonathan Ball, 2010), pp. 146-47.

17   It was republished in Frederik van Zyl Slabbert, *The System and the Struggle* (Johannesburg: Jonathan Ball, 1989), pp. 21-22.

18   Swart, *Progressive Odyssey*, p. 156.

ment of apartheid, he was less effective in presenting a concrete synthesis of the alternative.'[19]

In public Slabbert looked awkward when praise and admiration were bestowed on him. To a fawning admirer who commented on his charisma, Slabbert replied with a slight twinkle in his eye: 'Yes, I studied Charisma 1, Charisma 2 and Charisma 3 at university.' In many ways Slabbert was *the* Afrikaner golden boy of the 1960s: intelligent, articulate, principled, dynamic, witty, and, to cap it all, a fine rugby player who once played for Western Province. (Whenever this was mentioned, he was always quick to add: 'Only because Doug Hopwood was injured.')

Self-deprecation was one of his attractive qualities. Swart commented on his tendency to shun adulation: 'He remained very much a private person, never indulging in political backslapping and seemingly embarrassed when others were effusive in their praise ... I was never able to decide whether his conduct on these occasions was a reflection of humility or boredom.'[20]

If Slabbert had a failing, it was a lack of patience and staying power. Philip Myburgh, a PFP member of parliament between 1981 and 1987, observed: 'He lacked the ability Helen Suzman and Colin Eglin had, namely what we in Afrikaans call *vasbyt*: to sink your teeth in and refuse to let go. He had a five-year attention span.'

Indeed, in his career between 1964 and 1986 Slabbert never occupied a position for longer than five or six years. After leaving parliamentary politics in 1986, he turned to civil society and extra-parliamentary activity by founding the Institute for a Democratic Alternative in South Africa (Idasa), which was a forum for research and debate. During the 1990s he became a successful businessman but continued to long for a return to the kind of public role that only political leadership offers in South Africa. 'He does many things,' Eglin said of Slabbert in his final years, 'but a single theme or goal is lacking.'[21]

Progressive leader

As leader of the PFP Slabbert was a fresh breeze in the increasingly stale parliamentary politics, which attracted ever fewer of the best talents of white society. Forceful without being overbearing, he was a man with a razor-sharp analytical mind. 'His style is so utterly different,' a reporter observed. 'It is his unique ability to reduce politics to a series of simple, logical arguments that progress to a single, devastating conclusion.'[22] Time and again he ridiculed the huge gap between the promises of apartheid ideology and the sordid reality. He distinguished between sham and

---

19   Interview with Colin Eglin, 11 June 2011.
20   Swart, *Progressive Odyssey*, p. 157.
21   Interview with Colin Eglin, 11 June 2011.
22   Wilkins, 'This Man Who Guides the Ordinary People'.

genuine reforms, arguing that sham reforms were dangerous because they created the illusion of change and a false sense of security.

In parliament the NP did not quite know how to deal with Slabbert. He was comfortable in his skin as an Afrikaner and in speaking Afrikaans, yet he was sharply critical of Afrikaners who arrogantly extolled their identity and used colour to exclude and ostracise half of Afrikaans speakers. He believed the ethnic glue of Afrikanerdom was dissolving. His close friend, poet Breyten Breytenbach, summed up his view well: 'The sameness of the white-ish Afrikaners no longer exists, the blueprint has finally been broken down.'[23]

In the four years they were in parliament together, John Vorster refused to acknowledge Slabbert's greeting when they passed each other in the lobby. Here he was, among the best and brightest in the Afrikaner community, passionate about Afrikaans, the writings of NP van Wyk Louw and the poetry of Breyten Breytenbach, but repelled by Afrikaners' support for apartheid, which he saw as a dire threat to society and to Afrikaner culture.

The NP leadership found it impossible to dismiss such a man as *volksvreemd*, but as Vorster observed, Slabbert had a chink in his armour: he lacked staying power. When, in the mid-1970s, opposition newspapers raved about Slabbert and even spoke of him as a future prime minister, Vorster said caustically: 'If that is so, then that future is very, very far off indeed. I get the idea that being a back-bencher in a small party with limited time for debate is steadily killing Slabbert politically.'[24]

Although it sounded premature in 1975 when Vorster made the comment, the assessment turned out to be true. Nevertheless, Slabbert put matters on the agenda that most knew could not be avoided by killing the messenger. It was almost as if there was a feeling of sadness in the Afrikaner nationalist movement that he was not part of the ruling party, grappling as it was with awesome challenges.

This sentiment is reflected in the story told of Hans van Rensburg, leader of the paramilitary pro-German Ossewa-Brandwag (OB) movement in the war years. Asked by members of the movement what he thought of their main opponent, Prime Minister Jan Smuts, who had many OB followers detained, Van Rensburg replied: 'He has all the qualities of a great leader: the intellect, the experience, the magnetism, all the characteristics, except one: he is not on our side.'

In recounting the story in *Die Burger*, editor Piet Cillié said the same could be said of Bram Fischer, leader of the SA Communist Party, when he died: 'He was of the calibre a *volk*, a movement, a party would dearly have loved to have on their side. In his youth he fed the belief that he would remain on the side of the National[ist]

---

23   Breyten Breytenbach, Introduction to Van Zyl Slabbert, *Afrikaner Afrikaan* (Cape Town: Tafelberg, 1999).

24   John D'Oliveira, *Vorster – The Man* (Johannesburg: Ernest Stanton, 1977), p. 247.

Afrikaners.'[25] Privately, nationalists increasingly commented on Slabbert in the same terms.[26]

South Africa's options

The Soweto uprising of 1976 forced whites to consider alternatives to unadulterated white domination, but until 1990 they ruled out any system in which whites could be outvoted. As late as 1988 more than 90% of whites surveyed rejected the option of 'a single mixed Parliament with the majority in control'.[27] They dismissed the view that their fear of majority rule was unrealistic; they had made up their minds that the choice was between white control or black control.

Nevertheless, many people had come to understand that the white community, with its fast shrinking demographic base, could not hold out indefinitely against the demand for majority rule and that the real question was what kind of majority rule was most desirable. Democratic theory distinguishes between two kinds of majority rule in societies with deep racial or ethnic divisions. The first is ascriptive majority rule, where voters vote on the basis of racial or ethnic identity. There are few floating votes and the largest population segment wins. Elections turn into a racial or ethnic census and the minority community is locked out permanently.

The second kind of majority rule is one where the electoral system is designed to create a large enough floating vote to make the outcome of elections uncertain and the alternation of ruling parties a real possibility.[28]

To achieve a balanced form of majority rule, liberal politicians in South Africa encouraged a process that would first loosen the NP's grip on power. The next step was to create the conditions for a stable, negotiated settlement that would avoid the winner-takes-all element of the Westminster system. Slabbert's early political career revolved around these issues. He co-authored *South Africa's Options*, published in 1979, with University of Cape Town academic and fellow liberal David Welsh.[29] The book argues that increasing pressure and a shrinking demographic base meant whites would have to make painful choices. The alternatives were prolonged siege leading to a near-war situation with full-scale military and paramilitary mobilisation, on the one hand, or, on the other, all-party negotiations for a new constitution underwritten by parties across the spectrum.

25   Piet Cillié, *Tydgenote* (Cape Town: Tafelberg 1980), pp. 81-82.

26   For an illuminating account of these years see Paul Cassar, 'The Emergence and Impact of Dr F van Zyl Slabbert in South African Politics', Master's dissertation, UOFS, 1984.

27   Hermann Giliomee and Lawrence Schlemmer, *From Apartheid to Nation-building* (Cape Town: Oxford University Press, 1989), p. 156.

28   Elaine Spitz, *Majority Rule* (Chatham, NJ: Chatham House Publishers, 1984).

29   Frederik van Zyl Slabbert and David Welsh, *South Africa's Options* (Cape Town: David Philip, 1979).

In September 1978 Eglin asked Slabbert to chair a committee to revise the party's policy of a qualified franchise as proposed by the old Progressive Party. To a large degree these proposals corresponded with the proposals Slabbert and Welsh would later outline in their book, advocating abolition of a qualified vote but retaining the party's commitment to federalism and entrenched individual rights. The committee proposed proportional representation and free association, which would necessitate the abolition of population registration and other pillars of apartheid. It advocated a consociational democracy involving the sharing of executive power between the majority and the minority parties in a grand coalition. Minorities would have a veto on crucial issues. Welsh recounts that he wanted to use the term 'a consensus-driven system' rather than veto right, but Slabbert was firm: 'Call it a minority veto because that is what it is.'[30]

The interesting thing about *South Africa's Options* is that shortly after it was published Slabbert expunged any reference to his co-authorship from speeches, articles and books. No extract from it is included in the anthology of his writings of the 1980s, which appeared under the title *The System and the Struggle*. It is omitted from his list of publications listed in the book.

What happened?

The most likely explanation is that Slabbert had come to accept that, with political polarisation continuing apace, it was above all necessary to engage an increasingly alienated black leadership. Unobtrusively, he removed power sharing in cabinet and a minority veto as key pillars of the party's policy. Interviewed for this book, several members of the PFP caucus of the time said it was a prerogative of the leader to downplay certain policy pillars. Some admit that abandoning the notion of power sharing sharply reduced the party's chances of increasing its support at the polls.

Discarding a white veto

Why did Slabbert abandon the notions of power sharing and a minority veto? The main reason was the ushering in of a tricameral parliament. This increased the gulf between Slabbert and the NP government. With polls showing that more than half of the electorate believed society would be fully integrated in twenty years' time, Slabbert felt the government ought to have taken the bold step of incorporating everyone, including blacks, into the new system. He continued to argue that the tricameral parliament undermined the very idea of non-violent change and intensified the violence inherent in the system.[31]

Under Slabbert the PFP did well, winning 27 seats in the 1981 election to become the official opposition. But in 1982 Andries Treurnicht and 21 others walked out of

---

30 Communication from David Welsh, 18 June 2011.

31 Slabbert, *The System and the Struggle*, p. 87.

the NP caucus to form the Conservative Party (CP). With its rock-solid support of at least one third of the Afrikaner vote, pollsters confidently predicted that the CP would supplant the PFP as official opposition in the next election.

Slabbert felt boxed in. The tricameral system was bound to reduce the status and influence of Slabbert and his party. The coloured and Indian parties in the tricameral parliament demanded that they, rather than the PFP, should be recognised as spokesmen for their respective communities and as witnesses to the injustices of apartheid. Several English-speaking businessmen and editors propagated a yes vote in the referendum on the new constitution as 'a step in the right direction'. Government speakers branded the PFP opposition as 'spoilers'.

Slabbert was fighting on another front too; he was disappointed by the short-sightedness of some sections of his regular constituency, which could not accept his view that cooption of Indian and coloured minorities would fail as long as the African majority was excluded. The referendum yielded a victory of more than two thirds for the yes vote.

Slabbert had fought the scheme with everything he had and felt the result as a personal blow. Ray Swart, then a Natal PFP member of parliament, tells of a private conversation with Slabbert in 1983 during the latter part of the campaign. Slabbert expressed himself in strong terms as feeling 'politically dirty' as he contemplated the prospect of serving in a parliament under a constitution he believed to be totally flawed. He mooted the idea of the PFP making a dramatic gesture of refusing to participate in the new system. But, as Swart correctly pointed out, such a step would leave a gap for others less determined to resist apartheid.[32]

There were other reasons for abandoning mandatory power sharing. It was a device that drew vociferous opposition from the extra-parliamentary forces that had begun to organise on a large scale in the early 1980s. Increasingly, the demand was for what Nelson Mandela often called 'an ordinary democracy' in which the majority ruled. Disenchanted with parliamentary politics, Slabbert hated the prospect of championing a minority veto to the extra-parliamentary forces. ANC supporters considered the veto an expression of white determination to hang on to resources and of their mistrust of black commitment to real democracy. Democracy seldom succeeds in divided societies without recourse to something like a veto. However, such vetoes are rarely included in a formal constitution, depending instead on agreements between the main contenders for power.

Yet another reason for Slabbert's decision to abandon the idea of power sharing and a government of national unity was the NP's hijacking of these concepts. During the 1950s the NP had replaced the term 'races' with 'ethnic groups', and in the early 1980s it substituted 'minorities' for 'ethnic groups', but all within the context of the

---

32   Swart, *Progressive Odyssey*, p. 165.

apartheid system. By the mid-1980s, it began speaking of power sharing and consensual decision-making. Arend Lijphart, the main theorist of consociational democracy, pointed out their fundamental error: whereas his proposals were based on the voluntary association of individuals with groups, the NP government used the law to force all people into one of four statutory groups.

Between the referendum of 1983 and abandoning parliament as a vehicle for reform in 1986, Slabbert made two shifts. First, he turned away from trying to win enough votes to force a coalition committed to establishing a system in which minorities would not feel insecure. Second, he abandoned mandatory power sharing and increasingly put his faith in individual rights and an independent judiciary. Such shifts would signal a fundamental break with the system that had prevailed since 1910, in which parliament with a simple majority could, apart from two entrenched clauses, make any encroachment it chose on the life, liberty and property of any individual subject to its sway. Embracing the doctrine of positivism, the courts largely functioned to enforce parliament's will.[33]

A change of thinking

These shifts in Slabbert's thinking occurred against the background of major changes in the way the Western world saw human rights. The creators of the United Nations, particularly Britain, tried to use the UN to preserve the racial and imperial order of the pre-Second World War period. At the same time, the states that became independent in the first three decades after the war were more interested in their own sovereignty than in protecting the individual rights of their citizens. Initially, the West accepted a human rights regime as part of an attempt to establish a symbolic order against the Soviet Union. Slowly the situation changed. With a country such as India now playing an important role, the UN was turned into an instrument for ending empires and white supremacy in the developing world. However, human rights as a pressing concern for the international community only gained major prominence in the mid-1970s after democracy had turned sour in many African, Asian and Latin American states.[34]

In South Africa the concept of human rights made headway only haltingly. The Progressive Party, founded in 1959, favoured a rigid constitution and an entrenched bill of rights. In 1973 Progressive politicians, together with some black leaders, called for a bill of rights and a federal constitution. In 1978 a legal scholar published a book in which he argued that parliamentary sovereignty, together with what he called a

---

33 Serjeant at Arms, 'Power of Constitutional Review', *Mail & Guardian*, 10 February 2012.
34 Mark Mazower, *No Enchanted Palace: The End of Empire and the Ideological Origins of the United Nations* (Princeton: Princeton University Press, 2009); Samuel Moyn, *The Last Utopia: Human Rights in History* (Cambridge, MA: Harvard University Press, 2010).

'primitive positivist outlook' on the part of judges, had produced a system of law with no safeguards for individual liberty.[35]

Internationally, from the early 1980s, progressive lawyers and academics were increasingly articulating the new dogma that human rights, as part of a well-structured constitution, were enough to protect minority rights, making mandatory power sharing to protect the rights of minorities superfluous. Whereas democratic pluralists such as Arend Lijphart propagated power sharing as the best approach to ruling highly divided societies, the new doctrine of human rights claimed that properly entrenched individual rights, independent courts and a vigorous civil society were strong enough to safeguard a minority's rights and protect it from discrimination. But this was a novel, largely untested approach that by the mid-1980s had produced few encouraging results in deeply divided societies in the developing world. A common trend was for politics to bypass the legislature and migrate to the courts – to the increasing chagrin of the executive, which set out to destroy their independence.

Slabbert never explained why he abandoned minority rights and a veto power as suggested earlier in *South Africa's Options*. Perhaps the main reason was that, like so many other opinion formers, he expected the NP to remain powerful enough for quite some time to protect white interests. Virtually no one foresaw the NP disintegrating as a party in the 1990s and the ANC transforming the state into its tool.

While Slabbert did not make a major input towards ensuring greater countervailing powers in the future system, his contribution to bringing about the end of apartheid has been greatly underestimated. Economic sanctions hurt the economy, but they did not affect the lifestyle of whites. Diplomatic and sports sanctions were inconvenient, but hardly enough reason to give up power. Demographic realities weighed ever heavier, but few whites could see a way around them.

What made a difference in the NP government's calculus was Slabbert's success in demolishing the party's ideology. Without an ideology, apartheid's gratuitous cruelty, its greed and unfair privileges could no longer be justified. In the end the NP felt itself impelled to negotiate, not so much because sanctions threatened the economy, but because its leaders' moral conviction about the rightness of its ideology collapsed. Parliamentary debates, in which Slabbert shone, were vital in forcing the ruling party to accept that it no longer had any legitimating ideology.

A long history of selective condemnation of Afrikaners, starting with British missionaries in the early nineteenth century, inclined the NP to dismiss all criticism from English-speaking editors and politicians. Afrikaner nationalists in general tended to listen only to those critics who could genuinely use 'we' in reasoning with them. The two critics outside the NP who could do so best were Johan Degenaar,

---

35 John Dugard, *Human Rights and the South African Legal Order* (Princeton: Princeton University Press, 1978), pp. 34-48.

a philosophy lecturer revered by Slabbert, and Slabbert himself. Neither was an anti-apartheid moralist. Slabbert methodically exposed the stark contradiction between the official policy and the sordid practice, but he never adopted a superior tone and always debated issues in an open-minded way.

Although Afrikaners in general continued to hold Slabbert in high regard, there was little chance of the PFP gaining significant Afrikaner votes. Slabbert's removal of the power-sharing pillars of the party's policy would further reduce any chance of an electoral breakthrough.

A tale of two states

By the early 1980s the NP was no longer fuelled by the twin engines of apartheid and Afrikaner nationalism. It was now both the party of reform and the party that represented, much more powerfully than in the 1950s or 1960s, the interests of the semi-state corporations and the other business of the state. One could almost say that two overlapping states existed. There was a 'core state' in which Afrikaners occupied most of the senior positions in the central government, the security forces, three of the four provincial administrations, and public corporations such as Eskom and Iscor.[36] Beyond this Afrikaner core there also was a multiracial 'outer state' of business leaders, homeland governments with their bureaucracies and racially mixed security forces. The core and the outer state were steadily removing salary and wage disparities and reducing white privilege.

Until the late 1980s it was common for Afrikaners to talk about 'our' defence force, 'our' minister, and 'our' police force when referring to the core state. A study found that 95% of Afrikaner students were sympathetic to the state, measured by a range of indices, against only 65% of English speakers.[37] Slabbert was one of the politicians who moved easily between the two states. As Afrikaner nationalism began to unravel, he became increasingly popular among Afrikaner students and a younger generation of journalists. He also established firm links with Mangosuthu Buthelezi in the 'outer state'. He swiftly threw the PFP's weight behind the power-sharing proposals for the Natal-KwaZulu region presented by the Buthelezi Commission in 1982.

General Jannie Geldenhuys, who became chief of the defence force in 1985, recently remarked: 'The government heeded the criticism of people like Van Zyl Slabbert and one or two other Afrikaner commentators on the left much more than

---

36 For a fuller discussion see Annette Seegers, 'Towards an Understanding of the Afrikanerisation of the South African State', *Africa*, 63, 4, 1993, pp. 477-97.

37 Jannie Gagiano, 'Ruling Group Cohesion', Hermann Giliomee and Jannie Gagiano (eds), *The Elusive Search for Peace: South Africa, Israel and Northern Ireland* (Cape Town: Oxford University Press, 1990), pp. 191-208.

that coming from any English-speaking critic like Ken Owen or the official oppo-sition.'[38] In retirement Chris Heunis said that Slabbert's decision in 1986 to abandon parliament as an instrument of reform plunged him into deep despair about the future of parliamentary politics, because he had such a high regard for Slabbert.[39]

Repelled by parliament

On 2 September 1985 it was exactly a year since the start of a cycle of protests trigger-ing an increasingly lethal police response. This threatened to tear the country apart. Dismayed by the grim struggle for ascendancy, Slabbert had become thoroughly disenchanted with parliamentary politics. The state and the extra-parliamentary forces were battling one another with no end in sight and endgame scenarios abounded. He wrote: 'I am desperately bored by the "five-minutes-to-midnight-heavy-breathing-politics" at dinner parties where some angry black rolled his eyes at the assembled whites, promising the day of Armageddon and watched them get goose-pimples.'[40] He could not see either the state or the extra-parliamentary forces prevailing. No external factor like the sanctions campaign could decisively influence the power balance.

Seeing no solution, Slabbert staked his hopes on attempting the seemingly im-possible. The last chapter of *South Africa's Options* acknowledges that it was almost impossible to persuade the white electorate to give up its sole hold on power. It quotes Max Weber, who wrote that only by reaching out for the impossible could man attain the possible. 'It may be that politics in South Africa will be the art of the impossible. Is this not a challenge worth accepting?'[41] On the back cover of *The Last White Parliament*, published in the second half of 1985, a quote from Slabbert appears: '[Here] in South Africa [we] have problems for which the rest of the world has found no solutions. That in itself is a great challenge.'

These are noble sentiments, but the challenge was to come up with a practical plan to persuade white voters to surrender their monopoly of power. By the mid-1980s people within the political system started to consider negotiating with the ANC, but questioned whether it would stick to a pact that was agreed upon. Was it not more likely to become simply yet another one-party-dominant state in which corruption, inefficiency and the marginalisation of minorities would be widespread?

It was not far-fetched to suspect the ANC of some of these tendencies once it got into government. Its leadership was in exile or jail and for most of the time the Soviet Union was its only major sponsor. The available evidence suggested that the

38   Interview with Jannie Geldenhuys, 5 April 2008.
39   Jan, his son, confirms this: e-mail communication, 9 June 2011.
40   Slabbert, *The Last White Parliament*, p. 126.
41   Slabbert, *South Africa's Options*, p. 171.

exiled leaders took a special interest in the model of the Soviet Union and Eastern European countries. The difficulty was that Slabbert – like almost all white South Africans – knew so little about the ANC. The government's efforts to paint the ANC in the blackest colours had backfired among many liberals. Some thought virtually any alternative was better than the Botha government whose intransigence had landed the country in a state of siege.

In the course of 1985 Slabbert came to believe no solution was possible without the ANC-in-exile, although he was still entertaining the possibility of major change from within. He co-founded the National Convention Movement in South Africa. Others who took the lead were Mangosuthu Buthelezi, Archbishop Denis Hurley (the most significant Catholic leader in South Africa in the second half of the twentieth century) and a number of business leaders, of whom banker Chris Ball and supermarket tycoon Raymond Ackerman were the most prominent. The idea was to establish a broad front of leaders who could issue an appeal to stop the violence and start negotiations for a non-racial constitution.

For Slabbert it was a chastening experience to hear from leading South Africans that they would not participate in the Convention movement. Archbishop Desmond Tutu, patron of the United Democratic Front, turned down Slabbert's plea to attend or to speak to Buthelezi about stopping the violence. Slabbert told an interviewer in 1994 that the church leader had said: 'I will not speak to that man. He is beyond the pale.' As an aside, Slabbert commented: 'That is now our great Christian leader.'[42]

The idea of a Convention movement was not helped when Buthelezi fiercely attacked the ANC. There was a major setback just as the movement was about to be launched. Slabbert tells the story: 'The National Convention Movement bombed two days before the conference. The most embarrassing thing ... But it bombed because the ANC issued a statement from Lusaka saying that Slabbert was simply Botha's pawn, and trying to undermine the struggle. Just like that.' He continued: 'I had commitments three days before that all of them would be there. And the ANC issued this thing and that's when I said: "Okay, I'll take the PFP's executive and we'll go and talk to these guys." And that's when we went.'[43]

In October 1985 Slabbert led the PFP executive on a visit to Lusaka where it met with members of the ANC's executive. More than nine years later he told journalist Patti Waldmeir that he was 'charmed out of my pants'. He continued: 'They took us to the Lusaka polo club and we drank South African wine. Snot en trane. Wonderful stuff.' In his view the government's demonisation of the ANC leaders was completely counterproductive. 'You go there and it's completely different. I mean you

---

42   Interview with Van Zyl Slabbert by Patti Waldmeir, 11 November 1994.
43   Interview with Van Zyl Slabbert by Patti Waldmeir, 11 November 1994.

just can't believe it. And they are reasonable and they laugh and they chat and they talk about the domestic situation.'[44]

Colin Eglin of the PFP wrote positively but more soberly of the ANC leaders they met: 'They were certainly not agents of Moscow engaged in the "total onslaught" to which Botha constantly referred. Their desire was to be "home" one day.' He recalled the poignant words of Alfred Nzo at their departure. 'And so we say farewell to you as you go back to South Africa – our wonderful country – while we stay right here.'[45]

In his book *Tough Choices*, which appeared in 2000, Slabbert remained effusive. 'To say that I was overwhelmed would be putting it mildly. Mac Maharaj, Thabo Mbeki, Alfred Nzo and Gertrude Shope . . . a whole new era of history opened for me, an awareness of my insulation in the fight against apartheid, a feeling of intense camaraderie and common objectives.' He continued almost as if he were reliving a profound religious experience, citing the 'overwhelming moral validity' of the ANC's struggle and the 'doubtful value of anything tried from within "the system", especially from within white parliamentary politics'. [46]

The Botha interview

On a tour to Australia in mid-1985 Slabbert told Eglin he was thinking of leaving parliament, which he believed had become irrelevant. When Eglin could not persuade him to change his mind, he advised Slabbert to inform the president of his intentions.[47]

On 25 November 1985 a meeting took place between Botha and Slabbert at the latter's request. Slabbert intended to inform the president that he would resign from parliament because he had come to believe that parliamentary politics were futile. The discussion, however, took a quite different tack.

From the transcript it seems as if there was much common ground between the two. Slabbert said he believed there were certain things that could be done about the political crisis. 'The problem with the ANC is it is a myth. No, it is not a myth, it is a romantic image to people in the world . . . I honestly think – and I say that from my experience of the matter – you can pull out the teeth of the whole ANC story. But this is not a story I can discuss with cabinet committees.'

Slabbert asked to talk to Dr Niel Barnard, head of the National Intelligence Service, and Botha replied that he was welcome to talk to both Barnard and the special

44   Interview with Van Zyl Slabbert by Patti Waldmeir, 11 November 1994.

45   Colin Eglin, *Crossing the Borders of Power: The Memoirs of Colin Eglin* (Johannesburg: Jonathan Ball, 2007), p. 211.

46   Frederik Van Zyl Slabbert, *Tough Choices* (Cape Town: Tafelberg, 2000), p. 103.

47   Eglin, *Crossing the Borders of Power*, p. 214, and private communication, 6 September 2011.

cabinet committee on blacks. Slabbert asked for clarification on the NP's insistence that the white community needed to have 'self-determination' in the future. When Botha replied that a white person had to retain his 'cultural rights, the way of life, his languages and the right to have children educated in this way', Slabbert responded: 'I have no problem.'

Slabbert pointed out that there were few, if any, historical precedents for the peaceful transfer of power from a minority to a majority. Black liberation was impossible without white security. When Botha declared that he could not agree that the tricameral constitution must be destroyed in order to write a new one, Slabbert remarked: 'We will have to see how things go further because I think there is a political difference between us.'[48]

Slabbert did not know the conversation was being taped. Two months later, after he walked out of parliament stating that Botha's intransigence had precipitated his action, Botha asked his permission to publish a transcript of the interview. Two points need to be made here. First, it was outrageous of Botha to tape a conversation with the leader of the opposition without informing him beforehand. Second, Slabbert did not subsequently represent his opponent's views fairly. Some of Botha's remarks, it is true, must have exasperated Slabbert. The president spoke of the need to recognise the homelands because they represented 'minorities' who would not forego their 'rights'. Regarding urban blacks, the president made a weird comment. According to him, half of the black people 'do not want to throw the rights they have attained into a pot and leave them there'. He was probably referring to the independent homelands being reincorporated into the Republic.

Slabbert conveyed the impression that the president's intransigence made him quit politics, but judging by the transcript the meeting was friendly and constructive. Eglin is quite correct to observe: 'The meeting was not confrontational and the differences between Slabbert and Botha were no greater than one could have expected at the commencement of exploratory discussions . . . At no stage did Slabbert lay down any markers that would define reasons for his political resignation.' The president agreed to his request to talk to certain key committees in government to explain an initiative he had in mind, and even offered to attend such a meeting. 'The meeting ended with Slabbert saying: "Mr President, many thanks", and with farewell pleasantries.'[49]

If Botha had been a different kind of leader, he would have seized on Slabbert's remark that the ANC's teeth could be pulled and asked how that could be done. He would have asked Slabbert to act as his personal intermediary in getting negotia-

---

48   *Weekend Argus*, 15 February 1986 published the transcript in full. It was republished as a supplement to the *SA Digest*, 28 February 1986.

49   Eglin, *Crossing the Borders*, pp. 254-55.

tions started. But there was no chemistry between Botha and Slabbert, and Botha was far too confident of the government's ability to crush the ANC.

Slabbert's comments in the interview with Botha would have been unremarkable if not for the remark: 'You can pull out the teeth of the whole ANC story.' He knew the ANC in exile was trapped in a hopeless guerrilla war and hung up on an obsolete Stalinism. But Slabbert had learnt from his National Convention initiative that the ANC and its proxy, the United Democratic Front, were powerful enough to spoil or block any constitutional initiative that excluded them. There was no alternative to legalising the ANC and allowing it to participate in politics. Slabbert realised the state would be able to suppress the ANC for at least another decade, but he also understood that it was in the interests of whites to negotiate with the ANC and other extra-parliamentary movements before endemic instability took root.

A new partner

When Slabbert and his team met Mbeki and his colleagues in October 1985, negotiations were only a distant possibility for the ANC (see p. 205). The movement's official position, as communicated to the PFP executive in October 1985, was that the armed struggle was the only way forward. Frequently briefed by the South African military, Slabbert considered this strategy 'a bit of a joke'. The reality, as he stated in his public comments, was that the country had become stalemated between the politics of repression and the politics of revolt.

As they drove to the Lusaka airport after the ANC-PFP meeting, Slabbert and Mbeki discussed the prospects of negotiations. It was the first time they could talk privately. Slabbert in all probability expressed his grave concern about the possibility of South Africa descending into a state of prolonged siege that steadily turned into a low-level civil war. Mbeki put Slabbert's mind at rest by saying he had no doubt that talking would prevail if the ANC really had to choose between civil war and negotiations.[50] Slabbert recorded Mbeki's response as follows: 'Mbeki did make it personally clear to me that "talking is better than killing" and negotiations could be explored.'[51] A partnership was born.

In an article posted on the Web after Slabbert's death in 2010 the commentator RW Johnson speculated that Slabbert had indicated he wanted to promote dialogue with the ANC, to which Mbeki's reply was that Slabbert first had to leave parliament. The deal was: 'Van would resign, form Idasa and he would then be rewarded with public talks with the ANC – hence the famous Dakar meeting.' He goes on to speculate that Slabbert agreed to the condition, adding that Slabbert was just one more

---

50   Mark Gevisser, *Thabo Mbeki: The Dream Deferred* (Johannesburg: Jonathan Ball, 2007), pp. 496-98.
51   Frederik Van Zyl Slabbert, *The Other Side of History* (Johannesburg: Jonathan Ball, 2006), p. 46.

person 'who had been charmed and deceived by Mbeki: trusting him had been a fatal error'.[52]

Johnson's speculation is interesting, but I have reservations about any suggestion that Slabbert walked out of parliament to meet a demand by Mbeki. Ranged against it is the fact that ANC leaders had just met with the executive of the PFP, a white party. More importantly, Slabbert was not the kind of man who would have submitted to anyone's demands if he had wanted to stay on in parliament. The truth was he was more than ready to abandon parliament and now an excellent reason presented itself. In the preceding eleven years he had moved from the placid life of an academic into the turbulent world of parliamentary politics, but he had grown tired of it. What could be more noble and exciting than abandoning parliament to pursue the ideal of a negotiated settlement along liberal democratic lines? It was an ideal worth devoting all his energies to, even his career.

Was a deal between Mbeki and Slabbert struck in Lusaka? Undoubtedly Slabbert assumed that the ANC would draw on him when they came into power. Johnson writes: 'As I know from many conversations with Van, he had high hopes that this relationship would ultimately lead him to playing a significant role in making sure the new dispensation would work. "When the ANC takes over," he told me, "they are going to need all the help they can get. And it's vital for all of us that they succeed because only that way can the country succeed."'

At this stage Mbeki was too weak to sell the idea of open-ended talks to the ANC leadership. Slabbert sketched the ANC's position as follows: 'They were violently against any form of negotiations ... they were still exporting the revolution à la the African Solidarity Committee in Moscow.' At the Lusaka meeting the ANC delegation told the PFP executive: 'Look, we don't believe in negotiations. You have got to understand that.' Slabbert adds: 'Thabo may have been [in favour of talking], but Thabo was under intense pressure from the hardliners because of that ... Guys who are his closest allies now [in 1994] were fighting like crazy to prevent him from getting any position of authority.'[53]

As late as 1988 the dominant view within the ANC about the struggle's future course had not changed. Slabbert recounts a meeting in Germany where he gained the impression that Mbeki and Aziz Pahad were the only ones beginning to say: 'Well, maybe negotiation is possible. The others, however, were saying: "Nonsense. It's struggle."' Slabbert later asked Beyers Naudé, who was also at the meeting: 'Bey, what would happen to the ANC if they released Mandela?' He replied: 'Van Zyl, they are totally unprepared for that.'[54]

In the literature Mbeki is often portrayed as the ANC leader who 'seduced' Slab-

52   RW Johnson, 'Van Zyl Slabbert: What Went Wrong?', www.politicsweb.co.za, posted on 21 June 2010.
53   Interview with Van Zyl Slabbert by Patti Waldmeir, 11 November 1994.
54   Interview with Van Zyl Slabbert by Patti Waldmeir, 11 November 1994.

bert, but in 1985 his position in the ANC was too weak to engage in any seduction. ANC leader Oliver Tambo backed him, but someone like Chris Hani in the ANC's armed wing was openly critical of 'diplomacy' and talks. Far from being engaged in seduction, Mbeki was desperately soliciting help. Early in 1986 he sent a letter encouraging Slabbert to quit parliament. If he would do that, he went on to say, Slabbert would no longer be the leader of a small party, but one of the leaders of a movement to which the great majority of people of South Africa belonged.[55]

Slabbert by no means planned to join the ANC but rather carefully positioned himself as an independent. He would keep this stance for the next five to seven years. In 1991 Lawrence Schlemmer would depict him as one of four or five people who were considered independent enough to 'act as political mediators or arbitrators'.[56] But Slabbert did not mean to be a mediator or arbitrator for the rest of his public career. He was prepared to burn his bridges with respect to the tricameral parliament but had no intention of remaining in the political wilderness. The question was whether Mbeki would offer Slabbert a senior political post once politics normalised.

Getting out

In December 1985 Slabbert issued a press statement that displayed a profound alienation from the system. He called Botha's Rubicon speech four months earlier a 'non-event' with a 'cataclysmic effect' that showed the poverty of the government's vision. The government 'showed no ability to remove the flashpoints of popular discontent'.[57] The statement made no reference to the government's acceptance of the need to accommodate urban blacks in the same structures as the other groups, the repeal of the racial sex laws, and the flourishing of black and mixed trade unions within an inclusive system of industrial relations. Slabbert's opposition to the government had turned into revulsion.

In December came what Slabbert called the 'final straw'. He discovered the military was continuing to destabilise Mozambique despite the government's commitment in the Nkomati Accord to refrain from doing so. Ten years earlier, in 1975, when he was still a novice in parliament, he became very upset when he discovered South Africa was deeply involved in military operations in Angola without any approval from parliament and without the public being informed. In destabilising Mozambique in 1985 the Botha government was treating both parliament – and a diplomatic accord it had signed – with contempt, and he was not prepared to go along with that.[58] In *The Last White Parliament* he wrote with reference to the

55   Interviews conducted in February 2012 with sources that were close to Slabbert.
56   O'Malley Archives, Interview with Lawrence Schlemmer, 15 August 1991.
57   Slabbert, *The System and the Struggle*, pp. 82-83.
58   Slabbert, *The Last White Parliament*, pp. 39-42; Slabbert, *The Other Side of History*, pp. 46-47.

Angolan episode: 'If you were in opposition in South Africa, I began to understand, you needed iron in the soul not to lose faith in what you believed ... You have to keep plugging away patiently without the prospect of immediate reward and always be prepared for failure and disappointment.'[59]

Slabbert still had iron in his soul, but he no longer believed in parliament as a means to achieve his objectives. No longer part of the loyal opposition to government, he decided to become a critical ANC ally. It was a perilous road. The ANC leadership and Mbeki personally remained committed to an armed struggle and would only embark on talks with people or organisations in South Africa if they could weaken the enemy.

Starting informal talks with the ANC offered Slabbert something he desperately wanted: a way out of parliamentary politics. His scheme was to work with Mbeki on ending apartheid and on post-apartheid reconstruction. He envisaged a non-racial post-apartheid order that offered full opportunities for all, regardless of colour. Slabbert said on occasion that one had to prepare for failure and disappointment, but he did not think his journey would lead him into the political wilderness. He believed he had forged a liaison with Mbeki. Both men were bright, energetic and engaging, and in 1986 neither was yet 50 years old. They had time on their side.

His action represented an abrupt change of course. Eglin pointed out later that in Slabbert's *The Last White Parliament*, published towards the end of 1985, he had stated: 'Participation in the tricameral system is necessary because I believe that evolutionary constitutional change is both possible and desirable.'[60] Early in 1986 Slabbert told the top leadership of his caucus that he intended to resign as leader unless the entire PFP resigned their seats and then sought a mandate to boycott parliament until the law prohibiting racially mixed political parties was scrapped.[61] Slabbert received no support and in all likelihood left those present puzzled.

On 6 February 1986 Slabbert resigned as leader of the opposition and member of parliament. He denounced Botha's policy of reforms as a sham and parliamentary politics as 'a gross ritual of irrelevancy'. Alex Boraine walked out with him – but only after he had asked some senior members whether he should not make himself available as leader and discovered he had little support.[62] Undoubtedly delighted with the extreme terms with which Slabbert denounced parliament, Mbeki issued a statement calling Slabbert a modern-day 'new Voortrekker'.[63]

Initially it looked as if Slabbert's act of walking out of parliament seriously dam-

59   Slabbert, *The Last White Parliament*, p. 42.
60   Cited by Eglin, *Crossing the Borders*, p. 214.
61   Interview with Van Zyl Slabbert, *Leadership South Africa*, 1986, p. 1. For an extensive exposition of his scheme see his *The Other Side of History*, pp. 62-74.
62   Swart, *Progressive Odyssey*, p. 182.
63   Slabbert, *The Other Side of History*, p. 26.

aged the PFP, which people like Suzman and Eglin had so patiently built up. Eglin told Slabbert he considered the way in which Slabbert had left the party in the lurch 'shocking' – the party had even established the Van Zyl Slabbert Trust for elections. When Slabbert told Suzman he had given twelve years to his parliamentary career, she exclaimed, 'Twelve years!' She was then in her twenty-sixth year.

The implications of Slabbert's action were far from clear. In his final year in politics he increasingly depicted the conflict as one in which there was a simple juxtaposition between the 'system' and the 'struggle'. Implicitly he was telling those who remained in parliament they were part of a completely discredited system. Slabbert tried to correct that interpretation by stressing that the parliamentary opposition still played a valuable role.

Harry Oppenheimer publicly stated that Slabbert had 'gravely and perhaps irreparably damaged his own credibility'.[64] He hailed Colin Eglin, who was chosen as a replacement leader, 'as a man of courage, whose reliability and loyalty to his party has been tried in the fire'. Ken Owen correctly noted the implication that Slabbert lacked these virtues. More frivolously, Owen suggested that Slabbert was politically akin to the migrating Afrikaner *trekboers* of the eighteenth and nineteenth centuries, who continued to move on in search of better pastures. Slabbert was 'the Afrikaner child of the *veld*, always shifting to better ground'.[65] Despite the stereotype, there was some truth to it.

Slabbert and Boraine now founded the Institute for a Democratic Alternative in South Africa (Idasa) as a non-partisan organisation that aimed to promote an inclusive democracy by talking to a wide range of people in and outside South Africa. But funds trickled in only very slowly. Slabbert, in his own words, had no plans or strategies.[66]

Meeting at Dakar

When they met in New York in early 1986, Slabbert told Mbeki not to underestimate the importance of growing numbers of Afrikaners, particularly academics, breaking with Afrikaner nationalism and apartheid. Here the idea emerged of a meeting somewhere in Africa between a group of mainly Afrikaans-speaking South Africans and some leading members of the ANC.[67] A few months later Slabbert and Breyten Breytenbach, a poet and close friend who lived in Paris, met on the island of Gorée off the coast of Dakar, Senegal, and decided Dakar was a suitable venue. Slabbert and Boraine raised the funds in the United States and found well-known interna-

---

64   Anthony Sampson, *Black and Gold* (London: Hodder & Stoughton, 1988), p. 228.
65   Ken Owen, 'The Man Who Was Not There', *The Passion for Reason*, p. 128.
66   Slabbert, *The Other Side of History*, p. 46.
67   Graham Leach, *The Afrikaners: Their Last Great Trek* (London: Macmillan, 1989), p. 149.

tional financier George Soros willing to donate a substantial sum, although he feared South Africa was doomed and the conference futile.

Breytenbach used his contacts with Danielle Mitterand – the French president's wife and head of the France Liberté institute – to smooth the entry of conference participants into Senegal and get Senegalese President Abdou Diouf to welcome the participants officially. The Dakar conference was to be followed by meetings with political leaders in Burkina Faso and Ghana. Mbeki and a few other members of the ANC executive would travel with the Idasa delegation to these countries.

On 3 June 1987, just more than a year after the South African government proclaimed a national state of emergency, the press broke the news of an imminent meeting in Dakar between an ANC delegation of eleven senior members (more than half went on to become cabinet members) led by Thabo Mbeki, and a motley group of about sixty people personally invited by Slabbert or Boraine. Half were white Afrikaans-speaking academics, teachers, journalists, artists, directors, writers and professionals. The group also included several coloured Afrikaans speakers, ten English-speaking businessmen and academics, and three German political scientists working on South Africa. No one formally represented an organisation or party.

Apart from press briefings, Slabbert rarely spoke. As could be expected, the topic of violence dominated the discussions. Other topics included the quest for a democratic alternative, the ANC's commitment to an equitable non-racial future, economic policy in a post-apartheid society, and cultural and language rights, with particular emphasis on the future position of Afrikaans. The only known record of the Dakar conference, held from 9 to 12 July 1987, was a secretly prepared ANC document of 80 pages, written by Tony Trew and some anonymous ANC members.[68]

As the conference account makes clear, the ANC delegation was convinced it occupied the moral high ground on all issues, including that of violence. It depicted the organisation as one that had been in the vanguard of a long peaceful battle for rights and liberty against apartheid, turning to violence in the early 1960s only when its non-violent protests had fallen on deaf ears. It was committed to observing the Geneva protocols and its guiding principle of the 'proportionality of means' in using violence.[69]

Believing that 'victory was certain', the ANC delegation envisaged negotiations at a 'two-sided table' as an imminent prospect. On one side would be the representatives of the state and all other 'racist' forces (including Inkatha and other 'reactionary' organisations) and, on the other side, the forces for liberation and popular democracy under the ANC's leadership. Among the latter would be representatives of trade unions, churches and selected 'progressive [white] liberals'.[70]

68   African National Congress (ANC), 1987: Paris-Dakar meeting, Cape Town: Mayibuye Centre, University of the Western Cape, unpublished manuscript.
69   ANC 1987 document, pp. 67-69.
70   ANC 1987 document, pp. 67-68.

In political philosopher André du Toit's keynote speech on violence he took issue with the notion of two clearly defined sides waging battle, preferring instead to speak of a proliferation of internecine conflicts, and warning that indiscriminate violence and terror on the part of the insurgents could damage the political cause of resistance. He warned the ANC: 'Revolution is not around the corner – the heady assessments of recent years are gone.'[71] The state would never win legitimacy by using large-scale coercion, but there were also distinct limits to the ANC challenge to state power.[72]

On the question of a future political system, ANC head of research Pallo Jordan was clear: he rejected any form of decentralised power. There had to be unity and 'unity could only be demonstrated through unity in action'. He argued that all groups in South Africa had been 'created, sustained and nurtured by state policy. The cleavages can be unmade precisely because they were manufactured [by apartheid].' The emergence of a new nation had to be based on a rejection of the divisions on which apartheid was based. He warned that the future government would impose a policy of 'liberatory intolerance' towards organisations based on race or ethnicity. This was a characterisation of society as sweeping as the ideology of the apartheid state and as devoid of a proper understanding of multi-ethnic societies.

The other ANC delegates too were not prepared to make any significant concessions to minorities. They took the line that the ANC's commitment to non-racialism made minority or group rights superfluous. They did not think a bill of rights necessary to assuage fears and considered that the Freedom Charter offered enough guarantees for minorities. They also dismissed pleas for power sharing, federalism or the decentralisation of power, claiming that these devices would only serve to buttress existing privilege.[73]

On the language issue the discussion soon deadlocked. African governments in other parts of Africa wasted no time in elevating the colonial language to the only effective public language, but the conference took no note of this. ANC delegates would not concede any demand for enforceable language rights. Few members of the Idasa group questioned ANC assurances that it would not marginalise minorities. There was no reference to other countries in Africa where soon after coming to power nationalist movements ruthlessly displaced members of minorities from civil service jobs or expelled them from the country in the name of Africanisation.

In the discussion on a post-apartheid economy Leon Louw, executive director of the Free Market Foundation, entered a plea for massive decentralisation and privatisation. The ANC delegates countered with a strong insistence on state intervention

---

71   André du Toit, 'Beginning the Debate', *Die Suid-Afrikaan*, 11, 1987, pp. 18-20.
72   ANC 1987 document, pp. 6-7.
73   ANC 1987 document, pp. 18-19, 70.

to 'democratise' the economy. Some expressed the view that the system had to culminate in socialism. Appealing to the Freedom Charter, they demanded national-isation of the mining and banking sectors, redistribution of land and collectivised agriculture. The new South Africa would have to guarantee 'the masses of the people freedom from hunger, disease, ignorance, homelessness and poverty'. Social analyst Lawrence Schlemmer warned that all-or-nothing strategies could actually strength-en the regime.[74]

The Idasa group was silent about the extraordinary influence that communism and communist activists exercised on the ANC in exile. Breytenbach was the only participant who expressed a word of caution. Referring to communism, he warned against supporting a system 'which we have seen in neighbouring countries not to be successful'.[75] In his book *True Confessions of an Albino Terrorist*, published three years earlier, he had pulled no punches about the extraordinary strategic leverage of communists in the ANC-led movement. But at the conference none of the inter-nal South Africans quoted Breytenbach's view. Tending to dismiss the propaganda of the South African government too readily, they missed the opportunity to delve deeper into an important issue.

Remarkably, the conference did not discuss the rapid decline of democracy in Africa and the steady deterioration in state capacity in many independent African states by the 1980s, where all-powerful dominant parties strutted the stage and tol-erated little opposition. They rigged elections, emasculated the courts, cowed the press and stifled universities. Leaders made themselves exceedingly rich.[76] There was a tendency at the Dakar conference to assume the ANC was too smart and morally upstanding to fall into this trap.

The ANC gave little indication of how democracy and socialism would come about. Later a member of the internal group expressed his bafflement: 'Listening to the ANC was like reading Revelations 21. They had an apocalyptic vision of a Great Moment of Change, where all democratic forces would be on the one side of the negotiating table under the leadership of the ANC, with the government on the other side, working out the hand-over of power. It was not even a round-table con-cept, but a two-sided table.'[77] While using democratic language, the ANC delegation in fact practised what has been called 'democratic exclusion', which recognises only a single political identity and imperiously excludes other identities.[78]

At the end of the conference the participants issued a declaration stating their

---

74   ANC 1987 document, pp. 24-26, 75.

75   ANC 1987 document, p. 11.

76   Martin Meredith, *The State of Africa: A History of Fifty Years of Independence* (London: Free Press, 2005), p. 379.

77   Jacques Kriel, 'The Human Face of Dakar', *Frontline*, July 1987, p. 23.

78   Charles Taylor, 'The Dynamics of Democratic Exclusion', *Journal of Democracy*, 9, 4, 1998, p. 148.

preference for a negotiated solution for South Africa and depicting the South African government as the main obstacle. It expressed deep concern about the proliferation of uncontrolled violence.[79]

The Afrikaans press and *Die Burger* in particular denounced the conference, arguing that it was an attempt by Slabbert to embarrass the government, highlight parliament's lack of legitimacy and boost the ANC as an extra-parliamentary movement. The real problem, however, was that the government had become bogged down by indecision. All the Afrikaans press could do was to discredit Slabbert and the Idasa group as useful idiots.[80]

'I'd die for that bugger'

After the conference most of the participants travelled together to Burkina Faso and Ghana. At a meeting in Accra, Ghana, a hostile questioner challenged the motives and credibility of Slabbert's group. Mbeki responded: 'We are not fighting the white people. We are not fighting individuals, but as South Africans we would like to come together to destroy the apartheid system.' Slabbert later said he had his 'epiphany of loyalty' at that moment, adding 'I'd die for that bugger'.[81]

The ANC group was jubilant over the outcome of the conference. An ANC report stated that the Idasa group's 'ideological perception of themselves' had been dismantled by the 'emotional intensity of the event . . . They were overwhelmed intellectually, ideologically and emotionally'. Mbeki was slightly more circumspect. 'No punches were pulled', he wrote, but added that the Idasa group was 'overwhelmed' through debate and 'their horizons had been broadened'.[82]

Mbeki discovered at Dakar that giving non-binding assurances about a future ANC government fell on fertile soil among Afrikaners, who hoped they were all true. He was playing a double game. According to ANC stalwart Mac Maharaj, Mbeki, as one of the six members of the SA Communist Party's (SACP's) Politburo, was at the heart of planning the revolution the ANC hoped to unleash in South Africa. The longer-term goal was wresting control away from the security forces, the civil service and the media, and restoring the land to the people. The immediate task at hand was to target those working for a compromise settlement that would exclude the ANC and rescue the capitalist system. It rejected 'group rights' as a concept 'fraught with the danger of perpetuating inequality'.

In 1989 Mbeki, in the words of SACP leader Joe Slovo, 'brilliantly chaired' the SACP conference in Havana, where the party accepted the document 'The Path to

---

79   For the declaration see Slabbert, *The Other Side of History*, pp.75-78.
80   Chris Louw, 'SA pers oopgevlek', *Die Suid-Afrikaan*, 11, 1987, pp.26-29.
81   Gevisser, *Thabo Mbeki*, pp. 514-15.
82   Gevisser, *Thabo Mbeki*, pp. 512-13.

Power' as its manifesto.[83] This document had its roots in the SACP's thinking about 'National Democratic Revolution (NDR)'. The first extensive formulation of this idea dated back to the early 1960s when the SACP accepted it as policy. It envisaged a radical change to the political system as the first stage of a revolution. This had to create the conditions for the second stage, which was socialism. By the mid-1980s approximately three quarters of the ANC's national executive were SACP members.[84]

Reflecting on Dakar 30 years later, journalist Chris Louw said: 'Only much later did I realize how naive I was at Dakar. There was a kind of bravado among the younger Afrikaners, tired of the stereotyping of Afrikaners as rigid and racist . . . We wanted to show we were even more African than the ANC; in that sense the meeting on our part was more about show and symbolism than substance. We were so ashamed of our government, of PW Botha's boorish conduct, of the mishmash of NP policy, that we fell for the temptation to side with the ANC and its ideology. In that spirit we dismissed any reference to minority or group rights as being code language for NP support. We wanted to create as much distance as possible between us and the NP.'[85]

Michael Savage, fellow sociologist and close friend of Slabbert, later gave this account of the expedition from a liberal perspective: 'At Dakar, Thabo seemed to fool the whole darn lot of us, as he gave all the signs of being a true non-racial democrat, and was warm, open and approachable. My view is that Mbeki's commitment to full democratic non-racialism was a chimera, hiding behind a justified and enduring hatred of raw racism and a hidden belief that the new social order must be predicated on aggressive Africanism and affirmative action. My view is that Mbeki successfully hid his emergent Africanism and he was not what he seemed to be – a warm, open, true non-racial democrat.'[86]

In his later years Slabbert tended to agree with this view, but he continued to consider Dakar a path-breaking event that cleared the road for negotiations. However, neither of the main parties considered the informal talks to be important in breaking the logjam. In 1992 Niel Barnard, head of the National Intelligence Service (NIS), remarked that the process of negotiations was not facilitated by groups like Idasa, hoping to act as 'middlemen'.[87] The NIS wanted to establish direct contact to start informal talks.

---

83   South African Communist Party, 'The Path to Power', Programme of the SACP, adopted 1989, www.sacp.org.za.

84   S Ellis and T Sechaba, *Comrades Against Apartheid: The ANC and the South African Communist Party in Exile* (Oxford: James Currey, 1992), p. 37.

85   E-mail communication from Chris Louw, 29 May 2009.

86   E-mail communication from Michael Savage, 19 May 2011.

87   Alf Ries, 'NIS wou sonder middelman na die ANC gaan', *Die Burger*, 18 February 1992.

In 1995 Mike Louw, second in command at The NIS and one of the most consistent advocates of a negotiated settlement, dismissed the idea that Dakar acted as a catalyst for negotiations. He remarked: 'In the circles where the decisions were made it had a negative effect; it made our task [to persuade the government to talk] more difficult.' He was equally frank in rejecting the assumption that members of the Afrikaner intelligentsia sitting down to talk with an ANC delegation had a positive effect on the Afrikaner community. Louw believed it was definitely having the opposite effect: '[They were seen] as just selling out, they could not be trusted . . . These people were [seen as] going over to the other side . . . [it was] well planned by the ANC, who had these naive people coming to them in order to drive a wedge in the Afrikaans ranks and to break up Afrikaner hegemony which by that time was already broken up into pieces because of internal struggles.'[88]

Once in government, the ANC leadership made no or little mention of Dakar in its account of its path to power. In 1994 ANC master strategist Joe Slovo dismissed the notion that the Dakar meetings and subsequent conferences organised by Idasa and other bodies had a significant effect on either the government or the ANC in exile: 'Nothing serious emerged from that . . . I think it really got serious with Mandela's initiative from inside prison.'[89] There is no mention of Dakar in the historical introduction to a book of Mbeki's speeches, co-authored by his close friends Essop Pahad and Willie Esterhuyse, and published on the eve of Mbeki being sworn in as president in 1999.[90]

Calling for negotiations

Slabbert continued to call for negotiations throughout the final years of the 1980s. He pointed out that there were two kinds of negotiations. One was negotiation for capitulation, in which whites arranged for a peaceful abdication of power. The other was negotiation for participation, in which whites and blacks both approved a new constitution. The question, according to Slabbert, was whether the regime would be willing to initiate the second kind of negotiation.

There was good reason to ask how the NP government conceived of negotiations, but there was another question Slabbert did not pose: how did the ANC view negotiations? The organisation was fighting a classic 'war of position' in which it saw each concession as the platform for the next assault. But the ANC was subtle: in every case it would move only after the balance of power had shifted in its favour.[91]

88   Interview with Mike Louw by Patti Waldmeir, 29 May 1995.

89   Interview with Joe Slovo by Patti Waldmeir, February 1990.

90   Slabbert, *The Other Side of History*, p. 54.

91   ANC, 'Negotiations: A Strategic Perspective', NEC Paper, 4th Quarter, 1992; see also Pierre du Toit, 'Dis tyd vir 'n opvolg-skikking', *Die Burger*, 1 October 2000, and for an extended treatment see his inaugural lecture published by the University of Stellenbosch, 2002.

In the late 1980s Slabbert wrote extensively on the process of negotiations. He was strongly influenced by the literature on democratisation in the 1970s and 1980s, with its emphasis on Argentina and other Latin American countries where democracy was established as the product of different 'pacts' between the contending parties. Essentially, the parties undertook not to harm each other after the election. Security pacts dealt with handling violations of human rights in future; other pacts dealt with economic policy and the future political system.

Slabbert was correct in seeing that the need for democratic institutions in South Africa arose from a prolonged political struggle in which neither side could prevail. But there was a big problem in applying to South Africa insights from studies on democratisation in Latin American states. In Latin America the basic cleavage was class, and the political conflict was often between a populist government with working-class backing and the security forces protecting upper-class interests. The pacts served to reintroduce democracy as a system in which the outcome of elections was genuinely uncertain. There was, in other words, a real chance of the minority party becoming the majority in a future election.

In South Africa, by contrast, the huge disparities in wealth and income – largely along racial lines – would make it extremely difficult for a minority that ceded power ever to recover a significant share of it. Hence the need for pluralism, for checks and balances, or indeed for the minority veto, which Slabbert had supported back in 1979. In 1998, two years after the South African Constitution was adopted, Northern Ireland reached a settlement along quite different lines. The Good Friday agreement, which transferred legislative and executive authority to an elected Assembly, accepted the single transferable variant of proportional representation, which increases voters' choice (they can vote for up to six candidates in a constituency). In the Assembly all members must designate themselves in the first session as Unionist, Nationalist or Other. Key decisions can only be taken by cross-community support.

With polls indicating from the mid-1980s that the ANC would attract well over 60% support in an election, there was a real likelihood that democracy in the deeply divided South Africa could turn into a liberal veneer for racial domination. Pierre van den Berghe warned that majority rule had been the 'great moral alibi of Black Nationalism' in Africa. If a party can mobolise the largest racial or ethnic group in the electorate it can disguise its racism as democracy. A system where most of the leaders and representatives are supported on the basis of their race is radically different from a genuine democracy where voters are swayed by beliefs and interests.'[92]

---

92   Pierre van den Berghe, 'Introduction' to Pierre van den Berghe (ed.), *The Liberal Dilemma in South Africa* (London: Croom Helm, 1979), p. 7.

Slabbert showed little interest in such warnings and appeared to think a sound constitution and entrenched human rights would act as a buttress against the abuse of power. In a polemic with Slabbert, Lawrence Schlemmer argued that South Africa needed a constitution preventing simple majority rule to hold the ANC in check. Was it not better, Schlemmer asked, to work for a settlement in which all groups would enjoy security and in which whites did not have to 'write off their history'?[93] Slabbert replied that liberals who remained neutral in the white-black conflict and pinned their hopes on incremental change were fooling themselves. Implicitly, he rejected any alternative to ordinary majority rule within a constitution that safeguarded individual rights. He recognised the dangers of the ANC coming to power, but undertook to join the new struggle if the liberation movement became a tyranny.[94]

In October 1988 Slabbert led an Idasa team to a conference in Leverkusen, Germany, to debate the country's future economic policy with an ANC delegation that included SACP leader Joe Slovo. A delegation from the Soviet Union also participated. Russian academic Gleb Starushenko argued that a prerequisite for a settlement was a guarantee to whites that there would be no nationalisation of private property. He also proposed a minority veto in one of the legislative chambers where the four racial communities had to be equally represented. Slovo rejected this out of hand, on the grounds that whites would use a minority veto to keep their control over the means of production.[95]

The talks that Slabbert initiated using the Idasa forum performed a valuable service in helping the public accept that negotiation with the ANC was unavoidable. Yet at all the conferences, starting with Dakar, few people challenged the ANC's assumption that once in power it was entitled to rule without any checks except those provided for in the constitution. If the American 'founding father' James Madison was correct in describing a constitution as a mere 'parchment barrier', there was a huge risk attached to entrusting the ANC with the power that a landslide victory at the polls would deliver. The Idasa conferences amounted to a major public relations coup for the ANC. Putting their political differences aside and keeping their agenda hidden, the ANC leaders handled the groups from South Africa with great skill.

By 1989, isolating the NP government – which had long been the ANC's plan – suddenly seemed an attainable objective. In that year an Idasa conference of Afrikaans writers and an ANC delegation, chaired by Slabbert, even supported the ANC's call

93 Lawrence Schlemmer, 'Politieke keuses', *Die Suid-Afrikaan*, October 1988, pp. 20-22.

94 Van Zyl Slabbert, 'Hoe ry die boere sit-sit so', *Die Suid-Afrikaan*, October 1988, p. 24.

95 Hermann Giliomee, 'Die kommuniste by die ANC', *Die Suid-Afrikaan,* February 1989, pp. 6-11. This was based on an interview with Joe Slovo in Leverkusen.

for a cultural boycott. The climate had changed so much that some commentators cavalierly dismissed the NP government's call for minority rights as an obscene attempt to cling to the perks of office. At work was what British political theorist Bernard Crick in a different context called a combination of 'noble hopes and fatuous credulity'.

Where did Slabbert stand on all of this? He was well aware of the pitfalls of a negotiated settlement between a semi-revolutionary party and the representatives of a discredited political system. He also worried about the conflicting messages the ANC sent out, but he trusted that Mbeki's view would prevail. What animated him most was not so much his admiration for the ANC's commitment to its cause and his initial high opinion of Mbeki, but his outright rejection of the arrogance with which the NP leadership projected the party as the only organisation that could hold the country together. He considered PW Botha a blundering bully on some occasions, but was even more critical of FW de Klerk, someone who was intellectually on a par with him. He often recounted to me how De Klerk with the slightest of smiles would rise to his feet in parliament after a Slabbert speech, dismiss his analysis, and go on to present apartheid, with all its defects, as the best policy option for the country. The memory continued to rankle.

Slabbert cut off

After De Klerk's speech of 2 February 1990 Slabbert became a highly sought-after commentator on the process of negotiations. Maintaining an independent position, he carefully outlined the obstacles to a settlement and did not hesitate to criticise any major partner if it played a spoiling role or made unreasonable demands. He criticised the ANC demand for prompt transfer of power and showed understanding for De Klerk's role, which he described as that of 'participant referee' who had to retain the trust of the security forces while insisting that he remained politically impartial.[96]

Slabbert yearned for a political role, but soon discovered that neither the ANC nor the government had a meaningful role for him once negotiations started in all seriousness early in 1992. De Klerk made a clumsy effort to appoint him to the position of chairman of the board of the South African Broadcasting Corporation, but because Slabbert was not approached beforehand he turned the offer down. At the request of Danie Hough, administrator of the Transvaal, he became chairman of the Central Witwatersrand Metropolitan Chamber. It was tasked with multiple issues, including establishing a common tax base, ending the rent and service charge boycotts, and negotiating a new structure for an integrated metropolitan authority. Slabbert laboured conscientiously, serving as chairman for two and a half years.

Once the ban on the ANC was lifted, Slabbert helped set up Mbeki and his wife

---

96   O'Malley Archives, Interview with Van Zyl Slabbert, 18 August 1992.

in a Johannesburg penthouse, but he did not hear from him again for nearly three years. In 1993 Slabbert ran into him at Aziz Pahad's wedding. 'Van, where have you been?' Mbeki asked his old friend. Impatient to be invited to participate in the projects of the government-in-waiting, Slabbert replied. 'You are the busy one; all you need to do is pick up the phone.' The next day Slabbert went to Mbeki's new residence in Riviera. He told Mbeki: 'I am not asking for any rewards, but I am available. Use me.' Mbeki responded: 'If you were in my position, what would you do?' Slabbert replied: 'I would appoint a number of committees of experts in key areas to tell me how much I have to learn and how stupid I am.' Slabbert wrote later: 'This must have offended him. [It] was the end of our comfortable relationship. He is the only person I know who has demonstrated to me that my friendship was expendable.'[97]

Perhaps Mbeki simply asked Slabbert to realise that it would be very difficult for him, with his power base still weak, to take on board a very intelligent white politician who was not an ANC member. Another possibility is that Mbeki understood Slabbert to be saying he could not expect to govern effectively without leaning on a coterie of white experts.[98] Yet another hypothesis is that of Cyril Ramaphosa. He remarked that in contrast to the self-confident Nelson Mandela, who did not mind surrounding himself with clever advisers, Mbeki 'needed to be the brightest in the room'. He expressed the wish that Mbeki had been bold enough to draw on advice from diverse sources and not just people with the same views.[99]

It is unlikely that Mbeki ever envisaged a role for Slabbert after the ANC had won power. Slabbert was a highly intelligent, talented person with a gene for leadership. Mbeki had no desire to involve Slabbert in a free-for-all discussion on ANC policy and be outshone by his logic and reasoning. To grasp this point, imagine Mbeki trying to explain his HIV/Aids denialism or his support for Robert Mugabe with Slabbert sitting in on the discussion. While Mbeki knew precisely what he was doing in excluding Slabbert, it was Slabbert who was unrealistic about the possibilities of the ANC drawing him in. In his non-racial idealism Slabbert overlooked the ANC's exclusive nature. Just like the NP in virtually its entire history, the ANC had no room for independent outsiders.

Mbeki above all wanted the ANC to prove that blacks could successfully govern the most advanced economy in Africa. The role of whites was essentially that of contributing their skills, paying their taxes and keeping quiet. Slabbert, on the other hand, was much more aware than Mbeki of the immense difficulties the ANC would encounter in running the country and stimulating the economy.

---

97   Slabbert, *The Other Side of History*, p. 57.

98   Joseph Lelyveld, 'How Mbeki Failed', *New York Review of Books*, 9 April 2009, p. 27.

99   Alec Russell, *After Mandela: The Battle for the Soul of South Africa* (London: Hutchinson, 2009), p. 20.

In the negotiations for a new constitution Slabbert played no role. He was, in the words of ex-editor Ken Owen, 'the man who was not there'. There is no reason to believe Slabbert would have had any quarrel with the political part of the Interim Constitution agreed to by the end of 1993. It was not very different from the PFP policy of the 1980s, which he introduced after tacitly discarding the idea of power sharing. In all probability he would not have spoken up against the weak form of power sharing that the Interim Constitution represented.

Disillusionment

Slabbert's disillusionment with Mbeki and the ANC in general did not start immediately after the 1994 election. In a 1997 book he still gave the ANC the benefit of the doubt on the question of whether the new system could be described as a liberal democracy. He wrote: 'The general trend [for government] is more to observe liberal democratic principles than to subvert them.' He was clearly irritated by those engaged in 'abstract democratic model-building' that was 'unreflective of South African realities'.[100] He was, however, worried that the party bosses exerted too much control over the candidate lists in the system of proportional representation used in the elections of 1994 and 1999.

Because the Electoral Act under which these elections were held was not valid beyond 1999, the cabinet, responding to a proposal by Minister of Home Affairs Mangosuthu Buthelezi, appointed an Electoral Task Team (ETT) under Slabbert's chairmanship to review the system and propose an alternative if needed. The ETT was widely representative of civil society. It concluded that while the proportional representation list system used in 1994 and 1999 provided for fair representation and simplicity of voting, it was deficient in providing accountability – the most important element. Slabbert's team proposed a combination of constituency representation and proportional representation, as is the case in German elections. The commission drafted a bill and attached it to an extensive report. Some of the attachments were quite critical of the existing electoral system and presented arguments for an alternative.

When Buthelezi brought the report to cabinet an extraordinary thing happened. At the proposal of Minister Kader Asmal, the report was effectively censored. Although thousands of copies had been printed and bound, the cabinet instructed Buthelezi to have the report withdrawn and then to reprint it, omitting the attachments. As Buthelezi wrote: 'The government did the opposite of what the Van Zyl Slabbert Commission proposed: it left the voter disempowered.' The government stuck to the existing system, relying entirely on the party leadership to choose

---

100 Heribert Adam, Frederik van Zyl Slabbert and Kogila Moodley, *Comrades in Business: Post-Liberation Politics in South Africa* (Cape Town: Tafelberg, 1997), pp. 83, 86.

candidates and hold them accountable. Voters were effectively empowered for a fleeting moment every five years and immediately disempowered for the following five years.[101]

President Mbeki had made Slabbert wait for a year for his letter of appointment. While the ETT was at work, Slabbert received many hints that the ANC considered the exercise a waste of time and that party leaders had no intention of changing a system that suited them so well. Slabbert wrote afterwards: 'In all my years as a factotum/facilitator I have never felt so used, abused and insulted.'[102]

Asked just before Slabbert's death on 14 May 2010 why he spurned Slabbert's services, Mbeki replied that he was baffled by rumours of Slabbert's alleged antagonism towards him. 'The honest truth is that I do not have the slightest idea why Van Zyl had developed this attitude ... Why did he not tell me, and perhaps Mandela, what he would have liked to have done, within government, to serve the postapartheid order?'[103] This comes across as feigned innocence and a determination to play the role of devious seducer to the end.

'Looking for a saviour'

Before the 1999 election Slabbert briefly considered the idea of a political comeback and asked RW Johnson to investigate his options. Johnson told him he had no hope of attracting much support if he founded his own party. If he were to stand as Democratic Party (DP) candidate for the office of premier of the Western Cape, the support would be no more than 25%. A situation might arise where he would have to choose between throwing in his lot with the ANC or the NP.[104]

Meeting with DP leader Tony Leon, Slabbert emphasised that in the event of a hung parliament, he would insist that the DP in the Western Cape align itself with the ANC, not the NP. Leon notes: 'His loathing for the NP was still evident. I told him it would be a deal-breaker: our voters would never accept such a proposition.' Slabbert's demand was incompatible with the DP election call to 'fight back'.[105] After the election, with Mbeki now president, Slabbert hinted in a newspaper article that he had voted ANC. But the call, with perhaps an offer for a cabinet post, never came.

Slabbert knew he was charting a dangerous political course by aligning himself

101 Mangosuthu Buthelezi, 'How the Old ANC Scuppered Electoral Reform', www.politicsweb.co.za, first posted 7 March 2009.

102 Slabbert, *The Other Side of History*, p. 105.

103 Heribert Adam and Kogila Moodley, 'Slabbert's Opening of the Apartheid Mind', Le Maitre and Savage, *The Passion for Reason*, pp. 65-68.

104 Johnson, 'Van Zyl Slabbert: What Went Wrong?'

105 Tony Leon, *On the Contrary: Leading the Opposition in a Democratic South Africa* (Johannesburg: Jonathan Ball, 2008), p. 603.

so closely to Mbeki and the ANC in general. Asked by an interviewer in 1994 if he had been a 'useful idiot', as PW Botha called him after the Dakar conference, he replied with characteristic frankness: 'No question about it. I was a useful idiot.'[106] In his book *Tough Choices*, published in 2000, he recognised that he 'was not really perceived [by the ANC in exile] as being part of the struggle'. ANC members had left him in little doubt that 'if they could not make me a part of [their struggle] I should be neutralised'. Mocking himself, Slabbert observed: 'But a lot of water still had to flow under the bridge before this insight crystallized.'[107]

He went on: 'With hindsight one realises how infinitely more accomplished they [the ANC leaders] were as politicians; to what extent it was part of their daily existence to charm a variety of people over the world and to make them a part of the struggle. In a certain sense we were putty in their hands.' Yet the question is still: why did Slabbert risk so much by getting into bed with the ANC? His friend Breyten Breytenbach answered the question gently: 'He was too trusting of the ANC. He did not realise the ANC is neither about building a new nation nor about reconstruction and development, but about divvying up the spoils of victory.'[108]

Irina Filatova expressed tougher criticism of Slabbert. As head of the African Studies Department at Moscow State University in the late 1980s to the early 1990s, she often met ANC cadres visiting Moscow. She says it was impossible to overlook the authoritarian tendencies within the ANC leadership. 'From the way they treated the opposition both within their own ranks and outside them, and from the way the ANC tried [during the 1980s] to establish its complete control over certain areas of the country, it was obvious that these tendencies were there, and that they were not going to go away after the ANC had come to power. If anything, such tendencies might even become stronger.'

Filatova felt Slabbert should have grasped earlier that the ANC's intolerant 'democratic centralism' was in the DNA of all African nationalist movements. She added: 'I was amazed at the naivety of the attitudes of so many South Africans, particularly liberal whites, in that period, who expected liberal tolerance and benevolence from the ANC. To be frank, it was only partly because they had not seen the ANC in exile and did not know it. People seemed to look for a saviour, a heroic figure to die for, to lead them out of this vale of tears.'[109]

A shrewd Africanist pointed out: 'No African liberation movement ever successfully turned into a political party.' Casting itself as the representative of the entire

106 Interview with Van Zyl Slabbert by Patti Waldmeir, 11 November 1994.
107 Slabbert, *Tough Choices*, p. 103.
108 LeMaitre and Savage, *The Passion for Reason*, p. 14.
109 E-mail communication from Irina Filatova, 29 May 2009.

oppressed people, it presided over an increasingly undemocratic system once it assumed power.[110]

A last book

In 2006, four years before his death, Slabbert published a final book, *The Other Side of History*, which attacks some of the myths about the transition. More importantly, it briefly analyses where his scheme went wrong. He wrote that his idea had been to help Mbeki build a non-racial liberal democracy functioning under a constitution that 'does not celebrate majoritarianism, but [constrains] the use and abuse of power. That is why the separation of powers, rule of law and respect for human rights form such a distinctive part of liberal democracy.'[111] Slabbert now admitted that the ANC's 'non-racialism' was mainly a façade. He had 'more than a sneaking suspicion that Africanism *in an exclusive sense* is fast becoming the new dominant ideology'.[112] He also expressed serious concerns about the new order. He recognised that liberation movements tend to have a deep distaste for any constraint on their use, or even abuse, of power.

This meant, Slabbert continued, that one had to be on the lookout for how key constraining institutions were coopted, or how the executive ignored the legislature or other organs of government. He noted that serious tensions had developed between the demands of a liberal democracy and the tendency of the ruling party to establish democratic centralism, in which the ruling party controls virtually everything. It was, he remarked pointedly, a practice 'made famous by the government of the USSR'.

Finally, Slabbert pointed to the tension between those pursuing market-oriented growth and those in pursuit of a National Democratic Revolution, who called for nationalisation. But reaching for the impossible to the last, he concluded: 'Out of the current confusion, something extraordinarily creative may yet emerge.' He was 'not without hope for the future'.[113] By 1994 both the NP and the ANC had come to regard Dakar as an insignificant milestone in South Africa's journey to an inclusive democracy. Slabbert now found himself, as he put it, on the 'other side of history'. History, as the ANC wrote it, had indeed passed him by.

But he did become a symbol in a way he did not expect. A new generation of Afrikaners respected him as one of the first Afrikaner intellectuals to renounce apartheid unequivocally. Slabbert was comfortable in his skin as an Afrikaner. He actively

---

110 Marina Ottaway, *South Africa: The Struggle for a New Order* (Washington: Brookings Institution, 1993), p. 44.
111 Slabbert, *The Other Side of History*, p. 163.
112 Slabbert, *The Other Side of History*, p. 12.
113 Slabbert, *The Other Side of History*, pp. 163-65.

guided and supported Aardklop, an Afrikaans cultural festival in Potchefstroom, and spoke up for retaining Afrikaans as the main medium of instruction at the University of Stellenbosch. He was the first to dare to take a large group of Afrikaners to speak to the ANC in exile. The government did not consider it helpful, but as a symbolic act it gave hope to millions of South Africans who laboured under the yoke of apartheid.

As a politician there were in fact two Slabberts. One is an icon in the mould of John F Kennedy. The similarities are striking: the charm and charisma, the warmth, the self-deprecating humour, the intelligence and the ambition. Throughout Slabbert's life there was an element of impetuousness – almost a recklessness – that was epitomised by his dramatic act in 1986 of sacrificing his entire political base in the hope of returning to politics in the new system for which he was prepared to stake all.

The other Slabbert is the sombre, even sad figure of his final years. He saw the end of apartheid, for which he had worked, and knocked at the door of the new dispensation to help build the new order. But the ANC did not invite him in.

Chapter 9

'The Risk of Not Taking Risks':
Ending Empire

IN A FAMOUS BBC DEBATE WITH DUTCH HISTORIAN PIETER GEYL IN 1948,
Arnold Toynbee – who traced the rise and fall of more than twenty civilisations –
spoke of two 'formidable facts'. First, almost all civilisations the world had known ultimately collapsed. Second, trends could be detected, and also symptoms signifying
impending breakdown.[1] According to Toynbee, Western civilisation was heading
towards breakdown. He pointed out that once a civilisation reached its zenith, its
masters invariably believed history had come to an end. Little more than 40 years
later, an American scholar would duly produce a study based on the premise that
capitalist-liberal democracy, a system that originated in the West, indeed constituted
the end of the historical process.[2]

Unlike Oswald Spengler, whose famous book *The Decline of the West* predicted
the inevitable decline of all civilisations, Toynbee believed civilisations could go on
indefinitely. Their demise was due to human shortcomings such as complacency
and failure to recognise the burning resentment of the oppressed. But all too often,
he noted, the 'wrestlers with destiny' looked to scapegoats to account for their
inadequacies. In the aftermath of the Second World War, communism and capitalism performed this function for one another. But in Toynbee's view the real cause was
invariably either 'war' or 'class', or a combination of the two. (Toynbee subsumed
race and caste under the term 'class'.[3])

Geyl summed up Toynbee's view on the final phases of a civilisation's decline: 'It
enters on a period of disintegration, which even the most active, most original, most
courageous of its members are powerless to stop. The creative personality, or the
creative minority, can now do no more than fight rearguard actions and put off the
end without preventing the final catastrophe. Such a minority often turns despotic,
consumed by nationalism and militarism and increasingly loses its ability to rule.'[4]

---

1   P Geyl and A Toynbee, *Can We Know the Pattern of the Past?* (Bussum: FG Kroonder, 1958), p. 21.
    Historians rightly dismiss the notion that laws can be formulated about the rise and decline of civili-
    sations, but do take comparative observations seriously, if well grounded. There is another caveat:
    South Africa was never a 'civilisation'. Its white population was an offshoot of what constituted
    Western civilisation.
2   Francis Fukuyama, *The End of History and the Last Man* (New York: The Free Press, 1992).
3   Arnold Toynbee, *Civilisation on Trial* (Oxford: Oxford University Press, 1950), p. 23.
4   Geyl and Toynbee, *Can We Know the Pattern of the Past?*, pp. 7-8.

In European colonies settled in the second half of the second millennium, the settlers invariably tried to establish a white-dominated offshoot of their own civilisation. In colonies founded by the Portuguese and the Spanish, colonial rulers allowed the elite from among the oppressed into the ranks of the dominant group. Because there was no formal colour barrier, the end of colonial rule did not spell the end of domination by those of European descent.

In the colonies founded by the Dutch and the British, however, history took a different course. The colour bar that existed by the end of colonial rule was impermeable. When the subjugated population finally launched its assault against the colonial rulers, the latter could draw on no or few dependable allies from across the colour line. In South Africa most whites had no intention of returning to Europe, but they had left the task of getting black allies in government far too late. The government was quite unprepared when, in the late 1980s, both its erstwhile Western allies and the black opposition jointly demanded majority rule.

An elusive solution

In the 1970s the South African government admitted black trade unions into the statutory industrial relations framework. It wanted all workers to participate in a statutory system of dispute resolution in bargaining for wages. At the same time, it kept social spending on white people constant, narrowing the racial gap. Much-improved primary health care contributed to rapid black population growth, a sharp decline in the rate of infant mortality, and a substantial increase in black life expectancy. But it was unable to offer a political solution attractive to the black elite.

By the end of the 1980s the NP government no longer projected a tough and uncompromising image in defending its rule. Ton Vosloo, former newspaper editor and later managing director of Nasionale Pers, believed the will of the NP leadership had been sapped by endless squabbles within the party about 'reform' and unremitting world condemnation of apartheid. After the NP split of 1982, the party lost substantial Afrikaner support and, while it won considerable English backing, it was no longer the determined upholder of white self-determination. Vosloo noted: 'Under FW de Klerk the party no longer had any kick left in it. This explains its poor performance in the negotiations. Governing for too long and retreating into a laager where whites felt safe contributed greatly to the implosion of white rule. The emperor turned out to be a streaker.'[5]

'More embittered against us'

In September 1984 an uprising in some black townships in the south-eastern Transvaal signalled the start of a determined assault against white rule. Compared to the

---

5   E-mail communication from Ton Vosloo, 12 April 2007.

uprisings of 1960 and 1976–77, the township revolt of 1984–86 was much better directed. By the mid-1980s the ANC in exile, based in Lusaka, had established itself as the premier challenger of the apartheid state. The SA Communist Party led by Joe Slovo dominated the movement's strategic thinking and planning. In 1979 an ANC delegation had visited Vietnam to study the tactics the Vietcong had employed in the war against the forces of the US and the government of South Vietnam. It returned convinced of the appropriateness of a 'people's war' in the townships. In 1985 ANC leader Oliver Tambo issued a call from Lusaka to make South Africa 'ungovernable'.[6]

'People's war' combined high-profile armed attacks by trained units with mass campaigns of civil disobedience. Inside the country the United Democratic Front (UDF) was a large, amorphous body made up of a multitude of organisations. The state found it difficult to suppress, although it acted as the ANC's barely veiled surrogate. The unions had become well organised and militant. In the early 1970s only about 3% of the black workforce were members of trade unions. By 1988 at least a third had become organised. Strike action intensified, often dovetailing with political demonstrations. In 1987 more than 5.6 million workdays were lost as a result of strikes.[7]

Although the UDF leadership maintained their actions were spontaneous or provoked by harsh police action, new studies – particularly Anthea Jeffery's groundbreaking *People's War* – focus on the organised nature of the revolt and the ANC's considerable part in stewarding it. Slovo scoffed at suggestions that the ANC did not play a major role in the urban uprising that started in 1984. In a 1994 interview he said: 'Every major campaign, including the defiance campaign [which had started in 1987] came from Lusaka . . . Virtually every campaign emanated from the outside and not from inside – the strategic sort of concept of it. The UDF and so on were vitally important actors inside, but the strategic initiatives came from the leadership of the ANC.'

This did not mean, he said, that the ANC sat in Lusaka and decided there should be a demonstration in Khayelitsha on a particular day. But Lusaka gave 'the right lead at the right time' and put resources at activists' disposal. He added: 'A lot of initiative is taken by people on the ground, that's what always happens. So, what sometimes seems to be a spontaneous response is not really spontaneous in the absolute sense of the term.'[8]

Cyril Ramaphosa was forthright in characterising the power relationship between the external and the internal ANC. 'We would go for briefings to Lusaka and we

6   Anthea Jeffery, *People's War* (Johannesburg: Jonathan Ball, 2010), pp. 25-40.
7   David Welsh, *Whither South Africa?* (Port Elizabeth: University of Port Elizabeth, 1988), p. 4.
8   Interview with Joe Slovo by Patti Waldmeir, 14 November 1994.

would brief them on the situation ... and the National Executive Committee would discuss the matter and decide this was a new campaign that had to be launched. We knew that we were executing an important task ... but we always felt that we wanted to execute that task within the policy guidelines and parameters set out by the movement outside.'[9]

The ANC turned against Mangosuthu Buthelezi and his Inkatha Freedom Party after he refused to submit to the ANC leadership and support the armed struggle (see pp. 166-67). In parts of the country, particularly in rural Natal, a low-level, intra-black civil war raged from the early 1980s to the mid-1990s. But the ANC's fight was not only against Inkatha. Its goal was to be seen as the sole movement in charge of the liberation struggle. After the Black Consciousness Movement announced a plan in 1982 to form an umbrella organisation, the ANC urged its activists to block any such action.[10]

Those detained at times of urban protests or rebellions refused to be cowed, as they had been in the past. Instead, they became more determined to fight apartheid. After speaking to a number of detainees during the state of emergency of the late 1980s, Leon Wessels, deputy minister of law and order, told President Botha how strongly politicised the detainees had become. Botha replied: 'We have achieved nothing with the detentions. We have only made them more embittered against us.'[11] The empire was crumbling fast.

PW Botha tried to adapt apartheid, but kept a wary eye on his constituency. Soon after he came to power he said that while he considered mixed marriages socially undesirable, he could find no biblical injunction against them. Intending to abolish these laws as soon as possible, he asked the churches for advice. White Afrikaans churches, including the largest, the Dutch Reformed Church (DRC), were hopelessly divided on the issue. A spokesman for the white DRC Moderature told the president the church would not ask him to repeal the laws. But the coloured, black and Indian 'daughter churches' of the DRC family reacted with anger to the response of the 'mother' church (the white DRC).[12] In 1985 the government went ahead and abolished the laws banning 'mixed' marriages and sex across the colour bar.

Influx control was vital to maintain the fiction of a white state. From the beginning of the apartheid period the government had tried to argue that influx control did not discriminate against black people, but regulated the movements of migrants

---

9   Interview with Cyril Ramaphosa by Patti Waldmeir, 19 January 1995.

10   Jeremy Seekings, *A History of the United Democratic Front in South Africa, 1983-1991* (Cape Town: David Philip, 2000), pp. 44-45.

11   Interview with Leon Wessels, 8 June 1992; Leon Wessels, *Die einde van 'n era: Bevryding van 'n Afrikaner* (Cape Town: Tafelberg, 1994), p. 59.

12   T Dunbar Moodie, 'Confessing to Remorse About the Evils of Apartheid: The DRC in the 1980s', unpublished paper, 2011.

from the homelands, as with *Gastarbeiter* in Europe. In 1981 the state deported Xhosa residents from informal settlements in Cape Town under the laws covering aliens. Funds supplied to the homelands were classified as 'foreign aid'. Apartheid had entered its final, surrealistic phase.

In 1981 Piet Koornhof, minister of cooperation and development (the old Department of Native Affairs), spelled out the policy's political arithmetic: 7.8 million blacks were citizens of an 'independent country', and a further 5.6 million blacks were tied to homelands that wanted to become independent. According to Koornhof, the only homelands that refused to accept independence were KwaZulu and another homeland that was quite small. The combined population of these two homelands was 6.25 million, fewer than the combined 7.8 million whites, coloureds, and Indians living in the common area. Koornhof's startling conclusion was that 'with so many black people independent, it will be useless for South Africa's enemies to continue pleading for one man one vote'.[13]

The government was still toying with the idea of putting 'a roof over apartheid'. By this it meant an overarching structure that would accommodate both the homelands and the white state in a 'constellation' or 'commonwealth'. President Kenneth Kaunda of Zambia, who remained the most valued interlocutor between South Africa and its neighbouring states, told Botha: 'The constellation idea will not work with apartheid.'

Kaunda urged Botha to start meaningful dialogue with 'genuine leaders' such as Nelson Mandela, Oliver Tambo and Walter Sisulu. If South Africa did not capture the moment, there would be 'an upheaval in South Africa [that] will be catastrophic for all in Southern Africa.' Playing for time, Botha replied that because of Mandela's 'relationship with the Transkei' he first wanted to discuss the issue with the Transkei government, and Nelson Mandela's stand on the question of violence would also have to be considered.[14]

The government persevered with its homeland policy. In 1983 the state spent approximately 9% of its budget on the homelands. Of this, 60% could be considered regular expenditure channelled into education, health and infrastructure. This expenditure met apartheid's political and ideological objectives at a cost the government did not consider prohibitive.

A dismal end

Features of the homelands policy became increasingly weird. KwaNdebele, proclaimed a homeland in 1971, was nothing more than an extended dormitory town for workers commuting to Pretoria. Yet it received self-governing status in 1981.

---

13 Robert Schrire, *Adapt or Die: The End of White Politics in South Africa* (London: Hurst, 1991), p. 52.
14 Brand Fourie, *Brandpunte* (Cape Town: Tafelberg, 1991), pp. 69-71.

Bizarrely, Chief Minister SS Skosana pushed for independence in 1984, triggering strong resistance from civil servants, traditional leaders and most of the elected politicians in the homeland. Acting under instructions of the chief minister and his close associate Piet Ntuli, a small group of vigilantes terrorised dissidents. Some were assassinated, others disappeared or were flogged. KwaNdebele exhibited the most grotesque face of the homelands policy. One study noted: 'Its independence would have no significance beyond what it meant in benefits to a small, isolated coterie of politicians and white advisors.'[15]

The Botha government tried to keep its homelands policy alive through multi-plying bureaucratic structures on the second level of government. On 11 November 1982 Pretoria and the independent homelands signed an agreement establishing a secretariat, a council of ministers and working groups covering finance, economics and a range of other areas. It established regional committees linking the various independent homelands to adjoining regions to deal with matters of common concern.

Some government supporters tried to argue that political power would increasingly be 'decentralised and shared' in these committees. But the government itself declared that the initiative did not entail any sharing of power or revenue. The regional committees were only advisory. As Chris Heunis phrased it: 'Such bodies will serve as a channel through which the development needs and potential of a region can be made known to the national planning and implementation organizations ... It is, however, of cardinal importance that the political and fiscal sovereignty of the various states will not be diminished in this way. The advisory committees will have no negotiating or decision-making powers.'[16]

By the late 1980s the homelands had become a bureaucratic nightmare. Profligate spending, corruption and huge budget deficits were the order of the day. Since the homelands were nominally independent, the central government's ability to intervene was limited. The Transkei government employed 800 people in its Department of Foreign Affairs, more than the entire staff complement of the South African Department of Foreign Affairs.[17] Derek Keys, the last minister of finance of the NP government, said of the homelands policy: 'It was a failed system. The homeland elites raked off the system. There was a huge salary bill, but very little service

15 Brian Pottinger, *The Imperial Presidency: PW Botha – The First Ten Years* (Johannesburg: Southern Books, 1988), p. 268.

16 Hermann Giliomee, 'The Changing Political Functions of the Homelands', Hermann Giliomee and Lawrence Schlemmer (eds), *Up Against the Fences: Poverty, Passes and Privilege in South Africa* (Cape Town: David Philip, 1985), p. 54.

17 Interview with Pik Botha by Patti Waldmeir, 18 January 1995; Interview with Pik Botha, 14 August 2011.

delivery or tax returns. The national government got very little from these centres of administration.'[18]

The Department of Constitutional Development and Planning under Chris Heunis began dismantling the old 'native affairs empire' that controlled virtually every aspect of black people's daily lives. With the abolition of influx control on 1 July 1986, one of the most important functions of the department fell away. Blacks were no longer to be 'administered' by a separate department and black local government would no longer exist in an administrative limbo. Accordingly, the Administration Boards (see p. 111) were abolished and their functions transferred to the provinces. In the place of the four 'white' provincial councils came an administrator and an executive committee drawn from all the racial communities and appointed by the president. Regional Services Councils were introduced in the cities to provide an overarching structure for the racially segregated local authorities and to redistribute resources to the disadvantaged townships.

The tricameral parliament gave representation to the three 'minorities': the white, coloured and Indian communities. It did away with a whites-only parliament, but duplication or triplication of functions occurred in the 'own affairs' bureaucracies and homelands administrations. There were now 13 legislative assemblies apart from parliament, with a total of 1 270 members, 121 of whom were ministers of government. In total there were 151 government departments, including 18 departments of health and 14 departments of education. At the apex stood 11 presidents, chief ministers or prime ministers.[19] Apartheid in its final phase was an administrative morass.

Ideological collapse

In the course of the 1980s the ideological underpinnings of apartheid collapsed. The predominantly white DRC finally broke with apartheid at its 1986 and 1990 synods. In 1986 it declared the church was open to anyone regardless of colour. It formally decided to base its racial policy on the New Testament, reminding its members that race played no part whatsoever in this part of scripture. The synod admitted that the church had erred in biblically justifying forced separation and not pointing out this error much earlier.[20]

In 1986 the Afrikaner Broederbond sent a memorandum entitled 'Basiese staatkundige voorwaardes vir die voortbestaan van die Afrikaner' (Basic political con-

---

18 Interview with Derek Keys, 17 October 2010.

19 Michael Savage, *The Cost of Apartheid* (Cape Town: University of Cape Town inaugural lectures, 1988), p. 8.

20 Nederduits Gereformeerde Kerk, *Kerk en samelewing* (October 1986), especially pp. 16, 19, 52-57; *Church and Society* (Pretoria: General Synodical Committee, 1990), paragraphs 280-85; Willie Jonker, *Selfs die kerk kan verander* (Cape Town: Tafelberg, 1998).

ditions for the survival of the Afrikaner) to its divisions for comment. The document argued the very opposite of long-held core beliefs. It now defined the *exclusion* of blacks at the highest level of decision-making as a threat to the survival of whites. Blacks had to be represented and the head of the government might not necessarily be white. Executive Council chairman Pieter de Lange acknowledged that these steps entailed 'calculated risks', but stated: 'The greatest risk we currently run is not to take any risks. Our will to survive as Afrikaners and our energy and faith are the strongest guarantee [of our survival].'[21]

But the idea of a negotiated settlement had not yet gained ascendancy. Rejecting Afrikaner abdication, the document proposed mechanisms such as group vetoes that would hold classic majority rule in check. It also supported the division into 'own' and 'general' affairs based on the key apartheid measure, the Population Registration Act. (The idea of an additional group, based on voluntary identification, had just begun to gain ground.)[22]

Afrikaner business leaders concluded that the costs of apartheid had become far too steep. Anton Rupert strongly criticised the government's economic mismanagement. Since the early 1970s central government expenditure had doubled every five years in current prices and inflation was at its highest rate since the 1920s. Low economic growth led to spiralling unemployment. For several years there had been no net increase in black employment.[23] He warned: 'The biggest source of unrest is unemployment . . . It is a fertile ground for intimidation and subversion.'[24]

But what should come in apartheid's place? In the West, widespread pessimism about the prospects for democracy and broad-based prosperity in Africa had gathered pace since the early 1970s. This mood was encapsulated in the 13 May 2000 edition of *The Economist* with its cover story 'Africa: The Hopeless Continent'. Africa was falling further and further behind other continents. Its economies lagged, its share of world trade plummeted, investment and savings declined, life expectancy fell and unemployment worsened. In many countries corruption blighted state administration and business. *The Economist* stated: 'At the core of the crisis is the failure of African leaders to provide effective government.'[25]

---

21 Ernst Stals, 'Die geskiedenis van die Afrikaner Broederbond, 1918-1994', unpublished ms. commissioned by the Executive Council of the AB, 1998, p. 647. Donald Horowitz used an English translation in his discussion of the document in *A Democratic South Africa: Constitutional Engineering in a Divided Society* (Cape Town: Oxford University Press, 1991), p. 80.

22 Stals, 'Die geskiedenis van die Afrikaner Broederbond', p. 647; Horowitz, *A Democratic South Africa*, p. 80.

23 Rupert spoke of the preceding nine years, but the actual figure was four years. Personal communication, JL Sadie, 8 December 2001.

24 Rembrandt Corporation Archives, Letter from Anton Rupert to PW Botha, 24 January 1986.

25 Martin Meredith, *The State of Africa: A History of Fifty Years of Independence* (New York: Free Press, 2006), p. 286.

In South Africa the debt standstill after Botha's Rubicon speech compounded sluggish economic growth. Between 1980 and 1986 a fifth of British firms left South Africa and total British direct investment halved. But some perspective is needed. Sanctions alone could not bring the state to its knees. Very often disinvestment led to South African companies acquiring multinational corporations at bargain-basement prices. Trade ties with the West weakened, but those with Asia improved and the overall volume of foreign trade grew. By the end of 1986 the country had a trade surplus of R15 billion. Yet the ban on new foreign loans and investment severely dented business confidence. The hard fact was that South Africa, a developing country, was now in the desperate situation of having become an exporter of capital.[26]

Limits of reform

The public relations disaster of the Rubicon speech on 15 August 1985, followed by the decision of foreign banks to call in loans and terminate borrowing facilities, brought apartheid to a crossroads (see pp. 202-3). In the uprisings of 1960–61 and 1976–77 resistance had focused on aspects of apartheid, especially the pass laws, inferior education, discrimination in wages and salaries, the neglected state of urban townships, and so forth. This time, however, the revolt was directed at the entire apartheid system.

Between 1979 and 1986 the Botha government brought black unions into the industrial relations framework and abolished influx control, removing two of the main pillars of apartheid. Yet Botha received little credit for this. For the ANC and UDF it was impossible to reform apartheid. The 'constellation of states', the tricameral parliament and the narrowing of the gap in education spending were all premised on the maintenance of racial separation. Every 'reform' measure was a painful reminder of the reality of apartheid and the state's classification of its citizens into compulsory groups.[27]

The Botha government's vacillation and inconsistency stoked the fires of revolt. Since the early 1980s hopes had been raised that influx control would be abolished, but in September 1985 PW Botha dashed these hopes, retaining these hated measures – only to announce their abolition the following year. There was a strong expectation that population removals and land consolidation would come to an end, but in September 1985 the government announced new proposals for further consolidation. It rejected attempts by the KwaZulu government and the Natal Provincial Administration to devise a system of joint planning and decision-making that might have grown into an integrated regional government.

---

26   Charles H Feinstein, *An Economic History of South Africa* (Cambridge: Cambridge University Press, 2005), p. 230.

27   Lawrence Schlemmer, 'Just Why DID the Wheels Come Off?', *Sunday Times*, 29 September 1985.

Botha insisted that the four statutory groups entrenched in the Population Registration Act should remain despite reform and that these distinctions were not
discriminatory, but normal and 'natural'.[28] He nevertheless believed that his government was genuinely engaged in eliminating apartheid. For him the problem
lay in 'how to find the money, the expertise and the administrative resources to
remove inequality in practice' while maintaining the statutory groups prescribed
by apartheid.[29]

Botha was all too aware of the white electorate's demands. A 1984 survey found
that upwards of 80% of Afrikaners (and 35% to 45% of English speakers) supported
the key pillars of apartheid: the ban on sex between white and non-white; segregated
residential areas, schools and public amenities; separate voters' rolls for coloureds
and Indians; and homelands for blacks. The ANC and its policies were anathema
to white voters. In polls conducted in 1988–89 only 2% of Afrikaners and 7% of
English speakers preferred the option of a 'unitary state, one Parliament, and one
person, one vote', while only 3% of Afrikaners and 11% of English speakers wanted
'a single mixed Parliament with the majority in control'. Only 1% of Afrikaners and
3% of English speakers wanted Nelson Mandela in power, against 12% and 39%
respectively who preferred Mangosuthu Buthelezi in power.[30]

In stark contrast to all this was the ANC's view. Nelson Mandela would later speak
of an 'ordinary democracy' – a system in which the victorious party rules the country until a new election is held.[31] From the mid-1980s secret government polls showed
the ANC would receive more than 60% of the vote in a free election, while the NP
could rely on only 19% to 23%.[32]

Many better-educated whites had come round to accepting the prospect of blacks
in government, provided it was in a 'multiracial' order that guaranteed their security and property. They wanted a system with a balance between the black majority
and the other racial minorities. Analysts pointed out that their expectations of what
they would need to concede were quite unrealistic.[33]

A hostile world

PW Botha often came across as a quintessential Cold War warrior convinced of the
determined Soviet onslaught on trouble spots in the developing world and South

---

28 Koos van Wyk and Deon Geldenhuys, *Die groepsgebod in PW Botha se politieke oortuigings* (Johan-
    nesburg: Rand Afrikaans University, 1987), pp. 9-29.

29 Schlemmer, 'Just Why DID the Wheels Come Off?'

30 Hermann Giliomee and Lawrence Schlemmer, *From Apartheid to Nation-building* (Cape Town:
    Oxford University Press, 1989), p. 157.

31 SA Institute of Race Relations, *Race Relations Survey, 1984* (Johannesburg: SAIRR, 1985), pp. 360-61.

32 FW de Klerk, *Die laaste trek – 'n Nuwe begin* (Cape Town: Human & Rousseau, 1999), p. 207.

33 Lawrence Schlemmer, 'South Africa's National Party Government', Peter Berger and Bobby Godsell
    (eds), *A Future South Africa* (Cape Town: Tafelberg, 1988), pp. 7-28.

Africa as one of its prime targets. Along with the South African military, he launched an ideological offensive during the 1970s, speaking of a total onslaught requiring a total strategy. Jannie Roux, director-general in the prime minister's office, wrote a memorandum for Botha arguing that a total strategy presupposes something like a totalitarian state. Botha jotted down the comment 'an interesting view' in the margin. His rhetoric did become milder in the course of the 1980s. His intelligence officials even began talking to their Soviet counterparts (see pp. 176-177).[34]

The debacle of South Africa's incursion into Angola in 1975 made it imperative for the state to co-ordinate its intelligence gathering and its analysis of the shifting threats to security. The introduction of the National Intelligence Service in 1979 greatly improved the state's capacity, but it would only be towards the end of the 1980s that the advice of Dr Niel Barnard, the head, and Mike Louw, his second in command, began to gain ascendancy over that of the military. From the late 1970s the military adopted the formal position that there was no military solution to South Africa's problems. The task of the military was to bring about appropriate conditions for a political solution. But military command did not consider the ANC, with its close links to Moscow, part of the solution.

PW Botha considered the Carter administration's term (1976–1980) 'four years of hell'.[35] He was glad when the conservative Ronald Reagan won the presidential election in 1980, but when he first met Herman Nickel, the US ambassador to South Africa, Botha said his experience with Washington had not been encouraging, starting with the Clark Amendment in 1975 blocking aid to Unita. Nickel pointed out that the Reagan administration opposed the drive in the US Congress for increased sanctions against South Africa. Nickel recalls: 'PW Botha shot back: "I don't care which branch of your government does this to us. The effect is the same."'[36]

Soviet policy towards South Africa had become increasingly contradictory and remained an issue of concern. By the end of the 1980s Soviet military support and training was at its highest level ever and the ANC enjoyed full diplomatic privileges. The Soviets even gave assistance to the ANC's Operation Vula – aimed at establishing an ANC network inside South Africa – and this continued even after negotiations began in 1990.[37] At the same time, however, statements by Gorbachev and other high officials gave the impression that Soviet enthusiasm for the ANC's liberation struggle had waned and that they favoured a compromise solution.

---

34   Interview with Jannie Roux, 29 May 2008.
35   Dirk de Villiers and Johanna de Villiers, *PW* (Cape Town: Tafelberg, 1984), p. 322.
36   E-mail correspondence Herman Nickel and Howard Walker, 11 May 2011.
37   Vladimir Shubin, *The ANC: A View from Moscow* (Johannesburg: Jacana, 2008), pp. 259-66.

An Eminent Persons Group

Pik Botha believed South Africa would be at grave risk if the West completely turned its back. He continued to press the president to pursue reform. His first opportunity came two weeks after the Rubicon speech. The European Union (EU) had come under severe pressure from Asian and African countries to step up sanctions to end apartheid, but the EU was not prepared to stop importing South African minerals. To ward off the pressure it sent a delegation of the foreign ministers of Luxembourg, the Netherlands and Italy – the 'Troika' – to South Africa to urge radical reform.

The visit nearly turned into a disaster, with PW Botha losing his temper and shouting at the members of the EU delegation. To avert a crisis, Pik Botha asked Carl von Hirschberg of the Department of Foreign Affairs to draft a statement the visitors could take back. In this statement, dated 30 August 1985, the government committed itself 'to abolishing what the world perceives as apartheid'. It opposed apartheid, if by that was meant racial domination or exclusion, or unequal opportunities or the impairment of human dignity. It was striving towards a system where the different communities took 'co-responsibility on matters of common concern, coupled with protection of minority rights'.[38]

Delighted, Pik Botha wanted to give the document the grand name of the 'Westbrook Manifesto', but it is doubtful that the president attached any great value to it. When he was shown the draft still in Von Hirschberg's longhand, the president just nodded. Von Hirschberg noted: '[PW Botha] did not question a thing. It was weird; he never questioned it or wanted to discuss it; just nodded and gave it back to Pik, who said "Please get this typed"... Eventually a typed copy was given to each [member of the delegation] and they left. What happened in their meetings in Europe I do not know.'[39]

US President Reagan and British Prime Minister Thatcher were the two main bulwarks against the determined efforts to increase South Africa's isolation. In a letter to PW Botha, dated 6 September, Reagan urged initiatives that would bring 'representative black leaders to the table for open-ended talks on the elimination of all racial discrimination and the political participation of all groups'. Leaders in jail or detention had to be allowed to participate.[40]

At a meeting of the Commonwealth in Nassau in October 1985, Thatcher stood virtually alone in opposing a call for comprehensive economic and diplomatic

---

38 'Synopsis of the Main Elements of the South African Government Policy on Constitutional Reform', unpublished memorandum, not paginated.

39 Pieter Wolvaardt et al. (eds), *From Verwoerd to Mandela: South African Diplomats Remember* (no place: Crink, 2011), vol. 3, p. 336.

40 Letter from Ronald Reagan to PW Botha, 6 September 1985, www.aluka.org.

sanctions against South Africa. Afterwards she wrote to PW Botha that she had told the conference the Commonwealth needed to back 'dialogue between the South African government and representatives of the black community in the context of the suspension of violence by all sides'. Reminding Botha it was no small achievement on her part to get the Commonwealth to put its name to the suspension of violence, Thatcher asked him to receive a Commonwealth delegation. Botha appreciated her government's insistence that it would not meet with any ANC leader as long as the organisation would not renounce violence. Yet when Thatcher first mooted the idea of a visit by a Commonwealth group, later known as the Eminent Persons Group (EPG), he rejected this 'interference'. He only backed down after an angry Thatcher reminded him that in a group with representatives from nearly 50 countries she had managed virtually alone to deflect the call for drastic sanctions. Botha reluctantly relented after Thatcher assured him she would make it clear to the EPG that it was not its task to tell the South African government or people how to organise their own affairs.[41]

The EPG visited the country for four weeks during the first half of 1986. Consisting of seven people, it was co-chaired by the affable Olusegun Obasanjo, former head of a military government in Nigeria, and the brash and strident Malcolm Fraser, ex-premier of Australia. President Botha did his best to appear conciliatory, but privately he referred to the group as 'a bunch of old women'.[42]

Undoubtedly forewarned, the EPG did its best not to ignite the president's short fuse when it met with him. The transcript of the group's encounter with the president, in which Obasanjo acted as its main spokesman, gives the impression of the group virtually tiptoeing around the president. Both sides stuck to vague generalities.[43] The group's itinerary also included meetings with Nelson Mandela. As Obasanjo later told an interviewer, Mandela declared himself in favour of a government that 'has been negotiated before the election', by which he probably meant a government of national unity.[44]

Pik Botha saw the visit as an opportunity to achieve a real breakthrough and get down to real talks with the ANC. With both he and Obasanjo contributing input, the EPG developed what it called a 'Possible Negotiating Concept' aimed at clearing obstacles to negotiations. The EPG would take the concept to the ANC and other relevant parties if the Botha government approved. On 12 March the EPG proposed

41 Letters from Margaret Thatcher to PW Botha, 31 October and 17 November 1985, and 8 January 1986; Botha to Thatcher, 12 November 1985, www.aluka.org.
42 Interview with senior official in PW Botha's office, 23 September 2009.
43 Transcript of meeting of President PW Botha with the EPG, May 1986.
44 Interview with Olusegun Obasanjo by Patti Waldmeir, 8 November 1994; Roelof F (Pik) Botha, 'His South African Connection', Hans d'Orville (ed.), *Leadership for Africa: Essays in Honor of Olusegun Obasanjo* (no place or publisher, 1997), pp. 61-65.

the following prerequisites for negotiations: the government had to issue a declaration of intent; there had to be confidence-building measures to demonstrate the government's good faith; political prisoners had to be released; and the government had to spell out the link between their release and the initiation of a political process.

The 'Possible Negotiating Concept' that was finally produced consisted of two parts. The first half proposed that the government commit itself to removing the military from the townships, release Mandela, lift the ban on the ANC and other extra-parliamentary organisations, and free up political activity. It wanted the ANC to suspend its campaign of violence.

The second half contained a postscript based on a memorandum by Pik Botha that indicated how far the government was prepared to go. The 'indications' included a statement by the Botha government that it was not in principle opposed to the release of Mandela or the lifting of the ban on any organisation, and was willing to negotiate with an open agenda. Pik Botha later remarked: 'Eyebrows were lifted on our side, but I explained to my colleagues that I could substantiate each point from statements made by several government members over the past year.'[45]

Pik Botha's efforts to tie the cabinet to statements made by individual ministers in a different context demonstrate his desperation to break the political deadlock. The reality was that there was no consensus in government circles on black political rights, the release of Mandela and other prisoners, the lifting of the ban on the ANC, or making the cessation of violence a prerequisite for negotiations. PW Botha, for one, held a very different view on these issues from that of his foreign minister. Violence was a particularly difficult question. The ANC feared that if it renounced violence, the government would embark on protracted negotiations aimed at preserving as much of its power as possible, leaving the ANC with no or few levers to extract concessions. The government suspected the ANC would resume violence, or threaten to do so, if it did not get its way in negotiations.

Scuppering the EPG

By mid-May 1986 PW Botha had had enough. He had only allowed the EPG's visit to please Mrs Thatcher and had no intention of conceding on the sticking points. He agreed with Obasanjo's assessment that the South African conflict was 'between two nationalisms both wishing the best for the country,'[46] but unlike Obasanjo he did not believe a stable compromise between them was possible. He decided to end the EPG visit in the most emphatic way.

---

45 Botha, 'His South African Connection', p. 66.
46 Botha, 'His South African Connection', p. 64.

During the weekend of 16–18 May 1986 Pik Botha and Obasanjo were trying to reach a compromise position on the issue of violence, which they believed was the only outstanding matter. But the entire mission was terminated on the Sunday night when the South African defence force (SADF) launched commando and air raids on what it termed 'ANC bases' in Harare, Lusaka and Gaborone. Each of these cities was the capital of a member state of the Commonwealth, and each had been visited by the EPG as part of its mission. This military action effectively torpedoed the EPG mission.

Except for Magnus Malan, no minister had known these attacks would take place. Neither was the Department of Foreign Affairs informed. In the preceding six years Foreign Affairs had often been embarrassed by SADF cross-border raids ordered without any regard for its own initiatives. On 9 May 1986 agreement had at last been reached between Foreign Affairs and the Department of Defence that the former would be given 24 hours' notice of any raids.

Early on the morning of 18 May, the phone rang as Carl von Hirschberg, a senior Foreign Affairs official assigned to the EPG, walked into his office. An EPG staff member asked a single question: 'Is it true that the SADF bombed ANC targets last night?' Von Hirschberg hurried to the foreign minister's office where he found him 'hunched over his desk, clearly shell-shocked' and unable to talk. Von Hirschberg later commented that 'the raids were a deliberate, pre-planned act designed to ship-wreck and totally derail the EPG initiative. Which it did in no uncertain terms.'[47]

Later that morning the scheduled meeting of the EPG with ministers Chris Heunis, Magnus Malan and Gerrit Viljoen took place. Even Heunis, who had to chair it, had not known of the raid beforehand. His son Jan Heunis, who as a Department of Foreign Affairs official assigned to the EPG also attended the meeting, later said: 'We were dumbfounded.'[48] Chris Heunis, the senior minister, gave a lengthy explanation as to why the government could not accept interference in the affairs of the country – and by extension the EPG proposals. Jan Heunis recounted: 'The atmosphere was as heavy as lead. There were EPG remarks about the consequence of the collapse of the talks and we finally went our separate ways.' Von Hirschberg commented later that the meeting was a 'complete disaster'.[49]

On one level the breakdown seemed to turn on a single word. The government wanted the ANC to commit itself to *terminating* violence, while the ANC was not prepared to go beyond *suspending* violence.[50] Each side feared that yielding on this

---

47 Wolvaardt et al., *From Verwoerd to Mandela,* vol. 3, p. 338.

48 Communication from Jan Heunis, 10 July 2011.

49 Wolvaardt et al., *From Verwoerd to Mandela,* vol. 3, p. 338.

50 On the dispute that arose between Thatcher and Botha over 'renouncing' and 'suspending' violence see Jan Heunis, *Die binnekring: Terugblikke op die laaste dae van blanke regering* (Johannesburg: Jonathan Ball, 2007), pp. 64-65.

issue would irrevocably weaken its position. But on another level the breakdown was inevitable. At that point PW Botha had no desire to enter into negotiations, and certainly not with the EPG acting as intermediary.

Von Hirschberg viewed the collapse of the EPG initiative in stark terms: 'A huge opportunity to end the violence in the country and to defuse the pressure for sanctions, if not to end them, was simply thrown out of the window by the president and a few cohorts.'[51] The EPG flew out of the country shortly afterwards. Its only recommendation was for the Commonwealth to impose comprehensive and mandatory economic sanctions.

While Pik Botha received little credit from his colleagues, he and Von Hirschberg were right about one thing. South Africa would pay a heavy price for this action. It would give the anti-apartheid movement in the West increasing leverage in lobbying for radical action. PW Botha's defiance ignored the fundamental reality that the international community ultimately legitimised states.[52] The attacks accelerated the international de-legitimisation of South Africa. Pik Botha had every reason to be shell-shocked in hearing of the raids.

Taking charge

In mid-1986 PW Botha decided he would personally take charge and introduce a form of power sharing he considered prudent. On 6 June he called a meeting of the NP's Federal Council, the party's highest decision-making body. He told the council that the special cabinet committee (SCC) on constitutional reform had been unable to produce a concept. This was undoubtedly because of the deep divisions within the committee (see pp. 183-185). Botha proceeded to lay down policy directives for incorporating blacks politically. It is not clear whether the cabinet formally endorsed these directives beforehand, but it can be assumed that Chris Heunis and his department had assisted. Showing he was fully in control, Botha said he hoped the SCC would formulate policy accordingly. 'If they don't do this, I will be speaking before them at the federal congress.'[53] A tape recording of the meeting registers laughter at this point.

Botha pointed out that his directives would not 'undermine white South Africa's right to self-determination'; otherwise it would not take long for the country 'to land on the slippery slope of the Progressives on which our enemies wish to put us'. He warned (presciently, it turned out) that if the NP did indeed end up on such a

---

51 Wolvaardt et al., *From Verwoerd to Mandela*, vol. 3, pp. 338-45.

52 Chris Alden, *Apartheid's Last Stand: The Rise and Fall of the South African Security State* (London: Macmillan, 1996), pp. 275-76.

53 Tape recording of the proceedings of the NP Federal Council, 6 June 1986 (in the possession of Inus Aucamp, Bloemfontein); E-mail communication from Inus Aucamp, who attended the meeting, 10 August 2010.

headlong slide, 'it would not govern for long and will in fact perish'. He pointedly stated: 'There comes a time when one must take a stand against the Schultzes and Crockers [officials in the US State Department], for whom I don't have a minute's time.'

Botha's directives were incorporated almost verbatim into the motion accepted by the NP's Federal Congress in September 1986. It accepted universal franchise for 'citizens', the eradication of racial discrimination and the effective protection of minorities. In his speech to the congress FW de Klerk stuck closely to Botha's directives, saying the party was requesting a mandate for joint decision-making and power sharing in a system that included all population groups, but also protected communities and enabled them to conduct their lives without domination by another group.[54] This was a plea for the policy of own and general affairs to be extended to blacks.

It was a move typical of the NP in its final years. It meant different things to different followers. To reformists it heralded a further advance on the road to a real democracy; to conservatives it signalled that the essentials of apartheid – race classification, group areas and population registration – remained intact. No extra-parliamentary organisation showed any interest in Botha's moves. The NP failed yet again to turn towards federalism as a solution to the complex nature of South African society.

The heart of the problem was PW Botha's determination to protect whites against black domination. As Dr Jannie Roux, director-general in his office and keeper of the cabinet minutes, said: 'Botha could not understand why separate development could not provide a solution for the urban blacks. There was talk among the ministers of black city-states, but it went nowhere. Cabinet members who were concerned that no progress was being made with the issue of black rights realised that within the framework of separate development nothing could be offered that would be acceptable to the majority of blacks. The policy had landed in a cul-de-sac and some members of the cabinet realised that all too well.'[55]

'We have to fight a war'

Starting in Sebokeng in September 1984, the major rebellion that broke out in the townships seriously undermined both South Africa's foreign relations and the Nkomati Accord. The pace of change accelerated rapidly. After ten months of widespread revolt President Botha declared a state of emergency in some magisterial districts on 20 July 1985. After a two-day conference in Kabwe, leader of the ANC in exile Oliver Tambo called on 'the masses' in South Africa to make the country

---

54   De Klerk, *Die laaste trek*, pp. 128-29.
55   Interview with Jannie Roux, 29 May 2008.

'ungovernable'. The conference also decided to intensify the armed struggle. The ANC journal *Sechaba* stated that the conference's emphasis on the 'armed seizure of power' led to the 'realisation that we must attack not only inanimate objects but also enemy personnel'.

It was this ANC conference that would erase the distinction between 'hard' and 'soft' targets.[56] Afterwards the National Executive Committee issued this confident appraisal: 'Our conference will be remembered by our people as a council-of-war that planned the seizure of power . . . through the terrible but cleansing fires of revolutionary war.'[57]

Up to this point the Botha government had pursued a strategy of counter-insurgency, entrusted mainly to the police force. Now it decided to embark on counter-revolutionary warfare by turning to what was called the 'securocrat option'. This meant approving radical measures proposed by the military to re-establish stability and suppress the uprising. The trigger was the explosion in November 1985 of the first landmines the ANC had planted on rural roads in the northern Transvaal. Within the space of a few weeks eight mines claimed the lives of nine civilians, including a small child.[58]

The South African military began to arm Renamo again as part of the destabilisation of Mozambique, contrary to the Nkomati Accord. Botha reverted from diplomatic to military mode. As a study of Botha's presidency notes, this reversion was 'sudden and emphatic'.[59] Botha readied himself for a violent confrontation with the ANC and its supporters in neighbouring states. On two or three occasions he asked his cabinet: 'Is there anyone who would deny we have to fight a war to ensure our right to survival in this country?' Pik Botha recounted in an interview that the ministers just sat there, saying nothing.[60]

Allegations of the violation of the Nkomati Accord soon surfaced. Commentators assumed 'the military' had taken over, ignoring Botha. This is wrong: Botha remained fully in charge. General Geldenhuys, head of the defence force from 1985 to 1990, said wryly: 'I don't know anyone [among the military] brave enough to ignore PW. Nkomati was not concluded as a result of military or security considerations. We heard that Nkomati was concluded because Foreign Affairs wanted to end the diplomatic boycotts and because PW was keen to get invitations from the British and German heads of government for a visit to Europe.'

The military considered Mozambique a failed state that could not stop ANC in-

56   Cited by Herman Stadler, *The Other Side of the Story: A True Perspective* (Pretoria: Contact, 1997), pp. 66-67.

57   Alden, *Apartheid's Last Stand*, p. 215.

58   Pottinger, *The Imperial Presidency*, p. 330.

59   Pottinger, *The Imperial Presidency*, p. 232.

60   Interview with Pik Botha, 31 January 2008.

filtration. Geldenhuys asserted: 'We violated the Nkomati Accord, but only after it had been violated by the other side.'[61] Minister of Defence General Magnus Malan was a hawk who provided cover for the military. It could always rely on him to persuade Botha that an operation in Mozambique was strategically necessary if it became public.

In March 1986 Botha briefly lifted the partial state of emergency, but declared a national state of emergency on 12 June 1986. The state used massive force to crush the revolt. Between 20 000 and 30 000 people were detained at one point or another.

The ANC in exile soon realised the difficulties of directing a war from the outside. It was unable to properly control militant youths who fought pitched battles with the security forces in the townships. Like the guillotine in the French Revolution, the burning tyres of the 'necklace' murders defined the terror of township life in troubled areas. The necklace eliminated suspected collaborators, often on flimsy evidence, and struck fear in the hearts of those who wavered in their commitment to the struggle. Vigilantism became the dominant pattern rather than disciplined action following commands. The state of emergency and mass detentions dealt both ANC actions and vigilantism a heavy blow. In October 1986 the ANC's Political-Military Council admitted: 'Despite all our efforts, we have not come anywhere near the achievement of the objectives we have set ourselves.'[62]

A system for security

Suppressing the township revolt was only one part of what the Botha government tried to achieve. The other, much more difficult aim was to win the 'hearts and minds' of urban blacks. The military implemented what it called an 'oil-spot strategy'. An area would be 'stabilised' and uplifted socio-economically as a preparation for elections that would lead to 'good government'. General Malan, the main proponent of the system, described the difficulties in implementing the strategy: 'The main problem was black poverty. We had to build houses for them on a large scale. But we were handicapped by a lack of funds, bureaucratic red tape and cabinet ministers acting like little gods in protecting their respective territories. Chris Heunis would phone and bark: "Keep your hands off my territory."'[63]

Heunis felt aggrieved by military encroachment in its attempt to improve the living conditions in strife-torn townships. What aggravated the turf battles with Constitutional Affairs was the fact that most of the 'hearts and minds' money flowed to the military. In parliament Heunis said 'it cannot be the aim of security

---

61   Interview with Jannie Geldenhuys, 5 April 2008.
62   Alden, *Apartheid's Last Stand*, p. 216.
63   Interview with Magnus Malan, 9 February 2008; Magnus Malan, *My lewe saam met die SA Weer-mag* (Pretoria: Protea, 2006), pp. 207-17.

forces to take over state activities'. The financial means were in any case far too limited to effect real change.[64]

Central to the strategy of restoring order and improving conditions on the ground was the National Security Management System (NSMS). It divided the country into eleven Joint Management Centres (JMCs), each covering a region (such as the eastern Cape). Membership consisted of the heads of state departments stationed within a JMC region. Each JMC had four working groups: a committee for intelligence, one for constitutional, economic and social affairs, one for communication, and one for security matters. Underpinning the eleven JMCs were some 60 sub-JMCs and around 450 mini-JMCs.

All these JMC structures reported to a national office chaired by the deputy minister of law and order. When a partial state of emergency was proclaimed in 1985, PW Botha appointed Deputy Minister of Law and Order Adriaan Vlok as chairman. Roelf Meyer succeeded him and Leon Wessels followed after Meyer. These structures helped the state respond quickly to local-level threats to its security. Intended arrests and detentions were sometimes discussed on a need-to-know basis, but sensitive issues were rarely put on the table.

Johan Mostert, who provided intelligence briefings to the working committee of the NSMS, commented: 'To my best knowledge no illegal steps were planned or reported. Officials of the Department of Justice sat in on the discussions to act as watchdogs, and they took their task seriously. No activity that could be described as a serious violation of human rights was ever discussed in my presence or came to my attention. The structure succeeded exceptionally well in keeping the country as stable as possible.'[65] Leon Wessels wrote: 'As far as I am concerned we [in the NSMS] were not involved in illegal acts. We wished to maintain law and order to make possible a settlement that was negotiated at a table rather than unilaterally imposed by an AK47. In this the NSMS succeeded very well.'[66] Jakkie Cilliers, later head of an institute of strategic studies, passed this judgment as an outsider: 'On a day-to-day basis it [ran] the state of emergency, doing a very effective job.'[67]

At the top of the structure stood the State Security Council (SSC) as the main statutory body that deliberated on security. Chaired by the president, its statutory members included the ministers of justice, police and defence, and their respective heads of department (the head of the defence force, the commissioner of police and the director-general of justice). The minister of finance and the head of the

---

64 For a crisp analysis of the system see Annette Seegers, 'South Africa's National Security Management System, 1972-1990', *The Journal of Modern African Studies*, 29, 2, 1991, pp. 253-73.

65 E-mail communication from Johan Mostert, 8 September 2011.

66 Leon Wessels, *Vereeniging: Die onvoltooide vrede* (Cape Town: Umuzi, 2010), pp. 214-15.

67 Interview with Jakkie Cilliers by Patti Waldmeir, 7 December 1994.

National Intelligence Service were also full members. Cabinet ministers were occasionally invited to attend as co-opted members. Provincial leaders, including Transvaal NP leader FW de Klerk, occasionally attended. Loose language, like 'eliminating' opponents of the regime permanently, was used in documents that circulated at the lower levels of the NSMS, but there is no evidence that such proposals were put before the SSC.

Botha strongly believed that houses, medical care, proper schools, a firm grip on law and order and the availability of jobs would take much of the sting out of black alienation. But he did not disagree with the military view that the struggle was 80% political and 20% military. However, the only political solution that would satisfy him and most of the top command would have to entail 'white self-determination' in a number of areas. For most educated blacks the struggle was not a class struggle but one for national self-determination. They would settle only for a system that would give them a degree of dignity reflected in a strong black presence in government and other national institutions.

Deadlocked negotiations

PW Botha remained a civilian politician to the core, but he attached considerable importance to the decisions of the SSC, which had a full-time secretariat with representatives from the military, police, National Intelligence and the Department of Foreign Affairs. According to cabinet secretary Jannie Roux, the politicians dominated the discussions while the officials rarely spoke. This is confirmed by General Jannie Geldenhuys: 'It is nonsense that the so-called "securocrats" governed the land. As head of the defence force I sat on the SSC and spoke not more than 15 minutes in total. The politicians spoke 90% of the time.'

One of the reasons for the reluctance of the military to intervene in the debate was the virtual absence of a military enemy inside the borders. Geldenhuys stated: 'Umkhonto weSizwe, the ANC's military wing, was never a significant military factor. It had no impact on the struggle of the 1980s.' In addition, the SADF was far from comfortable with the role of the military in suppressing the revolt. Geldenhuys remarked: 'A force like the SADF that depended largely on conscripts had no alternative but to accept its limitations. One could not use conscripts in an offensive capacity against civilians and even deploying them in a defensive capacity in townships was problematic. We never liked it.'[68]

The rise of the military, particularly in the NSMS, together with the attempt to win hearts and minds, sidelined the Department of Constitutional Development and Planning and marginalised Chris Heunis, who had long been close to the president. The president broke up his department into a Department of Information

---

68   Interviews with Jannie Geldenhuys, 27 May and 24 June 2008.

and Constitutional Planning, and a Department of Development Planning, which concentrated on socio-economic issues. Two other steps signalled the declining influence of his department. First, the president appointed Stoffel van der Merwe to the cabinet to liaise with black leaders on the negotiating process and report directly to the president. Second, the security clearance for two senior officials of Heunis's department was removed.[69]

During 1987 and 1988 Chris Heunis spoke to more than 250 people to canvass support for a national council where a new constitution would be negotiated, but the idea failed to get off the ground. The reason, as he well knew, was the government's exclusion of the ANC from any talks. He told a meeting at the Rand Afrikaans University there might have been justification for the ANC to take up arms in the 1960s, because they had no alternative means of political expression. In 1990 Nelson Mandela would cite these words approvingly in the first meeting between the government and the ANC leadership.[70]

In 1989 Heunis told Botha he found it impossible to negotiate with blacks while at the same time being responsible for implementing the Group Areas Act.[71] He had discussed the issue before with Botha, but the president had forgotten about it. When a furious Botha berated him, Heunis resigned.

Heunis had advanced negotiations with blacks as far as was possible within the constraints imposed by Botha. In 1988 he told a researcher: 'I am happy with what I have achieved. Perhaps I have gone somewhat faster than the NP's constituency was able to absorb.'[72] Heunis would likely have offered tougher resistance to ANC demands for 'simple majority rule' than NP negotiators did in the second half of the talks. In retirement he said: 'Sanctions made it vitally important for South Africa to negotiate if it wanted to remain part of the Western trade and financial networks, but there was no need to negotiate only about the handover of power.'[73]

A deadlock ended

The war in Angola – where South African forces in alliance with Unita confronted an alliance of the MPLA and Cuban forces – remained deadlocked. There was no consensus on the South African side about the objectives. Minister of Foreign Affairs Pik Botha worked for the withdrawal of both South African and Cuban forces in order to create the conditions for a free and fair election, supervised by the UN. By contrast, although senior military officers also wished to rid the sub-

---

69   Alden, *Apartheid's Last Stand*, pp. 259-60.

70   Archive for Contemporary Affairs (ACA), Bloemfontein, Minutes of Meeting between the RSA government and an ANC delegation, 4 May 1990, p.12.

71   Jan Heunis, *Die binnekring*, p. 13.

72   ACA, Chris Heunis Collection, Interview with Chris Heunis by A Agenbach, 1998.

73   Interview with Chris Heunis, 15 December 2002.

continent of Cuban troops, they wanted to crush Swapo and enable anti-Swapo parties to win the election in South West Africa (later Namibia).

In 1982 Jannie Roux chaired an SSC sub-committee of senior officials that launched an in-depth investigation into the socio-economic circumstances in northern South West Africa. Privately Pik Botha asked Roux also to report on the political dimension since conflicting evidence was filtering through. The sub-committee found that Swapo was not a terrorist movement but an Ovambo people's movement. Most members wanted a UN-supervised election, which the Ovambo majority were convinced Swapo would win. PW Botha later discussed the report with Roux, who recalls: 'He said it was an illuminating report that made him lie awake for three nights. He came to the conclusion that the findings were correct.'[74]

Roux believes the South West African election result in 1989 came as a great shock to a large part of the military. Despite the military's intensive 'hearts and minds' campaign, Swapo won more than 90% of the votes in Ovamboland.[75] The war in Angola constituted a major obstacle to constitutional negotiations in South Africa. The presence in Angola of more than 30 000 Cuban troops and large numbers of Soviet advisers created considerable anxiety in the white community, driving the two white language groups in South Africa into each other's arms. It undoubtedly helped the NP capture nearly half of the English-speaking vote in the 1987 election. South Africa had a total territorial force of 20 000, but did not deploy more than 3 000 soldiers in Angola at any one stage.[76]

Much was at stake. Confronted by an aggressive right wing accusing it of selling out, the government would be severely hit by a humiliating retreat from Angola. The Soviet Union and Cuba seemed determined to record a victory in Angola and win a battle in the Cold War. Victory could open the way for a Swapo incursion into the northern parts of South West Africa. Botha refused to consider any retreat that might be seen as wavering in the face of communist aggression.

In 1988 the apparent stalemate in the war was suddenly broken. The Reagan administration received word from the Soviets that they were eager to get out of Africa. Both South Africa and Cuba prepared to withdraw. For South Africa the financial costs were high. Between 1985/86 and 1988/89, military expenditure increased by 25% at constant prices to make up 17.7% of the budget.[77] The fruits of this expenditure were ambiguous. South Africa had helped turn Unita into a formidable force and had thwarted Swapo attempts to establish a military presence in South West

---

74 Communication from Jannie Roux, 10 April 2012.

75 Comments by Jannie Roux, 27 March 2012.

76 Interview with Jannie Geldenhuys, 7 May 2008.

77 Sean Archer, 'Defence Expenditure and Arms Procurement', Jacklyn Cock and Lauwrie Nathan (eds), *War and Society: The Militarisation of South Africa* (Cape Town: David Philip ,1989), pp. 244-59.

Africa. However, Swapo had managed to survive politically and easily won the first free election.

Botha's last election

In 1987 PW Botha unexpectedly called another election. He had started his career as a party organiser and ended it a devout servant of the party. He always kept his eye carefully on his own constituency, one that wanted reform to be slow, deliberate and cautious. When a general election was called in 1987, there was speculation that the Conservative Party under Andries Treurnicht, founded in 1982, would come to within a whisker of victory.

Unexpectedly, the NP under Botha performed impressively. It won 123 of the seats (compared to 142 in 1981), while the Progressive Federal Party captured 19 (27 in 1981) and the Conservative Party 22. It was calculated that the NP won 52% of the overall vote, 59% of the Afrikaner vote and 43% of the English vote.[78] For the first time English speakers supported the NP in greater numbers than any other party. The war in Angola had united the two white communities in South Africa.

The election campaign resembled shadow-boxing. Botha seemed to be fighting in the first place against the ANC, which the NP identified as its main opponent.[79] This only increased the appeal of the ANC among black South Africans, and the organisation emerged as the government's main opponent in the political battle for the state. Simon Jenkins, a distinguished commentator in the British press, wrote afterwards that Botha was a leader in the classic mould described by Machiavelli, who argued that the prime interest of a leader ought to be restoring a society's equilibrium. In Jenkins's view Botha regarded order as an a priori virtue. 'Policy should be directed always to re-establishing order ... Sustaining such an equilibrium in a multiracial, more or less capitalist state without the spiralling level of bloodshed is no mean feat – State of Emergency or no. It demands every ounce of pragmatism in a leader.'[80]

Botha was indeed a pragmatist, but seemed to have reached his limits on extending political rights to blacks. Mike Louw of the National Intelligence Service commented: 'He was like a rubber band that was stretched to its very limits. He was playing games to extend the time.'[81] But his party was steadily changing. It was no longer an ethnic party committed to unity and policy consistency, but a pragmatic, catch-all party. The new caucus of the NP was much better educated than its pre-

---

78 Lawrence Schlemmer, 'Assessment', DJ van Vuuren et al. (eds), *South African Election 1987* (Pinetown: Owen Burgess, 1987), p. 322.

79 This was the view of Heribert Adam expressed in *Sunday Star*, 17 May 1987.

80 Simon Jenkins, 'Paradox of Botha's Legacy', *Die Suid-Afrikaan*, June 1988, p. 45.

81 Communication from Mike Louw, 21 February 2008.

decessor, younger (70% were now in the 30- to 50-year age group), and more interested in a settlement than previous NP caucuses. The new caucus was also much less responsive to dogmatic authority and the traditional call to blood ties.[82]

An intelligence assessment

By the end of the 1980s the Botha government had restored a large degree of equilibrium. In the view of the best-funded intelligence agency in the world, the US Central Intelligence Agency (CIA), no fundamental changes were imminent. In a 70-page report entitled 'South Africa into the 1990s', dated 20 January 1989, it concluded that the government 'has weathered more than four years of unprecedented domestic and international pressure'. Its aim was to delay fundamental change as long as possible, believing the security forces could guarantee continued white prosperity until well into the next century. Nelson Mandela was unlikely to be released unless the government was certain it could contain any black mobilisation. The ANC realised that majority rule was not around the corner.[83]

This CIA assessment correctly captured PW Botha's thinking. It was also correct in concluding that the United Democratic Front and Cosatu, the main internal black opposition groups, had not been decisively defeated. Despite the detention of many activists, the mass movement remained able to operate. The government's strategy of black cooptation had failed. Black people rejected government institutions, from the homeland governments down to black local authorities.

The state had managed to suppress the uprising, but found it impossible to broaden its legitimacy through reforms. Chester Crocker, US assistant secretary of state for Africa, succinctly summed up the state of play: '[The] government and its opposition had checkmated each other. Neither could move unilaterally: the black resistance had no hope of forcing the government to capitulate, but the government could no longer hope to regain the legitimacy it lost.'[84] A mutually harmful stalemate had set in.

Influential South Africans had begun exploring radical alternatives to the apartheid order. In September 1985 a delegation of business leaders headed by Anglo American's Gavin Relly visited Lusaka to meet with the leadership of the ANC in exile (Harry Oppenheimer thought it inadvisable to accompany the group). Consummate ANC diplomat Thabo Mbeki went to work to persuade the businessmen that they had no reason to fear an ANC government. The Progressive Federal

---

82 Hermann Giliomee, 'Nuwe gesig van die NP', *Die Suid-Afrikaan*, 17, 1988, pp. 8-9; Hermann Giliomee, 'Afrikaner Politics, 1977-1987', John D Brewer (ed.), *Can South Africa Survive? Five Minutes to Midnight* (London: Macmillan, 1989), pp. 108-35.

83 Martin Plaut, 'CIA Assessments of South Africa's Transition: How Accurate Were They?' everfasternews.com, first posted 22 July 2007.

84 Chester Crocker, *High Noon in Southern Africa* (New York: Norton, 1992), p. 491.

Party under the leadership of Van Zyl Slabbert also made a pilgrimage to Lusaka. The governments of Britain and the United States relaxed the ban on diplomatic contacts with ANC leaders. South Africa's diplomatic relations were gravely at risk. Government initiative was urgently needed to prevent severe damage.

New thinking

The National Intelligence Service (NIS), established in 1979 as a successor to the Bureau for State Security, played a prime role in breaking the impasse of the late 1980s. It correctly recognised that the gravest threat to South Africa's future prosperity was not an armed revolution, but general lawlessness and a breakdown of discipline and values, affecting workers, students and pupils alike. Alienated activists in the townships would sabotage any state effort to improve the general condition of township life. The productivity of workers would decline. The country's growth prospects would wane. South Africa would remain a country at war with itself, even if a semblance of public order prevailed. A severe clampdown would extinguish the fires, but some coals would continue to smoulder, ready to flare up at the slightest breeze.

Mike Louw, second in command at the NIS, recalls the situation in the late 1980s. 'Nowhere was the situation out of hand, but it was clear that politically and morally we were losing our grip. Everywhere in the townships we encountered intimidation and a strong political consciousness. The political system had become obsolete, and a long bloody struggle lay ahead. It became clear that the sooner we negotiated a new system the better.'[85] The danger was not a revolt, but growing anarchy. Louw added: 'Ungovernability is not something you can turn on and off like a tap; it creates an entire new mentality, a mentality … that we are struggling with today [in 1995], namely a total breakdown of authority and no respect for the law.'[86]

The NIS had pushed these views in the course of the 1980s, but failed to prevail in a tough turf battle with the military and Magnus Malan, minister of defence. There were other areas of disagreement. The military believed in maintaining a wide security cordon beyond South Africa's borders. Louw strongly disagreed. 'The enemy is here, watches over your child, prepares your food at your home, works in your garden, walks in the street every day – this is where the danger lies, not far away beyond our borders.'[87] Time was running out. The position of whites weakened with every year that passed.

---

85 Interview with Mike Louw, 21 November 1994; Interview with ex-Police Commissioner Johan van der Merwe of the South African Police, 22 November 1996.

86 Interview with Mike Louw by Patti Waldmeir, 29 May 1995; Patti Waldmeir, *Anatomy of a Miracle: The End of Apartheid and the Birth of the New South Africa* (New York: WW Norton, 1997), pp. 49-51.

87 Interview with Mike Louw, 2 September 2007.

Magnus Malan scoffed at Louw's criticism of the 'forward' policy of hitting insurgents at places far beyond South Africa's borders. 'Such people are ignorant about war. If we allowed ANC insurgents to come over the borders in large numbers we would have had a full-scale, bitter war with ten times the number killed. It would have made a settlement impossible.'[88]

The other area of disagreement was over the timetable for a negotiated settlement. The military believed there was no quick solution, or, as influential American strategist JJ McCuen formulated it, 'winning takes a long time – years rather than months'.[89] Malan had studied revolutionary warfare as a military cadet and visited the United States at the time of the Vietnam War. In his view, a revolutionary elite inspired by Karl Marx fomented the uprising in South Africa by exploiting the appalling conditions in which poor black people lived. To counter the revolutionary onslaught, the state had to study the Chinese revolution – Malan had a copy of Mao Zedong's *Red Book* on his desk – and do everything possible to meet the needs of the impoverished masses. With the revolutionaries inspired by communist doctrines, there was little room for compromise. In Malan's view the government would have to continue to fight them for a long time.[90]

Both Niel Barnard and Mike Louw, the two most senior NIS officials, believed it was in whites' interests to negotiate a deal as soon as possible. From about 1983 Pieter Swanepoel, NIS director of evaluations, advocated in in-house papers the release of Nelson Mandela and unbanning of the ANC. Swanepoel drew on studies showing that Mandela, virtually unknown in Soweto in the late 1970s, had become a household name by the mid-1980s as the result of an intense campaign overseas and at home. The figure of Nelson Mandela had to be demystified before his release, to avoid what happened when the Ayatollah Khomeini returned to Iran.[91] In 1986 JM Coetzee (later awarded the Nobel prize for literature) wrote: 'Mandela's face, on posters and T-shirts, was everywhere to be seen in the uprisings of 1985–86; the slogan "Free Mandela" was daubed on the walls of power.'[92]

From the mid-1980s NIS head Niel Barnard began nudging the president in the direction of 'talks about talks' with Mandela, arguing that 'there was no answer in trying to fight it out'.[93] Chris Heunis and Kobie Coetsee also told Botha that talking to Mandela was the only way to go.[94] In 1985 the president offered to set Mandela free on condition that he rejected violence as a political instrument. Mandela turned

---

88 Interview with Magnus Malan, 9 February 2008.
89 JJ McCuen, *The Art of Counter-revolutionary War* (London: Faber and Faber, 1966), pp. 195-96.
90 Hermann Giliomee, 'Onderhoud met Genl. Magnus Malan', *Die Suid-Afrikaan*, 7, 1986, pp. 12-13.
91 Communication from Pieter Swanepoel, 30 July 2011.
92 JM Coetzee, 'Waiting for Mandela', *New York Review of Books*, 8 May 1986, p. 3.
93 Riaan Labuschagne, *On South Africa's Secret Service* (Alberton: Galago, 2002), p. 23.
94 Interview with Niel Barnard by Patti Waldmeir, 25 November 1994.

him down. In a statement read out by his daughter Zindzi, Mandela said he would not give any undertaking 'at a time when you, the people, are not free'. Justice Minister Kobie Coetsee, who was also responsible for prisons, told George Bizos – Mandela's lawyer since the 1950s – that PW Botha had said to him: 'We have painted ourselves into a corner; can you get us out?'[95]

In November 1985 Coetsee visited Mandela in the Volkshospitaal in Cape Town, where he had been admitted for surgery. Coetsee later presented the visit as taking place at his initiative. It can be safely assumed, however, that the excessively cautious minister would not have acted without the president's authorisation. After returning to prison on 23 December 1985, Mandela came to a crucial decision. He jotted down his thoughts: 'I concluded that the time had come when the struggle could best be pushed forward through negotiations. If we did not start a dialogue soon, both sides would soon be plunged into a dark night of oppression and war ...' He went on: 'The enemy was strong and resolute ... [but] they must have sensed that they were on the wrong side of history. We had right on our side but not might ... It was time to talk.'[96]

Early in 1986 Mandela asked Bizos to come and see him. They discussed ways in which the issues between the government and the ANC could be settled. Mandela asked Bizos to inform Oliver Tambo in Lusaka about his intention to start talks. The only other person Mandela told was Walter Sisulu, who encouraged him to continue the conversation.[97] Coetsee met Mandela again when the EPG visited him in jail in February 1986. Although Mandela urged him to join the discussions, Coetsee left early.

The political crisis in South Africa entered its most acute stage with the failure of the EPG mission (see pp. 259-60) and the proclamation of a nationwide state of emergency on 12 June 1986. Although there was never any danger of the state losing control, the seething uprisings of the mid-1980s and the intransigence of the PW Botha government meant the prospect of a battle to the bitter end was no longer a far-fetched possibility.

On 24 January 1986 Anton Rupert, doyen of Afrikaner businessmen, wrote a letter to Botha. He referred to the president's earlier private comment that he would 'rather be poor than yield [to blacks]' and was not prepared to renounce apartheid. Rupert warned that any attempt to cling to apartheid would lead to a future that would be 'both poor and black'. The belief that apartheid guaranteed the white man's survival was a myth; in fact, 'it threatens his survival'. Rupert went on to say:

---

95 George Bizos, 'The Release of Nelson Mandela', undated ms., p. 2.

96 Nelson Mandela, *Long Walk to Freedom: The Autobiography of Nelson Mandela* (Randburg: Macdonald Purnell, 1994), pp. 512-13.

97 Bizos, 'The Release of Nelson Mandela', p. 3.

'[Apartheid] is crucifying us; it is destroying our language; it is relegating a once heroic nation to the position of the lepers of the world.' He warned Botha that if he failed in the task of removing apartheid 'then one day we shall surely end up with a Nuremberg'.[98]

The talking starts

Mandela made his move in July 1986. He wrote to General Willie Willemse, head of prisons, requesting to see Coetsee to discuss talks. Willemse phoned Coetsee, who asked him to bring Mandela to the minister's official home in Cape Town. Here Mandela and Coetsee talked for three hours, with Coetsee probing issues such as the ANC's willingness to suspend armed struggle and provide guarantees to minorities. Mandela asked to see the president, but for nearly two years he received no response.[99]

Meanwhile PW Botha had become interested in Mandela's strategic thinking. Strongly influenced by the military in the early 1980s, in the final years of the decade he turned increasingly to Barnard from the NIS for advice. Barnard in turn depended heavily on Louw's wise counsel. The president told Coetsee informal talks with Mandela could begin, but had to be kept a secret not shared even with his cabinet colleagues. In May 1988 Botha appointed four officials to meet regularly with Mandela in prison: Niel Barnard and Mike Louw of the NIS, Fanie van der Merwe, a senior official in the Department of Constitutional Development and Planning, and General Willie Willemse.

While friendly, Mandela was adamant he did not really wish to discuss matters with these officials who were not policy makers.[100] He wanted to talk directly to the president. Reluctantly, he explored the possibility of a negotiated settlement in these meetings, knowing that the gist of the talks would be reported to the president. On occasion the four officials met as a group with Mandela, but in most cases Barnard saw him alone, meticulously reporting every conversation to Botha. In these report-back sessions Barnard found the president to be sharp, attentive and open to argument. He recounted: 'One could be very frank with him and he would listen even to unpalatable views. There was only one rule: he had to believe you would not lie to him or mislead him.'[101]

Between May 1988 and 11 February 1990, when Mandela was released, talks were held on 48 different occasions. Above all, the president wanted Mandela's views on how to change a violent conflict into a political conflict. From the start Mandela

---

98   Letter from Anton Rupert to PW Botha, 24 January 1986.

99   Mandela, *Long Walk to Freedom*, pp. 518-19; Anthony Sampson, *Mandela: The Authorized Biography* (Johannesburg: Jonathan Ball, 1999), p. 352.

100 Jannie Roux, citing Willie Willemse in a communication of 10 April 2012.

101 Interview with Niel Barnard, 13 March 2012.

made a great impression on the government team. Commenting on his consistency and integrity, Louw said: 'You could listen to this man for hours and hours and hours and he just comes across as a very honest man, very dedicated and very hard-headed once he had made up his mind.'[102]

When the committee raised the issue of Mandela's alleged sympathy for communism and his refusal to break with the Communist Party, Mandela replied in a measured way that in his youth he had found aspects of communism attractive, but he was not a communist. Yet he refused to break with the SA Communist Party, the ANC's main ally: 'If I desert them now, who have been in the struggle with me all these years, what sort of ally would I be to you or to the government?' He answered his own question: '[People] would say that Mandela is a man who turns the way the wind blows; he is not to be trusted.'[103]

The officials also explored other issues. Was the ANC genuinely interested in a peaceful settlement? Mandela admitted the ANC did not have the capacity to overthrow the government and that he did not favour insurrection. The other main question was about a future political system. While Mandela considered majority rule non-negotiable, the new system had to be balanced and had to ensure white domination would not be replaced by black domination. 'Minorities have a legitimate interest in security,' he said.[104] Other issues discussed included the release of political prisoners, the opening up of street politics, the return of the exiles, the normalisation of political activities and the first election.

Gerrit Viljoen, at that stage minister of education and the main intellectual in cabinet, recounted that in the final months of 1988 cabinet accepted 'the inevitability of a negotiated settlement'. It was realised, Viljoen said, that 'we are not going to find a solution through violence; secondly, that the opponents are reasonable people, that they have a case; and thirdly, that those black leaders who are working within the system will not go any step further unless there is an unbanning and a release, and all these things I think led to the acceptance of a negotiated solution. And then [came] the illness of Botha.'

Botha next asked Gerrit Viljoen and Kobie Coetsee to take forward the discussion with Mandela at the political level. According to Viljoen, the meetings took place either at the end of 1988 or in January 1989. At about the same time Botha ordered the prison authorities to give Mandela 'an open phone to discuss matters with whomever he wanted in Harare, Lusaka or Pretoria or Johannesburg'.

The two ministers met twice with Mandela in the Victor Verster prison and once

102 Interview with Mike Louw by Patti Waldmeir, 29 May 1995.
103 Interview with Mike Louw by Patti Waldmeir, 29 May 1995.
104 Niel Barnard, 'NIS wou sonder middelman na ANC gaan', Die Burger, 18 February 1992.

in Tuynhuis while he was still a prisoner. But he was, as Viljoen noted of their first meeting, 'the head of the house, the host, he was not there as prisoner'. They told Mandela that Botha had accepted that a new constitution could be drafted legitimately only by negotiations and agreement. That, the ministers pointed out, 'needed talking with these people whom he [Botha] had earlier said he would never talk with because they represent the devil'. Hence the need for a formula that would enable both the government and the ANC leadership to sell the idea of negotiations to their respective constituencies. The ANC had to be able to justify the suspension of the armed struggle, while the government had to be able to say 'something in the line of the rejection of communism, the abandonment of revolution and the armed struggle' on the part of the ANC. Viljoen concluded after the sessions with Mandela: 'With Mandela in prison . . . we lose all the way. He is a figure with world acceptance and world respect.'[105]

Meeting the president

Mandela wanted an interview with the president, but the deadlock persisted. The president refused to receive a prisoner and certainly not one who had rejected his demand to renounce violence, and the prisoner refused to forswear violence unless there was an undertaking that he would be freed unconditionally. In an interview some years later Mandela simulated a conversation between him and the president in which the latter demanded he forswear violence before a real conversation could take place. Mandela said he would reply: 'Oh no, I am not coming to you cap in hand. I am coming to you as the leader of an organisation. Don't worry about my policy. Consider us discussing the question of the future of South Africa.' In the end it was the president who relented. As Mandela observed, 'We met as equals.'[106]

The two men met on 5 July 1989. Also present were General Willemse of prisons and Barnard of the NIS.[107] In retirement Botha maintained he told Mandela Marxism was one of the forces that had ruined Africa and it would destroy him as well. Mandela considered Botha to be a 'first-class gentleman', who treated him courteously. In prison he had steeled himself for very tough negotiations that he remained convinced would take place one day with the NP leader. He had heard from other black leaders that Botha did not negotiate with blacks, but 'merely shouts'. In a memorandum he sent to the president before their meeting, he warned that this would 'make the discussion very difficult'.[108]

105 Interview with Gerrit Viljoen by Patti Waldmeir, 20 October 1994; Interview with Lena Viljoen, 16 March 2012, in which his wife confirmed that Viljoen saw Mandela in prison.
106 Interview with Nelson Mandela, 12 March 1992.
107 No tape or transcript of the interview has yet emerged.
108 Interview with Nelson Mandela by Patti Waldmeir, 1 March 1995.

Mandela's fears were unfounded. He confessed later that he went into the meeting 'a bit frightened', expecting 'war' because of Botha's reputation as an ANC hater. But Botha was relaxed, open and friendly.[109] He said later: 'In our meeting, if you did not know the South African situation, you would not know who the State President was and who the prisoner.' Very little of substance was discussed, but Mandela made it clear that he was not willing to be freed before Walter Sisulu and others with whom he had spent many years in prison were also released.

The meeting was supposed to be kept quiet, but the president could not contain himself. On a hunting trip shortly afterwards he showed some cabinet members a photo of him, Mandela, Willemse and Barnard, and told the story of the prison talks. The secret of this momentous event – which with one or two exceptions not even the ministers knew about – was out.

Barnard was later criticised for his remark that Botha had laid the table for negotiations, leaving it to De Klerk to complete the process. However, by the end of 1988 Botha had accepted the idea of negotiations with the ANC; he sent Gerrit Viljoen and Kobie Coetsee to talk to Mandela about a framework for talks. But whether Botha and Mandela would have reached a settlement is difficult to say. As Barnard observes: 'The moment Mandela was free the situation was never the same again.'[110]

Mandela spelled out the basic framework for negotiations in a single line of a memorandum he sent to the president before their meeting. It had to reconcile the black desire for majority rule with the requirement of whites that this would not mean the subjugation of the white minority.[111] Botha had just barely crossed the barrier of power sharing with blacks. Majority rule could well have been a bridge too far.

Meeting the ANC abroad

Realising that a settlement with the ANC could not be built on Mandela alone, leading NIS officials began to contemplate meeting with the ANC leaders in exile. Mandela was opposed to the idea, suspecting a plot to drive a wedge between him and Oliver Tambo and other exiled ANC leaders. But the NIS continued to press for a meeting. In the course of 1989 the NIS under the leadership of Niel Barnard decided to find a way of meeting with the ANC abroad. Acting as a go-between was Stellenbosch academic Willie Esterhuyse, who between November 1987 and May 1990 arranged discussions on British soil between ANC delegates and NP-aligned

---

109 David Ottaway, *Chained Together: Mandela, De Klerk and the Struggle to Remake South Africa* (New York: Times Books, 1993), p. 39.

110 Interview with Niel Barnard, 13 March 2012.

111 Martin Meredith, *Nelson Mandela: A Biography* (London: Hamish Hamilton, 1997), pp. 387-89.

business leaders, journalists, clergymen and academics.[112] Twelve such discussions were held; several took place at Mells Park House near Bath in England.

PW Botha suffered a second stroke in February 1989. He retired as party leader and the caucus elected FW de Klerk to replace him. On 14 August 1989 Botha resigned as president after virtually the entire cabinet asked him to do so. De Klerk was sworn in as acting president on 15 August. The next day he chaired a meeting of the State Security Council. On the agenda was an NIS proposal that it be authorised to take 'direct action' to gather information about the ANC and the 'potential approachability of its different leaders and groupings'. No objection was raised. For the NIS this provided the cover it wanted.

Two NIS officials, Mike Louw and Maritz Spaarwater, flew out to meet Thabo Mbeki and Jacob Zuma in a hotel in Lucerne, Switzerland. The failure of the 'people's war' to topple the state or seriously challenge stability had greatly strengthened Mbeki's argument in ANC ranks that 'talking is better than fighting' (see p. 225). Mbeki greeted Louw and Spaarwater with the words: 'Well, here we are, bloody terrorists and for all you know fucking communists as well.' Louw recalls: 'That broke the ice and from that moment on there was no tension.'[113]

They reported back to De Klerk, who took over as president on 15 September 1989. At first the new president reacted with fury. Long irritated by the generous room his predecessor had given the security agencies, De Klerk believed the Lucerne mission was a challenge to his authority. Shown the State Security Council minutes, he calmed down and listened attentively.

Early in 1990, after the cabinet had decided to lift the ban on the ANC and a number of other organisations, Louw and other NIS officials met again in Europe with an ANC team under Mbeki. Agreement was reached about a process that included the return of exiles, suspension of the armed struggle and the pointing out of ANC caches inside the country. A period was set for the government and the ANC to prepare their respective supporters for negotiations.[114]

Political downfall

As leader, PW Botha straddled two eras. His early career coincided with the rise of a radical Afrikaner nationalism in the 1930s that would soon develop apartheid as its operational ideology. But he was also the man who spearheaded the modernisation

---

112 A feature film, *Endgame*' depicts these informal talks as a parallel channel that was decisive in settling disputes before real talks began. FW de Klerk rejected this, stating: 'The film even conjured up my brother Willem calling me from Mells Park to clear certain things with me. That never happened.' Interview with FW de Klerk, 28 May 2009.

113 Allister Sparks, *Tomorrow is Another Country: The Inside Story of South Africa's Negotiated Revolution* (Sandton: Struik, 1994), p. 113.

114 E-mail communication from Maritz Spaarwater, 22 July 2007.

of the political system that started in the mid-1970s and continued over the next ten years. He suffered a serious stroke early in 1985 and was no longer as effective a leader as he had been in his first six years. In the last four years of his term he was a highly divisive figure, who could at times become irrational and unpredictable. This upset De Klerk and Heunis so much that the former seriously considered resigning, while the latter actually did.[115]

Botha gave his last major public speech on 16 December 1988 on the occasion of the 150th commemoration of the battle of Blood River. He bewailed the failure of the world's major nations to guarantee the rights and security of small nations such as the Afrikaners. What he did not take into account was that large nations only protect small ones if they represent mutually cherished values. Apartheid made it impossible for Western nations to protect Afrikaners or the white community at large or to help them negotiate a power-sharing deal.

Botha's actions in his final years should not detract from his considerable achievements. He managed to retain the majority support of a conservative white electorate. He was the first NP leader to move away from the idea of an exclusive white nation as the foundation of the political order. He broke down the symbolism of an all-white parliament, removed discrimination in the defence force, and accepted the recommendation of the Wiehahn Commission to admit black trade unions to the statutory industrial relations framework. He took the initiative to abolish the racial sex laws. He also presided over a dramatic redistribution of income, while sharply increasing the already heavy burden on white taxpayers. According to the International Monetary Fund, the South African tax rate was exceptionally high for a middle-income country.[116] But Botha was unable to abandon the core apartheid pillars of group areas and population registration underpinning enforced group identities. Nor could he bring himself to abandon the homelands policy. Yet in his final year in office he came around to accepting the need to start negotiating with the ANC.

When Vorster was forced to retire he became an embittered man, but Botha remained defiant and scornful towards cabinet ministers who visited him at his home in Wilderness, George. He never forgave them for forcing him out and could not understand the haste with which the De Klerk government sought to negotiate a settlement, condemning their willingness to hand over power so meekly. He was furious with Niel Barnard for not keeping the tapes of the talk between him and Mandela. Perhaps considering the use Botha had made of his taped conversation with Van Zyl Slabbert, Barnard and Louw had prudently decided to destroy them.

There were two memories that cheered Botha up. He told Patti Waldmeir that

115 Daan Prinsloo, *Stem uit die Wilderness: 'n Biografie oor oud-pres PW Botha* (Mosselbaai: Vaandel, 1997), pp. 235-37.
116 De Klerk, *Die laaste trek*, p. 173.

ex-US Secretary of State Henry Kissinger, 'with his dark voice', paid him a visit and said: 'I owe you an apology for leaving you in the lurch in Angola.' Botha replied: 'Of course you owe me an apology. Because the United States, through the CIA, promised us that they would mine Luanda and that our forces together with [Jonas] Savimbi's forces would take Luanda and establish good order and government in Angola.' However, 'at the last moment they [the United States] dropped us'.

The other good memory was that of President Mandela asking him 'to once again play a role, else his work, my work and South Africa will be destroyed'.[117] But Botha was no longer fit to play any role. Mandela remarked that one of his greatest regrets in life was that he did not have the chance to negotiate with Botha. He believed he and Botha – they were both in their early seventies in 1989 – would 'have dragooned' their respective organisations forward.[118] He would never quite know what to make of FW de Klerk, twenty years his junior. Negotiations presided over by a fit PW Botha and a fit Nelson Mandela would have been a spectacle to behold. No one can really tell what the outcome would have been.[119]

117 Interview with PW Botha by Patti Waldmeir, 1 March 1995.
118 Interview with Nelson Mandela, 12 March 1992.
119 Communication from Jannie Roux, 12 April 2012.

Chapter 10
Time for a 'Quantum Leap': FW de Klerk's Venture

ON 18 JANUARY 1989 THE NEWS BROKE THAT PW BOTHA HAD BEEN HOSPI-
talised after a stroke and would be on sick leave for six weeks. On 2 February, just
before the NP's parliamentary caucus met, the chairman received a letter from Botha.
After proposing the separation of the offices of president and NP leader, Botha asked
the party to elect someone in his place as NP leader. Since he had not floated the idea
beforehand, the election took place in an atmosphere of high drama. The majority
accepted De Klerk's proposal to elect a new leader immediately to avoid a political
vacuum. Chris Heunis and Pik Botha were eliminated in the first round.

In the next round De Klerk came up against Barend du Plessis. Though Du Plessis
had been in cabinet for less than six years, he had made his name as a competent
minister of finance and an outspoken champion of reform. De Klerk squeezed home
by 8 votes, 69 to 61. As the more senior cabinet minister and also leader of the
Transvaal NP – which had a majority in the caucus – De Klerk's majority should
have been much bigger. Admitting that he had scored what he later called 'a nail-
biting victory', he concluded that Du Plessis's surprisingly strong showing was because of his reformist image – in contrast to his own 'conservative image'.

In his acceptance speech De Klerk said the party had to escape from the corner in
which it found itself. The time had come for a well-considered 'quantum leap'. He
added: 'Our goal is a new South Africa . . . free of domination and oppression in
whatever form.' Seven months later, addressing his old constituency in Vereeniging,
he said: 'Give me your hearts and I promise, as never before, to try to break through.'[1]

The sequence of speeches congratulating De Klerk strictly followed cabinet
seniority, with Du Plessis last in line. He welcomed De Klerk's commitment to reform as expressed in his acceptance speech, adding that after De Klerk had taken the
leap, he would find Du Plessis and all those who had voted for him already there
because they had made the jump long before.[2]

But the real problem the party faced was this: now that it had taken the leap, what
should it do next?

---

1 Patti Waldmeir, *Anatomy of a Miracle: The End of Apartheid and the Birth of the New South Africa*
   (New York: WW Norton, 1997), pp. 137-38; FW de Klerk, *Die laaste trek – 'n Nuwe begin* (Cape
   Town: Human & Rousseau, 1998), p. 152.
2 E-mail communication from Barend du Plessis, 19 September 2011.

A different kind of party

Between the general election of 1958, when De Klerk voted for the first time, and that of 1982, when he became NP leader of the Transvaal, the NP was based solidly on Afrikaner support and dominated the political system. Such a dominant-party regime often arises after a national group or class that forms a numerical majority has experienced a political trauma or suffered a long period in the political wilderness. Invariably it sets itself the task of executing a major project close to the heart of its constituency. Once in power, such parties tend to win successive elections by large margins and to dominate the formation of government and set the public agenda for an extended period. The distinction between ruling party and state, characteristic of liberal democracies, to a large extent dissolves.[3] Even a highly critical supporter is still likely to ask: 'Who but the government is in a position to do things for me?'[4]

As NP leaders, Hendrik Verwoerd, John Vorster and PW Botha all viewed political alternatives to apartheid in existential terms, believing that to give up power meant the demise of the Afrikaner *volk* as surely as the African sun rose every morning. At a meeting in Vienna in 1977 US Vice President Walter Mondale told Vorster the United States insisted on a system in South Africa under which 'every citizen should have the right to vote and every vote should be equally weighted'.[5] Vorster responded that succumbing to this demand would have exactly the same result as a Marxist victory. 'In the one case it will come about as the result of brute force, in the other it would be strangulation with finesse.'[6]

PW Botha declared that the 'Nationalist Afrikaner has resolved never to be subordinate again in his own country'.[7]

But apartheid was never an end in itself, particularly not after the high economic growth of the 1960s. Gerrit Viljoen, the government's chief negotiator in 1990 to 1992, expressed the view of reformists in 1977: 'Apartheid is neither an ideology nor a dogma. It is a method, a road along which we are moving and it is subject to fun-

---

3   This is the definition of TJ Pempel, editor of *Uncommon Democracies* (Ithaca: Cornell University Press, 1990), which covers such regimes in developed countries (Sweden, Italy and Japan, among others). For a comparative study of dominant-party regimes in developing countries (Mexico, India, Taiwan, Malaysia and South Africa), see Hermann Giliomee and Charles Simkins (eds), *The Awkward Embrace: One-Party Dominance and Democracy* (Cape Town: Tafelberg, 1999).

4   Giliomee and Simkins, *The Awkward Embrace*, p. 340.

5   SA Institute of Race Relations, *Survey of Race Relations, 1977* (Johannesburg: SAIRR, 1977), p. 573.

6   Deon Geldenhuys, *The Diplomacy of Isolation: South Africa's Foreign Policy Making* (Johannesburg: Macmillan, 1984), p. 243.

7   Dirk de Villiers and Johanna de Villiers, *PW* (Cape Town: Tafelberg, 1984), p. 23.

damental reassessment.'[8] De Klerk recounts that he strongly supported the proposed labour reforms of the Wiehahn Commission at the end of the 1970s: the
imperatives of growth and tackling the shortage of skilled labour weighed heavier
than the maintenance of orthodox apartheid[9] (see pp. 146-147).

This pragmatic tendency became even more pronounced after the Conservative
Party was founded in 1982. The NP became a catch-all party that drew increasing
numbers of English speakers. In the 1987 election most of the English vote went to
the NP. But the party's pragmatism had unintended consequences. The NP as an
interest-based party attractive to the middle class could no longer appeal to the
primordial values of blood and soil, or threaten to pull the pillars of the state down
if the *volk*'s survival was threatened. The demand for power sharing would lack
credibility if the minority party that wanted part of the power did not represent a
volk or a nation or a religious group, but a motley collection of voters.

Accustomed to power

FW de Klerk was a firm supporter of apartheid and of the mutation introduced in
the 1980s, which can be called reform apartheid. He was born in 1936 into a Transvaal political family. His uncle, JG Strijdom, was NP provincial leader from 1933
until his election as NP leader in 1954, serving as prime minister from 1954 to
1958. His father, Jan de Klerk, was a member of the cabinets of Strijdom, Verwoerd
and Vorster. His brother Willem was editor of the daily *Die Transvaler* and later of
the Sunday paper *Rapport*. In the early 1980s Piet Cillié, one-time editor of *Die
Burger*, likened FW de Klerk to a 'little prince' steeped in the ways of maintaining a
monarchy's status and power, and intent on keeping fights inside the court. Reforms
had to be delayed until the need for them had become imperative and sufficient
caucus support for them had been built up.

De Klerk's family were Doppers – members of the Gereformeerde Kerk. Father
Jan and sons FW and Willem studied at Potchefstroom University, the country's
only university with the right to instruct students within a Christian perspective.
The university stood for a 'principled approach' to politics and other spheres of
life. De Klerk would remark that as a law student he learnt to base his approach to
legal issues on principles rather than court judgements. He tried to apply this
approach to spheres beyond the law and also to his work as an attorney, always seeking solutions within the framework of a value system based on morally defensible
principles.[10]

---

8   John de St Jorre, *A House Divided* (New York: Carnegie Foundation, 1977), p. 13. For a discussion
    on apartheid as a radical survival plan formulated in the 1930s and 1940s see Hermann Giliomee,
    The Afrikaners: Biography of a People (Cape Town: Tafelberg, 2003), Chapter 13.

9   Interview with FW de Klerk, 30 May 2009.

10 De Klerk, *Die laaste trek*, p. 52.

After receiving a law degree, De Klerk practised for nearly twelve years as an attorney in Vereeniging before entering parliament in 1972. From the outset the NP leadership considered De Klerk cabinet material. He had a fine mind and excellent debating powers. Even his strongest critics acknowledged that he never stooped to personal attacks. He was engaging, forthright and sociable, and he enjoyed the cut and thrust of argument. John Vorster appointed him to the cabinet in 1978 without first imposing the 'internship' of serving as a deputy minister. In 1982 De Klerk was elected leader of the Transvaal NP after his predecessor Andries Treurnicht broke away to form the Conservative Party (CP). As Transvaal leader De Klerk performed well in stemming a formidable CP assault on the NP's Transvaal base during the 1980s. Between 1986 and 1989 he served as chairman of the Ministers' Council in the House of Assembly (the council administering white 'own affairs') at the same time as being national education minister.

De Klerk was the ultimate party loyalist. He avoided identification with either the *verligte* or the *verkrampte* wing of the party. While personally popular, he came across as someone who acted tactically and pragmatically rather than strategically or purely as a matter of principle. He once described himself as 'on the left flank of the party's right wing'.[11] His reform initiatives were always carefully calculated and, as Du Plessis later pointed out, never landed him in trouble with the party leadership.[12]

Vorster saw in De Klerk a future NP leader, and there were considerable similarities in their leadership styles. Both were superb at persuading the cabinet and the caucus through rational argument of the need for change or the need to stay put, as the case may be.[13] Derek Keys, who had extensive experience in managing corporations before he became finance minister in 1992, said of De Klerk: 'He is probably the best motivator that I have been able to work with. And just an excellent politician with a wonderful sense of how the currents were running and what could be harnessed and what could be ignored.'[14]

'White house' leader

The race for PW Botha's successor started immediately after the communications disaster of the Rubicon speech in August 1985 (see p. 199). Several cabinet ministers had begun to suspect the president had suffered a stroke. De Klerk positioned himself as a centrist with conservative leanings. When Chris Heunis proposed to cabinet in January 1986 that black representatives be accommodated in parliament, De Klerk opposed it. It was in this brittle political atmosphere that Pik Botha caused

---

11   Leon Wessels, *Die einde van 'n era: Bevryding van 'n Afrikaner* (Cape Town: Tafelberg, 1994), p. 126.
12   Communication from Barend du Plessis, 25 July 2011.
13   Communication from Koos van der Merwe, 26 July 2011.
14   Interview with Derek Keys by Patti Waldmeir, 21 January 1995.

a huge upheaval when, in a press interview shortly afterwards, he said there could be a future black president in structures that white and black representatives had agreed upon. Both Heunis and De Klerk privately asked the president to censure the foreign minister, warning that the party could split unless tough action was taken. In cabinet PW Botha told Pik Botha that he (Pik) would not survive, but shortly afterwards the president relented. He settled for reprimanding his foreign minister severely in parliament – for all practical purposes a political lynching.[15]

In his capacity as chairman of the Ministers' Council in the House of Assembly (the house for white representatives) De Klerk was one of the strongest supporters of the tricameral parliament. Under this system whites, coloureds and Indians controlled their 'own affairs' (residential areas, schools and cultural affairs), while general affairs (defence, foreign relations, etc) were discussed jointly. Representation was fixed according to population numbers and voting in parliament took place according to a fixed formula. There was never any chance of the main white party being outvoted. An NP pamphlet issued ahead of the 1983 referendum on the draft constitution explicitly stated that bringing blacks with their numbers into the system would mean that 'whites, within ten years, would not stand a chance'.[16] In fact, coloured and Indian members in the tricameral parliament implacably opposed both race classification and residential segregation, and there was virtually no support for the system in the black community.

From the start De Klerk was one of the most enthusiastic supporters of the tricameral system. In February 1986 he said his party believed that 'recognising the importance of group existence is not discriminatory per se', but a condition for peaceful existence. Each group 'should have a community life of its own', including its own residential areas, schools and other institutions that enabled it to look after its own interests and preserve its character.

De Klerk also supported race classification, which was the cornerstone of both apartheid and the tricameral parliament. In 1986 he said in parliament that the policy required 'certainty in regard to the definition of each group'. It also meant 'each group must have a power base of its own, a power base within which the group is able to take care of its own affairs by itself'. What De Klerk did not mention was that this group membership was not voluntary, but decreed and imposed by the state.[17] In 1987, at a point when other party leaders had accepted the inevitability of a few mixed suburbs, De Klerk urged whites at a public meeting to report people other than whites living in 'white' areas.[18]

---

15 Theresa Papenfus, *Pik Botha en sy tyd* (Pretoria: Litera, 2010), pp. 380-87.

16 *Die Afrikaner*, 29 April 1987.

17 *House of Assembly Debates*, 1986, vol.1, cols 145-46.

18 Waldmeir, *Anatomy of a Miracle*, p. 111.

In January 1986, De Klerk also clashed with his colleague Chris Heunis in a meeting of the special cabinet committee on blacks. De Klerk opposed accommodating black voters in parliament on the same basis as the three minority groups. White dominance would be surrendered to blacks as a result of numbers. The question of a black president also came up. De Klerk had previously asked Heunis how a democracy that included blacks could be established in South Africa, while still ensuring that the president remained white. Heunis replied that this was not possible. De Klerk said he could live with something like a rotating presidency, 'but somewhere there must be somebody who had enough power in his hands, somewhere in a good government there must be a PW Botha who had enough power and authority to ensure that things went right in a country'.[19]

In a meeting of the committee on 1 March 1986 the president stated that the big problem was the lack of unanimity in cabinet about the future political role of blacks. He was also worried that coloureds and Indians did not really accept the new dispensation. De Klerk remarked that negotiations with blacks were on the rocks and there were fundamental differences between the ministers over the question of where the NP and the country were heading. Heunis pointed out that it was impossible for him to negotiate in the absence of cabinet consensus. The only thing on which the cabinet agreed was that South Africa was one state. In the words of the *Sunday Times*, which had access to minutes of some of the meetings of the special cabinet committee, Heunis wanted to de-emphasise 'own affairs'. De Klerk wanted the opposite. The *Sunday Times* summed up De Klerk's position by the end of 1986 as follows: '(a) a new content to the concept of own powers for regional and group bodies, and (b) a greater geographical content for population groups to which own affairs could be devolved.'[20]

In mid-1986 the NP finally accepted that all those South Africans living outside the independent 'homelands' formed part of the South African state and shared a single citizenship. They had the right to participate in the institutions of the common area (previously called 'white South Africa').[21] In his speech to the 1986 federal congress in August De Klerk stated that any solution would have to be based on

---

19 *Sunday Times*, 28 August 1994. The passages in this and the following paragraph were based on the minutes of the special cabinet committee quoted by Daan Prinsloo, PW Botha's official biographer, in his manuscript, which had to be submitted to the state legal adviser. Acting in terms of the Protection of Information Act, De Klerk, in consultation with the state legal adviser, instructed Prinsloo to remove the passages before publishing the book. According to the paper, the legal adviser ordered the destruction of the verbatim report in the original manuscript because the quotations in them could not be verified against the original tapes. The relevant passages were leaked to the *Sunday Times*.

20 *Sunday Times*, 26 August 1994.

21 'Federale Kongres vir Vryheid en Stabiliteit', NP pamphlet, 1986.

the premise of 'self-determination for each population group' over its own affairs. He added: 'No people or group should be placed in a situation in which it is dominated by any other nation or population group.'[22] In its manifesto for the 1987 election the NP stated that any system had to enjoy the approval of all racial groups, including blacks: '[Any] solution that is arrived at has to be based on the premise of self-determination for each population group over its own affairs and joint decision-making in respect of general affairs.'[23]

But outside the NP there was little or no support for the government's proposals. In 1986 Minister of Justice Kobie Coetsee asked George Bizos, a lawyer close to ANC leaders both in jail and in exile, whether the ANC would accept a fourth chamber to represent blacks in parliament as a first step towards a political settlement and the ending of sanctions. Bizos's answer was an emphatic no: 'I reminded him [Coetsee] that the majority of the coloured and Indian people had rejected the 1983 constitution. [The ANC] would settle for nothing less than meaningful participation in the affairs of the country, universal suffrage, free and fair elections and a democratic constitution. He was visibly upset and told me not to preach to him.'[24] A similar response could have been expected from any leader of the United Democratic Front.

Mangosuthu Buthelezi, leader of the Inkatha movement and the most likely NP ally in a post-apartheid order, denounced the tricameral parliament as a 'mammoth betrayal' of blacks.[25] He initiated the Buthelezi Commission and the KwaZulu-Natal Indaba, both of which recommended regional integration based on proper consociational principles that included universal franchise, freedom of association and voluntary group membership. Buthelezi also refused to negotiate while Nelson Mandela and other ANC leaders remained in jail.

De Klerk later claimed the interim constitution of 1993 was the logical conclusion of NP decisions taken in 1986–87.[26] This view must be rejected. The 1986 decision accepted a common system, but did so within the framework of mandatory racial classification and a distinction between 'own' and 'general' affairs, the objective being a carefully crafted system that would prevent black domination through the sheer force of numbers.

In his speeches in the 1987 election campaign De Klerk rejected the allegation of the Conservative Party that the NP favoured black majority rule. NP policy, he said, was to move away from majority rule and negotiate a system in which no group

22   CRE Rencken, 'Speeches Made at the NP Federal Congress, 1986', unpublished ms., unpaginated.

23   'NP Policy: The Facts – Election 6 May', NP pamphlet, 1987.

24   George Bizos, 'The Release of Nelson Mandela,' undated ms., p. 6.

25   Ben Temkin, *Buthelezi: A Biography* (London: Frank Cass, 2003), p. 227.

26   Waldmeir, *Anatomy of a Miracle*, p. 113.

would dominate over another.[27] Although own affairs/general affairs was an important device to persuade whites to accept the tricameral parliament, it produced a dead end because it was impossible to extend the system to blacks. As De Klerk confessed ten years later, it would have been much better for the party if in 1986 it had developed a federal policy.[28]

A *verkrampte* image

Towards the end of the 1980s De Klerk privately asked Progressive Federal Party (PFP) leader Colin Eglin why he always referred to him as a *verkrampte*. Eglin, who enjoyed a good personal relationship with De Klerk, replied: 'My indictment against you is even greater than that ... You are aspiring to be the next state president. I am a fairly perceptive politician and I don't know whether you are *verlig* or *verkramp*, and I think that is worse.' To which De Klerk responded: 'I am not *verkramp*, but if you were the leader of the NP in the Transvaal, with Andries Treurnicht breathing down your neck in the Transvaal, you might even sound like me.'[29]

In his autobiography De Klerk argues that his conservative image was a consequence of his position in the tricameral system as chairman of the Ministers' Council for whites. It was in this capacity that he championed the own affairs policy and fought battles against ministers in charge of general affairs departments who tried to combine greater centralised control with de-racialisation.[30] But these words obscure the fact that he enthusiastically threw in his weight behind own affairs. Minister of Transport Eli Louw recalls: 'FW liked the system of a Tricameral Parliament [based on Own and General Affairs] very much. It suited him perfectly, because there was no consensus within the party how to tackle the issue of rights for black people.'[31]

Barend du Plessis, minister of finance, also recalls that De Klerk was an enthusiastic supporter of own affairs. He adds: 'I don't know what motivated him to jump. I was as surprised as everyone ... I only know that if he and his conservatives had not opposed us all along, we might have arrived earlier at certain solutions.'[32] Eli Louw tells a revealing story in his autobiography. In 1988 he gave an order for all apartheid signs on the trains to be removed. PW Botha agreed on condition that South African Transport Services (SATS) should be instructed to do this without any publicity. 'Just keep quiet and take the signs off,' the president said.

27 *Beeld*, 29 April 1987.
28 De Klerk, *Die laaste trek*, p. 127
29 Interview with Colin Eglin by Patti Waldmeir, 15 November 1994.
30 De Klerk, *Die laaste trek*, p. 114.
31 Interview with Eli Louw, 30 December 2010.
32 Interview with Barend du Plessis by Patti Waldmeir, 3 November 1994; Communication from Barend du Plessis, 20 July 2011.

Louw went ahead, but the *Cape Times* got wind of it and published a report with a banner headline 'SATS burns apartheid signs'. In the next cabinet meeting De Klerk complained that he had to read in the newspaper about a matter cabinet had not even discussed. He gave notice that he would take it further. After cabinet adjourned, an angry Louw told De Klerk: 'I'll tell you why I did not bring it before cabinet. It is because there are people like you who would shoot it down. Your problem is that you are too damn scared and that's why we do not get any further.'[33]

The main reason for De Klerk's conservative stance was his precarious position in the seat of Vereeniging, which he had held since 1972. The NP won the general election of 1987 convincingly, but the CP had made strong inroads in the Transvaal. It retained seven seats in the province and took fourteen mostly rural seats from the NP. De Klerk retained his Vereeniging seat by a mere 1 524 votes (compared to 4 329 votes in 1981) even though the CP still placed him on the NP's conservative wing. For De Klerk the political stakes had become very high. As Transvaal leader he was still the frontrunner in the race to succeed PW Botha, yet he was under threat in his own constituency.

He could, however, stand for president without representing a seat. In terms of section 7(5) of the Republic of South Africa Constitution, Act No. 110 of 1983, 'no person may be elected or serve as State President unless he is qualified to be nominated or elected and take his seat as a member of a House'. In other words, De Klerk qualified as a presidential candidate on the strength of his eligibility for parliament. If the constitution had stipulated that he had to be an elected member of parliament, De Klerk's political career may well have ended at age 53 in the general election of 1989. The NP candidate in the Vereeniging seat scraped home by five votes, but only after four recounts – the previous counts all showing a CP majority. Koos van der Merwe, who won the neighbouring constituency of Overvaal for the CP in 1987 by 1 074 votes, is adamant that if De Klerk had had a *verligte* image he would have lost his seat, perhaps in 1987 but almost certainly in 1989.

While in 1986 De Klerk accepted the need to incorporate blacks in common structures, he still thought some aspects of the homeland policy, particularly the independence of homelands, could be retained. He continued to believe that 'own affairs', especially for the minority communities, could serve as a stabilising mechanism. While the limits of this policy were becoming ever more starkly evident, the Transvaal NP, which he led, was under increasing pressure from the right wing, which resisted any further dilution of white power. De Klerk's model as leader was John Vorster between the years 1966 and 1974, when he used his personal popularity and debating skills to dismantle some of the crudest components of apartheid.

But unlike Vorster, whose 'summits' with black and coloured leaders were held

---

33   Eli Louw, *Oor my pad: 'n Outobiografie* (Potchefstroom: Andcork, 2009), pp. 138-39.

in private, De Klerk had to face coloured and Indian politicians in the tricameral parliament. This had an enormous educative impact on him and other NP politicians. It was no longer possible to speak about separate freedoms and the good intentions of apartheid once coloured MPs had spelled out the humiliations and injustices of this policy.

Kobus Meiring, a deputy cabinet minister, told of a speech he made at an NP 'team-building' meeting about the grave injustices brought about by the Group Areas Act. He slammed a colleague who had earlier boasted of being instrumental in the ejection of a married mixed couple from a white residential area. Meiring recalls that when PW Botha spoke later, he looked at him 'with those unbelievably penetrating eyes and said in a calm voice: "Colleagues, everything our colleague has just said is true and we will have to work on it."'[34]

De Klerk described his experience of the tricameral parliament as follows: 'I had to face the wrath and the bitterness of the coloured people, especially with regard to their education and their rejection, yes, it had a marked effect on me, and it made me sensitive, trying my conscience.'[35] During one of the heated debates in parliament Allan Hendrickse, leader of the coloured Labour Party, asked President Botha to return District Six in Cape Town to the coloured people. The way in which the coloured people had lost property under Group Areas removals, he said, amounted to 'theft'.[36]

De Klerk consistently denied that he had undergone a sudden, Damascus-type epiphany or that his decision was a purely moral one. There was no shattering moment of truth or a 'conversion', he claims, and there is no reason to doubt him on this score. For all his searching for principles, he was an adaptable politician, weighing up alternatives in a shifting demographic and political balance, all the while keeping his own electoral base in mind. He abandoned apartheid because the homelands policy had failed to achieve 'separate freedoms', not because it was wrong from the outset. He told a television interviewer: 'If one believes a policy is unworkable, it becomes immoral to advocate it.' Pragmatic survival instincts took priority over morality in De Klerk's decision to abandon apartheid.[37]

For De Klerk it was important to reject the notion that apartheid was evil in its conception and that Afrikaner nationalists, including his uncle and father as NP leaders, propagated and executed a policy they knew to be evil. It was also important to dispel the idea that personal conversion prompted him to abandon apartheid.

Niel Barnard, head of the National Intelligence Service (NIS) which became

---

34   Kobus Meiring, *In Interesting Company* (Cape Town, privately published, 2004), pp. 53-55.

35   Interview with FW de Klerk by Patti Waldmeir, 23 November 1994.

36   *Sunday Tribune*, 2 October 1988; Paul Bell, 'Our Only Sin', *Leadership*, vol. 7, no. 3, 1998, p. 57.

37   Interview with FW de Klerk by David Frost, 14 February 1993, official transcript.

increasingly influential after PW Botha brutally squashed the initiative of the Eminent Persons Group in May 1986 (see p. 270), also rejected the idea that morality was the decisive consideration. 'Not a moral feeling or a Damascus experience, but power politics played the decisive role.'[38] The existing system had broken down and a new leader had to strike out on a new course. Mike Louw, second in command at the NIS, described the situation during the second half of the 1980s as follows: 'It was clear that [apartheid] was in shreds ... We were left without anything really to guide the country except for the pragmatic manoeuvrings by PW and other people.'[39]

But it would be wrong to think that morality played no role in De Klerk's 1990 decision to lift the ban on the ANC and release Mandela. I interviewed him shortly afterwards. To be provocative, I asked, 'Why are you doing all of this? The government could have held out another ten years.' De Klerk responded angrily: 'We could have carried on for another ten years, but that would have involved killing a lot of people. Where is the morality in that?'[40] Johann Rupert, head of the Rembrandt Group, recounts De Klerk's words to him shortly after the release of Nelson Mandela: 'Don't you realise [that] for the first time in my life as an Afrikaner I can look people in the eye?'[41] Morality played its role, but only after the political need for change had become imperative.

Exploring alternatives

De Klerk dated the start of his political conversion back to 1986. Ig Vorster, one of De Klerk's best friends from their student days and who later became dean of the Potchefstroom law faculty, also believes a clear shift in De Klerk's thinking can be traced back to 1986. He reconstructed his friend's thinking as expressed in a private conversation during that year: 'We should have some form of negotiation, some form of rethink that eventually will end up not in majority rule in the ordinary sense of the word, but in majority rule coupled with a sensible, well-negotiated power-sharing basis.' Vorster added: 'In other words, he accepted majority rule but without the winner taking all. That still meant a white veto.'[42]

De Klerk remembers his own thinking back in 1986 differently: 'I accepted that it will be one man one vote, and the protection would have to be built in through checks and balances, and not through a veto. I advocated consensus.'[43] But to his

---

38   Liezl Steenkamp, 'Geen morele besluit nie', *Die Burger*, 11 February 2010.

39   Interview with Mike Louw by Patti Waldmeir, 29 May 1995.

40   This is taken verbatim from Patti Waldmeir's interview with British Ambassador Robin Renwick, 16 December 1994, where Renwick retells a story I had told him earlier.

41   Interview with Johann Rupert by Patti Waldmeir, 3 March 1995.

42   Interview with Ig Vorster by Patti Waldmeir, 16 February 1995.

43   Interview with FW de Klerk by Patti Waldmeir, 23 November 1994.

colleagues in cabinet there was little sign of a shift in his thinking. The reformers saw him as ultra-cautious and a stumbling block in the way of change. He was like John Vorster, who waited for sufficient consensus in the party before he moved.

While a conservative, De Klerk was what can be called a parliamentary democrat. He decided that if he succeeded Botha as president, he would not want to govern the country in Botha's style. He was virtually the only minister who spoke up in cabinet against the extension of the state of emergency in 1988. He resented the sidelining of cabinet by the State Security Council (SSC) on security matters. One of his first steps as president was the restoration of cabinet authority in all decisions. Botha had distributed among cabinet members only those matters in the SSC minutes that he felt they needed to know about. De Klerk, by contrast, had all SSC minutes circulated.[44] As president, De Klerk would use a participatory style of decision-making in cabinet, allowing a free exchange of views. Meetings were often twice as long as those under his predecessor.[45]

But the differences between him and Botha went further. Botha had introduced major socio-economic reforms and tried to manage the political consequences in a managerial style.[46] Behind this lay the assumption that if the government created enough social development and uplifted the black population, the cry for political dominance would fade. This was a fallacy, as Colin Eglin noted: 'The more Botha tried to reform – and Botha was a reformer in the socio-economic field way ahead of De Klerk – the more the political pressures built up and the more he tried to manage and clamp down, the more the pressure built up.'[47]

De Klerk, by contrast, was a parliamentarian, someone who tenaciously defended the political primacy of the institution. He stuck to the policy of own affairs and general affairs, but he could no longer deny the need for a settlement based on black inclusion in parliament. He also realised that genuine negotiations with credible black leaders had to take place as soon as possible. In 1987 he told British Ambassador Robin Renwick that the Rhodesian white leadership had 'left it much too late to negotiate with the real black leaders'. As the ambassador got to know De Klerk better, he discovered he strongly disliked 'the country being governed as a kind of security camp'.[48] Stoffel van der Merwe, a deputy minister for constitutional planning, claims that by the end of 1988 De Klerk had opted for fundamental constitutional change, recognising democratic principles but entailing negotiations to prevent the domination or subordination of any group.[49]

44 Communication from Jannie Roux, cabinet secretary, 5 September 2011.
45 De Klerk, *Die laaste trek*, p. 171.
46 See the essay on Botha's managerial style in Hermann Giliomee, *The Parting of the Ways: South African Politics, 1976-82* (Cape Town: David Philip, 1982), pp. 34-42; De Villiers and De Villiers, *PW*, p. 90.
47 Interview with Colin Eglin by Patti Waldmeir, 15 November 1994.
48 Interview with Robin Renwick by Patti Waldmeir, 16 December 1994.
49 Cited by David Welsh, *The Rise and Fall of Apartheid* (Johannesburg: Jonathan Ball, 2009), p. 356.

De Klerk enjoyed two advantages. First was solid conservative support. Barend du Plessis later graciously conceded that as the more *verligte* candidate he would have had to spend much more time with the conservatives to win their trust.[50] Second, De Klerk had seven months of 'internship' for the presidency. His elevation to the party's leadership seven months before his election as president was unique in South African political history. If he had succeeded Botha immediately, there would have been tremendous pressure on him to continue in Botha's managerial style. In addition, he would have experienced great problems in freeing himself from a pressure group such as the military, which had built up great influence.

'Internship' as leader

During his 'internship' as leader, which stretched from February to September 1989, De Klerk could put distance between himself and some of the pressure groups and gain greater clarity about his policy options. He could look back and acquire a historical perspective; he could look forward and decide what role he wanted to play. Did he want the role of a political manager or of a democratic leader committed to the autonomy of institutions such as the cabinet, parliament, the courts and the Reserve Bank? He could reflect on all these without having to think about the need to fight for his political life in a forthcoming election.

Above all, he could take time to study the South African situation carefully. One of the people who set up meetings for him was Pieter de Lange, chairman of the executive council of the Afrikaner Broederbond and rector of the Rand Afrikaans University. De Lange recalls that De Klerk first underwent 'economic instruction'. 'Wim de Villiers [executive chairman of Gencor] and others were tutoring him over weekends in the way the economy works.' De Lange added wryly: 'That is quite a basic thing for a new leader to learn, quite apart from the moral things.'[51] Derek Keys, minister of finance between 1992 and 1994, had high praise: 'He grasped at once what the issue was when I had to raise something . . . his sense of judgement [about economic issues] was top rate.'[52]

De Lange and De Klerk's brother, Willem, also set up private dinners with Nthato Motlana and other black leaders who were close to the United Democratic Front. FW de Klerk was in the fortunate position that he could meet them without having the final responsibility for what was happening in the country. He also kept in touch with his base. He was a member of the Afrikaner Broederbond from a young age and had served with Wim de Villiers and Nic Wiehahn on a sub-committee of the Broederbond on labour reform during the 1970s.

---

50 Communication from Barend du Plessis, 25 July 2011.
51 Interview with Pieter de Lange by Patti Waldmeir, 12 October 1994.
52 Interview with Derek Keys by Patti Waldmeir, 18 January 1995.

Towards the end of the 1980s the Broederbond recovered from the membership losses it had suffered after it had issued a letter mooting the possibility of a black president (see p. 252). By 1988 its membership stood at 17 369 in 1 212 divisions across the country – the highest figures for both categories ever. The divisions' responses to the head office's regular letters and their own inputs gave De Klerk a good idea of the thinking of an influential section of the Afrikaner community. He told De Lange that 'if the Broederbond had not done the work it did in the 1980s, he could not have made the speech he made on the second of February'. De Lange observed that De Klerk was 'thinking about the unthinkable, that is a situation where whites do not have a monopoly of power anymore, where everybody has full citizenship ... It was about building up trust between the races through talks on local, regional and national level.'[53]

De Klerk broadened his understanding of his challenges in meetings with the heads of government in African states, including Zambia, Zaire, Mozambique and Malawi. In June 1989 he visited Europe for talks with the heads of government of Britain, Germany, Portugal and Italy. With financial sanctions and capital flight dampening economic growth and exacerbating unemployment, the trip was important to establish what the expectations of Western leaders were. They all told De Klerk substantial political reform was necessary before they could start lifting some of the sanctions.[54] The meeting with British Prime Minister Margaret Thatcher went well. She backed him in his attempt to establish a form of power sharing on the model of the Swiss federal cabinet. In her memoirs she drew a comparison between De Klerk and the Soviet Union's Mikhail Gorbachev as leaders with vision and boldness.[55]

At this stage De Klerk had established firm control over the party. Outside the military, everyone was tired of PW Botha's imperious rule and his closeness to the military. De Klerk was quite different from his predecessors, who had each had a special adviser. Leon Wessels said: 'There was no clique around him ... Socially he was very active but he was not someone inclined to gossip. He liked to exchange viewpoints and arguments. He was prepared to concede a stronger argument. But in the party he was *die man wat die tamboer slaan* (the man who called the shots).'[56]

Gerrit Viljoen noted: 'International events in the first half of 1989 had a considerable effect on FW's sense of urgency and also on his sense that you cannot do it in a half-baked way, you have to go for it and do it very thoroughly and

53   Interview with Pieter de Lange by Patti Waldmeir, 12 October 1994.
54   Interview with Robin Renwick by Patti Waldmeir, 16 December 1994.
55   Margaret Thatcher, *The Downing Street Years* (London: HarperCollins, 1993), pp. 532-34. For a snide comment on De Klerk as 'just another bloody Boer' ascribed to Thatcher see Anthony Sampson, *Mandela: The Authorized Biography* (Johannesburg: Jonathan Ball, 1999), p. 386.
56   Interview with Leon Wessels, 8 June 1992.

fundamentally.'[57] De Klerk accepted that a settlement would have to be the product of negotiations. But he had not yet decided if it could include the ANC while the organisation pursued a two-track strategy of signalling a willingness to negotiate while preparing for armed insurrection.

National Democratic Revolution

By 1989 the ANC was still clinging to the theory of the National Democratic Revolution (NDR). The NDR was the key premise of the main theoretical document the SA Communist Party (SACP) adopted in 1962, *The Road to South African Freedom*. It located the NDR within its theory of colonialism of a special kind that postulated the existence of an 'oppressing white nation' occupying the same territory as the oppressed black nation and enjoying the wealth the latter produced. The NDR's objectives were to overthrow the 'colonial state', to introduce popular control over all institutions, to nationalise the main industries and to introduce radical land reform.

The SACP wanted to play a key role in the ANC, and the SACP leadership aimed to have all the strategic positions in the ANC filled by its members. By the mid-1980s approximately three quarters of the ANC's national executive were SACP members.[58] One of them was Thabo Mbeki, who had fled South Africa in 1962.

In 1989 Mbeki chaired the SACP congress, when it reiterated its commitment to the NDR objective of overthrowing the 'colonial state', establishing popular control over vital sectors of the economy and restoring the land to the people. It rejected 'group rights' as 'fraught with the danger of perpetuating inequality'.[59] By 1989 the NDR theory of 'colonialism of a special type' had been transplanted just about wholly into the ANC's programme.[60]

There was no sign that the ANC could achieve a revolutionary victory through military means. Chris Hani and other radical ANC leaders in fact rejected negotiations on the grounds that the movement's revolutionary underground had to be much stronger before talks could begin. The armed struggle had sustained the protests inside South Africa, but in military terms it was largely a bluff. During the 1980s the ANC and SACP together were consistently among the top ten out of some 80 organisations or movements receiving Soviet aid; other countries could not be

---

57 Interview with Gerrit Viljoen by Patti Waldmeir, 20 October 1994.

58 Stephen Ellis and Tsepo Sechaba, *Comrades Against Apartheid: The ANC and the South African Communist Party in Exile* (London: James Currey, 1992), p. 37.

59 'The Path to Power', Programme of the SACP, adopted 1989, www.sacp. org.za.

60 Irina Filatova, 'The Lasting Legacy: The Soviet Theory of the National Liberation Movement and South Africa', paper presented to the Centre for African Studies, University of Cape Town, 2008, pp. 16-18; Irina Filatova, 'The ANC and the Soviet Union,' www.politicsweb.co.za (first posted on 10 August 2011).

relied on for substantial support. As Russian historian Irina Filatova wrote: 'Without Soviet assistance the ANC, as we know it, would not have existed and South Africa's history would have been very different. There would have been no armed struggle or a much reduced armed struggle and without that the ANC would have had great difficulty becoming the main symbol of the black struggle.'[61] In 1991, with the break-up of the Soviet Union, financial assistance to the ANC would cease.

An ANC insider calculated that approximately half of a total of 12 000 trained guerrillas were infiltrated into South Africa. Of these 6 000, a third abandoned their mission, and many others were turned against the ANC by the security forces, killed, or convicted and sent to jail. In 1987 Mangosuthu Buthelezi commented on the lack of any significant success in the armed struggle. 'After twenty-five years of endeavour every bridge in the country is still intact and there is not a single factory out of production because of revolutionary activity. The classic circumstances in which the armed struggle wins the day . . . are just not present in South Africa.'[62]

In 1987 Govan Mbeki was released. After the September 1989 election Walter Sisulu and all other high-profile political prisoners except Mandela were released. Most white voters assumed that these leaders were released on compassionate grounds, not with a view to starting negotiations.

An electoral mandate

The caucus elected De Klerk NP leader in February 1989, but he lacked his own electoral mandate. With an election pending for all three houses of parliament before the end of the year, he immediately turned his attention to reformulating the party's policy programme. He appointed a five-man 'inner committee' to write the election manifesto and took an active role (see p. 310). The NP faced a serious challenge. For the first time in more than 30 years it faced the possibility of a hung parliament that would force it into a coalition.

An address by De Klerk in parliament in May 1989 was the first sign of a major break with Botha's policies. De Klerk envisaged the introduction of a just political, economic and social system. Speaking later, Gerrit Viljoen, minister for constitutional development, called for a system in which every South African had a right to participate in decision-making on all levels. The NP's manifesto for the election of 6 September was a plan of action the party undertook to strive towards during the following five years.

Large parts of the plan came across as a liberal democratic manifesto. It proposed a pluralist programme for a heterogeneous society, stating that democracy could only work if common values and areas of agreement existed among its citizens.

---

61   Irina Filatova, 'South Africa's Soviet Connection', *History Compass*, 6, 2, 2008, p. 401.

62   *Cape Times*, 17 September 1987.

It pledged the party to negotiations with leaders across the board with a view to creating a new order. Yet the document still contained much of what has been referred to as 'reform apartheid'. It stated that 'group diversity' had to be taken into account and the principle of self-determination over groups' own affairs had to be retained, along with power sharing for general affairs. Instead of prescribed group identities, people should be able to change their group, provided the 'receiving group' agreed. Group areas would have to be retained for the preservation of their own community life, but free settlement areas would be proclaimed after consultation with residents. The plan presented a new ideological framework for the political system that twenty years earlier might have launched the country on a new course. But the NP was already in a weakened state and the interim constitution of 1993 would be a far cry from this action plan, which supposedly constituted the party's mandate.

By July 1989 the NP's prospects still looked bleak. On the basis of opinion surveys, the analyst Lawrence Schlemmer stated that if voters were to go to the polls at that moment, 'the most dramatic shift in white public opinion since 1948' would occur. The number of NP seats would drop from 123 to 78, and the CP and the Democratic Party (DP) would win 52 and 36 seats respectively.[63] With the election campaign in full swing, the simmering conflict between Botha as president and De Klerk as party leader came to a head. On 14 August Botha's ministers asked him to retire, which he did on the same day. The NP may have fared even worse if it had fought the election under the leadership of PW Botha, who was now seen as old, cantankerous and bereft of new ideas.

Once Botha had resigned, the NP's marketing agency came up with the idea of projecting the party as 'under new management', with a new leader and new policies. It worked. According to the CP's Koos van der Merwe, the CP's polling showed that its support dropped by 30% in the final two weeks as floating voters defected to the NP with its 'new' image.[64] The NP won outright, but for the first time since 1958 attracted less than half the vote. In a parliament of 165 seats its share dropped from 120 seats to 93. Another 29 NP seats had now become marginal, with majorities of fewer than 1 500 votes. The CP won 39 seats and the DP, formed out of the Progressive Federal Party and some minor reformist parties, 33 seats.

If the NP had won eleven fewer seats, there would have been a hung parliament. Before the election the CP hoped that in a hung parliament it would come to power with the help of conservative NP members who rejected an NP-DP coalition. The CP coming to power would have been disastrous. It had campaigned under the

---

63 JM Aucamp, 'Die Nasionale Party van Suid-Afrika se laaste dekade as regerende party, 1984-1994', doctoral dissertation, University of the Free State, 2010, pp. 236-40.
64 Communication from Koos van der Merwe, 5 August 2011.

banner of a homeland where whites could exercise self-determination, but had no idea where this white homeland would be or how it could be established.

For De Klerk the election sent a strong message that most voters – probably at least 70% – wanted a new leader with fresh ideas for establishing a common system for whites and blacks. Up to the election he had given no strong signs in public that he was prepared to abandon some of the NP's shibboleths. Speaking privately two weeks before the election, DP leader Colin Eglin considered De Klerk 'not an initiator, not an out-in-front leader', and was convinced De Klerk was not 'going to be able to cross the Rubicon on his own'. The only way he could cross was 'if a few democrats push him across'.[65]

The NP triumphed but was unlikely to win an outright majority in any white election again. Support among its followers for negotiations was weak. The proportion of whites favouring negotiations with the ANC had dropped by four percentage points since 1986. Some 62% of whites (including 78% of Afrikaans-speaking whites) now opposed the idea. Secret polls conducted by a government agency showed that some 60% of blacks could be expected to support the ANC in a free election.[66] Judging by the polls, the political polarisation of South Africa seemed to be extreme.

Yet among the political elite there was a marked change of mood. Ton Vosloo, managing director of Nasionale Pers, observed that a fair measure of stability had been established in South Africa and beyond its borders. The talk was no longer of South Africa finding itself in a 'pre-revolutionary situation', but in a 'pre-negotiating situation'. It was increasingly accepted in the ranks of the elite that the ANC had to be one of the parties at the table.[67]

De Klerk was elected as president on 14 September 1989 and sworn in on 20 September. In his acceptance speech he pledged the government to promoting reconciliation and starting negotiations for a new constitution to bring about a generally acceptable solution. He also committed the government to tough action against terrorism and violence.[68] A few days after he was sworn in, Mike Louw and Maritz Spaarwater informed De Klerk of their meeting with Thabo Mbeki and Jacob Zuma in Switzerland (see p. 227).

The fall of the Berlin Wall

Between April and November 1989 South Africans closely watched two developments that directly affected the possibility of a peaceful settlement. First, the war in Angola ended in a peace settlement brokered by the United States and the Soviet

65   O'Malley Archives, Interview with Colin Eglin, 20 August 1989.
66   Welsh, *The Rise and Fall of Apartheid*, p. 347.
67   O'Malley Archives, Interview with Ton Vosloo, 21 August 1989.
68   De Klerk, *Die laaste trek*, p. 169.

Union. A UN-backed process ending with the proclamation of independence for South West Africa (later Namibia) could now begin. It got off to a shaky start on 1 April, with 2 000 Swapo belligerents streaming into South West Africa from Angola – in violation of the accords – in an attempt to seize the territory. This seemed to confirm white suspicion that no political pact with a liberation movement was worth the paper it was written on.

Peace in South West Africa was quickly restored after brief but fierce fighting, and implementation of the resolution proceeded without further hitches. The first free elections followed in November. Blacks and whites peacefully went to the polls after decades of bitter conflict. It made a deep impression on almost all South Africans. Hannes Smith, the fiery editor of the *Windhoek Observer*, observed: 'With an abruptness that surprised everyone the white man of South West Africa decided to accept independence and black majority government.'[69]

The second dramatic development was the turmoil in Eastern Europe where thousands of people openly challenged the communist regimes. In May 1989 the German Democratic Republic (GDR), or East Germany, looked stable and as if it would last for many decades, but the election results of that month – which produced 98% support for government candidates – were so blatantly fabricated that thousands of people were aroused to protest despite the risks.

On 2 May 10 000 East Germans in Leipzig staged the biggest demonstration since the 1953 uprising. Five days later Mikhail Gorbachev, attending the 40th anniversary of the founding of the GDR, said to his stony-faced host Erich Honecker: 'History punishes those who are late.' Demonstrators began holding regular demonstrations and 'vigils for change' in several cities. A week after Gorbachev's visit 90 000 people gathered in Leipzig shouting slogans like 'We are the people'. In October a crowd of 300 000 assembled in Leipzig and in the following month half a million gathered in Berlin demanding immediate reform. In a sheer panic Honecker's colleagues removed him in a coup and liberalised foreign travel. On 9 November the East German authorities announced that people could cross the border into West Germany without advance notice. The Wall had fallen.[70]

In South Africa, the Mass Democratic Movement, a mass movement of organisations that served as a front for the UDF and other organisations after they were severely restricted was inspired by events in Eastern Europe to organise 'a month of protests'. This included marches through town centres and white suburbs, and along white beaches. The police handled some of these marches with velvet gloves, but on 2 September broke up a Cape Town march with brutality. Activists and church

69   Hermann Giliomee, 'Vreugdevure en etniese spoke in Namibiaë, *Die Suid-Afrikaan*, 24, December 1989, p. 10.

70   Tony Judt, *Postwar: A History of Europe since 1945* (London: Vintage, 2010), pp. 613–14.

leaders, including Allan Boesak and Nobel Peace Prize winner Archbishop Desmond Tutu, decided to stage a mass march in Cape Town on 13 September. Some white public figures, including the mayor, academics and professionals, expressed their support. The organisers announced that they would not ask permission for the march and it would go ahead even if it ended in a blood bath.

Dirk Hattingh, moderator of the Western Cape Synod of the Dutch Reformed Church, feared a major confrontation. On 11 September he called Johan Heyns, moderator of the General Synod of the DRC, in Pretoria and three other DRC leaders. The next day they met with Tutu, Boesak and other church leaders. Hattingh wrote: 'The atmosphere was tense, even hostile to the white church leaders . . . The black churches and their leaders approved of the march. It was clearly an organised action that could not be stopped in any way . . . We realised no one could stop the march of so many people, not even with guns.' Accepting that there was no way the march could be stopped, the white church leaders asked Tutu for assurances that it would be peaceful, property would not be damaged and confrontation with the police would be avoided. When Tutu and his group agreed, the white church leaders undertook to ask De Klerk to allow the march to take place.

Meeting with De Klerk and some of his senior ministers immediately afterwards, they found the acting president 'firm but fair and open to persuasion'. For De Klerk it was one of the toughest decisions he had to take. Reflecting five years later on the momentous decision to permit the march, he said 'it was taken within the framework of legalising the position of prohibited political organisations. Secondly, there was an element of realising that if we did not allow such marches we might have seen instead thirty thousand people marching, half a million marching.'[71] Gerrit Viljoen, minister of constitutional development, remarked: 'It was really the big changes internationally that took place with regard to the Soviets and Eastern Europe that brought home the inevitability of a fundamental change.' Viljoen continued: 'FW said: "We cannot have a democracy without protest marches! These things will be part of a new dispensation."' According to Viljoen, De Klerk was scared that if these marches were not allowed, 'you could have a half a million or a million people coming together and then the question of legitimacy and control . . . becomes very, very acute'.[72]

In a vital intervention De Klerk publicly called on the marchers: 'Do not batter the door down. It is already open.' Leon Wessels told the leaders of the march: 'We may have good news for you, but if anything goes wrong, all hell will break loose.' He recalls: 'You pump adrenalin all the time.'[73]

---

71   Interview with FW de Klerk by Patti Waldmeir, 23 November 1994.
72   Interview with Gerrit Viljoen by Patti Waldmeir, 20 October 1994.
73   Interview with Leon Wessels, 8 June 1992.

De Klerk decided that the march the next day could go ahead with this proviso: '[The] route had to be discussed with Tutu, the protests had to be peaceful, and the police would not be visible.'[74] The following day 30 000 people marched slowly through the streets in a peaceful march. Tutu spoke from the City Hall balcony while the banned green, black and gold flag of the ANC was openly displayed. No property was destroyed, there was no police intervention, and no complaints were laid. In the following days peaceful marches followed in several towns and cities.

Along with the release of Mandela five months later, De Klerk's decision to permit the Cape Town march was a turning point. Both could have gone seriously wrong. Waldmeir remarks perceptively on De Klerk's gamble: 'He could only gamble that, once the lid was removed, [the revolutionary pressures] would dissipate rather than explode. He was right: The Cape Town crowd never exceeded the thirty thousand that he considered manageable. He began to believe – and it was crucial to his future plans – that he could manage not only protest marches but also the entire process of change.'[75]

A changing climate

In 1988 and 1989 the climate for a settlement in South Africa improved dramatically. In the Soviet Union the previous policy of providing substantial aid to liberation movements in the developing world as a way of weakening the West was on its way out. The new talk of *glasnost* and *perestroika* constituted a dramatic change from the old revolutionary rhetoric in which many ANC leaders in exile still believed.

The heads of African states in East and Central Africa increasingly pushed the ANC to consider liberation without political violence. At times ANC leader Oliver Tambo had been deeply offended by some of the actions of these leaders – in particular by the moves of President Kenneth Kaunda – but by mid-1989 it was clear that circumstances were ripe for the ANC to adopt a new strategy. On 21 August 1989 a sub-committee of the Organisation of African Unity issued the Harare Declaration. It was drafted under Tambo's supervision and received the backing of both the National Working Committee and the Frontline States.

The declaration called for an end to apartheid and a negotiated settlement that would transform the country into a non-racial state with citizens enjoying common and equal citizenship. There was no reference to minority rights, but people could join the party of their choice, provided it did not further racism. It was vague about economic policy and committed the ANC only to an 'economic order which shall promote and advance the well being of all of South Africa'. The government

---

74 Dirk Hattingh, 'Protesoptog, 13 September 1989', unpublished ms., 28 February 2009; Interview with Dirk Hattingh, 8 August 2011.

75 Waldmeir, *Anatomy of a Miracle*, p. 139.

had to prepare the climate for negotiations by lifting the ban on restricted persons and organisations, ending the state of emergency and repealing legislation that circumscribed political activity. Both the government and the ANC should suspend hostilities. Both parties should agree on constitutional principles and the introduction of an interim government that would supervise the drawing up of the new constitution.[76]

The declaration was bland enough on economic policy not to frighten investors. But the proposal for an interim government meant a rupture of constitutional continuity, signalling in effect a revolutionary victory. The state had not been defeated and De Klerk had no intention of conceding to this demand.

A major obstacle was the issue of violence. A formula had to be found for getting the ANC legalised and starting negotiations without making the symbolic concession of renouncing the armed struggle. The ANC in exile had long claimed for itself the mantle of leadership of the liberation struggle and had no intention of allowing competitors on its turf – except in the rural areas of KwaZulu and Natal, where Mangosuthu Buthelezi had shown from the early 1980s that he and his Inkatha movement would be a tough nut to crack. Abandoning the armed struggle would fatally weaken the ANC through internal schisms and create an opportunity for the Pan Africanist Congress to snipe at it from the radical left. In the memorandum Mandela sent to PW Botha prior to their meeting, he had written that there would be no easy compromise on violence. He described the government's insistence on the renunciation of violence as symptomatic of the continued commitment of whites to domination. Nor would the ANC break with the SACP.

'A window of opportunity'

De Klerk announced his new cabinet on 18 September. One of the main changes was that Gerrit Viljoen was moved to the portfolio of constitutional development. He was tasked with heading the government's negotiations with extra-parliamentary movements.[77] Hendrik Verwoerd used Werner Eiselen to test his ideas about the ethnic character and aspirations of African society; John Vorster relied heavily on Hendrik van den Bergh's advice in countering subversion; PW Botha paid most attention to his military advisers in his attempts to control and deflect mass protests and thwart insurgency. De Klerk now tasked Viljoen with negotiating with extra-parliamentary parties.[78] Another major change was the appointment of industrialist Wim de Villiers to the new portfolio of administration and privatisation. One of his main tasks was to scale down the state's role in the economy in order to

76   Hassen Ebrahim, *The Soul of a Nation*, Cape Town: Oxford University Press, 1998), pp. 451-55.
77   De Klerk, *Die laaste trek*, pp. 172-73.
78   De Klerk, *Die laaste trek*, p. 173.

promote rapid growth to tackle unemployment. De Klerk accepted the view that poverty in South Africa had become so acute that redistribution through fiscal measures would not be enough; the economy had to grow much faster to create enough jobs.

On 9 November the Berlin Wall fell, signalling the end of the Cold War. According to De Klerk's wife Marike, De Klerk made his decision to end apartheid and start negotiations a week after the Wall fell. She recalls: '[He] had what he called a window of opportunity . . . so he decided if you decide to cut a dog's tail, you don't cut it piecemeal, you cut it and get it done with.'[79] In fact, De Klerk's boldness was in sharp contrast to the way he had acted previously. In a newspaper article on doubts about De Klerk's political outlook, Rykie van Reenen, a gifted journalist, wrote the apt headline: *De Klerk: Verlig, Verkramp, Versigtig* (Enlightened, Arch-conservative, Cautious).[80]

It was undoubtedly true that the collapse of the Soviet Union created a unique opportunity that put the ANC under pressure, but De Klerk's decision was not a rash one. Since the beginning of that year he had immersed himself in the political challenges facing him. The Cape Town march had forced him to realise that attempts to restrict mass protests would meet with stiff resistance. The fall of the Berlin Wall enabled the government to tell its followers that there was no need to fear that Moscow was still conspiring to overthrow the government in South Africa.

To start negotiations and find political partners across the colour line were the most urgent priorities. Botha's attempt to negotiate on his terms had failed, and by the end of the 1980s relations between the NP government and Inkatha were severely strained. In 1989 a committee was formed consisting of four members each from the NP and Inkatha, with Roelf Meyer and Oscar Dhlomo as chairmen. In September 1989 the two parties made a joint proposal to break the deadlock on negotiations: Nelson Mandela had to be freed, the ban on the ANC and other organisations had to be lifted, and group areas had to be scrapped. The ANC made identical demands. There was virtually no argument left for excluding the ANC.

Between 3 and 5 December the cabinet, supplemented by deputy ministers and the provincial administrators, met for a *bosberaad* at the D'Nyala game reserve near the Botswana border. Gerrit Viljoen submitted a report on all-party negotiations and Minister of Finance Barend du Plessis put the hard economic facts on the table: sanctions were biting, oil was in short supply and the repayment of foreign debt was dragging the economy down. De Klerk said: 'We can hold out for another ten or fifteen years, but there will be sanctions, sabotage and terror. Do we want

79   Interview with Marike de Klerk by Patti Waldmeir, 2 March 1995.
80   Lizette Rabe, *Rykie* (Cape Town: Tafelberg, 2011), p. 242.

that? We must avoid negotiating at a point where we have to yield under pressure. We must use this golden opportunity.'[81]

According to De Klerk even the most conservative cabinet members were ready for the 'quantum leap' of a government-controlled process of which the ANC had to be part.[82] The meeting accepted the logical consequences of power sharing on condition that there was reasonable protection for minorities. The cabinet had to ensure that good and orderly government was maintained.[83] De Klerk told the meeting he had received conflicting advice from the securocrats on the possible release of Mandela. One faction said: 'Set him free and treat him as an important leader.' The other faction said: 'Set him free and tell the world he is a terrorist.' Pik Botha responded: 'Forget the latter nonsense. Make certain that you are photographed together after his release. The picture will tell the world the story.'[84]

Implicitly this meant lifting the ban on the ANC and other extra-parliamentary movements, but it was only a day or two before De Klerk would address parliament that the cabinet formally decided to do so and to release Mandela unconditionally. De Klerk recalls that lifting the ban on the SACP and Umkhonto weSizwe was his most difficult decision.[85]

Talking to the police

De Klerk thought it was important to prepare the security services for the far-reaching changes under way without spelling out the D'Nyala decisions. In 1990 both the police and the military came under new commanding officers. On 1 January 1990 General Johan van der Merwe, previously head of the security police, took office as the new commissioner of the police, and General André (Kat) Liebenberg replaced Johannes (Jannie) Geldenhuys as chief of the defence force.

At the Police College in Pretoria on 10 January, De Klerk met Van der Merwe and 800 police officers summoned from across the country. Many of the officers had had a tough six years combating the uprising. This was especially true of the security police. At one stage during the state of emergency 18 000 people were detained. All had to be questioned and – if sufficient evidence could be gathered – prosecuted.

It was the police who fought the battle on the ground and some had to do the dirty work in carrying out political orders. Some 175 policemen would later seek amnesty from the Truth and Reconciliation Commission, but only 15 soldiers applied for and were granted amnesty. In fighting the insurrection the police, under pressure

81 Interview with André Fourie, 12 December 2010.
82 De Klerk, *Die laaste trek*, p. 179.
83 De Klerk, *Die laaste trek*, p. 177; E-mail communication from Jannie Roux, who attended both the D'Nyala meeting and the cabinet meeting in a secretarial capacity.
84 Interview with Leon Wessels, 8 June 1992.
85 Interview with FW de Klerk by Patti Waldmeir, 23 November 1994.

from politicians, were compromised. In 1988 Minister of Police Adriaan Vlok instructed General Van der Merwe to destroy Khotso House, headquarters of the South African Council of Churches and a regular meeting place of activists, telling him he had received the order personally from the president. Van der Merwe later wrote that after the order had been executed, some cabinet ministers told him the action should have been undertaken earlier.[86]

But others were shocked when the full story was revealed. De Klerk was a member of the State Security Council, which discussed the state's response to the ANC-led uprising. He wrote later that, while he accepted the repressive measures as necessary to restore stability, none of the gross human rights violations perpetrated was ever discussed in meetings he attended.[87] Nevertheless, aggressive speeches by political leaders created the impression that the enemy had to be wiped out before it committed acts of terror.[88]

As a deputy minister of police at the time, Leon Wessels disagreed with the line of argument that 'we did not know'. In 1997 he said: 'I refuse to condemn them [the soldiers and policemen] because we were on the same side and fought for the same cause, namely law and order as we saw it, and also to ensure that this country would not be made ungovernable . . . I do not believe the political defence of "I did not know" is available to me because in many respects I did not want to know.'[89] This was true of ministers who controlled security departments, but those in other departments were never confronted with these facts in cabinet meetings.

In addressing the police officers in January 1990, De Klerk said: 'I would like to get across to you the sincere appreciation of the government with regard to the enormity of the tasks which rest on your shoulders and, on the other hand, the sincere appreciation of the government for the exemplary way in which the South African Police have handled these enormous tasks.' He signalled that momentous times lay ahead. 'A mighty battle is unfolding in which the country could be propelled in two quite different directions: it could become either a racist struggle, in which black and white people get locked in a battle determined in a bloody manner, or it will be a battle over civilised values and norms . . . A battle between the forces of destruction and the forces of peace.'

He told the police officers the government had opted for a new dispensation that would be fair and just. It had to be one in which no group found itself in a dominant position over another. That could only be done by way of negotiations and a

---

86 Johan van der Merwe, *Trou tot die dood toe: Die Suid-Afrikaanse Polisie* (Johannesburg: Praag, 2010), p. 132.

87 De Klerk, *Die laaste trek*, p. 140.

88 Van der Merwe, *Trou tot die dood toe*, p. 402.

89 *The Citizen*, 16 October 1997.

joint search for solutions. Using a sport metaphor, De Klerk said: 'A team that keeps defending its try line can never win; it has to break away and score tries in order to win.' South Africa, De Klerk continued, 'could not go on keeping the lid on the security crisis. It could not continue suppressing dissent and locking people up. The time has come for a normal process of open politics. This entails removing from the police the burden of preventing people from assembling and gathering support for their views ... The police must no longer be used as an instrument to attain political goals; the politicians must stop asking the police to lie in the front trenches of the political battlefield.'

He assured the police that the government had not become paralysed in the battle against communism and Marxism. It had no intention of allowing a system that would attack the free market, freedom of conscience and an independent judiciary, or would lead to the country sliding into lawlessness, licentiousness, anarchy and corruption, as had happened in some African countries. This generation had to choose between offering the next generation a reasonable settlement or a revolutionary situation, 'culminating in an Armageddon' with 'blood flowing ankle-deep in some streets and four to five million dead'. The challenge facing the police was to help bring about a profound change of mind in order to reach a peaceful settlement that would enable people to realise their true potential.[90]

General Van der Merwe understood the message to mean that the police would be taken out of the political arena. He later admitted this was a misunderstanding. 'We as the police became more embroiled in politics than ever before.'[91]

To make the task of providing a stable environment for negotiations even more difficult, apartheid South Africa was a remarkably under-policed state. In 1984 there were only 1.4 policemen per 1 000 of the population, compared with roughly 2.4 in the United Kingdom, 4.4 in Ulster, 5.7 in Algeria and 16 in the Soviet Union.[92] In 1988 there were 64 851 people in the permanent police force at a time when the population was approximately 35 million. Of these, between 3 000 and 4 000 were members of the security police.[93]

The police could also count on the support of the city and traffic police forces, many of whom passed information to the police. In addition, the police were assisted by a sophisticated network of intelligence gathering to which the National Intelligence Service, Military Intelligence and Military Counter-intelligence all contributed. But there were always tensions between the different branches of the security forces, and the situation worsened after De Klerk's momentous speech of 1990. From the

---

90   'Die rol van die Suid-Afrikaanse Polisie in die hervormingsproses', unpublished ms., January 1990.
91   E-mail communication from Johan van der Merwe, 29 August 2008.
92   Brian Pottinger, *The Imperial Presidency: PW Botha – The First Ten Years* (Johannesburg: Southern Book, 1988), p. 287; *Financial Mail*, 12 April 1985.
93   E-mail communication from Johan van der Merwe, 24 September 2011.

1990s these sources of support began to dry up as the coordination of the various intelligence agencies weakened and as the 'necklace murders' frightened informers. The police was the agency in the firing line. Unlike his predecessor De Klerk was very concerned about his image and at pains to avoid becoming an accomplice in something illegal.[94] After the transition it was the top command of the police who would have to face the Truth and Reconciliation Commission, while the military in effect would boycott the proceedings.

An ambivalent police force

From his first days in office De Klerk was confronted with allegations that he did not act firmly and expeditiously to root out rogue elements in the security forces – or agents paid by them – suspected of disrupting the ANC and assassinating targeted members. In the late 1980s the *Weekly Mail* and *Vrye Weekblad* regularly published reports in which sensational allegations were made of police death squads and extra-judicial killings. In 1989 evidence surfaced of a police hit squad stationed on the farm Vlakplaas, engaged in killings and in undermining the ANC, and of a covert SADF unit, the Civil Co-operation Bureau (CCB).

In 1990 De Klerk would appoint the Harms Commission (see p. 326) in response to public outrage over the murders committed by Dirk Coetzee and Butana Almond Nofemela, part of a police death squad stationed at Vlakplaas and working under the cover of the CCB. The CCB allegedly carried out several assassinations, including that of academic David Webster, who reputedly had evidence of South Africa's continued backing for Renamo and of death squads inside the country. During the 1980s its function was 'to cause maximum disruption to the enemy'. This could include murder, infiltration, bribery, compromise and blackmail. After reports had surfaced at the end of 1989 of clandestine CCB activities, General Magnus Malan disbanded the unit in 1990.[95]

With the Vlakplaas unit disbanded, its members were reassigned to conventional crime detection, but its commander Eugene de Kock and some other ex-members continued to sell guns to Inkatha on the strife-torn East Rand and fomented violence in other ways. It was only in 1994 that Judge Richard Goldstone – appointed to head a commission on the allegations of political violence – informed De Klerk of these activities. Goldstone concluded that De Kock and the people under him could not have carried out their activities without the connivance of some senior police generals.[96]

The police top command was ambivalent about De Klerk as the new leader. General Johan van der Merwe noted that in sharp contrast to that of his predecessor,

94 Van der Merwe, *Trou tot die dood toe*, p. 196.
95 Magnus Malan, *My Life with the SA defence force* (Pretoria: Protea, 2006), pp. 323-32.
96 Stephen Ellis, 'The Historical Significance of South Africa's Third Force', *Journal of Southern African Studies*, 24, 2, 1998, pp. 284-85.

De Klerk's management style was relaxed and accommodating. 'When he chaired a meeting he encouraged free and frank debate. Anyone could criticise his point of view or disagree with him.' But there was a major problem, Van der Merwe added: 'The far-reaching changes that he announced on 2 February 1990 put the security forces in the firing line, and the police had to bear the brunt of it.'[97] The police lost hundreds of officers targeted in the violence.

Van der Merwe remarks: 'De Klerk had no insight into the kind of battle the security forces had to wage. The ANC refused to renounce violence and to reveal its arms caches all over the country. We were expected to expose the underground activities of the ANC but at the same time treat it as the government's equals.' It was, he observes, 'very difficult to allay the mistrust of the police in the good faith of the ANC/SACP coalition'. During the preceding decades the police had been in touch with the security services of several independent African countries and had learnt much about the intrigues, maladministration, the coup d'états and the political excesses of movements they considered very similar to the ANC.[98]

De Klerk had no option but to work with the police force he had. Van der Merwe observes: 'De Klerk could not afford to alienate the Police or the defence force. At the same time, however, it would destroy him politically if it was revealed that he stood idle while the security forces were complicit in the political violence.'[99] He added: 'The government's decision to negotiate with the ANC launched it on a route from which there was no return. It suddenly found itself between a rock and a hard place. It could neither turn back nor, according to all indications, win another election under the existing constitution.'[100]

The military

Shortly after being sworn in as president eight months earlier, De Klerk had signalled that he would make only limited use of the military in his efforts to reach a constitutional settlement or to enforce stability. He reduced the period of military service for conscripts from two years to one, cutting back the size of the active military from 75 000 to 55 000. Of these, only 12 000 were full-time combat soldiers. He reduced the influence of the military and civilian bureaucrats by the decision that only politicians should be members of the State Security Council and by slashing its secretariat.[101]

---

97 E-mail communication from Johan van der Merwe, 29 August 2008.

98 Van der Merwe, *Trou tot die dood toe*, pp. 170-71.

99 Van der Merwe, *Trou tot die dood toe*, pp. 169-70.

100 E-mail communication from Johan van der Merwe, 8 January 2010.

101 Annette Seegers, 'South Africa's National Security Management System 1972-1990', *Journal of Modern African Studies*, 29, 2, 1991, pp. 253-273; Herbert Howe, 'The SADF Revisited', Helen Kitchen and J Coleman Kitchen (eds), *South Africa: Twelve Perspectives on the Transition* (Westport: Praeger, 1994), pp. 78-92.

The military got another hint of the major changes that were under way during a meeting at a military base in Phalaborwa in November 1989, when members of the top command met with De Klerk and a number of senior ministers. The military had planned to ask the cabinet to approve large-scale capital expenditure for the development of a new fighter plane to replace the outdated Mirages. Malan had asked that more than R1 billion be set aside for developing tanks locally to counter a possible invasion by tanks from Zimbabwe.[102] A number of the generals asked Johan Mostert, co-ordinator of the intelligence committees, to include in his security briefing a reference to fresh intelligence about a military escalation in Mozambique.[103] At the Phalaborwa meeting Barend du Plessis, as minister of finance, asked Mostert if his projection of an escalation of hostilities was based on the assumption that apartheid would remain in place. He also challenged the correctness of the military's claim that countries beyond South Africa's borders were in the process of building up increasing military capabilities and ever more sophisticated armaments.

Du Plessis argued that not a single one of those countries could afford such equipment on its own, or would be allowed to incur such expenses by the IMF and World Bank, to whom they all were heavily indebted. He requested the generals to inform the meeting where these armaments came from and who paid for them. They could not do so. Du Plessis adds: 'In PW Botha's time such questions would have been frowned upon if not summarily ruled out of order and the SADF would certainly have had most of their plans accepted and funded.' Nothing came of this presentation and it exposed the generals for not having done their homework properly. The cabinet turned down General Malan's request. For the military it had become clear that drastic changes were under way that would seriously affect their role and budgets.[104]

Since the early 1980s the military had argued that military force could not win the war; it could only create the conditions for government to negotiate a political solution, which was indispensable.[105] Now was clearly the time for politicians to take the bull by the horns. In January 1990 De Klerk, accompanied by Public Enterprises Minister Wim de Villiers, met with members of the military top structure and senior managers of Armscor. De Klerk gave notice that there could well be far-reaching political changes in South Africa that could end the country's global isolation, easing armaments procurement in international markets previously inaccessible.[106]

---

102 Confidential information from a participant in State Security Council meetings, 2 February 2009.

103 E-mail communication from Johan Mostert, 11 March 2009.

104 E-mail communication from Johan Mostert, 11 March 2009; E-mail communication from Barend du Plessis, 19 September 2011.

105 De Klerk, *Die laaste trek*, pp. 178-79.

106 E-mail communication from General Ian Gleeson, chief of staff at defence headquarters, 8 August 2011.

De Klerk was aware that the leadership of the army and the police were sceptical of his efforts to draw the ANC and SACP into a constitutional settlement. Some cabinet members saw Malan and Vlok as being too close to the top officers in their respective forces. Patti Waldmeir cites an unnamed minister who alleged that De Klerk confronted both Vlok and his successor, Hernus Kriel, about allegations of a Third Force. On these occasions he asked: 'How do you explain this?' But the un-named minister went on: 'They always had convincing answers. I think it was a question of trusting the people who advised him.'[107] (The source was in all proba-bility one of the cabinet's negotiators who faced stiff criticism from members of the cabinet, including Vlok and Kriel.)

There is no evidence of complicity by Kriel, who became minister of law and order on 29 July 1991. In 2007 Johan van der Merwe categorically stated that nei-ther De Klerk nor the State Security Council had ever given instructions for the il-legal use of violence. He implied that PW Botha did so but made it clear that Botha would not bring it before cabinet; he would talk separately to a minister or a head of a department.[108]

Towards 2 February

De Klerk estimates that about 90% of the speech he gave at the opening of parlia-ment on 2 February 1990 was finalised at the D'Nyala meeting, adding that he did not consider the remaining matters significant. Almost miraculously, there were no leaks of the momentous decision, something that had sunk the Rubicon speech in 1985. On 31 January the cabinet agreed to the final package and on the night before the speech a few officials checked the final draft in Jannie Roux's office in the presi-dency. Once the task had been completed, someone turned the bronze busts of the six previous heads of state on a mantelpiece to face the wall.[109] There was a general sense that a leader like Hendrik Verwoerd would not like to look on the proceedings.

In his 2 February 1990 speech De Klerk announced the lifting of the ban on the ANC, SACP, Pan Africanist Congress and their subsidiary organisations, the release of people who had been jailed for acts committed on behalf of these organisations, and the scrapping of emergency restrictions on the media and radical extra-parlia-mentary organisations. The state of emergency would be lifted as soon as possible. De Klerk gave notice of the government's determination to negotiate a democratic constitution based on equality before the law and the protection of minority and individual rights. He announced the pending release of Nelson Mandela, who, he said, could play an important role in 'achieving the goal of a new democratic order'.[110]

107 Waldmeir, *Anatomy of a Miracle*, p. 186.
108 Welsh, *The Rise and Fall of Apartheid*, p. 476.
109 De Klerk, *Die laaste trek*, p. 181.
110 De Klerk, *Die laaste trek*, pp. 182-89.

Mandela walked out of prison on 11 February. He paid tribute to Mangosuthu Buthelezi for his stand against negotiations before all political prisoners were released. Buthelezi said De Klerk's sincerity could no longer be doubted. The Conservative Party called talks with the ANC 'high treason' and its leader Andries Treurnicht demanded that an election be called immediately. An enraptured world looked on.[111]

Delivering on a promise

De Klerk made his speech of 2 February 1990 exactly a year after his election as NP leader, when he promised a quantum leap. Over the preceding year his public image had changed markedly. An apparatchik politician whose long public speeches were marked by their apartheid rhetoric had become a dynamic political leader, communicating his vision crisply and convincingly. During the preceding year he had taken the party from apartheid thinking, with state encroachment on the private sector and fervent anti-communism, to beginning to accept the idea of a common society built on shared beliefs and values, and a free market. The government had started reducing the role of the state in the economy in order to stimulate growth and create jobs. De Klerk used the fall of the Berlin Wall as an opportunity to start all-party negotiations with an open agenda.

How did De Klerk turn his party around? To understand this, we need to look at how he operated in the different contexts of the party – the parliamentary caucus, the party machinery and the cabinet. The following chapters cite the views of ministers who were highly impressed with De Klerk's leadership abilities. Here it would suffice to give the views of two members of the NP caucus.

One is Con Botha, a graduate of Stellenbosch University and representative of a Natal constituency, who served as the NP's chief information officer in 1989. He worked closely with De Klerk for seven months in 1989 as a member of the committee tasked to draw up the party's manifesto for the September election. Reflecting on the committee's work, Botha said later: 'From March to September I literally lived by his side as a member of the committee, which had to meet twice a week . . . So we really saw the man from day to day, and saw him growing in stature . . . [it] was such a quantum leap . . . This man was so supremely confident [as if] he never gave the thing a second thought. I must assume that there were many hours of painstaking introspection, but that he kept away from his colleagues.'[112]

Jacko Maree, a Stellenbosch University law graduate who practised as a lawyer in Ladysmith and represented the NP in parliament in that constituency from 1986 to 1994 and served as an NP MP in the new dispensation until 1999, shares Botha's views. He observes that while members of the caucus could sense from newspaper

111 Welsh, *The Rise and Fall of Apartheid*, pp. 382-86.
112 Interview with Con Botha by Patti Waldmeir, 24 January 1995.

reports in December and January that major changes were under way, De Klerk had not, as was the rule, submitted the package that would be presented on 2 February to the caucus beforehand. Normally such a breach of the rules would have angered the caucus, particularly with the CP breathing down the NP's neck. Maree states: 'The speech surprised us as much as it did the world ... Yet in a special meeting of the caucus just after the speech De Klerk received unanimous approval for his action. There was no criticism of his speech or his neglect to clear the package beforehand. Any leader with less support or abilities would have been cut to pieces.'

The response of the caucus was a tribute to De Klerk as leader. Its members had rallied behind him to a man. How did De Klerk do it? Maree states: 'He displayed the quiet confidence of someone who had carefully considered the options and had thoroughly studied them before coming to a conclusion. He was an analytical thinker and formidable debater, who came across as sincere and fair. Invariably, he set out the relevant facts, the choices, the pros and cons of any action and the reasons why he had reached a certain decision ... He spun such a strong logical web around the caucus that no one could escape. He was a kind of apostle that attracted the caucus members as disciples. It was remarkable how he turned the caucus into a tight unit despite the difficult political situation we faced.'[113]

Those entrusted with state security were much more critical of the new president. De Klerk soon signalled that he was not interested in ruling South Africa through using the 'securocrats' and the structures his predecessor had created. He had never done any military service and was never close to any of the 'security ministers', sharing the intense unhappiness about 'interference' by securocrats in the 'civilian departments'.

The lion and the fox

Five hundred years ago Niccolo Machiavelli set out in *The Prince* some of the realities of power. There are, he wrote, two ways of fighting: by law and by force. 'The first way is natural to men and the second to beasts. But as the first way often proves inadequate, one must needs have recourse to the second. So a prince must understand how to make nice use of the beast and the man.' Machiavelli went on: 'As a prince is forced to know how to act like a beast, he should learn from the fox and the lion; because the lion is defenceless against traps and a fox is defenceless against wolves. Therefore, one must be a fox in order to recognise traps and a lion to fight off wolves. Those who simply act like lions are stupid.'[114]

If PW Botha was a lion, FW de Klerk was a fox and everything depended on

---

113 Communication from Jacko Maree, 12 November 2010.
114 Niccolo Machiavelli, *The Prince* (Harmondsworth: Penguin Books, 1961), pp. 99-100.

whether he would see the traps the ANC would lay for him. He came to power disgusted with the way in which the government and its security forces had acted like lions. As a jurist, he believed that laws and a constitution could settle disputes and that judges would weigh up arguments judiciously and fairly before delivering an honest verdict. His entire attempt to bring about a constitutional settlement in South Africa hung on this belief – that a deal could be struck that balanced the interests of minorities with the aspirations of the majority.

'Liquidators of this firm'

'We are basically the liquidators of this firm,' President FW de Klerk said to Roelf Meyer, a deputy minister, as they stood alone one evening in mid-December 1989 on the stoep of Botha House, the presidential residence overlooking the Indian Ocean near Durban. A few days earlier the cabinet had decided at a *bosberaad* to release Nelson Mandela and start negotiations with parties and movements across the spectrum for an inclusive democratic system. Recalling the reference to liquidators, Meyer observed that De Klerk was aware that 'I would know the meaning of it, both [of us] being lawyers'. In mid-1992 De Klerk appointed Meyer as the NP's chief negotiator. After the 1994 election in which the ANC resoundingly defeated the NP, Meyer reminded De Klerk of his words on the Botha House stoep.[115]

Talking to *Financial Times* journalist Patti Waldmeir in 1994, Meyer said he saw the negotiations as a way of 'creating a new opportunity for ourselves [the Afrikaners]. Because it was quite clear that if we had to continue in the way that we were moving at that stage, we would have lost everything, culture, language, everything.' In the apartheid years the Afrikaners had been 'standing in one corner behind a closed door', but now they could 'come out and play in the whole field'.[116]

Meyer believed De Klerk's remark at Botha House signalled the end of the president's battle against majority rule, but this interpretation was wrong. De Klerk meant closing down the 'firm' of apartheid and putting in place a new 'firm' based on sound principles. Waldmeir, to whom Meyer recounted the Botha House remark, concluded that De Klerk had tried his best to prevent majority rule until the final days of his presidency. She adds: 'De Klerk joined the battle [in 1990] because he thought he had a fighting chance to outsmart and outmanoeuvre the ANC in negotiations; just possibly even to outvote them, by forming a coalition of moderate black leaders like Chief Buthelezi or, at the least to deny them an overwhelming majority; and if all else failed, to overrule them in a new power-sharing government.'[117]

115 Waldmeir, *Anatomy of a Miracle*, pp. 149-50.
116 Waldmeir, *Anatomy of a Miracle*, p. 209.
117 Waldmeir, *Anatomy of a Miracle*, p. 150.

Chapter 11
'Paddling into Dangerous Rapids': Drafting a New Constitution

LOOKING BACK IN 1997, FW DE KLERK DESCRIBED SETTING OUT IN 1990 ON the dangerous course of negotiating a new constitution: '[It] was rather like paddling a canoe into a long stretch of dangerous rapids. You may start the process and determine the initial direction. However, after that the canoe is seized by enormous and often uncontrollable forces. All that the canoeist can do is to maintain his balance, avoid the rocks and steer as best as he can – and right the canoe if it capsizes. It is a time for cool heads and firm, decisive action.'[1]

De Klerk did not set out on this journey to cede all power. A good judge of this is Nelson Mandela, who spent many hours in one-on-one negotiations with him. 'Mr De Klerk was by no means the great emancipator, but a gradualist, a cautious pragmatist. He did not make any of the reforms with the intention of putting himself out of power. He made them precisely for the opposite reason: to ensure power for Afrikaners in a future dispensation. He was decidedly opposed to majority rule, or "simple majoritarianism" as he sometimes called it, because that would end white domination in a single stroke.' Although he was prepared to allow the black majority to vote and create legislation, he wanted 'to create a system of power sharing, which would preserve a modified form of minority power in South Africa'.[2]

Patti Waldmeir, a journalist who interviewed both leaders, remarked aptly that Mandela censured De Klerk for being a politician, not a saint. De Klerk had embarked on his dangerous ride into 'the rapids' not only because he believed he was doing the right thing, but because he thought his party and constituency could win. Mandela seemed to think, she went on, that De Klerk was 'some kind of handmaiden who would help him to deliver the new South Africa. Only later did he realise – to his evident disgust – that he was facing a rival in politics.'[3]

Power of the powerless

At first glance the outcome of the negotiations, as reflected in the 1996 Constitution,

---

1 Verbatim copy of speech by FW de Klerk to Andersen Consulting, London, 21 January 1997.
2 Nelson Mandela, *No Easy Walk to Freedom: The Autobiography of Nelson Mandela* (London: Little, Brown, 1996), pp. 542-46; Patti Waldmeir, *Anatomy of a Miracle: The End of Apartheid and the Birth of the New South Africa* (New York: WW Norton, 1997), pp. 215-16.
3 Waldmeir, *Anatomy of a Miracle*, p. 150.

presents a puzzle. De Klerk led the party that held political power and had the backing of a powerful military loyal to the civilian leadership. Yet he failed to secure
mandatory power sharing, which is what he wanted above all. By contrast, the party
without power – the ANC – got what it wanted: majority rule. There are two expla-
nations for this outcome. One is that the NP failed to meet its objectives because it
negotiated poorly; the other is that the government's negotiating position was in
fact much weaker than was generally thought, while that of Mandela and the ANC
was much stronger. By 1990 the NP's strengths and the ANC's weaknesses were
more apparent than real.[4]

By 1990 De Klerk's government was operating under many constraints that were
not fully appreciated. First, the truth of the dictum that 'demography is destiny'
had begun to manifest itself with a vengeance. Between 1970 and 1996, the population doubled from 22 to 41 million. While the number of whites remained nearly
static at approximately 4 million, the black population more than doubled from 15
to 31 million. By 1990 whites formed less than one seventh of the population and
in the so-called 'white' areas they made up less than a fifth.

The white demographic position was precarious in more ways than one. Once a
politically dominant community's reproduction rate drops below 1.5, it faces serious problems in asserting itself.[5] In the case of white South Africans this rate had
indeed dropped to below 1.5 by the mid-1980s and its demographic structure now
resembled that of a developed country. The black population structure corresponded to that of developing countries in sub-Saharan Africa, Southeast Asia and
the Middle East, showing a pronounced 'youth bulge'.

Studies show that political violence is highly likely in countries with a 'youth
bulge' – where people in the age group 15 to 29 make up more than 30% of a particular community. Between 1970 and 1999 four fifths of violent conflicts in the
world occurred in countries where 60% or more of the population was under the
age of 30. The great majority of them were struggling to get a job, dependent on
their parents, despised by the dominant elite and suffering from low self-esteem.
By the end of the century more than 63% of the population of Soweto would be
younger than 30 years.[6]

In the uprising against the government, which reached its height from 1984 to
1986, black youths played a prominent role. They formed the shock troops in attacks on black policemen and suspected informers, supported mass rallies, and enforced school and consumer boycotts. Taking Cradock in the 1980s as case study,
we find black youths playing a prominent part in setting up 'self-defence units',

---

4 E-mail communication from JM Coetzee, 14 December 2009.
5 Lionel Beehner, 'The Effects of the Youth Bulge on Civil Conflicts', Council on Foreign Relations
   website, http://www.cfr.org, first posted 27 April 2007.
6 Interview with JL Sadie, 30 October 2003.

street committees and people's courts in an attempt to wrest control from the state on a local level. These youths succeeded in winning what could be called 'organised anarchy beyond government control'.[7]

On many occasions where people died, the subsequent court case or a Goldstone Commission report (see p. 328) found that the ANC, its supporters or anarchistic youths had had a major hand in triggering a conflict, provoking a furious response from Inkatha members. Invariably the police, who sided strongly with Inkatha, became embroiled in the conflict. The ANC framed almost every violent conflict in a way that all or most of the blame fell on Inkatha or the police. In many ways the war for the South African state was won by propaganda.

Initially the government thought the fall of the Berlin Wall would work strongly in its favour. Shortly after his 2 February 1990 speech (see pp. 309-11) De Klerk told Van Zyl Slabbert there had been two reasons why he ushered in all-party negotiations. Certainly, he had made a spiritual leap and now accepted that apartheid was morally untenable. But he added another reason: 'I would have been a fool not to take the gap that the fall of the Berlin Wall and the collapse of Communism gave me.' He was convinced, Slabbert wrote, that he had the ANC at a serious disadvantage.[8]

The fall of the Soviet Union would have been a deadly blow for the ANC if it had remained in exile, where it would have been out on a limb. It continued to get support and advice from Moscow, particularly about propaganda,[9] but started receiving substantial support and funding from the United States and some countries in Europe too. Nelson Mandela became an international icon. South Africa could no longer depend on a strong anti-communist lobby in Washington and other Western capitals. Decision makers and opinion formers in the West no longer feared a South Africa with many communists in leading positions – as long as they subscribed to a market-oriented economic policy.

The NP had failed to find strong black allies, except to some degree Mangosuthu Buthelezi and his Inkatha movement, which became the Inkatha Freedom Party (IFP) in 1990. Inkatha claimed to have 1.8 million members in 1990, 40% of whom lived and worked on the Witwatersrand. From the start the ANC resisted a deal in which Inkatha would be a major player, claiming Buthelezi was a mere government puppet. De Klerk failed to form a stable alliance with Buthelezi. The root of the problem was De Klerk's inability to make a firm choice between a pro-Buthelezi, pro-federalist

7 Philip Powell, 'A Study of Theoretical Aspects of ANC Mobilisational Methods in the Eastern Cape Townships of Cradock and Port Alfred, 1980-1988', Master's dissertation, Rand Afrikaans University, Johannesburg, 1991; Anthea Jeffery, *People's War: New Light on the Struggle for South Africa* (Johannesburg: Jonathan Ball, 2009), pp. 86-87.

8 Frederik Van Zyl Slabbert, *The Other Side of History* (Johannesburg: Jonathan Ball, 2006), p. 28.

9 Vladimir Shubin, *ANC: A View from Moscow* (Johannesburg: Jacana, 2008), pp. 236-49.

strategy and a pro-ANC, pro-centralist strategy – and stick to it. More than once he would alienate Buthelezi by an abrupt, unmotivated change of course. At the end of 1991 he would accept the idea of an elected body to draft a constitution after he and Buthelezi had rejected it out of hand for two years. In the Record of Understanding of September 1992, he would accept ANC demands that were designed to create a rift between the government and Inkatha. As a result, De Klerk ended up as Mandela's junior partner.

Buthelezi, for his part, considered De Klerk naive in his understanding of the ANC. After the transition he said: 'The ANC, it must be remembered, had most of their leaders trained in the Soviet Union. They have always wanted a one-party state. They have no tolerance for any opposition party. That is how they have eliminated the PAC. That is why they unleashed all the violence not only on the IFP, but also on the Pan Africanist Congress and Azapo.'[10]

Although lacking any formal power, the ANC held several strong cards. It soon became clear that the lifting of international sanctions depended on its consent. Western governments were loath to accept any constitution that did not carry Mandela's approval. It was almost as if the world was waiting with bated breath for his 'enthronement'. But there was a dark side to the ANC too. Like the guillotine that darkened the Paris sky during the French Revolution, the necklace murders in South Africa defined the terror of township life in troubled areas.[11] The ANC leadership in exile was in no hurry to distance itself from the necklace because it was a lethally effective way of eliminating or silencing police collaborators and intimidating those opposing ANC hegemony.

Finally, there was the economy, with black unemployment an issue of major concern. In 1986 business tycoon Anton Rupert had warned PW Botha there had been no increase in black employment over the preceding nine years.[12] The unemployed swelled the numbers of the crowd in rolling mass actions and street marches that on occasion turned the struggle into a carnival of the oppressed. Financial sanctions were almost impossible to circumvent. Derek Keys, chief executive of Gencor and minister of finance in the NP government from 1992 to 1994, explained that debt rescheduling normally operated without political participation. But after South Africa defaulted in 1985, the rules were changed and a representative of the ANC was included in the consortium. It made circumventing financial sanctions even more difficult.

---

10 Interview with Mangosuthu Buthelezi, 15 September 2010.
11 In a necklace murder, the person accused of being an informer to the police or of undermining ANC actions was usually accosted by a crowd; a tyre doused in petrol was put around the victim's neck and he or she was set on fire. More than 400 people were murdered in this way between 1984 and 1989.
12 Rembrandt Archives, Letter from Anton Rupert to PW Botha, 24 January 1986.

But the South African government had not been brought to its knees economically. Barend du Plessis, minister of finance from 1984 to 1992, puts the situation in perspective: 'We could carry on in our financial isolation for many more years to come, but at a maximum growth rate of 3% on condition that the real state expenditure did not increase by more than 1% a year ... With an existing backlog of black unemployed and terrible needs with regard to health and education, we could face growing numbers of angry black people who had nothing to lose.'[13] The stranglehold of financial sanctions would inevitably mean ever-greater unemployment, which would hit the rapidly growing black population – and young work seekers in particular – very hard.

Derek Keys sums up the situation by 1990 as follows: 'From a financial point of view, South Africa did not have to negotiate in 1990, but conditions were tightening ... [The] situation was serious but it is not as if we had fallen off the precipice. The economy could go on.' Over the long term, however, the situation was serious. Keys sketched it as follows: 'The main problem for the economy was the lack of fixed investment, both local and foreign. The economy needs at least 15% of GDP in fixed investment just to barely tick over. We were well below that, we were not getting nearly enough. A way had to be found to restore trust in order to attract investment.'[14]

It is possible that with PW Botha and Chris Heunis as negotiators a different deal could have been struck, but there were distinct limits to what they could have achieved. After the negotiations had been completed, Chris Heunis gave this assessment of the power balance by 1990: 'Sanctions made it vitally important for South Africa to negotiate a settlement if it wanted to remain part of the Western trading and financial networks, but the situation was not so desperate to negotiate the hand-over of power.'[15]

David Welsh made an astute assessment: 'When the process started the NP and the ANC ... had a rough parity of bargaining position, the NP having the advantage of incumbency, the power of state resources and extensive support of the white population, and the ANC having numbers and a mass-based following.'[16] Yet, as the process of seeking a settlement unfolded, some of the government's weaknesses became apparent. De Klerk decided not to rely on the advice of his military or (as will be pointed out later) a shrewd adviser on negotiation strategy. The government was also unable to counter the ANC's ability to influence large sections of the English press to accept its version of the conflicts in the townships. Finally, the

13   Interview with Barend du Plessis by Patti Waldmeir, 3 November 1994.
14   Interview with Derek Keys, 17 October 2010.
15   Interview with Chris Heunis, 15 December 2002.
16   David Welsh, *The Rise and Fall of Apartheid* (Johannesburg: Jonathan Ball, 2010), p. 488.

ANC could rely on large numbers of school dropouts and unemployed workers to keep stoking the flames of rebellion. Negotiations in such circumstances were sure to be tough, messy and protracted; much would depend on whose will was the first to crack.

'Chained together'

De Klerk and Mandela met for the first time on 13 December 1989. Jannie Roux, director-general in the president's office, attended the meeting and noted: 'There was no warmth between the two men.'[17] Nevertheless, until December 1996, when De Klerk led the NP out of the Government of National Unity, the two men were 'chained together'.[18] De Klerk considered Mandela a Thembu patriarch bearing the mantle of authority 'with the ease of those who are not troubled by self-doubt'. He was struck by Mandela's interest in Afrikaner history. 'He was very interested in the Afrikaners. He spoke about the Anglo-Boer War, about Generals De la Rey and De Wet. There was clearly an association of the struggle of the ANC and more specifically Umkhonto weSizwe with the anti-imperialist Boer fighters. He had great empathy with the Afrikaner freedom struggle.'[19] Initially De Klerk made few critical comments about Mandela, but in later years he depicted him as a leader who was principled but also as a 'cruel' and 'unfair' opponent.[20]

Both men had been shaped in a special way for their historic task. Mandela was the first member of his family to attend school. He left home for Johannesburg at a young age, and soon became a leader in extra-parliamentary politics. His 27 years in prison turned him into a man with extraordinary discipline, commitment and vision. Aged 71 in 1989, he still set great store by the traditional hierarchies, especially that of royal lineage, but was also attracted to communist doctrine. It now seems reasonably certain that in the early 1960s Mandela was a member of the executive of the SA Communist Party, but he soon allowed his membership of the party to lapse.[21] He was above all an African nationalist, committed to freedom for his people and equality with whites in a democratic state.

De Klerk was above all a parliamentary politician keenly aware of his political mandate and determined not to get too far ahead of his essentially white working-class constituency of Vereeniging. He became a cabinet minister at the young age of 43. When apartheid was still the law of the land, he was adept at tactical adapta-

---

17   Communication from Jannie Roux, 27 March 2012.

18   An elaboration of this theme is to be found in David Ottaway, *Chained Together: Mandela, De Klerk and the Struggle to Remake South Africa* (New York: Times Books, 1993).

19   Interview with FW de Klerk, 30 May 2009.

20   *Rapport*, 8 April 2012.

21   Stephen Ellis, 'The Genesis of the ANC's Armed Struggle in South Africa, 1948-1961', *Journal of Southern African Studies*, 37, 4, 2011, pp. 657-76; Personal interview, 19 April 2012.

tions to apartheid in a way that strengthened the system of political control. But negotiations with the ANC required quite different skills.

A tactician rather than a strategist, he was up against Mandela, who stuck to his core demand of 'ordinary majority rule'. De Klerk was, by his own admission, a peacemaker, a man who shied away from unnecessary conflict. He believed in his ability to reason with others and win them over to his side. In his memoirs he mentions that at the D'Nyala meeting (see p. 302) the cabinet discussed the risks of negotiating with the ANC as well as fall-back positions.[22] However, none of the ministers interviewed for this book knew what these fall-back positions were.

Dr Niel Barnard, head of the National Intelligence Service (NIS), later expressed criticism of De Klerk's negotiating style: '[He is] a very strong pragmatist. I think he believes he is clever enough to dodge around each issue and to manipulate and tactically out-manoeuvre other people and in the end he paid a heavy price for that . . . I think the old man [Nelson Mandela] very early on decided that De Klerk was a lightweight to a certain extent and he bullied and pushed him a lot of times . . . I think he quickly sensed that possibly on the other side was someone who would pragmatically be jumping around all the time on difficult issues, not giving him straight, clear answers.'[23]

De Klerk was facing a much more difficult situation than Mandela. The world – and the United States in particular – had turned against white rule in South Africa, expecting Mandela to be 'crowned' as soon as possible. Even the craftiest negotiator would have been tested to the limits if he had found himself in De Klerk's position as leader of white South Africa. Unlike Mandela, De Klerk knew how urgent a settlement was for the economy. Accordingly, he had a timescale for a settlement that was much shorter than Mandela's. In 1992 he appointed business leader Derek Keys to the cabinet. Keys struck up a good relationship with the ANC's economic policy makers. This turned out to be a masterstroke.

De Klerk also had to work with leaders of a police force and army he had not appointed. 'I have to play with the cards I have been dealt,' he told Mike Louw, who succeeded Niel Barnard at the NIS.[24] The government was unprepared for the waves of violence rolling over the country, arising mainly from intra-black political competition. In retrospect it would have been advisable to keep the State Security Council functioning to monitor the security situation, but as De Klerk told Barnard, he was in a hurry to restore cabinet rule 'in all its glory'.[25] De Klerk erred by failing to free some of his ministers to work full time on the negotiations with the ANC, which could draw on some top talents.

22 FW de Klerk, *Die laaste trek – 'n Nuwe begin* (Cape Town: Human & Rousseau, 1998), p. 178.
23 Interview with Niel Barnard by Patti Waldmeir, 8 December 1994.
24 Interview with Mike Louw, 21 November 1994.
25 Interview with Niel Barnard, 14 March 2012.

An unknown adversary

Under apartheid virtually the only contact De Klerk and most other cabinet ministers had with black leaders was with the homeland politicians who – with the exception of Mangosuthu Buthelezi – did not rattle their cages. In the ANC the government was facing an adversary for which it was quite unprepared. Most ANC leaders had been either in exile or in prison for twenty years or more. The vision of most ANC leaders in exile was extremely close to that of the Soviet Communist Party as 'the embodiment of progress and justice, the bright future of humanity'.[26] In exile the ANC rarely dressed itself in the garb of African or black nationalism. Instead it demanded 'non-racial majority rule'. At first glance 'non-racialism' provided an attractive opposite to the NP's talk of the 'group', the 'community' and 'own affairs', which were part of the apartheid policy of enforced group membership. The NP government did not commission any study of the treatment of minorities by African nationalist parties that had come to power on the continent twenty to thirty years before. Such studies would have shown that, once in power, such movements in most cases accepted minorities only grudgingly.

Mandela always revered the British parliament as the most democratic institution in the world. Based on the rule of 'the winner takes all', the Westminster system makes no provision for minority rights. For relatively homogeneous societies, Westminster is an effective system because regular turnover of the majority party in elections provides an essential corrective mechanism. In South Africa, where blacks form nearly 80% of the electorate, the ANC was unlikely to be defeated soon once it brought the black population under its control.

During the late 1980s there was increasing talk in Moscow of the need to assuage the fears of national minorities. In 1988 a seminar in the city was attended by a group of Soviet academics and bureaucrats and ANC representatives. The academics stressed the need for a future ANC government to recognise the salience of ethnicity and develop forms of political pluralism to hold the state together. But the ANC participants rejected any idea of making race or ethnicity building blocks of a new system. Pallo Jordan told the seminar that recognition of minority rights in the Soviet Union was 'progressive' and indeed 'the condition for empowerment and self-determination'. In South Africa, however, it was reactionary. 'It would subvert the rights of the majority and preserve the power of the oppressor minority.'[27]

In Mandela's letter to PW Botha in 1989 (see pp. 274-75) he touched on the issue of the majority and the minorities. He wrote that one of the key points in future negotiations would be 'the [ANC] demand for majority rule in a unitary state and the concern of white South Africa over this demand, as well as the insistence on

---

26 Irina Filatova, 'The ANC and the Soviet Union', www.politicsweb.co.za, first posted 10 August 2011.

27 *Report on the ANC-Soviet Social Scientists Seminar*, Moscow, 21-24 February 1988, part 1, p. 12.

structural guarantees that majority rule will not mean the domination of the white minority by blacks ... The most crucial task which will face the government and the ANC will be to reconcile these two positions. Such reconciliation will be achieved only if both parties are willing to compromise.'[28] In the first meeting between De Klerk and Mandela on 13 December 1989, the president told Mandela group rights would ease white concern over majority rule. Mandela replied that the ANC had not fought apartheid for 75 years to accept a disguised form of it.[29]

In a meeting with State Department officials in Washington on 13 November 1989 ANC chief diplomat Thabo Mbeki remarked that the 'political struggle in South Africa was between one party that was committed to a non-racial South Africa and those who seek the protection of groups'. He said he was convinced De Klerk 'was wedded to the group concept'. Schemes to protect white political power were 'unacceptable' to the ANC, but 'compromise on cultural and educational issues may be possible, though difficult'. He went on: 'The ideal situation for the South African population would be to mix, but the right to people's culture, language and religion must be guaranteed.' Their rights had to be codified without retreating to separate development. Mbeki told the meeting that each of the six homeland leaders was in the 'non-racial camp'.[30]

The ANC headed a loose conglomeration of bodies that included: an exiled leadership accustomed to a hierarchical form of leadership; a locally-based mass movement known as the United Democratic Front (UDF); NGOs and human rights organisations; the Cosatu-led trade unions with a strong tradition of mandates and leadership accountability; and youth organisations, many of whose members were militant, ill-disciplined and raring to challenge the state or any competitors of the ANC. But ultimately the organisations inside the country accepted the ANC's leadership and its definition of policies and goals. The UDF and Cosatu waited to be incorporated on terms the ANC would determine. By mid-1990 some order and some hierarchy had been imposed despite the seeming chaos.

The ANC faced huge challenges. The most daunting were the repatriation of thousands of exiles and the setting up of local, regional and national structures. Mandela was the ANC's greatest asset and the very personification of the struggle. Even without political organisation or political education, everyone knew who he was. It was a moot point whether the masses understood what drove Mandela, apart from ending apartheid, or with what he wished to replace white rule. He had become the

28　Hassen Ebrahim, *The Soul of a Nation: Constitution-making in South Africa* (Cape Town: Oxford University Press, 1998), p. 449.

29　Waldmeir, *Anatomy of a Miracle*, p. 148.

30　Wikileaks, Cable from US State Department to Selected US Embassies and Consulates, 16 November 1989.

icon of the black quest for freedom and, as analyst Marina Ottaway pointed out, 'symbols do not need analysis'. Without Mandela's presence, a million people would not have flocked to the ANC's first rallies in the first few months of 1990. Ottaway recorded a vivid image: 'A young woman struggling to maintain her footing in the crush of a crowd surging toward a rally in Port Elizabeth gasped to a friend: "Everybody has to see this man, everybody."'[31]

Groote Schuur talks

From 2 to 4 May 1990 a government delegation of fourteen people, led by FW de Klerk, sat down with an ANC delegation of fifteen members, led by Nelson Mandela. This was the historic first meeting between Afrikaner leaders and leaders of the African nationalist movement. It was a highly symbolic occasion that captivated the world. Yet the question arose of whether this was the best way to formally kick off negotiations. The press photograph of the participants conveyed the message that only two parties would count in the negotiations. One was the incumbent party on its way out, enjoying 20% support in polls; the other was the ascendant party on its way in, expected to attract at least 60% support. Inkatha, enjoying approximately 10% endorsement, was absent.[32] Buthelezi often pointed out that the Harare Declaration assumed 'the only negotiations of any importance . . . will be the negotiations between the ANC and the SA Government'.[33]

Like other liberation movements, the ANC claimed to embody the aspirations of the entire population. An analyst pointed out that no African nationalist movement had ever successfully turned itself into a regular political party.[34] The Harare Declaration of 1989 crowned the ANC as the only party apart from the South African government to deliberate over a new constitution. US State Department officials told Thabo Mbeki at the end of 1989 that the United States could not back the declaration, because 'it did not like language signifying that the ANC is the sole legitimate representative of the South African people'.[35]

De Klerk's entire team consisted of Afrikaner men – nine politicians and six government officials. The latter were Niel Barnard and Mike Louw of the National Intelligence Service, SSJ (Basie) Smit of the police, WH Willemse of prisons, Fanie

---

31   Marina Ottaway, 'The ANC: From Symbol to Political Party', Helen Kitchen and J Coleman Kitchen (eds), *South Africa: Twelve Perspectives on the Transition* (Westport: Praeger, 1994), p. 33.

32   De Klerk, *Die laaste trek*, p. 207.

33   MG Buthelezi, *South Africa: My Vision for the Future* (London: Weidenfeld and Nicholson, 1990), p. 132.

34   Marina Ottaway, *South Africa: The Struggle for a New Order* (Washington: Brookings Institution, 1993), p. 44.

35   Wikileaks, Cable from US State Department to Selected US Embassies and Consulates, 16 November 1989.

van der Merwe of the Department of Constitutional Development and Jannie Roux from the office of the state president. Neither Minister of Defence Magnus Malan nor any other military officer was included. In terms of symbolism, omitting a military figure was a blunder. De Klerk had clearly indicated that he staked everything on a constitutional solution.

Always attentive to symbolism, the ANC put together a team of ten black men, one black woman (Ruth Mompati), one Afrikaner man (Beyers Naudé), one Jewish man (Joe Slovo), one coloured woman (Cheryl Carolus) and one Indian man (Ahmed Kathrada). Nine of the ANC team gave a Lusaka address, and three (Mandela, Kathrada and Walter Sisulu) had recently been released from prison. It was an early sign that the ANC in exile, together with Mandela, would dominate the movement after the transfer of power, although the UDF and trade unions had borne the brunt of the struggle on the ground.

Despite the vast differences in political outlook and the bitter political struggle, the Groote Schuur meeting was marked by its conviviality. Fanie van der Merwe recalls: 'It went off famously. Everybody got on well: suddenly they are the same people . . . [They talked] about anything and everything, and they could laugh about it . . . the food they eat, everything, where they have been, it just opened up, how the police arrested them.' When Basie Smit remarked on how thin Matthews Phosa had become, Phosa joked it was because the police had been chasing him so hard.[36] Humour was a great binding force. Patti Waldmeir remarks: 'In reality, Groote Schuur was about bonding and being seen to bond . . . Nothing substantive was agreed there – except to keep on talking.'

Mandela was the ANC star, giving part of his opening address in correct if somewhat stilted Afrikaans. De Klerk expressed the hope that the discussions would not take place in a spirit of 'brinkmanship' but with a mutual commitment to 'compromise and reconciliation'. Mandela responded in kind. He told De Klerk he considered him an 'honest individual', but added: 'I am not so sure that in the direction that you have taken, you can carry along with you the National Party and your people.'[37]

From the start the sides were locked in a battle for the moral high ground, with Mandela stressing it was the ANC that had taken the initiative in seeking a settlement three years earlier. After Joe Slovo spoke, Gerrit Viljoen, the minister of constitutional development, responded: '[It] is almost unbelievable the extent to which the guilt apparently is all one side and the innocence on the other.'[38]

---

36 Interview with Fanie van der Merwe by Patti Waldmeir, 13 October 1994.
37 Archive for Contemporary Affairs (ACA), Bloemfontein, Kobie Coetsee Papers, PV357, 1/A1/8, Groote Schuur Meeting 2 – 4 May 1990, vol. 1, pp. 2-6.
38 ACA, Coetsee Papers, Groote Schuur Meeting, vol. 1, p. 35.

The main dividing issue was the violence that swept the country. A week previously the *Weekly Mail* had written that 'there was nowhere in the world where political deaths occur on the scale they do in South Africa now'. According to an official toll, there were 547 political deaths in the first three months of 1990. After the ANC's legalisation in 1990 Mandela used a speech in Durban to urge his followers to throw their weapons into the sea, but this had little effect. The UDF published a Programme of Action for its workshop in April 1990, which depicted negotiations as a 'means to the seizure of state power'. It described the building of 'dual power' as the most important strategic objective of the liberation movement.[39]

Gerrit Viljoen drew a picture of the turmoil and violence in the country, with black people being subjected to pressure 'not to go to schools, not to go to work, [not to] pay rents and rates, and [to support] business boycotts'. The government faced enormous pressure from its own constituency, which believed the police were bending over backwards to avoid clashes. A classical scholar, Viljoen issued a prescient warning: 'A system created by violence tends to live by violence. And this is exactly the opposite of what is envisaged by the notion of democracy, such as we are striving for . . . One cannot create a democracy, of which one of the essential features is that political disputes are settled peacefully, you cannot create a democracy by the use of violence.' He cautioned the ANC against double talk: on the one hand, it issued appeals for a peaceful process but, on the other, it used 'rhetoric for the maintenance of violence', which tended to mislead 'youthful leaders who may perhaps not be so well controlled.' Pik Botha warned about the 'perception' that the ANC was not interested in negotiations at all but only wanted to achieve the position of sole representation of all black people.[40]

The ANC wanted both the lifting of the state of emergency and stability but, as De Klerk pointed out, the use of emergency measures in a 'strong-handed way' had the desired effect in leading to a decrease in violence; the moment they were relaxed, the incidence of violence shot up again. If ending violence was the primary consideration, the state of emergency had to stay.[41]

The question arose whether more political prisoners could be released under a more liberal definition of political violence. But a long history of bitter racial struggle hung over the debate. Mandela tellingly pointed out that after the Afrikaner Rebellion of 1914–15 more than 300 rebels were released within two years. If the current political prisoners were not released promptly, it would only be 'because the current challenge to the government comes from blacks and not whites'.[42]

39   Ottaway, 'ANC: From Symbol to Political Party', p. 45.
40   ACA, Coetsee Papers, Groote Schuur Meeting, vol. 1, pp. 38-39, 42 and 44.
41   ACA, Coetsee Papers, Groote Schuur Meeting, vol. 2, p. 36.
42   ACA, Coetsee Papers, Groote Schuur Meeting, vol. 2, p. 13.

On the third day of the talks Mandela and De Klerk squared up against each other. This foreshadowed the bitter exchanges between the two over the following four years. Mandela stated a view he would repeat regularly: the government had to accept full responsibility for the fact that blacks and the ANC in particular had turned to violence, which he described as merely 'defensive'. He went on: 'The methods which an oppressed community uses in order to vent its political expressions, are determined by the methods used by its oppressor ... Just as the government forced us to resort to violence, they can create conditions for us to move away from violence ... Please create conditions for us where we can, with dignity, call off the armed struggle.'[43]

Seeing this as a sweeping moral condemnation of the entire history of white rule, De Klerk offered a defence that prompted Slovo to comment afterwards: 'One realised he was not going to be easy.'[44] De Klerk argued that the NP had always accepted that provision had to be made for all sections of the community to exercise political rights. He believed there had always been the will and determination in the NP to accommodate aspirations for political rights and economic opportunities for blacks. There was a 'perception' on the NP's part that the ANC in the past was 'unreasonable' in refusing to participate and move towards political development and full political rights.

But that, De Klerk went on to say, was in the past. The NP government was committed to working out a system of power sharing and full participation for all South Africans. Day by day the government was defending its policy of politically including all South Africans in a just and equitable way in its pursuit of *geregtigheid* (justness). De Klerk explained that this was a stronger word than *billikheid* or *regverdigheid*; it meant '*really* just, according to the norms also of the Bible'.[45]

Mandela replied in a dignified way: 'When 27 years ago I was sent to prison I had no hate. I have come out after nearly 27 years and I still have no hate. Our peaceful demonstrations ... have been suppressed by the police in [actions] in which lives had been lost. That was the position when I went to prison, that is the position today.'[46]

Both De Klerk and Viljoen went out of their way to appear reasonable after the meeting. Speaking more like an academic than a politician, Viljoen said the government 'did not question that the majority must govern, but it does ask if stability and nation-building – especially in a plural society – were served best by a majority that governs all by itself'. He added: 'The minority right that has to be protected is

---

43 ACA, Coetsee Papers, Groote Schuur Meeting, vol. 3, pp. 13-15.
44 Interview with Joe Slovo by Patti Waldmeir, 14 November 1994.
45 ACA, Coetsee Papers, Groote Schuur Meeting, vol. 3, pp. 21-22.
46 ACA, Coetsee Papers, Groote Schuur Meeting, vol. 3, p. 34.

the right to meaningful representation in and involvement in decision making in some important or sensitive matters.'[47] This position was a far cry from presenting power sharing as a non-negotiable demand.

The Groote Schuur talks were the last occasion on which the government and the ANC discussed the enormous task that lay ahead reasonably calmly and without recriminations.

Soon the escalating violence forced them to meet again in an atmosphere of crisis. On 6 August the two sides met and agreed to the Pretoria Minute. The government promised to release all political prisoners and indemnify the exiles, while the ANC suspended all armed actions with immediate effect. On television Mandela stated: 'We have started some form of alliance already.'[48] But the violence continued unabated and six months later, on 12 February 1991, the two parties signed an accord at DF Malan Airport in Cape Town in yet another attempt to bring about stability. The parties pledged to end armed attacks and other forms of hostilities, and commit themselves to peaceful participation in a democratic process.

The DF Malan Accord also failed to stamp out violence or bring about greater understanding. Ever since the Pretoria meeting De Klerk found himself under constant attack from Mandela, who accused the president of being unable or unwilling to curb a mysterious 'Third Force' that unleashed violence on ANC members and tried to disrupt the movement.

The Harms Commission

In February 1990 De Klerk appointed well-respected judge Louis Harms to investigate death squads and dirty-tricks operations in which a secret defence force unit, the Civil Co-operation Bureau (CCB), played a key role. According to a well-placed source, De Klerk hoped the commission would not only curtail the illegal operations on the part of state agents but also expose the ANC's complicity in much of the violence. However, investigating the ANC was not part of its brief.

Lacking the power to undertake a full-scale investigation, the Harms Commission was unable to make a comprehensive finding on the complicity of state agencies because no relevant evidence was put before it. The terms made it possible for senior officers to refuse to testify and for some CCB agents giving evidence to appear in bizarre disguises. Documents were shredded beforehand. Johan van der Merwe, chief of the police, made the revealing remark in his memoirs that Harms had done everything in his power to reveal the truth, but it was a hopeless task because 'the activities of the different units in the police and defence force were

---

47 *Die Burger,* 10 May 1990.

48 Anthony Sampson, *Mandela: The Authorized Biography* (Johannesburg: Jonathan Ball, 1999), p. 426.

cloaked in so much secrecy and because legal and illegal activities had become entangled in each other'.[49]

Harms found evidence linking the CCB to several conspiracies to murder. He concluded that the bureau's activities 'have contaminated the whole security arm of the state' and that an operative 'neither knows nor recognizes any higher authority'. He found it probable that the police may have committed violent crimes for political ends, but pointed out that no evidence had been laid before the commission of a political hit squad operating from the Vlakplaas police station. Harms found that Magnus Malan could not be held responsible for the activities of the CCB.[50]

After the report was published De Klerk expressed the wish that it would end the witch-hunt for individuals, but this was a vain hope. In some quarters the Harms report was dismissed as a whitewash because it did not dig deeply enough.

A year later, in October 1991, De Klerk came up with an imaginative response that would counter many of the allegations about the violence. He established a Standing Commission on Public Violence and Intimidation, chaired by Judge Richard Goldstone. He had cleared the appointment beforehand with other parties and provided the commission with proper investigative powers. De Klerk found Goldstone fair and thorough. He later wrote that as a result of the commission's work 'we were slowly able to escape from the miasma of unfounded allegations, accusations, disinformation and propaganda which had previously shrouded the question of violence'.[51]

De Klerk's willingness to appoint a tough-minded judge and provide him with adequate staff and resources should have dispelled the ANC's suspicion that he had a double agenda. But because De Klerk was by far the NP's greatest asset, the ANC, including Mandela, attacked him without initially accepting any culpability for the ANC's role in the violence. De Klerk repeatedly pointed out that most of the violence occurred between ANC and Inkatha supporters, and that the ANC was deeply involved in violence in Natal and other violence-racked parts of the country. The Goldstone Commission largely endorsed this view, but for the ANC leadership the belief in the government's complicity was so deeply rooted that it was unprepared to accept any evidence to the contrary.

A spiral of violence

By mid-1990 the violence in South Africa had reached ominous dimensions. De Klerk was attempting an impossible task: to resolve a conflict that in some areas

49   Johan van der Merwe, *Trou tot die dood toe: Die Suid-Afrikaanse Polisie* (Pretoria: Praag, 2009), p. 169.

50   South African Institute of Race Relations, *Survey 1990-91* (Johannesburg: SAIRR, 1991), p. 493; *Report of the Commission of Inquiry into Certain Alleged Murders*, 1990, pp. 189-96.

51   De Klerk, *Die laaste trek*, pp. 230-31.

had tipped into low-intensity civil war with a police force that had enforced apartheid but was now expected to be apolitical. De Klerk had not sat down at the end of 1989 with his military and police generals to work out a strategy for dealing with the political storm that could have been predicted. After the ANC was unbanned, the violence increased markedly. In the early 1990s two to three times as many people died in political violence per year than between 1985 and 1989.[52]

Undoubtedly, elements in the security forces stoked violence, as did elements in the ANC, which still saw itself as a revolutionary party. In 1990 the police uncovered 'Operation Vula', authorised by Oliver Tambo in the late 1980s to prepare for a revolutionary war if negotiations failed. Even after the exposure of Vula, the ANC followed a dual strategy of simultaneously preparing for negotiations and plotting an uprising.

The ANC placed newspaper advertisements telling its supporters that MK, its military wing, had not been dissolved. It continued to send cadres abroad for training and to smuggle arms into the country. It armed 'self-defence units' in conflict areas. In 1991 a police spokesman alleged that AK-47s caused most killings and injuries in townships. Even though the Inkatha Freedom Party (IFP) possessed some of these illegal firearms, most guns came from ANC arms caches set up in South Africa since the suspension of the armed struggle.[53]

The ANC brooked no opposition to its claim that it and it alone led the liberation struggle. Its strategy was not so much, as analyst Anthea Jeffery puts it, 'to hit at apartheid, which was crumbling in any event, but to eliminate rivals to the ANC'. It also attempted 'to drive out black local government, inhibit policing and create semi-liberated areas under the control of street committees, civic associations and people's courts. School boycotts and stay-aways helped to provide cover for attacks on local councillors, policemen and all deemed collaborators.'[54]

In April 1992 Goldstone issued a report that concluded the 'primary cause' of violence was 'the political battle between supporters of the ANC and IFP'.[55] In January 1993 he stressed that the violence was different from the violence of the 1980s. It was now about intra-black political competition. He said: 'The evidence still points to the primary trigger of the violence as being the political rivalry between the ANC and Inkatha.' Even if there was a Third Force, it could not have brought about the high levels of violence.[56] The state, or more specifically the police, tended to

---

52 These figures are taken from graphs in Herman Stadler, *The Other Side of the Story* (Pretoria: Contact, 1997), p. 183.

53 Jeffery, *People's War*, p. 277.

54 Letter from Anthea Jeffery, *Sunday Times*, 20 September 2009; for the early stages of the campaign see Jeffery, *People's War*, pp. 41-83.

55 Cited in Jeffery, *People's War*, p. 325.

56 O'Malley Archives, Interview with Richard Goldstone, 12 January 1993.

favour Inkatha, but as Colin Eglin pointed out, state agents did not necklace anyone.[57]

Mandela dismissed Goldstone's April 1992 report as 'superficial' and repeated
that the police and the army were responsible for fomenting violence in the country. Earlier he had said: 'In no other country would the government keep ministers
whose departments were responsible for the deaths of 8 000 people . . . killed by
death squads, by factional violence and by security force action.'[58]

Mandela invariably demanded prompt action after an atrocity, but when De Klerk
asked for evidence and names of witnesses, he would reply that it was the task of the
police to gather evidence. De Klerk commented that Mandela was clearly unaware
that the head of a state was powerless to order prosecutions without proper evidence. When in May 1991 De Klerk suggested a multi-party peace initiative, Mandela replied it would be pointless, 'since the government knew exactly what to do'.[59]

Richard Carter, De Klerk's private secretary from 1992 to 1994, remarked that
De Klerk's refusal to act on allegations was the result of his training: 'He is a jurist,
he goes by the law, he allows the law to take its course.' Carter emphatically rejected
Mandela's charge that De Klerk lacked compassion. 'I saw him on many occasions,
12, 15, 20 occasions, deeply disturbed [by information] that people's shacks had been
burned down, kids had got killed, I mean deeply disturbed, sitting with his head in
his hands saying no, no, reading a report and just his face in a grimace and reading
this . . . Nelson [Mandela] accusing him of being unperturbed [by] black deaths
was in my opinion one of the lowest levels that Nelson ever sank to.'[60]

It was only in 1993 that Mandela took a more considered view. At a funeral he
said: '[T]here are members of the ANC who are killing our people. We must face
the truth. Our people are just as involved as other organizations in committing
violence.' For De Klerk it was unclear whether Mandela's personal attacks on him
were intended to break down his image among blacks – in 1990 some 20% of
blacks indicated support for De Klerk as a leader – or whether he was genuinely
convinced of his complicity in the violence.[61]

De Klerk was confronted with a difficult balancing act. As he depicted his challenge later: 'On the one hand, the NP had to continue governing the country in the
face of escalating violence from the ANC, the Inkatha Freedom Party and elements
from within the security forces. It had to retain white support for the negotiations
despite alarming statements and acts by the ANC and other groupings. And it had to

57 O'Malley Archives, Interview with Colin Eglin, 24 November 1993.
58 Jeffery, *People's War*, p. 276.
59 Welsh, *Rise and Fall of Apartheid*, p. 418.
60 Interview with Richard Carter by Patti Waldmeir, 15 October 1995.
61 De Klerk, *Die laaste trek*, pp. 214-17.

try to get the best possible constitutional settlement despite the fact that the party's power base inevitably shrank in the run-up to the election.'[62]

At the same time he had to ensure that the state remained neutral in the political competition, to avoid the charge that he tried to be both player and referee. What made this last particular duty so onerous was the ANC leadership's assumption – which grew as the negotiations progressed – that the NP government's main obligation was to play handmaiden to the movement in attaining office.

In the meantime the NP had to prepare itself for negotiations. Speaking after the transition, Pieter de Lange, chairman of the Broederbond's executive council, remarked on the air of unreality in Afrikaner circles about the NP's bargaining position: 'I remember very distinctly – it was strange thinking, very superficial thinking. It was thought that, after De Klerk's speech [on 2 February 1990] ... we would have a lot of cards to play. For instance, the Group Areas Act, they would give us something, and [we would] say OK the Group Areas Act will go. Which was total nonsense.'[63] At the outset the ANC indicated that the government would have to remove the statutory foundations of apartheid without expecting any quid pro quo.

Opening parliament in 1991, De Klerk announced that the government intended to abolish the Group Areas Act and as many of the other racial laws as possible. It was even found to be possible to scrap the Population Registration Act on which the tricameral parliament was based. De Klerk told parliament it was no longer possible to use laws to discriminate in favour of certain communities and to force people into particular communities. A community could no longer rely on government to enforce their separateness by laws. A distinctive community life would have to depend on the will and means of its members.[64] The NP opened its membership to all races at the end of 1990.

'The true nature of violence'

In the first week of July 1991 the ANC held its first national conference since its unbanning. The conference decided to intensify the struggle and wrest power on the ground so the negotiations would simply set the seal on victories the ANC had already won. Delegates also resolved to 'embark on a publicity campaign ... to expose the true nature of the violence'.[65] Two weeks later a major political storm erupted when three newspapers revealed that in March the police had deposited R250 000 in an Inkatha account to fund two IFP rallies. One of the rallies had taken

---

62   E-mail communication from FW de Klerk, 20 April 2007.

63   Interview with Pieter de Lange by Patti Waldmeir, 12 October 1994.

64   House of Assembly Debates, 1 February 1991; JM Aucamp, 'Die Nasionale Party van Suid-Afrika: Die laaste dekade as regerende party, 1984 tot 1994', doctoral dissertation, University of the Free State, 2009, pp. 218-280.

65   Jeffery, People's War, pp. 283-84.

place shortly before prolonged fighting broke out between the IFP and the ANC in Pietermaritzburg. In large newspaper advertisements the ANC now claimed government agencies were 'drowning the country in blood'.[66] In newspapers aligned to the ANC this incident soon became known as Inkathagate.

There was no evidence the sum had been used for violent acts. Buthelezi denied any knowledge of the payment and said R250 000 was a mere drop in the ocean compared to the R300 million or more foreign donors had given to the ANC since it was unbanned. But for those looking for a smoking gun in the government's strategy this was conclusive evidence of police collusion with Inkatha. Put on the defensive, De Klerk removed Magnus Malan and Adriaan Vlok from the defence and the police portfolios respectively, and appointed Roelf Meyer and Hernus Kriel to replace them.

The *Weekly Mail* also published allegations that some 200 Inkatha members, who had been trained by the SADF seven years earlier in the Caprivi, were being used as part of a 'Third Force' against the ANC. The SADF was responding to intelligence that an ANC committee in Dresden, East Germany, had decided during the early 1980s to eliminate Inkatha leaders and Inkatha-aligned headmen. It was estimated that by the mid-1980s more than 100 Inkatha leaders had been assassinated.[67] Inkatha office-bearers were acting in state structures and were therefore entitled to state protection, so there was nothing sinister in the cabinet agreeing to the men being trained.

Chris Thirion, a senior officer in Military Intelligence, remarked: 'There was no problem with training the unit; the problem arose when the so-called Caprivi trainees were not placed under any proper command structure in the police force.'[68] They were let loose to respond to ANC attacks or hit suspected ANC operatives. After a thorough investigation the Goldstone Commission found no evidence to suggest the SADF provided training for the purpose of forming hit squads.[69]

'The realities of power'

In several interviews that Irish journalist Padraig O'Malley conducted with Afrikaner politicians and opinion makers in the winter of 1991 there was no sense that the government had lost the initiative to the ANC or that the roles would be reversed within a year. Van Zyl Slabbert, one of the most astute analysts, predicted in September 1991 that there would be no popular election under a new constitution over the next five or ten years. South Africa would first have to go through a 'fairly strong

66 Jeffery, *People's War*, pp. 284-85.
67 Jeffery, *People's War*, p. 301.
68 Interview with Chris Thirion, 15 September 2011.
69 Jeffery, *People's War*, p. 525.

experience of joint government'. He had little doubt that while the NP was willing to negotiate a democratic constitution, 'they want to play the game and win according to the new rules that they have negotiated'. He added: 'The ANC still looks at the whole transition as a morality play in which they deserve to be winners and this is unfortunate. It means that they don't take the realities of power too seriously at the moment.'[70]

On 22 to 23 July 1991 the cabinet met for a *bosberaad* at D'Nyala to review the prospects for negotiations. After eighteen months there were still very few signs that the ANC was able and willing to negotiate in good faith. De Klerk said the ANC was using negotiations merely as a means to usurp state power. The government followed a 'dualistic' approach to the ANC. On the one hand, it conceived of the possibility of governing the country with the ANC, Inkatha and other parties; on the other hand, it saw the ANC's connection with the SACP as an insuperable obstacle.

He added that the government was holding back on attacking the ANC, which was damaging for the trust that had to exist between the government and its followers. The government and the NP urgently needed new strategies for handling the ANC. 'It needed to go on the attack but not in such a way that it undermined or destroyed the negotiating process.' Viljoen remarked that the government tried so hard to understand the ANC with empathy that it tended to forgive the organisation's mistakes. Minister of Justice Kobie Coetsee pointed out that at its national conference the ANC still called itself a revolutionary organisation, which impaired state security. Minister of Health Rina Venter observed that the government's 'dualistic attitude' caused uncertainty among civil servants about the way in which they had to act towards the ANC.[71]

At the meeting De Klerk indicated what he thought needed to be done to get the negotiations started: 'consensus' had to be reached within the existing forums on how violence could be ended, thus 'depriving' the ANC of its precondition that violence had to cease before multi-party talks could begin; 'intensified pressure' had to be put on the ANC with respect to the violation of non-followers' rights during protest actions; and attempts had to be made to 'expose the senselessness' of the ANC still exerting pressure for a vote while the government had long accepted that point. The ANC had to be singled out as the party delaying the negotiations. The NP and the parties sympathetic to it had to 'put pressure' on the ANC to agree to a multi-party conference as soon as possible, and in speeches the ANC had to be singled out as a 'delaying factor'.[72]

---

70 O'Malley Archives, Interview with Van Zyl Slabbert, 23 September 1991.

71 ACA, Kobie Coetsee Papers, PV357, File 1/K2/9, Minutes of D'Nyala Cabinet Meeting, 22-23 July 1991, pp. 1-17.

72 ACA, Coetsee Papers, PV357, Minutes of D'Nyala Cabinet Meeting, 22-23 July 1991, pp. 23-25.

Having signalled that he had no intention of using the military to influence the process (by omitting Magnus Malan from the Groote Schuur talks, sacking him eighteen months later, and sharply reducing military service), De Klerk's negotiating strategy was essentially that of a parliamentary politician pointing out to the electorate the folly of the opponent's positions on the assumption that voters would punish those deemed to be dishonest spoilers.

The problem was that the ANC was no regular opposition party; in many ways it still functioned as a revolutionary organisation. Its leadership calculated that De Klerk had no fall-back position if the ANC persisted in being 'unreasonable'. There was also little De Klerk could do to loosen the ANC's hold on the black masses. Denied a vote for so long, they were unlikely to be persuaded by the NP government of the ANC's 'unreasonableness'. But there was a slim chance that the NP would impress the outside world if the government presented itself as the 'reasonable party'. The main strategy discussed at a *bosberaad* in 1992 was what was referred to as the 'acceleration of the negotiations process' (see Chapter 12).[73]

A new scheme

At the D'Nyala *bosberaad* in July 1991 De Klerk asked for a policy programme that could replace the set of proposals the NP had put before the voters in the 1989 election. In September 1991 the NP held a federal congress at which it accepted a set of constitutional guidelines published in a document called *Constitutional Rule in a Participatory Democracy*.[74] It proposed a two-legged scheme: a 'constitutional state' coupled with an entrenched bill of rights, and a 'participatory democracy'. In the constitutional state the constitution would enjoy higher authority than all other laws. An independent judiciary could declare an act of parliament null and void if it was in conflict with the constitution. The intention was to curtail arbitrary action on the part of the rulers and keep the process of government within proper bounds. This emphasis on a constitutional state was to be the NP's most important contribution to the constitutions that would be accepted in 1994 and 1996.

The 'participatory democracy' element entailed a proposed devolution of power to regional authorities that would enjoy the right to raise their own financial resources. This had to be constitutionally entrenched. For the local level it proposed two electoral rolls, one in which the names of all residents appeared, and one containing the names of owners, lessees and ratepayers. When a journalist challenged this, Roelf Meyer said: 'The argument could be that otherwise squatters can control. One must

---

73   ACA, Kobie Coetsee Papers, PV357, File 1/K2/9, Minutes of Cabinet *Bosberaad*, July 1992.

74   *Constitutional Rule in a Participatory Democracy: The National Party's Framework for a New Democratic South Africa*, with an introductory letter by FW de Klerk, dated 4 September 1991.

ensure that a balance of interest has been maintained, and if this does not work we must certainly find another formula.'[75]

On the regional level the NP proposed that the nine development regions should be used as a point of departure for planning a new system. For a legislative council it advocated electing representatives from electoral districts, complemented by members indirectly nominated by third-tier authorities. The executive authority should be made up of three to five leaders of political parties that have a predetermined level of support.

For a national legislature the NP proposed a bicameral system with the First House elected by universal franchise on the basis of proportional representation. The Second House would give representation to nine regions, each of which would get an equal number of seats to be filled by regional elections. Each party that won a specified minimum number of votes in a regional election would be given an equal number of seats. The Second House would vote on matters affecting regions and minorities, on an unspecified weighted majority.

On the executive level the NP proposed a presidency consisting of the leaders of the three biggest parties and a rotating chairmanship. Decisions, including the appointment of the cabinet, would be by consensus. The cabinet would be a collegial one, also operating on the basis of consensus. De Klerk described these proposals as an indication that power should not be vested solely in the hands of a single individual, political party or group – and as a rejection of domination of any kind. Gerrit Viljoen pointed out that the NP had changed its ideas about minority rights radically. It no longer accepted that race could be the basis for defining groups; this core of the apartheid policy had to be replaced by free association. Minorities had to pursue their interests through mobilising themselves in a political party. All parties with substantial support should form part of the executive.

The NP's opponents quickly put their finger on a major weakness that Colin Eglin formulated as follows: '[The] NP does not talk about special rights to minority groups; they are talking of minority political parties. Now what are we actually talking about? In what society do the minority political parties, when they lose elections [get treated as] co-equal with majority political parties?'[76] Joe Slovo mocked the Second House as the 'House of Losers'.

This system was almost a replica of the Swiss presidency. Gerrit Viljoen admitted later that the chances of getting the Swiss model of a rotating presidency accepted were 'slim', but the government nevertheless felt it had to propose it.[77] But it was fanciful to imagine that this system could be transplanted to South Africa with its

75 O'Malley Archives, Interview with Roelf Meyer, 2 September 1991.

76 O'Malley Archives, Interview with Colin Eglin, 3 August 1992.

77 Interview with Gerrit Viljoen by Patti Waldmeir, 20 October 1994.

tradition of polarised politics.[78] In Europe checks and balances had developed over 500 years and ways had been found whereby the majority of people could check the extreme powers of the aristocracy or all-powerful vested interests.

In South Africa, however, it was the minority that wanted checks and balances, and the majority that was unwilling to accept this. Ruling parties not only want to rule, but also want to continue to rule. There was every reason to expect that the ANC would win the election by a large margin and would display the same indifference towards the opposition as the NP did when it was in power.

Early in 1991 almost 9% of blacks backed the NP and a further 14% supported 'a party with De Klerk as leader'.[79] Respected analyst and pollster Lawrence Schlemmer pointed out that polls showed two thirds of black people accepted the idea of the NP forming part of government in a future government. A clear majority of ANC supporters backed it. An earlier poll showed that, of people who would vote for the ANC, 65% 'felt close' or 'very close' to the NP, against 34% who felt so to the SACP and 27% who felt so to the PAC.[80]

In the course of 1991 the NP's initial black support dwindled rapidly. The ANC managed to establish control over many townships, often through strong-arm methods. Mandela's stature as liberator had grown. As someone of royal stock, Mandela's support in the homelands was particularly strong. With the exception of Buthelezi, who had formed the Inkatha Freedom Party, none of the governments in the homelands had built up a strong party. Assured by Mandela that they would retain their rights and powers, traditional leaders in these areas threw their weight behind the ANC.[81] At the Convention for a Democratic South Africa (Codesa), which met in December 1991 to discuss the drafting of a constitution, more than half the homeland delegations would back the ANC positions. Homeland blacks became the ANC's strongest support base. At a crucial time the homeland policy had backfired for the NP government.

Within the ANC there were radical leaders for whom the idea of a power-sharing marriage with the hated NP government was too much to stomach. Most of the ANC leaders who had been in exile were SACP members, whose frame of reference was the socialist governments in Eastern Europe and the Soviet Union. They knew there was no chance that the NP, as part of a constitutionally prescribed Government of National Unity, would agree to proposals for nationalisation and the radical transformation of the public sector. To drive these projects they favoured a highly

78 Welsh, *Rise and Fall of Apartheid*, p. 426.

79 Communication from Lawrence Schlemmer, 23 February 1991.

80 Lawrence Schlemmer, 'Codesa after the Referendum', *Indicator SA*, 9, 2, 1992, pp. 7-8.

81 RW Johnson and Lawrence Schlemmer, 'National Issues and National Opinion', RW Johnson and Lawrence Schlemmer (eds), *Launching Democracy in South Africa* (New Haven: Yale University Press, 1996), p. 105.

centralised state with an all-powerful executive dominating parliament and the judicial branch.

Edging closer

By September 1991 the major parties had not yet agreed on how a new constitution had to be drawn up. The ANC considered itself bound by the Harare Declaration of 1989. This envisaged the suspension of the constitution and the formation of an interim government that would rule by decree and supervise the election of a constituent assembly. Both the NP and the IFP rejected the ANC's proposed route. In November 1990 Gerrit Viljoen, minister for constitutional affairs, said the government opposed both a constituent assembly and an interim government that ruled by decree. 'We are a sovereign independent country. We are not like colonies becoming independent and . . . there is no question of handing over power to an interim government.'[82] The government insisted that all parties with proven support should draw up a constitution before any election took place, and that the tricameral parliament should enact it in legislation.[83]

The main parties also kept sparring about the modalities of constitution making and forming an interim government. The government stuck to the idea of a non-elected, all-party convention to draft a constitution and an expanded cabinet by way of nomination. At first the ANC did not want to budge on its demand for an elected constituent assembly at the start of the process, but in January 1991 Mandela narrowed the gap between the two parties by calling for an 'all-party congress'. It had to draw up an interim constitution and lay down general binding principles restraining the drafters of the constitution, including the requirement of special majorities on special issues.

The parties slowly edged closer on the drafting of a constitution. The government signalled its willingness to consider some sort of transitional government, provided it did not imply a break in constitutional continuity. A National Peace Accord, signed by almost all the significant parties in September 1991, gave momentum to the idea of a constitutional convention. All the major parties except the Conservative Party and the Pan Africanist Congress signed a Declaration of Intent for the Codesa scheduled to meet on 20 to 21 December at Kempton Park.

In October the ANC's national executive committee announced its demand that an interim government of national unity should govern South Africa for no more than eighteen months, after which the election for a constituent assembly should take place.[84] It agreed to attend Codesa, but made clear its rejection of any attempt

---

82 Johannes Rantete, *The African National Congress and the Negotiated Settlement in South Africa* (Pretoria: JL van Schaik, 1998), p. 179.

83 Welsh, *Rise and Fall of Apartheid*, p. 424.

84 Allister Sparks, *Tomorrow is Another Country* (Cape Town: Struik, 1994), p. 129.

to turn it into a constitution-making body. It dismissed the idea of ANC members being coopted to the current cabinet, but it had begun to toy with the idea of an interim governing council made up of representatives of the major parties.[85]

In the end nineteen parties agreed to attend Codesa. It was decided to have five working groups and that each party could send two delegates and two advisers to each of the working groups. The main parties agreed that decisions would be taken by means of the vague concept of 'sufficient consensus'. That meant, De Klerk remarked, that the biggest parties – the ANC, NP and Inkatha – would have to agree before a decision could be taken.[86] Some observers believed there was a good chance the NP and Inkatha would agree on most issues, forcing the ANC either to withdraw or to suggest a compromise.

A confident cabinet

On 5 and 6 December 1991, two weeks before the opening meeting of Codesa, the cabinet held another *bosberaad* at D'Nyala at which Jannie Roux, from the office of the president, took the minutes. They show a government still confident of bending the ANC to its will. De Klerk told the meeting the government rejected an elected constituent assembly. 'The NP's September 1991 guidelines should serve as the foundation of a transitional government based on the [existing] constitution.' The government had to oppose the ANC's demand for an interim government, but it would signal its willingness to appoint blacks to the cabinet after it had changed the constitution. It planned to identify real leaders with genuine support as partners in a future government. A party becoming part of government would have to accept co-responsibility for government decisions.[87]

De Klerk's plan was that the transitional government would introduce the essential elements of a new constitution and in this way shape the final constitution and a future form of government.[88] He was adamant that the NP government could not be forced to accept anything with which it did not agree. It had to keep the initiative and reach out to all moderates. A referendum among whites could be won 'if a plan was held up for the voters and if sufficient assurances were given that domination or oppression would not happen'. De Klerk believed the government could 'cautiously consider the option' of announcing that, if it had not received certain decisive answers from the ANC by 30 April 1992, it would proceed unilaterally.[89]

De Klerk described the alliance between the ANC and the SACP as problematic

85   Rantete, *The ANC and the Negotiated Settlement*, p. 175.
86   De Klerk, *Die laaste trek*, p. 235.
87   ACA, Kobie Coetsee Papers, PV357 /A1/8, 'Byeenkoms van die Kabinet en ander politieke amps-bekleders by D'Nyala', 5-6 December 1991, pp. 7-8.
88   ACA, Coetsee Papers, 'Byeenkoms by D'Nyala', pp. 8, 18.
89   ACA, Coetsee Papers, 'Byeenkoms by D'Nyala', p. 14.

and contemplated demanding that no alliance could participate in an election. He was not quite happy about the NP's September 1991 proposal for a rotating presidency because it meant the ANC 'would necessarily have to be part of it'. He envisaged a referendum by the end of 1992, changing the existing constitution early in 1993, and holding an election at the end of that year.[90]

De Klerk was confident that white voters would approve the scheme if offered security against majority decision-making. He said: 'The NP would form such an important party in a transitional government that it would be in a position to influence decisions about the final constitution and the future political system in a decisive way.'[91] Dawie de Villiers urged his fellow cabinet ministers not to deviate from the September 1991 plan.[92] There was a general sense that burning issues had to be resolved before the referendum.

The minutes project an image of a confident cabinet, united in its resolve to pursue its goal of a transitional government resting on both power sharing and the free market. Van Zyl Slabbert was quite right about the government's intention to try to win, but not about its determination to realise its goals. Within the next nine months it would lose the initiative irreversibly.

A major shift

At the D'Nyala *bosberaad* the government was determined to have neither an elected interim government nor an elected constitution-drafting body. A week later, however, it suddenly decided on an important shift that drew a line through much of what was discussed at the *bosberaad*. In Gerrit Viljoen's words: 'It was decided to embark on a major shift in [the government's] negotiating strategy, namely to accept the idea of an election for both a constitution-making body and an interim government.' He explained the thinking behind the shift: it was necessary to get rid of the 'parties of straw' at Codesa and also to accommodate foreign pressures directed against a non-elected constitution-making body. Margaret Thatcher, British prime minister until 1990, was in favour of a non-elected constitution-making body, but both the Bush administration in the United States and British ambassador to South Africa, Robin Renwick, rejected the idea.[93]

Some cabinet ministers, with Pik Botha the most prominent, expressed the hope that the NP could win an election, but Viljoen noted this was not the reason for the government's change of course: 'This was not based on opinion surveys but on

---

90   ACA, Coetsee Papers, 'Byeenkoms by D'Nyala', p. 19.
91   ACA, Coetsee Papers, 'Byeenkoms by D'Nyala', p. 7.
92   ACA, Coetsee Papers, 'Byeenkoms by D'Nyala', pp. 8-9, 20.
93   Unless otherwise indicated this and the following paragraphs are based on the author's interview with Gerrit Viljoen, 13 January 1994.

impressionistic evidence of support in the coloured and Indian communities, and the belief that among many blacks there was a desire for an alternative to the ANC. There also was a hope that some of the homeland leaders could gather significant support that they could deliver to the NP.'

But the major reason for the shift was the government's fear of losing control of the process. Viljoen explained: 'The overwhelming feeling [was] that the longer an election was postponed, the worse the NP would fare at the ballot box. The government was encountering one crisis after the other in administering the country. It was necessary to involve the ANC in governing the country and to get them to accept responsibility. The government wanted as long a period as possible for the interim government (ten years plus) and that became an issue in negotiations with the ANC.'[94]

Mandela's attack on De Klerk at the opening of Codesa two weeks later (see the next section) overshadowed De Klerk's announcement of the shift. He proposed, as a first step, the drafting of a comprehensive constitution by Codesa, in terms of which a fully representative parliament would be elected. In the second step parliament, acting as a constitution-making body, could revise and adapt the Codesa constitution, but it would have to take into account some firm constitutional principles along with a bill of rights agreed to by all the parties at Codesa. The idea was floated that a heightened majority of at least 70% would be necessary to change the constitution and an even higher proportion to amend a bill of rights or a constitutional principle.

Once again De Klerk had come up with a shock announcement that could be expected to throw the opponents off balance. He probably calculated that the NP and IFP, along with some other parties, could attract well over a third of the votes in the next election. The ANC initially played along, happy with the concession that an elected body would draft the post-Codesa constitution.

According to Viljoen, the acceptance of an elected constitution-making body had not been cleared with the NP caucus despite the fact that De Klerk had long opposed the idea, even in public. Viljoen recounts: 'The result was great dismay among NP caucus members. FW tried to rectify the matter. His main argument was the urgent necessity for getting a joint government.'[95] An elected constitution-making body was anathema to Inkatha, which was the NP's most likely ally. Viljoen pointed out: 'FW had some rather shaky confrontations. The question of accepting an elected constitution-making body, that was a big turn [-around] and it was one which he did not properly finalise with this power base.'[96]

---

94   Interview with Gerrit Viljoen, 13 January 1994.
95   Interview with Gerrit Viljoen, 13 January 1994.
96   Interview with Gerrit Viljoen by Patti Waldmeir, 20 October 1994.

The move entailed great risks for the government. Unless Codesa produced a genuine power-sharing interim constitution, the ANC would win the first election handsomely and would be able to draft the constitution largely by itself. In that case it could credibly claim that De Klerk had also embraced the principle of an elected constitution-making body.

In retirement in 1994, Viljoen said: 'In retrospect the big mistake we made was that we did not immediately after the start of the negotiations set up a study commission to develop strong bottom lines for federalism, and also to conceptualise a blocking mechanism on cabinet-level decision-making and on other central government bodies. The result was that when we came to the actual negotiations we did not have any well-developed proposals.'[97]

'A vicious attack'

On 20 and 21 December 1991 some 300 delegates finally met at Kempton Park for the opening meeting of the Convention for a Democratic South Africa (Codesa). The idea was not to draft a constitution, but to decide on the next phase of the process of negotiation and transformation. Conflict over the ongoing violence exploded on the first day. Despite his growing international reputation, Mandela initially struggled to impose his authority on the ANC and hold the fractious parts together. He continued to talk as if the armed struggle had never stopped and drew a confusing distinction between 'action' and 'struggle'. In June 1991 he had said: 'We have suspended armed action, but we have not terminated the armed struggle, whether it is deployed inside the country or outside.'[98]

De Klerk watched with increasing alarm the spiral of violence and the ANC's refusal to admit its part in it. He was at the end of his patience with the ANC for keeping arms caches, maintaining Umkhonto weSizwe (MK) as a private army, and being knee-deep in the violence. De Klerk asked Minister of Justice Kobie Coetsee to alert Mandela that he would criticise the ANC for failing to meet its obligations under the Pretoria Minute. That De Klerk did not contact Mandela directly on such a critical issue was indicative of the poor relationship between the two men at that stage. Such an important and delicate statement should have been discussed personally between the two leaders instead of making use of a go-between.[99] Coetsee assured De Klerk he had spoken to Thabo Mbeki, who promised to pass the message on to Mandela, but either Coetsee or Mbeki failed to communicate the vital message to Mandela.

In his speech – the last one scheduled for the opening day – De Klerk slammed

---

97   Interview with Gerrit Viljoen, 13 January 1994.
98   Sampson, *Mandela*, p. 426.
99   E-mail communication from Jannie Roux, 13 April 2012.

the ANC for breaking its pledges to help end the violence and for maintaining a private army. He also asked if a movement still committed to violence could be trusted to keep to agreements that had been peacefully concluded. Suspecting the president of deviousness in using the opportunity to make the last speech before a world audience of television viewers, Mandela responded with controlled cold fury, stating that even the head of an 'illegitimate, discredited regime' had moral standards to uphold. He left no doubt that he thought De Klerk lacked such standards. He went on to say the ANC would not hand in their weapons before they were in power. He accused the government of arming Inkatha and other violent organisations. If De Klerk did not know about that, 'he is not fit to be the head of government'.[100]

On this and several other occasions Joe Slovo, despite his Stalinist background, was a strong voice for reason. That evening he told Mandela privately that he had publicly humiliated the Afrikaners' leader before millions of television viewers and should make some amends.[101] The next morning Mandela shook De Klerk's hand and promised to work with him, but the relationship between them was destroyed. De Klerk wrote seven years later: 'Mandela's vicious and unwarranted attack created a rift between us that never again fully healed.'[102] He could not respond to Mandela's unfair attack, but he pointed out afterwards that if the issue of MK's arms caches was not resolved, one party in the negotiations would have had a pen in one hand while demanding the right to have guns in the other. In retrospect, some of his closest advisers felt he should rather have suspended negotiations, telling the public he did not see his way open to have talks with a negotiating partner who had impugned his integrity in such a way.

A contentious mandate

From the outset the government envisaged a referendum that would give it a clear mandate for its constitutional proposals. The timing of that referendum was vital. (In the case of the conflict in Northern Ireland a referendum would later prove decisive in resolving the crisis. On 10 April 1998 the various parties ratified the Good Friday Agreement, which contained a complex series of provisions. Accordingly, the voters were fully informed about the future constitution when they ratified it six weeks later in a referendum.)

De Klerk had first mooted the idea of a referendum in March 1990 when he pledged that 'after the *completion* of the negotiations the constitutional proposals will be tested in a constitutional manner among the electorate. And only with their

---

100 Sampson, *Mandela*, p. 459.

101 Communication from a leader of one of the opposition parties, 23 September 2011.

102 De Klerk, *Die laaste trek*, p. 241.

support will a constitutional dispensation be introduced.'[103] Addressing the opening meeting of Codesa in December 1991, De Klerk said any substantive constitutional changes, even if they were transitional measures, had to be passed by parliament after a mandate had been received in a referendum.[104]

On 24 January 1992 De Klerk said the government mandate was the 1989 NP platform that provided for power sharing and universal franchise. The government was 'honour bound' to hold a referendum on any constitutional amendments in each of the white, black, coloured and Indian communities. He envisaged referendums 'in which every South African will be able to take part and which result may be determined globally as well as by the parliamentary community'.[105] If the four different voting blocs approved it, parliament would pass the necessary constitutional amendments and establish a transitional government.

Interviewed on the same day, Leon Wessels commented that if the proposals were voted down by the white community, 'you don't have a solution and then simply it will mean back to the drawing board, back to the negotiating table'. The same was true if any other community voted the proposals down.[106] The referendum was an important lever available to De Klerk to keep ANC demands in check.

On 17 February the course of history took a swift turn. The NP lost badly to the Conservative Party (CP) in a by-election in Potchefstroom. It was the latest of a series of defeats. Since 2 February 1990, when De Klerk launched his drive for a negotiated settlement, the CP had accused him and his party of treason and selling whites out. The CP could offer no alternative except Hendrik Verwoerd's discredited 'confederation of nations' and 'partition'. Nevertheless, it played very successfully on white fears that the NP sought a settlement that would wrest control of the defence force, the police force and all the government institutions from white hands. The NP's defeat in Potchefstroom at the hands of the CP was a heavy blow. The result projected nation-wide gave the CP 56% of votes and the NP a mere 44%.[107] It confirmed Mandela's greatest fear that 'De Klerk could lose his support base'.[108]

Suddenly De Klerk's quest for a negotiated settlement was in danger. His own political career hung in the balance. On 20 February he told the NP's federal council

---

103 *Die Burger*, 31 March 1990 (italics added).

104 FW de Klerk, 'Inleidende opmerkings tydens eerste sitting van KODESA, 20 Desember 1991', www. fwdeklerk.org.za, 7 June 2008; *The Star*, 29 January 1992; Aucamp, 'Die Nasionale Party van Suid-Afrika se laaste dekade as regerende party, 1984-1994', p. 348.

105 House of Assembly Debates, cols 36-37; *Die Burger*, 25 January 1992; *Cape Argus*, 24 January 1992.

106 O'Malley Archives, Interview with Leon Wessels, 24 January 1992.

107 Annette Strauss, 'The 1992 Referendum in South Africa', *Journal of Modern African Studies*, 31, 2, 1993, p. 340.

108 Koot Jonker, *Vegters teen politieke boelies* (no place: Griffel Media, 2009), p. 153.

and the party's parliamentary caucus that a question mark hung over the party's mandate to negotiate. He recommended a referendum rather than an election for a renewed mandate. After a long discussion the caucus agreed to a referendum.[109]

A referendum is a device used by parties to broaden their support when highly contentious ethno-national issues are at stake. The NP used a referendum in 1960 and 1983. In the 1960 referendum the NP asked for support for a republic within the Commonwealth, only to withdraw its application to remain in the Commonwealth a few months later. In 1982 the NP had split on the issue of power sharing, but when the government formulated the referendum question it avoided this term.[110]

Invariably the prerogative of formulating the referendum question is the chief advantage a ruling party enjoys over its opponents. This is the main reason why it usually wins a referendum and why the result is almost always controversial. But there are limits to the liberties a ruling party can allow itself.

The question the government did pose in 1992 was: 'Do you support the continuation of the reform process that the state president started on 2 February 1990 and which is aimed at a new constitution through negotiations?' It was a bland question that asked voters simply to endorse the principle of negotiations, not the outcome. A yes vote could certainly be taken as a rejection of the CP's stand, which offered no alternative to apartheid.

There was no mandate for open-ended negotiations. Lawrence Schlemmer pointed this out just after the referendum: 'Whites most certainly did not endorse negotiations with a future ANC government in mind. The NP gave as its most fundamental reassurance that there would be power sharing in the form of guaranteed coalition government for the foreseeable future. NP spokespeople also gave the assurance there would be no majority (or minority) domination.'[111]

While the referendum question asked only for endorsement of negotiations, the NP did indeed promise to take a certain stand in the talks. An advertisement was placed in papers under the bold headline: *As jy bang is vir meerderheidsregering stem Ja* (If you are afraid of majority rule vote Yes). It assured voters that by voting yes they could attain what white Rhodesians never could – namely, a constitution that prevented domination by the ruling party.[112] A 2008 study based on a close reading of the newspapers covering the referendum observes in an almost puzzled way: 'It is today difficult to believe, but it was power sharing for which a yes vote stood. It was pointedly brought to the voters' attention that nothing but power

---

109 Aucamp, 'Die Nasionale Party van Suid-Afrika se laaste dekade as regerende party', pp. 326-27.

110 Gary Sussman, 'The Referendum as an Electoral Device in NP Politics', *Politikon*, 33, 3, 2006, pp. 259-70.

111 Lawrence Schlemmer, 'Codesa after the Referendum', *Indicator SA*, 9, 2, 1992, p. 7.

112 *Die Burger*, 16 March 1992, Advertisement paid for by the NP.

sharing would be accepted. It was these promises . . . [of power sharing as a non-negotiable aspect] to which voters attached weight in bringing out their yes vote.'[113]

De Klerk himself told voters what they were voting for. In Cape Town he said: 'Our constitutional proposals were published last year [in September]. They have been accepted by all the congresses of our party. They are what we shall be negotiating for.'[114] Once or twice he qualified his pledge. On 2 March, while the referendum campaign was in progress, he said 'it would no longer be necessary to seek a new mandate in these matters in the event that his negotiators managed to secure the concessions in the NP's constitutional blueprint' of September 1991. De Klerk continued that while parties propagating a 'no' vote asked for a blank cheque, the NP did not do so. The cheque the NP was offering was 'filled in with the NP's constitutional proposals, which the voters were asked to sign'. It was a lie to 'depict the NP as ally of the ANC/SACP'.[115]

Colin Eglin said a few months later that De Klerk was being 'very naughty' in claiming he kept to undertakings he had given. In the referendum, he said, De Klerk referred to the party's September 1991 proposals 'and put them out saying I am not asking for a blank cheque, I am asking for this'.[116] Opinion surveys taken in the six months after the referendum made it clear that, as Lawrence Schlemmer formulated it, 'whites were essentially voting yes because they feared the consequences of a no vote on the economy, but their commitment was to negotiations and very little more'. There was not majority support among white voters for an interim government. Schlemmer observed: 'They were essentially voting to give [De Klerk] a mandate because of the very high trust they have in De Klerk not to sell them out.'[117]

The question of what could be called 'De Klerk's contentious mandate' would continue to haunt him and the party. In 1997 the issue blew up shortly after the NP had left the Government of National Unity, thus demonstrating that the system was based on majority rule. It had become clear that the NP as a minority party in the Government of National Unity had no effective power and the ANC had merely agreed to a unity government to assuage white fears. Ebbe Dommisse, editor of *Die Burger,* wrote that the mandate De Klerk had received was for power sharing, not majority rule. Implausibly, De Klerk rejected the charge that the voters did not

113 Amelma le Roux, '1992 Referendum: 'n Betekenislose gebeurtenis of een van die boustene van die nuwe demokratiese Suid-Afrika?', Honours thesis, University of Stellenbosch, 2008, p. 20.

114 *Die Burger,* 3 March 1992; ACA, FW de Klerk Collection, PV734, File M7/6/1, vol. 189; Gary Sussman, 'The Referendum in FW de Klerk's War of Manoeuvre: A Historical and Institutionalist Account', doctoral dissertation, London School of Economics, 2003, Postscript.

115 *Die Burger,* 3 March 1992.

116 O'Malley Archives, Interview with Colin Eglin, 3 August 1992.

117 O'Malley Archives, Interview with Lawrence Schlemmer, 2 October 1992.

know what they were voting for. He also denied that the NP had asked for a blank cheque.[118]

The supporters of a yes vote spanned the spectrum from far left (Jeremy Cronin of the SACP also voted), through to the moderate left, liberal politicians and business leaders, and sportsmen. The result was a huge victory for the yes vote, winning 69% of the votes in an 85% poll.[119] It was estimated that 62% of Afrikaners and 70% of English speakers voted yes. In his victory speech De Klerk said the outcome was a landslide victory for peace and justice in the country. The only viable policy was that of 'power sharing, [and] the building of one nation in one undivided South Africa'.[120]

The referendum result greatly enhanced De Klerk's reputation. He personally carried the yes vote and was magnanimous in victory. Yet the only thing that united the disparate yes vote was the simple realisation: 'There can be no turning back.'[121] Serious problems were lurking around the corner. Strong government pressure for minority rights and a white constitutional veto was likely to lead either to Codesa's collapse or to a split in ANC leadership ranks. There was a sense that time was running out. Achieving a settlement as quickly as possible had become De Klerk's overriding objective.

Deadlock

At the meeting of Codesa in December 1991 it was decided to task the five negotiating groups with working out agreements to be submitted to the next full meeting in May 1992. After the referendum in March 1992 the NP delegates arrived back at Codesa (now called Codesa 2) confident of winning as much as a third of the votes in a future election. This assumption would be a crucial consideration in the party's constitutional proposals. Late in 1991 the Democratic Party (DP), which acted as an important catalyst, had proposed that the interim constitution drawn up at Codesa 2 would have to enjoy the support of at least 70% of the members. The government believed there was a good prospect of the ANC and its allies receiving considerably less than 70% of the vote in the first general election, which meant there was a good chance of the interim constitution becoming the final constitution.

At Codesa, the execution of the government's agenda seemed to be on course. The Codesa setting favoured the government, with delegates from numerous parties all seeking a piece of the action. Some observers believed there were two broad camps of roughly equal numbers. With the backing of some homeland leaders, the NP

118 *Die Burger*, 14 February 1997.

119 Welsh, *Rise and Fall of Apartheid*, p. 441.

120 *The Star*, 19 March 1992.

121 Colin Eglin, *Crossing the Borders of Power* (Johannesburg: Jonathan Ball, 2007), p. 274.

seemed set to secure a fairly strong form of federalism with the appropriate functions and powers, including fiscal powers. But the great prize still eluded the government: agreement on power sharing.

Early in May De Klerk suffered a blow when Viljoen – his main constitutional and
political adviser and chairman of Working Group 2 which worked on the political
system – retired on account of ill health. Unlike De Klerk, Viljoen had entered politics late and did not quite take to it, but he impressed the Codesa delegates with his
gravitas, stature and authority. De Klerk appointed Tertius Delport, a former law
professor with a good grasp of constitutional issues, to replace Viljoen as chairman
of Working Group 2. Roelf Meyer became minister for constitutional affairs.

The main issue that concerned Working Group 2 was the percentages needed for
the elected Constituent Assembly (CA) to change the constitution that Codesa
would adopt. Delport, backed by De Klerk, suggested 75% for both the final constitution and the bill of rights, while the ANC's Cyril Ramaphosa upped the ANC's
66.7% to 70%. At a very late stage Ramaphosa added a rider: if the CA had not
accepted a constitution with the required majority after six months, there would
be a referendum on the draft constitution in which a simple majority would be sufficient. There was no way the government could accept this and it produced the
result the ANC desired: deadlock and a breakdown of the negotiations.[122]

The subsequent press debate focused on the NP's so-called blunder of insisting
on a higher percentage than the ANC wanted to concede, but in all probability this
was not the real cause of the breakdown. The *Sunday Times* published a report saying the ANC had already decided to scuttle the negotiations two weeks before the
breakdown on the apparent issue of percentages.[123] The ANC never denied this. In
some key areas the NP had performed quite well in the Codesa 2 negotiations.
Colin Eglin noted: 'The negotiating process took the ANC increasingly into the orbit
of the government's plan.' He felt the ANC's negotiators would have had trouble
gathering support from the grass roots for some of the agreements into which it
had been locked.[124]

Soon the deadlock at Codesa 2 escalated into a full-blown crisis. The ANC announced that on 16 June it would embark on a programme of rolling mass action
that would include demonstrations, marches, boycotts, factory occupations and a
general strike of at least three days. As in September 1989 with the Cape Town march,
ANC militants spread the idea of the 'Leipzig option' – a crowd of hundreds of thousands of demonstrators massing in Pretoria and Johannesburg, and forcing the
government out of power.

122 De Klerk, *Die laaste trek*, p. 255.
123 O'Malley Archives, Interview with Gerrit Viljoen, 7 August 1992.
124 Eglin, *Crossing the Borders*, p. 289.

Colin Eglin offered a more sober perspective: 'There was never any chance of the demonstrators succeeding in toppling the government, but after Codesa's breakdown the ANC leadership felt the need to return to its support base, which suspected it of selling out. Earlier the government did the same when it rallied and reassured its supporters in the referendum campaign.'[125]

Behind the mass action lay a tacit admission by the ANC that it had not managed to attain anything approaching unrestricted majority rule or meeting the demand for the nationalisation of sectors of the economy. ANC-aligned trade unions had become increasingly agitated by their absence from the negotiations.

On 17 June, a day after the ANC's mass action started, the negotiation process entered its darkest moment. IFP-supporting Zulus residing in a hostel attacked residents of the town of Boipatong and killed 45 people, mostly ANC supporters. It later emerged that the attack was driven by revenge against ANC comrades harassing hostel dwellers and murdering the girlfriend of one of them. Demonstrators foiled De Klerk's attempt to visit the township. Journalists tried to get the story, but the ANC allegedly ordered residents not to talk to the press. On 21 June Mandela accused De Klerk of shedding crocodile tears while the police had a hand in the atrocity. He said: 'They are killing our people to stop the ANC getting into power.'

De Klerk denied any police complicity and asked the ANC to account for its involvement in the murder of more than 6 000 people since 2 February 1990. Several independent investigations – including those of journalists Denis Beckett and Rian Malan, the Goldstone Commission, two senior investigators from the London police, and the Amnesty Committee of the Truth and Reconciliation Commission – could find no evidence of police involvement in the massacre.[126]

Mandela did not terminate the negotiation process, but said it was 'completely in tatters'. Relentlessly, he and other ANC leaders continued to accuse the government of involvement in Boipatong and other township atrocities and killings. Addressing the UN Security Council, he spoke of a 'cold-blooded strategy of state terrorism' by forces intending to entrench apartheid and impose their will 'on a weakened democratic movement at the negotiations table'.[127]

The ANC's propaganda victory after Boipatong turned the tables, putting the government on the defensive. For the proponents of the Leipzig option it was a heady moment. A crowd of 50 000 marched on the Union Buildings in Pretoria; chief negotiator and mass mobiliser Cyril Ramaphosa shouted: 'Next time FW de Klerk we are going to be inside your office.'[128]

---

125 Interview with Colin Eglin, 6 September 2011.

126 Jeffery, People's War, pp. 326-29; Welsh, Rise and Fall of Apartheid, pp. 450-53.

127 Rantete, The ANC and the Negotiated Settlement, p. 184; Steve Clark (ed.), Mandela Speaks (New York: Pathfinder, 1993), pp. 191-94.

128 Waldmeir, Anatomy of a Miracle, p. 207.

In this charged atmosphere the ANC faction bent on revolution decided to topple the military dictatorship of Ciskei. On 7 September a large crowd gathered in a stadium outside Bisho. A section broke away to storm the government's office, but soldiers opened fire and killed 29. The Goldstone Commission criticised both the ANC's flouting of the regulations and the trigger-happy soldiers. It noted that by now the police and organisers of mass marches had learnt how to cooperate so marches went off peacefully, 'which would have been unthinkable a short while ago'.[129]

Eglin told Mandela it was one thing for the ANC to rally its supporters through mass action, but quite another to try to overthrow the state. Mandela replied that insurrection was never the objective.[130] There was also growing concern over the huge losses business suffered as a result of the continued turmoil. The resumption of negotiations had become an urgent priority for both Mandela and De Klerk. Bisho had pushed the parties back to the negotiating table.[131]

An economic policy gulf

Although the ANC leaders scaled down their talk of nationalisation, there was good reason to be pessimistic about the prospects for a settlement. Politically the NP wanted a system that would divide and distribute power in such a way that no party would be able to dominate. It was also pushing for greater market-oriented policies, including privatisation. The ANC was afraid of being sucked into power in a way that would make it impossible for it to transform society economically and socially. Resolving bitter conflicts over economic policy was the ANC's greatest challenge while the movement was banned and most of its leadership lived in exile. Penuell Maduna, later an ANC cabinet minister, recounts: 'The most difficult issue was the economy. The other ones were not so hard. Not even multi-party democracy ... But the economy!'[132]

By the mid-1980s approximately three quarters of the ANC's national executive were SACP members.[133] In 1989 the SACP accepted the document 'The Path to Power', which spoke of establishing popular control over vital sectors of the economy and restoring the land to the people. It rejected 'group rights' as 'fraught with the danger of perpetuating inequality'.[134] There was no way an NP leader could reach a compromise with such a programme. But the SACP leadership was finding

---

129 Cited by Welsh, *Rise and Fall of Apartheid*, p. 454.

130 Interview with Colin Eglin, 6 September 2011.

131 Timothy Sisk, *Democratization in South Africa: The Elusive Social Contract* (Princeton: Princeton University Press, 1995), p. 219.

132 Mark Gevisser, *Thabo Mbeki: The Dream Deferred* (Johannesburg: Jonathan Ball, 2007), p. 539.

133 Stephen Ellis and Tsepo Sechaba, *Comrades Against Apartheid: The ANC and the South African Communist Party in Exile* (London: James Currey, 1992), p. 37.

134 'The Path to Power', Programme of the SACP, adopted 1989, www.sacp.org.za.

it increasingly difficult to ignore the attempts of Mikhail Gorbachev, general secretary of the Communist Party in the Soviet Union, to reform socialism.

In his final years in exile SACP leader Joe Slovo, long a Stalinist, expressed the fervent wish that Gorbachev would succeed. In 1988 he said in an interview in Leverkusen, Germany: 'We believe in socialism that can work ... What happened in the Soviet Union was an aberration, a criminal aberration.' He pointed out that the Freedom Charter did not advocate across-the-board nationalisation and continued: 'Wealth would have to be redistributed in a way that would not cause chaos.' In power, the ANC would have to provide material incentives to retain the skills of those who could contribute. He told me: 'Between me and you, we should retain all the whites and they have got an important part to play and we should give a lot of material incentives for them to stay. We have not only to redistribute wealth but also place blacks in positions where they can learn to run things. They are going to fuck things up, we know it. But it is a matter of balance.'[135]

Heated debate over economic policy continued in the ANC. Nationalisation as a policy option remained on the table. In 1990 Slovo admitted socialism's economic distortions and failures, but in his thinking there was always another opportunity when socialism could be applied 'more correctly' and with better results.[136] Mandela still clung to the Freedom Charter, which proposed breaking up 'monopolies' to redistribute wealth, and giving the land to those who work on it. After his release from prison he proposed anti-trust laws to break up the monopolies and help black businesses to 'flourish as never before'.

In February 1992 De Klerk and Buthelezi, arguing for free enterprise, overshadowed Mandela at the annual conference of political and business leaders at Davos, Switzerland. Leaders from China and Vietnam told Mandela that after the collapse of the Soviet Union they had abandoned socialism in their respective countries. He returned home to tell his colleagues: 'We either keep nationalisation and get no investment, or we modify our attitude and get investment.'[137] He could not get the word 'nationalisation' removed from the ANC's platform, but the ANC accepted privatisation as well as nationalisation.

Keys's 'dirty pictures'

When Minister of Finance Barend du Plessis retired in April 1992 on account of ill health, De Klerk replaced him with Derek Keys, chief executive of Gencor. Keys set out to convince some of the ANC leaders of the awesome challenges the government had to face to balance the budget and find a trade-off between the requirements of

---

135 Interview with Joe Slovo, 22 October 1988.
136 Joe Slovo, 'Has Socialism Failed?', http://www.sacp.org.za/docs/history/failed.html.
137 Sampson, *Mandela*, pp. 434-35.

redistribution and growth. With the war in Angola over, Keys was in a much better position than his predecessor to redirect expenditure from defence to social services and social upliftment. But as Du Plessis observed, the government – much to his and his colleagues' frustration – 'had to divert much of the money from defence to the expansion of the police force in order to counter the waves of violence'.[138]

Commentators generally considered the war in Angola, together with paying off foreign debt, as the root causes of the budget deficit, which peaked at 7.3% in 1992–93 (up from 1.4% in 1989). But other forms of expenditure also narrowed government options. Of major concern were unfunded liabilities connected to the state pension scheme that needed to be addressed with a major political transformation lying ahead. For many years, particularly in the 1960s and in the early 1970s, the annual contribution of state employees was lower than the accrued benefit. The state provided for the shortfall, but had left this off the budget. This now had to be brought onto the books before a new government took power.

The government also set about closing the racial gap in social benefits. Per capita social expenditure on blacks increased from 12% of the white level in 1975 to 69% in 1993. Settling the spiralling debt of the homelands added four points to the debt-to-GDP ratio. National government debt as a percentage of GDP rose from 36% in 1989 to nearly 50% in 1996.[139]

Derek Keys made several major contributions. First, he brought the state's liabilities with respect to the benefits of civil servants on budget, thus establishing the principle of transparency that his successors would continue. Second, he put the major structural problems of the economy on the agenda. Keys explained: 'For me the most important issue was the government consumption, which had nearly got out of hand. Fixed investment was at 14% of GDP and general consumption at 62%. Government consumption expenditure was at 21%, compared to 9% in a country like Japan. Investment at 14% is barely enough to cover wear and tear of the capital stock; real growth requires an additional 5% or more.'[140]

For Keys the solution was to restore economic growth by getting government current expenditure down and boosting fixed investment through offering investors attractive opportunities by, among other things, lowering tax on business. In contrast, the ANC proposed sharply increasing the tax burden on business, which was almost certain to lead to capital flight.

One of Keys's main tasks was to engage the ANC in a way that could lead to the

138 O'Malley Archives, Interview with Barend du Plessis, 20 August 1991.
139 Estian Calitz and F Krige Siebrits, 'Fiscal Policy', Stuart Jones and Robert W Vivian (eds), *South African Economy and Policy, 1990-2000: An Economy in Transition* (Manchester: University of Manchester Press, 2010), pp. 407-20; E Calitz, SA du Plessis and FK Siebrits, 'An Alternative Perspective on South Africa's Public Debt, 1960-1994', *SA Journal of Economics*, 79, 2, 2011, pp. 161-72.
140 Interview with Derek Keys, 17 October 2010.

forging of an economic pact underwritten by all the main parties. An opportunity came in August 1992, at a time when rolling mass action was at its height. Keys was paid a visit by the 'Mont Fleur group' under the leadership of Pieter le Roux of the University of the Western Cape, who had developed economic scenarios for South Africa. One of the members of the group was Trevor Manuel, who at that stage headed the ANC's Department of Economic Planning.

The group presented their set of four scenarios to Keys. First was the scenario of the 'ostrich in the sand': a recalcitrant white government rejecting a negotiated settlement. Second was the 'lame duck': a prolonged transition under a weak government, satisfying no one. Third was 'Icarus': a black government, unhampered by constitutional checks, embarking on a huge and unsustainable public spending programme that crashes the economy. Fourth was 'the flight of the flamingos' in which 'everyone rises together'.

Keys presented to the group a set of slides – which jokingly became known as 'Derek Keys's dirty pictures' – he had recently shown to cabinet. They were not very different from the Mont Fleur scenarios, but Keys could back them up with fresh, in-depth data. His talk greatly impressed the group, who began to realise in what dire straits South Africa found itself and how much worse the Icarus scenario would make it.[141] Manuel later told the story of the seminal meeting: 'It was very important because we were trying to understand the Icarus scenario and the dangers of macro-economic populism. That was certainly profound for me.'[142] The 'flight of the flamingos' seemed to be the only realistic option.

The emerging economic consensus was formalised by the establishment of an 'Economic Codesa' through the launch of the National Economic Forum, bringing together business, labour, government and the ANC. A commitment developed to create a welfare state as far as was possible for a developing country. Some welfare benefits had to be provided for the most disadvantaged. The *Financial Times* described this as incipient social democracy.[143]

Mandela's position also changed as a result of Manuel's briefing on the meeting with Keys. On 14 September he said: 'We want to break the deadlock [in the negotiations] because, if we don't, I fear the economy is going to be destroyed [and] that when a democratic government comes to power it will no longer be able to solve it. The longer it takes for democracy to be introduced, the more difficult it will be to repair the economy.' The realisation of the economic interdependence of white and black and employers and workers spurred increasing convergence between the par-

---

141 Interview with Derek Keys, 17 October 2010.
142 Dale Williams, 'Manuel: I Could Close My Eyes Now' in 'Thought Leader', *Mail & Guardian*, 14 June 2009.
143 *Financial Times*, 17 February 1993.

ties.[144] The question was whether this incipient economic pact could be accompanied by a political pact.

The formation of pacts

Much literature on the founding of a democratic system concentrates on the formation of pacts between the leaderships of an authoritarian state and the resistance movement. The idea is to provide guarantees to the outgoing government on future policy with respect to the economic system and private ownership in particular, as well as the security forces and cultural policy. Such guarantees must make it possible for the outgoing government to tell its followers there is no need to continue the fight because they would not be seriously disadvantaged in the new order. The talks between Derek Keys and some future policy-makers in the government on one side, and some ANC leaders on the other, represented an incipient economic pact, but several other major pacts still had to be forged.

By 1992 the ANC leadership had shelved nationalisation for the time being, thinking it would take at least twenty years before they could control 'all the levers of state power'.[145] But radical elements in the ANC, Cosatu and the SACP nevertheless remained committed to implementing the National Democratic Revolution, aiming for popular control over all institutions, nationalisation of the main industries and radical land reform. The immediate objective of the radicals was to establish ANC dominance in parliament and to begin the pursuit of a socialist alternative. It was accepted in ANC ranks that an ANC government would initially be unable to staff the senior positions in the civil service, parastatals, security forces and judiciary with its own cadres.

A civil service pact?

The civil service, dominated as it was by Afrikaners on the senior level, was a particularly sensitive area. The experience of decolonisation in Africa showed that new governments pledged to the liberation of their people made transforming the civil service one of their first priorities despite the loss of scarce skills and experience. In South Africa's much more advanced economy it was essential to prevent this from happening under a new government. With apartheid ready to be abolished, another

---

144 In his 1993 budget Derek Keys raised VAT rates from 10% to 14%, with some provision made for poorer citizens. The corporate tax rate was reduced from 48% to 40%. In the 1994 budget there was a further reduction in the corporate tax rate coupled with an increase in the dividend tax. A special levy on taxes raised the R4.6 billion spent on transition costs so the government would have a clean start. R2.5 billion was set aside to start the Reconstruction and Development Programme, which was a key ANC programme. Keys retired in September 1994, confident of the new government's ability to keep the ship on a steady course.

145 *Sunday Times*, 12 December 1993.

challenge was integrating into a single service some 650 000 civil servants employed in the homeland bureaucracies and the many thousands of white, coloured and Indian civil servants in the respective home affairs administrations. These employees had to be consolidated in nine or ten regional departments and one national department.

Some ministers saw it as a challenge to make good progress before serious negotiations had begun. For them a priority was a pact, concluded well before the NP government bowed out, about the introduction of affirmative action and the protection of expertise in the civil service over a period of time.[146] The recognition of Afrikaans as language, particularly in schools and universities, was also of major importance.

Early in 1990 De Klerk instructed all state departments to remove the vestiges of apartheid urgently and concentrate on effective service delivery, particularly for new voters. In some departments, like the Department of Health and Population Development, prompt action was possible because no apartheid laws were left on the books. By 1990 there were seventeen health departments under different authorities – a department for each of the four provinces, one for each of the three houses of parliament and one for each of the nine homelands, with a national department at the top.

Early in 1990 Dr Rina Venter, the national minister of health, and Dr Coen Slabber, director-general of the Department of Health and Population Development, embarked on drafting a plan to start the process of rationalisation in consultation with all the health departments. Aware of the urgency of attending to the HIV/Aids epidemic, Venter also tried to draw members of the ANC health department into meetings where they were briefed about the need for prompt action.

When Venter tabled the plan in cabinet in September 1990 Gerrit Viljoen, minister of constitutional affairs and chairman of the cabinet committee on negotiations, responded enthusiastically, especially because it gave substance to the party's federal policy. He felt rationalisation could start immediately. Agreeing with this, Minister of Foreign Affairs Pik Botha argued that such a step would signal that the government was in a hurry to shed apartheid.[147]

But opposition soon mounted from the provincial authorities to the rationalisation of the different administrations and the removal of some functions from the provinces to central government. They wanted to retain as many functions as possible for the provinces with their proven experience.[148] Fearing that once powers

---

146 E-mail communication from Rina Venter, 4 October 2010.
147 E-mail communication from Rina Venter, 29 September 2010.
148 E-mail communication from Kobus Meiring, 7 October 2010; E-mail communication from Con Botha to Kobus Meiring, 25 October 2010.

had moved up to the national level, an ANC government would devolve them downwards again, Venter and Slabber believed the greatest risk was to do nothing before power was transferred.

The stiffest opposition was from administrators and other members of the executive councils of Natal and the Cape Province where there was a reasonable chance that parties opposed to the ANC would win power on the provincial tier. These issues remained unresolved and would give the ANC, with no experience in governing, a free hand in the task of rationalising the highly fractured state administration. It would make it even easier to embark on the rapid displacement of whites in the civil service.[1]

By early 1991 Venter submitted to cabinet her department's plan for rationalising the health departments. As a result of opposition from some ministers the plan had to be shelved. Venter later said she received little help from De Klerk, who seemed to believe that rationalisation of the state administration, job security for whites, and retention of scarce skills and expertise could be left to the constitutional negotiations and to a power-sharing government.[2]

When the ANC took over in 1994, Coen Slabber, as the incumbent director-general of health, told Dr Nkosazana Zuma, the new minister of health, that the outgoing government had made no decision on the division of powers and functions. There also existed no implementation plans for restructuring health care and health provision. He stated later: 'There was nothing on the table.' He was sure his department could have done many things before 1994 with the ANC's approval.

Slabber also noted that the lack of real progress in the constitutional negotiations produced serious misgivings among civil servants. 'Civil servants took many courses in leadership development, especially on the middle level and top levels of management. They knew that if you go into negotiations you have to have a vision and some non-negotiable positions. We did not see that. For many civil servants it later looked as if the politicians were fighting only over their own positions and were leaving the civil servants to their own fate. The civil servants also did not have much faith in the government's negotiating team – they were not seen as strong.'[3]

The anxiety was reflected in a poll conducted among members of the white Vereniging van Staatsamptenare (Association of Civil Servants) in early 1992 when the referendum campaign was in progress. Most of the participants were Afrikaner males with a higher qualification than Standard Ten. The poll showed that more than half believed there would be black majority rule within two years. Two thirds of the participants who supported the NP or Democratic Party (DP) expected personnel

1   E-mail communications from Rina Venter, 6 and 8 November 2011.
2   E-mail communications from Rina Venter, 6 and 29 September 2010, 31 January 2011.
3   E-mail reply from Coen Slabber in response to questions of 5 September 2010.

to be replaced by political appointees. Only half trusted the current government and less than a quarter trusted negotiations at Codesa. Only 15% trusted an interim government. There was low trust in politicians in general, but more than three quarters of NP- or DP-supporting respondents trusted De Klerk.[4]

Sam de Beer, the minister responsible for the Commission on Administration and who took part in the negotiations about the future public administration, told cabinet the ANC had assured government negotiators it was 'eager to retain the efficiency of the civil service'.[5] He gave cabinet the assurance that no civil servant could be dismissed unlawfully. This opinion was mistaken. Piet Swart, legal adviser to the health department, pointed out to Venter that an ANC-led government could circumvent this simply by changing the job description of existing senior posts, which would compel all incumbents to reapply.[6]

This was just what happened after May 1994. The twelve senior directors of the national health department were forced to reapply and only one retained his job. An enormous loss of skills occurred throughout the civil service. Slabber stayed on for a while and offered his comments on the new minister's restructuring plan drawn up by her adviser. She promptly rejected it and appointed her own adviser in his place.[7] Soon the department was denuded of people with managerial expertise, which could have made a major difference in implementing the plan for fighting HIV/Aids drawn up before 1994.

The ANC's overwhelming victory at the polls in 1994 would greatly accelerate its plans to staff the public sector with its own loyal cadres by enforcing the principle of demographic representation in a way De Klerk and other senior ministers never foresaw. The ANC even insisted on extending the principle to private corporations although this was not in the constitution.

Between 1996 and 2002 some 120 000 civil servants, the overwhelming majority of them senior white civil servants, received packages to encourage them to leave the service. Some tried to stay on, but were cold shouldered, given no work to do or forced out of office. In 2007 Pik Botha stated that in the constitutional negotiations the NP would never have agreed to a process based solely on racial demography. De Klerk publicly agreed with Botha's stand, and two years later he said that in negotiating a constitution, the NP had not envisaged the ANC applying affirmative action and demographic representivity in an 'unconstitutional and racist' way. He observed: 'The Constitution makes provision for demographic "representivity"

4   JS Wessels and A Viljoen, *Waarde-oriëntasies en toekomsverwagtinge van die Vereniging van Staats-amptenare* (Pretoria: RGN, 1992), pp. 6-7, 44.
5   E-mail communication from Rina Venter, 31 January 2011.
6   E-mail communication from Rina Venter, 31 January 2011.
7   E-mail communication from Coen Slabber, 7 February 2011.

being applied only in the civil service and judiciary. Now it is applied also to civil society, business and the field of culture . . . An unbalanced application of demographic representation has no basis in the Constitution.'[8]

A cultural pact?

There were also vital cultural agreements to be reached. There was considerable antipathy among some ANC leaders to Afrikaans and Afrikaans-medium educational institutions. From the early 1970s black activists had focused on the use of Afrikaans as language of instruction as a symbol of the government's lack of sympathy for the needs of black pupils.

From 1987, the government introduced major changes in the governance of schools. Most important were 'Model C' schools in which governing bodies acquired the right to raise school fees and receive more freedom to control admission and maintain standards. Such schools could be defended as an attempt to lift the state's stifling hand and encourage parental involvement. Unwisely, some leading NP politicians clothed the policy change in terms that made it clear the school governors could use the policy to protect white schools.[9] In some schools in the northern provinces the insistence that Afrikaans be maintained as language of instruction soon became entangled with the demand for racial exclusivity.

There is no reason to doubt that effective protection for Afrikaans was an important issue for De Klerk. Yet the whole question of official languages received surprisingly little attention from government. The early failure to discuss some key issues, together with the changeover from Gerrit Viljoen to Roelf Meyer as chief negotiator, made later negotiations exceptionally difficult.

In June 1992 a delegation from the SA Akademie vir Wetenskap en Kuns – the main mouthpiece for Afrikaans in tertiary education – handed De Klerk a memorandum with proposals for a post-apartheid language policy, in the presence of some 50 Afrikaner leaders from all walks of life. The president pledged to keep the Afrikaans language community informed, using the Akademie as the main channel. But a year later, on 3 May 1993, chief NP negotiator Roelf Meyer told the Akademie's secretary he did not know of any document on Afrikaans that had been submitted. The only document he was aware of was the ANC's language proposals. This was startling news for the Akademie leadership, given that at least four Afrikaans bodies had prepared submissions.[10]

---

8   *Die Burger*, 21 May 2009.
9   Huw Davies, 'The Schooling Debate Immediately Before and During the Codesa Period', unpublished document, 4 December 2011, pp. 1-3.
10 Pieter Kapp, *Draer van 'n droom: Die geskiedenis van die Suid-Afrikaanse Akademie vir Wetenskap en Kuns, 1909-2009* (Hermanus: Hemel en See Boeke, 2009), pp. 139-42.

Later in 1993 the Akademie published its 'Language Plan for the Country'. It argued that there were eleven main languages, which it depicted as inherently of equal worth and entitled to protection. Citizens had to be given the opportunity to communicate with the government in any of the main languages. It urged retention of English and Afrikaans as official languages but proposed providing the opportunity for all nine other languages to attain official status. Language rights ought to be seen as a human right and incorporated in a bill of rights. These rights had to be expanded, not abridged.[11]

It was apparent from the start that the ANC paid lip service to multi-lingualism, but confidently expected making English the dominant public language once it was in power. The multi-party negotiating body finally decided to recognise eleven official languages. Lawrence Schlemmer commented that this decision 'was in fact a decision taken in bad faith'. Almost from the start the ANC 'back-tracked on its constitutional commitments, pleading costs and practicality, and it would continue to make very little [sic] resources available for effective multi-lingualism'.[12] The NP secured a clause providing that 'rights related to language and the status of languages existing at the commencement of [the Interim Constitution] shall not be diminished' but this provision would be omitted from the final constitution.[13]

The government and the ANC were soon at loggerheads over the language character of universities and university autonomy. Some ANC members – of whom Kader Asmal, a future minister of national education, was the most vociferous – soon indicated that the new government would have little patience with attempts by universities like Stellenbosch and Potchefstroom to maintain an Afrikaans character. Neither the government nor the Afrikaans universities collectively developed a comprehensive plan for the survival of Afrikaans at tertiary level. Stellenbosch and Potchefstroom simply assumed they could continue as an Afrikaans-medium institution. Rand Afrikaans University and the University of Pretoria made their own plans for dual-medium and parallel-medium instruction, while the University of Orange Free State opted for parallel medium.[14] As experience elsewhere demonstrates, both dual medium and parallel medium hold the real risk that English would drive out the regional or national language over the medium term.

On 16 September 1993 Minister of National Education Piet Marais warned De Klerk that 'education was not the priority among our negotiators, which it should be'. He added that in informal talks he had with ANC negotiators he gained the

11   SA Akademie vir Wetenskap en Kuns, *Nuusbrief*, 33, 3, 1993.
12   Lawrence Schlemmer, 'Liberalism in South Africa', Milton Shain (ed.), *Opposing Voices: Liberalism and Opposition in South Africa* (Johannesburg: Jonathan Ball, 2006), p. 86.
13   Welsh, *The Rise and Fall of Apartheid*, p. 540.
14   Hermann Giliomee and Lawrence Schlemmer, *'n Vaste plek vir Afrikaans: Taaluitdagings op kampus* (Stellenbosch: Sun Media), 2007, pp. 36-43.

clear impression they 'displayed an intolerance towards Afrikaans and to the demand that the Afrikaans universities could continue to imbue their mission with a
cultural content'. He urged De Klerk to have a list compiled of bottom lines and
undertakings the NP had given to its voters and to indicate which of them it had
met. At that stage all the main issues related to higher education had already been
settled.[15] De Klerk urged Marais to talk to the ANC negotiators about reopening
the issue, but Marais found no one interested.

As far as primary and secondary education were concerned, little progress was
made in planning for the new order. Early in 1993 a senior educationist lamented
that there were still fourteen education departments and one Department for National Education.[16] He asked government to put a strategic plan for education on
the table, but 'apartheid education' and Afrikaans were such emotional issues for
the ANC that no progress could be made before the election.

Afrikaans schools suddenly found themselves confronted with a major challenge
for which they were quite unprepared. Many principals and school boards simply
clung to what they were used to. In the more conservative regions, there was a strong
tendency to shun proposals to amalgamate Afrikaans-medium schools, many of
which were half empty, in order to ensure full enrolment. Some more progressive
schools switched to parallel medium, not anticipating the pressure for taking in
more children in the English stream than they could handle. The government could
have tried to give stronger leadership, but the language issue was only finalised in the
final rounds of the negotiations and the NP enjoyed the support of only half the
Afrikaner electorate.[17]

Demands for Afrikaans single-medium schools encountered opposition in negotiating forums from black bureaucrats and some English-speaking businessmen
and professionals who had aligned themselves to the ANC. They insisted on a new
order structured along 'progressive' lines with English as the de facto national language. Among these was the South African Democratic Teachers' Union, which had
already signed up many members. On the other side of the spectrum were conservative whites in the education establishment; believing the De Klerk government
had taken a fatal course, they made little effort to cooperate.

Holding the show together on the government side was the national education
minister Piet Marais, who had earned a reputation as a man of great commitment
and integrity. His department was showered with memoranda and position papers

---

15 Letter from PG Marais to FW de Klerk and a memo from Marais to H Giliomee, 16 September
    1993, and personal communication of the same date.
16 JF Steyn, 'Perspektiewe op 'n oorgangsbedeling vir die onderwys', text of a speech given on 15 Janu-
    ary 1993.
17 E-mail communication from Huw Davies, 18 December 2011.

from the white side, with sometimes unreasonable demands. Marais kept a cool head, with his eye on the national interest.[18]

The interim constitution fudged the main issues. It incorporated both the NP's demand for mother-tongue education and the ANC's demand for giving access to pupils of all races, but made no attempt to spell out how potential conflicts were to be resolved. This would give a future government the liberty to emphasise access in the language of instruction (invariably meaning English) at the expense of Afrikaans instruction.

The new government would soon put pressure on Afrikaans schools to offer English-medium classes parallel to those in Afrikaans where the numbers merited it. Over the next ten to fifteen years the number of single-medium schools would decline by nearly 40%. Most of them were located in the Western Cape. Nevertheless in vital areas – including the right to receive education in the language of choice, admissions and supplementary funding of education – the compromises reached between 1992 and 1996 held up well. As a previous head of a state agency for education remarked, things could have been better, but they also could have been far worse.[19]

Where the ANC government did impose its agenda was in ruthlessly dispensing with the services of senior white officials in various departments. In 1993 and 1994 De Klerk regularly met with senior civil servants of several departments, including the white education departments. On one occasion he promised to 'fight like a tiger' to protect the rights of all existing civil servants.[20] But as in the case of the Department of Health, the new government restructured the bureaucracy and required all senior officials to reapply for their jobs. With few exceptions senior officials were not reappointed. Among those not appointed were two senior education officials at the rank of director-general, Bernard Louw and Huw Davies. It was a development no one in the De Klerk government had anticipated.

18 Davies, 'The Schooling Debate', p. 3; Interview with Huw Davies, 6 December 2011.
19 Davies, 'The Schooling Debate', p. 5.
20 Davies, 'The Schooling Debate', p. 4.

Chapter 12

A Record of Understanding

ON 16 MAY 1992 THE ANC WALKED OUT OF CODESA 2 AND REVERTED TO ITS earlier demand for an elected constitution-making body empowered to pass a constitution by a two-thirds majority. At the opening of Codesa in December 1991 De Klerk, in a surprise move that he had canvassed with only a small group, proposed that an election be held for both a parliament and a constitution-drafting body. His ideal was a complete interim constitution that the elected constitution-making body could only change with a majority of 75% for decisions on the Bill of Rights, the regions and the structure of government, and 70% for the rest.[1]

The NP confidently expected to rally enough support for an interim constitution that would effectively curb the majority party's power. It was reasonable to expect that permanent power sharing and firm guarantees for single-medium schools would be incorporated in such a constitution. Though an ANC government with the required majority could still change the constitution after the election, a legitimate question would be: Why change a constitution on which so many parties spent so much effort at Codesa?

In the first week or two of May 1992 the ANC decided to get out of the Codesa forum as quickly as possible. SACP leader Joe Slovo is alleged to have said: 'We are in danger of being trapped in a constitution from which there will be no escape. We need a deadlock.'[2] On 15 May Codesa reached a deadlock ostensibly on the issue of percentages needed to write the final constitution after the election. The ANC now demanded that the elected constitution-making body had to be empowered to draft a new constitution, and that this document could be accepted with a two-thirds majority. Such an arrangement put the NP and Inkatha in a much weaker position than at Codesa 2.

The Record of Understanding between the ANC and the government that would be announced on 26 September 1992 would turn everything upside down. The NP, which was likely to get less than a quarter of the votes, would no longer be in a dominant position, and the ANC was likely to call the shots. Although it could be expected to agree to some constitutional principles or procedures before the election,

---

1   David Welsh, *The Rise and Fall of Apartheid* (Johannesburg: Jonathan Ball, 2009), p. 446.
2   Confidential interview with an NP cabinet minister, 11 November 2010.

it would be determined to avoid anything that would tie it down too firmly. And if it won the first election with a large majority, it would not feel obliged to respect the interim constitution.

By mid-1992 there was still no clarity about what was meant by a settlement agreed on by an elected assembly. The NP thought that it would be a mutually beneficial and stable settlement, one that the main parties would change only by mutual agreement. The ANC leaders who had been in exile believed they were fighting a classic 'war of position' in which each concession extracted from the government became the platform for the next assault in what the ANC called the 'National Democratic Revolution'. It would amend its position as soon as the balance of forces shifted in its favour.[3] In 1995 Thabo Mbeki, the deputy president, would tell an ANC conference that the negotiations for an interim constitution were 'contrived elements of a transition' necessary to end white domination. At no time did the ANC consider them 'as elements of permanence'.[4]

Confronting a crisis

The ANC's withdrawal from the negotiations in May 1992 confronted De Klerk with a serious crisis. He urgently wanted the ANC back at the table. He told an analyst that all along it was a matter of critical concern to him 'to get confidence in the economy restored and the whole sanctions package removed'.[5] For the business community this was a dismal time. Derek Keys privately said South Africa was 'a good way down the road to becoming one of Africa's basket cases'.[6] But there was also a ray of light: business had begun to believe it could do business with the ANC under Nelson Mandela. Helen Suzman told of a lunch she had arranged to enable Mandela to meet with some business tycoons: 'He charmed the bloody lot of them,' she recounted.[7]

Soon after the Codesa deadlock De Klerk indicated that his government was abandoning the idea of a Second House (or Senate) in which minority parties would be over-represented. It was also prepared to reduce the majority needed to change the interim constitution from 75% to 70%. He would soon accept that a two-thirds majority was enough. But the ANC refused to return. The economy was bleeding as a result of strikes, stay-aways and rolling mass action that would continue for

---

3 ANC, 'Negotiations: A strategic perspective', NEC Paper, 4th Quarter, 1992. See also Pierre du Toit, *Suid-Afrika op soek na 'n opvolg-skikking'* (University of Stellenbosch, 2002). See also his article in *Die Burger*, 1 October 2000.

4 SAPA PR Wire Service, Speech by Thabo Mbeki at ANC National Constitutional Conference, 31 March to 2 April 1995.

5 O'Malley Archives, Interviews with Lawrence Schlemmer, 21 August 1991 and 22 October 1992.

6 O'Malley Archives, Interview with Derek Keys, 27 August 1992.

7 Anthony Sampson, *Mandela: The Authorized Biography* (Johannesburg: Jonathan Ball, 1999), p. 434.

three months. Elements in the ANC leadership had heady plans for bringing the government to a fall through the 'Leipzig option'.

From the start of multi-party negotiations in December 1991 there had been tension between the ANC and the trade union federation because the ANC had not backed its demand for a seat at the negotiating table. Subjected to strong pressure from Western leaders and investors, the ANC was retreating from its commitment to nationalisation and this triggered unhappiness in Cosatu ranks. Cosatu was deeply concerned that the ANC might sell out the workers by accepting power sharing, an idea that some ANC negotiators had begun to nibble at. ANC hardliners also questioned several of the deals struck at Codesa 2.[8]

On 2 July 1992, six weeks after the ANC leadership had walked out of Codesa 2, De Klerk wrote to Mandela: 'Our information indicates that the SACP and Cosatu have played an important role in directing the ANC from negotiations to the politics of demands and confrontation, which are inherent in mass mobilisation. Insurrectionist thinking is currently flourishing within the ANC and is being propagated by a cabal with close links to Cosatu and the SACP.' He added: 'The stated ultimate goal of the ANC's mass action is the overthrow of government by coercion. This will not be tolerated.'[9]

An attachment to the letter, entitled 'The Current Influence of Marxism-Leninism within the ANC', stated that under SACP/Cosatu influence the ANC was pursuing an insurrectionist strategy aimed at forcing the government to 'meet certain bottom lines and/or transfer power to the ANC'. The ultimate aim was a communist system.[10]

Eli Louw, minister of manpower from 1987 to 1991, recalls: 'The trade unions were a formidable factor. Without them the ANC would never have got where they did. You could not ban or detain or arrest the trade union leaders. They were too many and too radical. They refused to be intimidated.' He added another important point: 'Without losing anything, the ANC could turn around to demand that an issue had to be renegotiated. That privilege our negotiators did not enjoy. The ANC had time and numbers on its side … We were isolated and the numbers had turned against us to such an extent that we simply had to get a settlement as soon as possible.'[11]

Considering the options

With South Africa plunged into a deep political crisis, De Klerk considered his options. The first was to push ahead without the ANC, hoping it would later be

---

8   O'Malley Archives, Interview with Lawrence Schlemmer, 2 October 1992.

9   Hassen Ebrahim, *The Soul of a Nation: Constitution-making in South Africa* (Cape Town: Oxford University Press, 1998), pp. 546-47.

10 Ebrahim, *Soul of a Nation*, p. 500.

11 Interview with Eli Louw, 30 December 2010.

forced to accept an interim constitution as a political reality. The second was to continue talking to the ANC, but stick to power sharing and minority rights as a bottom line. The third was to drop power sharing as one of the pillars of NP policy adopted in September 1991, and to stake everything on a constitutional state where individuals rather than groups enjoyed rights.

The first option found expression in a document submitted in July 1992 to cabinet at a *bosberaad*. Marked Top Secret, its core idea was for the government to take the initiative in putting a draft transitional constitution on the table and then proceeding to implement it. To attain international recognition, the transitional constitution had to be 'undeniably reasonable and unambiguously democratic' and based on the constitutional principles agreed to at Codesa. Such a constitution had to be published and passed by parliament by October. The government then had to announce preparations for either a referendum or an election. Only if the ANC returned to 'honourable negotiations' could the government reconsider the process.[12]

The De Klerk government did not want to pursue this option. Only a very determined government willing to force the constitution through parliament and call out the police, army and reservists for the election would have taken up this option.

The second option was to insist on power sharing with minority or group rights as the bottom line for a settlement. The NP's demand for power sharing went through different permutations. First there was the idea of white-black power sharing by way of a grand pact, followed by the proposal for a compulsory coalition of the main parties. This was later supplemented by the demand for proportional representation on every level, including appointments to cabinet and ambassadorships. The way in which the executive should function was left vague, but it certainly included the idea of a check on the power of the majority party in dealing with important issues. In addition to power sharing, the NP demanded minority rights, which included collective rights to determine language use in public and education, and a strong form of federalism. Until September 1992 the NP argued that individual rights did not constitute a strong enough form of protection for minorities.

The third option – which the government would choose against all expectations – was the constitutional state. In such a system the constitution rather than parliament is sovereign and, while it strongly protects individual rights, it does not accommodate the demand of minorities for collective rights. This was the policy that the Progressive Federal Party had adopted after the referendum of 1982, when it dropped the minority veto and opted to work for a liberal democracy based on majority rule and individual rights. By contrast, the NP's stated view since September 1991 was that the final constitution had to rest on two pillars: a constitutional state and participa-

---

12 Archive for Contemporary Affairs (ACA), Bloemfontein, Kobie Coetsee Collection, PV357, File 1/ K2/9, Cabinet *Bosberaad*, July 1992.

tory democracy/power sharing. De Klerk had spelled that out in a preface to the document 'Framework for a New South Africa' published before the meeting of the NP's federal congress in September 1991.

The NP government received little tangible support from friendly Western governments for any strong form of power sharing. British Ambassador Robin Renwick spelled out his government's position: 'We will support protection of minority rights, but we will not support a blocking minority … where the whites on their own could block all sorts of legislation.'[13] In July 1992 Herman Cohen, US under-secretary of state for Africa, declared that all sides had to recognise the 'right of the majority to govern'. No side could insist on 'overly complex arrangements intended to guarantee a share of power to particular groups, which will frustrate effective governance. Minorities have the right to safeguards; they cannot expect a veto.'[14] The ANC could not have phrased its key demand better.

Without any strong Western ally – and desperate to achieve a settlement as soon as possible to boost the economy – the government tried to persuade the ANC that conventional majority rule was ill-suited for addressing the problems of South Africa. An attachment to De Klerk's letter to Mandela of 2 July contended that 'the mere identification of the majority' was insufficient, and that the more fundamental feature of modern democratic states was the extent to which 'all citizens enjoy meaningful participation and fair representation in government institutions'.[15]

This was stretching the definition of a democracy. A defeated party in Britain's democratic system – on which the white democracy of South Africa between 1910 and 1984 was based – was not asked to nominate members to participate in cabinet unless the majority party needed this to form a coalition. And since the mid-1980s the polls had indicated that the ANC would get more than half of the votes.

De Klerk was adamant that power sharing as he envisaged it was not the same as a white veto, often pointing out that a vote was never taken in the four years he chaired the cabinet. If confronted with cabinet approval of something they disliked, ministers had to decide if they 'could live' with it or would have to resign. But this was a convention in the Westminster system, where a single party rules. In a coalition government dissent meant little unless it could lead to the fall of the government.

De Klerk failed to clear up an ambiguous situation. His mandate from his voters in the 1989 election, the September 1991 federal congress and the 1992 referendum was for power sharing. To the ANC he never made it clear that he could not underwrite a settlement unless this issue was resolved. He hoped to win the ANC over to

---

13   Interview with Robin Renwick by Patti Waldmeir, 16 December 1994.

14   Steven Friedman (ed.), *The Long Journey: South Africa's Quest for a Negotiated Settlement* (Johannesburg: Ravan Press, 1993), p. 157.

15   Ebrahim, *Soul of a Nation*, p. 555.

accepting power sharing for an indefinite period, but seemed to have dropped this as a non-negotiable issue by mid-1993. For him power sharing became an aspiration, a dearly hoped-for outcome, while his constituency thought it was his non-negotiable bottom line.

Superficially, the division between the ANC and the NP on power sharing seemed bridgeable. Assuaging the fears of minorities under an ANC government was always an important issue for Mandela. In Stellenbosch in May 1991 he gave a speech largely in Afrikaans in which he said simple majority rule might not work in South Africa. 'It may not be enough to work purely on one-person one-vote. Because every national group would like to see that the people of their flesh and blood are in government. The whites, for instance, have to be able to say: "There is Gerrit Viljoen, I have got representation."' He spoke of an 'in-built mechanism that makes it impossible for one group to suppress another.'[16] Among some ANC leaders a Government of National Unity – at least for an initial five or ten years – had gained ground.

In many ways the most crucial question was: How would a Government of National Unity function and how would it vote? It was as if the NP leadership was afraid to ask the question. One or two of the negotiators suggested privately that it all depended on whether the opposition could manage to draw at least a third of the vote in the founding election. But that ignored the logic of those democracies where the 'winner takes all'. The only way to counter this was an electoral system structured in such a way that it rewarded moderation, but the NP government paid little attention to this.[17]

Another question De Klerk failed to clarify was whether a Government of National Unity would require ministers to accept cabinet decisions and refrain from criticising them in public. After his resignation from cabinet in the Government of National Unity in 1997, De Klerk would often say to the federal executive of his party that the absence of a policy framework, underwritten by all parties in government, was the Achilles heel of the Government of National Unity. He would be openly critical of his colleagues in the cabinet, because he felt he was often the only one in cabinet who confronted the ANC.[18]

Nonracial majority rule

Rejecting power sharing, the ANC called for nonracial majority rule. The terms nonracialism and majority rule, as used by the ANC, have to be decoded. Social

---

16 Patti Waldmeir, *Anatomy of a Miracle: The End of Apartheid and the Birth of the New South Africa* (New York: WW Norton, 1997), p. 214.

17 A major study with this idea as its theme was published at the time but unwisely ignored by the government. See Donald Horowitz, *A Democratic South Africa? Constitutional Engineering in a Divided Society* (Cape Town: Oxford University Press, 1991).

18 E-mail communication from Inus Aucamp, former NP Free State leader, 18 May 2012.

analyst Pierre van den Berghe memorably pointed out that the liberal principle of majority rule represented the 'great moral alibi of black nationalism' in Africa. He warned that the term should not be accepted at face value. 'If your constituency has the good fortune to contain a demographic majority, racism can easily be disguised as democracy. The ideological sleight of hand, of course, is that an ascriptive, racially defined majority is a far cry from a majority made up of shifting coalitions of individuals on the basis of commonality of beliefs and interests. "Majority rule" in Africa can thus easily become a veneer for racial domination.'[19]

Eli Kedourie, a noted student of nationalism, observed after visiting South Africa that the principle of majority decision-making is 'workable only on condition that majorities are variable, not permanent': voters have to be willing to vote according to their interests and values rather than for candidates sharing their racial or ethnic identity. In divided societies, however, there is a pattern of the party representing the dominant racial or ethnic group being returned time after time. Kedourie pointed out that 'the worst effects of the tyranny of the majority are seen when the unalloyed Western model is introduced in countries divided by religion or language or race'.[20]

Vernon Bogdanor, a leading authority on comparative politics, noted that 'no divided society has been able to achieve stability without power sharing.'[21] The precise arrangements in successful societies differed, but in all of them there was some set of arrangements whereby no major segment felt permanently left out in the cold. The secret, he argued, lay less in constitutional provisions than in institutional arrangements – for instance, how the cabinet was composed and how it would operate.

David Welsh, who attended Codesa in 1992 as adviser to the Democratic Party, commented on the ANC's demand for a nonracial order: 'nonracialism (apart from the elimination of all discriminatory laws) was chimerical, an aspiration that had not been achieved in any multi-ethnic or multiracial situation. Group voting preferences would continue to dominate.'[22] That was a reality the NP knew all too well from its own history of mobilising the Afrikaners. The ANC, understandably, rejected it. Surprisingly, large numbers of liberals believed in the ANC's nonracial creed. Shortly after the 1994 election De Klerk too began to suggest that the time would soon come that voters would be swayed by their interests rather than their identity but he could offer no evidence for this.

19 Pierre van den Berghe, 'Introduction' in Van den Berghe (ed.), *The Liberal Dilemma in South Africa* (London: Croom Helm, 1979), p. 7.

20 Eli Kedourie, 'One-Man, One-Vote', *South Africa International*, 18, 7, 1987, p. 1.

21 Vernon Bogdanor, 'Forms of Autonomy and the Protection of Minorities', *Daedalus,* Spring 1997, p. 66.

22 Welsh, *The Rise and Fall of Apartheid*, p. 357.

Lacking strategists

The structure of Codesa – with its nineteen parties, some of them insignificant fringe organisations – was clumsy. This feature delayed the day that De Klerk would be forced to make some crucial decisions: How would the government's negotiating strategy be determined and who would negotiate on the government's behalf once it met face to face with the ANC in bilateral negotiations? The only experience NP leaders had acquired during the previous decades was in talks with the coloured, Indian and homeland leaders who, with the exception of Mangosuthu Buthelezi, had no strong base and very little power. No real skills in conducting negotiations with a formidable adversary had been developed. De Klerk had held no portfolio as a cabinet minister in which his parleying skills were really tested. He was above all a pragmatist seeking common ground where there were serious differences, and performing well in keeping his party together.

Two kinds of experts were needed. The first was strategists who could analyse the ANC's strategy as well as the movement's objectives once in government. Remarkably, the ANC spelled out its goals in great detail: to take control of all the major levers in society – the civil service, state corporations, the security forces, the intelligence community, the state broadcaster and the Reserve Bank. The government needed a strategy to forestall these objectives, if they were going to affect the capacity of the future political order to retain efficiency and provide security.

There were experienced and knowledgeable people on whom De Klerk could draw. During the 1970s and 1980s several senior military officers took negotiating courses in Israel, which the military believed had special expertise in this area. They introduced courses on negotiating strategy in the defence force. In the Department of Foreign Affairs both the minister, Pik Botha, and his director-general Neil van Heerden had acquired extensive experience in the Namibian negotiations. At the universities there were several outstanding academics with a sound analytical grasp of racial and ethnic conflicts and negotiated settlements. In large corporations and the Chamber of Mines were several people who had more than ten years experience of tough bargaining with trade unions.

Magnus Malan, minister of defence, believed De Klerk had made a serious error at the outset. 'He had at his disposal no profile analysis of the ANC's leaders and no analysis of the ANC's negotiating strategy or of the way in which a counter-strategy could be developed. FW and his negotiators thought the ANC thinks and feels just like us. There was no one with the experience of Cyril Ramaphosa. We won the war militarily but lost it politically.'[23] Malan was referring to the war of the 1980s. The situation of the early 1990s was, however, quite different. Military means were no longer as relevant or appropriate as before.

---

23 Interview with Magnus Malan, 9 February 2008.

Chris Thirion, second in command in Military Intelligence, agreed with De Klerk's move to negotiate, but later questioned his strategy. He felt De Klerk should have made it clear that the army would remain intact until the violence had subsided and public order had been properly established. This might have forced the ANC to reconsider its strategy of negotiating while stoking violence.[24]

De Klerk never used his military and national intelligence bases fully. He disapproved of the strong military influence on the PW Botha government and swung over to the other side. 'I want to restore cabinet and government to its full glory,' he told Niel Barnard of National Intelligence.[25] But this was premature: the ANC had not yet shown its commitment to a genuinely democratic order. A president in charge of the country in its gravest hour would have been better served if he had retained the State Security Council, where security issues could be thoroughly debated, the actions of the state agencies could be co-ordinated, and the commanding officers of the military and police could be put on the spot about allegations of illegal and extra-legal activities.

De Klerk erred in thinking his meetings with senior military and police officers in the first months of 1990 would be enough to make sure the security forces were fully behind him and his quest for a settlement. As the violence continued and evidence mounted that the ANC was responsible for most of it, sections in the top military command began to lose faith in De Klerk and the process he had initiated. Some of them authorised illegal acts to destabilise the ANC (see Chapter 13). But there was no coherent plan and in the end these actions only benefited the ANC, which used them to argue that there was a 'Third Force' De Klerk was either unwilling or unable to control.

De Klerk was confident that he could manage the transition process largely on his own and could restrict participation from the government's side to civilian politicians and officials. He also believed many of the trickier aspects of the transition could be resolved by a future Government of National Unity, in which he expected the NP to have an important say. So he left many key aspects undecided. Rina Venter, minister of health, believed the NP government could have proceeded far with the integration of the seventeen health departments.

But the matter was left hanging in the air, and by May 1994 the director-general of health had to report to the new minister that there were no systems or procedures in place for the rationalisation of the health departments.[26] Government ministers mislaid plans drawn up by Afrikaans organisations to protect Afrikaans as a public

---

24 Hilton Hamann, *Days of the Generals: The Untold Story of South Africa's Apartheid-era Military Generals* (Cape Town: Zebra, 2001), pp. 181-83.

25 Interview with Niel Barnard, 20 January 2012.

26 Interview with Rina Venter, 5 October 2010.

language and did not prepare a route for Afrikaans-medium schools and universities in the future. The most serious unresolved issue was that of indemnity for members of the security forces.

The second kind of expertise needed was in negotiating strategy and tactics. Cyril Ramaphosa, who became the ANC's chief negotiator after the collapse of Codesa, had cut his teeth as the general secretary of the National Union of Mineworkers (NUM) and was generally considered one of the shrewdest and toughest negotiators in the game. Naas Steenkamp, one-time president of the Chamber of Mines and chairman of its negotiating team, believes that what De Klerk needed above all was a negotiating plan and an expert on negotiating tactics comparable to Ramaphosa.

Roelf Meyer, the NP's chief negotiator after the collapse of Codesa, was impressed with Ramaphosa. Journalist Patti Waldmeir, who interviewed Meyer after the completion of negotiations for an interim constitution, said: 'He [Meyer] reflects on Ramaphosa's background with envy.' She quoted him as saying: 'These guys had an advantage over us; they had been through negotiations par excellence in the mining industry . . . while we had to learn through experience on a daily basis – you can't read these things in books.'[27]

A specialist negotiator would have been equipped with a mandate in which ideal outcomes, fall-back positions and bottom lines were clearly formulated. The negotiator would enjoy no decision-making power, but act as an adviser, making inputs in the mandating process and putting forward tactical and strategic options. He would be fully conversant with the views of the president and he would have no authority to deviate from his mandate. Such an approach would allow the mandate-giver to focus much more sharply on defining the mandate. An approach along the lines Steenkamp proposes would have avoided many of the government's woes in the negotiations.[28]

But De Klerk was reluctant to bring people from outside the NP caucus into key political roles. He had done so in the case of economic policy, where he made the smart move of appointing Wim de Villiers and Derek Keys to key economic portfolios, but he seemed to believe political negotiations had to be the preserve of politicians. After Gerrit Viljoen dropped out of the negotiations in May 1992 because of ill health, he chose Meyer as his chief negotiator, overlooking Tertius Delport, who had taken a tough line against the ANC. Speaking much later, Delport said he told cabinet after the collapse of Codesa that the issue was not about percentages: 'We have just got to tell them – the ANC – to stop. We have got to crush them.' He believed the ANC had no physical or military presence.[29]

---

27   Patti Waldmeir, *Anatomy of a Miracle*, p. 210.

28   Interview with Naas Steenkamp, 1 December 2011.

29   Anthony Butler, *Cyril Ramaphosa* (Johannesburg: Jacana, 2007), p. 294.

De Klerk's following still strongly opposed ANC demands and what it called the ANC's 'irresponsible' mass action. It believed the NP could win as much as 30% of the vote and Inkatha at least 10%. It had a vision of a strong opposition that could block the ANC's radical demands.

A new team

From May 1992 Roelf Meyer held the positions of minister of constitutional affairs, chairman of the cabinet sub-committee on negotiations, and chief negotiator. Both Viljoen and Tertius Delport, his understudy in Working Group 2 at Codesa, insisted it was the NP's duty to honour the commitment to power sharing that it had made in the referendum three months earlier. In August 1992 Viljoen repeated that the majority party must not dominate the future legislative and executive structures, limiting the minority parties to the role of opposition. He wanted power sharing to be written into both the interim and final constitutions.[30] Delport believed the government threw away a strong hand at Codesa because NP delegates were too anxious to appease the ANC.[31]

De Klerk would soon appoint two other ministers, Leon Wessels and Dawie de Villiers, to assist Meyer in the bilateral talks with the ANC. Until the end of August there was no sign that these three were taking a different line from Viljoen or Delport on power sharing. Interviewed on 13 August 1992, Meyer said the process was 'absolutely' about power sharing rather than transferring power to the majority party in government.[32] In Codesa's Working Group 3 he had explained how the NP viewed the transition. Advisory bodies would be introduced before an election for a power-sharing interim government was held. The existing constitution could not be changed until the government held a referendum to consult its electorate.[33] Wessels remarked: 'We would not allow people to wrest power from our hands but we would be prepared to work out a constitutional framework in which we could share power.'[34] Dawie de Villiers insisted there had to be power sharing rather than a system where the party with 51% of the vote had 100% of the power.[35]

Ministers who would later become strong critics of these three negotiators expressed their view in similar terms. In August 1992 Hernus Kriel, minister of law

---

30 O'Malley Archives, Interview with Gerrit Viljoen, 27 August 1992.
31 O'Malley Archives, Interview with Tertius Delport, 25 August 1992; Butler, *Ramaphosa*, p. 294.
32 O'Malley Archives, Interview with Roelf Meyer, 13 August 1992.
33 Friedman (ed.), *The Long Journey*, p. 91.
34 O'Malley Archives, Interview with Leon Wessels, 19 July 1990.
35 O'Malley Archives, Interview with Dawie de Villiers, 17 August 1992.

and order, said the government had not deviated from its commitment to power sharing and would not be intimidated by mass action.[36]

The question is: Why did De Klerk choose Meyer for the extremely challenging task? The answer lies in Meyer's definition of himself, when he spoke to a reporter in 1994. He said he was a 'loyalist rather than a radical'.[37] In 1998, after he had broken with De Klerk politically, Meyer suggested that De Klerk had chosen him – a fairly junior minister – as front man and fall guy to be ditched if the boat hit the rocks.[38] With the negotiations in a severe crisis, De Klerk wanted a chief negotiator who would execute his instructions faithfully rather than one with an independent mind who would insist strongly on points important to him.

Meyer followed the classic route for advancement in Afrikaner nationalist politics – Junior Rapportryers and Afrikaner Broederbond – before going to parliament. Pieter de Lange, vice-chancellor of the Rand Afrikaans University and chairman of the Afrikaner Broederbond's executive council, asked Minister of Health Rina Venter to convey to De Klerk his view that Meyer was not up to the task of chief negotiator, because he was not a profound thinker and lacked the ability to take a firm stand. Venter thought that, in dealing with political nettles, De Klerk tended to assemble like-minded people around him rather than strong individuals. When she conveyed these views to De Klerk, he shrugged and said there was no more suitable person in the party. He dismissed the suggestion that he should contract a specialist from the private sector.[39]

Meyer was a courteous man with good interpersonal relations, but he was a strange choice if De Klerk had wanted to make a strong stand on key issues. Unlike Delport, Meyer had not studied constitutional law, and he did not seem to have read any of the literature on deeply divided societies establishing a form of peaceful coexistence after prolonged strife.

When he attended a conference in 1996 in Belfast, Northern Ireland, after a settlement had been reached, Meyer said there was no comparison between the conflict situations in South Africa and Northern Ireland: 'We in South Africa had basically no differences to resolve … It was almost as simple a matter as colour or race that separated us. We had to remove the problem in order to reach out to each other, and to discover each other as human beings.'[40] This was non-racialism with an almost evangelical fervour.

In a booklet published in 1998 Meyer presented his thinking in a very different

---

36 O'Malley Archives, Interview with Hernus Kriel, 18 August 1992.
37 Waldmeir, *Anatomy of a Miracle*, p. 210.
38 Bantu Holomisa and Roelf Meyer, *A Better Future* (Arcadia: The United Democratic Movement, 1998), p. 18.
39 E-mail communication from Rina Venter, 29 September 2010.
40 Padraig O'Malley (ed.), *Ramaphosa and Meyer in Belfast* (Boston: McCormack Institute, 1996), p. 27.

way from his enthusiastic endorsement of power sharing back in August 1992. He stated that as chief negotiator he was 'determined not to have anything to do with the variety of unrealistic *slenters* [gimmicks] and tricks which were still thought by some on our side to be viable options'. He added: 'Loaded majorities, rotating presidents, weird protective mechanisms for minorities (meaning whites) and the like would simply not bring the stability a new constitution had to ensure – apart from having no chance of being accepted by other parties.'

Meyer continued: 'A truly democratic constitution, based on individual human rights and with all the necessary in-built checks and balances to ensure the separation of powers of the state, was the only option as far as I was concerned. And we had to accept the consequences of such a dispensation. It was not always easy to sell the concept to my colleagues.'[41] But Meyer ignores the NP leadership's promise of a referendum if the settlement deviated too much from party policy. Inus Aucamp, a member of the caucus and later NP leader in the Free State, emphasised that De Klerk had promised a referendum if the proposed settlement deviated too much from the September 1991 policy: 'If it [the proposals put forward after May 1992] indeed represented a paradigm shift, why did De Klerk not call a referendum, which he promised to do if the proposed settlement deviated fundamentally from NP policy?'[42]

Meyer's view, as expressed in 1998, represented no less than the collapse of demands for a pluralist system aimed at maintaining a measure of balance between the majority and minorities. It underwrote the calls for what ANC leaders called 'an ordinary' or 'nonracial democracy'. This is usually found in stable, prosperous countries without deep racial or ethnic divisions, where a significant part of the electorate switches votes readily in order to defeat a ruling party. From the middle of 1992, when the negotiations started, to their conclusion at the end of 1996 Meyer spoke as if he were a free agent, unencumbered by any party mandate. He was, of course, nothing of the sort; he remained bound by the party's September 1991 proposals and by the promise made to the voters in the referendum of March 1992 to negotiate a power-sharing constitution.

Secret negotiations

From the middle of May to the middle of September numerous secret meetings took place between representatives of the ANC and the government in what became known as 'The Channel'. In these meetings Meyer had at his side SS (Fanie) van der Merwe, a senior official from Constitutional Affairs, and Niel Barnard from

41 Holomisa and Meyer, *A Better Future*, p. 18.
42 JM Aucamp, 'Die Nasionale Party van Suid-Afrika se laaste dekade as regerende party, 1984–1994,' doctoral dissertation, University of the Free State, 2010, p. 377.

National Intelligence. On some occasions Dawie de Villiers and Leon Wessels joined the government's team. Jan Heunis (legal adviser) often sat in. On the ANC side was Cyril Ramaphosa, supported by Joe Slovo and Mac Maharaj. On some occasions Valli Moosa, Penuell Meduna and Mathews Phosa joined them. Arthur Chaskalson and Dullah Omar contributed on legal issues.

Mandela and De Klerk, their respective principals, were kept fully informed of these meetings. The key question confronting people from both sides in the Channel was: 'Do we want to start fighting all over again?' It was a tense time requiring cool heads and strong nerves.

The Venter memorandum

In the period of suspended negotiations De Klerk and Mandela exchanged views in letters. In a confidential letter to Mandela of 2 July 1992 De Klerk took up the issue of the cabinet in a future government. He proposed an executive council directly elected by the voters, which would in turn appoint the cabinet. In effect, the council would consist of the leaders of the three biggest parties (ANC, NP and Inkatha), with the underlying assumption that each of these leaders would be able to block an important law or government action they did not like. (The ANC's negotiators would later refer in dismissive terms to these proposals as a 'troika' in which every leader had a 'veto'.[43])

Francois Venter, a Potchefstroom-trained legal academic working for the Department of Constitutional Affairs, drafted an attachment to the letter, entitled 'Government Proposals regarding a Transitional Constitution for South Africa'. Reflecting some ideas that had been circulating for four years in a study group of the Afrikaner Broederbond, the document brought about a major shift in the constitution-making process. It proposed 'the fundamental replacement of the principles of the current Westminster system with those of a Constitutional State', and 'an independent judiciary, with judges being appointed by a non-political body'.[44] The transitional constitution could only be changed 'within the framework of general constitutional principles agreed on by Codesa', and the Constitutional Chamber of the Appellate Division had to certify this to be the case.

Meyer would later credit De Klerk's letter to Mandela, and in particular the constitutional proposals, with breaking the deadlock between the government and the ANC. He stated: 'The government's policy underwent a significant shift. That document establishes a democratic system based on respect for the individual and the recognition of equal rights for all. It was the most important moment in the entire process of negotiations.' Meyer spelled out the change: ' It replaced the con-

---

43   Padraig O'Malley, *Shades of Difference: Mac Maharaj and the Struggle for South Africa*, p. 63.
44   Ebrahim, *Soul of a Nation*, p. 570.

cepts of majority *versus* minority and power sharing as basis for the new government. It was to my mind the moment in which a paradigm shift in NP thinking occurred and in which the foundation for the constitutional negotiations was laid.'[45]

This view is not quite correct. The document spells out more fully the idea of a constitutional state, which the NP's federal congress had accepted in September 1991 as one of its two pillars for a constitutional democracy. But De Klerk had not yet abandoned the power-sharing pillar. The NP policy that the government would take to the negotiating table was the one, accepted back in September 1991, which proposed a presidency consisting of the leaders of the three biggest parties and a rotating chair. Decisions of the 'troika', including the appointment of the cabinet, would be by consensus. On 13 August 1992 Meyer himself still maintained the process was about power sharing rather than transferring power to the majority party in government.[46] Only in the course of 1993 did NP negotiators begin to believe that a constitutional state could replace, rather than supplement, power sharing as a way of protecting minorities.

A Record of Understanding

Always concerned about a 'heavyweight pact' between the NP and the ANC, Mangosuthu Buthelezi became increasingly worried when the government embarked on a series of bilateral meetings with the major parties in an urgent attempt to restart negotiations. Meeting De Klerk early in August, he expressed grave misgivings about the talks between the government and the ANC. He felt De Klerk should have made it clear that the ANC was only one party among several and that only multilateral negotiations could save the country. He asked De Klerk to stop behaving as if the key issues would be settled between him and Mandela, and urged him to demand the disbanding of Umkhonto weSizwe.[47]

When the negotiations began in 1990 the ANC had insisted on a 'heavyweight pact' between it and the government from the start. The government refused and in his letter to Mandela of 2 July 1992 De Klerk still dismissed the ANC/SACP's notion that the conflict was between the government and the ANC as 'the only adversaries'.[48] In 1994 Joe Slovo observed that 'the whole thing' could have been settled much sooner. 'The basic reason is Inkatha.'[49]

On 26 September 1992 the NP government and the ANC signed a Record of Understanding, clearing the way for the ANC to return to the negotiating table.

45   JM Aucamp Papers (private collection), Roelf Meyer to JM Aucamp, 13 March 2011.

46   O'Malley Archives, Interview with Roelf Meyer, 13 August 1992.

47   Ben Temkin, *Buthelezi: A Biography* (London: Frank Cass, 2003), p. 282.

48   Ebrahim, *Soul of a Nation*, p. 546.

49   Interview with Joe Slovo by Patti Waldmeir, 14 November 1994.

'They caved in on everything,' Joe Slovo exulted afterwards. To him this was a symbol that the government realised there would be no solution without the ANC.[50] On the other hand, Meyer stated later that the Record of Understanding was merely the 'smokescreen that enabled the ANC to resume negotiations without losing face'.[51] De Klerk dismissed the claim that the government had accepted the ANC's position on an interim government and constituent assembly. He claims that as early as December 1991 he had proposed the same 'concept'.[52]At that point, however, the government still had the initiative. The government dominated Codesa up to the point where the ANC walked out.

The Record of Understanding was a crucial turning point and it is important to understand what it signified. De Klerk is correct that the ANC abandoned its original position, articulated in its Harare Declaration of 1989. Here, in De Klerk's terms, it demanded an 'unstructured and immediate' transfer of power before a constitution was even negotiated. Such a break in constitutional continuity happens only after a revolution or a shattering defeat in war. It is also true that De Klerk had already in December 1991 called for an elected interim government that would also serve as a constitution-making body. In the Record the ANC used the phrase 'a government of national unity', which the government hoped was a veiled acceptance of power sharing on the ANC's part. So, too, the statement that the final constitution 'would be bound only by agreed constitutional principles' was more of a government idea than an ANC view.

But the Record of Understanding was important both for what it said and what it did not say. It stated that the elected body would 'draft and adopt the new constitution' and 'arrive at its decisions democratically with certain agreed to majorities'. There was no reference to the decisions taken at Codesa on an interim constitution or to any majority that would be needed to change these decisions. This was the key lever the NP had in its hands before the breakdown of Codesa. This lever was not lost. On some other issues the ANC also got its way in a dramatic fashion. Buthelezi had long claimed that the ANC was the main offender in the violence between Inkatha and the ANC. For its part, the ANC claimed Inkatha was the primary offender and that violence in the urban areas emanated largely from hostels where most of the inmates were Inkatha members. The Record stipulated that eight hostels had to be fenced and that the display and carrying of traditional weapons in public would be prohibited.

Another issue was the release of political prisoners on which Mandela and De Klerk had begun to spar at Groote Schuur in 1990. De Klerk was on firm ground by

---

50   Waldmeir, *Anatomy of a Miracle*, pp. 216-18.

51   Roelf Meyer, 'ANC het algehele ommeswaai gemaak', *Die Burger,* 20 February 1997.

52   FW de Klerk, *Die laaste trek – 'n Nuwe begin* (Cape Town: Human & Rousseau, 1998), p. 266.

insisting on the internationally accepted Norgaard principles that ruled out amnesty for the murder of civilians. A prominent case was that of Robert McBride, sentenced to jail for placing a bomb in a Durban bar. The ANC demanded that the Norgaard principles be waived, but De Klerk refused.

Meeting De Klerk privately in what could be seen as a leadership summit, Mandela insisted on the release of McBride and others. After De Klerk had said once again that he would never release prisoners who did not meet the requirements for amnesty, Mandela answered in patronising terms: 'You must never put forward a position of intransigence like saying "never" when you know in the end you are going to give in, because when you do give in, you will be humiliated and I am trying to save you from humiliation.'[53] Ramaphosa and Maharaj both strongly believed that Mandela used this point to establish his clear ascendancy over De Klerk.[54]

This issue caused De Klerk his greatest anguish, but he agreed to the demand in order to get the negotiations back on track. The government released prisoners on a list provided by the ANC. No Inkatha prisoners were released, but Barend Strydom, a white man who had shot and killed several blacks in the centre of Pretoria, was set free.

Yet another issue on which the ANC got its way was the use of mass action as an instrument of political pressure. The ANC's mass action during the winter of 1992 imposed severe costs on the economy and greatly harmed investor confidence. De Klerk wanted a clause in the Record that mass action could no longer be used for political purposes. He gave instructions to his negotiators, Niel Barnard and Fanie van der Merwe: 'In no way are you giving in on this issue.' But they and the ANC negotiators failed to settle the issue, leaving it to Mandela and De Klerk to seek a solution. Barnard recounts what happened: '[They] had a one-on-one and within five minutes – it could have been ten – they came back and scrapped the whole issue of mass action completely.'

De Klerk explained to the outraged Barnard: 'Well, I have found a compromise with Mr Mandela and it is not necessary anymore.' In assessing De Klerk's style in this and several other important issues, Barnard concludes: 'I have never seen him being very strong under difficult circumstances. He would always [be] looking out for a compromise, for the easiest way out … The point is this: it's easy to sit in your office in the Union Buildings, and give instructions on difficult issues, but if you are in the firing line and have to take the decisions it is a very different experience.' Barnard felt strongly that some issues a leader 'cannot handle by compromise'; he had to take a strong stand. That ability, in Barnard's view, ultimately determined trust between a leader and his followers.

---

53 Interview with Cyril Ramaphosa by Patti Waldmeir, 19 January 1995.
54 Interviews with Mac Maharaj by Patti Waldmeir, 31 January and 14 April 1995; Interview with Cyril Ramaphosa, 15 January 1995.

Barnard is convinced Mandela would not have acted in the same way in dealing with PW Botha and that Botha would not have acceded to Mandela's demands for the fencing of the hostels, a ban on the carrying of traditional weapons and the release of prisoners, but would have referred them back to the negotiators. He believes Botha would have sensed that Mandela's key objective was to sever the ties between the government and Inkatha, and would have refused to go along with this.[55]

Two scenarios

After the Record was signed, Hernus Kriel told cabinet: 'This is the end of our alliance with Inkatha.' Told of this remark some twenty years later, Buthelezi said: 'Well, Mr Kriel was quite right.'[56] Buthelezi was understandably very angry and broke off relations with the NP. In effect, De Klerk was beginning to accept the ANC's demand for a heavyweight pact between it and the NP. It was one in which the government would increasingly occupy a junior position.

Mandela emerged from this episode with a greatly enhanced stature in his own ranks. Ramaphosa could not hide his admiration: 'Mandela is a very stubborn man. He has nerves of steel. Once he has decided that a particular issue has to be pursued, everything else matters little.'[57] For De Klerk it was a searing experience. In his letter of 2 July he had fully explained to Mandela what progress was being made on all the issues and why the ANC's demands were unrealistic and unfair towards Inkatha. Mandela was not interested in arguing; he was setting non-negotiable preconditions for the ANC's return to the table.

It is often speculated whether negotiations could have taken a different course at this point. In cabinet Hernus Kriel insisted that the ANC should be forced to yield in order to get agreement.[58] At the time he told a journalist off the record that the government 'is not affected by the ANC mass action at all. We will not be forced through mass action to hand over the government to the ANC.'[59] A year later he would say that the NP made a fundamental mistake in not insisting on power sharing as one of the constitutional principles the two parties had to agree on.[60]

What would have happened if Kriel's view had triumphed? Two scenarios are possible. One is that the ANC might have found its following had become exhausted by disruptions and the loss of wages and less keen on mass action. The ANC might have returned to the negotiations divided and in a much weaker position. The other scenario is one of the government taking a much tougher line and calling a state of

55 Interviews with Niel Barnard by Patti Waldmeir, 8 December 1994 and 9 May 2012.
56 Interview with Mangosuthu Buthelezi, 15 September 2010.
57 Waldmeir, *Anatomy of a Miracle*, p. 218.
58 Allister Sparks, *Tomorrow is Another Country* (Johannesburg: Struik, 1994), p. 184.
59 O'Malley Archives, Interview with Hernus Kriel, 18 August 1992.
60 O'Malley Archives, Interview with Hernus Kriel, 27 July 1993.

emergency. The world would have responded with tougher action. The economy would have taken a nose dive and the negotiations would have resumed with the NP in a much weaker position. Of the two scenarios the second is more likely.

A 'summit' of sorts

The meeting between De Klerk and Mandela that would lead to the Record of Understanding could be compared to the summit parleys of national leaders who met one-on-one on crucial occasions, such as the Chamberlain-Hitler meeting in 1938, the Begin-Sadat meeting in 1978 or the Kennedy-Khrushchev meeting in Vienna in 1961. The latter encounter was the subject of a major book and a television series. The author makes an important point in a folksy way: 'Mr Nice Guy rarely walks away with much from the negotiating table; Mr Nasty may do better, but he has to guess how far to go without alienating his opponent.'[61]

Mandela had got away with humiliating De Klerk publicly at the opening of Codesa in December 1991. He knew he could do so again, if necessary. He was now in full control of the ANC. Niel Barnard, head of the National Intelligence Service, remarked: 'They [the ANC negotiators] would never dare to move in a fundamental way on any strategic issue if they hadn't discussed it with him.' He would also directly oppose De Klerk's position on power sharing, sticking to the principle he had enunciated at the start of the talks in prison: if the ANC wins the election, it would consult widely; but if it wins the election, it must govern the country.[62]

On the recommendation of the Channel it was decided that the talks between the government and the ANC would continue. It would only be on 1 April 1993 that the Multi-Party Negotiating Process started. In the meantime public support for De Klerk as leader had dropped from 60% in March 1991 to below 40% by November 1992. Support for the NP, which was about 40% in July 1992, slumped to just over 20% by March 1993. Black support for the NP declined from 8% in 1990 to just 2% by the end of 1992. ANC endorsement among blacks was rising steadily and would top 80% in the election.[63]

Turning point

The crucial turning point in the negotiations was the Record of Understanding. If the government wanted to retain the initiative in the constitutional negotiations and retain electoral support beyond white ranks, it had to stare down the rolling mass

---

61 David Reynolds, *Summits: Six Meetings that Shaped the Twentieth Century* (New York: Basic Books, 2007), p. 431.

62 Interview with Niel Barnard by Patti Waldmeir, 8 December 1994.

63 Chris de Kock, 'Movements in South African Mass Opinion', RW Johnson and Lawrence Schlemmer, (eds), *Launching Democracy in South Africa* (New Haven: Yale University Press, 1996), pp. 49-52.

action. It had to spread the message much more insistently that no settlement would be possible without the endorsement of the white electorate.

The Record of Understanding meant three things. First, the ANC would return to the negotiating table but under the conditions it had set. Second, the Record spelled the rupture of the NP-Inkatha alliance. Third, the NP was reduced to the role of a junior partner. Kobie Coetsee, minister of justice and generally a close ally of De Klerk, saw it as nothing short of disastrous. 'Today we have lost our country,' he told his cabinet colleague Rina Venter in hospital, where he was taken for chest pains.[64] Yet, significantly, Coetsee by all accounts took no action to reverse the direction the cabinet had taken,

De Klerk could still hope that power sharing would take root and grow under a Government of National Unity to which the ANC was committed. Mandela would dash this hope a little more than a year later when he insisted that decisions in cabinet would be taken with a mere majority. What remained was 'consensus seeking', as De Klerk called it, but that was between parties with substantially different views of how the country needed to be transformed.

In September 1992 the ANC knew it could not effect fundamental change on its own. Ramaphosa described the state of play succinctly: 'Government was in power and controlled the state, [while] the ANC represented the overwhelming majority of the population. It was these two major forces that needed to be bound together.'[65] As late as 1993 Mandela told the American ambassador that his greatest fear was that something would happen to De Klerk.[66] The ANC in fact needed De Klerk and the NP to attain full power in a Government of National Unity.

64 Interview with Rina Venter, 10 November 2011.
65 Butler, *Ramaphosa*, p. 292.
66 Interview with Princeton Lyman by Patti Waldmeir, 30 November 1994.

Chapter 13

A wary military

INITIALLY THE MILITARY REACTED POSITIVELY TO DE KLERK'S SPEECH OF 2 February 1990, welcoming the 'purification' of its role and stressing the defence force's professionalism, its apolitical nature and its reliance on citizen soldiers.[1] There appeared to be no chance of a military coup. General Jannie Geldenhuys, chief of the defence force from 1985 to 1990, formulated the traditional posture: 'The military stands in the British military tradition. It accepts the government of the day and does not interfere with politics. It was never the NP in uniform ... I never visited the politicians at home. When De Klerk became president he told me that I could get an interview at any moment, but I never felt the need.'[2]

Geldenhuys retired in 1990. General André (Kat) Liebenberg succeeded him as defence force chief. Liebenberg had previously been in charge of Special Forces and made little secret of his abhorrence of an ANC government with a substantial number of communists in its leadership ranks. General George Meiring, who was army chief from 1990 to 1993, was also very concerned about the communist influence in a future government. He became defence force chief in 1993.

From the start De Klerk was aware that some elements in the defence force, and in particular in its covert units, might try to undermine his project of dismantling white rule. He used a vivid metaphor to describe his challenge. He felt like a man 'who had been given two fully-grown watchdogs, say, a Rottweiler and bull terrier. Their previous owner [PW Botha] had doted on them ... and had allowed them to run free and chase cats all over the neighbourhood. I had to put a stop to all that. I knew that if I pulled too hard, I might choke them – or they may slip their collars and cause pandemonium in the neighbourhood.'[3]

On 2 March 1990 De Klerk met the top command of the military. According to some sources, the military had earlier advised against the release of Nelson Mandela on the grounds that 'it's going to cause havoc in the country'. De Klerk's retort was: 'I am going to release Mandela because in jail he can make no mistakes.'

---

1   Annette Seegers, *The Military in the Making of Modern South Africa* (London: IB Tauris, 1996), pp. 271-81.

2   Communication from Jannie Geldenhuys, 5 April 2008.

3   Cited by David Welsh, *The Rise and Fall of Apartheid* (Johannesburg: Jonathan Ball, 2009), p. 469.

The atmosphere was tense and De Klerk sensed scepticism or trepidation among some.[4]

De Klerk was quite right about unhappiness in military ranks. Reflecting on the four years following the unbanning of the ANC, General Meiring said: '[It] made life terrible for us ... When it happened we had a major problem on our hands ... We still had the increasing internal unrest to handle, but we had nothing – no more laws – to do it with because these people were now unbanned, and we could not take any preventative measures.'[5] He opposed halving white conscription before negotiations had even begun. The military widely respected Magnus Malan, minister of defence, and he could have stopped any of the criminal activities had he wanted to, but he was profoundly sceptical of the route De Klerk had taken and the quality of the government's negotiators.

De Klerk retained Malan as minister of defence. It could be read as an attempt to keep the military in his reform camp, but he did not include Malan or any senior military officer in the government delegation at the symbolic Groote Schuur meeting with the ANC in May 1990 (see Chapter 11). De Klerk was above all a parliamentary politician who opposed both the military's influence on the PW Botha government and the prospect of semi-permanent rule by emergency decree.

Peace in Angola and independence for Namibia allowed De Klerk to cut back drastically on defence spending. One of De Klerk's first steps as president was to halve conscription and replace the National Security Management System, which coordinated state actions, with the National Coordinating Mechanism. Its emphasis was socio-economic development rather than security. He radically modified the State Security Council (SSC) through stipulating that its members had to be elected and accountable politicians or bureaucrats. He also created a rival in the form of a special cabinet committee on security.[6] An insider remarked that he had reduced the SSC to the status of a 'toothless tiger'.[7] The military felt sidelined.

In January 1990 the National Intelligence Service (NIS) briefed De Klerk about possible unlawful activities by both the police and the military. In March 1990 it informed him about the official chemical and biological warfare (CBW) programme, named Project Coast, in which Dr Wouter Basson played a leading role. De Klerk ordered the termination of the offensive CBW programme and all research except for a new generation of tear gas. The NIS also warned him of a plot by elements in

---

4   See the different versions in Hilton Hamann, *Days of the Generals: The Untold Story of South Africa's Apartheid-era Military Generals* (Cape Town: Zebra, 2001), pp. 181-83, and FW de Klerk, *Die laaste trek – 'n Nuwe begin* (Cape Town: Human & Rousseau, 1998), p. 171.

5   Hamann, *Days of the Generals*, pp. 181-83.

6   Seegers, *The Military*, pp. 266-67.

7   Jan Heunis, *Die binnekring: Terugblikke op die laaste dae van blanke regering* (Johannesburg: Jonathan Ball, 2007), p. 148.

either the police or the army to assassinate Dirk Coetzee, who had told the press of death squads.

There were also alleged attempts by elements in the security forces to undermine the ANC, carry out counter-revolutionary projects in some of the homelands and supply arms to Inkatha. Overall, there had been what a military analyst called a 'gradual criminalisation' of the intelligence community, Special Forces (especially after the regime change in Zimbabwe) and Project Coast.[8] Only the naive would have expected that, with peace concluded in Namibia and the ANC no longer banned, there would be an abrupt end to all covert security forces projects. De Klerk wrote that the truth or falseness of some of the allegations was never properly established.[9]

In January 1990 De Klerk appointed a judge, Louis Harms, to investigate alleged dirty-tricks and death squad activities in the security forces. But the brief was far too limited to expose the illegal activities and flush out the offenders. After Harms had reported De Klerk expressed the hope that the investigations would put an end to 'witch-hunts on individuals'.[10] This was a vain hope in the existing climate.

In mid-1991 De Klerk removed Malan after the 'Inkathagate' episode, and ordered the police and the military to stop encroaching on the political terrain. His appointment of Roelf Meyer to the portfolio of defence was unlikely to help him get a firm grip on the military. The military leadership did not have a high opinion of Meyer's ability to hold his own in negotiating with the ANC. General Chris Thirion of Military Intelligence told of a meeting attended by both Meyer and General Meiring, who came across as a huge, menacing figure in altercations. Meiring asked Meyer: 'Do you know these people with whom you are negotiating?' Meyer responded furiously, telling the military to stick to its turf.[11]

This was a response that was rooted in the 1980s, when several members of the Botha cabinet were upset by what they deemed to be excessive military influence on civilian politics.

An unfortunate affair

The ANC's withdrawal from negotiations in May 1992, followed by months of political turbulence, seemed like the beginning of a new revolutionary challenge and the Record of Understanding heightened these concerns. Some generals felt power slipping away rapidly and believed De Klerk had no fall-back position. They had lost faith in De Klerk's ability to deliver on his promise of an orderly transition in

---

8   Jakkie Cilliers, 'Die hele storie is nog nie vertel nie', *Beeld*, 13 November 2011.

9   Cited by Theresa Papenfus, *Pik Botha en sy tyd* (Pretoria: Litera, 2010), p. 654.

10 Allister Sparks, *Tomorrow is Another Country* (Cape Town: Struik, 1994), p. 157.

11 Telephone communication, 29 November 2010.

which the army's professional standards were retained. Rumours began to circulate of a large-scale absorption of ANC 'soldiers' into the army.

General Pierre Steyn, defence force chief of staff who would be appointed to investigate illegal activities in the military, saw the divisions in the top ranks as follows: a progressive section believed the country had embarked on a transition and that the NP government would become part of a Government of National Unity that would enjoy support from all communities.

But, Steyn continued, there was another section that said: 'Nonsense, we can't afford this.'[12] Privately they expressed disdain about the politicians' judgement. In the latter camp were some other top-ranking officers with little enthusiasm for a form of regime change that would put a communist-led ANC in power.[13] General Liebenberg was convinced the negotiations were going terribly wrong. He thought the army might be called on to restore order and get negotiations on the right track. [14] But there is no evidence that, apart from disobeying the order not to employ Civil Co-operation Bureau (CCB) agents, he (or Meiring) authorised any unlawful acts.

Western governments had become worried that the turmoil in the country was increasingly jeopardising the chances of a settlement. Their intelligence agents working in the country reported that elements in the security forces were embroiled in some of the violence. Other aspects worried them even more. South Africa was known to have nuclear bombs and had developed a sophisticated response to the threat of biological and chemical warfare. There was concern that some of the weapons could be used for offensive purposes. The Western powers were especially alarmed about the possibility that, with the ANC poised to take over the reins of power, this technology could land in the hands of ANC allies – including the Irish Republican Army, the Palestinine Liberation Organisation and the Libyan government.[15]

After the signing of the Record of Understanding on 22 September 1992 rumours began to proliferate about the complicity of elements of the security forces in the violence. Unconfirmed reports stated that during a visit to Washington in 1992 US government officials confronted Roelf Meyer with allegations that a 'Third Force', buried in Military Intelligence, was out of control. Meyer allegedly called De Klerk to inform him about this.[16]

A senior American diplomat based in Pretoria believed that until that point De Klerk had not probed deeply into the allegations of security force involvement in the violence, because it was not expedient to do so. 'I don't think that De Klerk felt

---

12   Interview with Pierre Steyn by Patti Waldmeir, 2 December 1994.

13   Hamann, *Days of the Generals*, p. 196.

14   Interview with Pierre Steyn by Patti Waldmeir, 2 December 1994.

15   Communication from a senior official in Military Intelligence, 26 November 2011.

16   Interview with Chris Thirion, 1 December 2011.

at that point, when he needed the support of the security forces to pull this [the negotiations] off, that he could do that. So I think that he preferred to believe it was not true.'[17] General Steyn recalled that he found it 'inexplicable' that De Klerk did not take firm action at the outset. Using the intelligence reports, he should have acted swiftly 'and stopped the sedition in its tracks'.[18]

Herein lay the fundamental cause of the poor relationship between Mandela and De Klerk. Mandela was angered by De Klerk's refusal to investigate the security forces promptly and thoroughly, while De Klerk accused Mandela of turning a blind eye to the much wider complicity of ANC cadres in the violence.

Goldstone's raid

On 16 November 1992 Judge Goldstone, acting in all likelihood on tip-offs from both the police and NIS, raided the Pretoria offices of the Directorate of Covert Operations, a unit of Military Intelligence. Instead of proceeding quietly with his investigation, Goldstone – to De Klerk's dismay – sought maximum publicity. The *Weekly Mail* and *Vrye Weekblad*, which had published several other exposés, immediately dubbed it the 'smoking gun' that finally revealed the existence of the 'Third Force'. Among Goldstone's finds was the discovery that Military Intelligence had on its payroll nine or ten former CCB agents, including Ferdi Barnard, alleged murderer of David Webster. This was on the direct instruction of General Liebenberg, who had disregarded De Klerk's instruction that the state should never again employ a CCB agent.[19]

De Klerk appointed General Pierre Steyn to conduct an inquiry into all the allegations. After a month he was ready to submit an oral report together with a written 'staff report', prepared by two people, one from Military Intelligence and one from National Intelligence. The staff report of some 50 pages stated that the 'greater part of the information available is unverified allegations that need to be substantiated/ refuted before proper evaluation is possible'.[20]

Some of the top-ranking generals dismissed the inquiry as an exercise in smearing the defence force's reputation and set about covering their tracks as quickly as possible. Very few volunteered information. The police were not asked to launch a full-scale investigation into allegations that were flying about.

Much of the suspicion about irregular activities focused on Project Pastoor, originally established as a counter to conventional threats. It was alleged that there were

17 Interview with senior diplomat by Patti Waldmeir, 30 November 1994.
18 E-mail communication from Pierre Steyn, 29 November 2011.
19 Hamann, *Days of the Generals*, p. 197; Interview with Chris Thirion, 20 September 2011.
20 Staff Paper prepared for the Steyn Commission on Alleged Dangerous Activities of SADF Components, December 1992, pp. 1-2.

plans for an offensive chemical attack on Frelimo soldiers in Mozambique (such an attack never took place), and that secret agents planned to instigate violence and discredit the ANC. There were also allegations about elements in Military Intelligence using mercenaries, drawn from neighbouring countries and based in the Fifth Reconnaissance Unit at Phalaborwa. These mercenaries were allegedly responsible for some of the murders of train passengers (in total about 50 to 60 were murdered) and for incitement of violence at taxi ranks. Some people named in the report, for instance Dr Wouter Basson, would later be accused of using the police's forensic laboratories to produce poisons to be used against anti-apartheid activists.

The allegations in the staff report were alarming, meriting serious examination. But much of the evidence in the written reports was flawed, based on phone taps of conversations that were not transcribed but summarised. In 1994 the attorney general found on the basis of three written reports prepared for him that there was insufficient evidence to support the allegations.[21]

The staff report named six senior military officers – including Generals Liebenberg, Meiring and CP (Joffel) van der Westhuizen (chief of Military Intelligence) – as people who carried 'an albatross of the past around as an inescapable burden'. Another ten with the rank of brigadier, colonel or commandant were said to be 'engaged in apparent self-initiated activities' against the ANC. It recommended a refinement of the 'mandate' of some defence force components and a removal of some officers from their posts.[22]

Steyn concluded that secret operatives, acting on their own, could cause such disruption on trains and at taxi ranks that blacks would lose faith in the negotiations. In a subsequent interview he said he did not believe there was anything resembling a Third Force, but there was enough reason to fear an attempt to disrupt the ANC and put obstacles in the way of a settlement. He used a vivid metaphor: 'It's like someone in a very elegant performance on a cross-bar, all [one] needs to do is to just tap it and the person will come tumbling down.' He added that De Klerk felt a strong message needed to be sent to the military, and he supported him in that.[23]

The 'Night of the Generals'

On 19 December 1992 De Klerk summoned a few ministers who had not gone on holiday to an emergency meeting. Steyn was also present. De Klerk had decided to stamp out dissidence in the leadership ranks of the defence force, even though Steyn

---

21   Johan van der Merwe, *Trou tot die dood toe: Die Suid-Afrikaanse Polisie* (Pretoria: Praag, 2009), p. 202.

22   Staff Paper prepared for the Steyn Commission, pp. 1-8.

23   Interview with Pierre Steyn by Patti Waldmeir, 2 December 1994.

had not yet tabled a written report. He allegedly said: 'I don't want to fire captains or majors. Who is in the line of command, who is responsible?'[24]

Hernus Kriel, minister of law and order, recalled that the meeting considered the ANC's demand for the dismissal of the entire top structure of the defence force. One or two ministers supported this demand, but Kriel voiced his strong opposition: 'We are not playing with children. We are governing because the defence force allows us to do so. If we get rid of the top commanders from Kat Liebenberg downwards, the top command could decide to get rid of us and seize power. And where are we then?'[25]

Kriel was right to warn against rash action, but well-placed military analysts did not share his views about a possible coup. The regular army was no longer all white and the force greatly depended on white conscripts and the citizen force, both of which were divided along party and class lines.[26]

The group of ministers took no decision. De Klerk seriously considered dismissing Liebenberg, who had defied instructions not to employ any CCB agents, but decided against it. Instead he asked Liebenberg, Meiring and Van der Westhuizen to identify the officers who had to be removed. Using their list, De Klerk announced the next day that 23 senior army officers had been retired or suspended, adding that no evidence had been found of a Third Force.

Some of the names on the list of people that were to be dismissed or retired appeared as a result of the rivalry between Military Intelligence and National Intelligence. General Chris Thirion, a highly regarded officer who was known for his progressive views, was among those named. Thirion initiated libel proceedings and received a public apology from De Klerk, who called him a loyal soldier.

Steyn was put in an impossible situation. His investigation was far from completed but senior officers were dismissed on the basis of untested allegations. They were given no chance to state their case. Steyn later said this was 'a horrible denial of the *audi alteram partem* rule. It would have been far better to appoint a respected judge together with a team of top investigators and to charge suspects in court.' He said: 'I advised him [De Klerk] against it and I will say it in a court of law . . . I was considered to be a traitor. I was not allowed ever to talk to the press and tell them what had happened.'[27]

Steyn's colleagues in the defence force quickly sidelined him and he had to watch impotently as the dirt was swept under the carpet. 'My own organisation closed their doors on me. I was no longer able to function as defence force chief of staff. My

24   Hamann, *Days of the Generals*, p. 198.
25   Interview with Hernus Kriel, 8 September 1992.
26   Interview with Chris Thirion, 23 November 2011.
27   Interview with Pierre Steyn by Patti Waldmeir, 2 December 1994.

early retirement was inevitable.'[28]A grave injustice was committed against some honourable officers, notably Steyn and Thirion.

The 'Night of the Generals', as Pik Botha later called it, was 'a very unfortunate affair'. Kriel described it as a 'near catastrophe'.[29] One can only speculate why De Klerk acted in this manner. The *Weekly Mail,* with good sources in the ANC, wrote that the purge of the military was planned well in advance. A deal had been struck between the government and the ANC to allow joint control of the security forces and to enrol Umkhonto weSizwe members into the national army. Goldstone's raid had provided the pretext for setting up Steyn's probe.[30] To date no other source has appeared to back up the *Weekly Mail* report.

De Klerk's wife Marike later told Thirion that Mandela regularly confronted her husband with allegations about Military Intelligence's involvement in 'Third Force' activities, but he could not offer any details that could be investigated.[31] De Klerk later wrote in his memoirs that the events revealed the gulf between the political and military leadership, with the latter believing politicians naive about the ANC's true nature. According to him, the military command considered it unwise to dismantle secret units that could be used if negotiations failed.[32]

Years later a newspaper exchange between De Klerk and Thirion revealed the rift between De Klerk and many of the military leaders. Writing an open letter to De Klerk, Thirion stated that the security forces fought in 'a war of insurgency without rules' and provided a platform for a negotiated settlement. The politicians, however, for more than twenty years wasted the opportunity to use it. He took exception to De Klerk 'using a broad brush', claiming that the security forces were out of control and expressing regret that he (De Klerk) did not take stronger action to deal with those guilty of illegal actions. Reacting to the Steyn report, De Klerk took the 'wrong decision for the wrong reason and fired the wrong people'. He accused De Klerk of having a selective memory. It was irrelevant whether the president knew or did not know of all the transgressions. The point was 'you did not want to know'.

While conceding that the South African government fought a 'difficult revolutionary enemy that respected no rules', De Klerk in reply stated that it was 'unnecessary and unjustified' to resort to illegal actions, including murder and gross abuses of human rights.[33] The Steyn report showed something 'drastically wrong in the defence force', and he took instant action instead of leaving it to an inquiry that 'probably would be inefficient'.

---

28 E-mail communication from Pierre Steyn, 11 October 2011.

29 Papenfus, *Pik Botha en sy tyd*, p. 654.

30 *Weekly Mail,* 23 December 1992.

31 Hamann, *Days of the Generals*, p. 188.

32 De Klerk, *Die laaste trek*, pp. 276-85.

33 FW de Klerk, Response to Open Letter of Chris Thirion, 5 August 2007.

Robert Caro, biographer of President Lyndon Johnson, remarked that power does not so much corrupt but reveals.[34] De Klerk was a civilian politician comfortable with the political power that he had accumulated over the years and at home in parliament as a member of the majority party. His encounters with the military leadership reveal an almost visceral distaste for the kind of power the military held and for their conception of 'establishing order'. He was not a leader for times of conflict or war, but for peace, proper rules and harmony. He was never comfortable with the role of commander in chief – and the 'Night of the Generals' showed it.

Military integration

The military received another shock when news broke of the pending integration of Umkhonto weSizwe (MK), the military arm of the ANC, into the defence force. Jakkie Cilliers, a military officer who would later become an analyst of defence policy, believed that earlier the ANC may well have been willing to give up MK as a bargaining chip.[35] Even with Soviet aid, the actual number of ANC-trained fighters was remarkably low. According to a senior intelligence officer in the defence force, the ANC had a mere 3 000 armed fighters (compared to Swapo's 16 000) and never had more than a thousand combatants inside the country.[36]

An ANC delegation told a meeting in Moscow in 1990 that there were 600 to 700 fighters inside South Africa at that point and 2 000 outside the country. Yet in 1991 the ANC made the wild claim that it had brought 13 000 or more operatives back into the country. Undoubtedly there was a massive 'recruitment programme' in the space of a few months that was accompanied with very little training.[37] Together with the armies of the homelands, there were now some 16 000 troops available for integration. Although MK was still outnumbered by the SADF, it was unlikely MK would simply be absorbed into an untransformed defence force.[38]

In December it was announced that 6 000 officers, including colonels and brigadiers, would be retrenched and there would be a drive for the same number of recruits. While this step would add to the unhappiness in military ranks, it had become imperative to find work for some of the thousands of young black adults who were unemployed.

The *Weekly Mail* also reported the dismissal of a number of paid informers who

---

34 Bloomberg TV, Interview of Robert Caro by Charlie Rose, 29 May 2012.

35 Interview with Jakkie Cilliers by Patti Waldmeir, 7 December 1994.

36 Interview with Tienie Groenewald by Patti Waldmeir, 1 December 1994.

37 Vladimir Shubin, *ANC: A View from Moscow* (Johannesburg: Jacana, 2008), p. 305; Anthea Jeffery, *People's War: New Light on the Struggle for South Africa* (Johannesburg: Jonathan Ball, 2009), p. 274.

38 Mark Shaw, 'Biting the Bullet: Negotiating Democracy's Defence', in Steven Friedman and Doreen Atkinson (eds), *The Small Miracle: South Africa's Negotiated Settlement* (Johannesburg: Ravan Press, 1994), pp. 228-56.

had penetrated deep into the ranks of the ANC leadership. General Tienie Groene-wald, a former air force intelligence chief who would soon join the conservative Afri-kaner Volksfront, said the government had destroyed its power base by effectively 'neutralising the SADF's intelligence capacities'.[39]

A right-wing threat

About one million whites voted 'no' in the referendum of 1992, but they seemed without any significant leadership. This changed abruptly when General Constand Viljoen, who had retired as a highly respected chief of the defence force in 1985, entered politics. Called the last of the Boer generals, he was highly regarded in the defence force for his professionalism and personal integrity. He was convinced the ANC was still pursuing a revolutionary agenda and that De Klerk had caved in to their demands. Blunt, determined and committed to the Afrikaner cause, he was the sort of leader many Afrikaners would have flocked to if he had had a credible plan of action. Viljoen joined the Afrikaner Volksfront, a coalition of right-wing parties, or-ganisations and movements, all demanding an Afrikaner *volkstaat*, or ethnic state.

To further his goal Viljoen planned to disrupt the elections, have De Klerk re-moved as leader and restart the negotiations. Some people believed he could raise 50 000 men from the citizen force and some defence force units.[40] General Meiring, who succeeded Liebenberg in 1993 as chief of the defence force, warned the gov-ernment and the ANC of the dire consequences if Viljoen opposed the election. To dissuade Viljoen, for whom he had 'the highest regard', Meiring met him several times. At one of these meetings Viljoen said: 'You and I and our men can take this country in an afternoon,' to which Meiring replied: 'Yes, that is so, but what do we do the morning after the coup?' The internal resistance and foreign pressures and the stagnant economy would still be there.[41]

De Klerk was right in his calculation that no armed revolt from the right wing, even if led by Viljoen, would take place if the army remained neutral. The fractious-ness of the right wing and the leadership rivalry paralysed any concerted move. In March 1994 Viljoen mobilised 4 000 well-trained men to rush to the help of Presi-dent Lucas Mangope of Bophuthatswana, who believed the ANC was determined to overthrow his government. But the 'Ystergarde', an ill-disciplined rabble of Afrikaner Weerstandsbeweging (AWB) members, posing as a paramilitary movement, also converged on the scene and started shooting wildly. Viljoen, ever the professional

---

39 Jeffery, *People's War*, p. 362.
40 Johann van Rooyen, *Hard Right: The New White Power in South Africa* (London: IB Tauris, 1994); David Welsh, 'Right-wing Terrorism in South Africa', *Terrorism and Political Violence*, 7, 1, 1995, pp. 239-64.
41 Interview with George Meiring, 11 November 2002.

soldier, took one look at them before abandoning his plans and opting for the constitutional route.

To placate the right wing symbolically, Viljoen needed some agreement on an Afrikaner ethnic state, a *volkstaat* where Afrikaners could enjoy some form of territorial self-determination. Negotiations for including this in the constitution took place between the ANC's Thabo Mbeki and Jacob Zuma, Niel Barnard, Constand Viljoen and Wally Grant. Braam Viljoen, a brother of Constand, acted as a facilitator.

General Viljoen formed the Freedom Front as an alliance of right-wing organisations and registered for the election. The settlement entailed the establishment of a Volkstaatraad, where a future Afrikaner state could be debated. This council was indeed set up after the election, but the idea of a substantial ethnic state was stillborn. Ironically, De Klerk, who was regarded as the leader of the NP's conservative wing during the 1980s, played virtually no role in neutralising the right-wing threat.

'De Klerk and Viljoen had virtually nothing to say to each other,' Niel Barnard of NIS later observed. [42] From the start De Klerk dismissed the idea of an Afrikaner *volkstaat* and Viljoen later admitted: 'We could never get consensus among our people about where our *volkstaat* would be.'[43] Most favoured a state with Pretoria as its capital and including parts of the western Transvaal, eastern Transvaal and northern Free State. But while most whites in this area were Afrikaners, the great majority of people there were not Afrikaners. A 1993 poll showed that only one fifth of Afrikaners supported a *volkstaat* so strongly that they would consider moving there themselves; more than half either opposed it or were uncertain about it.[44]

A wary acceptance

George Meiring, chief of the defence force, states that on the day Nelson Mandela was inaugurated as president De Klerk said to him while they were watching the flypast: 'We really needn't have given in so easily.' (De Klerk strongly denied to me that he had used these words.)[45] According to Meiring, he responded to De Klerk: 'You never used your strong base to negotiate from, you never used the military as a base for strength, which you had available to you, you never wanted to use it.'[46]

Many of the senior police and military officers watched De Klerk's attempt to lock the ANC into a balanced settlement with deep misgivings. Some of them had had a leading hand in battling the ANC during the 1980s and had profound doubts about the possibility of the ANC becoming a regular political party. After 1990 small

---

42 Interview with Niel Barnard, 28 May 2012.

43 *Sunday Independent*, 25 March 2001.

44 Lawrence Schlemmer, 'The Depth and Scope of Support for a Volkstaat', unpublished report of a poll, February 1996.

45 Communication to author by De Klerk, 28 June 2002.

46 Hamann, *Days of the Generals*, p. 227.

sections in both the police and the military tried to destabilise the ANC and undermine the negotiations. But the large majority in the command levels of both the
police and the military stayed loyal to the government of the day and resisted the
calls that were undoubtedly made by more junior officers to resist. It was the top
military and police command that made a peaceful election day possible. As Niel
Barnard of NIS observed: 'They are the unsung heroes of the democratic "miracle"
in South Africa.'[47]

---

47   Interview with Niel Barnard, 28 May 2012.

Chapter 14

Negotiating the NP out of power

ALTHOUGH TALKS BETWEEN THE GOVERNMENT AND THE ANC BEGAN SHORTLY after the Record of Understanding was signed, they gained momentum only after the appearance in 1992 of an article by Joe Slovo entitled 'Negotiations: What Room for Compromise?'[1] Pointing out that 'there was no prospect of forcing the regime's unconditional surrender across the table', he proposed compulsory power sharing in a Government of National Unity for a fixed number of years. He made it clear, however, that 'no minority veto in any shape or form' would be tolerated, and that 'compulsory power-sharing as a permanent feature in a future constitution' was unacceptable. Nothing should be allowed to impede 'real democracy'.[2]

In Slovo's view South Africa was a 'sick' society with a 'sick logic' that could only be remedied by drastic action. In March 1992 he told an audience that blacks occupied only 14 of the 2 385 top-income positions in the central state departments and provinces. Whites held 98% of productive property and earned 85% of personal income. He firmly rejected a settlement that tied the majority's hands and entrenched the free market.[3] The alliance of the ANC, the SACP and Cosatu had made a huge concession when it agreed to abandon socialism and nationalisation and he was determined to resist any check on their ability to transform the civil service and provide a range of social benefits. That, for Slovo, constituted real democracy.

Most of FW de Klerk's constituency thought that by power sharing he meant an NP veto on critical issues in cabinet, but De Klerk's articulation of the policy the NP had accepted at its September 1991 congress was more subtle. The policy proposed a presidency consisting of the leaders of the three biggest parties with a rotating chair. Decisions by this body, including appointing the cabinet, would be by consensus. In an interview with British television, he gave the clearest exposition of his ideas. 'We don't want to frustrate majorities,' he said. He did not think that a party with 5% of the vote could say: 'I am as strong as a party with 45% of the

---

1   Johannes Rantete, *The ANC and a Negotiated Settlement in South Africa* (Pretoria: JL van Schaik, 1998), pp. 183-99.
2   Joe Slovo, 'Negotiations: What Room for Compromise?' *African Communist*, 3, September 1992, pp. 37-40.
3   Joe Slovo, 'We, Too, Have Bottom Lines', *Business Day*, 27 March 1992.

vote.' He conceived of power sharing as leaders of different parties 'jointly working together in the agreed upon programmes of the government of national unity'.[4]

The key to a power-sharing settlement was Nelson Mandela, and it was probably the collective ANC leadership who had asked Slovo to write the November 1992 article. Mandela had enough authority to forge a compromise on his own in which power sharing was accepted for a specified period. Initially De Klerk was confident that, with his experience in administration and his considerable persuasive powers, he could win Mandela over to the idea, but the longer the negotiations dragged on, the more resolutely Mandela rejected it.

In 1993 the ultimate prize for peacemaking was bestowed on De Klerk and Mandela when they were awarded the Nobel Prize 'for their work for the peaceful termination of apartheid'. The award was richly deserved: no one had done more to prevent the country from sliding into civil war. The remaining challenge was to write a constitution that would enable South Africa to reap a peace dividend in the form of increased opportunities for all.

Power curbing

It soon became clear that the ANC would refuse to include power sharing and voting in the cabinet in the new constitution. Instead, the new order would provide mechanisms that could curb the ruling party's power, including the so-called 'Chapter 9' institutions such as the auditor-general, the public protector and the Human Rights Commission.

A key clause in the Record of Understanding stated that the negotiators would be 'bound only by agreed constitutional principles'. Both the ANC and the NP as the ruling party had a chequered record on individual rights. The ANC wanted to keep the issue of rights off the table until it was in power, while the NP in power had trampled on individual rights and had unsuccessfully tried to don the garb of champion of minority rights despite holding a dominant position.

It was in the formulation of the constitutional principles that the government and the ANC, and later the Multi-Party Negotiating Forum, for the first time paid serious attention to writing entrenched rights into the constitution. In the course of 1993 a set of principles was defined that would be incorporated in the constitution.[5] The first ten principles made provision for classic democratic rights (regular elections, universal franchise, freedom of speech, freedom of information, etc) and the independence of key institutions (auditor-general, Public Service Commission, Reserve Bank and the judiciary).

---

4 Transcript of David Frost interview with President De Klerk on 'Newsline', 14 February 1993.
5 The following is based on Siri Gloppen, *South Africa: The Battle for the Constitution* (Dartmouth: Ashgate, 1997), pp. 202-05.

A second set of principles made a half-hearted bow in the direction of minorities. Minorities were assured of participation in the legislative process and of vaguely defined 'collective rights of self-determination' in the religious and cultural spheres.

A third set laid down principles for a quasi-federal system, setting out how powers were to be allocated to each tier of government and outlining the substantial power of national government to override provincial governments. The last set provided for the right to collective bargaining and for a public service that was both career-oriented and broadly representative of the community. Once in power, the ANC would use this last clause to impose demographic 'representativeness' on the civil service and 'cadre deployment'.

De Klerk would frequently refer to these mechanisms – the Chapter 9 institutions, the constitutional principles and the devolution of some power to the provinces – as 'checks and balances' that would safeguard the rights of minorities. To Rina Venter, minister of health, who had become increasingly concerned about the de-emphasising of power sharing, he said: 'We must look to the Constitutional Principles as our main safeguard.'[6]

But Jan Heunis, the government's own legal adviser, felt that most of these principles were vague and uncertain and did not signify much.[7] Nevertheless, a constitutional state that entrenched individual rights and established an independent judiciary went some way towards preventing minorities from being at the mercy of an all-powerful government. Ten years earlier Van Zyl Slabbert had already moved in that direction.

From the NP's point of view the most obvious shortcoming in the proposed constitution was the absence of power sharing.[8] While valuable, a constitutional state could not replace power sharing. On comparative evidence it could safely have been predicted that a ruling party with a large majority would soon attempt to load the bench with judges sympathetic towards the executive.

Holding the cabinet together

Formal multi-party negotiations resumed only in autumn 1993. On 1 April 26 parties met in a forum called the Multi-Party Negotiating Forum. Apart from these discussions, cabinet ministers and senior officials discussed the future constitution in several forums.

First there was the cabinet, which was divided: those who opposed the deals (called the 'anti's') were Hernus Kriel, André Fourie, Rina Venter, Tertius Delport,

---

6 Interview with Rina Venter, 10 November 2011.

7 Jan Heunis, *Die binnekring: Terugblikke op die laaste dae van blanke regering* (Johannesburg: Jonathan Ball, 2007), p. 201.

8 Gloppen, *South Africa*, pp. 202-05.

Danie Schutte, Japie van Wyk and Magnus Malan, who retired early in 1993; several ministers trimmed their sails to the wind.

On the other side of the spectrum stood three ministers: Roelf Meyer, Leon Wessels and Dawie de Villiers. Apart from performing their normal tasks as ministers, they attended numerous bilateral meetings between the government and the ANC between September 1992 and November 1993. They had to take any compromises forged there back to cabinet for a decision. Leon Wessels puts the total strength of those backing the compromises at not more than 'three and a half' out of the 23-member cabinet. But he adds: 'Three and a half with FW on their side could hold their own against the rest.'[9]

To thrash out the government's response to the compromises and develop policy options, De Klerk formed a cabinet sub-committee called the 'Beleidsgroep vir Hervorming' (Policy Group for Reform). This was the arena for heated debates. On the occasions when he attended, De Klerk participated vigorously. He summed up and persuaded his ministers to accept unpalatable decisions. Reflecting on how the cabinet functioned between September 1992 and November 1993, Delport said: 'Once De Klerk had swung behind Roelf, one had to challenge De Klerk's leadership if you opposed a particular deal. None of us was prepared to do that.'[10]

De Klerk did not lead the cabinet through intimidation or strict discipline. With his engaging personality and a good legal brain, he thrived on discussion and weighing up conflicting analyses in debate. His style had strengths and weaknesses. There was a remarkable openness and tolerance of dissent, and even junior ministers had ample opportunity to express their views.[11] At the same time there was a lack of focus. Cabinet meetings often ran on long over lunchtime (which had been the limit in PW Botha's time). Eli Louw, who was minister of transport, believed Botha was a much better chairman: 'PW quickly cut a long-winded person short. No memorandum longer than three pages was allowed.'[12]

Most cabinet ministers had a high regard for De Klerk's ability to hold the cabinet together in the face of major divisions over a political settlement. One of them was Derek Keys, executive director of the mining house Gencor from 1986 to 1992, and minister of finance from 1992 to 1994. Looking back, he stated: 'Taking business and politics together, De Klerk is far and away the best CEO I have seen. He is the best exponent of group dynamics I have seen in my experience. By that I mean a leader who strongly influences his board (or cabinet, in De Klerk's case), not by asserting or imposing his own views and threatening action in case of dissent, but by

---

9   Leon Wessels, *Vereeniging: Die onvoltooide vrede* (Cape Town: Umuzi, 2010), p. 258.
10   E-mail communication from Tertius Delport, 28 February 2012.
11   Leon Wessels, *Einde van 'n era* (Cape Town: Tafelberg, 1994), p. 127.
12   Interview with Eli Louw, 30 December 2010.

putting issues on the table. In allowing full opportunity for discussion but also shaping the debate, he made it possible for a consensus to form and a firm decision to be made on which there was no going back. To attend cabinet and watch him at work was sheer delight. FW carried the cabinet beautifully.'[13]

As the government was forced to make one major concession after the other, some ministers became more critical. They sensed the government was losing control of the process and that De Klerk was unable to stem the tide. When Meyer reported to cabinet that the ANC had rejected yet another aspect of the NP's negotiating position, De Klerk would thump the table, crying: 'That we cannot concede, that we cannot accept, here we draw the line.' But, according to Kriel, the ANC would persist in its demand and the cabinet would eventually accept it without demurral.[14]

André Fourie said: 'In the course of the negotiations, De Klerk changed his basic political philosophy. He no longer subscribed to group-based politics but accepted classic liberal individualism and common values in the place of minority rights and minority interests.' Fourie thought that De Klerk became convinced that the constitution and the values of a classic liberal, individual-based democracy might offer enough protection.[15]

Reflecting on this process some years later, Hernus Kriel described De Klerk as follows: 'Someone with a really smart legal brain, but not really a leader who can take a firm stand in a tough negotiating situation. He is constantly seeking a compromise, he tries to persuade but is unable to draw a line.' Kriel was highly critical of the performance of the NP negotiators, but in his view there was a much larger problem. 'We had no plan, no strategy, no bottom line where we would refuse to yield any further. We had no clarity on the goal at which we wanted to arrive.'[16]

Delport shared these views: 'There was no clear bottom line. On several occasions De Klerk said: "We shall never concede to this." And then, a few weeks later, we found ourselves conceding on that particular point. Kriel sometimes whispered in my ear when the statement was made that we would refuse to concede: "Yet another case of famous last words." On one occasion, when we expressed dissatisfaction about conceding something to the ANC, FW said: "But gentlemen, you don't understand. Nelson Mandela and I are going to govern the country."'[17]

Wessels, who was considered one of the strongest De Klerk supporters in cabinet, remarked in 1998: 'He [De Klerk] misread the situation completely. He thought

---

13   Interview with Derek Keys, 17 October 2010.
14   Interview with Hernus Kriel, 8 September 2010.
15   Interview with André Fourie, 5 December 2010.
16   Interview with Hernus Kriel, 8 September 2010.
17   Interview with Tertius Delport, 11 November 2010.

he could retain his authority, and share his power. When that failed, he had no fall-back position. He didn't understand black politics.'[18]

Fast-forwarding negotiations

The negotiations went into fast-forward on 10 April 1993, when a white man as-sassinated Chris Hani, the popular leader of the SA Communist Party. This trig-gered a crisis that jeopardised the entire attempt to reach a settlement. De Klerk remained at his holiday home, while Mandela addressed the nation on radio and television. At the time it seemed magnanimous for De Klerk to step aside for the good of the country. But the price was that Mandela sounded like the man who was actually in control and the country's real voice. It seemed as if he was already president.

In his address to the shocked nation Mandela spoke with gravitas and compo-sure and fostered interracial goodwill, but at the funeral he accused the govern-ment of creating the climate that led to Hani's assassination. He made the baseless assertion that the government was spending R9 billion per year to incite violence. Another untrue allegation was that the State Security Council had decided to mobilise 23 000 men to protect whites.[19] In the contest between the ANC and the NP, one side was pulling out all the stops in its use of rhetoric, while the other side seemed hesitant and uncertain of itself.

After Hani's death the public order was brittle. Both Niel Barnard and SS (Fanie) van der Merwe felt that the hope for a peaceful settlement was steadily fading and that spreading anarchy was a real possibility. They drew up a timetable in which 27 April 1994 was marked out as the election date. They urged De Klerk to accept it. At the same time, the ANC leadership was confronted with growing impatience and anger among its followers. Both De Klerk and Mandela decided to accept the dead-line suggested by Barnard and Van der Merwe.

The ANC leadership presented this as a major ANC victory. Mandela and De Klerk were scheduled to receive the Liberty Medal in Philadelphia, United States on 4 July and meet with President Clinton in the White House afterwards. Mandela now let it be known that he was not willing to travel to Philadelphia unless an elec-tion date was set. A senior US diplomat based in Pretoria recounts that Mandela indicated that without the election date 'it would not be a congenial situation at all, [threatening] the whole atmosphere of that thing'.[20]

But setting a date at a point when so many issues still had to be settled played badly in public. Waldmeir quotes an Afrikaner business leader who preferred to

---

18 Anthony Sampson, *Mandela: The Authorized Biography* (Johannesburg: Jonathan Ball, 1999), p. 464.

19 FW de Klerk, *Die laaste trek – 'n Nuwe begin* (Cape Town: Human & Rousseau, 1988), p. 295.

20 Interview with a senior American diplomat by Patti Waldmeir, 30 November 1994.

remain anonymous: 'It's like handing over the title deeds to your farm without first knowing the price.'[21] In the negotiating sessions in August, October and November 1993 the rush to meet the deadline would create a pressure-cooker effect that put the NP at a great disadvantage.

Collapsing pillars

Power sharing and the independence of the homelands, along with a strong form of federalism, were the pillars of the NP's negotiating position until the final rounds of talks. As late as May 1993 De Klerk said in an interview to the *Financial Times* that he would accept nothing less than power sharing in a permanent constitution. A few weeks later he envisaged an 'executive committee' composed of all parties that had won more than 15% of the votes running the cabinet on the basis of consensus.

In interviewing Roelf Meyer on 13 August 1993, journalist Padraig O'Malley quoted these remarks, pointing out that such talk had faded away. He said: 'I cannot understand how there could be such a dramatic switch in . . . the position of the State President.'

Meyer explained that in 'bilaterals' earlier in the year, the ANC negotiators had stated that they could not sell permanent power sharing to the party's constituency. In response the NP delegates had accepted power sharing for five years. They had also agreed not to force a deadlock by insisting on the inclusion of power sharing in the constitutional principles. According to Meyer, the NP, however, 'reserved the right to advocate this whenever it wished to do so'.

If Meyer's account is correct, this moment signified a crucial NP retreat: it sacrificed its core demand – power sharing – for the pittance of having the 'right' to propagate the principle. Still on the table, Meyer added, was the concept of a 'leadership core' in cabinet, comprising leaders of the main parties, who would be responsible for 'policy in general at the top'.[22]

By mid-1993 De Klerk started preparing cabinet for power sharing in an uncommon guise. At a cabinet *bosberaad* at D'Nyala in July 1993, Kobie Coetsee presented a position that those in cabinet critical of the NP retreat saw as a De Klerk flyer. He argued that power sharing took different forms and that various mechanisms could be used to divide power. These included what was called 'checks and balances': devolved powers to the regions in a federal system, a constitutional court that would adjudicate on the legality of legislation, and offices and bodies that

---

21   Patti Waldmeir, *Anatomy of a Miracle: The End of Apartheid and the Birth of the New South Africa* (New York: WW Norton, 1997), p. 226.

22   O'Malley Archives, Interview with Roelf Meyer, 13 August 1993.

would guard against corruption and the infringement of rights.[23]

On the independent homelands there was also a hasty retreat. The government's view until late in the negotiations was that the independent homelands could be reincorporated into the Republic of South Africa if they so wished, but they would not be forced to do so. The ANC was adamant that homelands had to be reincorporated before an election. Pik Botha was designated to negotiate the issue, but failed to reach an agreement with Ramaphosa. Jan Heunis, who was present as legal adviser, told Botha: 'You and Cyril are talking totally at cross-purposes. For the ANC it is a vital issue and it will sink the negotiations in order to get its way.' Botha then phoned the president, who agreed that the independent homelands could be compelled to return.[24]

All indications are that cabinet was not consulted. The homelands were the foundation of the government's racial policy, the subject of more than a hundred formal treaties and thousands of hours of debate in parliament. Yet the policy was abandoned in a brief conversation between the president and his foreign minister. With that went any hope the NP may have had of attracting votes from the approximately 600 000 black civil servants in the homelands.

With the homelands no longer clouding the discussion, the ANC and the government moved closer on federalism. This issue never produced strong emotions since there was no prospect of an Afrikaner homeland. Until very late in the day, NP leaders did not espouse federalism with much conviction. The Westminster system, in place until the early 1980s, had a powerful centralising effect that outlived its abolition in the 1983 constitution. The homelands were never anything more than a form of second-tier administration. By the late 1980s the government was sick of the extravagance and lack of accountability of the homeland authorities. Senior civil servants warned that South Africa lacked the administrative capacity for more than five provinces at most. But without any apparent deep reflection, the NP quietly discarded the strongly federalist proposals of its September 1991 policy.

Meyer attempted the impossible task of reconciling the government's new tack with the promises made during the referendum campaign. In the second half of 1992 he told a journalist: 'Power sharing can take many forms. Federalism is one.'[25] But the weak form of federalism, or regionalism, that would be accepted was a far cry from the power sharing in cabinet that the NP had promised in the referendum.[26]

Neither De Klerk nor Meyer pushed strongly for federalism during the negotiations. Maybe they sensed that the ANC would offer stout resistance and simply

23 Telephone interview with Rina Venter, 6 November 2011.
24 Interview with Jan Heunis, 25 January 2012.
25 Allister Sparks, *Tomorrow is Another Country* (Cape Town: Struik, 1994), p. 187.
26 David Welsh, *The Rise and Fall of Apartheid* (Johannesburg: Jonathan Ball, 2009), pp. 486-500.

did not want to take a strong stand on an issue the NP had long neglected. André Fourie, minister for land and regional affairs, felt that in the case of Meyer, passivity had turned into outright rejection. At a meeting attended by De Klerk, Meyer, Fourie, Mangosuthu Buthelezi and Lucas Mangope, Fourie found Meyer's attitude towards the two homeland leaders so offensive that he registered his disapproval.[27]

The strongest demand for federalism came from Mangosuthu Buthelezi, who had withdrawn from the negotiations after some of his demands were not met. At a late hour the negotiating parties accepted two ballots, one for the national government and one for the provincial governments, which would strengthen the federal character of the system. This helped to persuade Buthelezi to participate in the election.

Property rights

The ANC was forced to abandon its effort to circumscribe property rights in a way that would please its supporters on the left. Long influenced by communist and populist thinking, the fall of communism in Eastern Europe made it impossible for them to pursue the National Democratic Revolution openly. Ways had to be found to attract investors, mollify business and retain the efficiency of the private sector. A balance had to be found between the need for high economic growth, which required entrenched property rights and attracting skilled people, and the demand for redistribution, black empowerment and affirmative action. At the heart of the property rights issue was the question of whether market value would be paid in cases of expropriation.

In the negotiating forum, the committee was split between those who wanted property rights entrenched firmly and those who wanted a looser formulation, making expropriation easier. The NP's Sheila Camerer and the Democratic Party's (DP's) Tony Leon fought hard to have property rights recognised as a fundamental right in a liberal democratic system. After much haggling, Leon proposed a set of principles that an expert on the subject, Professor Carole Lewis of Witwatersrand University, had drafted for him.

Although the committee accepted this proposal, there was a second proposal on the table. The Technical Committee of the negotiating forum proposed that the entire bill be interpreted in a manner consistent with a democracy 'governed by the principle of equality'. After heated debate it was agreed that the term 'liberty' would appear alongside 'equality' in the relevant clauses.[28] Expressing a profound feeling of betrayal, radicals denounced the ANC's climb-down on property rights as a 'capitulation'.[29]

27 Interview with André Fourie, 1 December 2011.
28 Tony Leon, *On the Contrary: Leading the Opposition in a Democratic South Africa*, (Johannesburg: Jonathan Ball, 2008), p. 217.
29 Welsh, *Rise and Fall of Apartheid*, pp. 526-27.

Appointing judges

Then there was the matter of the appointment of judges to the Constitutional Court. Given the importance that De Klerk attached to the Constitutional Court in a future order, it is surprising that he initially paid little attention to this question. The negotiating forum accepted the DP's proposal that a new committee, the Judicial Service Commission (JSC), would recommend ordinary judges for appointment. The method by which judges of the all-important Constitutional Court would be appointed was not resolved. In a special back-room deal Kobie Coetsee, minister of justice, and his ANC counterpart, Dullah Omar, agreed that all ten judges to serve in the new Constitutional Court would be appointed by the president and cabinet, with the qualification that four positions would be reserved for serving judges. In effect, this would hand the Constitutional Court to the ANC.

Some of Coetsee's colleagues were outraged. In an attempt to back out of the deal, Coetsee faxed the details to Tony Leon and asked him to sound the alarm. A DP statement said it was 'profoundly wrong' that membership of an immensely powerful judicial body should be in the hands of the cabinet.[30] It was finally agreed that the president would appoint six of the judges from a list that the Judicial Service Commission would nominate. But a loophole remained. The appointment of the JSC's 23 members was not clarified. By 2011 there was an ANC-aligned bloc of 16 in the JSC, who, to all appearances, rigorously followed the party line on appointments to the bench.[31]

Fumbling amnesty

Another crucial issue was the granting of amnesty to members of both the liberation organisations and the security forces. The De Klerk government faltered on two occasions. In the meeting in August 1990 that led to the Pretoria Minute, the government and the ANC agreed that a general amnesty had to be granted immediately. A committee, consisting of Niel Barnard, Fanie van der Merwe, Thabo Mbeki and Mac Maharaj, was assigned the task of drafting a proposal. The committee was about to reach an agreement when De Klerk and Minister of Justice Kobie Coetsee intervened.

Barnard tells the story: 'Kobie [Coetsee] objected and said the issue had to be handled in a different way. He always wanted to look as if he was the one who made the important decision. I was angry because the issue was urgent and had to be settled decisively. I knew that Kobie invariably procrastinated. I followed him and De Klerk to an office in the building and repeated my arguments. But Coetsee persisted, and in the end De Klerk sided with him.' Understandably, the ANC was furious. As

---

30 Leon, *On the Contrary*, pp. 222-27.
31 E-mail communication from JH (Koos) van der Merwe, 17 October 2011.

Barnard phrased it, its view now was: '*Ons wou redelik wees, maar nou gaan ons die Boere braai.*' (We wanted to be reasonable but now we will fry the Boers.)[32]

Again in mid-1992 Hernus Kriel expressed grave concern in cabinet over the amnesty question. Coetsee had still not made up his mind. Kriel warned that a new government would not be able to control the security forces if they were treated as scapegoats, having to appear in court while others who had planted bombs would be walking around free.[33] Pik Botha, in cooperation with Cyrus Vance, special representative of the UN's secretary-general, pursued a general amnesty for all sides.

According to Jan Heunis, the ANC's proposal would have suited the government very well.[34] There was initial agreement, but Thabo Mbeki and Mathews Phosa warned that they expected resistance in ANC ranks and urged NP negotiators to settle the issue quickly. Yet De Klerk had handed the matter to Kobie Coetsee, notorious for his procrastination and indecision. He had hopelessly bungled the matter by failing to resolve it.

The government's performance on the issue of amnesty was shocking. Several cabinet members expressed puzzlement over De Klerk's refusal to reprimand Coetsee or to refer important tasks to other ministers. The amnesty issue was left hanging until late 1993, at the very end of the negotiations, when it was dealt with in a postscript to the constitution.[35]

Coetsee was also very critical of the way negotiations were conducted. On 15 August he scribbled a note on his pad: 'The more important an issue, the less time is devoted to it at the World Trade Centre in Kempton Park. Voters fear that what has been decided could [later] be overturned.' In November 1993, during the final days of the negotiations, he made another note: 'The most expensive farce in history for which we shall yet have to pay. Debate is window dressing.' He also wrote: 'The President is a poor chess player; he leaves his flank open.'[36]

Consternation in cabinet

By mid-1993 several cabinet ministers were deeply concerned about the turn that the negotiations had taken. *Rapport* newspaper dubbed them the 'anti's' – those opposed. 'Dissidents' is too strong a word to describe them, since they did not attempt to leak information or mount a collective response.

One of the main reasons why there was no open revolt was because the negotiating team never presented a comprehensive plan to the full cabinet that made it clear

32   Interview with Niel Barnard, 13 March 2012.
33   O'Malley Archives, Interview with Hernus Kriel, 18 August 1992.
34   Heunis, *Die binnekring*, p. 156.
35   Theresa Papenfus, *Pik Botha en sy tyd* (Pretoria: Litera, 2010), pp. 647-48.
36   Archive for Contemporary Affairs (ACA), Bloemfontein, Kobie Coetsee Collection, PV 357, Files 7/39 and 7/40, and File 1/N1/11 NP Federal Executive, 1993.

how everything fitted in. The negotiators laboriously devised walls for the new order, but the cabinet had made no decision on what would constitute the very foundation of the negotiated order. AA van Niekerk, minister of agriculture, who was
not committed to any camp, captured the cabinet's mood in a poem: 'We struggle
with the problem/ of approving the constitution piecemeal/ we first accepted those
parts where we were in agreement with the other [party]/ only to discover we were
technically out-manipulated.'[37]

The cabinet accepted contentious compromises, believing there would be power
sharing for at least the first five years during which the hard issues like affirmative
action, land reform and the transformation of the civil service and judiciary could
be properly resolved. Without power sharing, the majority in cabinet would settle
these matters.

From mid-1993 the split in De Klerk's cabinet began to widen. The 'anti's' felt the
negotiated deals, all put together, represented a settlement that they could not defend
to voters. But the negotiators pointed out that cabinet had approved every individual
deal and that opposition at such a late stage was not in good faith. *Rapport*, under the
headline 'Two Camps in Cabinet', alleged that some ministers who were not part of
the negotiating team were closed off from 'reality'. Their 'moment of truth' dawned
when the draft proposals for the interim constitution were published.

The anonymous source quoted in *Rapport* alleged that the 'anti's' had not been
following the negotiations closely. 'Now they suddenly see red lights flashing and . . .
wrongly suspect hidden motives on the ANC's part.'[38] In a letter to De Klerk, Rina
Venter protested strongly. She complained that no analysis of how the discrete deals
fitted into a larger picture had ever been put before cabinet.[39]

Van Zyl Slabbert remarked that by the end of the negotiations, 'De Klerk's negotiators were really part of Mandela's team in facilitating the transition to majority
rule'.[40] Legal adviser Jan Heunis felt De Klerk had failed to develop a clear vision
before the negotiations of 'what the cabinet intended to achieve and where negotiations would leave them'. In none of the negotiating sessions he attended did the
NP's negotiators insist on a point. They were not prepared to take a stand. When
they sensed the ANC found the government's view unacceptable, they did not press
for it strongly. 'I saw how non-negotiable aspects within a couple of minutes became negotiable.'[41]

At a private meeting with Meyer, Tony Leon pointed out that the government,

37   My translation from an Afrikaans poem Van Niekerk wrote in October 1993.

38   *Rapport*, 1 August 1993; see also the report 'Hier is die anti's se sewende antie', *Rapport*, 12 September 1993.

39   US Ms Collection, Kempton Park documents, Rina Venter to FW de Klerk, 2 August 1993.

40   Van Zyl Slabbert in a review of Waldmeir's *Anatomy of a Miracle*, *Sunday Independent*, 25 May 1997.

41   Heunis, *Die binnekring*, pp. 157, 160-61.

without reaching agreement on key issues, 'had yielded all the advantages to their opponents who simply had to wait it out'. Meyer replied that 'once the government lost control of the security situation it wasn't really in a situation to control much else'.[42] But this statement must be questioned. Those in command of the police and the military at the time claimed that at no point during the transition did they lose control. There is no reason not to believe them.

A final showdown

For the constitution to be promulgated in time for an election to be held on 27 April 1994, the draft constitution had to be completed by mid-November. On 30 August an NP policy document claimed that the party's policy of a 'participatory democracy' would be attained through the sharing of power. It added: 'Power sharing means effective participation by several parties in decision-making at cabinet and other levels.' De Klerk told the party: 'No party will be in the same position as the NP at present where it can take all the decisions or has untrammelled power in its hands.'[43] Delport formulated the position he believed his colleagues in cabinet shared since the break-up of Codesa: 'What majority [was needed] in cabinet for a decision? We said seventy-five per cent all along.'[44]

Most of the burning issues were still unresolved, among them power sharing in the Government of National Unity. These were finally tackled in a meeting deep into the night of 17–18 November 1993. De Klerk and Meyer represented the NP side, and Mandela and Ramaphosa the ANC. Decisions on the six outstanding issues, dubbed 'the six-pack', had to be taken.

The ANC conceded security of tenure to civil servants (it would later become clear that this did not mean that they would be retained in their posts). Provinces could write their own constitutions, but only if these were consistent with the national constitution, and whites could elect 30% of the representatives in the local government elections scheduled for 1996.

Two decisions went badly against the NP. Mandela demanded that if the future Constituent Assembly could not reach agreement, 60% support in a referendum would be sufficient for the adoption of the constitution. De Klerk agreed. As Ramaphosa's biographer remarks: 'The sixty per cent threshold was so low that a threat thereafter hung over the heads of NP negotiators.'[45]

It was also decided that eleven official languages would be proclaimed, ostensibly

---

42   Leon, *On the Contrary*, p. 219.

43   JM Aucamp, 'Die Nasionale Party van Suid-Afrika se laaste dekade as regerende party, 1984-1994', doctoral dissertation, University of the Free State, 2010, pp. 339-40.

44   Interview with Tertius Delport, 11 November 2010.

45   Anthony Butler, *Cyril Ramaphosa* (Johannesburg: Jacana, 2007), p. 308.

to protect Afrikaans. The sub-committee dealing with the issue consisted of Barnard and Professor Koos Pauw on the government side and Albie Sachs as the ANC's main representative. Initially Barnard and Pauw proposed two official languages (English and Afrikaans), with the nine other languages as national languages. Government would commit itself to develop these languages to the point where they could also become official languages. The ANC rejected this flatly. They also rejected the next proposal for four official languages (English, Afrikaans, Zulu and Tswana). It was decided that all eleven languages would have official status. According to Lawrence Schlemmer, this decision was taken in bad faith. The NP leadership seemed not to have taken the language issue very seriously. Neither did the demand for culture-specific schools and universities enjoy high priority.

Finally, there was the most crucial issue of all: decision-making in the cabinet of the Government of National Unity. According to Sampson's authorised biography of Mandela, De Klerk had demanded a two-thirds majority in cabinet on crucial issues. Some ANC negotiators were prepared to offer 60%, but on this fateful night Mandela drew the line at 50%. He added: 'We just hope we will never have to use it.' Slovo responded: 'We have won the battle for an executive based on majority decision-making – something we thought we would never win. None of us thought even a week before that we could win that.'[46]

De Klerk offered a different version in his memoirs. He wrote that he was in favour of a consensus model from the start, since avoiding confrontation or voting would make it easier for the members of cabinet to seek consensus.[47] But this does not square with the position he spelled out in the referendum campaign. On 18 November 1993 there was a frantic last-minute scramble to formulate the final agreement. Ramaphosa told Mac Maharaj and Fanie van der Merwe, who were drafting the formulations: 'We will not agree to any form of veto or troika control.' The final agreement read that the cabinet should function in the spirit of seeking consensus, but that when this failed, the majority would take the decision.[48]

Heunis remembers his shock when told that the NP had agreed to majority rule. It was not the agreement itself, but the fact that the NP had made an agreement for which it had no mandate. To Heunis, the mandate the NP had from the voters in the referendum was for a consensus-seeking model with built-in vetoes.[49]

The vexed amnesty issue was also resolved. The NP had made the fatal error of postponing the matter until the ANC had the upper hand. The ANC had earlier formulated a draft clause stating that there *could* be amnesty. This would leave the

---

46   Waldmeir, *Anatomy of a Miracle*, p. 232; Sampson, *Mandela*, p. 472.

47   De Klerk, *Die laaste trek*, p. 308.

48   Padraig O'Malley, *Shades of Difference* (Johannesburg: Penguin, 2007), p. 63.

49   Heunis, *Die binnekring*, p. 150.

members of the security forces who had committed serious human rights violations open to prosecution by a new government. At the very last minute the words 'there shall be amnesty' were inserted. According to Mac Maharaj, the NP negotiators were so relieved about the amnesty that they apparently did not worry much about majority decision-making in cabinet.[50]

The way amnesty was dealt with opened the door to the Truth and Reconciliation Commission, which would expose numerous human rights violations by members of the security forces. A large number of policemen had to appear before a body whose composition was slanted in the ANC's favour. This would not have happened if a general amnesty had been granted earlier. The commission was to become yet another nail in the NP's coffin.

'What have you done?'

Early on the morning of 18 November 1993 the cabinet met to hear the outcome of the decisive talks between De Klerk and Mandela the previous night. De Klerk told them he had accepted Mandela's demand for majority decision-making in cabinet and then adjourned the meeting briefly to allow cabinet to contemplate this. Delport recounted his shock at the announcement. 'I realised it was final, *die koeël is deur die kerk* (the die has been cast). We had given in on all six issues. I said to Dawie de Villiers, my provincial leader, "I cannot accept this, I am going to resign." Dawie said: "You will have to tell FW." I walked to FW's office and knocked on his door. When he opened it I grabbed him by his jacket's lapels and cried: "What have you done? You have given the country away. You have allowed children to negotiate. What we have now is not power sharing; it is conventional majority rule. We have lost all power."'

Delport was in such a state of anguish that he wept. De Klerk calmed his distraught colleague and then asked: 'What are you going to do?' Delport's response was: 'I intend to rally enough colleagues. Together with the Conservative Party caucus you will no longer have a majority.' De Klerk responded: 'Then there will be civil war.'[51]

Consulting like-minded colleagues, Delport formulated four options. They could tell the voters that the NP had failed to get what it wanted and that they opposed the compromises; they could tell the voters that they were unhappy but had decided to accept the situation; they could take the matter back to the caucus; or they could try to make the new system work 'and save what there was to save'. Delport remarked that, in the end, 'We decided to do nothing'.[52]

---

50   O'Malley, *Shades of Difference*, p. 402.

51   Interview with Tertius Deport, 11 November 2010.

52   Interview with Tertius Deport, 11 November 2010.

André Fourie, Hernus Kriel and Japie van Wyk deliberated with Delport after this confrontation. Fourie recounted: 'We just sat there. We were embarrassed. We realised we had allowed power to slip away. In cabinet De Klerk would talk of writing into the final constitution what was missing in the interim one, but we knew the battle was over; we had lost power and would never get it back again or share it. *Die Afrikaners is uitgelewer* (The Afrikaners have been abandoned to their fate).'[53]

It is interesting to ask why it took so long for any sign of revolt to manifest itself in the cabinet and the caucus. De Klerk had led his party in one of the most extraordinary ventures ever. He surrendered power even though the ruling party was not facing imminent defeat. As late as May 1992 it still looked as if the ANC would be locked into a power-sharing deal in which the NP would enjoy a major say. Eighteen months later the NP government was a lame duck with no prospect of ever regaining power. Yet only two caucus members and not a single minister resigned.

The answer must be sought in the popularity and authority De Klerk had acquired between February 1989 and September 1992. He had become the party. It was to him that all the ministers and all the party's representatives looked for a settlement that they could defend. To criticise him and to mobilise opposition was to call into question the entire project of finding a negotiated solution. There was simply no alternative leader, no alternative solution.

Telling the people

David Welsh sees the deal struck between 1992 and 1996 as one providing for political power for blacks, subject to constitutional constraint, while whites could continue to dominate the economy, subject to important qualifications aimed at redressing inequality.[54] Political analyst Steven Friedman perceptively remarked: 'The Nats got a pretty good deal for white South Africans, but not such a good deal for the party.'[55]

Among followers of both the NP and the ANC disillusionment soon set in. The leaders had failed to secure buy-in from their followers. On both sides growing numbers of people felt that their leaders had given away too much and consequently resented the settlement.[56] ANC followers objected to the abandonment of the socialist state, the affirmation of existing property rights, and the independence of the judiciary. Attempts would soon start to white-ant the settlement.

From the perspective of NP followers, the deal had major shortcomings. Language rights and the right to instruction in Afrikaans in schools and universities could

---

53   Interview with André Fourie, 1 December 2010.
54   Welsh, *The Rise and Fall of Apartheid*, p. 526.
55   Interview with Steven Friedman by Patti Waldmeir, 17 November 1994.
56   E-mail communication from JM Coetzee, 19 December 2011.

have been more tightly formulated. The majority in parliament was allowed to make appointments to institutions guarding rights and combating corruption, thus weakening these institutions. Affirmative action was not limited in time and scope. In the eyes of the security forces there was no proper provision for amnesty. With a majority on the Judicial Service Commission, the ruling party could pack the bench in the name of representivity and transformation. The issue of land redistribution was left hanging. NP followers could not understand why their party, which had entered negotiations with such a strong hand, came out with so little.

De Klerk would be in the centre of the storm when, after little more than a year, the NP pulled out of the Government of National Unity. He had interpreted the result of the referendum of March 1992 as an open-ended endorsement. But as Lawrence Schlemmer pointed out six months later, there was not even support for a multi-party interim government. 'They were essentially voting to give De Klerk a mandate because of the high trust they had in De Klerk not to sell them out.'[57]

The NP leadership had trouble explaining the final deal to their party. The NP's *dagbestuur* (executive) approved the final policy document only on 21 December, a day before parliament promulgated the interim constitution.[58] The leadership had negotiated a constitution and only afterwards brought party policy in line with the outcome of the negotiations. An NP pamphlet on the settlement maintained that in the first five years power would be shared 'in the legislative processes' and also 'in cabinet between those parties with substantive support'.[59] Nothing was said about what would happen after 1999. Given Mandela's position on decision-making in cabinet, any form of power sharing in the Government of National Unity would at best be very weak.

In the party's briefing for the election sent to NP ministers, candidates, speakers and canvassers there was a section entitled 'We keep our promises', based on extracts from De Klerk's speeches. Power sharing was one of the promises the leadership claimed it had kept.[60] This statement was stretching the party's credibility. A commentator warned in *Rapport* that the NP leadership would have to present a much stronger case before it would persuade its followers that the party was not on a suicide course.[61]

---

57   O'Malley Archives, Interview with Lawrence Schlemmer, 2 October 1992.

58   E-mail communication from Inus Aucamp, 18 May 2012.

59   NP pamphlet, 'Nasionale Party beleid', December 1992.

60   The New National Party, 'Briefing Notes', ms. dated 20 February 1994. There is some ambivalence in the document; on the one hand, it claims that power sharing was accepted, but on the other, it points out that this would be only for the first five years.

61   *Rapport*, 2 January 1994.

A free South Africa

Election day, 27 April 1994, went by peacefully. The ANC won 62.7% of the vote, the NP 20.4%, Buthelezi's IFP 10.5%, Viljoen's Freedom Front 2.2%, the DP 1.7% and the PAC 1.2%. The ANC attracted four fifths of the black vote and was for more than 94% dependent on black voters. The NP drew half its votes from people who were not white, emerging as the party with the support of more than 60% of the votes in the white, coloured and Indian communities. Afrikaners were split almost right down the middle between the NP and the Conservative Party. The NP won control of the new province of the Western Cape.[62]

De Klerk still hoped that after the first democratic election his party could exert power as a gatekeeper for strategic sectors. But the NP's ability to act as the agent for these sectors was soon questioned. The security forces had developed serious doubts about De Klerk soon after he came to power and his poor handling of the amnesty issue alienated them further. Business leaders had initially applauded De Klerk's moves, but when the ANC dropped nationalisation as a policy option, they quickly accepted it as a government with which they could do business and accordingly scaled down their support for De Klerk and the NP. Most white civil servants had decided early on that negotiations would result in black majority rule and the replacement of many of them by blacks. They gave up on the NP as the guarantor of their interests, particularly after the ANC promised to pay out satisfactory packages to retrenched civil servants.[63]

Unexpectedly Constand Viljoen, leader of the Freedom Front, became 'the flavour of the month', as Van Zyl Slabbert put it. Concerned about 'the Afrikaans language becoming a symbol of polarised mobilisation', Mandela asked Slabbert to talk to Viljoen about how this could be avoided. Viljoen mentioned three potential triggers. If there were forced integration of rural schools, there would be bloodshed. If inadequately trained, poor black farmers were settled among established farmers and there was stock theft, there would be bloodshed. And if a Truth and Reconciliation Commission led to an Afrikaner witch-hunt, there would be major trouble.[64]

The relationship between Mandela and De Klerk, never very good, deteriorated further. Some NP ministers felt themselves trapped in cabinet. They had to go along with decisions they did not approve of, but nevertheless had to stick to the convention prohibiting them from commenting critically on cabinet decisions. On one occasion when the NP office criticised a decision, a furious Mandela told De Klerk

---

62 For a full analysis see Johnson and Schlemmer, *Launching Democracy,* and Hermann Giliomee, 'The National Party's Campaign for a Liberation Election', Andrew Reynolds (ed.), *Election '94 South Africa* (Cape Town: David Philip, 1994), pp. 43-72.

63 JS Wessels and A Viljoen, *Waarde-oriëntasies en toekomsverwagtinge van die Vereniging van Staats-amptenare* (Pretoria: HSRC, 1992).

64 O'Malley Archives, Interview with Van Zyl Slabbert, 14 November 1994.

he should leave the cabinet along with his fellow NP ministers. De Klerk responded calmly that in terms of the constitution the president did not have the power to force the NP ministers to leave; the interim constitution entrenched the right of parties with substantial support to be in cabinet.[65]

De Klerk kept trying to influence his ANC colleagues in cabinet, but Mandela in particular, and other ANC cabinet members targeted De Klerk in concerted and seemingly orchestrated attacks. It was clear the ANC was barely tolerating the NP in cabinet. One day De Klerk arrived at a meeting of the executive of the NP federal council in an emotional state about Mandela's personal attacks on him. As an example, he told the meeting that the president's office had phoned him with a request to hang on for the president. After waiting for half an hour, he phoned Mandela to inquire what was going on. The president bluntly replied he no longer wanted to talk to him.[66]

Despite his pleas, the ANC refused to write power sharing into the final constitution. De Klerk told the federal council's executive that the other NP cabinet ministers could stay, but he was resigning from cabinet.

On 30 June 1996 De Klerk took the NP out of the Government of National Unity. In a speech in London on 21 January 1997 he declared that the balanced political settlement of the kind that the NP had sought had not come about, but rather the surrender of power and with it the loss of 'sovereignty'. He went on: 'The decision to surrender the right to national sovereignty is certainly one of the most painful any leader can be asked to take. Most nations are prepared to risk war and catastrophe rather than to surrender this right. Yet this was the decision we had to take. We had to accept the necessity of giving up on the ideal on which we had been nurtured and the dream for which so many generations had struggled and for which so many of our people had died.'[67]

In response, Die Burger, under the headline 'Oorgawe' (Surrender), asked whether the leader of a party that had fared so poorly in the negotiations could continue in a leadership position.[68] A spate of critical letters appeared in the Afrikaans press. One stated: 'The NP received a mandate from us to protect and secure our interests at all times. De Klerk did not get a mandate to lead, like a Judas goat, his unsuspecting people to the political abattoirs.'[69] De Klerk responded that he had never promised a white minority veto. He weathered the storm, but concluded that his political role had come to an end. With NP support dropping steadily in the polls, he retired on 26 August 1997.

65   Interview with AA van Niekerk, 3 March 2012.
66   JM Aucamp and Johan Swanepoel, Die einde van 'n groot party: 'n Vrystaatse perspektief op die NP (Allensnek: Befonds, 2007), pp. 27-28.
67   Verbatim copy of speech by FW de Klerk, 21 January 1997, issued by his office.
68   Die Burger, 6 February 1997; see also my column in Rapport, 2 February 1997.
69   Rapport, 16 February 1997.

Soon the bloc that voted NP began to disintegrate. English speakers drifted away after big business had made its peace with an ANC government. Afrikaners increasingly saw De Klerk as an opposition leader rather than the senior partner of Mandela. Middle-class Afrikaners were attracted to Tony Leon, the unabashed DP leader who as a staunch and unapologetic liberal had no objection to criticising the ANC.

From 1996 support for the NP (later renamed the New National Party, the NNP) steadily declined. It went into a coalition with the Democratic Party and then suffered an inglorious demise in 2004, with the ANC absorbing what remained of the party. A triumphant President Thabo Mbeki stated that the NNP understood its obligation to help eradicate 'the terrible legacy of its policies' and added that the ruling NP had at one time thought its rule was its 'Season of Light'. For blacks, however, it meant a 'Season of Darkness' that condemned the country to a future where they had nothing to look forward to. Calling the absorption of his old party by the ANC a case of *boedel oorgee* (surrendering of the estate), De Klerk urged minorities to fight for the rights provided by the constitution instead of snuggling up to the ANC. He resigned from the party on 13 August 2004.[70]

A tactician, not a strategist

De Klerk's finest moment was the year between his election as NP leader in February 1989 and 2 February 1990, when he made his famous speech. He quickly grew into the job, appeared decisive and determined, and wore the mantle of power with grace and dignity. His speech of 2 February was masterly – indeed, one of the big moments in South African history and unquestionably one of the great speeches in the history of the twentieth century. Nelson Mandela said: 'It was a breathtaking moment, for in one sweeping action he had virtually normalised the situation in South Africa. Our world was changed overnight.'[71] For his courage, De Klerk, along with Mandela, fully deserved the 1993 Nobel Peace Prize.

Overseeing the negotiations, De Klerk was essentially a tactician. He often reacted to a pressing challenge or looming crisis in bold and imaginative ways that –initially at least – caught his adversary off balance. His 2 February 1990 initiative caused disarray in ANC ranks for quite some time. So did his offer at Codesa in December 1991 for the election of a body serving both as an interim government and the drafter of an interim constitution. But in each case the ANC recovered to press its non-negotiable demands for an elected constitution-making body and majority rule. The

70   Hermann Giliomee, *The Afrikaners: Biography of a People* (Cape Town, Tafelberg, second edition, 2009), pp. 694-95.

71   Nelson Mandela, *Long Walk to Freedom: The Autobiography of Nelson Mandela* (Randburg: Macdonald Purnell, 1994), p. 594.

calling of a white referendum in February 1992 seemed like a brilliant move at the time, but it was held far too early in the process to allow voters to pass judgement on the settlement.

It was a fundamental mistake on De Klerk's part to assume in 1990 that peace had been established and the time had come for a democratic settlement conducted by politicians in an orderly environment. It would have been better if he had retained the State Security Council and its capacity to identify points of friction at an early stage and thwart any attempts to undermine a settlement.

This ties in with another point. Was it wise of South Africa to avoid all foreign mediation and assistance? De Klerk was forced into a situation where he constantly had to prove that he had no part in fomenting the violence, and that he was not trying to be both a player and an umpire. As a respected observer noted: 'It may have been better if the negotiations had been conducted under the auspices of a group of strong sponsors, including the United States, which had then become guarantors of the constitution arrived at. As people's memories of the dark years of the 1980s fade, the argument for the ANC to abide by the terms of the settlement would become weaker and weaker.'[72]

De Klerk lacked both a comprehensive plan for negotiations and an experienced negotiations strategist. There was no plan for dealing with key issues such as the retention of skills in the civil service, amnesty for members of the security forces and setting up a Judicial Service Commission that would ensure a balanced judiciary over the longer term.

Fixing an election date well before the constitution was completed was a major error. The final stages of the negotiations at times seemed more like a disorderly retreat on the part of the NP government than a dignified march to an inclusive democracy. Because minorities across a large spectrum trusted him, he played a major role in getting South Africans of all colours to unite behind the constitution in 1994.

De Klerk's scheme of power sharing failed to materialise. The constitutional state in South Africa was a fall-back position after the ANC government had spurned the power-sharing option. It enhanced and entrenched individual rights. But much would depend on the ruling party's continued commitment to the constitution in the face of power and policy making migrating to the courts.[73]

Democracy had escaped from white domination but would soon find itself in uncharted waters. A balance had to be found between the executive, relying on its majority in the legislature, and a judiciary committed to upholding the constitution.

---

72   E-mail communication from JM Coetzee, 20 April 2011.

73   Dennis Davies, 'Only Politics Can Change the Future', *Cape Times*, 28 December 2011 citing the work of social anthropologists John and Jean Comaroff.

The challenge did not seem insuperable, but in 1994, with the country under the charismatic leadership of Nelson Mandela, virtually no one found it wise to even raise the issue.

Concluding remarks

IN REASSESSING THE LEADERSHIP OF THE NATIONAL PARTY, ONE HAS TO ASK how the different apartheid-era leaders read the facts, and how they translated these interpretations into political schemes and visions. And most importantly, what was the outcome of their plans?

In the course of the 1950s Nationalist leaders were forced to accept some fundamental realities: partition was impossible, black labour was indispensable, black urbanisation irreversible, the growth in black numbers inexorable and the prospect of chaos not to be discounted. Eben Dönges, minister of the interior, acknowledged in 1953 that he and his colleagues realised that apartheid could 'protect' whites only over the short run.[1]

Though NP leaders had all along realised that they might need black allies, they without fail insisted on segregated structures. As Chapter 3 points out, Hendrik Verwoerd initially thought that blacks might be granted a form of self-rule and might perform meaningful white-collar jobs outside of the homelands. In his discussion in 1950 with members of the Natives Representative Council, among whom several ANC members, he said that the government wanted blacks to have 'the greatest possible measure of self-government' in the townships, along with opportunities for training so that they could competently serve their own people 'in many spheres'.[2] The NRC flatly rejected his proposal, insisting on representation in parliament and in provincial councils.

Verwoerd tried to develop the homelands policy so that it might be seen as a credible alternative to apartheid, but by the end of the 1960s, this policy was increasingly questioned. Nevertheless, on the eve of the Transkei's 'independence', Nelson Mandela wrote in prison that it would be a mistake to consider homeland independence merely a farce. 'For the first time since conquest, the people will run their own affairs,' he said, adding that with independence the 'heavy hand of oppression will have gone'. Instead of calling for a boycott of the elections it would be better to accept independence as 'an accomplished fact' and to persuade the Transkei government to join the ANC in the liberation struggle.[3]

---

1 John Hatch, *The Dilemma of South Africa* (London: Dennis Dobson, 1953), p. 93.

2 AN Pelzer ed., *Verwoerd Speaks: Speeches 1948–1966* (Johannesburg: APB Publishers, 1966), p. 28.

3 Nelson Mandela, 'Clear the Obstacles and Confront the Enemy', published on the O'Malley Archives blog and republished on www.politicsweb.co.za on 14 May 2012.

John Vorster envisaged a South Africa in which 'satellites', in the form of black and coloured sub-structures, orbited around the white nation's institutions. Occasionally he held 'summits' of leaders but nothing of significance ensued. Vorster added a new twist to racial legislation by removing South African citizenship from those blacks whose putative nation had taken independence. This simply exacerbated black rejection of apartheid. His flimsy scheme of a confederation of 'independent' white and black entities collapsed in the early 1980s when Mangosuthu Buthelezi of Kwa-Zulu rejected it.

PW Botha was the first Nationalist leader to consider all local groups part of a multi-racial South African nation. Before the nation was seen as exclusively white. Botha proposed a Confederation of Southern African States that would turn Verwoerd's vision into a reality, with an emphasis on providing jobs and food. However, this proposal did not address the fundamental flaw in the system. As Zambia's Kenneth Kaunda told him, a workable system could never be constructed upon the foundation of apartheid. In her splendid work *The March of Folly: From Troy to Vietnam*, Barbara Tuchman writes that at the core of all folly is not error, but persistence in error. Leaders get trapped in wars they cannot win or cling to policies that cannot work, not wanting to admit that they were wrong. In 1992 Derek Keys, minister of finance, described the homelands as 'failed', with the elites 'raking it off' and the national government getting very little in return.[4]

A major folly on the part of the NP leaders was the exclusion of the coloured people. Had coloured voters not been disenfranchised in the 1950s most of the then Cape Province could have developed into an autonomous region in a post-apartheid federation.

Economic integration

In 1975 South Africa was the world's 18th largest economy and the world's 15th trading nation. (It would fall to 28th and 37th years later.)[5] This ranking could not have been achieved without what a study of economists called the 'part-modernisation of black education'.[6] The number of black pupils rose from 800 000 in 1950 to 2,75 million in 1970. There was a sharp increase in the budget allocated to the education of all groups. From 1957-62 spending on black education increased by 32%, followed by increases of 33% in 1962-67 and 36% in 1967-72. In the same periods, spending on white education increased by 32%, 37% and 57%; on coloured education it was 23%, 18% and 98%, and in the case of Indians 40%, 31% and 94%.[7]

---

4 Interview with Derek Keys, 17 October 2010.

5 RW Johnson, *South Africa's Brave New World: The Beloved Country since the End of Apartheid* (London: Allen Lane, 2009), p. 598. The figures are from the World Trade Organisation.

6 JW Fedderke, R de Kadt and J Lutz, 'Uneducating South Africa: The Failure to Address the Need for Human Capital', *International Review of Education*, 46, 3, 2000, pp. 257-81.

7 Hermann Giliomee and Lawrence Schlemmer, *From Apartheid to Nation-Building* (Cape Town: Oxford University Press, 1990), p. 106.

Because of the rapid increase in intake, per capita spending declined and the racial gap in spending remained large. Initially the expanded black education system focused mainly on literacy and basic skills. But the high economic growth of the 1960s had momentous political consequences. It became essential that the skills and talents of the entire population were drawn on. After 1970 the government rapidly expanded secondary and tertiary education for black and coloured students, leading to a steady narrowing of the racial gap in per capita education spending.

South Africa was on an irreversible course of political as well as economic integration. The evidence was clear: the higher their level of education, the more emphatically black and coloured people rejected apartheid. Remarkably, the NP government never tried to reverse educational spending, even when it became clear that education had a radicalising effect.

More than 200 years ago Edmund Burke wrote that at times leaders have to take their followers not where they want to go, but where they have to go. The NP leadership faced two huge challenges. First, it had to bring all workers into a single industrial relations system, giving everyone the right to representation in the statutory industrial negotiating forums. Second, South Africa had to democratise the political system on the basis of universal franchise.

The government met the first challenge of labour reform reasonably well, but fell far short on the second. Workers who had industrial rights invariably demanded political rights even more emphatically. For this reason almost all democratic countries had granted their citizens political rights before they extended industrial rights to all workers.

In the mid-1980s South Africa was wracked by protests in which the black trade unions played a leading role. But violence and strife were not all that marked the country. It was preparing for that most unexpected development of all: an integrated non-racial democracy based on universal franchise. The average per capita income in South Africa was far below the level where successful democratisation had occurred in other countries, but on other indices South Africa had advanced far. Between 1960 and 1985 the number of black high school students rose from 55 000 to 1,2 million, while the black student numbers grew from 1 900 to 49 200. The number of newspaper readers jumped, trade union numbers skyrocketed and civil society blossomed.[8] It was no longer possible to force the genie back into the bottle.

Leadership compared

A major theme of this book is the crucial role played by individual leaders and the contingent nature of developments. David Lloyd George, who headed the wartime

---

8 For a fuller analysis see Hermann Giliomee and Lawrence Schlemmer, 'Can a South African Democracy Become Consolidated?', Giliomee and Schlemmer, eds., *The Bold Experiment: South Africa's New Democracy* (Johannesburg: Southern Books, 1994), pp. 168-202.

coalition government in Britain from 1916 to 1922, wrote: 'It is a mistaken view of history to assume that its episodes were entirely due to fundamental causes which could not be averted and that they were not precipitated or postponed by the intervention of personality. The appearance of one dominating individual position at a decisive moment has often altered the course of events for years or even generations.'[9] Fifty years later, after one of his Middle East diplomatic missions, Henry Kissinger commented likewise on the difference leaders make.[10] In most key political transformations in the second half of the twentieth century one can discern a single, towering leader who changed the course of politics. Charles de Gaulle, Mao Zedong, Deng Xiaoping, Margaret Thatcher, and Mikhail Gorbachev come to mind.

During the early 1960s the granting of independence to Algeria and of self-government to the Transkei prompted the liberal historian CW de Kiewiet to draw a comparison between De Gaulle and Verwoerd. Neither De Gaulle nor Verwoerd was a professional politician. Both intimately and passionately identified with their people, and more than most leaders claimed to speak for their people, its history and its honour. Both had very few advisers on grand political strategy. Verwoerd took seriously the views of Werner Eiselen on black ethnicity and education. He also established the Economic Advisory Council, but representatives from the state dominated it. However, he and his successors bluntly dismissed all attempts of organised business to push for political reforms.[11]

Both Verwoerd and De Gaulle took huge political gambles. De Gaulle took France out of the North Atlantic Treaty Organisation without informing his party's caucus; in Canada he called for a free Quebec without consulting his cabinet. Virtually on his own he plotted the course of freeing France from the Algerian albatross. Verwoerd called a referendum on a republic despite research showing there was no majority support. It was not apartheid, but winning the referendum virtually on his own, taking the country out of the Commonwealth and realising the long-cherished ideal of a republic that secured for Verwoerd his almost untouchable position among Afrikaners.

It is often stated that Verwoerd was so obsessed with the principles of his racial policy that he was unable to change course. But in 1959 he opened up the possibility of independent homelands – which shortly before he had rejected – without consulting his caucus. Whether he would have changed course if in 1966 he had survived the knife of his assassin is pure speculation. But it is clear that he possessed the intelligence, the audacity and authority to do the unexpected.

---

9 Alan Jamieson, *Leaders of the Twentieth Century* (London: G Bell and Sons, 1970), Preface.

10 Michael Leventhal, *The Hand of History* (Johannesburg: Jonathan Ball, 2011), p. 263.

11 Louwrens Pretorius, 'The Head of Government and Organised Business' in Robert Schrire, ed., *Leadership in the Apartheid State* (Cape Town: Oxford University Press, 1994), pp. 209-44.

John Vorster and his successors remained in the thrall of Verwoerd's vision of self-governing black homelands and a South African 'Commonwealth' of black and white states. Kissinger, who met Vorster in 1976, considered him 'highly intelligent', but dismissed his secret scheme to establish one or two white homelands along with some subservient black homelands. NP leaders all made the error of judging the policies they espoused by their intentions rather than by the results.[12] Kissinger nevertheless concluded after his talks with Vorster that Afrikaners were 'not circling their wagons as they had been obliged to do too often in their difficult history'.[13]

Vorster was influenced by family dynamics and by his coterie of close advisers. He married into a family closely connected to the more moderate Cape nationalism. (His father-in-law, PA Malan, was director of both Nasionale Pers and Sanlam). Among his allies the most prominent were General Hendrik van den Bergh, whom he appointed head of the Bureau of State Security, and Piet Riekert, whom he made head of a commission on using black labour in urban areas. Third was Eschel Rhoodie, secretary of the department of information, who persuaded him to embark on a secret, illegal campaign to buy support for apartheid in foreign countries.

In contrast to Verwoerd's tight control of his cabinet, Vorster allowed his ministers great scope to pursue their own course, provided it remained within the ambit of government policy. This soon degenerated into rampant 'departmentalism'. An extreme case was the decision by a small number of politicians and officials to impose Afrikaans as medium of instruction in black schools in Soweto and elsewhere in the southern Transvaal. Neither the cabinet minutes nor the responsible minister's diary mentions a cabinet decision. This step triggered the black uprising of 1976.

Another thrust of this book is the unpredictable, contingent nature of political developments. Although the doubling of the black population from 15 million to 31 million between 1970 and 1996 constituted a massive change, by the mid-1970s it was by no means a foregone conclusion that all blacks except for those in rural Natal would form a consolidated political bloc supporting the African National Congress by 1994. But NP leaders were incapable of offering anything that could break up this bloc. Their policies had the effect of forcing the great majority of black South Africans into a single camp, which the ANC would control.

Of all their attempted reforms, the Tricameral Constitution was the most fatal. When in 1977 the Vorster government embarked on drafting a new constitution, Van Zyl Slabbert correctly argued that it would be far better to include blacks from the start in any new dispensation. Excluding them would create the impression of the rest of South Africa ganging up against blacks. Slabbert's anger at being spurned

---

12　Milton Friedman's comment on the regulation of markets, cited by Niall Ferguson, 'Friedman's Century', *The Spectator*, 14 July 2012, p. 18.

13　Henry Kissinger, *Years of Renewal* (London: Weidenfeld and Nicolson, 1999), pp. 968-69.

led to his estrangement from the political establishment. He could have made a major contribution in the early 1990s when serious negotiations finally started.

There are strong parallels between Vorster and Leonid Brezhnev of the Soviet Union. Both had accumulated massive power, with no chance of being voted out. Both attempted to govern without meaningful internal reforms and, in an attempt to deflect pressure, both pursued détente (Brezhnev with the West and Vorster with the independent African states to the north). Brezhnev's decision to authorise a full invasion in Afghanistan angered the United States, and fatally undermined his pursuit of détente. Similarly, Vorster's decision to support an incursion into Angola wrecked his outward policy and his attempt to establish détente with African states to the north.[14] As Jamie Miller will show in a forthcoming study, PW Botha was primarily responsible for cajoling Vorster into supporting the ill-fated incursion. Arnold Toynbee observed as early as 1950 that leaders suddenly faced by radical challenges tend to look for scapegoats such as 'communism' to account for their inadequacies.[15] Fearing communism in the region and ignorant of the American political system, Vorster and Botha suspended their critical faculties.

Yet Botha's contribution has been underestimated inside South Africa. After his visit to South Africa in the early 1980s UN Secretary General Perez de Cuellar remarked that two leaders had impressed him greatly because they understood power: PW Botha and China's Deng Xiaoping.[16] Botha tried to free up the private sector to accelerate growth and create jobs. Chris Heunis, minister for constitutional affairs, initially managed to persuade him to incorporate blacks in some common structures. He integrated the army, granted black workers full industrial rights, and established a well-staffed National Intelligence Service, which in a much more sophisticated way than its predecessor (BOSS) gathered and assessed intelligence.

Botha was also a far better manager than Vorster, particularly in running the cabinet as a tight ship and improving the administration of the state and the proper regulation of labour relations. He relied heavily on the advice of business leaders, particularly Wim de Villiers (later minister of economic co-operation in the cabinet of FW de Klerk), and on certain members of the Defence Force, notably General Magnus Malan, head of the defence force and later minister of defence. A National Strategic Management System with the National Security Council at the top – the brainchild of Malan and Botha – did a remarkable job in deflecting the ANC-led challenge to the state and providing a stable platform for negotiations.

But Botha made some fatal errors. First, he was unable to move beyond the homeland policy in meeting black demands. For too long he bought into the military's

---

14 E-mail communication from Jamie Milller, 31 July 2012.
15 Arnold Toynbee, *Civilization on Trial* (Oxford: Oxford University Press, 1950), p. 23.
16 Alf Ries and Ebbe Dommisse, *Leierstryd* (Cape Town: Tafelberg, 1990), p. 45.

perspective that the Communist threat rather than black political exclusion and widespread poverty caused the instability. He gave far too long a leash to the military to circumvent the Nkomati Accord and continue with aggressive action in Mozambique against the ANC. He kept Mandela in jail up to a point where he became a symbol not only of the freedom struggle but also of apartheid's inhumanity.[17]

During the second half of the 1980s Van Zyl Slabbert, with his unique debating and analytical skills, became one of the first white leaders to hold up the ideal of a non-racial democracy and the need for negotiating with representative leaders. He tended to accept in good faith ANC assurances of non-racialism and a commitment to a liberal, non-racial democracy. In the late 1980s few wanted to be seen as spoilers of a dream that might be unfolding. It was only by the early years of the new century that Slabbert became disillusioned when the ANC to all intents and purposes had become a typical black populist movement with no real place for minorities in the political system.

The last Afrikaner leader

FW de Klerk was the leader who finally accepted an inclusive democracy. Nothing in the first part of his political career suggested that he would be the leader to reform the race-based order. He resembles Lyndon B Johnson, Majority Leader in the US Senate, whose compassion for the downtrodden was qualified by his ambition to become president.[18] When PW Botha suffered a second stroke and resigned as NP leader early in 1989, De Klerk only narrowly won the leadership contest. Like Johnson, many and maybe most in his party considered him too conservative on racial issues.

As leader De Klerk was suddenly presented with a unique opportunity to reshape the political system. As the conflict between the offices of NP leader and president became increasingly untenable, De Klerk was sure he would succeed the ailing Botha as president and, more importantly, he did not have to contest his marginal parliamentary seat in Vereeniging in the 1989 election.[19] The quite unexpected fall of the Berlin Wall made it much easier for De Klerk to embark on negotiations with an ANC whose main backer was still the Soviet Union.

De Klerk was up against a formidable adversary in the person of Nelson Mandela. The very embodiment of the black freedom struggle, he exercised a mesmerising

---

17 Maritz Spaarwater, *A Spook's Progress: From Making War to Making Peace* (Cape Town: Zebra Press, 2012), pp. 85-86.

18 Robert A Caro, *Lyndon Johnson: The Passage of Power* (New York: Alfred A Knopf, 2012), pp. 8-11.

19 De Klerk did not have to contest his seat in Vereeniging in the parliamentary election of 1989 because he was the party's candidate for the presidential election. He qualified for the post as a member of parliament. In the election of September 1989 the NP's majority in his old seat was five.

influence. Mandela's disavowal of nationalisation and the fall of communism in Eastern Europe led to the mistaken conclusion that the ANC had discarded the idea of a revolutionary African nationalism. As late as 1989 the South African Communist Party (to which leaders like Thabo Mbeki and Jacob Zuma still belonged), supported radical policies that would undercut property rights and extend the ANC's political control over the judiciary, the media, and the security forces.

During the 1990s the ANC and SACP ostensibly retreated from many of their earlier commitments. However, once political power had been secured their leaders made clear that they regarded the political settlement merely as a bridgehead for a programme of comprehensive social and economic transformation. From 1996 onwards, the ANC was completely open about its intention to capture all 'all levers of state power' – even going so far as publish its policy documents on the Internet. However, by that point the myth of the ANC as a non-racial and democratic organisation had taken such hold that these overt statements of intent tended to be ignored or discounted by Western public opinion.

From the available minutes of cabinet *bosberade*, the De Klerk cabinet never seemed to have spent much time on the possibility that once in power the ANC could embark on a radical path. Unlike his predecessor, De Klerk apparently did not seek much advice on security matters from the military, which entertained few illusions about the ANC. Instead he strove, as he called it, to restore civilian government to its full glory. He appointed Wim de Villiers and subsequently he made Derek Keys minister of finance, who closed the financial books of the old order in a way applauded by all sides. In the opening phase of the negotiations he relied heavily on Gerrit Viljoen, who was respected across party ranks as a man of integrity and *gravitas*, but Viljoen had to retire for health reasons in May 1992. During the difficult last half of the negotiations De Klerk was a lonely figure who did not appear to have any confidantes.

De Klerk could never choose between the two tendencies in his cabinet: those favouring aligning the party with the ANC and a strong centralist approach, and those preferring an alliance with Inkatha along with a federalist approach. He failed to get Mandela to abandon rolling mass action to press political points or to give any meaningful say to representatives of minorities in the government of national unity. De Klerk had to renege on the commitment he gave white voters in the referendum of 1992 that he would not accept anything short of power sharing. However, the constitutional state, an idea that some divisions of the Afrikaner Broederbond had been propagating since the early 1990s, offered a measure of protection.

In her memoirs Margaret Thatcher described De Klerk and the Soviet Union's Mikhail Gorbachev as leaders with vision and boldness.[20] De Klerk, like Mikhail

---

20 Margaret Thatcher, *The Downing Street Years* (London: HarperCollins, 1993), pp. 532-34. For a snide comment on De Klerk ascribed to Thatcher see Anthony Sampson, *Mandela: The Authorised Biography* (Johannesburg: Jonathan Ball, 1999), p. 386.

Gorbachev, is correctly praised for freeing his country from a structure of severe repression and control. Both wrongly, as it turned out, believed their party would be an integral part of a future political order. Both greatly underestimated the forces they unleashed and the extent to which their adversaries would exploit the new opportunities that opened up. As politicians both were creatures of their parties, but both were sidelined politically, and their respective parties would soon disintegrate.

The settlement spelled the end of Afrikaner power and of leaders who were unambiguously Afrikaner leaders. Afrikaner leadership had developed in a constituency-based system and electorate in which Afrikaners formed the majority. It made for close ties between leaders and voters, but it also made the Afrikaner leaders introspective and unable to realise that since the early 1970s both the world and South Africa were set on a course of rapid change. The settlement that De Klerk negotiated fell well short of his constituency's expectations and the ANC, as it later turned out, refused to throw the National Democratic Revolution, adopted by the South African Communist Party in the early 1960s, into the dustbin where it belonged.

Apartheid, as Anton Rupert, doyen of Afrikaner business, wrote in a letter to PW Botha in 1986, 'is crucifying us, is destroying our language; it is degrading for a once heroic nation to be the lepers of the world.'[21] Between 1990 and 1992 the Afrikaners through their historic vehicle, the National Party, abolished all the statutory pillars of apartheid, and after 1994 there was no real Afrikaner resistance to the new order. But the Afrikaans language and the Afrikaner community faced an uncertain future. Much would depend on their self-belief, their initiative and above all, on their ability to come to terms with their history as a source of strength – but in such a way that they and their fellow South Africans discover a sense of common purpose and the confidence to forge a successful nation.

---

21 Rembrandt Corporation Archives, Stellenbosch, Letter from Anton Rupert to PW Both, 24 January 1986.

Acknowledgements

AS IS INVARIABLY THE CASE IN A BOOK SUCH AS THIS ONE, THE AUTHOR cannot sign off without acknowledging important contributions made by several people by way of granting interviews or offering criticism, suggestions, advice and critical comments.

I am grateful to JM Coetzee, Johannes Grosskopf, Albert Grundlingh and Stanley Uys, who read all the draft chapters and offered important comments and criticism on my treatment of the political figures that affected the lives of all of us.

Thanks also go to the following who offered the wonderful gift of friendship together with critical engagement and a love for social and historical inquiry: Heribert Adam and Kogila Moodley, Neville Alexander, Breyten Breytenbach, Pierre du Toit, Fanie Cilliers, Irina Filatova, Rick Elphick, Johan and Jeannette Groenewald, Chris and Marié Heese, Jan Heunis, RW Johnson, Jacko Maree, Maritz Spaarwater, Francois van der Merwe, Charles van Onselen, Mike Savage, Ton Vosloo, David Welsh and Virginia van Vliet, and Monica Bot and the late Lawrence Schlemmer.

I wish to express gratitude to the following people who offered important insights into the workings of different arms of the state apparatus: Niel Barnard (National Intelligence), Jannie Geldenhuys (the military), Johan van der Merwe (the police), and Jannie Roux (the cabinet secretariat). I was fortunate in securing interviews with many politicians and I thank them for their time. It would be invidious to single anyone out.

A warm thanks to Inus Aucamp and Johan Swanepoel, who uncovered, copied, and sent to me a collection of important and as yet not utilised documents from the Archive for Contemporary Affairs in Bloemfontein. Liesl du Preez did sterling work in the archives of the old Department of Foreign Affairs in Pretoria.

A special word of thanks goes to Naas Steenkamp for the important part he played in the conceptualisation and actual writing of the book. It was he who pointed out the appositeness of Robbie Burns's famous lines to the South African situation:

The best-laid schemes o' mice an' men
Gang aft agley

One National Party scheme after the other went 'agley', in Burns's words. The section in Chapter 6 dealing with the Wiehahn Commission, of which Steenkamp is one of only two surviving members, is largely a joint effort by the two of us. He also made valuable stylistic suggestions on virtually every page of the manuscript.

Except where indicated otherwise I conducted the interviews cited in the footnotes and was the recipient of the e-mail messages. I wish to thank Patti Waldmeir, a superb *Financial Times* journalist and author of *Anatomy of a Miracle: The End of Apartheid and the Birth of the New South Africa* (New York: Norton, 1997), an illuminating book on the transition, who gave me access to copies of the transcriptions of numerous interviews conducted by her between 1993 and 1995. I lodged copies of all the Waldmeir interviews, along with some other papers connected to the transition, in the Jagger Library of the University of Cape Town. Copies of my interviews will be lodged in the Manuscripts Section of the library of the University of Stellenbosch. I have also consulted the valuable texts of the interviews of Padraig O'Malley, which are posted on the Web.

I have a special debt to the University of Stellenbosch, and the Department of History in particular, which appointed me as a research associate and provided funding for research.

I thank the following publishers' editorial committees: The Editorial Advisory Committee of the journal *New Contree* for permission to publish material that first appeared in the article 'Great Expectations: Pres Botha's Rubicon Speech of 1985' in issue no. 55, May 2008; John Wiley & Sons for permission to republish the section on Bantu education, which originally appeared as 'A Note on Bantu Education, 1953–1970, *South African Journal of Economics,* vol. 77 no.1, March 2009; and Jonathan Ball Publishers for permission to publish material in the chapter on Van Zyl Slabbert that originally appeared in Alfred LeMaitre and Michael Savage (eds.), *The Passion for Reason* (Johannesburg: Jonathan Ball, 2010).

Baie dankie to Erika Oosthuysen, an exceptional publisher with great professional and personal skills and almost infinite patience with an author who does not know when to stop revising; and to Linde Dietrich, Roxanne Reid and Edwin Hees, who individually did much to improve the text.

Francine and Ryan Lake and Adrienne and Julian Lea showed genuine interest in and sympathy with the labour of writing. My greatest debt is to my wife, Annette, who gave constant encouragement and succour. It is to her that I dedicate the book with sincere apologies for prolonged spells of absent-mindedness and with all my love. *Tweesaam is veel beter as eensaam.*

In line with recent trends in history publishing, a bibliograhy does not appear at the end of this book. In each chapter a source is cited in full when first referred to.

Hermann Giliomee
Autumn 2012, Stellenbosch/Stilbaai

About the author

PROF. HERMANN GILIOMEE STUDIED AT THE UNIversity of Stellenbosch, where he completed his doctorate in History and lectured in the subject. From 1982 to 1998 he was Professor of Political Science at the University of Cape Town's. He was a Fellow at, among others, Yale, Cambridge and the Woodrow Wilson Centre for International Scholars in Washington. Currently he is Research Associate in the Department of History at the University of Stellenbosch.

His magnum opus, *The Afrikaners: Biography of a People* (2003), was published in South Africa by Tafelberg, in the USA by the University Press of Virginia and in the United Kingdom by Christopher Hurst & Company. In 2004 it appeared in Afrikaans as *Die Afrikaners: 'n Biografie* and became a South African top seller. The international English edition was listed by *The Economist* as one of its 'Books of the Year' for 2003, while the London *Sunday Times* called it 'fascinating' and 'indispensable'.

In 2007 Giliomee and Herbert Mbenga compiled and wrote the popular *New History of South Africa*, which was published simultaneously in Afrikaans as *Nuwe geskiedenis van Suid-Afrika*. His history of a Stellenbosch community, *Nog altyd hier gewees*, was also published in 2007.

He is married to Annette van Coller. They live in Stellenbosch and have two daughters and five grandchildren.

About *The Last Afrikaner Leaders*

This book breaks new ground . . . it is both illuminating and judicious, providing new slants on former National Party leaders. The great strength of the book is that the author does not shy away from challenging existing assumptions or prejudices. This is bound to set up interesting controversies that will enrich the debate about South Africa's tangled, disputed past. As an Afrikaner, though never a supporter of apartheid, Giliomee is able to write as what could be termed an 'ethnic insider'. His stature as an historian has enabled him to gain easy access to many of the key people involved in the issues about which he writes. Informants probably felt comfortable talking to a trusted and honest scholar like Giliomee . . . There is no other person in the world who could have come close to producing the impressively substantiated story of Afrikaner politics in the late 20th century.   DAVID WELSH

'Hermann Giliomee has taken a much traversed subject, and with new, invaluable insights into the personalities of the NP's leaders, turned it into what many will call the conclusive version of why apartheid began, its journey over 46 years, and why it handed over so abruptly to the ANC. Others may say that the narrative of apartheid's rise and fall is now even more controversial. Here is a hugely stimulating read, moving at a clipping pace – and with some very good touches on PW's temper and rages.'
                                                                                    STANLEY UYS

'Hermann Giliomee has the abiding virtue of a boundless intellectual curiosity, allied to a complete indifference to ideology, political correctness or intellectual fashion. A man who is proud to be an Afrikaner, regretting only the besmirching of his people's name by both Afrikaner Nationalists and their enemies, Giliomee is perfectly positioned to tell from the inside the story of one of the 20th century's greatest conundrums: how could the tiny Afrikaner people, taking power after they had been thoroughly defeated not long before, first build a major industrial state and then, against all expectations, negotiate themselves peacefully out of power?

Giliomee believes that the job of the historian is to explain, not apologise. His account is sober, intimately informed and invaluable. No one interested in the history of South Africa can neglect any book by Hermann Giliomee – and this book, based mainly on exhaustive interviews with many of the main actors, is an instant "must buy".'
                                                                                    RW JOHNSON

Index

Reconsiderations in Southern African History

Milton Shain
The Roots of Antisemitism in South Africa

Timothy Keegan
Colonial South Africa and the Origins of the Racial Order

Ineke van Kessel
"Beyond Our Wildest Dreams": The United Democratic Front and the Transformation of South Africa

Benedict Carton
Blood from Your Children: The Colonial Origins of Generational Conflict in South Africa

Diana Wylie
Starving on a Full Stomach: Hunger and the Triumph of Cultural Racism in Modern South Africa

Jeff Guy
The View across the River: Harriette Colenso and the Zulu Struggle against Imperialism

John Edwin Mason
Social Death and Resurrection: Slavery and Emancipation in South Africa

Hermann Giliomee
The Afrikaners: Biography of a People

Tim Couzens
Murder at Morija: Faith, Mystery, and Tragedy on an African Mission

Diana Wylie
Art and Revolution: The Life and Death of Thami Mnyele, South African Artist

David Welsh
The Rise and Fall of Apartheid

John Edwin Mason
One Love, Ghoema Beat: Inside the Cape Town Carnival

Eric Allina
Slavery by Any Other Name: African Life under Company Rule in Colonial Mozambique

Richard Elphick
The Equality of Believers: Protestant Missionaries and the Racial Politics of South Africa

Hermann Giliomee
The Last Afrikaner Leaders: A Supreme Test of Power